The Human Condition:

an evolutionary experience

Volume II

Ernest Dyer

Paperback ISBN: 978-1-80031-335-4
Hardback ISBN: 978-1-80031-334-7

www.newgeneration-publishing.com

New Generation Publishing

Contents

PART TWO

The pre-modern period

Chapter 5 1750 – 1900

'Before a revolution happens, it is perceived as impossible; after it happens, it is seen as inevitable.'

Rosa Luxemburg

World pop. 1750 approx 800m
World pop. 1900 approx 1,670m

At 1750 we can see the precocious foundations of what became a series of transformational innovations that would make such a dramatic difference to the ways in which the process of civilization would develop. The two most significant, and interlinked, innovations would be industrialization and the advance of the sciences. The progressive institutionalization of the sciences can be marked by the founding in 1660, of The Royal Society of London for the Improving of Natural Knowledge - shortened as the 'Royal Society'.

In relation to a wider aim of this book, in these two innovations we see a further acceleration in the rate of the generation of novel information, so further expanding the horizon of 'Reality'; of the phenomenal content that is the very essence of producing the bio-psychological entities, primarily involving consciousness, drawing evolution forward into the ever-widening terrain of the possible. Expanding the total 'amount' of information (ideas, knowledge, and facts) that humankind as a whole has potential access to, so offering the evolution of life (as consciousness) new levels of realizable possibility

Over the previous three hundred years of a European history, characterized by political hegemony dynastic machinations, and conflict, many people were only directly affected by the turmoil of warfare if it swept over their locality. Most of those living outside of the swaths of conflict endeavoured to live their lives pretty much as their forefathers had lived theirs. Their social and geographic horizons were generally local, extending not much further than farmstead or village and, only on occasion reaching to a nearby town. Up to mid-eighteenth-century Europe was still predominately an agricultural economy, with millions of people directly and indirectly dependent on seasonal fluctuations and soil fertility. Experiencing the economic conditions covering those that led to starvation to those that led to prosperity, and the range of outcomes in between. Up to the middle of the eighteenth century nine out of ten people in Europe were still economically dependent on agriculture and closely related industries. Few would have eaten meat more than once a week, most were illiterate, and all were vulnerable to a range of diseases. The mass of people stoically endured the uncertainties of a seasonally dependent economy, with at least some compensation being offered by the relative certainties of long-established social relations characterized by tradition obligations and occasional celebrations.

In order to get a closer sense of the impact of industrialization I will focus primarily on just one country (England), not least due to its being accepted as leading the way into industrialization. In most important areas - impact on agriculture and manufacture - the growth of urban centers and city life - pollution - poverty - trade - financial systems - technological innovations - workers resistance to exploitation - class divisions - elite power - political change - there was a sufficiency of a shared experience to make using just one county serve as a model for the progressively internationalized process of industrialization.

I use England as the model for the process of industrialization that, before the nineteenth century came to an end, would spread to central Scotland, south Wales, the Low Countries, Germany (united in 1871), Scandinavia, France, Russia, United States, Japan, Catalonian Spain, and to a lesser extent to a number of other European, South American, Middle-Eastern and Far Eastern countries. Britain was at the forefront of this new feature of humankind's historical narrative but it trod a developmental path along which these other nations would also travel, even if there were variations based on local environmental, as well as on political and social, conditions

The population of Britain (and most of Europe) was growing apace during the eighteenth century, with labour being displaced from the countryside at least partly due to the enclosures of common land. A process that dramatically transformed the way land was worked when between 1750-1830 4,000 Enclosure Acts enabled the 'legalized theft' of about 7m acres of land to take place in Britain. Enclosure being, in effect, the privatization of land previously held in common; land that had provided a significant supplementary means of subsistence for thousands of peasants and their families. Generations of illiterate peasantry had at best only poor documentary evidence of land-rights stretching back to Anglo-Saxon times whereas the wealthy landowners had access to a legal system with a willingness and the means to offer documentary 'proof' to support their claims. Thousands of rural families, at a scratchy stroke of a parliamentary commissioner's quill-pen, found themselves denied access to the means of making a decent living and for many denied even the means to survive. Similar transfers of access to productive land from the poor to the rich took place across much of Europe during the 18th and 19th centuries, as land began a process of commodification, with its value evermore closely calculated according to market-based profitability.

Karl Marx (in 'Capital') highlighted the importance of enclosures in the transformation from feudalism to capitalism. And the historian E.P. Thompson noted that: 'Enclosure (when all the sophistications are allowed for) was a plain enough case of class robbery, played according to fair rule of property and law laid down by a parliament of property owners and lawyers.' (Thompson, 1968, p237)

The average farm size in 1700 was estimated to be about 65 acres but by 1800 this had risen to 125 acres and 25% of all the land in England was held in estates of over 3000 acres. The aristocratic landowner tended to use the increasing profits from farm-rents for fairly conspicuous consumption rather than re-investment in agricultural improvement. It was their tenants and other smaller farmers that were at the leading edge of agricultural innovation and consequently they were the drivers of the increased production required to at least go some way towards meeting the demands of the growing populations in the towns and cities. But the importation of cereals and meat from Ireland was still required to make up England's deficit in internally produced foodstuffs.

Tradition had to some extent normalized class distinctions in the countryside, allowing at least some sense of unified local communities held together by traditional rights and assumed obligations. But increasingly, in large parts of Britain, a more ridged separation emerged with five broad 'classes': wealthy aristocratic landlords, bankers, and wealthy merchants – more substantial tenant farmers and middling merchants, landlords, and those in the better paid legal and administrative occupations – artisans, small-scale farmers and traders, along with scribes, skilled artisans - various types of respectable labourers and peasants, fisherman, builders, carters, and those serving in the military – and an underclass including groups such as those in rural and urban locations living in near abject poverty, criminals, prostitutes, and the otherwise destitute. With the substantial farmer-class increasingly endeavouring to maximize income by introducing more efficient farming methods, and their wealthy landlords keen to encourage this (for most short of supplying funding) in order to enjoy the higher rental values this gave rise to.

A range of new crops including maize, clover, potatoes and turnips, were planted according to a three-crop rotation plan and this on more efficiently drained soils. A more systematic approach was also taken to animal husbandry and the recognition that the better the quality of fodder and grasslands the better the meat, the more milk produced, and greater number of animals can be supported on available land.

These improvements saw landowners benefiting from increased productively on their own directly managed farmlands and from higher rents of farms occupied by their tenants. Available capital (as accrued profit or forms of credit) led to investment in technology. An extended process of mechanization 'freeing up' more labour from work on the land. Including such innovations as Jethro Tull's horse-drawn seed drill, allowing seeds to be planted in rows and covered with soil as planting progressed, rather than the more wasteful broadcast method; Arthur Ransome's (1770s onwards) improvement in various agricultural tools, including an all iron plough that was able to furrow through a wider range of soil types. These two innovations were generally neutral in terms of labour power, but the introduction of the threshing (1750s) and flailing machines (1784) meant that a growing proportion of farm labourers were no longer required for work on the land.[1] With much of the labour that was left now becoming weekly 'waged labour' rather than employed on the basis of mutually agreed annually renewed 'hire'. Workers displaced by mechanization had to choose between abject poverty in the countryside or to seek work in the towns and cities that were beginning to grow in size and number.

---

[1] At around this time the invention, by Eli Whitney (in 1794), of the 'cotton gin', with its enthusiastic take up in the USA transforming the production costs of cotton – also leading to a significant increase in imported slave labour to meet increased demand for this now cheaper cotton. In1785 Britain was importing 11 million lbs of raw cotton to process in its mills and by 1850 this would rise to 588 million lbs, mostly from the USA – at about the same time the export of cotton goods constituted, by value, up to 50% of Britain's exports.

Prior to the eighteenth century industries such as mining and quarrying, leather-working, cart-making, weaving, spinning, and other textile-related activities, were operating across European states, including Britain, France, the Low Countries, and Germany. In the early eighteenth century these industries - offering goods within a guild-based market system (craftsmen and merchants guilds, there were over 100 guilds in seventeenth century City of London) - were mostly producing for local markets in cities and towns of modest size; maintaining quality standards and setting prices as well as passing on skills via apprenticeship-type training systems. The guild system was coming under increasing pressure due to the introduction of the patent system (1624) and also the political advance of early 'free-traders'; an economic perspective that would be given some academic justification with Adam Smith's 1776 'Wealth of Nations', then later by the writings of the economist David Ricardo.

By 1700 a financial system had been developed involving financiers, merchants, and investors who were able to accrue capital; and this by people who understood the longer term benefits of investing large sums in ventures that potentially offered even greater returns. Capital steadily accrued during the seventeenth-century, then in the eighteenth was further increased due partly to a significant contribution from the trade in slaves and the profits from the mines and plantations in which they worked. A stock of capital was becoming available within a society characterized by a growing middle-class that increasingly valued investment for their savings. Between 1760 and 1790 investment in the British economy doubled relative to the proportion of Britain's national wealth. In the colonies, especially the Americas, new markets for goods were opening up and established ones expanding.

Retrospectively, we can see that a series of developments, driven by economic and technological innovations, were to take civil life in a distinctly new direction. These can be identified as beginning during the eighteenth century, when relatively disparate 16/17th financial, technological, and from these, social processes, merged to offer the ground conditions necessary for the economic adaptation termed 'industrialization'. A concept that most easily encompasses these interlinked developments, with all of their economic and social implications.

As the relationship between employers and workers (and landlords and tenants) changed, for the most part becoming more polarized and with an increasingly market approach being taken to economic management, a context of rumbling discontent lay just beneath the surface of eighteenth-century life. Food shortages, disruptive technological changes, forced enclosures, turnpike roads, profiteering, the incompetence and corruption of officials, the workhouse system (2,000 workhouses in Wales and England by 1770) – each generated their own problems and resentments. In addition, problems would arise when soldiers, no longer required by the military were cast off. A group brutalized by the harshness of campaigning and the bloody reality of close-fought warfare. Many of these desperate men, resentful of their immediate plight one exacerbated by long-since dislocation from birth-place, would roam the land seeking work to survive. If this was denied, then having to resort to begging or crime.

Throughout the eighteenth-century fear of criminal activity and general unrest led to evermore legal statutes being introduced by Parliament. By the century's end there were 200 capital offences; a person could be hanged, not just for stealing a sheep or horse but for stealing anything (even a handkerchief) from a person, or goods to the value of 5 shillings from a shop or a stable. This penal code of heavy punishments for what were viewed by many of those citizens making up juries as relatively minor offences, often resulted in not guilty verdicts being returned in spite of convincing evidence to the contrary.

Most employers considered that the primary role of government was to tax and regulate them lightly but to maintain the peace forcibly. This meant a heavy bias towards protecting their interests rather than those of their workers, but even so some local magistrates and judges regularly exercised judgments based upon more traditional expectations. In general, successive governments introduced laws that favoured employing over employed groups. This generated a sense of unfairness among common people who tended to view many types of criminal - poachers, smugglers, food thieves, breakers of industrial machinery, evaders of tithes and taxes - as more sinned against than sinners.

When the harvests were poor, causing prices of basic foodstuffs to rise, the reaction of the people could often be direct, effective, and generally quite well organized. In the late summer of 1766 Honiton lace-makers removed corn from farmers engaged in hording, sold it at a fair price then returned both the money and the empty sacks to the farmers. 'Riots' against rising food prices took place in Halifax, Abingdon, Nottingham, Maidstone, and in most other parts of Britain. Skilled workers especially, protested about attempts to introduce changes in working practices including, abuses in training (such as curtailed apprenticeships, and 'colting'), downward pressure on wages, the increasing alienation of mechanized work, and generally poor working conditions.

According to E.P.Thompson: '.....the final years of the eighteenth century saw a last desperate effort by the people to reimpose the older moral economy as against the economy of the 'free-market'.' (1968 ed., p73, 'The Making of the English Working Class')

Between 1700-1770 the export of finished cotton goods from Europe to Africa and the Americas increased seven fold – An increase in demand that had led to some more ambitious manufacturers collecting workers together in 'factories' in order to increase output and make transport of large amounts of goods to sea-ports easier. This began a slow process of change from the putting out system, with its at least nominally independent, one or two loom owning, operatives producing cotton goods in their homes. Family working units with a relative flexibility in working arrangements, and at least some sense of control over their lives.

The first English textile factory was established as early as 1721 by John Lome in Derby, producing finely textured silk cloth, using machinery powered by water from the River Derwent. Silk manufacturing factories had already been operating in China and Italy, and it is thought that Lome gained the idea of a 'factory' as a base for silk manufacturing with water-powered machinery when on a visit to Italy, in turn it seems that the Italian silk-makers had gained their own knowledge from China. Lome's factory employed up to 300 operatives at its peak of production.

To drive the fairly simple machinery of the early times these factories had to be sited with access to water-power, ideally fast flowing streams in generally 'damp' localities. Suitable conditions were found in the English counties of Lancashire and Yorkshire. By the early years of the eighteenth-century the use of water as a source of energy was well understood. It is estimated that by 1800 there were about 500,000 watermills in Europe, driving machinery for a range of purposes – cotton spinning, grinding corn, sawing wood, polishing precious stones, and even one driving the fountains in the garden of the Palace of Versailles.

Water was a significant source of power, Clive Ponting commenting on the use of water-power in the US and Germany noted that: 'The scale of operations possible with water can be judged from the Mastodon Mill on the Mohawk river [US] which took water in 102-inch diameter pipes to turbines that generated 1,200 horsepower and drove two miles of shafting, turning ten miles of belts, 70,000 spindles, and 1,500 looms, producing 60,000 yards of cotton a day. As late as 1900 Nuremberg still had 180 operational water-mills'. (op cit, 2000, p646)

Water-power played an important role in driving the early stages of the Industrial Revolution and was able to hold its own for some time against other forms of power, even steam. It was aided in this by a series of improvements including John Smeaton's (1750) breast-wheel water mill which, by taking the water midway in the top-to-bottom cycle of the wheel, combined the most useful aspects of the traditional undershot and overshot designs, and also the water-driven turbine of Benoit Fourneyron 1827. These, were further improved on with the engineer John Rennie's sliding hatch used to improve the efficiency of Smeaton's breast-wheel, and Jean Poncelet's use of curved blades to feed water though an incline hatch; innovations that continued to make water power a cost effective means of driving machinery. (see Roderick Floud and Donald McCloskey eds. 1994)

Between 1766 and 1787 the output of cotton goods in Britain increased five-fold. Up until about this time wood had been the principle source of power (other than water and wind) available to manufacturers, house, and ship builders, as well as used in the smelting of iron. But increasing domestic and manufacturing usage had led to a significant shortage of this material. Coal had only been used on a very small scale as it was less easily available and not as efficient as wood on open fires. The translation of heat into work-power by burning coal had already been practiced in order to supplement local shortages of wood and peat for domestic heating and cooking; initially using sea-coal and pit-coal found on or close to the surface.

Some industries continued to use wind- or water-power into the nineteenth-century. But the uncertain nature of these two, and the shortages of wood (hence high prices - by the middle 1750s with up to 600,000 trees having to be imported annually to Britain from Russia), meant that coal was increasingly in demand and with potential rewards making the challenge of 'mining' for it more attractive. Throughout the eighteenth-century coal sent from Newcastle by coastal passage to London had risen, to reach half a million tons a year. As both domestic and manufacturing demand grew pits were dug deeper and the areas that had a conjunction of easy access to coal, available labour, established or easy to build transport links, and with sites suited to manufacture (such as the damp climate of Lancashire for textiles) began to grow. The cities of Glasgow, Newcastle, Manchester, and Birmingham, each became centres for basic heavy industry, manufacturing, and for housing the workers that enabled industrial production.

Coal had been used to produce glass from 1610, brick-making 1620, and coke (coal reduced by heating to a more pure form of carbon) was being used from about 1640 to create the level of heat required to dry malt. The value of coke as a source of power had been known for some centuries when in the eighteenth-century it began to replace charcoal for smelting of iron (the Chinese had been using coke to smelt iron since about 700 CE). Whereas early on price was probably a minor factor in leading to the preference of coke over wood, a more significant advantage was that its production required far less labour than did charcoal made from wood.

Abraham Derby (a Quaker of Coalbrookedale) was using coke to heat a blast furnace as early as 1709 in order to produce 'pig-iron' – a hard, if brittle, form of iron. Up to the 1750s, techniques to work iron had not progressed much beyond the working and casting techniques undertaken by practical men taking more of a problem-solving approach to technological improvement. At this time the more useful 'wrought-iron', a refined form of pig-iron (decarbonized), was in fairly short supply. This shortage was overcome in 1784 by the ironmaster Henry Cort's method of 'puddling and rolling', which also made a much better quality of pig-iron ('forged iron') and this was further improved to make high quality wrought iron. This being the processed form of iron that would provide the type of versatile metal so important for the industrial revolution. Wrought iron formed the basic material for structural uses such as bridges, engine bodies and railways, wheels, and in buildings. But for small metal parts this was not easily worked, nor really strong enough to make the smaller working parts for engines and for much of the machinery they drove. For the tools that produced and maintained these steel – a metal combining the hardness of pig-iron and the versatility of wrought iron - would be required. Forged steel had been made since early in the

17th century ('blister steel') and in the 1740s a refined form of this ('crucible' or 'cast steel') was available. The process for producing higher quality steel would not be developed until the nineteenth-century when Henry Bessemer, in 1856, used a new cooling technique ('The Bessemer Process') to cast steel on a larger scale – Siemens then developed the Open Hearth Method to rival Bessemer – both methods were only successful if they could use fairly pure iron ores which did not contain too much phosphorous. It wasn't until 1879 that Sidney Gilcrest-Thomas, applying a more scientific approach, used a lining that was able to absorb the phosphorous from the ore. From when the 'Age of Steel' really accelerated and according to J.D.Bernal 'Cheap steel became the basis on which the imperialism of the late nineteenth century was to be built…..' (Bernal, 1969 ed., Vol. 2, p598).

Most of the mechanical innovations introduced into manufacturing and in agriculture had been significantly improved by the use of cast iron, then later of hardened steel. Iron and steel forged in furnaces that were progressively heated by using coke rather than wood for fuel. Coke being not only able to rise the temperature in the furnaces (and so increasing the purity of the finished metals) but produced from a material (coal) that could more easily be shipped to the sites of metal manufacturing plants rather than these having to be sited within forests with ever-depleting supplies of wood. The early refinements in metal production was given practicable form in the iron bridge built by Abraham Derby (scion of a three-generation family of ironmasters), at Coalbrookdale in 1770, to span the River Seven.

A series of inventions made in the eighteenth century enabled the operation of textile production to take place in factories rather than in homes as in the traditional putting-out system, Key early inventions being John Kay's 'Flying Shuttle' (patented 1733), a device making the weaving of thread easier and James Hargraves 'Spinning Jenny' (patented 1764), allowing workers to spin up to 120 spools of wool at a time. By the end of the century the Flying Shuttle was being used across the north of England with 20,000 Spinning Jennies operating in water-powered factories. The invention of the 'Powerloom' by Edward Cartwright (1785) enabled one worker to produce about the same amount of yarn in the same time as about 40 workers operating under the putting-out system. Arkwright's 'Water-Frame Spinning Machine' (1769), being able to spin 100s of strands at a time, continued the broader process of deskilling textile production, further opening up the opportunity to employ untrained and much cheaper women and children. Samuel Crompton's (1775) 'Spinning Mule' combined the processes of the 'Spinning Jenny' and the 'Water-Frame Spinning Machine', producing a strong but finely spun yarn especially suitable for the popular muslin textiles – a highly productive machine that could run up to 400 spindles at a time. In terms of productivity, it has been calculated that around 1710 it took about 50,000 hrs to spin (by hand) 100 lbs of cotton but in the mechanized factory of 1790 this had fallen to 300 hrs (Floud and McCluskey, sec, ed. 1994). These innovations, and some other technological refinements, provided the mechanical mean of establishing the Industrial Revolution in Britain.

The textile factories were originally fairly small-scale operations, employing a dozen or so workers at sites located beside fast-flowing rivers usually near country villages some that, over the following hundred years, were to grow into the large northern conurbations, housing low-paid workers working long hours and living in often appalling conditions. In the factories children as young as five years were used to keep production costs down and from a family's point of view could contribute some income to what were generally just about subsistence living conditions. It would take the Parliamentary Act of 1819 before there was a ban on children under nine years from working in cotton mills. But the use of child labour was not exclusive to factory production, children had worked in the putting-out system as part of the family unit, and of course children were employed in a range of domestic as well as commercial settings during the early nineteenth-century. It was the actual conditions: dust, heat, long hours, physical confinement, and constant risk of injury – that made factory and mine-working even more difficult. In 1815 parliamentary commissioners reported that girls as young as eight years old were working in flax mills for up to 15hrs per day, suffering physical punishment if they slacked in their work and long term ill-health from undertaking it. In many towns, including Colchester in Essex and Taunton in Somerset, children from the age of five years were considered as potential workers. Factory owners tended to favour women and children as workers, their being cheaper and more manageable than men. It would not be until as late as the Act of 1833 (the same year that Britain abolished slavery) that legal limits began to be set on the working hours of children, with factory inspectors appointed to enforce the law. Increasing public outrage at the appalling conditions in which women and children worked in coal mines led to the Mines Act of 1842 banning the employment underground of women and of children under the age of ten years.

The move to factory-based production allowed further efficiencies, including increased specialization of worker roles, the easier use of non-human power and, significantly for the previously independent weavers, workers could be more easily supervised. Even as late in the century as 1849 a normal male working week was over 70 hours. The factory system itself brought changes to the working lives of individuals – the iron discipline of the time-clock, the alienation of repetitive machine work, and other dehumanizing conditions of the factory, meant that the space for any sense of fulfillment in work drained away.

Government, concerned about possible social discontent, with beggars and paupers wandering the countryside and idle in the cities, sought to address the outcome of poverty by a series of 'Poor Laws'. Notably that of 1782 which introduced parish relief and expanded the 'workhouse' system as places of last resort for the elderly, unmarried mothers, orphaned children or those whose parents could no longer support them, along with the disabled or destitute. The workhouses were institutions which served to provide individuals with the basic means of subsistence in exchange for their freedom and personal dignity, even to the extent of separating families. On arrival at the workhouse an inmate had to give up their own clothes and would be forced to wear a standard workhouse uniform, impacting on a person's identity as well as their dignity. The 'Poor Law' of 1834 established workhouses in each district. The whole system could be viewed as being less about official generosity and rather more about controlling populations (using degrading physical containment and the fear of it), an addition to the various structures of conformity that already operated to channel and control groups within society.

Up to about 1800 land transport relied on the power of the horse, ox, or man, hauling people and goods over poor road surfaces, most of which turned to mud (becoming impassable) during the winter months or following summer storms. In Britain at the start of the nineteenth century men such as John Macadam and Thomas Telford were overseeing significant improvements in the surface and the drainage of roads linking the main cities, ports, and towns. The requirements of manufacture, the possibility of needing to move militias hastily to suppress worker unrest, and the opportunity to charge for passage along Turnpike roads provided the incentives for improvement. To the extent that Arthur Young, a commentator on England who favoured rural over city life, would bemoan the subsequent improvements in roads as being a significant factor in drawing young men and women towards the 'attraction' of cities like London. For Young an attraction that could '….induce them to quit their healthy clean fields for a region of dirt, stink and noise.'

By mid-century a network of about 23,000 miles of tarmac-surfaced roads (almost all run by turnpike companies) connected English cities. The trains of packhorses which trekked to and fro as they carried the bulk of the goods across the country at the start of the century, gave way to a range of heavy wagons that enjoyed priority over most other traffic on the highways. Telford (who held the position of the Surveyor General of the City of Bristol) also excelled in canal-building; his work included the Ellesmere and the Caledonian canals. It was the use of rivers and canals that, along with road building, and coastal shipping, represented movement in the early industrial revolution. Rivers and canals allowed for passages unaffected by all but very severe weather conditions and the flotation effect of water facilitated the movement of heavy loads at relatively low cost of energy input. For Britain the construction of canals along with the necessary locks, pump buildings, tunnels, aqueducts, and the barge building and servicing industry, began seriously from about the middle of the eighteenth-century. The Duke of Bridgewater, known as the 'father of inland navigation' had canals built on which to transport coal dug from his own mines. Until the advent of railways, canals would provide high returns for investors – the Bridgewater Canal alone was making an annual profit of £100,000, a considerable 50% annual return on investment.

The canal-boats (barges), with their mostly family crews, transported manufactured goods from the industrial heartlands to ports from which they could be carried across the world; with the barges returning up river loaded down with raw materials and parts for machinery to continue the cycle of production. It was the imaginative brilliance of those who planned the routes, designed and oversaw the construction, along with the more practical work of talented surveyors, engineers, and supervisors that built the canals. But also required was the hard physical work of construction – the millions of tons of earth moved by direct human labour, the millions of bricks made and used to contain the water or shore up miles and miles of tunnels – to be undertaken by nameless hordes of tough navvies labouring alongside a range of semi-skilled and skilled workmen.

Chris Harman (op cit, p319) noted that: *'Vast armies of labourers using relatively cheap steel picks and shovels were put to work building canals and the first solid, smooth-surfaced roads to link major towns.'*

It was the same mixture of skilled and semi-skilled workers, along with teams of tough navvies, all working under the guidance of technically gifted engineers and surveyors who, from about 1820s, would move on to begin the building of the railways. A form of transport that was to provide the means of faster overland travel than even the swiftest of horse-drawn coaches; carrying loads that would be far in excess of those carried on the barges between many more towns and cities than those linked by waterways.

Construction at this time was markedly influenced by the invention, by the bricklayer turned builder Joseph Aspdi (in 1824), of the chemical processes that produced Portland Cement and Concrete – materials that would transform the contruction industry from midd. century; notable constructions using these being the Thames Tunnnel and the extensive London sewage system.

Even before the 1820s, Britain had increasingly enjoyed a series of economic advantages, including greater access to overseas markets as well as an increasing home demand for consumer goods. To satisfy these demands old industries at first expanded their production, indeed the three decades leading up to 1820 even saw a boom in the hand-loom weaving trade; there were still 500,000 hand-workers operating within the putting-out system in 1820. But this increased demand also gave an impetus for innovation in techniques and to improvements in the means of production. If, up to the 1820s, the mechanization of industry within a factory system was still in the process of becoming established rather than its dominating manufacturing. Manufacturing of particular products often became a local specialitality – cotton mils in the largest northen cities, cutlery in Sheffield, pottery in Stoke and some nearby towns, shoes in Nottingham, etc.

In the fast growing cities such as Glasgow, Manchester, and Liverpool, populations lived packed closely together in rows of shabby streets adjacent to factories and workshops belching smoke into the dank air and pouring liquid waste into what had once been clear culverts, streams, and rivers, running through open countryside. Areas of the cities became heaving, steaming slums, with individuals and families endeavouring to carve some sort of acceptable lives out of quite miserable living conditions; ones that encouraged disease and infection. Air pollution caused a rise in a range of respiratory illness (asthma, bronchitis, pneumonia), and poor sanitation, along with high population density, led to the rapid spread of transmissible diseases (tuberculosis, cholera, smallpox, typhus). In addition, there were the sexually transmitted diseases that were a feature of a mass of humans, in close contact within a money economy, combined with a weak structure of normative social mores. Poor diet exacerbated by adulterated food-stuffs (noted by Fredrick Engels, 1845) made adults, and more so children, vulnerable to distorted bodies (rickets), and to cognitive impairment due to brain under-development - a vulnerability to physical deformation added to that caused by the working conditions (up to 16hr working days) in factories.

There was also the danger of childbirth taking place in the too often fetid conditions of nineteenth-century working-class homes. People that had genetic constitutions (especially their immune systems) formed through generations of living in the countryside became exposed on moving to the cities to types of germs (viral and bacterial) that they had little/no resistance too. As late as 1850 the average life expectancy of a male child was only 25 years. Even dead the bodies were packed tightly together in overflowing cemeteries.

The historian Roger Osborne suggested that: *'Industrialization subjected millions of people to virtual slave labour in factories and mines. It brought a largely rural population into cities where filth, squalor and disease made their lives miserable and dangerous.'* Going on to add: *'Conditions for working-class people in urban districts remained dire throughout the 1830s and 40s and remained so for decades in many cities'* (Osborne, 2006, p347)

In 1801 16% of the English population (for Europe generally the fig. was 10%) lived in cities and towns but by 1891 this figure had reached 53% of what was a larger total population, rising to 75% by 1900. Across Europe a similar pattern of the increasing number and size of towns and cities is illustrated by Berlin's population increasing by ten times and Vienna's by eight times during the century.

If the living conditions were generally poor then the working conditions for many were at least as bad. As a 'capitalist' economic system was developing so too did a system of the commodification of the relationship between workers who had only their labour to sell and owners endeavouring to maximize the returns for their (or shareholders) capital investment. A relationship often mediated by factory managers, supervisors, and foremen, intent on keeping their relatively privileged positions and if necessary tirelessly driving the workforce to do so.

Abject poverty for the unemployed, elderly and sick, and generally poor living conditions even for many of those in work, stimulated unrest and a willingness of those in work to withhold labour (strike) or even to riot, and this, along with rising levels of crime, caused concern amongst the middle and upper classes. These being especially fearful of the 'mob' – the more immediate collective expression of working class anger mostly in response to mainly local unfairness or injustice, with no democratic means of action, and an obdurate ruling class determined to maintain its own material comforts and social and political privileges. The Gordon riots of 1780, causing some material damage and much upper class alarm in London, had allowed a glimpse for those in power of how difficult it could be to control the righteous indignation of a populace quick to action as tempers rose when inflamed by injustice. The revolutionary activity that was taking place in France as the eighteenth century came to an end cast a long shadow of possible reckoning and demands for wrongs to be addressed ('equality', 'liberty', and 'fraternity') if the fever of revolution was ever to follow its shadow and cross the Channel to stimulate revolutionary ambitions amongst the oppressed classes in England.

Even in the very early stage of capitalist industrialization we can clearly view the asymmetric power relationship pertaining between employer and employee that has endured throughout the process, especially in 18/19th century Britain but throughout the world ever since (an enduringly obvious feature of Global versions of capitalism). An asymmetry that has to a significant extent been a central characteristic of the industrialization process and one that has been fostered by the various elite groups aided by a propagandist mass media that they have mostly owned and effectively controlled. Elites acting as if some sort of overwhelming power over the lives of others was some 'natural' right for those able to deploy capital, without any consideration of who actually creates this resource, and of the democratic rights that might be judged to be involved in sharing out the profits gained.

The common model of capitalist economic structures constructed by the more powerful, including their fellow-traveler political allies, had circumscribed and prioritized the power of 'ownership' (private property) and enshrined this in individuals rather than in all of the wider social interests involved in any industry. At its very heart industrial capitalism has been about exercising power over others even if via an anonymity mediated by limited liability company status, seeking justification on some assumed neutrality of the 'market'. And this primarily in order to maximize profit for individual company owners and shareholders. Even accepting that for our own twenty-first century version of capitalism, the 'shareholders' can now include a wide section the population who have been steadily inveigled into the current system via pension and other types of saving schemes.

Workers who make the most substantial contribution to creating 'primary' wealth and if, along the way, they are sufficiently organized or have the skills that allow a certain measure of 'market-power', then reasonable standards of living have been obtained. But when lacking the strength of unity, or the market power of valued skills, workers tend to gain but minimal standards; minimal being relative to any particular historical context.

Two key social changes were firstly, the shaping of the 'worker' and of the family structure to the time and motion frameworks that were judged as suitably efficient for the regular, relentless, pace of mechanized production – the waged worker, hired by the hour or paid by the 'piece-rate'. Secondly, workers continued to migrate to the towns and cities where the factories were situated to add to the thousands of their fellows, with distance dramatically reducing generational connections.

The densely-packed slum conditions of the cities and larger towns did bring people together and in places engendered some sense of shared interests; including the daily awareness of being exploited. A more tangible outcome of this situation was the founding of various lower middle and working class organizations determined on radical political reform. In Sheffield, in 1791, there was the Sheffield Constitutional Society (committed to universal suffrage and annual parliaments); with similar bodies soon being formed in cities such as Coventry, Norwich, Manchester and Birmingham. In London, the 'London Corresponding Society' (LCS) was founded, in 1792, by the shoemaker Thomas Hardy and a small group of skilled workers. The

LCS reached a membership of over 3,000, organized in nearly 50 local branches; it was able to draw thousands to its open air demonstrations. C.A.Bayly (2004, p102) described the LCS as being '....a reforming organization of intelligentsia and artisans,.......true great-grandparent of British socialism.'

They were amongst the people famously described by Edmund Burke as '......the swinish multitude'.

Different types of 'corresponding societies' (CS) were established across Britain. These groups formed various types of debating, corresponding, and campaigning societies, and they constituted a vibrant network of radicalism, with streams of letters and individual speakers passing between them. The societies were in effect the vanguard of the organized voice for reform of the lower middle and working classes. Some of them were also in regular correspondence with sympathetic groups in France; hence the repeated charge of their spreading Jacobinism in Britain.....they were called the 'Jacobin Army' by William Pit. The British radicals did draw encouragement from the French revolution, a connection symbolized by the practice in some groups of members addressing each other as 'citizens'.

The CS's had been a development on the earlier 'debating societies' that were a feature of some cities and large towns, especially in Scotland and northern England. Meetings of workers such as artisans, small shop-keepers, mechanics that would provide a model for the more organized network of CS. Debates within the Societies were generally educational, introducing members to historical contexts for contemporary events and to the arguments in support of political reform.

The Societies also produced publications, including magazines such as LCS's 'The Moral and Political Magazine', they also produced pamphlets on a range of subjects; if some were satirical and personally insulting to reactionary individuals such as Burke. Who, in his book 'Reflections on the French Revolution' 1790, had argued against the masses having any democratic rights and for them to respect British traditions and elite authority in order that their base 'human nature' could be controlled. Leading members of the aristocracy, and some parliamentarians, were challenged in mostly articulate and reasoned pamphlets and in newspapers such as the *'Sheffield Register'*. Many CS members also saw an important aspect of their role being to publicize the seditious writings of a Tom Paine. Especially powerful was Paine's 'Rights of Man' in which he attacked the concept of monarchy (as '.....debasing the dignity of man'), called for representative democracy, and suggested a higher level of taxation for the rich in order to alleviate the conditions of the poor and to fund the education of all children.

Characteristic of their campaigning activities was one undertaken by the LCS in the late eighteenth century when its leaders had organized a large demonstration on the outskirts of London (100,000-150,000 attended). The tone of the meeting was set by an appeal to the king 'Whenceforth, in the midst of apparent plenty, are we thus compelled to starve? Why, when we incessantly toil and labour, must we pine in misery and want......'

In 1794 the LCS had 40,000 copies of a leaflet containing an address given by 'citizen' John Martin to a packed meeting of its members held in the Globe Tavern, London. This was a radical address: '.....we must now choose at once liberty or slavery for ourselves and our posterity....' This articulate clarion call to organize was distributed across Britain and helped to re-invigorate older, and establish new, Corresponding Societies – From Birmingham, Bristol, Manchester, Maidstone, Halifax, Derby, Portsmouth, Newcastle, Gt. Yarmouth ...etc building perhaps the first nation-wide structure of British working class organization.

In addition to the Corresponding Societies, there were also the Hampden Clubs (30 such clubs in Leicestershire by 1816) and the many Political Unions and Chartists Lodges campaigning for political reform across the country.

Initial government reaction to these organizations had been relative low-key, although it did deploy a fairly extensive network of spies in an attempt to monitor the progress and assess the extent of dissent ('Citizen Groves' being one of the more infamous). But, towards the end of 1792 government concern was heightened, partly due to reports of popular support for the French revolutionaries (crowds in Sheffield had celebrated the successes of the French at the Battle of Valmy) but also shaken by the Gordon riots of 1780.

Across the country 'Church and King' mobs were formed to oppose the groundswell of calls for political reform, with thugs breaking up reform meetings and in places groups burning effigies and staging mock executions of Tom Paine. The government was responsible for a number of legislative acts being introduced to deal with what were viewed as seditious activities. Measures aimed to prevent, or at least inhibit, organized radicalism and or deter authors of the many pamphlets that were widening the awareness of legitimate dissent. From May 1794 the government began a more determined course of action against the more active radical groups.

In the face of this determined persecution the upward trend of organized radicalism petered out but throughout Britain workers and middle-class sympathizers continued at least some level of much less organized opposition to the worst excesses of industrialization and in support of political reform. The reform-focused activities of the early 1790s had laid the foundations for later, more successful, attempts at organizing working class economic and political resistance.

Up to mid nineteenth century governments in Britain and across Europe did little to alleviate the conditions in either workplace or city slum. Thomas Malthus's ideas on population could be cited by the ruling classes as spurious justification for their resistance to introducing measures to alleviate poverty. The pseudo-scientific view (and its dubious moral assumptions) that over-population would 'naturally' be regulated so why improve the conditions of the poor if this would only lead to more children and so more misery. Attempts to increase wages, improve living conditions, or for the masses to take part in legislative functions (governance) were viewed by many in the upper classes as insurrectionary; and even more evidence that the dreaded 'Jacobinism' had crossed the channel.

In Britain, it was a government of highly conservative, mainly large, landowners used to reacting to events in ways that protected their own interests. Interests that were in effect institutionalized in law, access to education, networks of nepotism, and the more subtle advantages of other forms of 'social capital'. Beginning in the late eighteenth-century the advancing manufacturing and merchant groups were able to influence the more aristocratic ruling elite; indeed some gradually to be incorporated within it. This influence proved effective, at least to some extent, in areas such as protection from the competition of imported goods, securing colonial sources of raw materials, and more generally with the government being persuaded to take a 'hands-off' approach to various aspects of industrialization except for controlling workers; for which they were confrontational and authoritarian.

Initially governments dominated by aristocrats only grudgingly conceded to the demands of the large merchants and investors in manufacturing for legislative conditions that would provide for an obedient workforce, and for the freedoms required to maximize profits. Demands that advocated an approach by government of 'laissez faire' in relation to business and robust authoritarianism in relation to dealing with worker unrest. Intellectually, supporters of the government's approach could draw political justification from Edmund Burke, social justification from Thomas Malthus, and economic justification from (an importantly selective misinterpretation of) Adam Smith.

The early stage of industrialization was very much driven by technological innovations introduced by a generation of engineers and some amateur inventors, if sometimes in collaboration with merchants and manufacturers. This collaboration can be illustrated by the process towards the development of the steam engine. More generally, the advance in the natural sciences (mathematics, astronomy, physics, mechanics) provided a fertile context for discovery and innovation; for the technological dynamism driving progress.

We can also begin to see the practical influence of a more theoretical perspective. Individuals such as James Watt and George Stephenson worked within an intellectual milieu in which those of a more technological mindset were in regular contact with individuals that can fairly be described (if not yet named) as 'scientists', mostly sharing membership of local scientific societies - the leading ones being: The Lunar Society in Birmingham (1765) (of which both Watt and his business partner Mathew Bolton were members), The Literary and Philosophical Society of Manchester,(1660), the Linnaean Society of London (1788) The Philosophical Society of Edinburgh (1731) 'The Royal Society for the Establishment of Arts, Manufacturing, and Commerce' (1754) (Benjamin Franklin and Karl Marx were Fellows) and 'The Royal Society' (1660). Across Europe and in the US, similar academies and societies of science were being established. From about the mid nineteenth-century, it would be the rise of university-based science that would begin to vie with most of the more local societies in holding the leading role in scientific advance.

It was a series of relatively incremental processes that enabled theoretical advances in the sciences and practical applications in technology to form an evermore productive (and profitable) alliance. One created to serve the interests of industries such as drugs, chemicals, weapons, agriculture, and other areas of manufacturing for private profit. The natural sciences, especially astronomy, chemistry, physics, biology, and geology, made significant progress, in terms of widening the understanding of human experience, during the eighteenth and early nineteenth centuries.

In the natural sciences technology-based inventions including: improved lenses and telescopes, microscopes, and laboratory equipment such as the mercury thermometer (1724), the Leyden Jar (1745), the Voltaic pile battery (1799), and not least 'spectacles'; This type of endeavour also resulted in increasing the clarity of the applied methodologies, that underpinned advance. The role of the printed book/journal was also a central aspect of progress in science; not least in forging the 'culture of science' (retrospectively seen as being based on somewhat idealized 'shared values') within a growing community of scientists. A series of landmark books, along with a proliferation of journals, marked the lift-off in the generation of academic and popular scientific information. In both quantitative and novel (qualitative) terms, the following two to three hundred years of accumulating scientific information has arguably - as a circumscribed method-based approach to gaining information - made the most significant contribution to extending the accessible 'Reality' within which humankind lives. The relentless production of information in terms of modes of knowledge.

Until towards the end of the nineteenth century (and then only very partially) the sciences did little to improve the living conditions for mass populations, even adding to their plight with the scientist's role in industrializing conflict as its military-related inventions enhanced the power of the already powerful.

In town and country the Poor Laws continued to bear down upon the dignity of workers at a time when, especially in the countryside, machinery was beginning to replace labourers, with many more aware that their own displacement might also not be long in coming. But groups of skilled workers were organizing themselves stimulated, not just by awareness of their own increasing industrial importance but also by the enlightened ideas of both the French revolution and the writings of men like Tom Paine and William Godwin. Robert Southey wrote in his book 'Letters from England' (1807) about the working people being 'victims of civilization'.

A collection of ideas infused the discussion of within, mainly self-educated, groups of workers – liberty, equality, fraternity, social justice, fair wages, the right to have a say in the future.....the right to have 'rights. They also considered examples of direct action, at one extreme the revolutionary action in France but also actions undertaken to progress the more modest aspirations of early trades unionism and other forms of working class organization. Within some groups, especially the lower-middle classes and skilled workers, there was a growing sense of solidarity around common interests and the idea that something could and should be done.

In the countryside the first quarter of the century saw a series of protests: the 'Blanketeers' (1817) centered on actions of Lancashire weavers whose wages had been progressively reduced and who were initially seeking a minimum wage (this in fact did have the support of some employers). A request rejected by Parliament in 1818. In response, strike action was called and a meeting of up to 15,000 textile workers and their supporters (possible 50,000 in all) met in St Georges Field Manchester with the intention of setting off on a march to London where they would present a petition to the Prince Regent. The plan was that along the route the march would gather support from groups of textile workers in districts to the south. The petition drew attention to the plight of Lancashire textile workers and called upon 'his majesty' to find ways to alleviate the workers conditions. Each of the marchers (mainly spinners and weavers) had a blanket tied to their backs. In practical terms this would be of use during the nightly stopovers but symbolically, the blanket represented the products of the textile workers on whose behalf the appeal (petition) was being made.

Even before this entirely peaceful meeting has seen the marchers off a magistrate (kept informed by government spies that had infiltrated the marchers) read the Riot Act and a force of mounted King's Dragoon Guards attacked the meeting. The two leaders, of the marchers, Samuel Drummond and John Bagguley, were arrested. Nevertheless, a few hundred determined souls set off in the steady rain, but even this denuded march was repeatedly harassed by the military and got no further than Stockport where it was violently dispersed. Treatment that embittered the previously generally royalist textile workers and had shown other workers that peaceful, reasoned, action was of little use in persuading obdurate and reactionary governments to reform.The brutal treatment of these Manchester Blanketeers would be repeated two years later on a similar, if larger, demonstration with an even bloodier outcome (see below).

Across Europe throughout the eighteenth and nineteenth centuries we can see the repeated out-breaks of protest against both local grievances, and the outcome of national economic policies impacting on poorer sections of societies. Local protests, national campaigns, the more direct action of strikes, and very occasionally more revolutionary outbursts, were evidence of an underlying potential in cities, towns, and in the countryside, for a significant challenge to governments. With the grounds for grievance being: poverty, injustice, general oppression and the lived uncertainties that were common across industrializing Europe.

In the early part of the century London had one third of its population living in poverty, Dundee two thirds; a pattern of disadvantage to be seen in many other cities as they grew into industrialization. Even for those in reasonably well paid work the shadow of falling into poverty was always present; when the only support available beyond what the wider family might be able to offer was the workhouse, charity, or from criminal activity. What often triggered action was anger at these conditions combined with a perception of the opportunity for change. Or, on occasion, when such were the forces of authority ranged against a group that change was an impossibility, a protest was simply a kind of noble quixotic act arising from despair and a sense of dignity denied. It was in the activities involved in organizing for carrying out numerous acts of collective protests, agitation, and political campaigning that forged the ambitions and built the structures (as well as gaining the experience) of working class organizations that would have some incremental success from the middle to the end of the century. And more so in the twentieth, when an elite controlled form of democracy would offer the working class a certain amount of influence. But the same processes that saw a limited success (mainly some material improvement rather than much substantial political power) diluted most of the more radical aspirations (to do with universal brother and sister hood) that had infused early working class organizations. Perhaps the discourse had been radical whilst the motivation of most people involved was only for modest improvements in material circumstances, and who would condemn this type of resigned accommodation to systemically unjust systems, given the circumstances that then prevailed.

It terms of governance, it would be judiciously judged reform that would be deployed to manage the competing dynamics of class interests in nineteenth-century Britain. In the run up to the hard fought passage of the 1832 Reform Bill both Earl Grey (Whig leader who became PM in 1830 on a 'reform' ticket) and the Duke of Wellington (Leader of the opposition) were 'instinctively' adverse to the idea of democracy but Grey at least had the foresight to realize that some concessions were a necessary step to take if their class was to maintain its privileged position in the longer-term. Concessions required to manage the expectations of a growing 'middle class'..... a change in the composition of society due to the dramatic growth in clerical, supervisory, managerial and professional employment along with the less dramatic but still significant increase in the number of small and medium sized family owned businesses. A class that by the 1830s made up between 20-30% of the employed and a class that was becoming more aware of its own importance to the progress of industrialization and of its potential power to influence government. Representatives of this class soon came to run the provincial towns and the newly growing cities of the industrializing regions - they were self-aware, generally had a strong sense of self-importance, and would endeavour to determine the work-ethic and social norms that would characterize Victorian Britain. At the local level it would be more enlightened individuals from the municipal middle classes that would at least begin the drawn-out process of improving the slum conditions in the larger towns and growing cities. Progress was slowly made in providing sanitation, clean drinking water, waste collection, some controls on the very worst air polluters, building regulations, and often setting up charities that funded schools and hospitals along with arms-houses for the elderly poor. These leaders of local governance might have been somewhat patronizing, generally confirmed in a sense of self-importance, and in morality many were hypocrites, but they did at least foster a sense of civic pride in their communities. As Victoria's reign unfolded they came to represent the idealized body of the citizenry of Britain, a body certain of British international supremacy and also a body comfortable with the idea of progress.

Europe of the first half of the nineteenth century (up to the landmark year of 1848) saw some insurrectionary protests and outbursts of collective anger, mainly based in the countryside. In Britain the Captain Swing disturbances (1830s -agricultural workers) and the Luddites (1811-13 - textile workers) both focused on protests against unemployment and the introduction of machinery. The basis of a historical misunderstanding that reverberates down to today is with Luddism being simplistically associated with anti-technology, whereas a truer (more sensible) understanding shows that they were in fact opposed to the starvation of their families simply in the cause of increased profit for factory owners and shareholders![2] – An ineffective refusal to meekly accept the sacrifice of their wives, babies and children so that shareholders and owners could keep theirs in luxury. For Luddism it was weaving frames, and for the Swing disturbances the introduction of threshing machines. Across Britain there were numerous 'food riots'. Such protests were usually local and were mostly quite spontaneous outbursts of collective anger in reaction to a sense of immediate injustice.

Not surprisingly 'unlawful' action did take place, with machinery being destroyed and the homes of those viewed as bad employers being attacked: colliers, coal heavers, tailors, and weavers, were amongst the more militant groups of workers. Although the more studied Luddite actions did not take place until the early part of the nineteenth-century there were many cases of machine breaking earlier than this, with 1717, 1720, 1738, 1792, being active years. Actions met with often vicious repression rather than any practical attempts to understand of the plight of workers.

The government of Britain exercised its ability to pass repressive or restrictive legislation and its reactionary system of magistrates, special commissions, judges, local militias, Hussars, (and from 1820 London and from 1830s the rest of Britain.....police forces) enforced the laws; as well operating a system of spies, covert agents, and agent provocateurs. The Combinations Acts (of 1799 and 1800 – repealed in 1824-5) inhibited workers from organizing to plan any effective form of collective action. These Acts were intended to prevent combinations of both masters was well as workers if viewed as

---

[2] The translation of the weavers, self-referenced as being represented by the fictional 'Ned Ludd', into an irrational opposition to any form of technological development (as 'Luddites') clearly illustrates the way in which events can be grossly distorted by the pens of maliciously intended politicians and journalists and repeated by those too lazy to consider the historical truths behind the intentionally demeaning labels they glibly apply. The misrepresentation of groups of desperate men, having to witness their families being forced to starve in order to advance profitability for a small number of uncaring factory owners, is a distortion of justice as well as of historical truth. A distortion operating to serve a broader (anti-worker) narrative required by powerful elites, with the enduring mediation of 200 years of a compliant, disingenuous, press, producing some supposed truth of unreasonable opposition to technological innovation; indeed to progress itself.

possibly being obstructive to economic progress. But their enforcement focused on any attempt of the workers to organize while combinations of employers were pretty much left alone. Trade unionism, as an expression of collective organization, did slowly advanced in spite of the legislative restrictions, during the first quarter of the nineteenth century, especially in trades such as cordwainers, shipwrights, woolcombers, shoemakers, and tailors, and indeed most of the craft-groups based in the larger cities.

Attempts by workers to organize also had to confront a state system that included industrial spies, agent provocateurs, and compliant magistrates (such as Frampton, noted below), all given military support by a government well aware of the difficult living conditions of a significant proportion of its population. Active repression, backed by government legislation and if necessary military action, was the instinctive response to any attempt at serious social or industrial improvement for the urban and rural working classes. If any action looked to be effective (usually if gaining the support of middle-class spokespeople) then a strategy of grudging concession usually coated in the language of liberal generosity was adopted. This pressure for political reform and better conditions for the working classes in the face of intransigent but clever (obstructive and reluctant) ruling elites was a feature of the nineteenth century, first in Britain then across Europe, the US, and elsewhere, as a the industrial revolution spread, with a significant impact on economic and social structures.

From early on the democratic fault-line of private ownership of industry and asymmetrical power relations between owners of capital and the (propertyless) workers placed the economic dynamism of industrialization on a conflictual basis that has continued down to today.

With a repressive legal system and economic circumstances ranged against them, the mass of working people could do little but resentfully conform unless that is, their own local group came under specific attack. In these local cases we see generally futile railing against the reality of unequal power relationships. Those in control of 'capital' were favoured by government and government had the power of laws, traditional deference, the mass media of the time, as well as support from the more economically powerful sections of the community. It also had the means to prevent popular action – a compliant judiciary, a conservative established Church, militias, the dragons, political spies and the use of agent provocateurs.

William Pitt initiated a barrack-building programme that placed the military at convenient centres of possible popular uprisings; a well-known fact being that by 1808 there were more troops mobilized against the Luddites in the midlands and the north than under Wellington's command during the Peninsular War. Strikes were common by miners, and textiles workers, but the loss of vital income would have deterred many others who had genuine grievances from taking industrial action.

Throughout the period of 18th/19th century industrialization, we see a series of governments (in Britain and across industrializing Europe) introducing laws that were specifically intended to prevent the effective organization of labour whilst at the same time being prepared to let employers organize in pretty much any way they wished.

In the year 1834 six agricultural labourers from the Dorset village of Tolpuddle joined together in order to attempt to maintain their wages. They had tried to form the *'Friendly Society of Agricultural Labourers',* which would have resembled more a friendly society than a trade union as we now understand these....... to defend themselves and other agricultural workers from wage cuts. Their already low wage of 10 shillings per week had been reduced to 7 shillings, with the threat of a further reduction hanging over them. James Frampton, a local landowner and magistrate contacted Lord Melbourne, the then Home Secretary, about this modest action, who ordered the arrest and subsequent prosecution of the six workers.

As the Combination Acts had been repealed 1824/25 the six were prosecuted under the 1797 'Unlawful Oaths Act'; an Act specifically introduced following the naval mutinies at Spithead and the Nore. One of the six, George Lovelass, said during their trial: "My lord, if we had violated any law it was not done intentionally. We were uniting together to save ourselves, our wives and families from starvation." Lovelass later in his prison cell wrote down the poem 'The Gathering of the Unions' that ends with the powerful two line cri-de-coeur:

> 'We raise the watchword liberty
> We will, we will, we will be free'

These six men were found guilty by a jury made up mainly of farmers (backed by large landowners) of 'swearing an illegal oath' and

564

sentenced to transportation to a penal colony in Australia for a period of 7 years (the maximum possible sentence); in effect sentenced to conditions amounting to slavery. The plight of six desperately poor men merely trying to defend their families gained the sympathy of a significant proportion of the population and public outrage, with protest marches and a petition signed by 800,000, led to the Tolpuddle Martyrs (as they became known) being granted a pardon in 1836 - if conditional on future good behavior - and to their being brought home.

In line with the broad strategy of minor concessions to accompany more general repression, a series of Parliamentary Acts were enacted to alleviate the conditions in factories. An 1802 Act had banned children from night-working, limited them to a max of a 12 hour day, and ordered some very basic educational provision. Under a 1819 Act no child under 9 years old could be employed and set a limit of 16 hour working day for those up to 16 years of age. But there was no properly organized system of inspection, just a responsibility passed to some magistrates and clergy to 'visit' factories which were very often owned by their neighbours and social acquaintances. A 1844 Act set limits on working hours for women. Later in the century the main provisions of a series of subsequent Acts of 1847, 1850, and 1853, included the limiting of the working day to 10 hours for all workers, and a range of regulations on ventilation, sanitation, and generally safer working conditions. Although a system of inspection was by now established the number of inspectors was small and the large number of factories made compliance with the Acts pretty much a voluntary affair.

The 'Sweeps Act' of 1864 brought an end to the practice of sending small children up chimneys to suffer ill-health from the intensely sooty, stifling, atmosphere and injury or death from falling. There was a more humane sentiment beginning to permeate sections of the middle and upper classes, a sense that the poor and low-paid might be more than simply beasts of burden whose purpose was to work, reproduce, and obey. This more enlightened attitude was also perhaps stimulated by ideas of what the 'beasts' might do if pushed too far. These legislative improvements in working conditions were due partly to pressure from middle-class philanthropists, and from a few more enlightened factory owners (sensitive to the accusation of using 'slave' labour), and also to the ruling class's fear of mass insurrection, rather than from any benevolent motives of politicians and capitalist investors as a body.

In politics it would be a combination of progressive working and middle-class leaders that would organize the sustained campaign for reform that led to the 1832 Reform Act. An Act that reformed the 'rotten boroughs', introduced sixty-seven more parliamentary constituencies, extended the franchise to tenant farmers, more modest landowners, small shopkeepers, and to heads of householders paying more than £10 per year in rent. So, democratic rights for most of the middle-class but an Act that still left the bulk of the working population without the right to vote.

The 1832 Reform Bill was eventually past despite attempts by Tory peers to thwart its passage through parliament and in due course was signed into legislation by a King whose support was luke-warm at best. The Bill was modest, in that it set a property qualification for voters that only extended the franchise to include one in seven adult males; still leaving thirty-five parliamentary constituencies with less than 300 electors each. It was seen as a 'great betrayal' by many workers who had thought that they and the middle-class had been campaigning together, being united in a commitment to more substantial reform. The Bill offered some increase in political power to the rising class of industrialists but, by omission, denied this to their workers.

Following the Napoleonic wars (1815) the government decreased the overall tax on the rich as well as easing the system of payment of dividends (and yet were faced a national debt rising to a massive £848 million by the War's end), whilst heavily increasing taxes on basic goods such as soap. With the Corn Laws increasing the price of bread (to the benefit of larger landowners) impacting disproportionately on the poorer sections. The mass of the population faced increase taxes, a succession of poor harvests, and rising rural unemployment due to mechanization. Unemployment was further exacerbated by the addition to the workforce of 300,000 ex soldiers and sailors demobilized at the War's end. Nelson, Wellington, and some other senior officers, were showered with state-provided financial rewards and exuberant praise, whereas most of those in the ranks were simply cast aside - to become retrospective heroes in due course when the British state required a convenient trope for recruiting the masses to support future wars. A passionately told, flag-wrapped, drum and bugle sounding, narrative of British heroes of a series of bloody conflicts as somehow representing some sense of 'genetic' British bravery expressed from Agincourt through to the Napoleonic Wars, and to fuel the propaganda for recruitment for the Boer War, and even more so with WWI.

From the second quarter of the century a range of technological innovations, mechanization of production processes, increased market opportunities, developments in transport and communications, urbanization, growth of credit-based banking (wider use of paper money), and the solidification of social and economic classes[3] began to gain a momentum that was to see a patterning of new forms of human activities spreading throughout the world. Or rather more specifically industrializing versions of pre-existing patterns of civil life, related mainly to: speed of communication, manufacturing productivity, intensified trading links, and the deployment of power by elite groups.

In Britain, the essence of this patterning could be identified in factories producing a range of goods, now powered more by steam, located in cities or on sites of early factory-based manufacturing which had seen towns and then cities growing around them. Cities that themselves provided local markets for the diverse range of tradesmen that economic opportunity and technological innovation created. In terms of technological innovation, the second stage of industrialization (from about 1825 onwards) is considered to have been based on the introduction of the steam engine and its range of potential applications.

The use of heat to produce the energy for 'work' had been utilized in the propulsion of shot in firearms, and of projectiles fired from cannons, for some time in Europe before the eighteenth century. It was Otto von Guericke (1602-86) mayor of Magdeburg who, in a series of rather dramatic experiments, demonstrated the power inherent in a vacuum. Then in 1698, Thomas Slavery (165-1715 - improving on initial work by De Caus 1576-1626) was the first person recorded as designing and having built a working steam 'engine'. One based on two vessels, with each vessel in turn being heated to convert water into steam and, when the steam was expelled out of a cylinder it left behind a vacuum which then allowed the water to be drawn up (Nature, 'abhorring a vacuum'); a process applied to drawing up

---

[3] The 'interest groups' of Max Weber, or, for Marx class divisions based on any group's relationship to the means of production.

water from mineshafts. Slavery's patent application was titled 'The Miners Friend'. Although useful in clearing water from the bottom of mine-shafts, it was a rather dangerous machine being prone to explode and, owing to the way it operated it had to be sited near to the bottom of a shaft.

Denis Papin (1690) went from turning De Caus's early heat into mechanical energy process, to build a type of 'pressure cooker' before going on to design a machine based on the principle of using heat to produce motive power. But he was thwarted by the unwillingness of the Royal Society to provide financial support for its further development.

In the early eighteenth-century, Thomas Newcomen designed a steam pump that was able to more practically exploit the potential of steam power in a way that was also suitable for pumping water out of mineshafts. This was a much safer machine than Slavery's and could be located at the top of a shaft. It used steam to drive an engine with a piston but was somewhat inefficient as the cylinder had to be reheated following each stroke. Given that it was mainly used to pump water from mineshafts, there was usually plenty of fuel (coal) for the reheating in situ.

In 1768 James Watt, a Glasgow instrument maker, designed an engine that used a separate steam condenser to overcame the cooling problems and hence produced a more efficient engine (achieving a fourfold improvement in energy efficiency compared with Newcomen's engine), one that proved economically viable to use away from coal-mines.

Over the next decade Watt introduced a number of minor improvements including: smoother cylinder surfaces – automatic regulators – double-acting expansion - steam jacketing – transmission gears. Arriving at a sophisticated 'steam' engine that allowed the conversion of vertical motion of the engine into the rotary motion necessary to drive manufacturing machines; hence it was soon introduced in textile manufacturing.

Slavery and Newcomen were practical men, exploiting known techniques to solve practical problems, but with Watt we see a more scientific approach, theoretical principles of efficiency were considered and finer working parts used. Watt was aware of the discoveries made by Dr Joseph Black (1728-99) a Scottish Doctor who had shown that different substances have different capacities to retain heat, a measure expressed as 'specific heat', and that steam had a significant capacity to retain the latent heat of water, and also that this heat could be recovered when the steam condensed. To better exploit this, Watt was able to produce more accurate machinery by adopting machining equipment similar to that used by John Wilkinson to bore the barrels of high quality cannons. This technique gave Watt the accurately shaped cylinders that he was looking for. He also introduced a series of further innovations one of which - combining flywheel, throttle, and centrifugal governor - allowed the operation to continue at a steady speed, even with variable load rates. An early example of self-regulation via mechanical feedback.

Watt formed a commercial partnership with Mathew Boulton, a Birmingham-based manufacturer, establishing a connection that flourished and made Watt's efficient and relatively cheaply produced engine the foremost commercially available steam engine; of the approx 2,500 steam engines made before 1800 this partnership built about 800 (Floud and McCloskey sec. ed. 1994) and sold them throughout Britain and in France, Germany, and Russia.

From the expiry of Watt's patent in 1800 the opportunity was open for different types of steam engines to be developed. The most successful being that of the engineer Richard Trevithick's whose lighter and higher powered 'high-pressure' engine, competed successfully with Watts engine in transport (a precursor to the locomotive engine of George Stevenson) and for draining mines, if not in manufacturing.

The steam engine would provide the motive force for moving goods and people on the 'railways', and these in turn were a substantial element of the second phase of industrialization. Railways, along with canals, shared a common purpose as both were originally developed to serve the needs of coal-mining. The canals were built to convey coal from pithead to city for use, or from pithead to port for export. And it was initially wooden railed 'ways' along which the trucks of coal were trundled down tunnels leading from coal-face to lift-shaft and so to the surface.

The development from short distance wooden railways to the iron railroads that would thread their way across countries and continents was made possible when steam power could replace human and horse power. The necessary improvements in the use of stream engines had been developing in the late eighteenth and early nineteenth century in the form of improvements in pistons, boilers, and in the gearing systems that assisted in the efficient transfer of raw power into controlled motion.

Wooden rails had been used to haul truck-loads of coal during the sixteenth century then in the seventeenth cast iron sides were attached to the wooden rails so making them more durable and able to bear heavier loads. By 1767 the foundry of Adam Derby at Coalbrookdale was producing fully cast iron rails. At the end of the eighteenth-century, along with the steady expansion of coal-mining, the use of 'railed ways' had spread to many of the industrial areas of Britain. What seems to have been the first public railway (horse drawn - the 'Surrey Iron Railway') was built to allow freight to be hauled from Wandsworth to Croydon in south London in 1803. It delivered and collected its loads, at a speed up to about 3 mph, to factories along the 8½ mile stretch of railway. A number of engineers had the insight to conceive the potential of applying the improving efficiency of stream to power the forward motion required to carry loads over distance. The locomotive (basically a mobile steam engine) had been incrementally improved and by 1785 William Murdoch had designed and had built a locomotive capable of 8 mph. The company he worked for, Mathew Bolton's of Birmingham (Watts later partner), declined to develop this further.

The potential of the steam engine, beyond the mines, factories, and railways, was realized in its use initially to power river and coastal shipping but, by as early as 1819, a steam-powered ship had 'paddled' its way across the Atlantic, and by the century's end steam powered ships would be criss-crossing all of the world's oceans. Steam was also being tried out to power vehicles along the improved road surfaces (tarmac from 1830, asphalt from 1835), with steam-driven coaches conveying fare-paying passengers on inner-city routes around London and Glasgow.

By 1801 there had been 19 parliamentary acts sanctioning the construction of extended railways. Men such as Richard Trevithick (1804) and George Stevenson (1814) had further improved the efficiency of steam engines (especially Trevithick) and built various types of steam driven locomotives for use in hauling coal if over fairly modest distances. In 1822 Stevenson's Hetton to Sunderland railway was the first to only use steam power, if aided at times by gravity. It was the competition set by the promoters of the Liverpool-Manchester railway which involved a prize for the best design of locomotive, a prize won in 1829 by Stevenson's Rocket that effectively settled the fixed engine or locomotive engine issue.

A number of private railway companies were formed via limited liability status, a mechanism that would serve as a model of business ownership for many of the pioneering industries that would develop during the nineteenth and twentieth centuries. This legal status allowed for a spread of general risk but also for any overall loss (or liability) to be limited. But it was a financial mechanism that further separated the workers from the owners of a company, usually by a body of managers whose own income and job security depended on their ability to maximize profits for effectively anonymous shareholders.

By 1840 the main cities and ports of Britain were connected by a railway network covering 5,000 miles. Twenty years later this would be 16,000, by when many of the larger towns would be connected to a transport system that not only transported people, manufactured goods, raw materials and agricultural produce, but also allowed faster communication of personal, national and international news and ideas; both the letter-post and newspapers soon came to use rail transport for distribution. From about the 1830s other countries soon realized the value of this form of transport and before the century's end railways would criss-cross most of Europe and both North and South America. By 1900 Britain and Europe together would have 220,000 miles of railways linking the capitals and most of the other large cities (in an iron-wired network); there would be 70,000 locomotives in operation across the world. As early as the 1850s trains had been able to attain speeds of 60 miles per hour and were hauling millions of tons of freight and carrying millions of passengers each year.

In some European countries the advantage of the railways was speed rather than cost compared to the use of waterways and both canals and rivers such as the Danube, Elbe, Rhine, and Rhone, would continue to carry a substantial proportion of manufactured goods and raw materials until well into the twentieth century.

The operating of the railways required a substantial supporting infrastructure. There was the construction of passenger carriages, goods trucks, and of the locomotives. Then the means to efficiently maintain moving parts including oiling, timely servicing and necessary repair work, along with those engaged in providing the basic support for the motive power; bringing coals and water to the locomotives. There was the fixed assets of stations, complex signaling systems, and the massive task of constructing the 'permanent ways' themselves, along which the trains would run – the bridges spanning rivers and valleys, carrying the 'iron road' over and under roadways, and along the tunnels that burrowed through hillsides. Building a railway system involved a monumental task of design, and construction using pick, shovel, heavy hammer, wheelbarrow, and later on dynamite.

There was also the human element of operating the system, including the people who ran the trains: the drivers, footplate men, guards, signalmen, those who carefully planned the precise timetables, those in the vast workforce who manned the stations; porters, ticket staff, cleaners, station masters and a host of administrative workers and managers in what were generally fairly efficient hierarchical organizations. Taken as a whole the railways of the world are potent examples of human ingenuity harnessing collective effort allied to a sense of pride in the job and in the social value of the enterprise.

The engineering industry itself advanced as the process of continuous improvement in engine, carriage, and signaling design, in machine-made parts and also in the improvement in the quality of iron, and later the more durable steel. The advent of the railway gave a significant economic impetus in speeding up the transport of manufactured goods and agricultural products and in being able to move masses of people at relatively low cost. Railways were also an important part of the formation of trades unions; by 1844 the French railway union had 44,000 members – a relatively small proportion of the total workforce but an indication of how organized industrialized labour was co-operating to defend or even improve their working conditions.

In Britain, the year prior to the opening of the line between Manchester and London saw 500 passengers a day were being carried on the stage-coaches but 1200 per day were carried on trains during the first year of the line's operation, reducing the journey time between these two cities by half. By 1875 18 European countries, 15 countries in the Americas, 5 in Asia, and 4 in Africa, had railways, most with over 1000 kms of track.

One renowned railway builder, Thomas Brassy, employed eighty thousand men building railways on five continents (E.Hobsbawm, 1975). Geographic and geological features such as rivers, mountains, hard rocks, and swampy plains, became little more than challenges to the engineers who designed the permanent ways and the surveyors, managers and workers (foremen and labourers) who built them. The economic benefits of railways were soon realized by powerful groups of investors and in turn by governments, and over the rest of the nineteenth century railways (along with steam-powered shipping) became a defining feature of globalizing industrialization.

Across Europe, wind would continue to be an important source of power throughout the nineteenth-century for shipping as well as driving mills for both corn grinding and for land drainage. Whilst on roads, canals, and the land, the use of horses and oxen endured into the twentieth-century. But taking the varied forms of transport, and the overall increased activity into account, the historical observer would also gain a strong sense of accelerated change and continuous movement. There was a massive increase in the tonnage of goods, often over much longer (intercontinental) distances - with people travelling to find work but increasingly also for leisure and to visit family and friends separated as, for many, traditional localized family ties were uprooted and spread far and wide to serve the needs of industrialization.

In manufacturing industry, ever greater accuracy was being applied to the design and construction of machines; with an engineering industry being created to build, service, and repair machinery. Steam-power had allowed factories to be located in places with easier access to canals, ports, and within reach of towns and cities whose larger populations were able to provide a steady flow of workers as well as increasing the demand for manufactured products.

The success of British industrialization was celebrated in the Great Exhibition of 1851 - housed in a magnificent 'Crystal Palace', sited within the expansive greenery of Hyde Park, London, and enhanced by the glittering spray produced by the array of fountains arranged around it. The visitors (of which there were over 6 million) past through colourful halls showing machinery from across the industrializing world. Halls containing looms, lathes, drills and other machinery used to manufacture the goods: textiles, toys, cash registers, armaments, typewriters, clocks, and a myriad of other items that were exported around the world. It was a showcase of Britain's industrial eminence; a glorious (and glorified) illustration of how far it had advanced and hinting at a future of continuous technology driven 'progress'. Taken as a whole, the Exhibition sent a message of Britain's control of a vast global trading empire and of its leading place in the relentless advance of industrial innovation. Similar festivals of national 'success' took place elsewhere: Paris in 1855 and 1867, London again in 1862, Vienna 1873, Philadelphia 1876.

The Industrial Revolution provided an economic framework within which practical technology and the theoretical sciences would develop and it was increasingly commercial factors that gave incentive and so direction to research. From the wider perspective of this book we see an expansion of empirical information becoming available to humankind – allowing the human imagination and practical ingenuity to realize the productive potential inherent in the natural world; albeit with the massive and relentless despoliation of it.

In addition, the idea of 'progress' became embedded into the collective civil psyche. The idea of questioning this by posing such questions as: 'Progress for what?' 'To what benefit for humans?' 'At what cost to humans?' 'At what cost to the environment?' and similar, more considered implications, of industrial progress - seem rarely to have surfaced into serious public debate. Although Adam Smith had himself considered moral responsibility (see his book 'The Theory of Moral Sentiments', 1759), and on the occasions when such questions did rise into the public consciousness they were effectively treated more with the debating equivalent of shuffled feet and polite coughs of embarrassment rather with much serious consideration. Commercially, progress was 'more money, more goods, more speed, and evermore consumption'. For the economically less powerful their social circumstances too often had to adjust to this very limited conception of progress.

The mechanization of agriculture continued throughout the nineteenth-century with such innovations as: improved iron plough 1814, mechanical reaper 1830, threshing machine 1837, clay drainage pipes 1840, cable plough 1850, steam plough 1858.

But even with all the investment and consequent increased productivity, mainland British farming continued to be unable to meet the growing demand for food of the increasing population (10m in 1800, 20m 1851, 37m by 1901). The answer was to supplement production in mainland Britain with the importation of food, in particular from British controlled Ireland, especially from the large Irish estates owned by mostly absentee English landlords. By 1800 Ireland was the source of about 16% of British food but this was at a cost to many of the Irish peasantry. During this period a range of foodstuffs including butter, corn, and meat, was being shipped across the Irish Sea to Britain while the majority of the Irish peasantry were having to exist on potatoes as the staple element of generally meagre diets. An economic policy that would have serious implications for the poorest people (40% of the population were reliant on the potato crop) of Ireland when, between 1845-1853, potato blight ravaged the crop. Even during years when the potato crop failed the exportation of vast amounts of food (mainly grain) to Britain continued, whilst many of the Irish starved or, if they had the means, migrated across the Atlantic.

In factories, the introduction of gas lighting – developed by William Murdock overseer at the Birmingham factory of Matthew Bolton – meant that production could continue throughout the hours of darkness. The machinery itself became more reliable and more durable as wood structures were replaced by iron, which in turn was to give way to steel as a preferred material. Accurate machine tooling methods made the tools which made the parts for the improving machines. The precision engineering industry that world-wide would provide the means of ever faster, more reliable, machines undertaking increasingly intricate mechanical operations has been described for Britain as an industry that: '……lies at the very foundation of mechanization, and without accuracy and uniformity, modern mechanical technology could not exist' (Floud and McCloskey, eds. 1991)

Thousands of engineers, whose backgrounds were usually in instrument or tool-making, were employed in designing and making 'Milling machines, planing machines, screw-cutting lathes, boring and sawing machines, and accurate measuring machines…' (Floud and McCloskey, 1991)

In the growing cities of the industrial heartlands, financially astute speculators invested in the construction of housing units - vast numbers of closely packed rows of cheaply built terraced housing, with waste disposal for most being via open sewers in the muddy lanes running between rows, with some more 'fortunate' tenants having access to usually grossly overused privies. Given the low level of most incomes, houses in many areas of these cities soon become occupied by more than a single family and densely packed localities that developed were noted so starkly by novelists such as Charles Dickens and Mrs Gaskell, and by social critics such as Fredrick Engels, who noted that: '……*we must admit that 350,000 working people of Manchester and its environs live, almost all of them, in wretched, damp, filthy cottages, that the streets which surround them are usually in the most miserable and filthy condition, laid out without the slightest reference to ventilation, solely to the profit secured by the contractor'* – (Engels,1845, p75).

But even within these miserable living conditions, with all the many stresses of humanity packed closely together, we see the working and lower middle class continuing to organize themselves. In 1833 the Rochdale Pioneers established the first co-operative society. Such is the enduring brilliance of cooperates that it has survived the corrosive blast of the neoliberal ideology of the late twentieth century and is continuing to flourish in various forms across the world in the twenty-first.

Following the disappointment of the 1832 Reform Act the main working class focus for political reform became the Chartist movement. A movement that saw the coming together of a number of different groups campaigning, initially for political change and later for economic improvement. Chartism could be seen to have begun as an organization in 1836 with the founding - by William Lovett, James Watson and Henry Hetherington - of the 'London Working Men's Association'. Other groups with a wide working class base included the East London Democratic Association (founded 1837) and the Birmingham Political Union (re-launched following a period of inactivity due in part to disillusionment with the 1832 Reform Bill). The wider movement came to publish a number of newspapers, most notably the 'Northern Star' established by Feargus O'Conner at Leeds in 1837 and with the Great Northern Union, also being founded in Leeds. Chartism was a movement that mobilized mass action of the kind not seen previously in Britain (or indeed Europe). Mass meetings, along with thousands undertaking military-type training in preparation for what was felt by some would be a popular uprising, and for strike action; the first general strike being the one of 1842.

Initially Chartism was not a socialist movement but rather one campaigning principally for democratic change based on the widening of the franchise. It drew support from many of the middle and lower-middle classes, a factor that was to become a strongly moderating influence within the movement. Attempts to form even closer links to middle-class campaigners would, from the early 1850s, split Chartism. The most substantial division was between a more moderate group, led by Fergus O'Conner, seeking close ties to the middle class radicals, and a more socialist group, led by George Julian

Harney, which came to take control of the National Charter Association.

Chartism was generally well-organized with clear aims being set out in the 'Charter' of 1837 launched in London in 1838 (William Lovett was the principle author), along with the setting up of a national petition to demand:

'The right of voting for Members of Parliament by every male from twenty-one years of age and of sound mind; Annual Elections; Vote by Ballot; no property qualifications for members of Parliament; Payment for members; and a division of the kingdom into Electoral Districts; giving to each district a proportionate number of Representatives according to the numbers of electors' (David Jones 'Chartism and the Chartists' Allen lane, London 1975). During 1838 Chartist rallies were held in Glasgow, Birmingham, and Manchester, as well as London.

The primary focus of Chartism was parliamentary reform and opposition to the work-house system, whereas improved wages and working conditions were the main focus of the emerging trades unions. John Doherty (leader of the textile workers) saw the potential of trade unions combining and he was instrumental in establishing (Dec. 1829) the 'Grand General Union of the Operative Spinners of Great Britain and Ireland' and in 1830 the more ambitious 'National Association for the Protection of Labour', an association based on a local structure of trade clubs affiliated to a central body located in Manchester. Doherty even had the foresight to imagine the creation of a political 'Labour Party'; an achievement that was to take 70 years to become a reality.

The 'National Union of the Working Classes' (NUWC), founded 1831, was 'the birth-place of Chartism'. But the debates around Chartism also clarified differences in class interests, and its development can be seen in the 'Poor Man's Guardian' a publication sympathetic to the interests of working people. The NUWC was preceded by the formation in 1829 of the 'British Union for the Diffusion of Knowledge' a more radical organization where, according to Max Beer: '....the tone of the speeches was full of a fighting spirit and revolutionary verve. The wage system was denounced as obnoxious and execrable, whilst labour and co-operation were regarded as the pillars of civilization'. (Beer, 1919, p235)

The NUWC proved fairly popular and early on increased its

membership – William Lovett and Henry Hetherington drew up a constitution very similar to the French 'Rights of Man' of 1789, with aims including: '...to avail itself of every opportunity in the progress of society, for securing for every working man the full value of his labour and....' - 'To protect working men against the tyranny of masters and manufacturers by all just means as circumstances may determine' - '......an effectual reform in the House of the British parliament' - 'To prepare petitions, addresses and remonstrations, to the Crown and both Houses of Parliament' - '.........the National Union feeling assured that the submission of the people to misrule and oppression arises from the absence of sound moral and political knowledge amongst the mass of the community'. (Beer, 1919, page 236)

Again here, as with Chartism, we see the mixture of fairly radical demands with peaceful means being advocated to pursue their attainment; as well as an underlying belief in the value of knowledge. There were ongoing tensions between the lower middle and the working classes on how best to co-operate in order to widen the franchise and improve working and living conditions. With most of the middle class (along with many skilled workers) being prepared to accept relatively minor concessions made to improve their conditions; a pattern that continued throughout the century and was an aspect of the progressive political reconfigurations that would be an on-going feature of industrializing countries across Europe and the USA. Yes, the working class in Britain did eventually gain politically and economically but, on balance, I think we would conclude that this was achieved by their mobilizing - through TUs and political parties. Initially the Liberal Party and then, in 1900, the Labour Coordinating Committee out of which came the formation of their own Labour Party. Albeit aided by small groups of middle class intellectuals who were prominent in the vanguard of the working class movement for change.

Later in the century Chartist groups came together for social as well as political activity, organizing: dances, tea parties, poetry readings, discussions and lectures on a range of non political subjects, and even Sunday schools. They often owned the buildings in which they met, with many of these maintaining a library and offering education classes in subjects such as general literacy, grammar, history, science, and logic applied to argument.

Women, even given the difficulties (childcare responsibilities, general social expectations, and significant male resistance), also became involved with Chartism. There were about 80 female Political Unions and Chartist Associations established between 1837 and 1844.

Similar attempts to organize the masses were a feature throughout industrializing Europe and the USA., and later on for South America. Such was the momentum toward effective organization, along with the high level of economic injustice and social oppression that, as Ponting notes: '.....perhaps the only surprising aspect of European history in the 19th century is that there was no major social revolution.' (op cit, 2001, p669)

The working class movement in Britain generally used 'constitutional' methods to advance their aims, including the use of petitions and the calling of conventions out of which a modest 'address' would be agreed; with both the petitions and the addresses being offered to the Queen and Parliament. In 1839 a petition calling for the acceptance of the Charter was rejected by Parliament; it was signed by possibly as many as 1,250,000 people following over 500 meetings of local groups. In 1842 another petition signed by 3,000,000 people (inspired by an earlier French example which had gained 5m signatures - it took 16 men to carry the 'peoples petition' into the House of Commons) was also rejected by an obdurate Parliament. National conventions were held in 1839, 1842, 1848, 1851, 1858, but routinely, these expressions of dissatisfaction from mostly disenfranchised citizens were effectively ignored. A final petition, submitted in 1848, following a mass meeting in Kennington, London, was signed by 2 million workers; although substantially more than this number was claimed. An interesting 'foot-note' re. Britain's social history being that one of the organizers of this mid nineteenth-century demonstration was William Cuffay, a black man who was later arrested and put on trial for '......levying war against the Queen' - he was sentenced to transportation.

These activities did serve to foster a certain unity amongst Chartist groups across Britain, but in relation to outcomes, had little direct political impact; if they were an important aspect of a gathering 'force' which would lead to a series of incremental reforms continuing up to 1918, when a measure of women's suffrage for those aged 30 years and over was introduced (an age lowered to 21 in 1928).

Chartist leaders were aware of the power of the printed word, and indeed a number were themselves journalists or booksellers. From the late eighteenth-century the radical press had been struggling with the high cost of production and the additional tax levied on newspapers. The latter made even worse by a significant increase following the introduction, in 1819, of the 'Gag Acts' - a series of six Acts of Parliament intended to suppress anti-government activities. One of these increased the tax on newspapers, so that any paper costing less than 6 pence per copy (so all of the radical newspapers and news-sheets) was subject to a 4 pence tax. The six Acts were a reaction by Parliament to an increasing number of riots, demonstrations, and strikes, by workers seeking economic improvement and/or parliamentary reform.

An upsurge in working class and lower middle class radicalism was infamously marked early in the century by the Peterloo Massacre, when, on the order of magistrates, troops rode into a demonstrators gathered in St. Peter's Field in Manchester to call for parliamentary reform. By the end of the day estimates are of between 10-20 demonstrators having been killed and 500 (including 100 women) injured. One of the main speakers on the day was Richard Carlile, a London-based journalist who returned to London to cover the massacre in his paper 'Sherwin's Political Register'. This action incited the government to order the paper's Fleet Street office to be raided and all of Carlile's stock of newspapers and pamphlets were confiscated. Carlile's response was to change the name of the paper to 'The Register', with the first edition covering the Massacre in even more gory detail. Carlile was arrested and put on trial charged with blasphemy and seditious libel - he was found guilty, sentenced to three years imprisonment, and fined the then massive sum of £1,500. Such was his tenacity that he continued to publish 'The Register' from prison and such became his popular notoriety that the paper was soon outselling most of the pro-government newspapers, including the 'Times'.

By the middle of the century Chartism benefited from technical advances in the printing industry, the removal in 1855 of stamp duty (Manchester Guardian reduced from 6 to 2 pence) and the increasing spread of literacy. Chartism had the support of about 50 newspapers; most of which were regional but a few having a national circulation. The 'Northern Star' was selling 50,000 copies per week at one point – and other popular Chartist-friendly publications included: 'Northern Liberator', 'English Chartist Liberator' plus a Scottish counterpart, the cheaper (1/2 penny) 'English Chartist Circular', 'The

Charter', 'Political Register', 'Regenerator', London Mercury', London Dispatch' - along with a veritable industry of pamphlet and the longer tract production. By the 1850s a radical press was fairly booming in Britain.

Sections of the Christian Church also made the connection between the moral teachings of their religion, the suffering of many sections of the working class, and the dehumanizing aspects of industrialization and urban-based living; especially so with the nonconformist and independent churches (such as: Quakers, Methodists, Congregationalists, Baptists, and the Salvation Army). There were many Chartist prayers including: 'From the loom, the factory, and the mine, good Lord deliver us'.

The Chartists focus had been primarily on electoral reform, with the expectation that economic and social reform would follow, but from the 1830s a strong strand of more radical socialism became prominent. Robert Owen (1771-1858) son of a tradesman, was one of the first to assert that the problems of poverty and exploitation, two defining features of early industrialization, could be overcome and that the productive potential of machinery could be harnessed to abolish the evils of poverty – Owen was himself a factory owner but the factory he set up in New Lanark offered relatively enlightened conditions for workers. Again, as with Chartism, we see the recognition of the importance of self-education and in most of the larger cities in Britain there were socialist 'schools' teaching political awareness, basic education, history, and the sciences.

By mid century education had become a central strand of Chartism, Socialism, and Trades Unionism; many of the leaders were self-taught, gaining hard-won education due to their determination to learn more about economics, history, and more radical political ideas. A number of Chartist leaders had faith in the potential of working class people to empower themselves through education and more general self-improvements. The book that did most to promote this type of knowledge Chartism was 'Chartism: A New Organization for the People', by William Lovett and John Collins, completed while they were both imprisoned during 1839. It argued for a comprehensive education system based in modern buildings, offering an enlightened science-based curriculum. In 1841 a National Association was established to promote the idea of universal education.

These and other campaigners highlighted the fact that wealth accrued to individuals not on the basis of the social value of the work undertaken but rather owing to the economic structures which had been progressively constructed to protect and advance the interests of those that owned property and invested capital, not in the interest of the masses who only owned and invested their labour. This strand of Chartism advocated a more gradualist approach to reform and as such was subject to vociferous criticism of more radical Chartist leaders such as Fergus O'Conner who saw knowledge Chartism as being a distraction from the central cause and was set on his ambition of a 'People's Parliament'.

Owen, along with William Benbow and others, campaigned for the formation of a more general trades union (a union of the unions). He considered trades unionism to be a vehicle for both improving the pay and conditions in the workplace and also a means of progressing more fundamental political and economic changes. The formation of national trades unions was not really practical until the 1830s with the spread of railways making communication between regions quicker and cheaper – even then, local and trade loyalties remained strong and in some ways inhibited national organization.- The Grand National Consolidated Trades Union founded in 1834 was, partly at least, a response to the 1832 Reform Act and its disappointing outcome making many (sections of) working-class people aware that their own interests differed from those of the middle and upper middle-class beside whom they had together campaigned for electoral reform (even after the act only one in six working men had the vote). Up until the middle of the nineteenth century most union members were skilled craftsmen whose monopoly of economically valuable skills gave them some power in the face of the pervasive antipathy of employers (and of Tory, and more so Whig, governments). If revolutionary fever had cooled somewhat, at least in the last two decades of the century the leading industrializing nations of Europe did see an upsurge in working class national organizations claiming allegiance to some level of socialist aspirations; national organizations, but ones acknowledging the international dimension of socialist possibility.

Chartism effectively came to an end in 1858 with the founding of the moderate 'Political Reform League', a move absorbing much of its motivational spirit. Some Chartists regarded this as a 'sell-out' and established the more radical 'National Political Union for the Obtainment of the Peoples Charter'. But the popular head of steam had now left the Chartist movement, even if its ideas were retained in the consciousness of many individuals and so fed into the aims of the on-going working class political movement. The 1870s saw a period of general economic improvements, apart from two short more depressed years of 1857 and 1866, contributing to a dampening of the spirt of radicalism..

I have been concentrating on a more detailed consideration of the industrialization of Britain. On the exploitative and oppressive structures of the capitalist mode of these developments and on attempts by the mass of workers on organizing to resist these. I felt that this would enable readers to gain a closer sense of the human dynamism of protest and of the more often obdurate response from the ruling elites; if, in effect, aided by the inherent conservatism of the bourgeoisie elements in both the middle and working classes. But, accepting variations related to historical circumstances and local conditions, these were processes that can been seen operating across much of Europe and parts of the Americas during this time. And we can see the tendency towards conflict within the process of capitalist industrialization becoming manifest during the fateful year of 1848.

The European political world was thrown into something of a turmoil during the revolutionary upheavals that took place in 1848 and after. The economic ground conditions for working and middle-class dissatisfaction (these were each different, the former related more to living conditions and satisfaction of basic needs the latter to political power) were present, but the ideas inherited from various sources gave this an idealistic focus as well as a practical direction. Ideas such as those taken from the writings of Tom Paine, the French revolutions of 1789 and 1830 with their 'equality fraternity, and liberty', and more immediately by such works as Marx and Engel's Communist Manifesto, along with the many left-wing/radical newspapers and pamphlets circulating at the time.

It is clearly misleading to separate industrial relations (master and worker relationship) from governance, not least because the latter sets the legislative framework for the former. The period covering the middle decades of the nineteenth century was in Britain characterized by the increasing political power of the middle classes but also the awareness of the ruling class that the views of the masses (or at least its more skilled and organized sections) did need to be at considered and, to some extent, responded too.

Across industrializing mainland Europe the masses were generally less patient than most of their British counterparts and direct insurrectionary actions were common - peaking in the 1848 attempts at revolution and culminating in the Paris Commune of 1871 from when change in Western Europe would be sought primarily through constitutional means - even if revolution remained an ongoing threat; more imagined as a danger by the upper classes and optimistically hoped for by the small radical vanguard of the workers. The embers of revolution would at least continue to glow, especially in Germany, and were later to flare up to engulf dictatorial aristocracy during the Russian revolution (early 20th century).

Although most of the 1840s in France was a period of relative political stability (with a government led by the monarchist Francois Guizot) there was a upsurge of socialist writing, providing ideas and inspiration for the workers: Bathelemy-Prosper, Charles Fourier, August Blanque, Pierre Joseph Proudhon, Louis Blanc, Etienne Cabet and others. These mainly advocated change by peaceful measures but they were clearly promoting the idea of a socialist future for France. Due mainly to the King's intransigence, supported by his chief minister Guizot, middle-class attempts to widen the franchise further were unsuccessful. As the end of the 1840s approached a series of sexual scandals involving the King's ministers became public knowledge and, of more relevance to subsequent events, an economic crisis was developing in a context that included a series of poor harvests.

Early on in 1848 sporadic clashes took place between police and workers and disorder spread rapidly, escalating in places into rioting. As an initial attempt to placate the 'mob' the King (Louis Philippe) dismissed Guizot but on the evening of the 23rd Feb. forty demonstrators were shot down by soldiers. On the morning of 24th, with his Palace besieged by angry workers, the King abdicated and fled to England.

This rapid success rather took the 'revolutionaries' by surprise and the provisional government that was in effect forced upon the Chamber of Deputies still reflected a range of political views if it soon co-opted four of the radical leaders, including the socialist Louis Blanc. A republic was declared and the new government introduced a number of measures intended more to appease popular opinion, and to gain some time to reorganize, than out of real conviction. A right-to-work order saw the new government taking on the responsibility to provide work for the unemployed, the franchise was increased from 200,000 to 9 million voters (almost universal 'manhood' suffrage), and the setting up of the Luxemburg Commission (with Louis Blanc as its President) to consider a range of social reforms.

This was a time when Paris was a veritable hotbed of left-wing political activity, with dozens of political clubs and newspapers (as well as pamphlets) reflecting a range of radical political views. The election of April 1848 was to show that the rest of the country was more 'conservative' in its politics. This election to the Assembly saw only 60 radical/socialist members elected against 500 bourgeois republicans and 300 constitutional monarchists – the success of the bourgeois presaged the political direction to be taken by France in the longer term. In the short term (Feb—March 1848) Alexis de Tocqueville, reflecting on the mood on the streets of Paris, wrote of the '...uniquely and exclusively popular character of the recent revolution...' Chris Harmon (1999, p335) writes of even this mild revolution being '.....a bomb beneath every throne in Europe'.

The new Assembly being composed mainly of representatives of the middle-classes, the financiers, capitalist manufacturers, merchants, civil servants, and professions, saw their short-term interests being in unity with their traditional opponents, the aristocrats. As being united against the workers who appeared to threaten their property. At the Assembly's first meeting in May the Luxemburg Commission was abolished, the government reneged on the commitment to provide work for the unemployed, and the call of the workers for a 'living wage' was ignored. Parisian workers took to the barricades, but the combined power of a state hungry to revenge the humiliation it had suffered and intent on deterring any future attempt at serious civil disobedience stood against them. Forty thousand of the insurgents, including many women, faced 125,000 well armed combatants under the command of General Cavigna. The outcome of one week's fighting was 1,500 workers dead and thousands more arrested. So, even a fairly weak spark of social reform had been extinguished by force of arms wielded on behalf of a government composed of members of a mostly republican middle-class and a disparate collection of monarchists. The two groups united perhaps by their fear of the workers or, if we judge them more generously, by a fear of what they felt would be complete social breakdown.

With its workers dispirited, if not completely cowed, their

organizations weakened by the loss of leaders and with its capitalist industrialists, merchants, and financiers in the ascendancy, France was now in a position to accelerate its own version of the industrial revolution. But the action of the Parisian workers had served as an example of resistance to people in other European countries. To the extent that it surely contributed to the wave of revolutionary insurrection that rippled across much of the continent.

In Vienna, 2,000 insurrectionists were killed, and in southern Germany a revolutionary army was formed (advised by Fredrick Engels) and uprisings also took place in Sicily, Milan, Venice, and Prague. Even if for most of those involved their anger was directed at those institutions of the ruling elite (Church and State) who they felt to be the cause of their more immediate practical troubles (increasing shortages of food, unemployment, and poverty), the ideological inspiration was for many drawn from the revolutionary ideas of the first French revolution. But the liberal middle-class leadership of the continental uprisings were mostly only seeking to gain some level of political power, and their erstwhile bourgeoisie supporters were not prepared to take an active part in progressing more revolutionary change. These looked more to the British model – pragmatic, respectful of private property, and of laws passed by a succession of bourgeoisie parliaments (most retaining an aristocratic spine) operating mainly to support the interests of the upper middle-classes and with at least some general commitment to the idea of 'free trade'. With constitutional arrangements modeled on some form of traditional structures (presidential republicanism or with a constitutional monarchy) but with a system of checks and balances that in general protected the interests of those such as: industrialists, shareholders, merchants, prosperous tradesmen, financiers, substantial farmers, large landowners, and of the Church.

Most of Europe's ruling elites made concessions: grudgingly extending suffrage, allowing some freedom of the press, bringing an end to the more obvious aristocratic privileges and to some more onerous feudal obligations; which did little to improve the circumstances of most peasants and industrial workers. In effect the, in terms of numbers, predominately working class (and peasant) actions enabled the middle classes to gain in power; a middle class that, whilst wanting to end the excessive privileges of the aristocracies, did not want to put their own property and position at risk.

To some extent the outcome of the political upheavals of 1848, and the counter revolutions that were victorious by the summer of 1849, was to modernize the social and political structures of a number of European nations and so enable them to accelerate their own capitalist-based industrialization. This was especially apparent in Germany where, in the decades from 1850, investment rose markedly and the production of coal, iron, and steel, increased dramatically; clear markers of a Germany being propelled forward towards its industrial transformation.

By 1870 most European countries were advancing along the road of industrial development. Sections of city-based industrial workers had organized themselves into trades unions and, when the political conditions were amenable, into political parties. But there were large areas - all of Portugal, most of Spain, southern Italy, and more rural regions of Germany, France, Scandinavia, Russia and middle Europe - seemingly unaffected by these developments. Feudalism and serfdom might have officially ended[4] but the tradition of large landowners exploiting and oppressing agricultural labourers – squeezing as much surplus out of their labours as possible – continued. Indeed, for many had become worse as, along with the ending of serfdom, so too did much sense of obligation on the part of the landowners to protect their workers.

I am sure that to a greater or lesser extent there were individuals in the middle and upper classes, appalled by the conditions of many working people and their families, who were motivated by a sense of social justice. I think we can be equally sure that many others in each group were fearful that if concessions were not to be made then the spectre of revolution that hovered over Europe would settle and spread.

If confirmation of these fears were needed it would be provided by the revolutionary spirit of the people of Paris who would rise again if in an original way in 1871, at a time when half of its population lived in or on the edge of destitution. The City itself was at the time being besieged by the Prussian army, with many of the workers and the poorer sections of the community having to eat rats and dogs in order to survive. The French government, led by Alodphe Thiers, had relocated to Versailles having negotiated a humiliating peace with the

---

[4] Serfdom ended: France 1793, Spain 1803, Prussia mostly by 1811 completely by 1848, Austria 1848, Hungry 1853, Russia 1861 and for all of Europe by 1864.

Prussians, embodied in the 'Treaty of Frankfurt'.

The people of a Paris, in the grip of winter, angry at what was felt as the Government's sell-out to the Prussians, held out for five months. It was the working people, labourers, semi-skilled, artisans, and their families who united to defend their city. A city alive with insurrectionary potential – dissatisfaction with the government and with their lot, and memories of 1789 and 1848 - revolutionary news-sheets and radical clubs flourished. Much of the National Guard was sympathetic to the workers and when Thiers ordered troops to take control of the National Guard's canons sited in Montmartre, the government troops were repelled in what was a bloody if minor skirmish With two generals taken prisoner by the mob being summarily executed. This action was the flame that ignited a general uprising and, as violence spread across the city, Thiers withdrew his troops and remaining civil servants to Versailles to join the government. Nearly 80,000, mainly members of the Parisian elites, fled the City.

The workers took control and straight away organized an election to a Central Committee. The committee that was duly formed was made up of a disparate band of socialists, left-wing republicans, and anarchists; it adopted the title of the 'Commune'. Then followed a remarkable, if very short, period of municipal self-government......by the people and for the people. Workers in metal working, jewelry-making, as well as tailors, shoe-making, typographers, printers, and other trades, took over workshops that had been abandoned by their owners. Those elected to the Commune were paid only the average wage of a skilled worker, pensions were paid to widows, children were provided with free education, and a series of measures were introduced to improve working conditions, and of more symbolic effect...... throughout the City monuments to militarism were taken down. The Commune endeavoured to inspire workers across France with a vision of a country based on autonomous but inter-linked communes controlled by, and in the interests of, the working classes. Few rallied to the idea but some attempts were made to emulate the Parisians in cities such as Lyons, Marseilles, and Narbonne. The social experiment that was the Commune was only to last for a couple of months; time during which the French Government had been re-grouping and organizing its own forces with a view to crushing the Commune. When ready, and with the passive collusion of the Prussians, it moved against the Parisian workers. In seven days of bloody street fighting the Communards were defeated; with the final act of resistance taking place in the Pere-Lanchaise Cemetery.

Then followed a terrible retribution, with 1900 Communards being shot in two days and government troops roaming through the City streets killing those they even only suspected - by their style of clothes or their demeanor - of being sympathetic to the Commune. Even the right-wing London Times described the revengeful orgy of violence against men, women, and children, as 'sickening'.

The number of government troops and supporters killed was 1,100, with about one hundred hostages (including the Arch-Bishop of Paris) being killed by the Communards. Estimates of the number of Parisian workers killed vary from 20,000-30,000; 43,000 were taken prisoner with about 5,000 of these being sent to a penal colonies.

Although the Commune was a short-lived social experiment of socialism in practice that had little immediate political impact, it was to have a symbolism that would permeate the mythology of socialism and communism for the following 100 years (influencing leaders of the Russian and Chinese revolutions, and some of the left wing combatants in the Spanish Civil War). Karl Marx saw the Commune as being '...the first great proletarian uprising'. But in the immediate decades following the terrible defeat of the Commune at the hands of a vengeful state a message had been sent to organized working people across the continent that revolutionary action would be costly, and that perhaps more could be gained from industry-specific industrial action.

A number of political parties were formed with ideological bases ranging from extreme left to extreme right but with most more or less committed to 'capitalism' i.e. unlimited accumulation of wealth, protection of private property, and private ownership of industry; as well as low taxes and a hegemonic form of 'free' market economics. But others connected to socialism and some to syndicalism, anarchism, and communism, constituted an enduring core of left-wing/radical ideologies. In countries such as Germany, France, Italy, Britain (and indeed in the US and Canada) it would be centre-left versions of political ideology that would prevail. Workers whose leaders believed in a planning and regulatory role for central government, supported attempts to redistribute wealth by progressive personal income and inheritance tax systems, and campaigned for various social welfare measures.

Western European Governments, in addition to providing the

infrastructure that enabled manufacturing and marketing to operate, became involved in providing necessary, if minimal, services such as education, housing, the legal system, health-care, and protecting the health/safety of workers. Even these relatively modest ambitions were only to be achieved to more or less some extent later on during the twentieth century. As a crucial factor in relation to how the world was to develop, the working class movement in Europe as in the Americas, Australia, Japan, China, never seriously progressed an international agenda and instead remained for the most part nationalist in focus - a focus that not only increasingly facilitated global capitalist hegemony (e.g. chasing low-wage settings – under the guise of 'relative advantage') but made war between them, with workers killing workers, acceptable for many.

In Britain, a Trades Union Congress of unions met annually from 1868. But even by 1900 only 191 of a possible 1,323 unions were affiliated, even accepting that these 191 did include over half of all trades union members. Post 1850s saw a period of 'new model unionism' - a time of the consolidation and creation of craft unions such as 'Amalgamated Society of Engineers' 1851, the 'Amalgamated Society of Carpenters and Joiners' 1860 and the 'Amalgamated Society of Railway Servants' 1872. Unions with a strategy of advance by negotiation rather than direct confrontation, and with an emphasis on maintaining pay and status differentials between skilled, semi-skilled and un-skilled groups. This aspect of inter-working class tension was taken advantage of by ruling elites who alternated between flattering the skilled (aspirational) workers whilst whenever possible facilitating the introduction of technological innovations that would undermine their skills and so also their negotiating power in the work-place. The propensity of working class groups in Britain, and other industrializing countries, to focus on promoting their own partial interests - if necessary to the detriment of other groups (especially so if the other group was in another country) has regularly and significantly undermined attempts at working class unity, to the benefit of traditional ruling elites. This has fatally disabled trades union effectiveness within and between industrializing countries: an enduring propensity to seek short-term self-interest that has inhibited working class solidarity.

'Workers of the World Unite' was a telling phrase but one more idealistic in the light of in-nation worker disunity and also the (easily fostered) nationalistic tendencies of workers across the world. Both aspects of the working class 'mindset' that the elite groups learnt how to skillfully manipulate and exploit, much to their own longer-term advantage.

In Britain, trade union membership in 1850 at about 100,000 rose to over a million by 1874 by which time the movement had its own newspaper, 'The Beehive'. Women were generally unwelcome in the larger TUs so they established their own groups including: 'Women's Protective and Provident League' 1874, 'National Federation of Women Workers' 1906, the 'Co-operative Women's Guild' 1883 (with a focus on suffrage) and also the 'Women's Trades Union League' 1888, with its central demand of women and men to have equal pay for equal work.

The 1884 Reform Act (formally the 'Representation of the People Act') extended reforms initially introduced in the 1867 Reform Act by extending the franchise for the urban boroughs, to the countryside.[5] And the 1885 'Redistribution of Seats Act' brought a degree of fairness to the larger towns and cities in relation to the population size of constituencies. This series of reforms did result in the widening of the franchise to include the higher paid workers (the skilled 'aristocracy' of the working class), and soon both Liberal and Tory politicians realized the need to gain the support of these newly franchised (higher paid) workers, but they still left all women and about 40% of adult males without the vote.

Two Royal Commissions of Enquiry were set up to consider trades unionism in 1867 and 1884. Outcomes from the deliberation of these commissions included the recognition of trade unions as legal entities and so entitled to legal protection (from 1871), and a number of industrial relations measures (including the 10 hr day and the right to sue employers for breach of contract). These, along with the wider franchise, enhanced the position of 'respectable' TUs, even if this did not mean any significant increase in actual constitutional political power.

By the 1870s trades unionism was firmly established in Britain, if still with a fairly narrowly based membership. But then followed an

---

[5] The novel 'Felix Holt' first pub. 1866 is a perceptive account of the times and of the experiences of a working class English 'radical' written by George Eliot – and its later added Appendix A 'Address to Working Men by Felix Holt' is Eliot's well-presented outline of what the character Felix would have said in response to the 1867 Reform Bill.

end to the years of relative economic prosperity - due in large part to competition from Germany and USA. - and an increase in the number of industrial disputes. The years up to 1914 were to see a rapid growth in trades unions (with a widening of the membership to include previously unorganized groups - 750,000 members in 1888 grew to 6,500,000 by 1918) and also a period of industrial militancy. With famous strikes such as the women of the 'Bryant and Mays' factory in 1888 (1400 women - low pay, 14 hour working days, liable to fines, and seriously harmful working conditions) and the 'Gas-workers and Dockers' strike of 1889 (in demand of an 8-hr day). The rate of militancy intensified, with a wave of strikes between 1910-1914. The print-workers strike in 1911, led indirectly to the setting up of a workers newspaper 'The Daily Herald'; initially a strike bulletin established by the TUC. George Lansbury, later the leader of the Labour Party, became its editor in 1912.

Certain, more radically minded, members of the middle-class (including Sidney and Beatrice Webb, Annie Besant, H.G. Wells, Emmeline Pankhurst, Ramsay MacDonald) came together in 1884 to form the Fabian Society, a body determined to outline theoretical ideas supporting reform backed up by the use of accurate statistical information. This was initially an intellectual pressure group advocating a gradualist, reformist, rather than revolutionary, approach to gaining a socialist society (amongst other changes calling for abolition of hereditary peerages, a national health-care system, and a minimum wage), within the Liberal Party. But it steadily moved towards the more avowedly working class political movement including the Labour Representative Committee. This Committee was formed by an alliance of groups - the Fabians, the Independent Labour Party, the Scottish Labour Party, and the Social Democratic Federation. In order to advance the collection and analysis of statistical information generated by research, some of these middle-class fairly moderate radicals - led by Beatrice Webb, George Bernard Shaw and Graham Wallas - founded the London School of Economics and Political Science (LSE) in 1895. A public research university committed to '…..the betterment of society.'

A number of trades unions set up libraries offering a book lending service, and some offered education classes. Trades such as potters and glass-makers had their own journals, containing quite polished articles on a range of subjects. Many in these groups recognized that education was both an activity that is in itself enriching and one that is also empowering; the power to argue on an equal basis with your political opponents and the power to negotiate from a more equal knowledge base with employers.

For the most part the trades unions were focused on more immediate improvement of the wages and working conditions of their members but ideas of revolutionary possibility still circulated and in places were a central aspect of the discourse of working class aspirations. But for the average working person these aspirations would have seemed unobtainable (and perhaps even to be feared as potentially disruptive); a merely utopian possibility shimmering on some distant horizon. A utopianism that did inspire the early ambitions of the Labour Party most obviously embodied in two parts of Clause IV of a Constitution adopted in 1918 that expressed the Party's socialist ideology/principles.

'4. To secure for the workers by hand or by brain the full fruits of their industry and the most equitable distribution thereof that may be possible upon the basis of the common ownership of the means of production, distribution, and exchange, and the best obtainable system of popular administration and control of each industry or service.

5. Generally to promote the political, social and economic emancipation of the people, and more particularly of those who depend directly upon their own exertions by hand or by brain for the means of life.'

Clause four would be significantly amended in 1995 by the 'New Labour Party' led by the neoliberal inclined Tony Blair and his political allies, presumably embarrassed by its aspirations.

The 1860s saw an upsurge of trades union organization across Europe, as well as more spontaneous incidents of labour dissatisfaction which included numerous strike actions in Germany, Russia, France, Belgium, Austria, northern Italy; a wave of industrial action that reached Britain by early 1871; disturbing the political complacency that had settled there. The instinct of the ruling elites was to stand firm but most had the sense to see that their survival would lay in concessions; the instincts of most industrialists was to call on governments to crush the organization of workers but again a certain pragmatism suggested that at least some labour grievances might need to be addressed; and a more conciliatory approach was suggested by groups of liberal intellectuals (such as the Society for Social Policy in Germany and the Liberal Party in Britain). Trade unionism in its more conservative forms increasingly became an accepted, if hardy ever welcomed by those in power, aspect of industrialization. And yet, having what has been in effect a constitutional 'safety valve' (deflection mechanism) for mass dissatisfaction probably provided the means to avoid revolution in 19th and 20th century Britain, and in industrializing Western Europe.

Eric Hobsbawm noted that: 'As capital and bourgeois society triumphed [1870s], the prospects of alternatives to it receded, in spite of the emergence of popular politics and labour movements'. (Hobsbawm, 1975, p187)

Consideration of the nineteenth-century working-class struggle against the living and working conditions in which they found themselves, illustrates the range of methods that were argued for. From seeking moderate incremental progress to calling for decisive revolutionary action, using methods ranging from restrained petitioning to advocating violent insurrection. The differences in aims and methods was another contributory factor to dissipating the potential political strength of the working class. Arguably, it might be that the ruling elites gave way gradually to the demands just because the calls for revolution scared them so much that they took the view that tactical concessions of a relatively minor kind made to the moderates was a price worth paying in order to retain their overall advantages and privileges.

The British economy grew as a result of rising wages, with surplus income for many creating an internal 'demand' for goods that in turn generated further economic growth. A generator of growth substantially increased by demand for manufactured goods from the US, Europe, and especially the extensive British Empire with its 'protected' markets.

British working class organizations did to some extent reach out to those pursuing similar aims in their own lands but despite a number of attempts the insularity of nationhood has obstructed the formation of any effective international organization of workers. Britain in the mid-late nineteenth century was a refuge for émigrés including Major Beniowski (Polish ELDA), Robert le Blond (Frenchman of NCA), Pierre-Joseph Proudhon (exiled French libertarian socialist), and of course Karl Marx. Going the other way, British representatives of trades unions and chartists groups, along with some left-wing journalists, travelled abroad seeking to maintain or establish some European wide links of more radical solidarity. The NUWC, with a broadly socialist leadership, was also strongly in favour of international links and was of considerable influence as an organization representing the working classes and had been at the centre of the increase in agitation and protests at the time when the 1832 Reform Bill was being progressed.

One group, the 'Fraternal Democrats' was an organization having been active in the mid 1840s brought together a fairly loose grouping of Chartists, trade unionists, socialists, social democrats and others on the left, along with representatives of a range of émigré groups. It drew up a 'Declaration of Principles'.

A pithily eloquent condemnation of inequality and call for the recognition of the unity of the human 'race', that continued:

'In accordance with the above declaration of the brotherhood [sic] of the human race, we renounce, repudiate and condemn all political hereditary inequalities and distinctions of 'caste'; consequently we regard kings, aristocracies, and classes monopolizing political privileges in virtue of their possession of property, as usurpers and violators of the principle of human brotherhood. Governments elected by and responsible to, the entire people is our political creed.

We declare that the earth with all its natural productions is the common property of all; we therefore denounce all infractions of this evidently just and natural law, as robbery and usurpation. We declare that the present state of society, which permits idlers and schemers to monopolise the fruits of the earth and the productions of industry, and compels the working classes to labour for inadequate rewards, and even condemns them to social slavery, destitution and degradation, is essentially unjust.

.........We condemn the 'National' hatreds which have hitherto divided mankind as foolish and wicked; foolish because no one can decide for himself the country he will be born in; and wicked, as proved by the feuds and bloody wars that have desolated the earth, in consequence of these national vanities.........this society repudiates the term 'Foreigner' no matter by whom or too whom applied. Our moral creed is to receive our fellow men [sic], without regard to country, as members of one family, the human race; and citizens of one great commonwealth – the world.'

Accepting the then taken for granted misogynistic orientation of this declaration, it does express sentiments that are of value today in relation to 'evil' in the world. It was within this political and social context that Marx wrote his deterministic analysis of the capitalist economic system ('Das Kapital' 1st Vol. pub. 1867 – last Vol. finally completed by Engels in 1894) as an outcome of historical development and as a temporary phase of human relationships - predicted by Marx to come to an end due to its own internal 'contradictions' and to give way to a socialist phase. A more enduring idea of Marx still considered as relevant, was the link between the stage of a country's economic development and the forms of social institutions such as the education system, laws, principle form of religion, and indeed a society's dominant ideas, that this gave rise to.

Although Das Capital contains the body of evidence supporting an extended argument for Marx's theory, his much shorter book 'The Communist Manifesto' (more a declarative pamphlet) is much more accessible and has certainly had a far greater impact on individual activists – as well as on members of the ruling elites who felt threatened by its powerful language and the signs of a nascent internationalization of working-class unity. It was written for a mass working class audience with a specific purpose of adding direction to revolutionary fervor and offering a focus for more general political dissatisfaction. Written by an intellectually confident young man, aided by an even younger Engels, their text was produced in some haste within the context of the excitement of a working class Europe seemingly gripped with the ferment of the late 1840s revolutionary milieu – the sense of a Europe on the edge of transformation, with a number of countries seemingly ripe for revolutionary change. The first print run of a thousand (German text) was undertaken in 1848.

Marx was involved in the organization of a conference of the Communist League in 1847 attended by delegates sent by (European-wide) groups sympathetic to the ideas of Marxism, plus some interested Chartists – bringing the number of attendees to about 100. On his return to Brussels, following a generally successful conference at which he agreed to write a declaration of principles for the Communist League, Marx considered three documents: a copy of the 'Communist Journal', an at times impassioned declaration on socialism written to two London sympathizers, and a draft outline by Engels of the 'Principles of Communism'. Engel's suggested that any new declaration should be called a 'manifesto'.

The final 'Manifesto of the Communist Party' was a 12,000 word class-based blast of criticism of the capitalist system, with a prediction that the proletarian class would in effect 'inherit' the earth and ending with the famous phrase: 'Let the ruling classes tremble at a Communistic revolution. The proletarians have nothing to lose but their chains. They have a world to win. WORKING MEN OF ALL COUNTRIES UNITE!'

The manifesto begins with the phrase 'A spectre is haunting Europe – the spectre of Communism', with the first section starting with the sentence 'The history of all hitherto existing society is the history of class struggle' - a beginning that clearly flags up the tone of the extended cri-de-coeur that follows.

European uprisings in 1848 were mostly undertaken by the more economically disadvantaged ('Lumpenproletariat' class), not the more skilled and semi-skilled working class as predicted by Marx. But probably the most significant aspect of social change that Marx under-rated was the ability of 'capitalism' – or rather the political systems that supported this – to 'flex', and so able to balance the threat of force and punishment with incremental social reforms; and more subtlety, to associate socialism with uncertainty, with being unrealistic, being in opposition to 'human nature', of out of touch idealism, etc. If the 'flex' of many European states was limited to minor reforms at times accompanied by harsh military repression.

The First International of the 'International Working Men's Association' – although its actual support amongst working people, and even the larger TUs, was low - did cause some concern amongst European governments aware that the grounds for general dissatisfaction were present across the continent and that the potential for revolution was obvious in the conditions of working class life. Governments became nervous about working class organization and some recognized that the International might be the catalyst to develop into the organizational structure that could provide the impetus and the means to advance revolutionary change.

Not untypically for left-wing political groups, the International was prone to internal dissent and broke up over the issue of support for the Paris Commune of 1871 (Marx was keen to support this uprising). In addition, Marx himself does seem to have been rather precious about his place as the intellectual head of the revolutionary communist/socialist movement and was generally antagonistic towards would-be sympathizers, such as Ferdinand Lassalle and Mikhail Bukunin, who were less respectful of the master than was

Engels.

Marx's ideas had little direct impact on political change in the nineteenth-century but, if somewhat differently interpreted, they did feed into the ideas contributing towards some dramatic changes that took place in Russia, East Germany GDR, China, Yugoslavia, Poland, Czechoslovakia, Albania, Vietnam, Cambodia, and Cuba, in the following one. Even if the lived experience of the working classes in most of these countries suggests that it would be difficult to convincingly argue that workers did 'win a world' or even 'lose their chains'. The material conditions of many did progressively improve but the relative inequalities and the essential power structures continued to consistently favour elite groups, even if the personnel of these changed. Marxism would also influence some of the first leaders of 1950s post-colonial African countries.

As the countries of Europe progressed their own individual paths of industrial development they also saw the emergence of independent working-class movements. From the middle of the century most of these generally had socialist orientations, at least theoretically. Germany had the German Social Democratic Party established in 1875, made an illegal party by the anti-socialist legislation introduced by the authoritarian German government in1878. It would serve as a model for European social democratic parties as it moved from being a revolutionary to a reformist party under the leadership of Ferdinand Bebel and William Liebkneckt. It had won 12 Reichstag seats in the 1877 election before being banned and then was legalized again 1890 from when it grew rapidly and, by 1912, it would have the highest number of Reichstag seats of any single party. In France, the more revolutionary French Workers Party (POF) established in 1879 by Jules Guesde, shared a similar Marxist ideology. As did the Spanish Socialist Workers Party (PSOE) 1879, the Czech Peoples Socialists, Polish Social Party (although these last two also had strong nationalist leanings), and the more radical 'Social Democratic Party of the Kingdom of Poland ('.....and Lithuania' added later). One outstanding individual arguing for political action in the early twentieth century was the intelligent and brave Rosa Luxemburg; a women incisive in analysis and determinedly clear on how to progress revolutionary change, active until her murder by those who feared what she might achieve with her determination, intelligence, and bravery.

As the nineteenth-century drew to an end trades unions gained strength in terms of membership levels and with this some industrial power as well as political influence. In Britain groups such as the Fabian Society and the Co-operative movement had some influence on the direction to be taken to pursue working class political ambitions. In 1889 the Fabian Society published a collection of essays edited by G.B.Shaw, the 'Fabian Essays in Socialism', which laid down markers for the future. James Kier Hardie (self-educated socialist from a poor working class background in Scotland) was instrumental in forming the Scottish Labour Party (1888) then, on moving to England, won a parliamentary seat in east London as an Independent Labour candidate. In 1893 he was one of the prime movers of the formation of the Independent Labour Party (ILP) (1893), and in 1900 the ILP formed an alliance with trades unions to become the Labour Representation Committee (noted above), that in turn became the Labour Party.

In the 1906 general election the Labour Party gained 29 members of parliament, constitutionally signally its arrival. For the rest of the twentieth century this party was to enjoy significant political influence, even if socialist principles were more for idealistic gloss than ever enacted when the Labour Party was in government; it was essentially a party of reformed capitalism. Even the seemingly radical 1945-51 Labour Government, elected on a tide of populist socialist expectation, would not be prepared to significantly challenge the dense layers of social and economic advantages of the 'establishment'. But it was at least to show the state taking a direct role in introducing measures that they expected to improve the conditions (health, housing, poverty, education, employment) for the population of the UK and in this sense important – but it represented Social Democracy rather than Democratic Socialism. The success of the British Labour Party at the 1906 election had been a significant step in the separation of the radical working class movements of socialism and communism (with their revolutionary ambitions) and the gradualist approach to achieving social democracy that would be taken by a Labour Party drawing leadership mainly from the middle-class and support from mostly conservative TUs.

A distinguishing feature of European industrial development had been a significant expansion of the 'middle class'. Meant here in a broad way, reflecting various combinations of: a level of income, a family's social status, and their patterns of consumption as distinguishable from similarly identified collective groupings of the working class and the upper class. A middle class made up in part by increasing numbers of people living on relative modest sums of invested income, taking advantage of bonds issued to finance government debt as well as publically issued shares in the increasing number of publicly quoted limited liability companies. In addition this class, with a collective awareness of its growing importance, was the outcome of the growth in occupational divisions: lawyer, doctors, managers, superior tradesman, engineers, shop-keepers, clergymen, and a profusion of clerks and administrators working in both public and private organizations. A body composed of individuals able to enjoy the benefits of having incomes that allowed the basic means of subsistence ('needs') to be fairly easily supported, so leaving a significant disposable residue that could be used to fund their 'wants'. Wants that included: more stylish clothing, ornate furniture, soft furnishing, colourful ornamental pottery, the latest mechanical kitchen and scullery equipment, for some even servants, and for many having pianos around which the family gathered in the comfortable front parlours of the substantial houses which graced the residential streets and squares and of the expanding suburbs of cities across Europe and North America.

In Britain rows of bay windowed 'villas' housing families taking a certain kind of pride in accoutrements heralding their social status and fashionably bourgeoisie taste. A burgeoning market in more ephemeral goods such as printed magazines, books, postcards, the paraphernalia of writing materials with which families, friends and businesses communicated with each other via the expanding postal service (began in 1840s). Certain newspapers such as The London Times (1785), The Daily Telegraph (1855), and The Daily Mail (1896) sought to reflect, and to some extent inform, the political interests and at least the 'public' moral outlook of this rising class. The main fears of the middle-classes was of the potential for insurrectionary, and even revolutionary, disturbance by the working masses, or of themselves having the misfortune to 'fall' into this class.

Intellectually, there was a liberal element in the middle-class that would have a significant influence in the social and political (if less so on economic) development of Britain. Into this eclectic intellectual mix went the political writings of James Stuart Mill and his son John, David Hartley, David Hume, David Hartley, Thomas Carlyle, John Ruskin - poetry by William Wordsworth and Robert Browning - novels by Anthony Trollope, Charles Dickens, William Thackeray,

Charlotte Bronte, George Eliot and Mrs. Gaskell and more general books such as Lecky's 'History of Rationalism' (1865), Buckle's 'History of Civilization', and the landmark 'Dictionary of National Biography' (1890s) that was, according to G.M.Trevelyan (1944): '.....the best record of a nation's past that any civilization has produced'.

If improvements in the living and working conditions as well as opportunities for most working class women were quite limited, at least the lives of many middle-class women were improving; from a position pretty much of tight if hypocritical patriarchal moral restraint and contrived economic dependence. Women's colleges were founded in Oxford and Cambridge; significant as much in terms of the symbolic recognition that women had the ability to succeed at the highest academic level than in relation to the number able to access the opportunity. The two parliamentary acts 'The Married Women's Property Acts' of 1882 and 1893 meant that a women's property would no longer become that of her husband on marriage and also that she could retain any personal income earned or gifted to her during a marriage. Books such as John Stuart Mill's 'Subjection of Women' (1869) argued the case for free women in a free society and for individual rights. Many women braved provincial social approbation and took to sporting activities such as tennis, golf, hill-walking, angling, and to the roads on bicycles. A relatively few women's clubs and debating societies were formed. But most professions (including medicine and law) remained closed to women and birth control continued as a subject for hushed discussion. In 1877 Charles Bradlaugh and Mrs Annie Besant were prosecuted for publishing a pamphlet on birth control.

Writers such as the Bronte sisters (the 'Bells') and Mary Ann Evans ('George Eliot') had to assume male pen-names in order to get published. But perhaps the most significant barrier to individual freedom and opportunity for women was the sheer weight of normative patriarchy - taken for granted if not actively supported by many women - and the narrow gendered expectations that pervaded most aspects of life in Britain, and indeed all industrializing countries in the nineteenth-century.

If some women made modest gains in access to education the vast majority were denied much beyond a basic (primary) level and socially all were expected to be modest in behaviour and quietly obedient to males. But apart from the contribution they made to reproducing the next generation many were also, by the second half of the century, making a significant contribution in areas such as light manufacturing, food processing, agriculture, domestic service, shop-work, and in the burgeoning sex industry. A range of normative and political pressures meant that women were in general effectively excluded from public life. The bourgeoisie image of ideal womanhood, illustrated in the family photographs prominently displayed on the mantle-shelves of even quite modest middle-class suburban villas, was of a modestly dressed married lady (matron) seated with a brood of healthy-looking children ranged around her full skirts, the youngest in her ample lap, as she gazes appreciatively up at her provider husband. But it was a marriage that she would be 'chained' too. Divorce was a mark of shame and usually resulted in social exclusion; being illegal in most European countries and against normative values in all of them

Small groups of women campaigned for the right to higher education and for access to the professions; and, of more importance for the longer-term, began to come together and organize. In 1858 Barbara Leigh Bodichon led a group of women who founded 'The English Women's Journal', which publicized women's issues, such as the promotion of women's education, and the campaign for women's property rights. These last were granted to British women in an Act of Parliament passed in1870. In France the 'Society for the Amelioration of the Conditions of Women' est. 1875 (becoming the 'League for Women's rights in 1882) argued for women's rights as did the 'German Women's Association' 1865 in Germany, which also promoted women's education and job opportunities. In the US, the 'International Council of Women' campaigned for women's civil rights.

As the end of the century approached, a number of women's groups in the industrializing countries campaigned for women's suffrage. In Britain Millicent Fawcett led the way in her leadership of 'The National Union of Women Suffrage Societies' (the 'suffragists'). This group advocated change via peaceful and legal means, unlike the 'Women's Social and political Union' (the 'suffragettes') that undertook considerably more militant direct action. The women's movement for political representation was given an international dimension with, in 1904, the formation of the 'International Women's Suffrage Alliance'.

But it was mostly middle-class women that engaged in these

campaigning activities and who would be best placed to benefit from reform. The lives of the mass of working class women were characterized by resigned acceptance of the denial of opportunities impacting (and in an experiential sense taken for granted as their 'lot' by most women) from early childhood into old age. Lives marked for most by relentless toil, social repression, and lack of the civil rights that most civil societies would today take for granted. Women and their movements, whilst supported by some individual males, had to confront the oppressive patriarchal economic, political, and social structures, along with the general intransigence of most men determined to retain their dominance. Perversely, they also had to face hostility from some women from all social classes.

Middle-class males generally had high moral expectations of their wives and female children and for most of these there was a relatively good standard of living. Family life was constructed assuming more traditional stereotypical images of women-hood which were created and idealized in newspapers, books and magazines. The values of which were broadcast from the pulpit at the Sunday services, whilst from the political lectern speeches were made railing against declining moral standards. The personally unambitious middle-class women, content with her useful but subordinate position and fortunate enough to enjoy a reasonable household income, could no doubt live a happy life, with aspirations focused on home and children. But life for most working class women during the nineteenth-century was often a struggle – working for a low wage in unhealthy factory conditions, keep a home together, and having to bear children with the dangers to health and life that continued to characterized this experience. The human spirit (by this I mean a type of transcendental humanness that can infuse individuals with a determination to endure) is a powerful force that can carry people though the most difficult of times – the day to day struggle against adverse circumstances sustained by brief days in the warmth of the sun, a humorous exchange with a neighbour, the occasional celebration, the glimpses of a child at play or a baby asleep. No doubt for some, a caring husband, and perhaps some even if only limited progress in economic conditions experienced or perhaps hoped for. But poverty, unemployment, domestic violence, ill-health, and child mortality were the brooding shadows that played over most of their lives.

By the end of the century the involvement of government in many aspects of civil life had become an assumed fact. In Britain (continuing as a model for the economic, political, and social processes of industrialization), there was the Local Government Act of 1888 which established County Councils, then a few years later Urban and District Councils. A network of municipal institutions responsible for a range of community level support services including sanitation (sewerage disposal and bathhouses), libraries, education, street lighting, waste disposal, building regulations and planning, and in the twentieth century the provision of housing. Cities such as Manchester, Birmingham, Liverpool, and Leeds, 'came of age', exemplified in a time of municipal pride that constructed the substantial town halls, oversaw the setting of parks and sports-fields, commissioning of statues, and building of a range of civic offices and utility buildings such as, libraries, schools, colleges, that were felt to reflect the high-water mark of Britain's 'success' in the world. But it was a pride that in general ignored the appalling slum housing conditions of many working people and of the basic needs of the poorest.

Mechanized transport and the early stage of what has become a food 'industry' are closely linked as, in the nineteenth-century, the benefits of mechanization and a more scientific approach to the production and preservation of foodstuffs developed. But as with the exploitation of technological possibilities and scientific ideas in most early industries the stimulus to develop was in demand. In the case of food a significant increase in demand caused principally by a rising middle-class with the sufficient surplus income to be able to purchase a more varied diet as well as a more general need to feed the increasing mass of people living in cities. The initial stimulus of home grown demand especially in Britain, Germany, and the US, encouraged the development of food processing and preservation techniques which in turn allowed trade in food over long distances. Older preservation techniques such as pickling, smoking, drying, salting, and the use of natural ice (and of underground 'cold stores') could now be added too with the significant improvement in preservation of meat and fish by refrigeration and in the canning of these, as well as of fruit and vegetables. The first demonstration of artificial refrigeration was given by the Scotsman William Cullen (Glasgow University) in 1748. But mechanized refrigeration as a practical invention began with James Harrison, an Australian, who in 1850 made an ice-making machine; a machine that was improved upon by a Frenchman, Ferdinand Carre. By 1870 refrigerated railway wagons could be made and from 1877 ships with refrigerated storage capacity were crossing the Atlantic carrying beef from Argentina. By the end of the century ice-making machines and refrigerators became available to the domestic market.

Refrigeration, canning, a much improved understanding of bacterial action on foodstuffs (Louis Pasteur), and innovations in how to avoid deterioration of food whilst in transit, brought far-flung areas of the world into the global food market; if most of this was produced in the interests of the industrialized nations. Local, or even national, markets would now have less influence in setting food prices and in determining its availability. Vast profits could be made from agriculture in frontier territories with the foundations for corporate agribusiness - companies such as United Fruit, Cargill, and Del Monte – being laid about this time. Indigenous peoples and virgin forests would be cleared to make way for the types of practices characterizing the new industrial-type agriculture.

The state-sponsored 'theft', of common land by various types of enclosure - including the enclosure of prairie grasslands in US, South America, and Australia - and the improvement in drainage in lowland and marshy areas, made more land available to landowners (increasingly investors as absent landlords living far from the land they owned) who were coming to see their land more as a capital asset to be fully exploited rather than as yes, a source of business income, but one with a focus on some community responsibilities. In Britain fencing and hedging had been used to enclose fields that were still relatively modest in size. But on the vast open lands of the Americas and Australia, effective control of livestock required the invention of 'barbed' wire to transform uneconomic if unfenced into highly profitable enclosed land.

In most of Europe food production had been improving from the seventeenth-century as techniques of soil improvement, crop rotation, and animal husbandry pioneered in the Low-countries spread; benefiting further from a general more scientific approach being introduced during the nineteenth-century. There was more knowledge about the growing of crops beneficial to fertility; including those such as peas, beans and clover which were able to fix nitrogen in the soil. Root crops were grown specifically as animal fodder, increasing the size and contributing to the overall improvement of the health of farmed animals. Improved systems of drainage were introduced, with wind-driven pumps drawing water from low lying areas to drain away in rivers and canals. Progressively, in line with a developing chemical industry, there was the introduction of artificial fertilizers with nitrogen, potash, and phosphates, making the most significant contribution to increased productivity.

More was becoming known about bacterial life in the soils and of animal diseases and their possible treatments. The approach taken to agricultural improvement was geographically piecemeal, with some parts of the developing world still retaining eighteenth century practices well into the nineteenth. The uneven introduction of agricultural improvements was reflected in the take up of mechanical inventions. The mechanized reaper was available from 1830 (by 1880 Germany had 20,000 and by 1914 300,000), the threshing machine from 1815[6], and stronger iron ploughs from at least as early as 1814. Jethro Wood's cast-iron 'moldboard' plough, with the innovation of replaceable parts, provided a means of opening up heavy soils that had previously only been of use to the farmer for the grazing of stock.

Mechanized agriculture benefited from an accumulation of small improvements in design, and in quality of materials used in construction. It was the US, driven by the stimulus of market demand, the challenge of different terrains, and a relatively small agricultural work-force, that led to the rapid take-up of agricultural machinery.

The more obvious feature of industrialization in the final quarter of the nineteenth century was the extent to which these changes were spreading across the world. By the 1890s the US had overtaken Britain in terms of share of world manufacturing output, as would Germany early in the twentieth century.

On the expansive continents of America and Australia, lands that had provided the sustenance for indigenous peoples were swallowed up as the mechanized plough trundled and clanked its way across virgin landscapes and barbed wire fences trailed over hill and across valley; the means deployed to provide profit as the primary return and to produce food as but the means to achieve this. The American Great Plains, romanticized as the 'Wild West' became according to Eric Hobsbawn '...essentially a cattle economy' (Hobsbawn, 1975) with tens of thousands of cattle, increasing to hundreds of thousands after the Civil War, pouring into the stockyards of Chicago each year from 1865.

---

[6] Significantly improved by Hiram Pitts 1837 in US – producing a machine that could undertake the equivalent amount of work that could be done by 120 men.

In the final quarter of the century the links between science and food production increased further, especially in the area of food processing. Science informed the means of improving the storage and preservation of traditional products, and also of developing a range of new processed foodstuffs where added value could mean additional profit. An example of the interlinking of science and food production being illustrated by the career of J. von Liebig, a research scientist in organic chemistry who's book 'Chemistry and its Applications to Agriculture and Physiology' published in 1846, was one of the earliest to categorize foodstuffs into carbohydrates, fats, and proteins; and identified the essential involvement of air-borne carbon dioxide in the first two and of nitrogen (in the soil) with the last. He (von Liebig) also formed a company which produced and marketed a meat extract named 'Lemco', promoted as 'The health of the prairies brought to your door'. Interestingly, we also see this scientist turned manufacturer's signature on his adverts, a practice that would be followed by many manufacturers who controlled private companies – indicating a willingness to personally endorse a product, '…trust me, I am prepared to personally confirm the claims made in this advertisement'.

This type of pictorial promotion and personal endorsement of manufactured products was to signal the beginning of a massive product promotion industry that would spread and grow to inveigle itself into all aspects of civil life from food to leisure activities, sex and dying, transport and weapons; even the 'selling' of politicians. An industry whose success to a significant extent depends on its ability to persuade consumers to accept the veracity of exaggerated and misleading claims and on occasion straight lies. An industry that has employed some of the most imaginative and intelligent people and then deployed this valuable resource to create a glossy virtual world of: perfections, improvements, satisfactions, value for money products, bargains, 'essential' goods, sharing in positive identity images (a process of 'interpellation' – noted by Louis Althusser)….etc.. All wrapped up in attractive and attracting imagery, operating in an historically mostly only lightly regulated media environment. To find evermore imaginative ways of making people feel that their looks or possessions are in need of some 'product' - a continuous process of inducing a sense of dissatisfaction with most aspect of our bodies and material lives.

As transport across the developing world improved, and links between markets consolidated, we can see the pampas of South America, prairies of North America and even the wide-horizoned farmlands of Australia, serving as vast 'fields' to produce crops such as wheat and cotton, and as grazing lands that supplied meat (especially lamb and beef) to Britain and Europe. The significant increase in the meat export trade from Australia and the Americas began a process of incremental intensification of: breeding, fattening, slaughter and processing. By the end of the nineteenth-century producing food in what had become a factory system that treated animals as but potential profit on the 'hoof'.

Wherever humankind has used domesticated animals for food there has been little in the way of sentiment; contain, feed, kill, and eat. But in societies where there has been a closer relationship to the animals in the field, or to those in the wild, there has been the expression of a certain respect for the animal's dying so that the humans might enjoy their, usually cooked, flesh and benefit from the complex nutrients available in meat. - the human/animal disconnect which characterized the commodification of meat from about the mid nineteenth-century was not dissimilar to the disconnected employee/employer relationship that was also a characteristic of industrialization.

The rising demand, not just in Britain but across the then industrializing areas of the World, stimulated continuous 'improvements' in agriculture. Land was gained by legal privatization, but on the frontiers of civil life often illegal land-grabs were inflicted on peoples that were demonized and dehumanized by a politically and socially constructed discourse that sought to picture native people as engaging in acts that were threatening and behaviour that made them seem inhuman; closer to the animals than to the humans. Doing so by the invention of activities (scalping – cannibalism - thieving) that were rarely if ever engaged in, and certainly to a far lesser extent than by some in the dominant culture. Framing fictionalized accounts of the godless and immoral dark-skinned 'native' who roams across the land, stealing as a way of life, raping whenever opportunity offered, and capable of killing women and children in the most barbaric ways. Along with these much repeated inventions and distortions the dominant cultural 'voices', including politicians, industrialists, big agriculture, and the mass media….. were supporting expansion and the necessary land-grabbing. These medacious accounts of native peoples purposefully ignored the accumulation of certain kinds of wisdom, often expressed in naïve but inherently strong languages infused with ideas of spirits and the conceptualization of natural forces. Languages enriched with concepts, images, and ideas, that were the outcome of centuries of complex cultural life produced by peoples who lived close to natural landscapes and so to dangers and uncertainties set within the circularity of seasonal rhythms. Native languages from across the world expressed the accrued experience of cultures redolent of ancestral livedness. Yes, invariably, there would have been the evils of tribal conflict, of inter-personal and inter-group persecutions, and much of the ancestral wisdom would have been shrouded in the mythical, infused with the imaginative. But the relentless destruction of cultures seen as a barrier to developing capitalist industrialization was an evil the impact of which continues. An historical evil that for peoples such as the indigenous peoples of north and south American, Africans taken as slaves, natives of Australasia, and many others, has expressed evils the impact of which resonate down to today as crimes against all of our humanity.

To seek to form a collective miss-identity encompassing a diverse range of people was an act generated by the most base of motives. Those who 'civilized' peoples wish to destroy they first make other, and others who were characterized as ignorant, immoral, and dangerous. A crude discourse weaving together lies, fictionalized accounts of contacts, exaggerations, harsh images, as but incremental steps towards the social construction of 'inhuman'; a concluding conceptualization that makes general persecution, rape, ethnic cleansing, and even massacre, acceptable, or at least 'unseen' by the masses of the (covetous) industrializing nations.

C.A.Bayly suggests that western Europeans countries were successful at dominating native peoples and gaining colonial territory due to their developing financial systems that were suitable to funding prolonged (and distant) military expeditions, as well as the centuries-long honing of military skills and of adopting a ruthless mentality toward the 'enemy'. Systems and abilities gained during the bitter and numerous seventeenth century European conflicts. As Bayly notes: 'Crudely put, Europeans became much better at killing people.' (2004, p62)

As the century progressed the railways opened up the pampas and the prairies of the Americas, making it possible to transport agricultural products such as meat and cereals but also to haul raw materials from inland forests, mines, and quarries, to towns and cities for internal use and to coastal ports for export. The coming of railways created a social and economic 'buzz' generated by a sense of movement and speed and also the practical benefits of being able to haul a wide range of goods and people over long distances, including across some pretty inhospitable terrains. The railways more easily allowed for the satisfaction of demand in consumer goods as well as providing the means for people to travel for business and for leisure. Globally, the stations themselves became a symbol of a town's progress and impressive terminal stations were constructed in city centres; just some being: Grand Central, New York (US) – Peterhof, St Petersburg (Russia) - St Pancreas, London (England) - Gare du Nord, Paris (France) - Chhatrapati Shivagi in Bombay (Mumbai – India) – Zhengyangmen, Beijing (China) – Buenavista, Mexico City (Mexico). Impressive buildings with vaulting glass, cast iron or steel spanned roofs, and ornate (even for some monumental) architecture, declaring the substance and importance of the activity they were a part of.

The funding of railways was often problematic, many investors made very good returns on capital invested; a few in France and the US even made fortunes. But some railway companies ran at a loss, with many railroad ventures offering tempting opportunities for speculation and even for the downright crooked. From early on governments realized the economic importance of this new form of transport and so were prepared to support them in a range of ways. For each country that initiated a railway building programme the enterprise itself was usually undertaken by private companies but in all countries governments were involved in some way. Belgium by 1840s operated a government owned railway system, whereas in North America federal aid played a significant role in funding and in facilitating rights of way and grants in land (- in the face of strong resistance from turnpike and canal companies), subsidies for what, in effect, came to be run as a private monopolies.

By 1869 North America was spanned east to west by a railroad completed with significant federal support; the final link to opening up the vast lands in the west. A railway had been operating across the Isthmus of Panama since 1855 (the Panama Railroad), allowing easy access to the west coast of North America for gold prospectors. Further north, the Canadian Pacific Railway was completed by 1886 and, in 1837, Tsar Nicolas of Russia enjoyed his first ride on a Russian train running the 27km route from St. Petersburg to Starkey

Selo. By the end of the century a rail-link was under construction from Moscow via the Caspian Sea, reaching Vladivostok in the far east of the country by 1916. This, the Trans-Siberian Railroad, completed an over 9,000 kms iron road across Russia.

The railways continued to spread; over bridges spanning rivers, viaducts crossing valleys, along cuttings between hills, and through tunnels under mountains - a relentless run out of the iron rails. By the 1880s France and Russia would have a similar mileage of railways as did Britain, with Germany and the US having even more. Globally at this time there were 32 countries, each with more than 1,000 miles of track, 70,000 locomotives carrying 1,371 million passengers and 71 million tons of goods each year.

The social effects of railways should not be underestimated. Being linked to a national railway system made possible an expansion of the 'leisure industry'. Exemplified by the rise in Britain and mainland Europe of the costal holiday resort, at first for the middle classes but later on also for workers benefiting from the advent of the 'annual holiday' in the factories. Railways came to carry the better paid workers from their comfortable homes in the suburbs to work in the centre of cities and towns but they also carried many of the lower-paid the other way to enjoy walking and cycling in the countryside. And all could seek work further afield and either 'commute' daily, or at least visit with families at weekends. As the century progressed railways, over and underground, were extensively used for within city transit systems.

Some of those engineers who were involved in the development of the railways soon saw the potential of steam to power shipping. The first serious attempt to use steam to power ships had been made by Bengnot and Jouffrey in 1770s, and in 1783 Jouffroy d'Abbans travelled up the river Saône in a paddle streamer named Pyroscaphe; a boat with 183 paddles fixed to a rotating drum, driving the boat forward. Steam ships were being used to tow barges on the Forth-Clyde canal in Scotland from 1790-1803, but this was soon suspended owing to damage to the canal-bank from the wash of the steamers. Five steam-driven boats were being used on the river Thames by 1815, one of which had travelled by sea from Scotland to take up work in the south. Further afield Robert Fulton's Clermont was on the Hudson River in 1807, steam-driven boats were soon cruising the Great Lakes, and from 1817 the Mississippi river. These contributing to the supply system available for colonists.

By 1825 steamboats were cruising on the Rhine and in the Baltic, steam-driven boats had crossed the English Channel, and their use on inland water ways, lakes, as well as for short sea crossings, had been accepted. The use of steam for ocean navigation developed slowly; facing the problem of coaling and a continuing preference of influential sections of the maritime industry (especially the British Royal Navy) for sail over steam. Bear in mind that the latest two-masted sailing clippers could cross the Atlantic (if fair winds) in 12-14 days and that wind was 'free'. For merchant and naval shipping steam initially served more as a supplement to sail rather than a clear alternative. Even as late as 1847 British merchant marine tonnage of steam shipping was only 16,000 out of a total tonnage of all merchant shipping of 3,000,000. It would take until 1900 before a greater tonnage of steam shipping was registered than sailing ships. Although, by as early as 1882, there were an estimated 22,000 steam ships operating across the world..

The Atlantic was crossed by a steam-driven paddle boat as early as 1819 (the 'Savannah' – New York to Liverpool in 25 days) with the crossing time from England to the US being reduced to 14 days by 1839, using a combination of steam and sail. A steam/sailing boat had taken only 103 days (63 of these under steam alone) to travel from Falmouth to Calcutta. The use of steam gained a significant advance from the 1840s when the more fuel efficient propellers (now designed to cope with the power of larger engines) replaced paddles as a means of transferring the driving force from the engine to the water. By the middle of the century the magnificent 'Great Eastern' designed by the visionary engineer Isambard Kingdom Brunel, at 680 feet long with engines producing 1600 horse-power, indicated how far the use of steam power had come from the earliest engines of Denis Papin and James Watt. Brunel's ship also symbolized the power of the of the technology that would shape the future of sea-borne transportation into the next century.

The first steam boats continued to use wood for their hull construction, later on merchant marine and warships would become 'iron-clad' and then progressively iron replaced wooden hulls completely. From the 1860s in the US, and the 1870s in Britain, iron gave way to the much lighter steel. By this time steamships were carrying goods and passengers across all of the world's oceans; in larger ships, able to run to more reliable timetables and to reduce journey time to about 50% that of sail.

Precision engineering and the use of high quality steel improved the efficiency and reliability of steam-driven engines, with boilers able to maintain higher pressures. Improvements such as the compound engine and the triple-expansion engine were developed to more easily push the screw-driven ships through the waves. Then, in 1894, the steam turbine was introduced, able to power larger ships more efficiently to and fro across the world's oceans; transporting ever-increasing amounts of raw materials, manufactured goods, and large numbers of passengers. With longer distances being made possible by the positioning of coaling stations along extended routes. A process of movement was foundational in creating a sense of globalization going beyond the trading links established by sailing ships. But wind was free and coal expensive so sail continued to be important throughout the Victorian period. It was only when capacity, speed, and regular timetabling became more important that steam began a gradual process of displacing sail if, even as late as the 1930s large sailing ships would be preferred to steam for carrying wheat from Australia to Great Britain.

There were also other improvements in marine technology; including those made to maritime infrastructure such as harbours, docks, lighthouses, and in navigational aids more generally. The building of the Suez Canal by Ferdinand de Lesseps in 1869 reduced sea journey times to the Middle and Far East and the building of the Panama Canal in 1914 would mean that ships could travel to the west coast of the Americas and beyond in much shorter times and without the risks of having to pass round the often stormy southern tip of South America (Cape Horn).

Taken together, steam driven trains and ships transformed the transportation of increasing amounts of raw materials, manufactured goods, and people, over both short and long distances in relatively short times. These improvements in transport were another significant factor – along with changes such as those in financial systems, machine production, precision engineering, colonial expansion, communication technologies, and in political accommodations – contributing to nineteenth-century industrial development and economic growth.

In cities towards the end of the century the horse-drawn omnibus, delivery wagons, Hackney carriages, private carts, gigs and carriages were giving way to transit systems and electric trams (Glasgow 1884). With an underground railway system opening in London in 1863; at first using steam engines but soon electrified, followed by similar urban mass transit systems in Boston, New York, Paris, and Berlin

This rise in mechanized transport contributed to the pollution that was another feature of industrializing city life bearing down more heavily on the working classes; that section of a city's population that usually occupied housing huddled in the smoky shadows of the factories in which they made their living.

The primary pollutants were in the discharges into the air from hundreds of small manufacturing units as well as the larger factories. Their smoke contained a range of toxic particles adding to the generally polluted air whilst the discharge of industrial effluent turned many rivers into sludgy toxin-laden soup. For much of the first half of the century human sewerage was poured directly into the open channels in the streets and via these into the streams and rivers passing through conurbations. Add to this the tons and tons of animal sewerage, produced mainly by the large number of horses whose energy proved the main means of moving goods and people through cities and towns during much of the nineteenth century. The number of horses in use in Britain by 1900 being 3.5 million. This animal waste material would be valuable manure if made available for the land but a raw pollutant if left (as much was) to 'mature' on city streets, then rain-washed into the rivers to mix with the human waste and the range of effluents produced in industrial processes. A toxic mixture and an ongoing example of the many negative externalities that would accrue as industrialization spread across the globe. Added to this was the range of discarded by-products of the industrial processes forming fetid tips at the expanding fringe of cities; if these also provided 'homes' for the waste-pickers who drew a living from combing the piles of waste.

In London, 'smogs' caused by the smoke pouring from thousands of factories and well over 3 million coal burning domestic fires were a significant health hazard, one that would continue until the clean air Act of 1956. Not surprisingly, health-related statistics support this outline. In Manchester of the 1840s 6 out of 10 children born to working class parents died before the age of 5 years, and average life expectancy for the working classes was but 25 years. The 'acid rain', so corrosive to human health, was noted as a feature of life in Manchester as early as 1872.

The costs of supporting a healthy population was one, as with pollution, that industry sought to avoid if it could. Indeed, as noted above, success in a raw-edged capitalist economy depends on the externalization of as many costs as possible. A cynic might suggest that the conditions of the working classes only began to improve when those in control of industry and government realized that a certain level of health (and increasingly as industrialization advanced, education) was a prerequisite for the continued development of a capitalist economy; not least in going to war to defend national self-interest.

The first significant purely scientific discovery to be developed for practical use was electricity. Gas had been used to light factories from 1805, for street lighting early in the century, and by 1885 the invention of the gas mantel led to gas being used in the homes of the better off. But by the 1880s electric powered arc lamps were beginning to be used to illuminate at least the central avenues of the world largest cities, famously so with Paris at the time of the Exposition of 1878. The incandescent light bulb was patented 1875, with an improved version in 1879. The first factory for making light bulbs opened in England in 1881, and by 1890 3 million electric light bulbs were lighting offices and houses in the US.

What had previously been horse-drawn or steam-driven trams gave way to electric powered systems from 1880 St Petersburg (Russia), 1881 Berlin (Germany), 1884 Cleveland Ohio (US), 1885 Blackpool (England), and were soon operating in most industrializing countries. Electricity offered the cheapest form of transferring energy over distance than the alternatives of: cables in motion (telodynamic), pressured air (pneumatic), or pressured fluids (hydraulic).

Electricity was also the basis of accelerating communication systems, not least the land-based telegraph and its undersea continuation in the long distance ocean cables connecting continents. By the final decade of the century the telephone was being introduced in the major cities of the industrializing world. In 1895 Berlin had 16 telephones per 1000 residents, New York 6, London 2, and Stockholm 41; miniscule by today's rate of use but the beginning of the widespread take-up of telephone-based technologies.

Starting in the eighteenth-century and continuing into the nineteenth there were a number of incremental innovations made to mechanical engines leading, in 1860, to J.J.E. Lenoir's invention of an engine that substituted gas for steam to drive the pistons. The efficiency of Lenoir's engine was improved upon by other engineers, with a four cylinder engine being patented in 1861 by Alphonse Beau de Rcha. In 1862 Siegfried Marcus was the first to use gasoline to fuel an engine that he had mounted on a handcart. The potential of this, the 'internal combustion engine', was fairly obvious, and a landmark was reached in 1878 with the patenting by Karl Benz of firstly, a two-stroke engine then, in 1885, a four-stroke engine that he used to provide the power for his 'automobiles'. By 1884 a series of inventions by Edward Butler - carburetor, ignition system, and spark plug - made the use of the internal combustion engine more viable. By 1900, with the addition of the supercharger, rotary engine, and the (in-line cylinder) diesel engine, the basic means of providing mechanical power for a machine that came to dominate terrestrial transportation during the twentieth century had been made available; rubber tyres and types of suspension were soon introduced to provide a softer ride.

In terms of the mechanical transport for the masses, the bicycle had also benefited from nineteenth-century technologies including: pneumatic tyres, gearing, ball-bearing races, hollow metal frames, and lighter ancillary components. It had begun the century as a 'running machine' (such as the hobby horse, and the velocipede), developed in stages into the safety bicycle of 1876 and more modern designs such as the 'Rover' safety bicycle of 1885. The first cycle race took place in Paris in 1868 and in 1884 Thomas Stevens took just over three months to cycle a 3,700 mile route west to east across America; the first use of the bicycle in war was in the 1899 Boer War. The bicycle, with its highly efficient use of human muscle power, freed up the masses (especially women) to travel far and wide; offering an affordable sense of freedom and making the countryside more easily accessible to the town or city dweller.

In Britain from the 1850s real wages for most groups improved and more leisure time became available as the working week was reduced, with a half-day holiday on Saturday afternoons for many. Spare time and surplus income to spend led to the growth of a range of leisure-time activities, from hobbies such as stamp (philately) and coin (numismatics) collecting, amateur interest in natural history (especially ornithology and botany), to a wide range of already established and newly devised board and card games.

There was a significant rise the level of spectating and participation in sports such as cricket, rugby, and association football. The English Football Association (FA) was established in 1863, Scotland's FA by 1880, Wales and Ireland had their own FAs in 1897. The first F.A Cup final was watched by 6,600 spectators with similar tournaments established in Switzerland 1860s, Denmark 1879, Italy 1898, and even Argentina by 1870s. The introduction of soccer to these and other countries was mostly begun by British expatriates. Other popular sports included rugby league in the north and rugby union in the south of England, bicycle racing (especially popular in Britain, Italy and France (1st Tour de France was held in 1903 with 20,000 francs in prize money), prize fighting (under the Queensbury rules in Britain), athletics (Britain), gymnastics (especially popular in Germany and Czechoslovakia), swimming and fencing. Sport more generally receiving a boost from 1896 when the 1st Olympic Games of the modern era was held in Athens. Golf, a game that had been played for some time began to increase in popularity, especially in Scotland. Lawn Tennis, derived from the much older game of 'real tennis' became popular amongst the middle and upper classes, with the first lawn tennis club being established in Leamington Spa, England, in 1874, and at about this time tennis was also being played in New York. The first Wimbledon Championships was held in 1877, first US Open in 1881, first French Open in 1889 and the first Australian Open in 1905. Billiards was popular from the mid. nineteenth-century, such that 8,000 elephants were being slaughtered annually in order to supply the ivory, mainly for the European billiard-ball market. From 1869 the balls began to be made from synthetic materials.

Across the Atlantic, local versions of baseball were being played from early in the century, with the first modern baseball field being laid out in 1845 and, by the 1860s, the game was perhaps the most popular spectator sport in the US. American football (with roots in the game of rugby played at the English public school of that name from 1823) was played in a very basic form from the 1820s, but really only began to increase in popularity in US colleges from the 1870s; with an initial attempt to formulate some rules being made at Princeton. Basketball was devised by Canadian born Dr James Naismith and played originally at the YMCA Training School based in Massachusetts. Also maintaining their popularity were the older sports of horseracing and the activities associated with hunting small animals with horse and dog, trapping, shooting, and otherwise catching and killing various species of creatures found in the countryside.

In sum: the nineteenth-century saw the introduction and development of a range of hobbies, games, other leisure interests, and the beginning of most of the sports that have global popularity (and a central aspect of the popular entertainment industry) in the world today.

In Britain and most industrializing countries, as well as taking part in these sporting and leisure activities, more people began to follow an interest in travel. Whether walking on moorland or hillsides, through forests and around lakes, bicycling out of the towns and cities for a day or two's relief from the polluted, overcrowded living conditions of home. The expanding rail network allowed trains to be filled with day-trippers and holiday-makers. For the British this meant trips to seaside locations such as Blackpool, Bournemouth, Scarborough, Southend, Llandudno, Margate, and to the Lake District. As the century progressed, more people travelled further afield – to walk in Germany, Austria, Switzerland, to ski in Austria, Switzerland, Italy, and to absorb the historical experience and visit the 'sights' in countries across Europe and Scandinavia and even further afield to Egypt and Palestine (Cooks tours). For the better off members of the working class, the annual 'holiday' developed to become a regular item in the calendar, as they followed the routes taken earlier in the century by the middle classes, who had themselves progressed to follow in the footsteps of European 'grand tours' made in the seventeenth and eighteenth-centuries by the upper classes.

In towns and cities public entertainment was on offer in colourful music halls, in theatres, and amateur choral and drama societies blossomed. In Germany, tavern theatres offered often rowdy, and sometimes risqué, entertainment. France favoured 'Café-concerts', with the popular Moulin Rouge being opened in 1889. By the end of the century the various opportunities for live entertainment was supplemented by the communal experience of watching pre-recorded entertainment when the 'Vistascope' had been invented (1895 US), a machine that could project film images onto a screen. It was first used to entertain the public in 1896 and from the first decade of the twentieth century 23,000 Americans a week were paying a nickel each to view these film-shows in the 10,000 'Nickel-Odeons' that had opened across the US. The year 1896 saw the first news-reels and the showing of major sporting events. From about 1900 feature films were being made with subject-matter including; sports and entertainment, news and more documentary subjects, and pornography.

These leisure opportunities, along with improvements in working conditions and for many in economic prospects, contributed to diverting the attention of most of the masses from ideas of revolutionary change and instead created a societal context increasingly more suitable for the 'constitutional' (conservative) trades unionism that developed in Britain and most of the industrializing nations.

The technical advances of printing: US double cylinder rotary press 1828 – Stereotypes for easy duplication of printing page blocks 1861, producing 15,000-25,000 sheets per hour – continuous reel 'webs' of paper producing 96,000 eight page sections per hour 1890s – type-setting machines, typewriters, photographers and pre-press reproduction of pictorial images, with the telegraph and telephone transforming the editorial side of newspapers and magazines.

These technical innovations and the market of an increasingly more literate society[7] led to news and information on leisure activities becoming available in specialist magazines for hobbies, sports, and for travelling. In addition, newspapers and magazines carried adverts for products related to these activities; all making a significant contribution to stimulate interest and also to contribute to the founding of the mass consumer society that would develop more obviously during the twentieth century. Cheap literature such as the 'penny thriller' pamphlets sold widely. In Britain stories of highwaymen, smugglers, and pirates, were popular as were those of cowboys and crime imported from the US. Gossipy papers, focusing on the trivial, such as Tit-bits (1880), Answers (1888) and Comic Cuts (1890), were popular. Numerous cheap editions of classic novels were being published by the 1890s. The Daily Mail (often used as a vehicle for its founder, Lord Alfred Harmsworth's jingoistic views) was founded in 1896 and sold at a cost of half-penny when compared to the three pence of the Times, by 1900 the Mail's circulation was 1,250,000 copies per day. From 1880 pictures were introduced into newspapers, marking the beginning of the photo-journalism that facilitated high impact news and current affairs journalism. The final decade of the century saw the (dramatic) expansion in the publication of cheap newspapers, magazines, pamphlets, and novels.

Advertisements proclaiming the attractiveness of a range of consumer goods and services were appearing in newspapers and

---

[7] The 1870 Education Act had brought primary education to all children in Britain and similar by the end of the century to most European countries.

magazines; yet another industry to begin in the nineteenth-century. Photography had developed during the second half of the century and it provided the technical means of fixing/freezing moments of time and of recording pastimes and travels as well as news. Framed photographs would be added to the objects, ornaments, and soft and hard furnishing, that were intended to enhance the homes of more affluent workers. Homes that were increasingly, from the second half of the century, spreading out from city and town centres to form the more comfortable 'suburban' housing estates that would be found attractive by many of the families of lower middle class and of skilled workers.

The projection (indeed 'creation') in the mass media of popular 'heroes', with carefully edited versions of heroic events and of the 'hero's' own involvement in these proved popular with the Victorian public – Wellington, Marlborough, Nelson[8] and later in the century, David Livingston and General Gordon. An unrealistic version of 'Britishness' reflected in Rudyard Kipling's tales of daring-do on the frontiers of empire and the myths of Britain's role in 'civilizing' colonial peoples.

The nineteenth century also saw the development in Britain and other industrializing countries, of 'childhood'; a period of play and education for more than just the children of the wealthy. There were idealized images depicted in novels and magazines of well-dressed children being gently but firmly shepherded by nannies, hunched dutifully over school books, or brought together with parents for musical entertainments; images intended to invoke an impression of a country such as Britain at ease with itself. A toys and games industry expanded to cater for children. Books specifically aimed at their entertainment were written by authors such as Charles Kingsley ('Water babies' 1862), Lewis Carroll ('Alice in Wonderland' 1865), and J.M.Barrie ('Peter Pan' 1902), as well as more acceptable versions of the 'fairy tales' of Hans Anderson and the brothers Grimm. All kinds of traditionally upper-class activities permeated down to many in the middle and lower middle classes, not least as sources of images with which to inform their own aspirational identities.

The economic and social impact of industrialization was overlaid

---

[8] Nelson was a gifted and determined self-publicist - even to the extent of himself having pamphlets, in which his 'character and exploits' were dramatically depicted and lauded, printed and distributed throughout Britain.

with the shadow of conflict, not just the ongoing wars waged against indigenous peoples on all of the inhabited continents but also both within and between the industrializing nations. The process of mechanization was extended to the means to wage war during the century. The Crimean War and the US Civil War stand out.

At the beginning of the century Europe experienced the military expression of rival national factions in Britain, Russia, Prussia, and Austria, faced with the territorial ambitions of Napoleon Bonaparte. The bloody and destructive outcomes for the participating nations were played out at the battles of: Marengo (1800), Trafalgar (1805), Ulm (1805), Austerlitz (1805), Jena (1806), Eylau (1807), Friedland (1807), the drawn out Peninsular Wars (1808-1813), Wargram (1809), Borodino (1812). Then a pause for Napoleon's resignation, later escape from open imprisonment on Elba, and his return for a series of relatively minor engagements leading to the French defeat by the British and Prussian armies at the Battle of Waterloo in 1815. The Vienna Settlement of 1815 resulted in an uneasy peace, one bristling with inter-nation suspicions, and with nations each still seeking to advance their own interests during a time when 1.5 million men formed the standing armies of France, Britain, Russia, Prussia/Germany and the Hapsburg Empire.

Russia was the first to let discontent with the European status quo show as it translated its long held ambitions (or rather the ambition of Tsar Nicolas I and the coterie of aristocratic and military self-interest that surrounded him) for control in the Balkans into warfare. It found an excuse to provoke the Turks when the Ottoman-Turkish Empire granted France religious (Catholic) concessions in Palestine. In July 1853 Russia advanced into the Danubian principalities of Walachia and Moldavia; in response the Turks declared war. They were anticipating support (even if somewhat reluctant) from Britain and France, assuming that they would want to protect their own economic interests in the Middle-East. The French military leaders were still harbouring a collective resentment of the Russians who, aided by the winter weather, transformed defeat by the French at Borodino into victory as the Grand Armée of 500,000 men had made an inglorious retreat back to France. England and France did join the conflict by late spring 1854, reinforced the following year by troops from the Kingdom of Sardinia whose leaders were expecting to gain British and French support to drive the Austrians from northern Italy.

The Crimean war of 1854-55 highlighted Russia's military weakness, a result of its relative lack of military industrialization. Even though, in the lead-up to conflict, Russia was dedicating four-fifths of state revenue to the military it was a military trained and equipped to fight eighteenth-century battles. A military soldiered mainly by serfs, many having been reluctantly wrenched from the their homeland and officered by privileged and mostly militarily unproven sons of the upper classes; often distracted by the appeal of impressive uniforms and being lionized within a vibrant social scene (depicted in Tolstoy's 'War and Peace', a novel set earlier in the century). The Russian assault was starved of supplies as its horse-drawn wagon trains became bogged down in the muddy terrain that stretched from Moscow to the battle front. Whereas forces that the French/British alliance had mobilized to stop Russian expansion benefitted from trained standing armies, modern weapons, railways to transport men and supplies, and experienced officers trained to approach war in a more strategic way; such as disrupting Russian supply lines by naval blockade in the Black Sea. The firepower of modern steel-barreled artillery laid down a marker for military conflict for the next 100 years as the weakness of cavalry and massed infantry, as well as traditional fortifications, were exposed to the relentless destruction of accurate cannonade.

Innovation such as the use of the electric telegraph enabled the co-ordination of forces. An innovation noted by American observers who had travelled to the Crimea and which would contribute to how their own civil war (of 1861-65) would be fought. By the War's end 480,000 (possible as many as a million) Russians had died, many from dysentery, cholera, and infected wounds, and 500 million rubles had been spent; France lost 100,000 men and Britain 25,000, with disease taking a heavy toll. The populations of all of the combatant nations paid the financial cost in rising taxes and in generally higher food prices. This was perhaps the first 'media' war, with the dispatches of journalists such as the London Times reporter William Howard Russell becoming available to British public within hours of actions and the vibrant photographs taken by Roger Fenton providing an immediacy of images illustrating life at the front.

The Treaty of Paris signed by the combatants in March 1856 was pretty much a humiliation for a financially exhausted Russia and a further step towards the dismantling of the Ottoman, and the remnants of the Hapsburg, empires. Other outcomes were to make a united

Germany certain and a united Italy more likely. The continued repression of the nationalistic ambitions of ethnic groups within the central European part of the Empire contributed to tensions that would in turn make a significant contribution to the causes of the First World War. Indeed, adding to disparate narratives of ethnic and nationalistic tensions that continue in places like Chechnya today.

When Alexander II became Tsar in 1856 he took the lessons from the humiliation in the Crimea to be that: industrialization should proceed at a pace, serfdom brought to an end, and the military modernized.

A German State was established in 1871 with a Kaiser as its Head of State; the head of a nation industrializing at a rapid pace and fiercely proud of its (Prussian) military tradition; a new nation led by an elite group grounded in an ideology of warfare. One feature of the new Germany that would haunt relations between it and France well into the next century was the annexation by the new Germany of the French territory of Alsace-Lorraine.

In Europe by 1860 there were 2.25 million men under arms, with Britain alone spending £15.6 million per year on the military by 1856. The nineteenth-century saw the beginnings of national expenditure being systematically allotted to fund the military, primarily from taxation and government borrowing. Now the world was set on a future of what would be in effect institutionalized warfare, the assumed normality of conflict as a central aspect of international relations based upon each of the more powerful nations progressing their leader's perception of self-interest, at pretty much any cost to others. Morality was only introduced, and then loudly, to assess the actions of other nations rather the actions of those doing the assessing.

This institutionalization of conflict included: large standing armies, a significant proportion of a nation's financial wealth being spent on weaponry, and a populist narrative of jingoistic nationalism being promoted by governments, national religions, and most of the national mass media. The foundations of the 20th/21st centuries 'war industry' had been laid.

Many of Europe's politicians and much of the mass media mendaciously endeavored to foster nationalistic collective identities formed out of the bundle of ragbag ideas, half-truths, imaginative historical narratives and mostly miss-constructed outlines of shared heritage. The central institutions of the state were aided by the mainstream media in fostering a spurious set of shared interests in some 'imagined community' as noted by Benedict Anderson (1983). Drawing all classes and other social groupings into a belief that they shared some 'common interest', detailed knowledge of which was being held by wise.... politicians, industrialists, church, and military leadership. A toxic mix of disparate national loyalties, expressed in jingoism, national chauvinism, and in times of crisis providing an international setting characterized by heightened forms of antagonistic xenophobia.

In trade, the three dominant European nations of Europe: Britain, France, and Germany, along with the US, would by the end of the century be responsible for 75% of the world's production of marketable goods, and a significant proportion of their national incomes would be siphoned off to be spent on developing their military forces.

The US was to face its own bitter internal conflict as it too experienced the drawn out legacy of the birth-pains of nationhood. The generally accepted (and historically convenient) cause of the American Civil War was the resistance of the southern states to the abolition of slavery and the determination of the northern states to bring this change about but also to hold the Union together, and to do both by force if necessary.

By 1860 there were 4 million people held in slavery in the US, the property of white owners, with each slave assessed as being 'worth' on average $1,000. Some political leaders in the Confederate states suggested that their resistance to ending slavery was more about the right of individual states to make their own decisions on certain types of issue rather than only that of slavery; a constitutional principle rather than a matter of economic self-interest. For the north, the abolition of slavery was not entirely motivated by humanitarian concerns for the well-being of some of the poorest most exploited of people, there was also consideration of the rapidly expanding northern industrializing states need for cheap 'free' labour.

A case involving slavery in relation to the US Constitution making news at the time involved Dred Scot, a Virginian Slave who in 1857 claimed that due to his having spent some time in a non-slave state it was unconstitutional for him to be held in slavery......the case went to the Supreme Court and the ruling was that as Scott could not be considered a US citizen (due to his status as a slave) he had no right to bring a case of any sort before the Supreme Court and, in addition, the court confirmed that he was the property of his master.

The opinion of Chief Justice Roger B. Taney declared that Scott was not entitled to rights as a US citizen and, in fact, had "no rights which any white man was bound to respect". Taney and six other justices ruled that Congress did not have the power to prohibit slavery in the territories. The ruling was a victory for the South but one that increased Northern antislavery sentiment, strengthened the newly formed Republic Party, whilst also exacerbating tensions between north and south.

Lines of implacable disagreement between some northern and southern states had been emerging for some time and came to a head with the election in 1860, of a more liberal Republican President, Abraham Lincoln (although he was against whites marrying blacks). In February 1861, seven southern states ceded from the Union (later to be joined by four more), with Jefferson Davis becoming President of the Confederate States of America. The first military clash came in April when the Confederate General Beauregard ordered his troops to fire on the Union soldiers in Fort Sumter; more a symbolic act of intention than an act of war, with the only casualty being a horse.

The outcome of the war was pretty much predetermined, the unknowns were how long would it last and how much it would cost in lives and money. The southern alliance could not come close to matching the north in terms of industrial resources and available manpower. The north's population being 20,000,000 - plus 800,000 immigrants between 1861-65 - whilst the south had a population of 6,000,000 and negligible immigration. The Union army 1,000,000, the Confederate army with 464,000 at start of the war (falling to about 150,000 by the war's end).......in 1860 the north had 110,000 manufacturing establishments, the south 18,000. The south could find no European allies who might have been able to assist either diplomatically or with breaking the north's blockade of southern ports. The main export income for the south came from cotton, but the blockade of southern ports – the north had a far superior navy with its 671 warships - significantly reduced exports from the south and so limited the income available to pay the costs of sustaining a war. The north, along with all of its other advantages, was aided by thousands of black slaves who fled from plantations, some to act as guides for Union troops, others to fight in northern regiments. By the end of the war 180,000 black soldiers were serving in Union regiments.

In Robert E. Lee and Patrick R Cleburne the south had two militarily gifted generals but realistically their only achievable aim could have been to make the war so difficult for the north that they would have negotiated a settlement that at least went some way to protect the interests of southern business people and the plantation aristocracy. As with most civil wars, this was a nasty, bloody, affair, with 359,000 Union and 258,000 Confederate soldiers having to die (about one third in battle, two-thirds from disease) and swathes of the southern territory laid waste before General Lee accepted the inevitable when he surrendered to General Ulysses Grant at Appomattox on the 9th April 1865.

Mechanized warfare had provided the material means for a series of senseless engagements of the type that would later characterize the European theatre in the First World War. With most engagements having indefinite military outcomes apart that is, from the slaughter of thousands of young men as they marched into a hailstorm of bullets and the thunderous roar of cannonades.

The historian Howard Giles noted that:

'Most battles quickly degenerated into murderous firefights at close range, each side blazing away until one or the other withdrew. Even later in the war when tactics had been refined and the spade took over as the main "weapon" as the armies dug in, generals often needlessly threw away the lives of their men in massed attacks......As such, most actions rarely seemed to achieve more than another pile of bodies. Even when a decisive victory was achieved, the enemy nearly always managed to limp away to fight another day. Inevitably, it became a dreadful war of attrition.' (Giles, 2003)

The soldiers' experience being brought vividly to life in Stephen Crane's novel The 'Red Badge of Courage': 'The battle was like the grinding of an immense and terrible machine....' '....men, punched by bullets, fell in grotesque agonies. The regiment left a coherent trail of bodies.' 'They accepted the pelting of the bullets with bowed and weary heads. It was of no purpose to strive against walls.' (Crane, 1895)

'Four score and seven years ago our fathers brought forth on this continent, a new nation, conceived in Liberty, and dedicated to the proposition that all men are created equal.'

These are the opening words of the Address delivered by President Lincoln on the Battlefield of Gettysburg, Pennsylvania, on 19th February 1863 – apart from the obvious omission of women, the proposition, as embodied in the American Constitution, also excluded Native American Indians. And, as the Supreme Court had ruled in 1857 (see above), black slaves were 'property' rather than citizens and they too were in effect excluded in the Address.

The Gettysburg Address cleverly (it was a skillfully 'crafted' rally cry) echoed the words in the second sentence of the American 'Declaration of Independence': 'We hold these truths to be self-evident, that all men are created equal, that they are endowed by their Creator with certain unalienable Rights, that among these are Life, Liberty and the pursuit of Happiness'.

This is just the sort of Americanese, writ large, of exaggerated but brilliant humanitarian ideals that owes more to the free-flying imagination of single-minded politicians, unbridled by any sense of moderation, as shaped by the cynical art of the speechwriter, than to the reality of human social relationships within the context being described. Wonderful, inspiring phrases, if only those who produced them and those that cheered them could live up to these ideals!

A telling positive correlation can be made between the rising tide of death and the rising profits of the financiers, bankers, and munitions companies, who between them produced the munitions and other materials necessary for the continuation of warfare and the commission gained for arranging the government loans to pay for these. As the old socialist soar goes 'War is extremely horrible but it is also extremely profitable!'

With this civil war we can more easily begin to identify those who benefit markedly from preparing for and indulging in the activity of modern warfare. During the conflict millions of rounds of ammunition was used, tens of thousands of tons of pig-ion, coal, and steel, hundreds of thousands of rifles, thousands of artillery pieces, a range of food and animal feed, blankets, uniforms, barracks, tents, railway engines and carriages, wagons, horses - bankers negotiated government loans, traders arranged imported war-goods - many of the workers in munitions factories, those making uniforms, boot-makers, and those making other war materials were on overtime etc. etc. Massive profits were made during this war.......a message not lost on arms manufacturers, suppliers, and investors for the future.

In the late nineteenth century the US, along with most of the governments of Europe, spent a massive amount on building their military capability. Military planning became a central feature of government, the art of diplomacy ostensibly intended to avoid war continued to be no more than a means deployed to prevaricate, persuade allies to a cause, to mislead (by direct threats or by identifying common enemies), and to negotiate time for further military preparation. Economic industrialization had been accompanied by the industrialization of the military, with military expenditure being in effect an important economic stimulus (a Keynesian 'demand-led' approach, if a means to this that he would not generally have approved of). But the same economic impact could have been made if instead of being spent on military preparedness, the same level of investment had been made in building schools, hospitals, libraries, scientific research centres, improved social services and similar non-military infrastructure. The claim that we need a strong military to protect our civil life is undermined by any rational consideration and will be considered in the concluding chapter below.

Companies such as Nobles, Armstrong, Krupps, Smith and Wesson, Tzhmash, Mauser, Daher, and many others, supplied ever-improved (in killing 'efficiency') munitions. The killing power of rifles, machine-guns, and artillery was undergoing continuous development, (steel cannons were produced with a range of up to 5,000 metres). And in the later part of the nineteenth-century hundreds of new warships were eased down slipways of Europe, the US, and Japan; bristling with cannons, and some with armour plating up to 24 inches thick.

Between1874-96 the leading European nations increased military spending by 50% and between 1880-1914 military spending by France increased by 100%, of Britain and Russia by 200%, and Germany by 400%. Throughout the history of organized human conflict there had always been some competition between combatants involving weaponry and tactics, but by the end of the nineteenth-century leading nations were engaged in a veritable arms 'race' that continues down to today. If any weapon was possible (however horrific its effect), be it machine gun, armour-piercing shell, poison gas, chemical weapon, most 'civilized' nations felt they could not be without it. Vast resources were from now on to be diverted to supply the means to kill and maim, and so the means of gaining massive profits for the arms and finance industries; recourse to war had become 'inevitable'.

Apart from the human carnage and wasted material resources resulting from civil and international conflicts there was the also the evil inflicted due to the civil powers pursuing their colonizing ambitions and trading interests. In Britain there was some condemnation by representatives of the middle and working classes of the brutality, corruption, and avarice that was a central feature of colonization but there was also many prepared to defend (indeed glorify) colonialism; of more selfishly just wanting their representatives to argue for a greater share of the plunder gained from the possession of colonized lands, for themselves.

Across the British Empire, millions lived a day-to-day existence focused on survival and whose knowledge of Britain was of some grand if nebulous, entity, far, far, away. Their direct contact with it being mostly limited to dealings with generally rapacious traders, free-booting hunters of precious metals or other valued goods, stiff tax collection officers, Christian missionaries, various types of 'scientific' collectors pursuing the collection and cataloguing of exotic plants, butterflies, and birds, and a military led by officers mostly lacking any sympathetic understanding of local customs and intent on subduing any of the indigenous peoples that expressed the least resistance to co-operating with the needs of the Empire. Some of the native peoples worked as servants to British, or British appointed officials; serving white managers and settlers engaged in overseeing plantations and maintaining infrastructure. Few individuals came from Britain seeking any form of genuine friendship and mutually beneficial trade links, and even some of those fleeing poverty or religious persecution at home travelled to the colonies motivated by the prospect of material acquisition.

As industrialization developed in mainland Europe the US, and Britain, these countries adopted a number of strategies for engaging with international markets, not least a range of tariffs on imported goods and controls on merchant shipping (e.g. Britain's Navigation Acts). The Pauline-like conversion of Britain from its strongly protectionist policies to become a bullish advocate of free trade, not surprisingly, occurred when the government - backed by leading bankers, industrialists and manufacturers - felt they had strong global market advantages as well as protected colonial markets, allowing them an advantageous position in international trade.

In Britain and mainland Europe itself many workers still trudged wearily through the working day in cities where crowded conditions and industrial pollution continued to make the home environment mostly uncomfortable and generally unhealthy. Due to both migration from countryside and a balance favouring births over deaths in residential populations, the rate of urbanization increased markedly across the industrializing areas of Europe from about the 1850s. Cities such as London, Paris, Vienna, and Berlin, doubled in population over the next 30 years, with an even greater rate of growth in civil areas of North and South America and Australia. In Britain, cities that had been involved in the early stages of industrialization such as Manchester, Birmingham, and Liverpool, saw some modest improvement in living conditions, with many city-dwellers gaining access to safe drinking water and some progress in sanitation, even if homes for most continued to be overcrowded. But for those still living in slum-like and overcrowded homes, their general health and mortality rates hardly improved. Fortunes continued to be made by 'jerry-builders', and their speculative investor backers, as they endeavored to pack as many homes as possible into each plot of land and to then set rents at as high a level as the 'market' could stand. But a market whose basic conditions encouraged over-occupation due to the high rent of each dwelling meaning that they had to be shared between as many families or individuals as possible. In effect, engaging in the very 'social engineering' (if by rent-price mechanisms) that the entrepreneurial types argued against when it comes to government trying to more sensibly plan a city's development, including the introduction of building regulations.

A prominent feature of industrialization had been the progressive advance of the centuries-long practices of economic and actual colonialism. Predominantly by leading European states but also in the late nineteenth-century by Japan and US. These states had by 1900 between them carved up most of the world. Even South America, where countries remained at least nominally independent states there were various forms of economic colonialism, maintained by the power of foreign investors and increasing dependence on export markets. An example of foreign influence can been seen in what happened in Paraguay. A country ruled from 1814-1840 by the paternalistic dictator Gaspar Rodriguez de Francia, brought to power primarily with the support of the peasantry over an aristocratic oligarchy. He attempted to take Paraguay on an independent route to development, overseeing a county that by 1840 had eradicated poverty, had achieved a low crime rate, and with free basic education for all children. These being quite novel features of South American countries of the time.

Francia was succeeded by another fairly radical if more belligerent leader in President Fransico Solano Lopez, who intensified Paraguay's internal development and, rather than simply conforming to the pattern of development taking place across the rest of the continent – a pattern based on enriching investors and companies of the imperial powers - Lopez chose another developmental strategy. He obstructed foreign investments, settled high tariffs on imported goods, and allowed the development of railroad, canal and telegraph systems whilst protecting a range of indigenous manufacturing companies, including a ship-building industry; in addition 98% of Paraguay's land was in public hands.

Whether due to President Lopez's wish to fulfill territorial ambitions or to preempt Argentina and Brazil's claims on Paraguayan territory, Lopez recklessly declared war, initially on Brazil then on Argentina. Brazil, Argentina and also Uruguay, formed a 'triple-alliance' and a bloody war - lasting from 1864 -1867 (some would say 1870) ensued, a war that ended with the killing of President Lopez and in humiliating defeat for Paraguay. Some historians have suggested that Britain was involved on the triple-alliance side. There is no clear evidence to support this claim, but there is some circumstantial evidence in that Britain did offer local diplomatic support and the outcome fortuitously generously benefitted Britain's commercial interests in the region. Not least British banks, including Baring Brothers and Rothschilds, who made loans available (if at very high interest rates) to enable the nations of the triple alliance to progress the war.

The years of war saw the armed conflict become genocidal (the Paysandú massacre coming at the war's end) as the three invading nations ruthlessly put the population of Paraguay to the 'sword' - almost 50% of Paraguay's people fled the county. The Triple Alliance set up a puppet government in Montevideo that progressively rolled-back the social and economic progress made by the Francia and Lopez regimes. The country was ransacked, and the victors adjusted their own borders to encompass some extensive and juicy bits of Paraguan territory. But the victor-nations ended the war deep in hock to British bankers. And the future of Paraguay was then to follow the same model of development as pertained across most of the rest of the sub-continent; one focused on serving the investment and trading interests of Europe and the US.

I intend completing this chapter with a closer, if quite condensed, consideration of colonization – that element of industrialization that has left a series of scars on much of the world's peoples. And if we are to gain some sense of perspective on colonialism circa 1900, we need to step back to allow some understanding of historical context.

We can note that from the earliest periods of humankind's civil history people from one area have endeavored to wield power, control, and influence, over neighbouring groups and many have been able to do so due to quite marked imbalances of power. Whether these were due to technological advantages, greater economic prosperity, traditionally accepted social stratification, or cultures of aggression allied to acquisitive natures. Even if these types of advantage were often credited to the power of the aggressor's sides 'God/s' or to the bravery of its combatants, and often to both.

The wish to create spheres of influence, or even more directly control empires, has been an almost defining feature of civil life.... just a few examples would be the violent formation of Akkadian, Assyrian, and Mycenaean, empires - the Phoenician colonization of north Africa - the periods of Pharonic control of Nubia - the geographically extensive Macedonian Empire brought together by Alexander - the equally extensive Roman Empire - Scandinavian peoples attempts to colonize areas of the north Atlantic and Great Britain during the 'Viking' period – the Aztecs control of much of Mexico and central America - The Qin Empire of China – the extensive Mongol empire across Eurasia and China - the Muslim empire of Mogul India – and Saladin's Arab empire in the Mediterranean region - as well as the Ashanti and Zulu empires in Africa - and the Polynesian and Maori in the south Pacific. Just a few more notable examples of humankind's propensity to seek to acquire the territorial resources, stored wealth, and even the enslavement, of others.

In more recent times it has been European countries seeking to colonize distant lands long-occupied by other, less economically developed, peoples. This began as early as the fifthteenth-century with Spanish and Portuguese exploits in the Americas – displacing or controlling the local ruling groups, looting the gold and silver and, along with the British, French and Dutch, establishing plantations. Enslaving, murdering, forcing religious conversion, and the relentless economic exploitation of native peoples in the process of extracting wealth from their lands. Wealth mainly in the form of very cheap labour (slavery), precious metals, gemstones, valued raw materials, and agricultural produce including sugar, then later on cotton, tobacco, opium, and meat, being the primary ones.

It was in 1498 that the 'Cape of Good Hope' (southern tip of Africa) was first rounded by the Portuguese (if Africa had been circumnavigated long before). The Portuguese and to a limited extent the Spanish, then later the Dutch and the British, used this as a route to the east and each successively established regular trading links with regions of the Middle and Far East. Trading initially in the much valued, and so very profitable spices such as: clove, cinnamon, cardamom, nutmeg, ginger, turmeric, and pepper; this last being used to mask the smell and taste of decomposing meat; a fairly common condition of this food.

Spices that had previously been traded to Europe as far back as Roman times after a lengthy journey from the areas in which they were grown. A journey beginning the goods being carried by pack animals to the main ports of Indonesia, Ceylon, India, and China, then carried by local and Arabian sailing ships, with fairly limited carrying capacity, to ports in Arabia and Persia. From where merchants organized caravans to transport the precious loads along the extended overland 'spice routes' to the Mediterranean-facing Middle-East. The City of Constantinople had an Italian quarter whose main activity was arranging the onward passage of spices carried in Venetian and Genoan ships to Italy then on to France, Spain and, after yet another long journey to countries of northern and western Europe. The primary routes being either overland from China and India, taking months to make the trip or the series of passages from the 'Spice Islands' (the Moluccas) and the ports of the Malayan Archipelago. This last taking in sea crossings, or traversing often difficult terrain and sometimes a passage through mountain ranges that could take up to two years, with the goods being bought and sold a number of times along the way hence, up until the seventeenth-century spices were only affordable by the wealthy.

From the early seventeenth-century the Dutch had sought to challenge the Portuguese and Spanish dominance of Far Eastern trade. An ambition made easier when, in 1616, the Dutchman Willem Schouten also found the route round the Cape. Soon the English would also be using this route (a route 'rutters' which the Portuguese and Spanish had endeavoured to keep secret) and both nations then competed with the Portuguese and Spanish and with each other for the lucrative trade in the east, trade that now included cotton, porcelain, precious metals, and other commodities valued on European markets, in addition to the trade in spices.

The Dutch brought a Protestant thoroughness to their methods of drawing wealth from their mercantile activities in the east. Illustrated in the progress of the Dutch East Indian Company (VOC – Vernige Oost-indische Compagnie), a joint-stock entity receiving its charter from the States-General (parliament) in 1602. A charter that provided for a monopoly of navigation rights east of the Cape of Good Hope (and west through the straights of Magellen). The company was run by 17 directors (Heren Zeventien or Gentlemen XVII) a group that would only meet a couple of times a year, to pour over balance sheets, and to consider the risks of its various enterprises in relation to potential profits. Although more modest versions of this type of joint-stock company had been established in Northern Italy, the VOC was an innovative extension of this basic arrangement with a specific purpose of accruing collective and personal wealth. This purpose was successful to the extent that this would make the Dutch East India Company the largest enterprise in Europe by the end of the seventeenth-century. Its charter gave it the right to make (and the freedom to break) treaties with native leaders, to build forts and to appoint local governors, who in turn could oversee imposed systems of 'justice'. In effect, the right to use force to further its own financial interests and even, if necessary, to wage war and occupy foreign territory!

The Company established its first base in Bantam, Java, in 1607 before re-locating to Djakata (re-named Batavia) from where it endeavoured, with a relentless determination fueled by avarice, to control both local trade and the trade back to Europe – trade extending to Ceylon, China, Formosa and Japan. Just one incident to illustrate the Company's methods was action taken in 1621 by Jan Peterszoon Coen the ruthless Governor General who did more than any other single individual to establish, mainly by force of arms, - wielded against both other European traders and indigenous peoples - Dutch control of the Far East. When the people of Great Banda (now part of Indonesia) resisted the Company's attempt to control production and trade (in effect control of the world's supply) in the most valuable spice of nutmeg, Coen had 2,500 of its inhabitants massacred and 800 others transported to Batavia.

The Dutch also used Batavia as a base from which to explore the

Southern Ocean. In the 1640s Able Tasman was dispatched to seek the great land to the south that had been noted by ships that had strayed off the routes to the east. He succeeded in this task– sailing round Australia 'discovering' Tasmania, New Zealand, and the Islands of Fiji and Tonga. Naming what we now know as Tasmania as Van Diemen's Land after the Dutch Governor-general who had ordered Tasman south. In Tasman's assessment the prospects for wealth so far south did not look promising so the Dutch lost interest in the southern lands.

The Europeans enabling the Dutch occupation in the Far East were a collection of merchants, plantation owners, administrators, soldiers, sailors, and some protestant clergymen. A significant proportion of each occupational group were freebooters, fortune hunters, and thieves. Life in these colonies was often hard (with the constant danger of disease) but, if fortunate, the potential rewards were great. Rewards that could more successfully be extracted by a ruthless approach to advancing their own as well as the Company's interests. According to one historian quoted by Mike Dash '...The Company as a body was avaricious, and its employees were often demoralized by its institutionalized greed....every able-bodied man from the Councillor [Governor-general] of the Indies down to the simple solider considered it an absolute must to care for himself first.' (Dash 2002, 'Batavia's Graveyard').

If they managed to survive the often harsh conditions these individuals could hope to return home in one of the many *retourchips* that carried trade good and supplies between Europe and the Dutch possessions in the east. Towards the end of the seventeenth-century (at the peak of its 'success') the Company had 10,000 soldiers under arms, along with 150 merchant ships and 40 warships to protect them. Each returning ship would have a cargo on which profits of up to 1,000% was being made.

Throughout the eighteenth-century the Company increasingly faced direct competition from the British whose navy had become the most powerful in the world. From the middle of the seventeenth-century England's parliament had introduced a series of Navigation Acts which permitted only English ships to carry any trade goods landed in any territory controlled by the English Crown; Acts specifically aimed to inhibit the Dutch. Serious financial problems and a wave of corruption scandals led to the Company ceasing to trade in 1798, with the Dutch Government taking possession of the

Company's overseas territories. In 1814 Britain captured the small Dutch colony (established in 1652) at the Cape of Good Hope; a strategically important stopping place on the route east. By which time the power-balance in the Far East had shifted decisively to favour the British. In 1800 European nations and their overseas possessions amounted to 55% of the Earth's land surface. This would grow to 67% by the last quarter of the century. It has been estimated that between 1820 and 1920 55,000,000 Europeans migrated overseas, 'pushed' by such factors as unemployment, religious persecution, poverty, and 'pulled' by the prospect of economic prosperity and the excitement of opportunities available in these 'underexploited' regions.

The progress of European industrialization, with its increasing need for raw materials for its factories and new markets for its manufactured goods, provided additional incentives to establish links with lands from India and further east to China. By the nineteenth century European countries had already seen the potential of taking seeds or cuttings of valued plants from one region of the world to take advantage of suitable climates, soils, and available labour, in another. Obvious examples being tea from China to India and Ceylon, cocoa and coffee from South America to various parts of Africa, rubber from Brazil to Malaya, the chichona tree (source of quinine which could be extracted from the bark) from South America to Java, and tobacco from the Americas to Africa.

During the eighteenth and nineteenth centuries Britain's most important overseas colony was the sub-continent of India. As with the Dutch and the Dutch East India Company in the Far East, so too did Britain allow its interests in India to be progressed via a chartered joint-stock company; in this case the English East India Company (EEIC) initially named 'The Company of Merchants of London trading into the East Indies'. The EEIC had received its first Royal Charter in Dec. 1600 from Queen Elizabeth I with a further Royal charter granted in 1609 extending the company's monopoly of Indian and South-East Asian Trade. A further charter was issued in 1656 by the Lord Protector (Oliver Cromwell) in which the company was given '...the authority to hold, fortify, and settle overseas territory'. The highest body in the EEIC was the General Court, composed of all the investors, but this body had little to do with the day-to-day running of the Company and available evidence suggests that the maximization of profits was the sole motivation for these 'gentleman'. The executive body was the Court of Committee, composed of 24 Directors elected by the General Court and headed by a Governor and a Deputy Governor.

The EEIC applied the same motivation, and used similar methods, as the Dutch EIC to set about drawing wealth from the Far East. From early in the 17th century the Company's main rivals were the Portuguese, French and Dutch with a plethora of other 'East India' companies being spawned in Europe, including:

Swedish East India Company
Danish East India Company
French East India Company

And the Imperial or Ostend Company charted in Vienna. A company given protection by the Hapsburg Empire under the Treaty of Utrecht (an 'East Indies' company in all but name).

James Lancaster was given command of the first EEIC fleet to reach its far eastern destination in 1602 with the lead ship, the Red Dragon, armed with 38 cannon; so prepared as much for conflict as for trade and as such a clear symbol of the methods to be used by the Company. A letter, ostensibly from Queen Elizabeth (in fact drafted by the merchants themselves), notes the aims of the company to be 'trade and friendship' but the subsequent operation of the company suggests that the emphasis was significantly more on trade than on friendship, with the latter being dependent on the extent to which native peoples (or their rulers) were prepared to collude in their own exploitation. Lancaster was able to negotiate the establishment of a 'factory' in the port of Bantum in Java. This provided a strategically well-placed base from which to trade directly with Chinese merchants when they made their annual visit to the port with a large fleet of junks laden with silks, porcelain, and other high value goods.

By the application of a clever strategy of playing local and regional native interests against each other, and if this failed having recourse to the ruthless use of military force, the Company gradually extended its control over the sub-continent. A significant stage in this expansion followed the Battle of Plassy in 1757 which gave the Company control of Bengal. The main sources of wealth were land taxes, customs revenue, and trade. Company profits from revenue collection alone had reached £7.5m by 1765. At the end of the eighteenth century India was contributing £500,000 annually to the

British Treasury, and the trading monopoly with China returned £3m per year in tea duties alone.

The behaviour of two of the Company's principle employees, Robert Clive and Warren Hastings, illustrate the way in which the Company pursued its interests. Clive seems to have been dedicated to the ruthless accumulation of personal wealth and glory, and although initially Hastings showed some sympathy with the Indian people (he felt that they should administer their own country) he also ensured that he was able to amass a large personal fortune (£175,000, equivalent to many millions today, by the time he retired in 1785). Following the battle of Gheriah in 1756, in which European forces had overwhelming manpower and weaponry advantages, the usual practice of plundering a captured city or town took place, with soldiers taking a share based on rank. Clive's share as a Lieutenant Colonel was £5,000. (Felipe Fernadez-Armesto 1995 p365 noted the 'great man' Clive, as: '......great in this case as, at least in greed and grasp and grip.').

In 1756 the Newab of Bengal, upset at the behaviour of the Company, attacked and took control of the City of Calcutta. Following this action a large group of British prisoners of war were locked up in a prison cell in the basement of Fort William for three days. Due to the heat and appalling overcrowding 120 people died of suffocation. The propaganda potential of this episode was not lost on the British press, soon reporting the event with the headline the 'Black Hole of Calcutta.' One of the survivors, John Holwell turned out to be a brilliant publicist and he sent graphic (and probably grossly exaggerated) accounts of what had happened back to the British newspapers. This gave the Company the support of an outraged section of Britain's population and fuelled a national sense of exasperation with these 'natives' to whom Britain mainly only wished to bring trade, Christianity and, in fact all of the benefits of civil life itself. The fact that the 'trade' was a one-way extraction of valuable goods and raw materials while what went the other way was a range of cheaply produced goods such as the textiles that all but destroyed India's own textile industry, that Christianity (as interpreted by British Anglican clerics) suited neither the cultural milieu nor the temperament of most of the population, and that the civil life exported to India consisted of the imposition of a new social hierarchy and a taxation system that was more a charge on being alive rather than a payment for any useful services being supplied. Most employees of the company took their lead from the stockholders and used the advantages employment with the Company allowed to gain wealth by means that were occasionally legitimate (within the context of their employment) but were more often based on corrupt practices. Along with the process of wealth extraction undertaken by the company so also the corrupt administration of its employees, gave no benefit to the mass of Indian people.

The historian Thomas Pakenham asked the pertinent question: 'Was it constitutional for a consortium of London businessmen to govern overseas territories, construct forts, dispense justice, raise revenues, coin money, wage war [engage in drug dealing!] and yet be outside direct control of parliament and answerable only to and indirectly (through the royal charter) to the crown?' (Pakenham, 1991, p169)

And the historian John Keay noted that: 'Imperial conceit would demand a glorious pedigree for 'our Indian Empire' but the plight of India's indigenous peoples in the eighteenth century scarcely affords it.' (Keay, 1993, p292)

It wasn't only the indigenous people of India and south-east Asia that were exploited by the EEIC, it was a company that also profited from the use of and the trade in slaves; mainly from Indonesia and West Africa.

By the end of the eighteenth century the Company's behaviour included breaking treaties, wholesale corruption, and excessive cruelty - exposed by, or rather brought to the attention of, a select committee of parliament - became too much even for the British Government; and the India Act (1785) and the India Charter (1793) introduced more state control, giving the British Crown the power to appoint the Governor General and a Board of Control (six Commissioners – including a British Secretary of State and the Chancellor of the Exchequer) whose remit was to control and direct the Company. At the same time as a 'sweetener' to the Company, and to send a conciliatory message to other joint-stock companies, the Government made a significant reduction in the duties on tea, so offering the prospect of a useful increase in the profits to be made from the China tea trade. According to Keay (ibid,1993) 'In return for surrendering administrative independence in India the Company was rewarded with the most important commercial opportunity in its history.'

By 1817 Britain was effectively in control of all of the sub-continent, apart from the fractious tribesman in the North West frontier, and of the Sindh province, who would only be subdued by 1842. The British Indian Army had 120,000 troops (mostly Indian 'Sepoys') led by British officers, plus 3,000 mercenary Ghurkhas, to control around 300 million Indians. According to one historian '........the British waged more or less continuous war against the Indian people' (Britannica 1974 Vol. 4, page 891). A prolonged campaign to conquer Afghanistan had ended in a humiliating defeat for the British. But Indian served as a secure base from which to enable further British expansion in Java, Borneo, Sumartra, Sri Lanka (Ceylon), and large parts of Burma.

Trade with China not only involved tea, silks and porcelain, (and the 'dumping' of cheap European textiles) but also the narcotic 'opium'. A drug that sends those taking it into a euphoric state where cares are diminished and a sense of well-being attained. This as but a transitory state, the maintenance of which comes at a cost, personal and for society, as the pleasant pastime activity becomes an addiction and the occasional escape from everyday reality becomes a narrow 'world-view' in which the addict can focus only on seeking the pleasurable escapes. For the addict, the 'fixes', that had initially brought pleasure would now only bring relief; and this the transitory relief of the temporarily satiated addict. Few addicts have any ability to contribute usefully to society.

As the heavy use of opium spread from the trading centres, the Chinese Government noted with alarm the detrimental impact it was having on whole communities (and also the increasing drain from China of silver used, along with tea, to pay for the drug) and so it decided to ban the drug's import. China moved to make the trade illegal from 1796, but in response the British East India Company (EEIC) turned to smuggling. Possible as much as 5000 cases of the drug a year were smuggled into China up to 1830 when the Company progressively increased this highly profitable activity to up to 40,000 cases per year. In 1839 the Chinese authorities confiscated 20,000 cases of the drug in Canton and expelled British merchants from the City. The British Government reacted by coming to the merchants' aid and in effect going to war ('The Opium War') with a trading partner. Amongst other acts of aggression it sent an armed fleet up the Yangese River to attack Nanking. The military strength of the British forced the Chinese to capitulate and pay an indemnity of 21 million silver dollars, open up five 'Treaty' ports, sign the 'Treaty of

Nanking' which leased Hong Kong to Britain, and also having to make other concessions to ease trading conditions. Perhaps worst of all (because the most humiliating), the Chinese were forced to accept the continuance of the opium trade - which reached 100,000 cases per year by the 1870s.

British control of India (still dominated by the EEIC) continued to be based on the unprincipled but clever playing off of one native interest (elite group) against another, and the use of military force when required. All the while extracting as much wealth as possible by such measures as the land tax – Pakenham (1991, p169) noted that: ' .....the Company's men lived by the ledger and ruled by the quill.' Or rather, they meticulously recorded their 'legalized pillaging' in this way.

Native troops (Sepoys) serving in the Company's Bengal Army had some awareness of the central role they played in maintaining the Company's position. In the year 1857, a combination of factors including a peasant rebellion against the hated land tax, and a simmering if general dislike of the Company in groups whose families had had land confiscated during protests earlier in the nineteenth-century, contributed to offer an opportunity for rebellion within the British Army. An army whose native members were confronted with an ultimatum to agree to serve overseas (General Enlistment Act 1856); in effect to contribute to the force for consolidating British colonial interests further east. But it was the infamous introduction of new Lee-Enfield rifles, whose greased cartridges were believed to be covered in cow-grease (risking religious pollution for the Hindu troops), that set the uprising in motion. Conflict spread throughout much of the army and the opportunistic Mughal Emperor, Bahadur Shah (along with some other dispossessed local rulers), gave his support and so helped to provide a legitimizing focus for the Sepoys and other groups rising against the British.

The rebellion (termed a 'mutiny' by British officialdom, partly at least in order to justify the harsh treatment of sections of the army - including rebellious soldiers being fired from cannon) failed, due to a significant extent to British support from the Punjabi Sikhs. But the cost to the British included the loss of income from the land tax, the disruption of the opium trade, the more general reduction in economic activity, and also in terms of casualties (40,000 native peoples in the siege of Delhi alone), was significant. Two key outcomes were the ending of the centuries long Mughal Empire in India and the final end of the East Indian Company. In future British India would be controlled from the India Office in London, a control locally exercised by a Viceroy appointed by the Crown and based in Delhi.

By the end of the eighteenth century, the British had established the occupation of Australia, Tasmania, New Zealand, and the western Pacific islands of Fiji, Tonga and the Gilbert Islands. Whilst other European nations laid claim to New Caledonia, the Marquesas, and Tahiti (French), and Mariana (German).

Russia sent military forces, and in their wake settlers, to gain and colonize Siberia and lands further east to China; with some Russian businessmen even casting acquisitive eyes over this border. The emancipation of Russian serfs in 1861 had perversely made many of them more vulnerable to exploitation and led to large numbers of peasants migrating east. As in the US, if on a much smaller scale, colonial expansion from Russia and Ukraine eastwards displaced indigenous peoples. The motivation was furs, timber, as well as land, and in places 'loot'. Following the completion of the trans-Siberian railway, a significant increase in trade in manufactured goods went eastwards and a range of raw materials returned westward.

By 1900 pretty much the whole of the Far East was either directly controlled or under the indirect influence of European Powers if a few areas that did not offer much potential for exploitation were relatively unaffected. Globally, any piece of accessible land, whether island or on a continental landmass, was likely to be brought under the 'protection' of some colonizing industrialized nation.

One of these, Japan, started on the road to industrialization a bit later than had the most European nartions. Following the civil war in 1868, the restoration of the Emperor and the ending of feudalism, astute Japanese businessmen and others of the ruling groups advanced the development of a financial system that was tailored to finance the process of industrialization. As this progressed, and with it the capacity to wage war, the Japanese looked to create their own mini empire. Expanding first to neighbouring islands of Ryukyu, Bonin, and Kuril, going on to force China to cede interests in Taiwan and southern Manchuria. Then, early in the twentieth century (1904-5), Japan defeated Russia and was able to gain control of Liatung, and part of the large island of Sakhalin.

If we suggest some balance to the emphasis that I have placed on exploitation, cruelty, and greed to frame colonialism, I would need to include what would be, at least claimed as, a benefit to 'civil' colonization. That in the longer term this allowed the colonized peoples to gain access to global civil history and to the knowledge that inheres within this; including the natural and social sciences, and western philosophy. Colonial peoples would also be provided with the technological advantages such as: modern agricultural techniques, railways, the telegraph, modern printing techniques, the 'medical model' of medicine, and indeed the mechanization of production and distribution processes. The overall benefit of each of these could be contended but not here.

Clearly, it could still be pointed out that these potential benefits could all have been offered in a mutually beneficial way – with knowledge flowing both ways – rather than any benefit being more the longer-term incidental outcome of European nations' attempts to wring as much wealth and assumed national prestige from their colonies as possible. The colonial powers acted in ways that were based on exploitation, were often cruel, and were throughout oppressive. We might accept that the indigenous elite groups displaced by the major powers had mostly taken a similar self-interested approach to their own governing and their passing was rarely mourned by the indigenous populations. This hardly justifies the ways in which the European colonizers behaved but it should make us aware that, in relation to good and evil - it is perhaps not 'who' rules but rather 'how' people are ruled that matters; or rather the system of 'governance', as we would now suggest

South America was to experience a different type of control by European (and later the US) power after its first European colonizers, Spain and Portugal, had become fatally weakened. Firstly, by their inability to support colonies at a distance when the Iberian Peninsula was being occupied by the French from 1807-14. Then secondly, by the disruption caused during the drawn-out period of the Peninsular Wars as Napoleon's army fought an increasingly rearguard action against Wellington's forces and Spanish guerillas; along with the generally debilitated condition of once powerful nations in decline.

The South American colonies were rarely governed wisely by Spanish and Portuguese administrators, merchants, and many others, most greedy for silver and gold, along with a Catholic Church greedy for converts as well as at least a share of the loot. The disruption in the European home nations allowed the colonized, especially Creole elites, an opportunity to be free of the colonizers. Nationalist movements made progress in some countries, and civil conflicts, at times breaking out into war in others, showed not just the weakness of the colonizing powers but also the fact of bitter rivalries between competing elite groups competing for control within countries across the continent. The main division was Creole against those of the merchant class and descendants of the administrators loyal to, Spain or Portugal. These groups came together on occasions when their combined strength was required to put down more popular uprisings or slave revolts (as in Cuba and Mexico).

During the period of the wars of independence, or of internal national conflict, the military came to the fore and gained a level of power that would be retained following independence. In many of the newly independent countries 'independence' meant only that colonization had been replaced by indigenous military dictatorships supported by powerful large landowners. By the time in 1825 that Bolivia was declared a Republic the whole of Spanish South America had freed itself of direct colonial control; at least politically rather than economically. The disruption of this period in the first quarter of the century left a legacy of armed rebel bands and gangs of bandits roaming the countryside and living off the land right up to 1850s. Most countries of Spanish South America experienced prolonged political turmoil.

Some countries fragmented, as smaller nationalisms emerged and demanded their own independence. And although in places peasants were mobilized to fight, outside of the cities in countries such as Mexico, Guatemala, Peru, and Bolivia, most Indian communities continued their lives relatively unaffected by the political upheavals. But when the interests of merchants, financiers, miners, and big farmers, came up against the interest of Indians it was invariably the former that got their way. According to Tulio Halperin Donghi (1993 p100): '....whether directed at the Church or at Indian communities, the dissolution of collective ownership was a goal of most "progressive" governments of the period'.

This conflict of interests became increasingly apparent in the latter half of the century when big landowners used clever lawyers to wrest land traditionally held in common by villagers from them; not dissimilar to the various types of 'enclosures' of common land that had been taking place in Britain and across Europe, and the taking of 'common' lands' from the native peoples of North America.

By the time the political landscape of nationhood was settling down the military had a significant degree of influence, even when not in direct control. The cost of supporting standing armies placed a heavy burden on national budgets, for some countries this amounted to nearly 50% of total government income. It was this situation of some economic instability overseen by politically weak governments that the next wave of colonizers would take advantage of. These European colonizers, were wiser than those being displaced and measured success in terms of economic profit rather than more simply in controlling vast swaths of land. European nations were also dissuaded from obvious political interference in South America when, in 1823, in a speech made to Congress and the House of Representatives, US President James Munroe warned European nations against attempting any direct colonization in South America *'In the discussions to which this interest has given rise and in the arrangements by which they may terminate the occasion has been judged proper for asserting, as a principle in which the rights and interests of the United States are involved that the American continents, by the free and independent condition which they have assumed and maintain, are henceforth not to be considered as subjects for future colonization by any European powers.'*

In setting out this US Government perspective Munroe was motivated by the fact that the US was looking to extend its own influence in the area; influence extending to both the annexation of territory and the advance of its political and trading interests.

This warning was timely but it also chimed with what Britain was learning from its experience as a colonizing nation. Its imperial presence in India was one of controlling territory, introducing and collecting taxes and endeavouring to maintain a firm monopoly grip on economic activity. Contrary to this, British imperialism across South America was to take a form of control that focused on advancing British economic interests by mostly shrewd economic investments and by cultivating and providing financial backing for the likely victors from the various elite groups seeking power.

According to Donghi (1993, p84): 'The beneficiaries [mainly Britain] of this informal empire avoided the complication and expense of administering it. They bore no responsibility for arbitrating the violent clashes among the various local interests. Instead they left those dubious honours to the Spanish American elites and concentrated on their profit margins.'

The US did not become a significant threat to Britain's global economic dominance until the 1850s; and then mainly only in Central America and some of the Caribbean Islands. In countries such as Mexico, Brazil and Argentina, British (and other European nations, especially French) businessmen and the agents of mainly British companies gave support to this or that elite group's attempt to gain power. Throughout the nineteenth-century the imports of British manufactured goods rose. Here, as had previously been the case in India, the import of cheaply made British cotton goods resulted in the near destruction of the indigenous textile industry.

As well as being able to profit by developing the local economies – mining, extraction of oil and hardwoods, construction, utilities, railways, and in a range of other capital projects - British businessmen, and to a lesser extent those from Germany and France, developed an export trade back to Europe in beef, mutton (refrigerated shipping from1883), wheat, sugar, maize, hardwoods, and coffee, as large swaths of rain forest and pampas was turned into grazing lands or for the cultivation of crops. Although British merchants and manufacturers had established themselves across the continent during the first half of the century the more significant capital investment was made from the 1850s, and between 1870 and 1913 British investment rose from £85m to £757m, and 50% of the shipping (by tonnage) using the ports of Argentina and Brazil was controlled by British companies. British banks were predominant by the 1860s. On very rare occasions the British did resort to 'gunboat diplomacy' to advance its interests… joining forces with France in the 1850s to blockade Rio de la Plata. Italy and Germany also joined forces to blockade Venezuela at the end of the century; initially with US collusion if later, partly in response to public opinion, the US came to oppose this action.

Filipe Fernandez-Armesto notes that the British businessman Weetman Pearson (later Lord Cowdray) '…was said to have looted more from Mexico than any man since Cortes'. A suggestion that he attempts to mitigate by noting that Pearson was also something of a philanthropist.

As the century progressed it was the US to the north that brought aspects of both classic forms of colonization – control of land and economic control – together as it progressed the consolidation of its the borders. A process that in the first half of the nineteenth century had included the Louisiana Settlement, Britain and Russia giving up claims to territory in the North West (Oregon), and Spain abandoning its claim to Florida; then the US annexing Texas in 1836 and further Mexican territory in 1846-48.

The opening of the California Goldfields in 1848 gave a real impetus to completing the Panama Canal. A project first suggested in the early sixteenth-century by both Spain and France. It was the French engineer Ferdinand de Lesseps, builder of the Suez Canal, who took the lead on behalf of a French construction company and between 1881and 1888 the first stage of the extremely difficult project was completed. Difficult in both engineering terms and the effect on the labourers of malaria and yellow fever; between 25,000-35,000 being said to have died during construction. When the French company gave up in 1899 the US took up the task and between 1904 and 1914 the final stage of the 51 mile canal was completed – reducing the journey from California to New York by 18,000 miles. Since then the US has effectively controlled the important 10 mile wide strip known as the 'Canal Zone' a right purchased from Panama on a perpetual lease for a down payment of $10m and $250,000 a year and in addition the US guaranteed the independence of the then newly created country.

The nineteenth-century saw the creation of a series of (nominally) independent South American nation-states but an independence subject to significant, if varying, degrees of control by US, Britain, and France (if French influence was mostly restricted to Caribbean Islands such as Haiti and Martinique). A financial system had been developed to serve the needs of capitalist economic requirements, including that of the need to factor in the costs of buying the cooperation of corrupt government ministers. Economically, the continent was increasingly drawn into a developing world economic system, illustrated by the rise of direct capital investment by European and US interests and the raising of capital by Latin American governments issuing bonds to be traded on the Europeans bond markets. There had been a significant broadening of the range of goods flowing between South American countries and Europe. From South America came food stuffs and raw materials such as – coffee, meat, hides, grain, timber, rubber, guano, copper - added to bullion and sugar. From Europe a range of standardized, manufactured goods, engineered metal products (machine tools, armaments, ships, trains, and a range of products to support utilities such as water, sewerage, and electricity plants), communication technology (typewriter, telegraph, submarine cables), and luxury goods for members of the wealthy elites. And of course a significant amount of financial capital invested, and of foreign banking expertise brought in to facilitate the industrial exploitation of the continent.

For Donghi (1993) 'Essentially, Latin America became a producer of primary products for European markets, while Europe traded its manufactures in return'

I accept that I have not conveyed any real sense of the economic, social and political complexities of nineteenth-century South America, which included the support of elite groups friendly to foreign investors. Elites that were themselves in a position to benefit from open trade, and able to deploy the military power to quell the resistance that occurred at a range of levels… from local peasant uprisings, industrial action in the cities, and slave revolts[9]. More significant political actions were also undertaken in support of idealistic aspirations, such as those expounded by Bernardo O'Higgins in Chile and the serial fighter for independent South American countries – Venezuela, Peru, Columbia, Ecuador, and the land that became Bolivia - Simon Bolivar.

Although Bolivar was highly critical of colonialism, he was in favor of only limited electoral franchise and of quite authoritarian forms of government; with parliamentary systems but with a life-long president. He set out and justified his political views in his 'Letter From Jamaica' (1815), suggesting that such autocratic systems were necessary to pragmatically reflect the type of government required by the then contemporary South American societies.

As the century developed, there was a continued influx of European and US businessmen, diplomats, and merchants, along with their liberalist (perhaps better described as 'acquisitive') economic ideas underpinned by the inter-linking of capitalist industrialization and free-trade with the concept of progress; most governments came to accept and promote the idea of this version of progress as an unquestioned good in itself.

Nineteenth century European colonization extended into the Pacific Ocean, including island groups (such as the Gilbert Islands, Papua New Guinea, Polynesia) and the southern continent which included the lands of Australia, Tasmania, and New Zealand. Lands that had perhaps been visited in the fifteenth-century by Chinese

---

[9] Britain itself did by then oppose the slave trade and Brazil finally succumbed to British pressure to bring this trade to an end in 1851.

seaman, with the west coast of Australia being noted from the seventeenth-century by Portuguese and Dutch sailors who had lost their way and strayed too far east whilst on the passage from The Cape of Good Hope to their Indonesia trading posts. One noted visit being made by the Dutch ship 'Eendracht', from which sailors landed in October 1616, leaving a memorial at Shark Bay in Western Australia. More organized expeditions were undertaken by the Dutch using their Indonesian base at Bantam as a starting point. In 1626/7 The Dutchman Pietr Nuyt led an expedition that explored a long stretch of the west coast and in 1642 Abel Tasman ventured as far south as New Zealand, giving the name Van Diemen's Land to what would be come Tasmania and later the name New Holland to what was to become Australia.

During the eighteenth-century the British Government became increasingly interested in the southern continent, and in the 1770s the government sent Captain James Cook on the first of a series of voyages, during which he carried out meticulous charting operations. Actual occupation began in 1788 when a fleet of 11 ships reached Botany Bay carrying about 1000 people – 570 male convicts, 160 female convicts, and 250 free citizens. A second fleet arrived in 1790, with a settlement being established in Sydney Cove. Exploration of this vast new territory and its progressive settlement went hand in hand throughout the nineteenth century. Notable expeditions being those undertaken in 1790s by George Bass and Mathew Flinders, the latter changing the name of the continent from New Holland to Australia in 1817; a move that signified the shift in the balance of naval power between the two European nations. By early in the nineteenth-century the coastline of the southern continent had been charted and the early settlers were learning to cope with the often harsh environment, with a steady stream of convict and voluntary settlers continuing to arrive.

From the very first contact the relationship between settlers and indigenous peoples, 'Aborigines', was antagonistic. By the time that the European colonists first landed aboriginal people had occupied the continent for over 40,000 years, an occupation begun by people migrating from southern Indonesia and spreading out across the vast continent.

These were a people that would develop a rather special world-view, one that integrated the living and the dead in a way that reflected the ways in which the land and its animal life supported their own existence – they saw living interconnections, real and imagined merged together, densely intertwined within all aspects of their environments. They believed that their ancestors were created out of the water, sky, and animals, during a 'dream time' when the natural world was infused with an animalistic spirituality. On death the ancestors had been absorbed into rivers, rocks, and other natural features, so assuming an enduring spiritual presence in the landscapes. When contact was first made with Europeans some Aboriginal groups considered them to be the returning spirits of their Aboriginal ancestors.

It is difficult to obtain exact figures but very rough estimates suggest that the continent was occupied by possibly over 1,000,000 Aboriginal peoples at the time of initial colonization, divided into possibly 500 distinct tribal groups. There was an element of inter-group conflict (more especially apparent with the Maoris of New Zealand), over hunting lands and other resources, but the cost of losing men-folk in conflict would have such an impact on small groups occupying fragile environments that negotiations and compromise, or the acceptance of another group's superiority, would probably have been the more usual ways of containing conflict.

These technologically primitive but culturally rich peoples, with little sense of ownership and of regular industry, would suffer a similar fate to indigenous people elsewhere in the world when advancing 'industrial civilization' sailed or marched over their horizons.

The systemic racism that was a contributory factor in making the ill-treatment more acceptable to the perpetrators was signaled by Britain declaring the whole continent 'Terra Nullius' – basically indicating that it was a land uninhabited by human beings and therefore not 'owned'. The 'non-human' inhabitants were treated in-humanly from the very beginning. Treatment illustrated by the reprisal inflicted for a minor insult to Britain, when the commander of the first fleet to arrive to establish the penal colony at Sydney Cove and the first British Governor of New South Wales, Arthur Phillip – who is thought to have generally taken a kindly if paternalistic approach to the aborigines – decided in response to some perceived insult to randomly select ten Aborigine men and to have them beheaded in public.

The coverting of land that the Aboriginal peoples were sustained by, along with the underlying racism of the European mindset towards native peoples, were the two main factors that set the background context within which the colonizers approached their relationship to the indigenous peoples of Australia, Tasmania, New Zealand, and other islands of the region.

In places Aboriginals fought back...... notably at Parramatta, Pinjarra, and Battle Hill, among others, following leaders such as Pemulwuy, Calyute and Yegan. A mostly untold history of colonization would be of resistance, of those that refused to bow. But the technological advantages, the ability to provision larger numbers of fighters, plus their ruthlessness, easily favoured the Europeans. In Australia the notorious Native Police forces (often using Aboriginal trackers to track Aborigines) engaged in massacres, and some farmers ventured out on murderous punitive expeditions in response to the theft of stock; often taken by a people whose own means of subsistence was being stolen from them by those now seeking their extermination.

In 1824 settlers were given official permission to shoot Aboriginals. During a time when in Britain childhood was being created 'factory laws, some general education, and the idea of 'play''......aboriginal children were being forced into labour. Aboriginal women were routinely raped by Europeans and, along with their men-folk, were often poisoned, tortured, or shot. Europeans hunted aboriginals simply for sport and at times settler groups also engaged in the wholesale slaughter of men, women and children.

In Queensland alone, between 1824 and 1898, 10,000 Aborigines were murdered, both casually and systematically; perhaps not surprising when the language infusing the discourse used in the anti-aboriginal propaganda included descriptive concepts such as 'wild animals', 'nuisance', 'thieves', 'vermin', 'primitive' (meant as an insult), and suggested that they were 'fair game'. A report by a Royal Commission, tasked to consider the situation, noted that: 'The treatment of Cape York people was a shame to our common humanity'. During the hundred years from 1788-1888 it is thought that the Aboriginal population of Australia was reduced from 1,000,000 to 100,000.

The island of Tasmania stands out in the bleak legacy of genocides carried out by 'civil' peoples in that the original 6,000 natives were completely wiped out by the end of the nineteenth-century – they were in effect hunted out.

The Maoris of New Zealand, with a significant militaristic element to their own culture, took longer to subdue but this was effectively completed by the end of the mid century Maori wars. A population of over 150,000 in 1800 (with groups living in approx. 600 fortified 'camps') being reduced to 42,000 by 1893; if this conflict was more of a 'draw' between the Maoris and the British. Most of the violence involved land disputes – as settlers endeavoured to transfer ownership from native peoples to themselves (to transform the status of land from being a common resource to a privately owned commodity), using a legal framework designed by the British and so favouring the settlers. Along with the actual violence used on the native peoples of Australia, Tasmania, and New Zealand, settlers also brought diseases such as small pox and venereal disease. Every possible degradation, humiliation, and cruelty was inflicted on these peoples by their 'civilized' colonizers.

Whilst the on-going persecution of the native peoples continued, the nineteenth century also saw the social and economic development of the southern continent. By 1830 58,000 convicts had been landed in Australia and thousands of immigrant settlers had established farms, a fishing industry (including hunting of whales and seals), and had laid the basis of mining, construction, and manufacturing industries. Explorers and naturalists travelled along coasts and ventured far into the interior ('Out-back') of the continent, identifying the course of the rivers, the extent of mountain ranges, and generally contributing to mapping the land and the recording of the great variety of the flora and fauna. Up until 1831 land had been granted to colonists but from this date it would be sold. The lands that had but 30 years previously been roamed over, and felt as but a nurturing landscape, within which the native peoples were spiritually attached by naturalistic links to the 'living' presence of ancestors and to the immediate daily sustenance, would from now be but another commodity – inveigled into the money economy – yet another example of a common resource transformed into private property. Indigenous peoples in European colonies with a significant 'white' presence elsewhere in the world - Canada, and sub-Saharan Africa, especially South Africa and Rhodesia – experienced similar processes of economic, social, and political, development.

The increasing needs of capitalist economic development required new sources of raw materials and expanding markets for manufactured goods. This, allied to the acquisitive characteristics of the merchant and of the imperialist national state, was to bring the vast continent of Africa into the sphere of expanding European civil life. A continent whose interior territory was pretty much unknown to outsiders until the nineteenth-century. The northern coastal regions had been involved with the development of civil life from its efflorescence in the Mediterranean region circa 2000 years BCE and in Egypt from even earlier as one of the civilizations contributing to knowledge of astronomy, mathematics, medicine, trade, architecture, religion, agriculture, the arts and to the administration of civil life. It is possible that as early as 600 BCE a Phoenician ship, at the request of the Egyptian King Necho, undertook the approx. 17,000 mile circumnavigation of the continent (as recorded by the Greek Historian Herodotus). And around 460 BCE a fleet under the command of the Phoenician, Henno the Navigator, set off west from Carthage with the intention of repeating this 'mythical' feat. Henno sailed down the west coast at least as far as the Senegal River and then ventured some way up the river into the interior. He returned with colourful stories describing exotic animals such as crocodile and hippopotami, and bringing back the skins of three female apes (probably gorillas). From early on Arab caravans had trekked deep into the Saharan and sub-Saharan regions engaging in trade, both in precious metals, manufactured goods, and in slaves.

Portuguese sailors voyaged south in the 14th and 15th, centuries, establishing trading forts in the more hospitable places along the western coast, with again the main trade being in slaves. The Africa of the time had already seen quite significant development in civil societies, going back perhaps as early as 3,000 BCE with the Kerma settlements in the region that became known as Nubia and certainly with the later Napatan settlement in the same region about 500 BCE. More recent and more substantial civil settlements included a Mali Empire begun perhaps as early as the first millennium CE but certainly consolidated by around 1230 CE when the Malinke people organized themselves to repel the encroachment of a southern aggressor (Soninki) from Ghana on the River Niger. The Mali Empire was a civilization whose prosperity was closely connected to the River Niger and its hinterland; the fertility of which was released due to a significant contribution of slave labour working on the land. It also benefited from a monopoly control of gold-fields and salt-mines, both of which provided valuable products with which to trade with their northern neighbours. The ability to organize an effective civil administration enabled the efficient collection of taxes – tax on all trade into and out of the vast region over which the Malinki came to rule. A rule to which the many subject tribal groups paid annual tribute in such goods as rice, millet, and weapons. Contact with northern Muslims led to the Mali upper classes adopting Islam as their preferred religion and there is a record of one king of Mali, Mansa Musa, undertaking a pilgrimage to Mecca (Haji) in 1324 with a vast caravan of 60,000 people. He is reputed to have had 500 slaves, each carrying a solid gold bar weighing four pounds. Musa's entourage distributed gold in exchange for hospitality as they travelled north to Timbuktu, east to Cairo, then on to Mecca. At its civil peak towards the end of the fourteenth-century, the Mali Empire had an administration based on provincial governorships with local mayors controlling the larger towns and cities and a huge standing army ready to move swiftly to put down any attempt at rebellion. It also developed its own distinctive art forms and had a level of scholarship admired by counterparts of the Southern European universities with whom there was contact.

In the east of the continent, with its heartland nestled within the highlands of Ethiopia, the Kingdom of Axum enjoyed a thousand-year ascendancy. Emerging in the 3rd century BCE, it exerted a significant regional influence extending at times as far north as the southern Mediterranean shore. Its Emperor converted to Christianity in the 4th century, thus establishing a firm cultural link to the Middle East and to southern Europe. A period of relative isolation set in during the rise of Islam, when the Empire was surrounded by generally hostile neighbours, and it never regained is central role in east African trade. A further factor in the Empire's demise involved climate change and the erosion of much of its most fertile soils. As the shrinking Empire reduced to the status of a modest kingdom, dynasties came and went until the restoration of the Solomonic Dynasty in 1270 (Yekuno Amlak who claimed direct descent from Solomon and the Queen of Sheba) establishing a line of dynastic decent that would last until 1974 when Haile Selassie died. The 17/18th centuries were ones of relative isolation and general decline, with the remains of the Empire separating into fractious regional power-bases. In 1855 Tewodros II (Ras Kassa) seized power and set about bringing unity to what had become a disintegrating state and introduced some aspects of modern civil society.

An uneasy alliance was maintained with the Portuguese who, from about 1520, helped to defend the kingdom against the Jewish

Falasaha and the Ottoman Muslims. The religious links with the Catholic Church, reinforced by the presence of zealous Jesuits, continued to overlie trading and diplomatic links with countries to the north. Following decades of religious factionalism all Christian missionaries were expelled early in the seventeenth century and the Empire reverted to its own original version of Christianity (Monophysite). Although mainly an agrarian economy, if with one characterized by extensive trading links to the north and east, the Ethiopian Empire had institutions of administration and culture that would fairly be describe as civil. It developed its own Ethiopic syllabary from roots in the Southern Arabian alphabet.

From the Christian era down to 1440 various kingdoms and modest empires have come and gone during the long history of Zimbabwe, some leaving enduring evidence of their achievements in the ruins of what once were significant – mainly granite stone buildings at: Khami, Great Zimbabwe, Natetale, and Dhlo-Dhlo (renamed Danangombe). Probably the most impressive monument being the *Imba Huru,* at about 32 feet in height and 800 feet in length, requiring 15,000 tons of granite blocks in its construction – and the skills of the architects, the stone-masons, and other craftsmen, as well as the sweat of the labourers. And of course also required was the administrative efficiency to organize the material and human resources for such a monumental undertaking and the necessary complex social structure to give rise to it. Many of the impressive stone buildings were constructed without the use of mortar. This civilization had been brought together by the ancestors of the Shona peoples attaining a period of marked prosperity by about the fifteenth century

In the mid 1440s King Mutota of the Mwene Mutapa (or Monomatapas) had established a kingdom extending across the vast Rhodesian Plateau and east into what is today's Mozambique. Although a largely agrarian region, there was a variety of small-scale economic activity, including iron-working and textile production. These commodities, as well as gold and cooper, and slaves, were the basic trade-goods exchanged with Arab and Swahili merchants based in the cities.

The City of Greater Zimbabwe itself has been estimated to have had a population of approx. 18,000 in the fourteenth-century, comparable to some late medieval European cities. Greater Zimbabwe was a centre of much commercial and administrative activity. One historian, D. Beach, offered a picture of aspects of the living conditions of the settlement of Zimbabwe, including the noise, smoke, and smells, that the densely packed population would have generated; noting hundreds if not thousands of cooking fires creating a veritable 'smog' over the town (cited in G. Connah, 2001 edition).

There is evidence of trade with places as far away at Syria (glassware), Persia (textiles) and China (ceramics and cattle) from perhaps as early as the fourteenth-century. Conflict with the Portuguese (mostly over trading competition) during the sixteenth-century led to a period of decline in economic activity. A situation only reversed when a confederation of the Shona people gradually formed the Rozwi Empire. An empire that was to oversee a period of prosperity until conflict with Europeans expanding from the south in the mid-nineteenth century symbolically brought an end to indigenous rule when, exhibiting his usual self-effacing modesty, Cecil Rhodes had the country named after himself! As he noted in his book 'Confession of Faith':

"We know the size of the world we know the total extent. Africa is still lying ready for us it is our duty to take it. It is our duty to seize every opportunity of acquiring more territory and we should keep this one idea steadily before our eyes that more territory simply means more of the Anglo-Saxon race, more of the best the most human most honourable race the world possesses."

We can see, writ large in Rhodes's revealing comment, both the racism that reflected the mindset of many Europeans of the time and also the underlying personal greed that used assumed racial superiority as a justification for the aggressive approach taken to pursue the accumulation of wealth. We can also note the use of the proactive word 'duty', suggesting a moral weakness, a dereliction of duty, if the spread of Rhodes's version of some fictional 'Anglo-Saxon race' isn't undertaken.

So this brief overview of civil life in sub-Saharan Africa, up to the time of colonization by the leading European powers, shows the aptitude to develop a level of civil life that the economic resources and the social conditions of the time could sustain. A level of civil life that colonizers and covetous adventurers such as Rhodes tried to deny. Even if within the indigenous civil life this aptitude was just as mired in the evils of self-consciousness – at the 'tribal' level the waging of war and widespread involvement in the institution of slavery - as was the civil life in the northern hemisphere. Empires such as those of the Ashanti, Yoruba, and Dahomey, gained a significant proportion of their wealth from the slave trade and in turn used some of this to purchase arms from the Portuguese, the Dutch, and later on the English, and to engage in armed conflict with their neighbours. The historians Jane Burbank and Fredrick Cooper suggest that the military peoples of: 'Ashanti, Dahomey, Oyo, Benin, produced... efficient slave trading mechanisms.' (Burbank and Cooper, 2010, p179) A 'commodity' gained in warring or by more specific raiding to the south seeking captives.

The cruelty of the Zulus under their leader Shaka is well-attested too. The Zulus (not showing such a level of civil development as the empires that had developed elsewhere in Africa) rose in 1816, from a relatively small clan (like the Matabele, the Zulus were also a confederacy of widely dispersed Bantu peoples) able to field about 350 warriors, to become, by the 1850s, a nation able to field a ferocious and well-trained army 50,000 strong, one armed with the short stabbing assegai so effective in hand-to-hand combat. They were a people who gloried in violence and who allowed themselves to be led by a militaristic elite that had little respect for the cultures and lives of other tribal groups.

What even this brief account of civil Africa does is clearly contradict any claim of little pre-colonial civil development beyond Egypt. We can note that for at least four millennia, the African continent had been developing its own versions of civil life, if also versions that included quite wide-spread civil strife.

In the sixteenth century the Dutch showed interest in the east coast of Africa and began to displace the Portuguese as the main traders; building trading forts at favourable places along the coast, The Dutch also established a stopover for the 'retourschips' (the East Indies bound 'return ships') for replenishing water and other stores on the long journey to the East Indies - at the Cape of Good Hope. Building a fort there and establishing the basis of a colony in the 1650s. At around the same time the British were showing an interest in the west coast, an interest that, prior to its being brought to an end within the British Empire, had focused on supplying the slave trade. Little was then known in Europe about sub-Saharan Africa beyond the more accessible coastal regions. The penetration into the interior of the 'dark continent' was pursued, mainly by tracing the source of the major rivers - a means of travelling inland made much easier with the invention of steam-powered gunboats and the discovery that quinine[10] could cure, or at least alleviate, the symptoms of malaria; the death rates of Europeans fell by 80% following the widespread use of quinine.

In 1788 The 'Africa Association' (full name 'Association for Promoting the Discovery of the Interior Parts of Africa') was founded in London by a group of English scientists, including the explorer Mungo Parks, and early on it sponsored an expedition to explore the River Niger and, in the 17 years to 1805, promoted further exploration. In 1857 the ill-matched pair Richard Burton and John Speake set out to find the source of the Nile and in 1869 Speake and J.A.Grant confirmed the source to be Lake Victoria. The Zambesi River was explored by David Livingston, and the Rivers Congo and Lualaba by Henry Morton Stanley, the Welsh born American citizen and journalist – who would later became notorious for his cruelty to the native peoples whilst working for the Belgium King Leopold II in the Congo.

From about the 1850s European interest in the continent increased to become what has been described as 'The Scramble for Africa' (repeated by Thomas Pakenham 1919, in the title of his substantial book 'The Scramble for Africa'). A scramble characterized by the leading European powers competing with each other to grab or at least control as much territory as possible. The evils that resulted in this approach can be seen at their worst in the way that King Leopold II took part in the scramble with some self-seeking enthusiasm. Leopold seemed to have been a man whose thoughts were focused on his own ego to the extent of it displacing any sense of humanity. This narrowing of interest led him to seek aggrandizement for his relatively modest European kingdom and the accumulation of as much personal wealth as possible. From his gaining the throne in 1865 he travelled widely in the Middle and Far East and took an interest in territories that might offer the potential to become colonies of Belgium. Leopold read with increasing interest about what was happening in Africa. Including his learning about the journey of the British Lieutenant Verney Cameron, the explorer who took three difficult years to cross Africa from east to west. A journey that he wrote up in letters home and in articles sent back to The Times

---

[10] Extracted from bark of the Cinchona tree by two chemists from 1820s and was being manufactured on a large scale by 1830s.

newspaper in London (read each day by Leopold). Cameron suggested that the land presented a veritable honey-pot of wealth in minerals and precious metals just waiting for the brave investor. Leopold offered, via the Royal Geographic Society of London, to pay Cameron's expenses and in 1876 he gathered members of the Society, some explorers, and other interested parties, at a conference in Brussels. This conference on Central Africa was ostensibly a scientific debate framed in the language of informed geographers but in fact, as subsequent developments revealed, it was but another step in advancing Leopold's personal ambitions.

The 'opening up', or rather the mapping and assessment of the potential of the central and south areas of the continent, was continued at a pace. Henry Morten Stanley, whose already harsh treatment of tribal groups had preceded his setting off, in 1876, to repeat Cameron's earlier journey crossing the continent from east to west. Stanley himself had boasted of his party having in 1875 killed 33 and wounded over 100 Bumbireh tribesmen that he felt had 'insulted' him. An incident that took place on his return from a trip which included the circumnavigation of Lake Victoria. A trip during which he met King Mtesea, the cruel Kabaka of Buganda, who was reputed to have had 30 of his full and half brothers murdered when he acceded to the throne.

In order to gain guides, bearers to carry his portable boat The Lady Alice, and for armed protection, Stanley formed an alliance with the notorious slaver Tippu Tip who was the owner of a number of extensive plantations tended by thousands of slaves; although a significant slave trader he also enjoyed a near monopoly of the west coast ivory trade. Stanley initially paid Tippu Tip the then enormous sum of $5,000 to supply about 450 men and women for the expedition and later on an additional $2,600 to persuade him to continue. The 700 strong party set out from Nyangwe (about 900 miles from the east coast of Africa) on the river Lualaba on 5th Nov. 1876 but found it difficult to make progress through the dense rain-forest, with sickness (small-pox, dysentery, typhoid) and exhaustion taking a toll; and increasingly meagre rations further reducing morale. After about the first four weeks some of the party were able to take to the Lualaba River in the Lady Alice whilst the rest progressed along the river bank. Although physically the journey became slightly easier, they found that the tribes living along the way were increasingly hostile, assuming that Stanley's party was just another people hunting expedition being made by slave traders. At the end of Dec. 1876 Tippu Tip decided he had had enough and he and his own group left Stanley to struggle on with a much reduced party. But in his customary style of dogged determination, allied to the willingness to liberally deploy their snider rifles, Stanley's group made steady if slow progress west. Having to negotiate several huge waterfalls and to hack their way through mile after mile of dense tropical jungle. It took Stanley 10 months to complete his journey and his exhausted, near starving, group of 115 men, women, and children, (left from the 700 who had set out) were just about finished when they managed to get a message announcing their 'success' through to the trading post at Boma, situated in the estuary of the River Congo.

It was in June 1877 that King Leopold heard the news of Stanley's successful crossing of Africa, during which he had confirmed the extent of the River Congo and also that it wound its way into the heart of a sprawling treasure-trove of potential wealth.

Media distortion (and Stanley's shameless approach to self-publicity, aided by and the public's propensity to 'hero worship') and the highly selective reporting of Stanley's travels in Africa led to his being feted when he returned to England in January 1878. But his attempts to garner business and political interest in significantly increasing the British presence in central Africa were generally unsuccessful. Frustrated with Britain's lack of interest in taking up the opportunities offered in the Congo, and having completed a book on his journey through the heart of the 'Dark Continent'; Stanley travelled to Brussels to meet King Leopold. The outcome of this meeting being that by late 1878 Stanley and Leopold arranged to work together to advance their shared interest in the Congo, or rather Stanley agreed to work for the King for the next five years. The mindset of covetousness invoked fears of being preempted by others and so Stanley agreed to the King's request to keep their plans as secret as possible. He returned to the Congo in Feb 1879 and began to establish the first few of an intended chain of trading stations – a task involving driving a path into dense jungle and dynamiting through rocky obstacles along the way.

But by now Britain was also taking a closer interest in central and west Africa, and the French were consolidating their own interests in the north-west of the continent, each signing treaties with a number of local kings. Treaties which gave the French significant trading rights in exchange for offers of protection for compliant tribal groups.

The French presence in the Niger Delta included a gunboat, the Voltigeur. That, in addition to protecting French local interests, was able to allow passage further afield to extend its influence by signing treaties with some local kings and chieftains further inland.

The successful advance of French control caused increasing concern to Britain, its reaction being to step up its own activities along the west coast, especially in the Niger region. It had been influential in the region for some time and the number of British traders increased steadily. Most of these being middlemen were working for the North Africa Company (NAC), a trading group specifically established to take full advantage of any opportunity to gain profit, mainly to be made in the lucrative palm oil trade. The NAC was a company run and owned by a group of aggressive and greedy stakeholders whose local agents had been active mainly in areas accessible to the River Niger, and so areas where they could gain some level of protection and threaten locals with gunboats. A threat made actual during a number of punitive expeditions that left whole villages destroyed and the inhabitants - men, women, and children - dead or mutilated.

Whilst generally given a friendly reception, the British representative, Edward Hewett, ('Her Majesty's Consul for the Bights of Benin and Biafra') encountered a less than enthusiastic response from some native leaders with one chief, King Ja-Ja of Opobo, in particular, being a man who had a shrewd understanding of trade and of the value of the resources under his control. Especially of his local monopoly in the palm oil trade, to maintain which he was prepared to use violence against any individual or group who threatened this. Hewett's response to opposition from leaders such as Ja-Ja was to use their obstructive approach as justification for Britain adopting even more aggressive methods. Hewett deployed gunboats to shell villages and towns, and machine guns (Maxim guns) against the civilian populations of any of the settlements that were deemed to be unfriendly to Britain; or rather the economic interests of British traders, meaning in effect the NAC. During the early years of the 1880s the British and French competed to gain influence and control in West Africa. At about this time the Germans also began to take a closer interest in the region and, through surreptitious and clever diplomacy, they were able to take control of Cameroon in the name of the Kaiser.

The generally fairly chaotic competition for large parts of Africa was seen by the stronger European powers (encouraged by national politicians who were in turn pressured by leaders of industry and trade, as well as jingoistic elements in their populations) to be an impediment to progressing their economic interests and so their representatives were brought together for the Berlin Conference which began in autumn 1884. The venue was the German Chancellor Otto Von Bismarck's impressive Berlin residence with representatives of 14 European governments attending, plus observers from the US. The outcome of the Conference was the division by European powers of vast regions of Africa, and included a statement of the principles that should guide their commercial and civilizing activities.

Article 11 of 'The General Act of Berlin' Feb.26th 1885

'The Signatory Powers exercising sovereign rights or authority in African territories will continue to watch over the preservation of the native populations and to supervise the improvement of the conditions of their moral and material well-being. They will, in particular, endeavour to secure the complete suppression of slavery in all its forms and of the slave trade by land and sea'.

For mendacious statements this is about as misleading as they come - in terms of slavery alone, the actual changes would be made in who were to be the slave owners, along with the expansion of those enslaved to the whole population in territories such as the 'Free Congo'!

Article 11 continues: *'They will protect and favour, without distinction of nationality or of religion, the religious, scientific or charitable institutions and undertakings created and organized by the nationals of the other Signatory Powers and of States, Members of the League of Nations, which may adhere to the present Convention, which aim at leading the natives in the path of progress and civilization. Scientific missions, their property and their collections, shall likewise be the objects of special solicitude.'*

The subsequent action of the signatory powers highlights Article 11 as representing the very highest level of diplomatic hypocrisy. The primary aim of the Berlin Conference was, in effect, to 'legalize' the crimes against humanity that the theft of African territory represented. An international attempt at legitimizing a 'theft', and the means used to carrying it out, that had already taken place.

At this time all of Africa excluding Ethiopia, Liberia, and nominally at least Egypt, was under the control of European nation-states or, in the case of the Congo Free State the personal control of King Leopold II. Germany controlled Togo, Cameroon, Tanganyika, and South-west Africa – Portugal: Mozambique and Angola – Spain: a region on the North-east coast and Spanish Morocco – Italy: Libya and Italian Somaliland – France: most of West Africa and northern central region (including the vast French Equatorial Africa) French Somalia, and most of the north of the continent (Algeria, Morocco, Tunisia) – Britain: Kenya, Sudan, Nigeria, Gold Coast, Uganda, British Somaliland, Nyasaland, Northern and Southern Rhodesia, Bechuanaland, and The Union of South Africa - Belgium (or rather, at that time, Leopold): The Congo Free State (would become the 'Belgium Congo').

The Berlin conference, and subsequent negotiations, agreed borders on the basis of carving up the land in line with their own economic interests balanced against what they could get away with – the traditional lands and the interests of native peoples were in effect ignored; arrangements that have contributed to the exacerbation of tribally-based conflicts into post colonial times. The long and continuing tradition of including high-flying humanitarian phrases in treaty documents was clearly apparent in Article 11 of the Berlin Treaty, but its irrelevance to actual behaviour was no more clearly illustrated than in the Belgium King's personal fiefdom of the Congo.

The tasty joint of the whole continent had been set before the Conference and was now being nicely carved up; the spoils of determinedly acquisitive aggression. It had already been lightly seasoned with some initial contacts, making natives peoples fully aware of the intentions and the potential power of the would-be colonists, and was ready to be devoured by the predatory nation-states of Europe. Commerce, Christianity, and Western civilization - were to be gifted to Africans' in exchange for the more nourishing fare of vast wealth for the Europeans. In the Congo the King, through his agents in the 'International Association' on the ground, set out to squeeze his 'share' ('share' being in practice as much as possible) of this wealth by in effect enslaving all of the native people living within the 1½ million sq miles of territory under his 'protection'. At first the king's agents employed the infamous trader and erstwhile friend of Stanley, Tippu Tip. An unsavory individual whose own past expertise in trade - having made a personal fortune from exchanging trade goods including guns for slaves with African chiefs in the east of the continent - made him well qualified to apply slave conditions to native peoples. Leopold made a fortune from selling land and mineral concessions to a number of European-based companies. But it was the forced labour of the Congolese native peoples where we see the expression of the most terrible of evils. The population was forced to kill enormous numbers of elephants (for their ivory tusks), and to build the infrastructure including roads, railroads, a network of trading posts, homesteads, and other buildings that would enable Leopold's agents and those of the private companies, to more efficiently extract the resources that they garnered - or rather the booty that they looted - from the land and its peoples.

The native chiefs had generally used their traditional power (backed by 'customs' and 'laws') to accrue relatively modest wealth and advantages for themselves and their family members but Leopold's agents took this exploitation to a considerably higher level. Whole villages were burnt to the ground if the natives were not malleable enough to conform to the demands of capitalist production, and resource extraction. A people whose lives had been framed within the patterns of day-light and night-dark and in the rhythm of the seasons, were expected to adapt to the iron discipline of regular, measured, time and of quantified production. Wives were taken hostage and sexually and physically abused until their husbands had returned with sufficient wild rubber. Think of any possible abuse that can be inflicted on a people and it happened in Leopold's Congo. Men such as E.D.Morel and Roger Casement reacted with horror at what they saw and endeavoured to bring the situation to the attention of the western world. Casement's Report of 1904 estimated 3 million people starved, shot, tortured to death......in sum 'murdered'. But later, better informed, reports estimate the figure to have been about 10 million.

The extent of the crimes (of enslavement, torture, mass murder.... in effect genocide) being perpetrated on behalf of Leopold became both an international embarrassment to the government of Belgium as well as prompting moral outrage in some European countries. In Nov. 1907, Belgium's parliament voted to annex the territory, and the Congo became a colony controlled by the State rather than one owned by the monarch. This change did lead to a significant reduction in the worst excesses, to some modest improvements in education (mainly

Roman Catholic schools) and in public health. But the relationship of colonizing state to colonized peoples continued to be based on the former endeavouring to ruthlessly exploit the latter.

For the sake of gaining a more balanced perspective it should be kept in mind that – although in the longer term, given the mindset of ruling elites in Europe western, colonialism was probably inevitable - the process of colonization was to some extent facilitated by the willingness of elites of favoured tribal groups in most African 'territories' to form alliances with the potential colonizers. What were initially mostly more equal voluntary alliances became much less equal forced allegiances as the presence of the colonizing nations became more entrenched.

A much less known (in the West) colonization was that undertaken by Russia. For centuries Russia had extended a fairly loose type of control over its neighbouring lands, a control extending at times as far east as the border with China. But during the nineteenth century there appears to have been an intention to match Western European countries and to impose a more 'formal' system of control, allied to this was the wish to gain a warm-water seaport facing the Pacific; this would be Vladivostok (means 'to rule', or 'ruler of') in the east. Siberia, the Caucasus, and large parts of central Asia were taken over and wealth gained, mainly via a poorly administered system of taxation (more akin to 'tribute') and control of trade. Especially the trade in furs and timber along with, if opportunity allowed, the looting of valuables from occupied lands. The low density of indigenous population levels made it difficult to organize much resistance to Russian expansion. Expansion which would only be halted due to its rubbing up against the Far-Eastern interests of other, more powerful, industrializing states.

The momentum of Russian expansion was thwarted by other industrialized countries such as Britain (in Southern Central Asia and China) and Japan (in China) with potential control over Northern China and the Korean Peninsula being curtailed by Russia's defeat in the Russo-Japanese war of 1905.

To the west of Europe the colonization of North America continued throughout the nineteenth-century. In 1803 the US paid $11,250,000 and cancelled nearly $4m of debt for 828,000 square miles, a wide swath of land running through the centre of the North American continent. This, the Louisiana Purchase, in effect what was already a colony being sold on to other colonists, opened up the central area of North America to the settlers from Europe who would travel in a steady stream of wagon trains (and later in the century the railroads) west across the Mississippi. The Purchase covered a large area in the centre of the continent... covering the whole of what became Iowa, Arkansas, Nebraska, Missouri, Kansas, Oklahoma, North and South Dakota, most of the area that was to become Louisiana, and Minnesota, and parts of what would become Montana, Wyoming, Texas, Colorado, and North and South Dakota.

The main outcome of war with Britain in 1812 was the European state giving up its claim to land south of the 45 (degrees) parallel and to Oregon territory. It was during this period that the cartoon version of 'Uncle Sam', and the tune that was to become the national anthem 'The Star Spangled Banner', along with colourful emblematic images of America, began to take shape. Florida was gained from Spain in 1819, and most of Texas from Mexico in 1836; with the US/Mexican war of 1846-48 resulting in the US annexing large parts of the south west.

These conflicts between neighbouring nation-states led to the creation of a vast new country; one whose national flag flew over the homelands of people whose ancestors had drawn sustenance directly from the land, who had for eons been able to watch red-skied sunsets draw in over rolling prairies across which contented herds of buffalo grazed, and over tree covered hunting grounds as the Sun set on distant horizons. Diverse groups of native peoples who had developed rich and complex cultural legacies unaware of the dark clouds of humanity drifting across the Atlantic to engulf and then destroy their traditional ways of life.

The US government adopted a particular model that was applied to ensure the transfer of land occupied by native peoples to white settlers and to corporate bodies. A model of relentless occupation based on signing treaties to cover an area of territory in which the rights of each party were outlined and then the US either directly finding an excuse to break the treaty or in their coming to the 'defense' of settlers, miners, hunters, and other groups who had themselves broken treaty conditions. The US army killing or forcibly – and in as much as treaties voluntarily entered into are legal documents, illegally - removing vast numbers of native Indians from their traditional homelands, was the central mechanism by which settlers gained land as 'civilization' marched west.

The killing included planned starvation and infection by European disease. These including smallpox, cholera, tuberculosis, disease sometimes inadvertently spread but at other times actually used as a killing tool; presents of small-pox infected blankets were given to natives. In places forced migration and actual massacres were justified on the basis of aggressive actions by Indians responding to their ill-treatment. But this was not just some economically motivated action (although this invariably was the main driver), the Indians were set up as part of the frontier culture of the newly emerging US nation. Painters then photographers, newspapers and magazines, without much sense of obligation to offer the truth and a bit later the cinema industry, as well as the populist narratives echoed by local and national politicians, all contributed to framing the image of the American Indian as an impediment to progress itself. The characterization of Indians as lacking intelligence, unreliable, violent, promiscuous, heathen, uncultured, and when possible as 'inhuman'. Similar to attempts made to characterize black Africans, Australian aborigines and indeed, native peoples whenever they were encountered by 'civil' peoples, so seeking to endorse and justify their persecution. Those who killed Indians and 'stole' their lands were projected as heroic, god-fearing Christians, bravely engaging in furthering the interests of the US.

A simplistic conceptual framework for summing up the view of native Indian peoples being the phraseology redolent of the American way that 'The only good Indian is a dead Indian' – a phrase that came along with many other simplistic notions of western prairie life. Another being the image of the 'cowboy', created from overly romanticized versions of the lives of the cowhands who, from the early 1860s, were employed in moving large numbers of cattle from range to railheads (Abilene, Dodge City,) on their journey to the mechanized abattoirs of the growing cities. Men whose working lives would have been hard, lonely, low-paid, and even no-paid during the times when they would have been laid off due to lack of work. With most not even being able to afford a side-arm (let alone a stylish Colt 45), the ever-present adornment of the fake movie 'cowboy'. The cowhand more often faced a relentlessly hard working life and an old age of poverty.

All cultures are prone to mythologizing their past, and to inventing national heroes, but the mass culture of the USA, using the newly emerging mass media and communication systems, attained a new level of meta-fictional invention. This mythologizing was economically underpinned by the idea of 'products', the commodification of mythology. It has created marketable 'products' - films, TV shows, magazines, clothes, toys, guns, etc.- from mythologies linked to a purposefully imagined history. Not least, when western movie scripts made their contribution to the mythology of 'winning the west', as if it were a deserved prize rather than having been the home-lands of many collectivities of native peoples from time immemorial.

In the late 1860s, when the persecution of Native American Indian peoples was at its height, General Carleton, at the time engaged in a campaign to clear the south west for settlers, ordered that 'There is to be no council held with the Indians, nor any talks. The men are to be slain whenever and wherever they can be found.'

Whilst the threat or use of military force was the most commonly used means of clearing territory of indigenous peoples, the systematic and cynical killing of the buffalo was just as effective in terms of genocidal outcomes. The buffalo represented 'life' for many of the plains Indians such as the tribes of the Arapaho and Cheyenne and those of the Sioux Nation. Buffalo were a productive source of images and colourful narratives that were indelibly imprinted into native cultures. They had for centuries provided the tribes with food, fabrics, tools (bone), decorations (bodily adornments), and the hunting stories which had enriched the cultural imagination for generation following generation; tales told, and hunting scenarios re-enacted, in vibrant dances in the musty glow of smoky campfires.

Between 1870 and 1880 about 15 million buffalo were systematically slain by hunters. William Cody, as 'Buffalo Bill' the national hero, was in reality a brilliant self-publicist who became famous on the strength of an ability to shoot a rifle at generally placid animals whose bodies made a large enough target. He had the entrepreneurial foresight to put a fictionalized idea of the 'winning of the west' into a circus-like stage show with which he toured the US and Europe. General Sheridan, tasked with clearing the Great Plains of Indians, suggested that the extermination of the buffalo was a prerequisite to obtaining peace and to advancing 'civilization'. There was the implicit promotion of an idea that the relatively newly created nation of the United States had some assumed (or rather invented) god-given right, to control the continent from the Atlantic to the Pacific coasts.

Taken on its own, the idea of the US state having some god-given right to expand its borders seems just stupid – and could be used by any covetous nation wishing to encroach upon neighbouring territory – but when we realize that the idea of some 'Manifold Destiny', (first used in an article in the July-August 1845 edition of the 'Democratic Review') is of the type of mendacious invention used historically by those who intend on implementing (or justifying) actions that 'normal' laws would not allow. Seeking to draw some spurious authority by inventing a link to some or other 'god's will'. Some attempt to link the obviously unacceptable to a 'higher' authority'. In the context of the US state marching west seeming to absolve the actor (thief) from the action (theft).

Key Indian wars took place between1865-90: with the Red River wars in the south east of 1865-85, the Apaches campaigns of 1865-1886, the campaigns in the North West in 1865-1890 and the Sioux campaign 1865 -1890. During this 25 year period the Fourteenth Amendment was added to the US constitution, an amendment that gave equal rights to all citizens of the United States apart, that is, from Native American Indians and slaves. By the last decade of the century Indian resistance was all but ended, and with the corralling of remaining groups onto impoverished reservations whole ways of living disappeared. The now yellowed paper treaties and the faded records of disingenuous speeches made by white leaders are but remnants of the institutional bad faith, avarice, and greed of US politicians - operating in the interests of cattle-ranchers, prospectors, land speculators, traders, and settlers - who were influential in setting the direction of the country for the next 150 years.

Again, when we consider evil, as with other colonized lands, we need to temper moral outrage at injustice with some sense of realism in relation to the motivational forces of self-conscious humankind. Rarely was the process of overrunning north America simply one of an evil colonizer using superior technology and a more murderous, acquisitive, national temperament to take control of lands occupied by peaceful native groups living some idyllically peaceful lives – tribes (as most groups living in proximity during the self-conscious stages of human evolution) had at times fought each other, with themselves forming alliances to more successfully wage inter-tribal war. These more local conflicts did have a generally limited impact on the people and even less impact upon the land itself but they would count as evil and would have continued even if the 'white man' had not arrived. Indeed, even during the persecution of tribes some Native Americans worked for and with the persecutors (at times taking an active part in the killing) usually against their own traditional enemies – such is the moral complexity characterized by observing the range of behaviours arising from human thinking at the level of self-consciousness.

The industrialized technology, deployed by people motivated by land clearance and territorial control, led to the native peoples of north America being brought close to annihilation (with whole tribal groups being killed off – in effect genocide) and to the cultures being practiced remaining in but much denuded forms. With more of this ancestral heritage only being retained in progressively thinner traces of collective memories, the display cases and scholarly publications of some ethnological museums, and more recently being re-invented for tourists. If, beginning in the late nineteenth century in the work of individuals such as Lewis Henry Morgan, American Indian culture, has also become a subject for the scholarly researcher (including by 20th century descendents of native peoples), determined to set out and preserve as much of these native tribal cultures as possible.

The approach to colonialism taken on the ground by individual Europeans, private corporations, and the agents of national governments, were each but local adaptations of a more general approach taken across in the world as the blight of self-conscious civilization encompassed almost all its peoples. An approach formulated from a collective mindset that assumed the 'foreign' as but a source of wealth; and for states some dubious international prestige and a contribution to national identity. An approach given determined authority by uneven levels of technological development. Crudely summed in the pithy phrase of Hilare Belloc: 'Whatever happens we have the Maxim gun and they have not'.

But colonization was not simply the replacement of ideal lives lived by peaceful peoples by the aggressive perpetrators of gross exploitation. Colonization was generally evil in intent and practice, but it often replaced, or colluded in 'partnership' with, local elites - kings, princes, tribal chiefs, favoured families, dominant castes, and other elite ruling groups - who had themselves exercised power over tribes and of tribal and ethnic groups in conflict with their neighbours. What colonization did was to 'industrialize', and increasingly globalize (de-localize), the exploitation; expanding the types of evil inflicted, and of significantly increasing its quantified level of expression. Economic and actual colonization displaced numerous types of the centuries-old adaptations to a range of natural environments.....by peoples' conscious of intimate links to the seasons and to the fauna, flora, and the natural features of the land. Displaced by a civilization determined on a relatively more recent type of adaptation to the environment based on using up, control, domination, and of the commodification of almost all aspects of the natural environment. An adaptation of mass manufacturing, of the exchange of goods between people involving some abstract values measured by money. Money representing alienated value (alienated from the fundamental relationships of exchange that non-monetary systems were based upon) and as such can be accumulated and its power to control deployed.

Each broad type of adaptation - industrialization and traditional native - had their own risks to survival and it can be argued that in a modern industrialized society, with some commitment to universal welfare, the benefit of the reliable production of foodstuffs, of scientific medicine, of efficient economic organization, can provide for longer, physically healthier, can offer the potential for more fulfilling, lives. But for most now ex-colonized countries the benefits of industrialization has not been delivered. Peoples living relatively non-materialistic lives were touched by evil when their very presence clashed with the relentlessly driving forces of capitalist-types, and later dictatorial communist-forms, of industrialization.

Local markets were distorted as cheap manufactured goods from the west replaced indigenous producers, local rulers were bullied, patronized, or bribed as the historian J.M.Robert's (1993, p359) noted 'In many places the arrival of European or American traders, prospectors and financiers led to economic concessions by formally independent local rulers which in fact, though not in name, soon tied their subjects to the wheels of the western chariot, whether this was intended or not'.

But western influence went further than disruption in the economic and cultural spheres, it also included the idea of nation-statehood; spreading the potential for the same mindless nationalism that usually accompanies the socio/political construct of nationhood. The synthetic creation of 'nation-hood' during colonial times has enlarged the potential for conflict inherent in the false aura of power, usually comingled with some sense of some past injustice or an imagined national destiny. In the Middle-East, Far-East, Africa, and South American, nation-states were initially created to suit strategies of global-politics by powers pursuing economic and imperial ambitions, rather than in the interests of the indigenous populations. Borders were drawn on behalf of the colonial powers by agents lacking much if any understanding of tribal occupation and traditional patterns of land use; so seeding future generations of disputes.

Colonization was a key element in determining the pattern of global politics from the late nineteenth-century onwards. The experience of colonization gave further advantage to the already advantaged members of the elite groups in the leading European nation states and the US.

Chapter 6 'The Natural Sciences, the Social Sciences, Medicine and Philosophy: 1750 – 1900'

Science as the: '....search for a solution to the mystery of the universe'

William Berkson (1974)

World pop: 1800 = 991 million
World pop: 1900 = 1,671 million

Prior to the late eighteenth-century activities that we might justifiably term scientific – in areas such as astronomy, mathematics, chemistry, as well reasoned speculations and experimental investigation involving the underlying constitution of matter and the forces that attract or repel, had been increasingly taken up by individuals driven by a curiosity in the natural world who were economically well-placed to progress their interests. During this earlier period technological improvements had also been made in more practical areas such as agriculture, transport, construction, and in the incremental mechanization of manufacturing crafts. We might even, if crudely, identify a class difference in those initiating the progress in science and those introducing technological innovation in the practical trades. But during the second half of the eighteenth-century we can clearly identify (not least in the personnel involved in the 'scientific' societies that were meeting at this time) the beginning of a convergence of interests between the two areas. A convergence accelerated as the men of industry realized the financial benefit accruing from the application of relevant science and the men of science seeing the benefit in terms of available funding for research, potential public good, and an elevation of their own social standing. This was a convergence of activities that had never been entirely separate but it was a convergence that would significantly increase and become formalized as the eighteenth and nineteenth-century unfolded. Not least, driven by manufacturers and engineers, who could see the potential commercial benefits from having scientists and technologists working together. It was a gradual series of processes based upon the mutual realization that each area could benefit from co-operating with the other. Of course, as European governments saw the benefits, in war and in industry, of this combination of the theoretical (scientific) and the practical (technological) they encouraged and themselves sponsored cooperation. A co-operative approach would also provide the basis of a feedback loop between application to improvement with this stimulating further theoretical innovation and practical invention.

It would be the intellectual dynamic of this mutually beneficial relationship that would significantly accelerate the creation of novel 'information', and so realize a qualitative enlargement of the horizons of human Reality. Obviously so with a re-conceptualization of the size and other properties of the Universe and of the subatomic realm but also novel information that would lead, by the twentieth-century to a dramatic re-contextualization of what it means to be human.

The 'Age of Enlightenment' has also been termed the 'Age of Classification' due to the practice of collecting and collating knowledge (mainly factual) and arranging this in classificatory systems. A practice that can be seen in a number of ambitious publishing initiatives of the eighteenth-century: Ephraim Chambers 'Cyclopedia' and the Scottish 'Encyclopedia Britannica' being examples. But perhaps the most wide-ranging of these was the project of the 'Encyclopedia of Sciences, Arts and Trades' published in seventeen volumes of text and eleven volumes of illustrations ('plates' – initially 4000 copies sold at a then massive £14 per copy) between 1751-1772, in which Dennis Diderot and Jean d'Alembert endeavoured to bring together the advances in knowledge made up to that time, giving as significant a place to technological as it did to scientific knowledge.

Eighteenth-century pioneers in scientific and technological advance included Joseph Black and Gabriel Fahrenheit. Black made significant progress in the introduction of measurement into understanding what takes place during chemical reactions, and Fahrenheit invented the mercury thermometer (1714), allowing more control over the heating of chemicals during a range of experiments. There were also the many 'craftsmen' that utilized the accumulation of knowledge in optics to produce improved telescopes, microscopes, and various types of magnifying glasses. The invention of engines and their improvement in the utilization of steam by individuals such as Thomas Newcomen and James Watt; Watt's approach in particular illustrated the way that science (thermodynamics) and mechanics (the steam engine as a mechanism) came together to stimulate improvement in technology (application). Later on, Ludwig Mond

(1839-1905) trained as a chemist in Germany and moved to England to become a central figure in the chemical industry with his work for the private chemical company Imperial Chemical Industry (ICI). Work that included the development of soda and ammonia, both substances with important industrial uses in a range of processes, obviously illustrating a direct link between research and industrial development in the nineteenth-century chemical industry. All the many pre-nineteenth century disparate strands of what had fused into a more general scientific and technological quest were to come together in more formal ways during the nineteenth.

A more modern understanding of what might broadly be termed the 'scientific method' was a significant outcome of the Enlightenment period. A period that valued learning more generally, as Francis Bacon famously observed in his essay 'Of Studies' (1597)

'Read not to contradict and confute, nor to believe and take for granted, nor to find talk and discourse, but to weigh and consider.'

Sums up the best (if idealized) spirit of the Enlightenment if more generally only involving relatively small groups of people in Western Europe (and even smaller sections in Eastern Europe). Literacy rates were increasing, although more so in countries such as England, France, Germany, than in Spain, Italy, Poland, and Russia. These literacy 'markets' generated the increasing availability of magazines, journals, pamphlets, news-sheets, and books. More enlightened ideas would during the nineteenth century progressively percolate through all classes of European society, at least to some extent in each. A central change in perspective was the idea of 'change' in itself, including the view that knowledge could accumulate; the static world claimed by the authority of the Church would no longer satisfy the intellectual curiosity of increasing numbers of people. And these people via direct personal contacts, publications, and the interaction of the debating salons, universities (there were 37 of these within the territory of the Holy Roman Empire alone) scientific academies, societies, and clubs.

Reading through the works of Enlightenment thinkers such as Voltaire, Montesquieu, Rousseau, Descartes, Locke, Spinoza, Hume, and Newton (and indeed pretty much the whole of Diderot's 'Encyclopedia') would allow us to gain some sense of the expansiveness of intellectual outlook that had developed during these three centuries (17th/18th/19th). The Church retained an influential presence (not least due to the religious beliefs of most intellectuals and scientists) but this influence was much more social than intellectual. Whilst it continued to act as a brake on the spread of any ideas considered to challenge the Bible - similar for Jewish and Islamic intellectuals and their own religious authorities - it could no longer inhibit intellectuals from reflecting on the world of experience (both social and scientific) and from determinedly pursuing their own interests within a wider scientific endeavour.

Towards the end of the Enlightenment period we see Kant's magnificent productions (especially the three Critiques) offering a clear sense of the Enlightenment advance in reasoning as considered by the acutest of minds. Kant was able to apply reasoned speculation to outline separate realms, and yet provide a basis of underlying unity, for reason and for feeling. A separation most clearly expressed in two of his Critiques. The 'Critique of Pure Reason' (the realm of rational consideration - with a focus on the limits to the psychological structure of clear reasoning) and the 'Critique of Practical Reason' (the realm of inner feelings - with a focus on ethics). On the Enlightenment itself Kant offered a cautionary note, suggesting that: 'If it is now asked, "Do we presently live in an enlightened age?" the answer is "No, but we do live in an age of enlightenment." (1784, essay 'What is Enlightenment?'). Kant's other writings at this time suggest that he viewed the lack of actual enlightenment as referring to the wider international political situation and the gains primarily in terms of the sciences, philosophy, and literature.

A more lasting outcome of the Enlightenment period was the beginning of a more marked separation of the speculations of philosophers on the world of experience from the activity of more practical individuals pursuing the various branches of the natural and social sciences. I will only consider a few of these – Physics, Chemistry, Astronomy, Geology, Biology, Sociology, Psychology, Anthropology, Medicine – to allow some sense of the widening knowledge-base of human Reality. Prior to a consideration of pre-twentieth century philosophy. Concluding this chapter with a summary of the nineteenth century.

Physics

The aspect of science that was to become the specialism of physics was, as would astronomy, chemistry, and mathematics, by based on ideas inherited from the Greeks; if their own work had itself been informed by work undertaken elsewhere, primarily Babylonia, Egypt (and possibly India and China). Aristotle himself brought together the insights of past philosophers, mostly to highlight their logical and/or empirical shortcomings - and then made his own suggestions, almost all of which offered improved explanatory frameworks.

Advances in understanding of the natural world made during the 'Greek efflorescence', were subsequently enhanced by Chinese, Indian, and Arabic, scholars. Aristotle framed his approach in relation to ideas such as: why is there an ordered natural world of regularities out of what he thought would have been an original primal chaos.[1]

Other framing problems which contributed to the context for post-medieval science would be the relationship between form and matter and the causes of change and of motion. Problems to which Aristotle himself had made some attempt to provide answers – and to which his authority (latterly supported by the authority of the Roman Catholic Church as well as most Protestant Churches) would accrue for almost 2000 years. For some historians of science this is deemed to have held up the advance of science, but we might ask, what would have taken Aristotle's place? I can imagine an argument to suggest that the need to overthrow viewpoints that had been accorded such authority meant the work involving a challenge to the Aristotelian worldview would have been more thoroughly tested and thought-through than it might otherwise have been. Even that the psychology of individual scientists was such that the sense of showing the 'weaknesses in authority', whether intellectual or religious, would itself have been a driving force motivating the activities of experiment-based discovery and theory construction. The idea that the Church, by its obstinate support for some Aristotelian interpretations, might have inadvertently contributed positively to the development of scientific rigor is ironic. The fact that Aristotle would not have been aware of any possible (dialectical) contribution he had made, and that the Church would have been an unwitting contributor to the advance of theories that made its own dogmas on the natural world and the universe seem nonsensical, hardy matters. Intentions and outcomes involving ideas on this scale rarely coincide. I just think

---

[1] Today we might say why a universe out of 'nothing', but then we would go on to consider what can we mean by nothing in this seemingly unique situation.

that we have too easily come to except the mantra of Aristotle's intellectual authority and the Church's fear-induced obstinacy without due consideration that a benefit might accrue to scientific endeavours if these are forged in the creative cauldron of opposition – claims of theory and discovery tempered by opposition beyond just peer review – both the Church and Aristotle provided structural frameworks of ideas that observation, advancing knowledge, and rational endeavour had increasingly shown to be flawed. Whether this is the opposition of past scientific authority (see Kuhn 'Structure of Scientific Revolutions') or that of religious, or ideological, or even common sense, viewpoints.

This is obviously an area that only a complex analysis could offer a fairly drawn balance on the role of wider 'social' (extra–scientific) opposition to new scientific ideas. But I felt the need to temper the enthusiasm of the historians of science to frame Aristotelian authority in 'science', and Church 'dogma' in almost everything, as forces that operated to inhibit the development of the sciences when I suspect the individual psychological and wider social dynamics would have been significantly more complex. What more significant progress would the sciences of the sixteenth century and beyond have attained without the challenge of ecclesiastical and Aristotelian authority?

In physics, Aristotle had suggested a world of matter and form, each dependent on the other. Without form matter would be chaotic and without matter form would be empty. It was a world-view that all individual expressions of form 'advance' towards the best possible design and in this sense it was a teleological world-view. Aristotle's advance on his predecessors involved the introduction of mechanical causes suggesting that it was the responsibility of philosophers to investigate these. He also asserted that form 'impels' towards improvement, whilst matter 'obstructs' and 'retards'. When form overcomes the negative aspects of matter we have the 'natural', when matter overcomes the positive aspects of form we have the 'un-natural' (monstrosities, deformity, the abnormal). Aristotle considered fundamental aspects of the material world: space, time, and motion. Viewing space as continuous, if limited; time as the transition from earlier to later; motion as that which take place as matter becomes form. He was interested in change, and suggested that different types of change implied different causes of the changes. One important source of change was caused by motion, and he had the insight to link the motion of a body in a proportional way to the forces that produced the motion and the forces of resistance of the medium through which a body was moving. A consequence of this being that there would be no empty space, no void. Aristotle is recorded as noting two types of motion, one being upwards/downwards motion which was a feature of motion on Earth; with heavy bodies tending to move downwards and light bodies tending to move upwards, the other being uniform circular motion, characteristic of the celestial, as shown in the movement of the heavenly bodies.

Advances in physics down to the Renaissance were incremental, mostly building on Greek foundations rather than making advances that involved significant new ideas. From about the fifteenth century scientifically minded individuals began to provide ideas that challenged the authority of Aristotle as they focused on mechanics and the projection of bodies (artillery/cannons) and began to contribute to a framework that moved beyond most aspects of Greek science. Galileo in particular, combined mechanical and mathematical explanations for the acceleration of falling bodies and the trajectory of projected bodies; he conducted experiments to better understand this behaviour and so bringing theory and experimental observation together.

In the seventeenth-century Rene Descartes attempted to explain the natural world by suggesting a 'mechanical philosophy' – He offered a wide-ranging theoretical framework involving concepts such as: inertia, impact, and circular motion. Underlying the mechanical was a mathematical superstructure. One including Descartes' suggestion of 'multi-dimensional co-ordinates' allowing a mathematical explanation of the position and shape of any object to be described. Descartes was at the forefront of the development of explanations of the natural world in terms of quantification. It would be quantification that would be a fundamental mode of methodology, and so explanation, that science would apply to natural phenomena.

Quantification informs one 'level' of explanation, albeit one that from practical and rational perspectives can be adequate, but there might be other 'levels' of explanation where a quantified language of science becomes less useful – its ability to explain involves limiting explanatory structures rather than ones that liberate – and here we are not just considering the social aspects of scientific explanations but also the philosophical ones. There is a debate to be had around the idea of the natural world actually only being made accessible to our understanding if quantified, much else would be understanding by appeal to authority (religious) or appeal to some sort of mystical intuition. But is there another way that links our understanding to a more humanistic approach. Here we move into the area of 'tacit' knowledge (outlined by Michael Polanyi, 1969), the less easily explained precognitive 'knowledge' - a kind of pre-conscious insight) that might form the basis for more 'explicit' understanding; clearly the thought content of tacit knowledge could also pre-form the type of knowledge that would be more amenable to quantification.

The empirical, mechanistic, (primarily reductionist) approach is clear in the perspective taken by Isaac Newton. Building on the work of late medieval scientists such as Johannes Kepler. Newton employed Kepler's ideas of the inverse square law in relation to the elliptical motion of planets, and deriving his gravitational laws from Kepler's law of motion. Benefitting from the work of mathematicians such as Descartes, Newton designed the infinitesimal calculus, a mathematical tool enabling him to solve some problems in physics. The credit for devising the infinitesimal calculus is shared by Gottfried Leibniz. Newton's work brought a unity to physics as he advanced the mechanical philosophy within a mathematical framework. His *'Philosophiae Naturalis Principia Mathematica'* published in 1687 is generally considered to have laid the foundations of physics for the following 200 years.

Of primary importance, Newton outlined three laws of motion derived from his own universal law of gravitation and in doing so he unified celestial and terrestrial motion, the forms of motion that Aristotle had kept apart. The Aristotelian search for causes of this or that particular phenomenon gave way to a search for universal laws underlying the phenomena of the natural world. Newton's view that nature operated in a mechanistic way included the suggestion that matter was made up of tiny indestructible particles (atoms) in empty space. Newton had a place for God but more as an initial creation and cause of motion, with a continuing role in very occasionally intervening to maintain the smooth running of the Universe.

Newton also made significant advances in the physics of light – he made use of prisms to separate light into its constituent components (wavelengths) and this he combined with a further prism to diffract the light beam, using lenses to focus it. For his experiments he increased (by a factor of 5 - 22ft on preceding scientists such as Robert Hooke and Robert Boyle) the distance between the prism onto which light was directed and the surface on which the diffracted white light was projected so allowing him to more clearly show the constituent (rainbow) colours of 'white' light. His experiments confirmed that light was made up of colours that differed in some characteristic way. He showed that the refractive index of glass was different according to the colour of light beam that was passed through it. And, through a series of imaginative experiments, he was also able to confirm his theoretical view that the colour of objects depended on the material of which they were made; this being based upon a difference in the reflective power (the colour they appeared to an observer) and the absorptive power, the 'colours' absorbed by the material.

Newton suggested that light was made up of a stream of particles. This 'corpuscular theory' (1690 – arguably a wave/particle duality) being an alternative to a wave theory initially suggested by Robert Hooke (1660s) and a bit later the improved wave theory of Christian Huygens (1678). This latter theory being tested in an experiment carried out by Thomas Young; in his two-slit experiment (1803), in which light was shone through a screen in which two 'slits' had been cut. The light propagated from the slits in line with what would have been predicted by Huygen's theory. Young also identified three (colour sensitive) receptors in the human eye and suggested that it was difference in wave length that produced the different colours.

Newton's view of the properties of 'matter' was quite complex, and in addition to his corpuscular theory of light there was also a place for a continuous aether (a type of background medium composing 'empty' space) and used this to explain an aspect of gravity. An explanation that is considered to be an early attempt at a 'curved-space' model of gravity.

Huygen's wave theory was more adequate in relation to explaining experimental findings than was Newton's corpuscular theory. But for most of the experimental outcomes being considered, the difference between the two theories did not matter all that much (at that time) and Newton's authority tended towards the promotion of his theory. So it would be a particle rather than a wave theory of light that would be the conventional approach for at least another 100 years. It was to take the mathematical genius and experimental insight of Augustin Fresnel who, following a series of experiments begun in 1815, was able to present a mathematical explanation for the puzzling polarization effect by means of a wave theory. Fresnel presented his own wave theory to the French Académie des Sciences in 1817 and, following further mathematical work on wave theory by Simeon Denis Poisson, the wave theory of the propagation of light displaced Newton's particle theory. This priority given to wave theory was reinforced in 1850 when Léon Foucault assumed the wave theory to propose a way to accurately (at least sufficiently) measure the speed of light.

Moving from the seen in itself to the seen only by effect, it was in 1600 that William Gilbert's published his book 'De Magnete' in 1600, in which he reviewed the published material covering most of what was then known of magnetism but also describing what was probably the first instrument designed to 'note' the signs of electrical activity; the forerunner of electroscopes and galvanometers.

In the early eighteenth century F.Hauksbee (an assistant to Isaac Newton) showed that electricity could be produced by friction, and around the same time Stephen Gray was undertaking a series of experiments demonstrating that electricity could be transmitted over distances. This culminated in Gray transmitting electricity along a fine thread running around his garden – and so making the discovery that electric current could 'flow' along suitable conductors. Gray went on to distinguished between 'electrics', materials that could be used to store electricity and 'non-electrics', materials that could not store electricity but along which it could be conducted. These early pioneers revealed some interesting phenomena of electricity - not a liquid but it 'flowed', it need not touch an object and yet could effect its behaviour, so 'action at a distance'.

During the eighteenth century a number of serious 'scientists', along with some other individuals with intentions to amuse, took an interest in the study of electricity. In 1745 a clergyman named von Kleist (a Pomeranian) received an electric shock whilst endeavouring to store electricity in a bottle, as did an experimenter attempting to do something similar in an experiment in Holland. The experiment undertaken in Holland was reported by Musschenbrok, a Dutch instrument maker who has also been credited with the invention of the Leyden Jar; a device for accumulating an electric charge, so an early 'battery'. The Leyden Jar was a useful piece of experimental apparatus that would continue to be used until the end of the eighteenth century.

The idea of giving electric shocks was found to be amusing and it became fashionable amongst the upper classes to discuss the phenomenon of electricity and to observe people receiving shocks;

even to the extent of the then King of France having a whole brigade of his soldiers being subjected to electric shocks, his being able to observe the men all 'jumping' in unison as the shocks were administered. Benjamin Franklin (1706-90), ever the curious and clear-headed intellect (in the world or science if not always in that of politics), carried out some interesting experiments with lightening and demonstrated its connection with electricity. In 1753 he invented the lightning conductor that we now take for granted but which has provided useful protection to large buildings ever since. He also provided a more theoretical explanation for the understanding of electricity when he suggested that electricity existed 'potentially' in all bodies at levels that had a natural balance of neutral charge, but that, if more charge was added or some charge taken away the object would then become either positively or negatively charged.

By the end of the eighteenth-century the study of the phenomena of electricity and magnetism was occupying the interest and time of many of the scientifically minded in Europe and the US. This work made a contribution to the sense of science exhibiting an international unity of endeavour.

The next important step taken was the invention, by Charles Coulomb, of a way of measuring electricity. His success was an outcome of his using the link between electricity and magnetism – he utilized the force that existed between two magnetic poles and so was able to measure the difference between levels of electrical charge. In 1795 the Italian, Alessandro Volta, conducted an experiment which, by placing two types of metal together with a damp cloth between them, could by itself produce a continuous electric current and that this current could be stored in a battery. As a related development, we see William Nicholson using power supplied by a battery to separate the constituent elements of water; oxygen and hydrogen and this, for J.D.Bernal (1954), initiated the study of electro-chemistry.

The Galvanic and Voltaic batteries[2] were a distinct improvement on the Leyden Jar for storing electricity and they were used in various ways in laboratories across Europe and North America. In 1820 Hans Ørstead (Danish) conclusively established the link between electricity and magnetism, and just five years later William Sturgeon invented the electromagnet. An invention that would enable the technical

---

[2] Both utilizing the same principle to store electricity derived from the transfer of electrons that takes place during the redox reaction – batteries named after their inventors Luigi Galvani and Alessandro Volta.

ground conditions for the development of the electric telegraph and the electric motor. The experimental work of scientists including Andre Marie Ampére, Carl Friedrich Gauss, and Georg Simon Ohm, increased the understanding of the flow of electricity through conductors. We retain recognition of some of the early pioneers in electricity with a number of scientific units – volt, amphere, ohm, joule.

In 1831 Michael Faraday was asked to complete an overview of the study of electromagnetism and this reinforced his commitment to further developing the understanding of the various effects of magnetism and electrical forces. In a landmark experiment in 1831 Faraday produced an electric current by a process of 'induction' and in doing so demonstrated the possibility of generating electricity. The significant progress in understanding made by Faraday was soon to set the path to commercial exploitation by Werner Siemens and Charles Wheatstone (the latter being a friend and sometime collaborator of Faraday). By the 1870s, the generation of electricity was to provide a source of power that would drive the economic development, and progressively the domestic convenience, of civil society.

Faraday's interests in the unseen forces of electric current, magnetism, and also gravity (identified by their effects) had primarily built on the work of Isaac Newton and he also significantly advanced the study of 'Field Theory' as a theory of the physical world; encompassing elusive aspects of the natural world (involving 'unseen forces') that would provide a focus of interest for generations of scientists that followed him. Faraday suggested the idea of 'fields' of force that surrounded electric currents and magnetized objects, an idea that James Clerk Maxwell would later translate into the language of mathematics ('Maxwell's equations'). This being a significant further advance that would have fundamental implications for the development of the physics in the twentieth-century.

Electricity was the first branch of science to develop into an industry in its own right. An industry that from the 1830s introduced the telegraph, electroplating, as well as lighting for streets, factories, and in 1881 for the British 'House of Commons'. Along with lighting for domestic use; a practical incandescent filament light bulb being made by Joseph Swan in 1878.

As investors were becoming more aware of the commercial potential of electricity a range of developments took place including the invention of the dynamo and, perhaps of greater longer-term importance, of the 'power station' (Edison, 1881) from which electric power could be distributed to any number of customers. A mark of the social acceptance of the importance of work generated by discoveries related to electricity was the founding in 1871 of a professional body that in 1889 became the 'Institution of Electrical Engineers'. The story of the scientific understanding of electricity can serve as an example of science incrementally producing theoretical knowledge that contributes directly to technical innovation, with practical benefits for society.

In relation to the social recognition of science more generally, it was William Wherwell who, in about 1833, introduced the word 'scientist' to describe the people who undertook the work of science; work which included observation, experiment, theorizing and, for some, teaching; all contributing to our understanding of the 'natural' world. With many of the outcomes of the accumulating knowledge being translated by designers, engineers, and craftsmen, into useful products such as lighting, transit systems, powered machinery, the telegraph, and wireless comunication.

Until well into the eighteenth-century British science was mostly the preserve of gifted amateurs. But the founding in 1799 of the Royal Institution was a sign of increasing recognition of the importance of the endeavour and of the potential of collective collaboration to advance these. The founders (especially Sir Benjamin Thompson 1753-1814 – 'Count Rumford of the Holy Roman Empire') of The Royal Society saw its role as being the promotion of those working in science, and via publications and media reports, the diffusion of scientific knowledge to a wider public. The latter aim was early on subverted by the society's first Director, the brilliant scientist but inveterate snob Humphrey Davy (1778-1829). He was an admirer of elitist French scientific institutions such as the Academy of Sciences and the Ecole Polytechnique, and used these as models for The Royal Society.

As a working scientist Davy made advances in the understanding of gases – almost at the cost of his own life during an experiment that involved his breathing a mixture of gases, including carbon monoxide. His experimental findings showed that molecules of matter (solid, liquid, and gaseous) are held together by electrical forces. Using the technique of electrolysis he was able to discover a number of elements including two, sodium and potassium, which are fundamental to the organization of living organisms and indeed play an essential role in facilitating the transfer of 'informational patterns' between neurons in the human brain.

Davy's approach to science as a discipline was intellectually elitist and, in relation to social structure, he favoured economic inequality and social ranking. Even though he invented the Minor's Safety Lamp in 1815, a life-saving invention for which he did not accept any fee, he seems to have had little time for working people's aspiring beyond their 'social station'. He ensured that steps were taken to physically exclude 'mechanics' from the Royal Society's impressive buildings. Ironic given that he himself had progressed from quite modest origins. The Society provided then quite modern laboratory facilities and also served as a focus for scientific debate in Britain. It could fairly be argued that Davy's domination of its business during the first two decades of the nineteenth-century was one of the factors that held back the advance of British science when compared to Germany or France.

It would be Davy's assistant Michael Faraday (1791-1867), also a man of relatively humble origins who began his working life at 14 years of age as a bookbinder's apprentice[3] who would take the Society forward. I have noted above, his contribution to understanding electricity and magnetism, and in Faraday we see an example of the potential of intelligence allied to motivation in an individual determined to seek out and find the opportunity to advance themselves and also, in Faraday's case, to advance the scientific enterprise. He worked at the Society for over 40 years and his obvious ability, capacity for hard work, and brilliance at explaining scientific ideas to public audiences, saw him significantly develop the Society's work.

In 1825 he was appointed Director of the Society's laboratory and rarely can a workplace have offered a more conducive environment for any person as did the Society's building - containing its laboratory, library, and lecture hall - for Faraday. He even made his home on the top floor. Unlike Davy, Faraday was a brilliant publicist for science, prepared to deliver interesting and stimulating lectures to a wide range of audiences including school children. The Institution's Christmas Lecture series initiated by Faraday – aimed at school-

---

[3] Faraday's parents were members of a sect of religious dissenters 'the Sandemanians' and of modest means – his father was a blacksmith.

children - continues to this day.

We have noted above that early in the nineteenth-century scientists such as Ampere and Øersted were beginning to better understand the relationship between electricity and magnetism and when, in 1843, James Joule discovered an equivalence between heat and mechanical power ('the conservation of energy') it started to suggest the possibility of an underlying unity in the various 'forces' of the natural world. Advances in the understanding of the unity of heat and energy being embodied in the laws of thermodynamics. The relationship between the theories of heat and mechanics was outlined in detail by William Thompson (Lord Kelvin) in his book 'The Dynamical Equivalent of Heat' published in 1851. The work on light (linking it to electricity and magnetism) undertaken from about 1855 by James Clerk Maxwell offered compelling support for this suggestion. His 'electromagnetic theory' was of profound importance in the development of modern physics. Maxwell's four differential equations would receive some experimental confirmation in 1886 with the work of Heinrich Hertz, during the period of his discovering radio waves whilst he was a professor at the Techische Hochschule in Karlsruhe.

Hertz also confirmed Maxwell's prediction that electromagnetic 'waves' of longer wave-length than visible light existed, and that they travelled at the speed of light at right angles to the source of their propagation; as with all electromagnetic waves – the constant 'c' in Maxwell's equations. Hertz had been a student of Herman von Helmholtz – Director of the Berlin Institute of Physics - who, with his friend Werner von Siemens, made a great deal of money by the technological development that used the theoretical insight of Faraday's work on electricity to produce electric power generated in a way convenient for public consumption. In the second half of the century Maxwell's formulation of electromagnetism began to cast a shadow of doubt over the explanatory power (scope) of the fairly static Newtonian scientific world-view.

For Thomas Crump (2001, p393) '....four equations, fundamental in classic electrodynamics first stated by James Clerk Maxwell in the 1860s, which describe mathematically the changes in an *electromagnetic* field over time'. These equations highlighting the underlying unity of electric and magnetic forces were set out in Maxwell's 'A Dynamical Theory of the Electromagnetic Field'.

For John Gribben, Maxwell's equations showed that: 'Every

problem involving electricity and magnetism can be solved using these equations, except for certain quantum phenomena' and 'Between them, Newton's Laws and his theory of gravity, and Maxwell's equations, explained everything known to physics at the end of the 1860s'. (Gribbin, 2002, pps. 431-332)

In 1878 Hendrik Lorentz, building on Maxwell's work, proposed an electromagnetic theory of light, suggesting that light is a result of electric oscillations just like electromagnetic radiation. Maxwell's equations had described how charged particles are the substance of electricity and magnetism, and Lorentz enlarged the understanding of these by identifying the force (the 'Lorentz force q') that acted on charged particles in the presence of an electromagnetic field. Thereby introducing an idea that would lead in the next century to the notion of electrons as constituents of the atom. The foundations of a fundamental challenge to the Newtonian world-view had been laid down.

It was the theoretical basis of understanding electromagnetic waves (radiation), and their empirical identification by Heinrich Hertz, that allowed the development in 1896 of radio communication by Guglielmo Marconi, leading to radio communication across the English Channel in 1899 and across the Atlantic in 1901. An innovation in communication soon exploited by the navies of Britain and Germany.

In 1879 Albert Michelson improved the accuracy of Leon Foucault's fairly accurate measurement of the speed of light (achieved by Foucault in a series of ingenious experiments involving mirrors), and went on to measure the speed of light as it passed through a vacuum tube, a measurement that would prove to be of significant value to twentieth-century physics.

Albert Einstein was to use Maxwell's differential equations, especially the constant speed of the electromagnetic 'light' waves that they described (minus Maxwell's 'molecular vortices'), as the initial point of reference for his theory of special relativity (1905). But Einstein focused on the fact that the then (pre-1905) concept of the speed of light was based (as was Maxwell's) on some notional fixed point of measurement and so did not take into account the position (and so 'relative' movement) of the observer.

Maxwell's equations also implied the presence of an 'aether' through which electromagnetic waves could be propagated, and so a substance that could presumably be detected as the Earth travelled through space. In a landmark experiment in 1887 undertaken by Albert Michelson and Edward Morley (the 'Michelson-Morley experiment'), the outome produced a negative result, in that no aether was detected, but also a positive one in that it confirmed that light traveled at a constant speed. As noted above, a characteristic of light central to Einstein's theory of 'Special Relativity'.

According to John Priestly (2015, p112): 'This experiment, "to test the aether wind" is in fact the most famous in all of physics'.

The experimental apparatus for studying electricity (and electromagnetic waves) also developed during this scientifically productive period, in particular with the use of the vacuum tube. The German Heinrich Geissler had the technical skills to construct a glass tube from which all the air had been expelled with an electrode fitted at each end – one positive (anode) the other negative (cathode). Passing an electric current between the two electrodes resulted in mysterious 'rays' being emitted from the cathode end of the tube. These 'cathode rays' drew the attention of scientists working in Germany and Britain. William Crookes designed and made an improved version of the vacuum tube in 1878. Using this he discovered that illuminated rays travelling through the tube could be 'bent' when passing through a magnetic field; suggesting that they could not be light rays. A somewhat confused (perhaps more bemused) Crooks simply termed these cathode rays 'radiant matter'. Thomas Crump cites with agreement a view common to historians of physics that considers the vacuum tube and its improved versions were technological breakthroughs facilitating: '..... the enormous stream of discoveries at the end of the nineteenth century that gave us such insights as the discovery of X-rays, [and] working with radioactivity...' (Crump, 2001, p204). The cathode ray tube, a development of the vacuum pump (tube), was initially designed and used by Johann Hittork in 1869. But it wasn't until Arthur Schuster demonstrated the deflection of cathode rays by electric fields and William Crookes and Jean Perrin each demonstrated that they could also be deflected by magnetic fields (so behaving as if electrical particles), that the potential for this technique begun to be more fully realized. It was shown that cathode rays were generated (formed) when an electric current passes through a vacuum tube. Although at first thought to be a form of electromagnetic radiation it was shown by J.J.Thomson (in 1897) that cathode rays moved at a speed slower than that of light and so could not therefore be electromagnetic radiation. Decades later, a version of the cathode ray tube would be a vital component of tele-visual communication and of computer screens.

In 1895 Charles Rees Wilson had invented the 'cloud chamber' to allow investigation into the formation of clouds (in particular the effect of 'adiabatic expansion') he soon realized that his chamber could also be used to study the behavior of charged particles (ions). Improved versions of the cloud chamber would later on be used to study sub-atomic particles. Famously so with its use by Thomson to in 1899 measure the charge (negative) and the mass of the electron (constituting $1/2000^{th}$ the mass of a hydrogen atom). Then later on (1911) a much improved version was used to enable photographic images to record the passage of single electrons through a mixture of air and ethanol vapour and its doing so marked the opening up of access to sub-atomic events for decades to come until its replacement in the 1970s by the particle accelerator.

With the dramatic finding of the 'electron', another traditional edifice of physics (and indeed 'common knowledge'), the integrity of the atom, had to be reassessed. The idea of an indivisible atom of Dalton (and Democritus before him) – had fallen to the ongoing progress of experimental science.

The integrity of the atom would be under further scrutiny with the discovery, using an improved version of the vacuum tube, by Wilhelm Conrad Rontgen in 1895 of X-rays (high energy electromagnetic waves). Whilst engaged in developing the method used by Hertz to investigate cathode rays, Rontgen covered his tube in black card in the expectation that this might allow him to detect the faint passage of the rays as they passed through the tube's skin. By one of those happy accidents that occur from time to time in scientific investigation Rontgen had left a sheet of paper coated with barium platinocyanide out of what he assumed would be the passage of any cathode rays exiting from the tube. To Rontgen's surprise, once his experiment began the coated paper began to fluoresce even though this could not have been caused by cathode rays. He followed up this initial 'accident' with a serious of careful investigations and concluded that he had discovered a new form of radiation one that, with ease, passed through some substances but not so easily through others. He went on to show that these 'X-rays' can penetrate a range of substances and can actually 'remove' electrons from these substances on the way through. And that these rays could cause photographic plates to fog even if these were covered in black paper. The discovery of X-rays caused quite a stir with the public – by 1898 archaeologists were using X-rays to examine Egyptian mummies, and photographic images of Rontgen's wife's hand along with other X-ray photographs were being carried in newspapers; causing a similar public stir, akin to that caused by electricity in the eighteenth-century.

This happy 'accident', as in most cases of unplanned scientific discovery, was so only in a relative sense because the enabling conditions were still, if indirectly, related to the investigation being undertaken and of course the presence of a trained mind able to interpret the unexpected phenomenon.

The medical potential for X-rays was soon being exploited (if the dangers associated with exposure was then unknown), as was their value for ionizing gases. In relation to the specific advance of theoretical physics, it would be the linking of X-rays with other forms of radiation that would be more significant.

In the process of investigating whether fluorescent materials were themselves the source of X-rays Antoine-Henri Becquerel, in 1898, found that the substance uranium (in the molecular form of uranium nitrate) emitted radiation under any experimental condition, the first demonstration of 'natural' radioactivity. A discovery that, as with X-rays, had a certain element of chance – Becquerel's father had been collecting luminous (phosphorescent) substances and so the uranium nitrate was at hand for the son to use.

So now there was evidence of a substance 'spontaneously' able to emit radiation and, unlike cathode and X-rays, no discharge or other tubes were required to generate this radiation. Not only were atoms now shown to be divisible but it seemed that even the immutability of elements (an immutable property of matter set by Lavoisier) was now in question. The discovery of radioactivity stimulated the interest of Pierre and Marie Curie and, following a series of experiments to measure the energy given off by a range of elements, they showed that radioactivity was spontaneously emitted by single atoms. This finding was announced in their 1898 paper 'On a New Radio-Active Substance Contained in Pitchblende'. By the early years of the twentieth century Marie had identified two new chemical elements – radium and polonium - that were even more 'radioactive' than uranium. The two new elements had been predicted by the periodic table of elements so two more pieces of the 'missing' elements of the table had been identified. Marie Curie was an outstanding research scientist, officially recognized by her becoming the first women to be awarded a Nobel Prize for physics (jointly with her husband and shared with Becquerel in 1903) and The Nobel Prize for chemistry (in 1911).

One of the implications of the spontaneous generation of radiation from within atoms (radioactivity) was that the associated 'energy' seemed to defy the then current scientific view on its conservation – here was not wood, coal, or oil, as sources of energy, but instead the tiniest amounts of matter generating relative (to their size) enormous amounts of energy.

As the nineteenth century closed three discoveries: The electron, X-rays and radioactivity – along with the study of black-body radiation[4] - had thrown the science of physics into some turmoil – with the authority of Newton and others under threat. But it was a turmoil pervaded with the excitement of the potential for more experimental discovery and new theory building.

Chemistry

Chemistry was another branch of science that would make significant advances during the nineteenth-century; as a pure science in itself but also one that would quite easily and increasingly link too and stimulate industrial developments. Even accepting that chemistry was probably the branch of science that for longest retained the influence of the magical and mystical with its links to alchemy; especially the centuries-long association with the possibility of finding the secret of making gold.

There would be advances in identifying underlying structures as well as the characteristics of the behaviour of matter, and also a separation made between organic and inorganic chemistry. Advances in chemistry were closely associated with the progress of the Industrial Revolution. It was textiles that underpinned the demand-side of the mechanizing economy and it was the textile industry that was able to identify and incorporate developments in chemistry such as the discovery of chlorine (as bleach) in 1774, and later on the manufacture of artificial dyes to replace expensive natural dyes used

---

[4] This being a theoretical description of a body that can absorb light without reflecting it - but that will emit radiation. A key phenomenon for the development of twentieth century quantum mechanics.

to colour textile products.

Useful advances had been made in the seventeenth century by John Mayow and in the eighteenth with the work of individuals such as Robert Boyle and Robert Hooke. Although chemistry was at this stage the least amenable of the physical sciences to the advances made in mathematics, this tool 'hovered' in the background to be gradually brought to bear and enable the accurate quantification of chemical combinations and reactions as the eighteenth-century, and a better understanding of chemical processes, progressed.

One of the chemical processes that stimulated advance involved the phenomenon of combustion; the changes in chemical composition taking place when substances were burnt (or later heated). About the mid seventeenth-century chemists such as Johann Joachim Becher (1635-1682) and Georg Stahl (1660-1734), focusing on an idea that had interested 'chemists' throughout the medieval period, had identified a substance (or rather something more nebulous that would perhaps be better described as a characteristic of substances) that they noted as being lost during the burning process – named as 'phlogiston' by Stahl. They suggested that substances rich in phlogiston (such as coal and wood) would burn well, whereas substances that contained little or no phlogiston (such as metals and damp materials) were difficult if not impossible to burn. They also suggested that phlogiston could actually transfer between substances. Although superseded by later advances, the phlogiston theory provided a useful explanatory framework, especially in its suggestion that some universal substance was involved in the process of combustion.

This idea was initially undermined when experimental findings challenged the central ideas of the phlogiston theory, that a substance would 'give–off' phlogiston when burnt and consequently would therefore weigh less. Joseph Black, applying accurate measurement to experiments on combustion, showed that matter can actually get heavier following combustion. It would be the work of the outstanding chemist Antoine Lavoisier that completed the displacement of the phlogiston theory.

Progress was also made in the study of other 'gases'; a name given to invisible substances that chemists were aware existed and which they were able to see the effects of in such natural phenomena as spontaneous fires occurring in mines and with the wispy flares of marsh gas. It was Stephen Hales who had shown that it was possible to collect and measure the volume of gases using a technique that was later improved by Henry Cavendish (1731-1810). Cavendish was a careful experimenter with different gases, identifying (if wrongly) phlogiston as hydrogen - called by him 'inflammable air', and showing that water was not an elementary substance but a compound of two other substances. The Swedish chemist Carl Steele had earlier suggested that air itself is a mixture of two gases. It was Joseph Priestley who (repeating the work of Steele) released a gas (by heating red oxide of mercury) that he found significantly improved the burning of materials. Although he himself did not realize the significance and felt he was still working within the phlogiston model, he also demonstrated that this gas (later identified as oxygen) was given off by green plants as part of their metabolic process. An energetic experimenter, Priestley would also identify ten other gases. By this time the authority of Aristotle and his four primary elements: fire, earth, water, air had been irreparably undermined after its 2,000 years of ascendancy.

It was a revolutionary France that took the lead in the advance of chemistry in the early years of the nineteenth-century. The foundations for this were laid down during and immediately following the period of the Enlightenment when France had seen advances in mathematics made by French mathematicians such as Pierre-Simon Laplace (1749-1827), Joseph Lagrange (1736-1813), J.B.J. Fourier (1768-1830) and Simeon-Denis Poisson (1781-1840). The Frenchman Antoine Lavoisier (1743-94) contributed to the significant advance of chemistry by applying an organizing rationality and the precision of mathematics to the interpretation of thoughtful observation allied to careful experiment. Such was the quality (and vision) of Lavoisier's work that he stood out even from a number of outstanding early scientific chemists (of the 18th century) such as Joseph Black (1728-99), Priestley, Steele, and Cavendish. It was the work of these that Lavoisier contributed to bringing together and to identify the wider implications of the progress they had made.

Following pioneering work as a geological surveyor, Lavoisier became one of only 55 members of the Academy of Sciences (in 1678) at the young age of 25. He brought some measure of order to the rather disorganized state of early eighteenth-century theoretical and experimental chemistry. Lavoisier (and by implication the science of chemistry) benefited from a combination of fortunate circumstances that included a good education in mathematics and in the main branches of the natural sciences. He also enjoyed the advantage of large personal (inherited) wealth, and he was a member of a society that was generally encouraging to scientific debate. Lavoisier conducted a series of experiments that led him to identify combustion as a process whereby the object being burnt requires oxygen (Priestley's 'pure air', named as oxygen by Lavoisier in 1779) from the air in order to initiate and maintain the combustion process (the process of 'oxidation'). He showed that experimental findings did not need the concept of phlogiston to explain them.

In 1775 he was appointed by King Louis XVI to became a member (commissioner) of the 'Gunpowder Committee' ('Royal Gunpowder and Saltpeter Administration') and he set up a laboratory in the Arsenal, Paris, described by Bernal as: '.....probably the best laboratory for the time in the world' (Bernal, 1969, Vol II, p534). Lavoisier, in collaboration with his colleague Pierre Laplace, continued to experiment with gases and on the effect of heating as they searched to identify the constituent properties of air. As a result of some ingeniously designed experiments involving guinea pigs, they came to identify the process by which animals maintain their body temperature by utilizing oxygen in a slow process of combustion (respiration). In 1774 Priestley travelled to Paris and showed Lavoisier how to produce a seemingly interesting gas by heating red participate of metallic mercury. Lavoisier found that this gas was much more efficient in the combustion process than common 'air' and concluded that therefore 'air' must be composed of oxygen plus another gas. A gas later identified by Priestley as nitrogen.

If it was the Englishman Joseph Priestley that actually discovered oxygen it was the Frenchman Lavoisier who was able to explain what it was and indeed to name it. Another Englishman, Joseph Black,[5] had identified carbon dioxide as a constituent of air (1754) and another, Henry Cavendish, who (noted above) had discovered that air also contained hydrogen (1766).

Lavoisier's work on oxygen included his becoming aware of its role in animal (and human) respiration and that it was transported from the lungs throughout the body by blood. His landmark paper 'Memoir on the General Nature of Combustion' (1786) brought together suggestive explanations for what happens during both

---

[5] James Watt, who significantly improved the early steam engines, was one of the technicians in Black's laboratory in Glasgow University.

combustion and in respiration for animals. He also showed the central weakness of the phlogiston theory, even if his alternative 'caloric theory' raised its own problems for the advance of understanding.

As well as being in the forefront of the science of chemistry, Lavoisier was appointed to a commission set up to devise a standardized system of weights and measures; France at that time, 1788, had up to about 2000, mainly localized units of measurement. He was one of six leading scientists on a commission (including Coulomb and Laplace) that recognized the need, for both science and a rapidly developing economy, to have a standardized system of measurement. Owing to then current political tensions Prussia, and most English-speaking countries, (Britain and US) were not invited to send representatives. The culmination of the work carried out to determine accurate units of length and weights being overseen by the commission was presented at an international scientific congress (in 1798) whose only substantive agenda item was the adoption of a metric system of measurement. A system based on units of 10; expressing a rational approach to measurement that only the most hard-headed devotee of traditional forms of measurement (e.g. the British Imperial 'system') would chose to ignore. This relatively bold attempt to bring order to measurement on an international level was a small but significant step in the advance of the scientific approach to dealing with the 'natural' world. France was in the forefront of the development of chemistry during the late 18th early 19th centuries. The progress was facilitated yes, by the interest, intelligence, and usually the favourable personal financial circumstances of individuals, but also by the patronage of Napoleon, and the good sense of some educationalists and politicians to promote its study.

John Dalton (1766-1844), another individual from modest origins (his family were Quakers, his father a weaver) who after a varied beginning (from the age of 12) to his working life, was able to benefit from an opportunity to gain some education and, in 1785, he qualified as a teacher. Dalton developed an interest in science which included an active interest in meteorology. He progressed to become a teacher at the recently founded New College Manchester, where he taught mathematics and basic science to a variety of pupils, including many sons of mechanics and others who were aspiring to be part of the booming Manchester manufacturing industry. Manchester at this time offered quite a thriving location for scientists. As well as an institution such as New College, there were also a range of debating and other types of literary and scientific groups. The foremost of which being the Manchester Literary and Philosophical Society and it was at a meeting of this group, in Oct 1794, that Dalton read a paper on colour-blindness (he himself suffered from this) and the condition of 'Daltonism' was introduced into the medical lexicon. The most significant long-term advance made by Dalton was his suggestion, based partly at least on his own experimental work on gases, was the revival of the atomic theory. He proposed that each element was made of a different type of indivisible, indestructible, particle and that different particles (atoms) could group together in pairs, threes, and fours and so be able to form 'compound atoms' (molecules) and that each type of these fundamental particles had their own atomic weight. Whilst the idea of 'atoms' as basic constituents of matter had been around since the Greeks (Leucippus and his pupil Democritus). Dalton's insight was a triumph in theory formation and one that would gradually provide a relatively simple theoretical framework for advancing both chemistry and physics. These ideas also suggested a possible way of classifying elements; in fact Dalton himself made an attempt at just such a table, based on an 'atomic weight' of these elemental particles. Thus laying the intellectual path towards the Russian chemist Dimitry Mendeleyev's (1834-1907) more systematic (and more accurate) periodic table of the elements that would be developed in 1869 around 50 years after Dalton's own version.

Mendeleyev was another brilliant scientist of quick intelligence and a determination to follow his interest in chemistry. At the age of 23, after qualifying at a teacher training college in St Petersburg, he moved to Germany to undertake research on molecular cohesion. Mendeleyev's work on the periodic table built on the work of Dalton and a number of other men of science. The Frenchman Alexandre Béguyer de Chancourtious, the Englishman John Newlands and the German Lothar Meyer all of whom, prior to Mendeleyev, were aware that it was possible to group elements according to atomic weight, that hydrogen was the simplest (lightest) element, and that the groupings were multiples of this. Mendeleyev's renown was due partly to his boldness, the relative clarity in his tables, and the underlying theory on which it was based; but also because his precursors had to an extent intellectually 'softened up' an influential section of the scientific community.

Mendeleyev had already established a certain authority as a chemist with his book 'Organic Chemistry' (pub. 1861) in which he tried to show that all of organic life was based on natural (physical) processes; no need for any 'soul-substance' or 'élan vital' type of force underlying the processes that organize and sustain living things. By 1867 he was a professor at St. Petersburg's Technological Institute, whilst also lecturing in organic chemistry at the City's University and, like Faraday, Mendeleyev was a brilliant and stimulating lecturer. One able to range widely over his subject-matter whilst making imaginative links between common-place phenomena to illustrate the points being made. In 1867 he began work on a manual of chemistry which was intended to meet the needs of his students, published in two volumes in 1868 and 1870. It was during this period of active reflection on fundamental aspects of chemistry that the idea of arranging elements according to their atomic weight, which was linked to their chemical characteristics, came to him in a dream that he was supposed to have had on the night of 17th Feb 1869.

The first presentation of this idea took place when he presented a paper - 'On the Relation of the Properties to the Atomic Weights of Elements' - to the Russian Chemistry Society only a month after the inspirational dream. The idea of a periodic table was then re-stated in a book 'The Foundations of Chemistry' published in 1869; and in this form it became available to a wider scientific public. Although chemistry was more receptive to the idea of some form of categorizing chemical elements, and Mendeleyev had already gained some authority within the scientific community, it was a key aspect of his theory, periodicy, that would have made it attractive for those scientists who gave a priority to science as a predictive method rather than more simply as an activity based on the collection of, facts, ideas and discoveries. The final version of Mendeyev's periodic table was based on an arrangement of the 61-63 then known elements.

His theory of periodicy made predictions of what could be discovered that would be in-line with (and therefore support) his theoretical arrangement of the elements – in effect his table left 'gaps' (at least six 'missing' atomic weights, gaps - between some of the 61 elements), the prediction being that there must exist elements waiting to be discovered whose atomic weight would be such that they would 'fit' into the gaps. The predicative aspect of the table must have recommended it to those scientists who saw science as an activity based on certain methods of observation and discovery – predictions fulfilled reinforcing the strength of a theory, whereas those unfulfilled leaving it open to doubt. For Mendeyev, it was the satisfaction of fulfillment that would be experienced when three elements were soon identified each having an atomic weight (and chemical properties) that allowed them to fit three of the gaps, these being: – Gallium 1875 - Scandium 1879 – Germanium 1886.

The persuasive confirmation of predictions fulfilled the utility value in having a way of categorizing the elements, and a natural propensity of the scientific mind to prefer the rational ordering of phenomena, were also in the theory's favour. With gaps being filled the systematic arrangement of elements based on Mendeyev's Table was accepted throughout the community of natural scientists.

If you, as did Mendeyev and the science of his time, consider atoms to be the smallest possible particle of matter then it would seem reasonable to attribute differing chemical properties to the differing weight of the atom of each element. It was later discovered that atoms themselves were made up of even smaller particles, including protons and neutrons held together in the nucleus of atoms and that it is the combined number of protons and neutrons rather than a 'weight' (based on protons) that was linked to an element's chemical properties. So today's preferred periodic table is based on an element's atomic number rather than atomic weight – although this revision actually only resulted in a small number of the elements of Mendeyev's Table having to change their position.

In 1848 the young Louis Pasteur had shown that molecules had characteristics which gave them a three-dimensional shape and that they must have chemical structures that are either right-handed or left-handed (their 'chirality'). Revealing the characteristics of atoms and molecules further, the German Chemist Friedrich Kekule in 1865 (echoing ideas first suggested by the Englishman Edward Frankland and the Scotsman Achibald Couper) suggested that a molecule of benzene (6H6) was composed of a ring of six carbon atoms. The implication being that molecules could be quantified, not just in terms of how many atoms they contain, but also in terms of their overall chemical structure. An explanation in terms of structural form, showing the number of atoms and the links between them in each molecule.

This opened the way for understanding atoms of different elements to be characterized by the number of links (valences) they could make with other atoms. Further progress was made by Svank Arrhenius (1859-1927) who, in 1889 publicized the results of his investigations into the role played by heat (energy) in the initiation of chemical reactions. He produced a mathematical formula, the 'Arrhenius equation' that described the relationship between 'activation energy' and 'reaction rate'. The study of chemical compounds, and chemical activity more generally, was to generate a stream of information that would provide the basis for an ever widening range of industrial applications.

A key tool for chemists invented in the 19th century (and significantly improved during the early 20th by William Crookes) was the spectrometer, used to identify different chemical elements. It was the two friends, Robert Bunsen and Gustav Kirchhoff, who noted that if chemical substances were heated a (barcode-like) pattern of bright lines could be detected in the radiated light. It was also found that when chemical substances were cooled a pattern of dark lines (the 'Fraunhofer lines') could be detected and further, that both forms of spectral radiation (bright and dark lines) were propagated at the same wavelength (see more on this under astronomy below). The discovery of these element-specific spectra soon led to the identification of a number of new elements (especially 'noble gases' such as helium, argon, krypton, neon and xenon) and spectral analysis as a sub-branch of chemistry was to serve as a fertile source of scientific knowledge in chemistry, physics, and especially astronomy, throughout the twentieth-century.

Early in the nineteenth century chemistry had been separated (initially in 1807 by the Swede Jons Berzelius) into inorganic and organic branches, but as the century unfolded a deeper understanding of the chemical nature of molecules showed that so-called organic materials were only made of more complex ('many atoms of usually different elements') compounds than so-called inorganic materials, and that there was no mysterious 'life-force' in one type of material (organic) that was missing in the other type (inorganic). The complexity of organic materials being mainly due to their all containing the complex and flexible (in terms of valency) element of carbon. But for the most part the two branches did maintain a difference, if not in theoretical understanding of their basic material and appropriate level of analysis, at least in the central focus of practitioners and increasingly of the research funders. If anything differentiates inorganic and organic chemistry it would be the latter's central focus on the properties of carbon based molecules and compounds.

A focus on carbon had been advanced by the work of Justus von

Liebig (1803-74) and his demonstrating the multiple ways in which elements vital for life - Carbon, Nitrogen, Oxygen, Hydrogen can form compounds. At around the same time in the 1850s Friedrich August Kehule's 'principle of catenation' identified how carbon atoms can link together to form chains making them even more amenable to combine with other elements.

The central issues that would occupy chemists during the twentieth-century had been identified by 1900 – these being the study of materials for inorganic chemistry, and the chemistry of life for organic chemistry.

Astronomy

Up until the end of the fifteenth-century the astronomical views of Aristotle and Ptolemy, with their static Earth and the heavenly bodies moving around it in a series of spheres, held centre-stage – especially in the influential Catholic Church. With the Church (Pseudo Dionysius) devising its own motive base for the Universe, including a celestial hierarchy composed of nine choirs of angels – seraphim, cherubim, archangels, etc. each with a specific function in maintaining the Universe; its motion and its order.

The period when significant advances were to be made in astronomy was also a time of European expansion across the world and mapping and measuring (seeking a sense of understanding though graphic representation) were included in both geography and astronomy. In their fifteenth-century revision of the Alphonsine Tables (star charts used for astrological purposes) Peurbach and Regiomontanus, aided by the use of the Arabic trigonometry of Levi ben Gerson, also improved ocean navigation. But into the medieval period the flat-earth view predominated and when even at the time that Columbus set sail west in 1492 there were serious suggestions that his ships might fall over the edge of the world.

Although the advances made in the sixteenth-century by the Polish astronomer Nicholas Copernicus have been seen as revolutionary, he did in fact return to some early Greek astronomy in his re-presenting the idea of a rotating Earth and of a heliocentric Solar System. Although his contribution was not in itself a revolution, it was felt as one in the context of 15th/16th century scientific/religious milieu and it was the act of an intellectually brave man to introduce it. Even if we accept that the book was published after his death and it has a 'religious apology-type' clause in the introduction, albeit this addition is not thought to have been written by Copernicus himself. Such was his belief in the value of exact calculation for explaining celestial (and other) motions that he suggested that 'The book of nature is written in the mathematical language'.

A clear strength of Copernicus's suggestion, making it difficult for the scientific community of the time to ignore, was its general match to the astronomical observations and in the improvements it allowed to astronomical tables. But it would take the wider circulation of his book 'The Revolution of the Celestial Orbs' (pub. in 1543), and the confirmation of Galileo's later view, to remove the most substantial intellectual objection to the Copernican universe.

One man, Giordano Bruno, paid a high price for, amongst other things (including suggesting an infinite Universe that implied numerous inhabited worlds - contrary to religious doctrine), promoting the Copernican theory, when in 1600 he was burnt alive by the Inquisition on the grounds of heresy. But the flames that consumed his body could not destroy the potential for a fundamental shift in world-view necessitated by Copernicus's ideas – thanks to Bruno and others this theory now needed to be taken into account by any serious astronomer.

It was the astronomers Tycho Brahe (1546-1601) and Johannes Kepler (1571-1630) who improved on the work of Copernicus by setting out to accurately describe planetary motion. Brahe established what was in effect the first modern astronomical observatory, Uraniborg, on an island off the Danish coast. It was here that Brahe and Kepler carried out most of their work. Brahe's theory included the retrograde step of placing the Sun in orbit round the Earth even if he retained the idea of the other planets revolving round the Sun. Brahe's system was a modified version of the one proposed originally by the ancient Greek philosopher Aristarchus of Samos, but the real value of his work was in the careful observation and detailed recording of planetary and stellar positions. He also fatally undermined the Aristotelian system which had placed all stars in a fixed unchanging outer sphere when he discovered a 'New Star' (B Cassiopeiae) in 1572.

Kepler, focusing more on the underlying planetary motion and using observational data collected at Uraniburg, set out three 'laws' of planetary motion in his book 'Tabulae Rudolphinae' (pub. 1627). Firstly, that the planets travel round the Sun in elliptical orbits (and so directly challenging the authority of Plato's and Aristotle's circular orbits) – with the actual observed movement of Mars offering convincing proof. Secondly, that planetary motion was such that a line drawn from any planet to the Sun would, as the planet moved, sweep through equal distances in equal times. Thirdly, that the '…square of the orbital period of a planet is directly proportional to the cube of the semi-major axis of its orbit.' This last law identifies a link between the distance between any planet and the Sun, and their orbital period.

Kepler also suggested that the force sustaining planetary motion was one similar to magnetism (in William Gilbert's 'De Magnete', 1600, the Earth itself is described as a magnet) a suggestion to be later taken up by Newton and made an important link between astronomy and physics – a precursor of the science of astrophysics.

The use of telescopes for astronomy had begun in 1609 and within 50 years it was a standard tool of observation. Their use provided a whole new perspective on celestial bodies and - even accepting further developments such as of spectral analysis, photography and radio telescopes - the improvement in lens and mirrors of telescopes and in their use has continued down to today. As professor of physics and military engineering at Padua University, Galileo Gelilei (1564-1642) had already undertaken work on the study of the motion of projectiles and of falling bodies. He was sympathetic to the views of both Copernicus and Kepler; indeed, after only reading the preface to Kepler's 'Mysterium Cosmographicum' he wrote a letter of congratulations to the author. Within days of using his first (x8 magnification) self-made telescope in 1609 Galileo had made observations that showed the new instrument to be a powerful tool for the practicing astronomer. He was able to note a moonscape of dusty seas and hills on what had previously been thought to have been a smooth surface. Within a year he was using an improved instrument giving x20 magnification. With these improved telescopes he went on to discover that the Milky Way (the 'Heavenly Nile' of the Egyptians) was in fact made up of thousands of stars, that Jupiter had four moons, that there were sunspots, and that the planets reflected light from the Sun .

In terms of theoretical contributions, Galileo's enduring work as an astronomer was in disproving most of the views of Aristotle and Ptolemy and in confirming some of those of Copernicus and Kepler. He also made important contributions to the application of mathematics to the study of planetary motion. But his contribution to the development of the telescope was also significant, allowing the Universe to be seen from a stunningly revealing perspective. Another advance was made in the 1670s by Giovanni Cassini (in France) and John Flamstead (in England – the 'Astronomer Royal') each of whom used the phenomenon of parallax to calculate the distance from Earth to Mars

It was Isaac Newton, scientific genius if flawed man, who completed the process, began nearly 150 years earlier by Copernicus (Newton was born 100 years after the publication of 'The Revolution of the Celestial Orbs'), finally completing the freeing of astronomy from the restrictive framework set by Plato, Aristotle, and Ptolemy, when he applied his powerful mind to resolving the problems that remained in reconciling astronomical theory to the then actual observational knowledge. He provided mathematical proofs for Kepler's three laws and also, with the law of universal gravitation unifying terrestrial and cosmological forces; set out in his dense and difficult book 'Philosophiae Naturalis Principia Mathematica' 1687 (translated as: 'Mathematical Principles of Natural Philosophy').

Empirical support for his theory of celestial dynamics was confirmed in 1846 with the discovery of Neptune. On the other hand he also held to the belief that the Universe was created by the Christian God and that the Earth was created in 4004 BCE (as had been calculated by Bishop Ussher following the genealogical lines set out in the Biblical book of Genesis).

The astronomical world-view that Newton left behind had clearly superseded that of the Greeks. He had deduced the motion of the Sun and planets from his understanding of gravitational forces. His law: '......the force between two bodies if directed along a line connecting them, is directly proportional to the product of their masses, and is inversely proportional to the square of their separation' (Cambridge Encyclopedia of Astronomy', 1979, p.400), had shown that on the level of the Solar System (and by implication all celestial bodies) that action at a distance (gravitation) could be used to explain their motion.

Edmund Halley (1656-1742) understood and publicized the scientific implications of the inverse square law, as it relates to gravitation, set out by Newton – that it was a 'universal law', so one that applied all across the Universe. In a busy and productive career in science Halley also made advances in astronomical measurement, and of course in predicting the return of a comet. He also questioned Ussher's claim of the Earth being created in 4004 BCE. Whilst his own suggestions did not place the age much further back it did serve as a challenge to the calculations based on the genealogy of the people in the Book of Genesis; he also attempted to calculate the size of the Universe. Halley was preceded as Astronomer Royal by John Flamstead[6] who had already made a significant contribution to accurately surveying celestial bodies seen in the northern sky (drawing up a catalogue of about 3000 stars). During an expedition to St Helena in 1676 Halley endeavoured to undertake a less comprehensive survey, focusing on just 300 of the brightest stars visible in the southern sky. Halley advanced his chosen branch of science in numerous ways during his life – including using the transit of Venus to identify the fact that the motion of stars is not fixed relative to one another (in direct contradiction to any residual respect still being given to the authority of Aristotle) and that this small change in positions relative to one another could be used to measure the speed of travel of stars as well as their distance from the Earth.

In 1761 the French astronomer Joseph Delisle (1688-1768), developing an idea initially suggested in 1663 by the Scotsman James Gregory, coordinated an ambitious scientific venture, one aim of which was to more accurately measure the duration of the transit of Venus. This was also a useful example of the early internationalization of science, with 120 astronomers from nine nations taking readings from primary 'cones of visibility' located across the world, attempting to record simultaneous observations. Mainly due to poor weather conditions the attempt failed, but a marker had been laid in relation to scientific co-operation. A more successful attempt was made in 1769 during a scientific expedition to Tahiti led by Captain James Cook. Information gained during this second attempt to measure the duration of the transit of Venus also enabled the distance between the Sun and the Earth to be measured as 95,000,000 miles (just slightly over 3 million miles more than today's accepted distance).

By this time the first 'modern' national observatories had been established in: Paris 1667, followed by London (Greenwich 1675)

---

[6] Flamstead was the first Astronomer Royal based at Greenwich Royal Observatory, appointed 1675, Halley was appointed as Astronomer Royal in 1720.

which, especially Greenwich, were to became the principle astronomical research establishments during the following centuries. Each of these observatories made use of the reflective telescope, mainly due to its optical advantages over the refracting telescope that had been used by Galileo. If from about the middle of the nineteenth-century, improvements in the quality of lenses and of the optical systems based on these, did result in a return to the use by many professional astronomers of refracting telescopes. By far the main focus of these state-sponsored observatories was recording the stellar and lunar positions. Throughout the eighteenth century we see the consolidation of advances made by post-Copernican astronomers, with individuals such as John Flamstead, Edmund Halley, and James Bradley, continuing the process of carefully identifying and locating celestial bodies and identifying their orbits.

As well as improvements continuing to be made in the technology of optical systems, developments in mathematics enabled more accurate measurement and also more reliable predictions. Mathematicians such as Laplace, (French), Euler (Swiss), and Alexis

Clairaut (French 1713-65) stand out. Clairaut made important contributions to explaining the sun-moon-earth system and travelled to Lapland on a 'scientific' expedition that included his establishing (by measurement) that, just as predicted by Newtonian theory, the Earth is flatter at the poles. He predicted (with an accuracy of 32 days) the return of Halley's Comet in April 1759. He also introduced Newtonian dynamics into France (then probably the leading nation in terms of science), a direct and successful challenge to the then influential Cartesian theory of vortices.

James Bradley (1693-1762) as the third Astronomer Royal based at Greenwich, outlined a method of determining the speed of light based on the time that it took for light to travel from a star to the Earth (Halley and Clairaut had shown how to measure the distance of stars from Earth) – at 308,300 km per sec. In 1746 the brilliant Swiss mathematician Leonhard Euler made the precocious assumption that light travelled in waves and that every colour had its own specific wavelength. From this he provided a mathematical description of the refraction of light. By 1762, when he died, Bradley had also completed an impressive star catalogue, locating 60,000 individual stars and, by allowing for the effect of barometric pressure and of temperature on his observations, had made a significant improvement in the accuracy of their recorded positions – the immensity of the

Universe was revealing itself at a pace.

John Mitchell (1724-1793) was another scientist who suggested an idea in advance of its time (and the means to test it) with his suggestion that there were celestial entities similar in gravitational effect to 'black holes'. These entities being areas of space that contained a star 500 times bigger than the Sun and that these massive objects would have such a powerful gravitational pull that nothing, not even its own light, could escape its gravitational field. This was an idea also suggested by Pierre Simon Laplace who in his two-volume 'Exposition du systeme du moude' ('The System of the World') published in 1796 (as part of his work on modernizing the teaching of science in France) suggested the possibility of 'bodies' 250 times bigger than the Sun and, as with Mitchell's slightly earlier idea, from which nothing could 'escape'. This idea was only included in the first edition of Laplace's book; a significant book in the history of science; perhaps it was omitted from the numerous later editions owing to the lack of interest in what might have seemed to have been a somewhat fantastical idea. Laplace's more significant contribution to the growing published scientific genre was his five volume 'Celestial Mechanics' ('Mécanique Céleste'), in which he summarized and extended the most important work of those who preceded him.

Yet another advance in the understanding of celestial bodies was the determination of a body's density. This was facilitated by the work of the single-minded scientist Henry Cavendish, who was in fact applying theoretical ideas and an experimental method suggested by his friend Mitchell, whose death in1793 had prevented him from completing his own work. A series of well-designed experiments involving a 'torsion balance' led to Cavendish calculating a figure for the density of the Earth of 5.48 times the density of water (the actual figure, obtained later using more sophisticated equipment, is 5.52). This work produced a standard measurement that enabled the calculation of the density of a solar, or indeed any, celestial body.

In 1838, the German astronomer Friedrich Bessel (1784-1846) discovered that the phenomenon of stellar parallax was a useful technique for improving the accuracy of estimating the distance to a star (the Greek Hipparcus had used parallax to measure the distance to the Moon as early as 189 BCE). Bessel went on to compile a catalogue of 63,000 stars. The 'mapping' of celestial bodies continued to advance with the bright clouds of gaseous materials, nebulae, drawing the attention of William Herschel and his sister Caroline (born in Hanover but worked in England – William was George III's personal astronomer). In addition to discovering the planet Uranus in 1781, the first new planet in the solar system to be discovered for at least 2000 years, William also added about 30 more nebulae to the catalogue began by Charles Messier (French 1730-1817), bringing this to just over 100. After his death Caroline, using much of William's data, went on to meticulously expand the catalogue to 2,500 nebulae and star clusters. William had also shown that nebulae, previously thought to be just gaseous clouds, in fact contained thousands of stars. The observation of nebulae gave rise to the nebulae hypotheses of planetary formation. The suggestion that planets could be formed out of the gaseous materials surrounding stars; a view that twentieth century astrophysics would confirm.

If by then if not already dead, then the final demise of the edifice that was based on the authority of Aristotle's cosmology came in 1782 with the discovery, by the eighteen year old English astronomer John Goodricke (who was both deaf and mute), that the star Algol ('b'Persci) was in fact two stars orbiting round a common centre of mass. This indicated that stars could have different luminosities due to their own intrinsic properties rather than this being an observational effect due to each star's distance from the Earth. This difference in luminosities allowed the distance between the Earth and a star to be measured and confirmed that the Universe was (at least) three dimensional. This measuring method, based on 'trigonometrical parallax', was the one noted above used in 1837 by Bessel to measure the distance from Earth to the star 61 Cygni. By mid nineteenth-century knowledge of stars was limited to the relative position of many, the apparent magnitude of some, and the distance from Earth of a few of them.

The late nineteenth-century enrichment of astronomy by the development of astrophysics (not least the increasing application of suitable mathematics) not only allowed a significant increase in the information related to the Universe but this also further stimulated humankind's imagination of the context of space, distance, and time.

Over tens of thousands of years the human mind (with its remarkable ability to 'imagine') had evolved to consider spatial environments confined to quite local territories, then regional, then continental, then oceanic (transcontinental). These same type of minds had to confront the implications of 19/20th century astronomy;

having to cope with the speed of light, with measurement of distance in terms of light-years, with infinities, and later with such exotic ideas as the curvature of space, dark energy and matter, black holes and cosmic radiation, and of an expanding Universe billions of year old containing trillions of stars.

Humankind would, over the 19th and 20th centuries, have come to terms with dimensions and times never before considered. Not just the conceptual 'furniture' of our minds but also the very space-time in which it was situated would need to undergo a seismic shift in perspective and understanding if were ever to gain some sense of the immensities with which we are confronted.

The use of spectral analysis that was of such value to chemists (noted above) also provided astronomers with a tool to investigate the elemental composition of celestial bodies. This method was able to interpret information from the electromagnetic radiation being emitted by celestial bodies. Being based on the characteristic differences in the patterns or frequencies (wavelengths) of light emitted, or absorbed by individual atoms and molecules. In 1802 the Englishman William Wollaston had observed that the light from the Sun separated by a spectroscope showed a spectrum crossed by dark lines. These were later termed 'Fraunhofer lines' following the German Joseph von Fraunhofer's systematic mapping of solar spectral lines and those produced by other bodies in the Solar System. Fraunhofer, as an instrument maker, had access to advanced optical instruments and he designed a 'diffraction grating' that enabled light to be spread out to reveal its spectrum. These lines were similar to those that had been noted during laboratory experiments on the spectra produced by chemical elements. This conjunction of observations created quite a bit of scientific interest, and generated a number of experiments, but it was not until 1859 when, following a series of experiments, Gustav Kirchhoff, outlined three 'laws' of spectroscopy.[7]

The first being that, when any substance is heated the flame changes colour, and the colour shown is a specific characteristic of the substance being heated. The spectrum produced in this way contains a pattern of bright lines that allows the elements in any

---

[7] Kirchhoff also worked with Robert Bunsen who had invented his eponymous Bunsen burner, used in laboratories throughout the world for generations.

substance to be identified. Each pattern of bright lines is unique to particular substances. Conversly, when a substance is cooled, instead of producing bright lines, it would produce patterns of dark lines. It would now be absorbing rather than (as when hot) radiating light and so producing patterns of dark rather than bright lines, but the light absorbed would be at precisely the same wavelength as the light radiated when hot. So now the light from a star and any gaseous material could be analyzed ('spectral analysis') to reveal the elements that were present.

Kirchhoff's law being that '...each element is capable of absorbing the same radiation that it emits' (Mitton, ed, 1979, p 406 – Cambridge Encylo. Astron.). The value of the understanding of the link between spectral characteristics of chemical elements in a laboratory and spectral characteristics of light produced by celestial bodies soon showed the potential of spectroscopy for making advances in astronomy.

Using spectral analysis, William Huggins and W.A.Miller made a significant contribution to the understanding of the chemical composition of stars. They published a paper in 1864 that outlined the spectral analysis of 50 stars and were able to identify that these 'bright stars' had a similar chemical composition to the Sun – and that some of the elements detected such as: hydrogen, calcium, iron, sodium, were important for organic life. Huggins was the first astronomer to use a spectroscope to study nebulae and in 1864 he noted the existence of two types of spectral characteristics and was able to distinguish between true stars and clouds of tenuous gases.

Between 1863-67 Angelo Secchi (Italian) used spectral analysis to classify 4000 stars according to their spectral 'footprints'. Grouped into four different groups in relation to the successive stages of a star's life – White stars, Yellow stars, Orange/reddish stars, and Faint red stars. A number of astronomers made contributions to the classification of stars, gifting a mass of data to the astronomers that followed.

E.C.Pickering and Antonia Maury (working in the United States) produced a detailed classification system set out in the 'Draper catalogue' (1st pub 1890 with a revised edition in 1897), a text that became a standard reference work. The culmination of this stage of using spectral analysis were the series of catalogues compiled by Annie J. Cannon, published between 1918-1924 in which 225,000 stars were classified.

As the century drew to an end a wide-ranging categorization system of star spectra had been devised, based on a alphabetical system on a scale of decreasing temperature:

O,B,A,F,G,K,M,R,N,S and each of these being sub-divided into numerically organized groups. As part of this interest in spectral analysis the phenomenon of colour-shift was noted; this 'Doppler effect' causing light from stars moving away from the Earth to 'shift' in wavelength toward red and light from stars moving towards the Earth (albeit relatively few of these) to 'shift' in wavelength toward blue. This is a phenomenon, to which Albert Einstein would turn during the twentieth-century, was part of an important 'shift' from the Newtonian understanding space and of time.

Another invention made and developed during the nineteenth-century was that of photography, the ability to use the chemical sensitivity to light of certain solutions (containing sliver halides) to record images passing through an aperture; images that soon came to be focused by a lens. From the 1870s, when dry gelatin plates replaced the wet collodion process, photographic cameras were adapted to work through telescopes, and photography soon came to be used to produce images of sections of the night sky; to 'freeze' and track the changing position of celestial bodies. Photographic plates could also be used to record the ultraviolet wavelength of light unseen by the naked eye. This new tool improved not just the study and mapping of stars but also enabled astronomers to record and study the spectra that are produced, and to study both of these aspects of astronomical investigation at leisure.

At the end of the nineteenth century interest in astronomy, stimulated by the tools of spectral analysis, photography, and evermore sophisticated mathematics, led to the construction of bigger and better telescopes located at sites of high elevation, and so ones offering more nights of clear skies. These included the Lick Observatory 1888 California, and the Yerkes Observatory 1898 Illinois, being just two of the more impressive. It would be the use and further development of telescopes, and also theoretical advance in astrophysics, that would underlie the significant progress in astronomy made during the twentieth century.

Unlike many of their predecessors, 'western' astronomers working in the nineteenth century did not have to be continually looking over their shoulder in fear of religious persecution, the threat of excommunication, or worse. Even if, to avoid a measure of social approbation, they did still need to be cautious when interpreting their discoveries and related implications if these challenged Biblical 'cosmology'. This, degree of intellectual freedom was a factor contributing to the freeing up of theoretical imagination and technical innovation.

Geology

For thousands of years there had been individuals who were curious about the Earth as a body, its creation, and the types of rock found beneath the surface as well as those exposed to view. Layers of the Earth into which they had quarried for stone, mined for precious minerals, metals and for fuel, and dug into for burial chambers; then, in the 18th/19th centuries, had burrowed into when constructing railways, canals, and the tunnels necessary for their progress across the land. In Britain, during this time such activities attracted a more detailed interest in the rocks beneath the Earth's surface. Appropriate then that the first geological society was founded in Britain in 1807.

Curiosity, as well as practical considerations, had motivated an interest in differences between rock formations and in the constitution of soils, as well as in the fossilized remains of strange animals to be found, some on but most beneath the surface of the land. The strangeness of these fossils coming not necessarily from their anatomy, in which they often resembled animals alive at the time, but a strangeness that came from the locations at which they were to be found: the remains of sea creatures found inland, of birdlike creatures found deep in the soil, seemingly native African animals found in Europe (sabre-toothed tigers, woolly mammoth). Some explanations were available in terms of religious catastrophes such as the Gilgamesh Epic flood and the Biblical Noah's flood. But for the more scientifically minded of the 17th and 18th centuries these imaginative explanations became less satisfactory in that, they failed to explain the fact that fossils were to be found at some depth, and why were the bones of animals only known to be native to one continent at that time found so far into another.

In 1669 Niels Stensen ('Steno') suggested that rock strata, even if now perpendicular to the horizontal or otherwise angled away from it, was initially deposited (under water in the oceans and rivers) in a series of horizontal layers. Subsequent changes in angle to the Earth being due to processes of various types of geological movement. For

Gabriel Gohau: 'Despite all his limitations, Steno provided a considerable leap forward in methodology for histories of the earth', (Gohau, 1991, p66). A century later Giovanni Arduino (1760) proposed three groupings for rocks:

1) Primary: crystalline rocks with metallic cores
2) Secondary: stratified rocks, often fossil-bearing
3) Tertiary: the less consolidated stratified rocks, the fossil marker for these being marine organisms.

And Johann Gottlob Lehmann (1756) proposed three similar categories:

1) Crystalline
2) Stratified
3) Alluvial

These categories were time-related in that the assumption (erroneous) was that the harder the rock the earlier it must have been formed.

In Europe the growing number of interested individuals that we can fairly describe as early 'geologists' generally accepted these types of crude categorization. Meanwhile the background explanatory framework for geological features was still in terms of the biblical creation story, and the accepted age of the Earth being that calculated by Bishop Ussher. In 1620 Ussher had, using the hereditary line from Adam as set out in the Book of Genesis, calculated the age of the Earth to be about 6,000 years, with the initial creation taking place in 4004 BCE.

The first serious challenge to Ussher's calculations was probably that of James Hutton (1726-1797) who, in 1779, suggested that the formation of the different types of rock (and indeed many of the Earth's geological features) was the outcome of the various natural processes of deposition, compaction, and erosion, taking place over long periods of time. And that these were natural processes that could currently be observed in action. He suggested that high temperatures generated deep within the Earth had caused violent earthquakes which pushed up dry land, with the slow process of weathering shaping the exposed rocks. He also suggested that valleys had been cut by rivers, and the plains formed by the accumulation of the deposition of materials washed down the rivers – and that some rocks (e.g. Arthur's Seat in the centre of Hutton's native City of Edinburgh) were formed by the solidification of lava from long extinct volcanoes. His view being that the outcome of these processes would have required far longer than Ussher's 6,000 years.

A significant step forward in the method of identifying the age of deposits was made by William Smith (1769-1839). Smith made the connection between fossilized animal (organic) materials and the layers of strata in which they were deposited and suggested that these were linked to the relative age of the materials. Smith's pioneering work on the use of 'fossil markers' (faunal succession) was refined by George Cuvier (1769-1832), who undertook a detailed study of the stratigraphical sequence of both land-based vertebrate and of marine fossils buried in deposits of the tertiary strata across the wide basin in which lies the City of Paris (co-written with Alexandre Brongniart as *'Essay on mineralogical geography of the surroundings of Paris'* 1808). By 1812 Cuvier had shown (as also had Smith) the possibility of using these as 'fossil markers' to determine the relative age of layers within strata at different locations, but Cuvier also identified a range of fossil organisms for which no contemporary specimens could be found, suggesting that many species must have become extinct; so offering a clear challenge to the Church's view of species survival. Cuvier's methods allowed the relative dating of different types of strata located long-distances apart.

Smith had been a surveyor, employed on the construction of canals and so well-placed to see the layers of rock, soils, minerals and other strata across Britain. He spent a considerable part of his life in undertaking the compilation of one of the first 'geological maps', recording the patterns of layers of strata across most of southern England and Wales (pub.1815).

A key aspect of the advancing knowledge of straigraphy, and of the fossil record, was an awareness of the amount of time that must have been taken to lay the strata down; the slow processes of deposition, consolidation, and compaction, as well as the formation of the more significant geological features such as mountain ranges, river valleys and oceans. By 1799 Cuvier had advanced to become professor of natural history at the Museum of Natural History in Paris and his methodical approach to the study of natural history included his making significant advances in comparative anatomy; on both contemporary organisms and on fossil specimens. One of his landmark insights was the linking of an organism's body (morphological structure) to its diet – plant eaters would have the wide fairly blunt teeth required for mastication and hoofed feet for plodding long distances to find suitable grazing rather than the fearsome array of sharp teeth and the clawed paws of the hunting 'sprinters' that preyed on them. Cuvier made outstanding contributions to geology and also laid the foundations for a new branch of the natural sciences that would be paleontology, just one highlight being his identification and naming of the bird-like Pterodactyl.

Cuvier suggested that there was a time when there would have been no life on Earth. He noted types of organisms that had become extinct and was aware of the significance of this as well as the amount of time required for the formation of rock strata by the operation of natural forces. But he did suggest that God must have created all of the species originally and that during the hundreds of thousands of years required for the age of the Earth a number of catastrophes (including Noah's flood) had occurred, with these being the cause of species extinction.

By the 1830s the science of geology was becoming more organized, not least as mining interests increasingly benefited from the knowledge of geologists, enabling them to identify types of strata that could be 'lode-bearing' whatever that lode - coal, precious metals, and as the century progressed oil - happened to be.

Charles Lyell (1797-1875) followed up suggestions on geological formations made earlier by Hutton and his 'The Principles of Geology' (three vols. pub. 1830, - Lyell was significantly assisted by his wife, Mary Horner, in this work) contained the results of extensive field-work and served as an overview of the science of geology at the time. Key aspects of this being the recognition that each stratum was deposited during a certain geological time and that each layer had distinctive fossil markers. He went further and suggested that, although species were fixed, each geological age was a period in which a completely new fauna was created, some showing progressive development of what seemed to be closely related species, with much of this fauna in turn becoming extinct as one period gave way to another. Lyell also suggested that a progression could be seen in the changing forms of life, a key aspect of 'uniformitarianism'; the theory that geological processes have operated in the same way in the past as they do now and that this can account for all geological change. By this time the opposing 'catastrophic' theory, based on a historically quite dramatic (including supernatural) events as recorded in the Bible, was looking increasingly unsatisfactory for the scientifically informed.

Increasingly, the rocks, soils, and other principle geological features of the world were seen as another potentially interesting field for the inquisitive and rationally minded to observe, collect data from, and upon which to offer theoretical explanations as to causes and constitution. Throughout the nineteenth-century a few individuals, with the leisure time and interest, tramped over the foothills of the Alps, the Pyrenees, and other European mountain ranges (then later the Appalachian and the Andes in the Americas), along steep-sided river valleys, descended into cave systems, and visited areas of high volcanic activity such as the Bay of Naples (Mt. Vesuvius).

Prior to the dramatic changes in the understanding of the biological world that would happen from the middle of the nineteenth-century, advances had also been made in showing the age of the Earth. An essential aspect of the wider context of the discoveries in biology that were to come. George Louis Leclerc (Comte de Buffon - 1707-1788) suggested that the Earth had been created out of a collision between a comet and the Sun, with the debris thrown off by the impact providing the material from which the Earth was formed. And that this super-hot material would have been molten at the start and had gradually cooled and solidified to the point where it could support life. With the perspective of the physicist (Buffon had originally trained as one) he applied this theoretical idea to experiments that might enable the determination of the age of the Earth. He heated balls of iron of different dimensions and then recorded the time taken for these to cool. He then extrapolated from these findings to calculate how long it would take have taken a 'ball' of iron the size of the Earth to cool. This was a crude experiment but it did illustrate a simple truth; that if the Earth had began as an extremely hot object it would have taken a very long time to cool down to become hospitable for life. Although Buffon's calculation of 75,000 years falls significantly short of the 4.5 billion years now accepted it did in the eighteenth century offer a strong challenge to the Church's own dogmatic contention. Buffon himself did not wish to make this challenge and felt his findings to be 'mere speculations'.

The brilliant mathematician Jean Fourier (1768-1830) applied mathematics to a number of complex natural processes, including the transfer of heat from a hot to a cooler object. He conducted a series of experiments and was able to formulate a range of equations that described this transfer of heat; he was aware that these could be used to calculate the age of the Earth. Like Buffon he also assumed that it had begun as a very hot object. Fourier calculated the age of the Earth at 100 million years, a significant advance on Buffon's figure. The equation-based method of Fourier's analysis was able to take into account a greater range of relevant factors, including the insulating effect of the formation of a surface crust as the Earth cooled. Buffon had an enduring influence on nineteenth-century geology (and indeed paleontology and biology), not least due to his 41 years as Keeper of the 'Jardin du Roi' in Paris (the botanical gardens) and his monumental 'Histoire Naturelle' (44 vols. published between 1749-1804).

In the work of Buffon, Fourier, and some others, the positivistic intellectual milieu had been provided with ideas that offered a more rational explanatory framework for geological phenomena. And it was from within this wider framework that geologists would be able to appeal for ideas and authority as the eighteenth century progressed.

The naval ships of Britain, and some other countries, had been surveying coasts and landmasses across the world for some time. Famously with the surveying expeditions led by James Cook, and with the voyage of the Beagle (1831-39), that was such a seminal experience for the young Charles Darwin, sent to complete a survey of the coastline of South America (along the coastline of Patagonia and Tierra del Fuego) that had began from 1826-30 by a previous expedition .

But the voyage of HMS Challenger beginning later on (1872) was a significant step in the more comprehensive development of the sciences of geology and oceanography. The Challenger had been launched in 1858 as an 18 gun corvette (it was a sailing ship with auxiliary steam power) and was converted - guns removed - into a state of the art floating scientific expedition ship. It carried biologists, chemists, physicists, and surveyors (in one of the first multidisciplinary expeditions), and a range of scientific instruments. It offered a well-equipped chemistry laboratory for the chemists and physicists, and an equally well-equipped natural history laboratory for the dissecting and preserving work of the biologists. In addition, for all of these scientists, and for the marine surveyors, there was a range of below surface and bottom sampling tools, measuring equipment, trawls nets, along with 144 miles of sounding line with which to plumb, and gain other data to map, the depths. Over a four year voyage the Challenger steered a zigzag course as it circumnavigated the globe, visiting every continent including Antarctica. In March 1875 the Challenger was stationed over an area of the North Pacific Ocean, having let out five miles of sounding line but still not managed to hit the ocean floor. It was over the Mariana Trench and so the deepest part of the world's oceans – at 6.78 miles deep (the equivalent of Mount Everest with over a one mile depth of water above the peak).

The findings of the Challenger expedition, including quite a bit of anthropological information on the many different and sometimes colourful peoples that were met with along the way, were collected in 50 volumes. A landmark publication reflecting a mass of information compiled from data gathered and observations noted during the course of this expedition.

The nineteenth-century geologists (along with paleontologists) had progressively pushed an awareness of the age of the Earth well beyond the Bible-based calculation of 6,000 years and a few had recognized that a significant part on this time saw the Earth devoid of humankind or any life-forms yet to emerge. Cuvier (1812) had suggested tens of thousands of centuries, Marcel de Serres (1838) millions of years, William Buckland (circa. 1818) millions and millions of years, expressing the extent that this was still based on informed guesswork rather than enlightened calculation.

The identification of radioactive isotopes initially by Henri Becquerel in 1896, then in the work of Pierre and Marie Curie, led to the work on aging the Earth undertaken by Ernest Rutherford (1871-1937) who used the phenomenon of radioactive decay to offer a calculation of it age. As rocks age the radioactive elements within them release helium which is trapped in the surrounding rock – consequently if you measure the amount of helium trapped within a measured amount of rock its age can be calculated. Using this relatively crude method Rutherford calculated an estimate of 500 million years for the age of the Earth.

Radioactivity now offered a means for geologists (geophysicists) to determine the age of rocks and, as the techniques were refined, the accuracy of this method improved significantly upon the previously used relative measures (i.e. the position of a stratigraphic layer relative to others), allowing increasingly more accurate quantification of the age of rocks and so of geological features.

Towards the century's end a number of theories had been suggested to account for the geological structure of the Earth. The main one mentioned above assumed that the Earth was cooling (that its molten core cooling very slowly) and consequently that the Earth was shrinking by minute amounts over long periods of time; so cooling and contracting. Eduard Suess (1831-1914 - appointed professor of paleontology at the University of Vienna and later professor of geology) noted the ways in which the coastlines of the continents seemed to 'fit' together. He suggested that the continents of Africa, Australia, and India, were once joined together in a landmass which he named Gondwanaland; but that forces related to the cooling, contracting, of the planet had caused them to separate. This theory suggested periods of relative calm interspersed with dramatic geological activity during which new oceans (driving landmasses apart), deep valleys and mountain ranges were formed. With this important contribution to constituting the foundations for the twentieth century, mainly summed up in his 'The Face of the Earth' published in three volumes between 1883-1909 (in which is the first reference to the 'biosphere'), Suess can be seen as a leading figure in bridging the two centuries.

The discovery of radiation and the implication of the massive amount of energy contained in atoms and released during radioactive decay, suggested that the molten mass at the centre of the Earth could maintain its heat for thousands of years, cooling only very very slowly. Early in the twentieth century (1912) Alfred Wegener was the first to suggest a more adequate 'continental drift' theory (as a mechanism for the movement of landmasses) in his book, published in 1915, 'The Origins of Continents and Oceans'.

A marker of how far geology was progressing was the First International Geological Congress, held in Paris in 1878. The conference was attended by about 300 individuals from 22 countries – mostly European but also the US, Australia, and India. A sense of the stage of the science's development can be seen from the conference agenda – this included the recognition of the need to standardize geological mapping and its nomenclature and also to find agreement on the characteristics of rock systems, including the place of flora and fauna in delineating these.

Biology

In the lead up to the modern period, the take up and development of ideas centered on the age and range of life on Earth continued to be inhibited by the dogmatism of the Church with its insistence on the literal truth of the account of creation outline in the Book of Genesis. Individual scientists socialized to respect the authority of the Church found it difficult to challenge its teachings. An individual somewhat less inhibited was the Swede, Carl Linnaeus (1707-1778) who, even as a Christian, came to express doubts about the Biblical age of the Earth. He accepted the Biblical account of the Flood but suggested that the distance from the oceans to the inland locations, where remains of marine creatures could be found, must have taken more than the biblical 200 days from the deluge setting Norah's Ark adrift to the waters receding and the Ark's landfall. Linnaeus suggested that the whole Earth must once have been covered with water and that this was currently undergoing a slow process of gradually receding. Hence sea-living organisms, inhabiting seas that once covered today's continents died and sunk to the ocean floor to undergo the long process of fossilization, becoming entombment in the layers of mud and other sediment that accumulated over them. During the eighteen century there was some historical evidence, provided by Jesuit Missionaries returning to Europe from the Far East, suggesting that civilizations had existed at a time at least 1000 years older than the date of the Earth's creation as recognized by the Church.

Many of the early scientific naturalists were amateurs pursuing an interest in plants and animals due to their being drawn by simple curiosity to the 'beauty' of the natural world, but with some others seeking knowledge of medicinal qualities, a feature which had long been recognized in plants. It was during the age of exploration linked in the 15th and 16th centuries with reports of overseas adventurer's encounters with the strange and exotic that gave an impetus to more organized study. The mutually favourable conjunction of the developing printing industry, and across Europe of a growing segment of an increasingly better educated public showing an interest in natural history, led to the successful publication of numerous texts, many enhanced with fine illustrations. These containing reports from abroad, as well as some quite ambitious surveys of local natural histories; all in the spirit of curiosity about the natural world that been pioneered much earlier by those such as Aristotle (384-322 BCE),

Theophrastus (371-287 BCE), Lucretius Carus (99-55 BCE) and later on Pliny the Elder (22-78 CE) and Dioscorides (40-80 CE).

Christopher Columbus, when not completely distracted by his obsession with gold, took some interest in the natural world, making notes on exotic and more mundane flora that he found on islands such as Hispaniola. As early at the fifteenth century Gonzalo Fernandez de Oviedo (1478-1557) - initially an inspector of mines - travelled to the East Indies and sent a stream of descriptive accounts of plant and tree species back to Europe. His book on the natural history of the Indies became one of the first of many natural history best sellers. He descriptive accounts included details of at least two specimens - tobacco plants and rubber trees - that would become important during the industrial revolution. A bit later Francisco Hernández (1517-1587) took part in a voyage to South America sponsored by King Philip II Spain for which he was tasked by the King to make a record of the natural history of New Spain (mainly comprised of Mexico). His completed 'record' ran to 38 volumes of text and he also sent back boxes and boxes of seeds, cuttings, and root stocks. Even the sometimes 'piratical' Walter Rayleigh took the artist-naturalist John White on a voyage to North America in 1584. And Ulisse Aldrovandi (1522-1605) organized a team of artists and engravers who would produce about 3,000 wood blocks, each depicting a different 'natural image'. The entomologist, Maria Sybilla Merian (1647-1717) travelled to the Dutch colony of Surinam and in 1679 published her 'Book of Caterpillars', with a focus on the dramatic metamorphosis that is a central aspect of the butterfly life-cycle. This type of more detailed study of a single (or just a few related) genera was to be added too the more wide ranging characteristics of the 'natural histories' complied by earlier naturalists.

These were just a few of the hundreds, possibly thousands, of individuals collecting information on plant and animal life. But increasingly the growing interest in natural history was taking institutional form in many European cities. As early as the first half of the sixteenth century some universities (notably Padua in 1533, and Bologna in 1534) had established a chair of medicinal studies, with the primary subject being botany. By the century's end many universities had similar chairs of medicine and many more had included the subject of botany in their curricula. Most of the university cities had also established their own botanical gardens to which at least some sections of the general population had access.

Up to the eighteenth century, naturalists were more interested in plant and animal anatomy, bodily function, breeding habits, lifecycles, and habitat, as well as any medicinal properties of plants. Increasingly into the nineteenth century, for some the interest was in the commercial potential of species.

Given the relentless accumulation of data on flora and fauna some pre-eighteenth century naturalists saw that a system of categorization was required if the information was to be better managed. During the sixteenth and seventeenth centuries, collections of plants had been organized in herbariums - large leafed 'books' within which plant specimens were pressed and so preserved - that, in terms of detail and anatomical similarity, were an advance on the relatively crude categories of earlier Greek, Roman, and Arab, naturalists.

Probably the most systematic classification prior to the eighteenth century was that was undertaken by Casper Bauhin, as set out in his 'Index of a Botanical Theatre' (1623). The text contained descriptions of over 6,000 species. In the late eighteenth century, the prolific writer on natural history, John Ray (1627-1795), although praising Bauhin and suggesting a clear utility value in classification, did warn about the synthetic nature of over-strict systems, and their potential to misrepresent connectedness. However, such was his belief in the utility value of classification that he did himself suggest a system based on morphological characteristics that could be applied to both plants and animals.

In addition to his work on geology noted above, Carl Linnaeus also made a number of significant contributions to the development of natural history, not just in terms of observations and suggestions related to fossils and geological formations. His greatest contribution was primarily in his ambitious attempt to categorize all of the minerals, fauna, and flora, then known. The advance introduced by Linnaeus was not only in devising a system that allowed for the categorization of all of the then known species but a system that would allow species found in the future to be assigned an appropriate classificatory category. His text 'System of Nature' (1735) set out his system of classification and was a landmark text in establishing the science of biology.

For the world of plants he had the insight to see, following a suggestion by Camerarius (1665-1721), that the sexual organs of plants were contained in the flower heads – the number of stamens and pistils - and his 24 broad divisions (classes) were a useful way by which to group plants with shared characteristics. His use of Latin double-names for any species, for example 'Linnaea borealis' (an evergreen shrub) would allow any plant species then known or yet to be discovered to have an individual name within this system. Linnaeus's system was modified to allow it to take into account differences in the floral phenomena that it sought to categorize but it was one with the potential for thorough-going systemization, so providing a valuable tool for the growing community of naturalists. Linnaeus himself did undertake some limited fieldwork but the vast bulk of his data came from his sending out teams of naturalists to gather information. The main practical focus of his life's work was centered on the magnificent and systematic collection of plants for the botanical gardens in Uppsala. As early as 1788, a Linnaean Society had been founded in London; the oldest natural history society still in existence.

The systematic arrangement of plant and animal life appeals to a human propensity to favour systematic order, if this adequately reflects categorization based on species (or whatever biological level) markers it can allow an improved understanding within a wider context of that which is being categorized.

Advances in bio-chemistry would later identify shortcomings in the Linnaean system but it did represent a system of classification that improved considerably in terms of adequacy on earlier attempts. More generally, systemization based on both morphological, and later on genetic, characteristics allows naturalists to have a sharable framework that identifies the possible, probable, and actual relationships between species.

One man who took issue with the determination of most naturalists to separate species, to classify and categorize with priority given to identifying differences, was Alexander von Humboldt (1769-1859). In 1799 von Humboldt travelled to South America and it is hard to imagine that any individual could have been more driven by an intense curiosity about the natural world. During his extended journey on the sub-continent he undertook detailed mapping and measurement of a range of natural features, even noting altitudes, air pressures, and weather patterns. He collected masses of plant and animal specimens and made detailed notes on many more. Prior to making his journey Humboldt had undertaken numerous excursions, with his measuring equipment and notebooks, within Europe. He was also a keen student of all natural history, keeping up-to-date with the geology, biology, and meteorology, of the time. His knowledge, and his field-work in Europe and South America, along with his keen intellect, enabled Humboldt to see the natural world in a novel way - in terms of connections rather than differences, and overall to view nature as an interdependent unity of life, expressed in his concept of *Naturgemälde*. Humboldt understood the relevance of the concept of Gaia long before James Lovelock. He emphasized the relevance of environmental conditions (including altitudes), so implicitly suggesting species adapting to different eco-systems. His three foot by two foot pictorial representation of the *Naturgemälde* was structured in 'zones' arranged according to such factors as altitude, temperature, and atmospheric pressure. This chart identified the flora and fauna occupying each zone; offering a means of comprehending similar ecosystems on separate continents and so further emphasizing the underlying unity in nature on a global scale.

.Erasmus Darwin (1731-1802) contributed to the species debate by identifying species characteristics as the outcome of generations of adaptation to different environments. In his book 'Zoonomia' he endeavoured to trace the changes in living forms from some original primitive organism ('filament').

The intellectual environment for naturalists of the mid-nineteenth century was invigorated with suggestive ideas from geology, botany, and zoology, ideas that would come together in Charles Darwin's theory of evolution. Credit here also needs also to be given to Alfred Russell Wallace who identified (initially realized during a bout of fever) the same biological mechanism underlying natural selection as did Darwin but who did not have the mass of evidence that Darwin had assiduously accumulated to support it.

By the time that Darwin (then aged 21/22) embarked on his life-changing round the world voyage on the Beagle (1831-36) it was generally accepted by natural scientists that the Earth was very old and that many species of organism had lived at one time but that many had died out whilst many others had survived, but he had also been exposed to the ideas of Thomas Malthus on human populations. Malthus had written 'Essay on the Principle of Population' (first pub. 1798) in which he framed life as a struggle for existence, a competition for limited resources with a strong possibility of individuals falling victim to disease or even being killed in wars. Darwin also was an admirer of von Humboldt, suggesting that without his stimulating ideas he would not have embarked on his formative voyage on the Beagle, nor would he have written the 'Origin of Species'.

It was the ideas, of Malthus and Humboldt, as well as the early evolutionary ideas current at the time, that Darwin brought to bear on his consideration of the varieties of life he was able to observe during the course of the voyage, especially time spent on the Galapagos Islands. Darwin himself wrote of his journey: 'The voyage of the Beagle, had been by far the most important event of my life, and has determined my whole career'. But it was also a career that benefited from the fact that he had inherited private wealth, and had married into even more, thus allowing him the time and the means to afford a comfortable home in a quite rural location for him to pursue his interests. Darwin's most significant contribution to the theory of evolution is in outlining a mechanism by which species can change, and more generally how biological development could occur. His central idea was that in any population of a species individuals can have slightly different characteristics; a few might have longer than average legs, a few others sharper than average beaks, colouring that made them less obvious to predators, etc. A population would live in a particular environment and those individuals who had the good fortune to possess slightly different characteristics that were better able to take advantage (were adapted to) of available resources would thrive and so would on average produce more offspring. They would therefore have a selective advantage over individuals who do not possess the advantageous characteristics. Over time, assuming the environment remains the same in terms of available resources and risks, the proportion of the population with any favoured characteristics would increase and the proportion of those without would decrease. Over many generations the advantageous characteristics would become fixed and possibly 'improve' further and might, (especially if the original population was geographically separated from other groups) accumulate to a point when a new species could be identified; and interbreeding between members of the original and the 'new' species could no longer give rise to fertile progeny. This, very simply put, is the kernel of Darwin's (and indeed Wallace's) theory of evolution of species by the process of natural selection.

For over nearly 20 years (from 1842), following his initial insight into the possible cause of species change taking place during his trip on the Beagle, Darwin worked quietly at his comfortable Victorian home set in the pleasant countryside of North Kent (on the outskirts of the small village of Downe, now within Greater London). Through numerous experiments, the study of scientific literature, and reflection on these as well as recourse to the copious notes made during and following the Beagle voyage, he amassed an impressive evidence-based 'argument' to support his theory. An argument that would be set out in his book 'The Origin of Species – by means of Natural Selection' first published in 1859.

Towards the end of this book (p452 of the 1968 Penguin edition) he wrote:

'I have now recapitulated the chief facts and considerations which have thoroughly convinced me that species have changed, and are still slowly changing by the preservation and accumulation of successive slight favourable variations'

Perhaps his most challenging suggestion, is that this would by implication include 'man', was made on page 455 '.....Therefore I should infer from analogy that probably all the organic beings which have ever lived on this earth have descended from some one primordial form, into which life was first breathed'

Darwin was not the first to suggest the idea of evolution, indeed versions could be traced back to the Greeks (see Lucretius 'On the Nature of Things'), and in the seventeenth century the polymath Richard Hooke (1635-1703) suggested that fossils were the remains of animals that had died a very long time before and that there might even have been whole species that had died out.

Another type of evolutionary theory, preceding that of Darwin/Wallace, was suggested by Jean-Baptiste Lamarck (who in 1802 coined the term 'biology' - as the study (ology) of life (bio)). Lamarck's theory of species change was based on ever-increasing complexity in terms of body-plan. His ideas were derived partly from alchemical influences allowing for the continuous spontaneous generation of lower forms of life. He identified the dynamic driving the complexification ('transmutation') as a process of adaptation to environmental conditions. Not in relation to Darwinian natural selection, rather that the body plan of individuals can change during their lives and that they then pass this on to their progeny - the most obvious example being the long neck of giraffes being due to some 'giraffe-like' creatures once finding themselves in an environment with favoured food being located high up is trees, causing them to reach ever higher as they sought the desired leaves; hence extending the neck, a feature then passed on to their descendants. An evolutionary explanation that in the twentieth century was suited to the ideological requirements of Joseph Stalin, and was accorded spurious scientific credibility by his Director of Biology, Trofim Lysenko.

There was a book anonymously published in 1844 as 'Vestiges of the Natural History of Creation'; the author was quite soon identified as the journalist Robert Chambers. The book set out an original theory of evolution and sales of 20,000 reflected a growing interest in the subject; suggesting that there was a popular 'educated interest' in and preparedness to accept the more fully-formed theory later suggested by Darwin.

Darwin had published papers on geology and in 1839 he had already published his 'Journal of Researches' a book that set out his experiences on the Beagle voyage (later republished as 'The Voyage of the Beagle'), he had been elected a Fellow of the Geological Society in 1837 and a Fellow of the Zoological Society of London and of the Royal Society in 1839. Even given a prevailing 'scientific mood' that was generally favourable to evolutionary ideas and his own authority in natural science, Darwin – who seems to have been a religious person with a wife who certainly was – was reluctant to publish. It took a letter from Alfred Russell Wallace (currently then collecting specimens on the Island of Ternate in the Moluccas for European collectors) to focus his attention on doing so.

Wallace had travelled extensively; studying the varieties of life he had encountered, and he was aware of the current scientific debate on evolution, including Darwin's contribution to this. The two men had been engaged in correspondence since a chance meeting at a scientific event held in London in 1854, but their ongoing contact seems to have been stimulated even more by Darwin's having read a paper written by Wallace on species of butterfly that he had found in the lower reaches of the Amazon River system. There is evidence that he, as had Darwin, had also read Malthus's book on populations. Darwin was generally encouraging to Wallace and the pair engaged in fairly regular correspondence. At that point Wallace had not identified the way it which species change came about (Darwin's bio-mechanism of 'natural selection') and it was in Feb. 1858 that he came to the idea of 'suitability' or 'fitness' (a concept applied later on) for survival in an environment.

Wallace then wrote a paper 'On the Tendency of Varieties to

Depart Indefinitely from the Original Type' in which he outlined and developed his ideas. When Darwin received this paper he was apparently quite shocked to see how close the ideas set out were to his own theory. To his credit Darwin did pass on Wallace's paper to Lyell who then (along with other friends of Darwin such as Hooker) appears to have taken control of the situation, the outcome being that a joint Darwin/Wallace paper was presented to a meeting of the Linnaean Society of London in July 1858. Wallace had not been consulted on this action but he appears to have been happy with the presentation and was prepared to concede the priority of the theory of natural selection to Darwin; he himself was to use the term 'Darwinism' as shorthand for the theory.

The publication in 1859 of Darwin's book and its implications for Church teachings caused a strong critical reaction from those whose beliefs were felt to be threatened. An interest in the theory, and perhaps more so in the 'raging' debate that it provoked, even reached into the popular press of the day. Darwin had provided an evidence-based explanation for species change and finally established the understanding of biological life as a continuous process of change; as well as placing humankind within the animal world and so subject to the same evolutionary processes. He had not identified the basic underlying cause of the biological differences upon which natural selection could operate to stimulate evolutionary development, and this was to come later when the work of Gregor Mendel (genetics) came to the attention of biologists.

A Moravian monk Mendel had become a priest in 1843 and, whilst progressing studies for a teaching diploma at the University of Vienna undertaken in his 20s, he was judged as being not all that bright, failing the oral part of his teaching examination. It was later suggested that this failure was due more to nerves than any lack of intelligence, a view which his subsequent progress would support. He was sent back to the monastery, labeled a failure at the age of 31 (1853). The Augustinian monastery offered an environment with a strong tradition of plant growing (market gardening) and also a library suitable for members of a religious order with significant teaching responsibilities. On his return to the monastery, encouraged by the scientifically minded Abbot C.F. Napp, he began his study of the natural world, progressing a well-organized (dogged and relentless) regime of study focused on an understanding of heredity, using the common pea plant as the means of observing this.

Mendel identified seven characteristics of the pea plant, including colour and shape, and suggested that the expression of each of these in any plant involved two 'particles', one gained from each parent. And that if any pair of particles were different one would be dominant – and so expressed, the other recessive - and so not expressed. His training in mathematics had given him knowledge of statistical methods sufficient to analyze quite complex sets of results. His research over a seven year period suggested that inherited characteristics were not a 'blend' of each parent but rather they came from one or the other. The fact that he had identified the biological (information) transmission mechanism underlying the operation of Darwinian natural selection did not initially make any impact on mainstream biology. The findings of this research, set out in two papers, were presented, in 1865, to the Natural History Society in Brünn, and they were also published in a fairly local circulation natural history journal. But the significance of his findings seems initially not to have been understood.

It is interesting that this 'failed' teaching student, judged to have a poor intellect, was promoted to the position of Abbot on Abbot Napp's death in 1867. Perhaps a flair for administration, including planning and recordkeeping (as well as some training in statistics) that led to his promotion, were the same attributes suited to his experimental programme. But Mendel also had the insight to see the value of understanding heredity and the ability to interpret his results in relation to how it might operate.

Due at least partly to increasing responsibility in relation to monastic life, Mendel effectively ended his active interest in the study of heredity. It was to take the work of Hugo de Viris (Dutch botanist 1848-1935) in Holland and Walter Bateson (1861-1926) in England before this biological mechanism was again identified and the name of 'genetics' given (by Bateson) to the study of the biological mechanism of hereditary. It was de Viris who in 1899 was preparing his own findings for publication and, whilst undertaking a literary review, he came across Mendel's two papers and was immediately aware that Mendel had been the first discoverer of what became known as gene theory. At the same time (around 1900) Erich Tschermak von Seysenegg in Austria and Karl Correns in Germany had also made this discovery of how hereditary operated. Mendel had died in 1884 over a decade before he gained the credit deserved for the years of careful experimental work and the principle discovery this made possible.

It was whilst using a microscope to examine a small piece of cork that Robert Hooke had identified discrete, seemingly self-contained, entities, and in 1664 he named these 'cells'. Later studies showed that the shape of cells differed depending on their function; square for liver cells, long cells for muscles, even longer cells for some nerves, etc. Hooke only had access to compound lens microscopes but from 1830 biologists had access to instruments using achromatic lenses and, from 1878, to the higher resolution obtainable by the achromatic compound microscope invented by Ernst Abbe.

The ideas of cellular reproduction and of aggregations (colonies) of cells were put forward by Matthias Schleiden and Theodor Schwann in the late 1830s early 1840s. Schwann had suggested in 1839 that all living entities are composed of cells, establishing similar basic 'bio-units' for plant and animal life. In 1833 Robert Brown was able to describe the 'nucleus' as a primary structure within cells. A particular type of nerve cell (Purkinje cells) was identified by Jan Purkinje in 1837. Further advance in the understanding of living processes, including reproduction, was made in 1875 with the identification by Walter Flemming of his finding, within the nucleus of cells, tiny strings of material that would later be termed chromosomes.

Early in the new century biologists were aware that the 'genes (units of heredity) were to be found in the chromosomes and that these were composed of nucleic acids. These compounds had been isolated by Friedrich Miescher in 1869, but at that time their central role in heredity was not recognized. To complete the picture of the biological carrier for the material of inheritance, early in the 1900 century the chromosomes would be identified as the carriers of genes for species whose reproduction was sexually generated; each parent contributing one set of chromosomes (the gamete – sex cells i.e. the egg and the sperm).

Late in the nineteenth century William Sutton offered a theory of heredity based on genes as located on paired chromosomes. By 1882 Walter Flemming was using a staining technique to distinguish the chromosomes within the nucleus of cells and was able to observe and describe the way in which they divide during cell division (mitosis). The central role of the nucleus in heredity was suggested by three

German scientists in the mid 1880s (confirmed by 1902). And in 1890/1 Hermann Henking, when studying the process of sperm formation, noticed that one form of chromosome did not come as one of a pair, he named this the X chromosome (the male determinant).

Improving optical microscopy, along with staining techniques developed by Camillo Gogli, led to productive work on identifying other structures (organelles) within the cell. The resulting increase in the understanding can be illustrated by the work of Albrect Kossel who, towards the latter part of the nineteenth century, was able to identify discrete types of organelles composed of large and of small molecules; amongst the former would be DNA nucleotides. By the end of the century knowledge of the cell included: the identification (not the understanding of function) of organelles within cells, including ribosomes, mitochondrion, chromosomes, the nucleus, endoplasmic reticulum, and the Golgi apparatus. The identification of the cell's role as the building block of organisms, and of its nucleus in heredity, generated a keen interest in the life sciences; an interest that would drive intensive and productive research throughout the twentieth century.

The year 1900 had seen the` rediscovery of the Mendel's work with 'genetics' and this, the bio-transmission of information system, would be a central focus for biology throughout the 20th and early 21st centuries.

Sociology

Since early civil life commentators – not least as ever the Greeks! – have made observations on the social life of their fellow humans. From about the early eighteenth century the empirical and technological success in advancing a certain way of understanding the 'natural' world was becoming known. This way, or method, of understanding included within the wide range of human intellectual activity called 'science' had began to influence a body of intellectuals whose area of interest was human behaviour and human society itself. The wide range of activities subsumed under the concept of science were brought together owing to certain similarities in method and increasingly the formation by participants of a collective identity fostered by co-working, institutional recognition, and their own sense of intellectually travelling in the same broad direction. The sciences as a general method were becoming a significant means of humankinds' generation and accumulation of 'information', as knowledge. It was from this method of knowledge accumulation – theorizing, experiment, observation, and increasingly quantification - that the modern social sciences such as sociology, psychology, and anthropology, developed. Each in turn adding their own identifiable contributions to an understanding of the human condition; to the contribution already made by the then more established social sciences of economics and history.

In tracing the foundational origins of the social sciences (with a determinate bias towards 'western' history) we invariably begin with the Greeks. Principally Plato and Aristotle, but a number of others (including Herodotus, Thucydides and Polybius) also contributed to an intellectual milieu, enhanced by sometimes challenging debate, which mostly endeavoured to eschew religious explanations for social and political conditions and instead drew more reasonable conclusions following the application of more rational thought processes.

Plato's book, 'The Republic', had a significant role in setting the terms by which political and social arrangements would be discussed. In it he outlined a division of labour (divisions made in the name of economic efficiency) based on 'natural' differences, and he set out the nature and conditions required for a just society. A broad conception of justice being for Plato a priority for any society, with law-makers being tasked to maintain this. His analysis included the assumption that human-beings are drawn into social relations due to a natural need to come together for mutual satisfaction. His aim being to design the ideal political and social arrangements that would ensure a very conservative version of justice, and so for him contribute to social cohesion.

Aristotle contributed a further development of analytical tools and tended towards the practical and material; 'empirical', as compared to Plato's more 'idealistic' tendencies. Aristotle's book 'Politics' includes a consideration of various political constitutions based on the then quite novel 'comparative method'. The basis of society being for Aristotle 'associations'; at base the association of female and male (primarily for the procreation of children) and the wider association between the rulers and the ruled; to the mutual advantage of both in providing the framework for well-ordered social stability. These primary associations are 'natural' forms of social relationships. Aristotle's social science-related considerations ranged across laws, customs, political constitutions, and social institutions, with the latter including an appropriate system of education.

The value of Aristotle's designation of the 'natural' is somewhat undermined by his narrow view of male and female abilities, by his acceptance of political inequality ('democratic elitism'), and the assumption of slavery, as all being 'natural' conditions.

In relation to the social sciences, it was the intellectual legitimacy of discussing social and political arrangements, and doing so using a methodology based on more rational analysis, that was a key aspect of Plato and Aristotle's enduring legacy.

About 700 years later St Augustine (354-430 CE) followed Plato in terms of admiring his approach to reasoning - if he mostly differed in terms of outcomes. With Plato's own outline of an 'ideal society' (the Republic) being a key influence on Augustine. It might be more useful to consider Augustine in relation to early psychology given the intensity of his self-analysis (especially in his 'Confessions') with its focus on guilt, memory, language, intentionality, and on consciousness experienced in time. But he also made a contribution to social science more broadly in his consideration of social relationships. A key aspect of this being contained in a number of chapters within the nineteenth book of the 'City of God'. Here Augustine set out a system based on four domains (or grades) - the domus, the civitas, the orbis, the mundus - encompassing social relationships that are essential for human happiness; if the final domain was more spiritual than social. The basic domain (the domas) is based on the household, the next (the civitus) on the city and the state, then the whole world (the orbis) and the range of human societies within it, finally, but for Augustine most importantly, there is the overarching Universe (the mundus) encompassing the heavenly bodies (including the Earth) and also God, the Angels, and the souls of those who have died. It is in the last (the mundus) that the City of God is to be found. The earthly city within which humans life is mostly pervaded with sin but within it the Christian Church stands out as a beacon of hope. His commitment to the Christian Church (the institutional means of God's earthy mediation with the world) as the ultimate source of truth biased Augustine towards prioritizing the metaphysical over the rational. But his work did broaden the acceptable field of academic study beyond the theological to include more mundane aspects of the human condition and its network of social and political relationships.

In the early medieval Islamic world, Arabic scholarship included elements of social science within its wider scientific endeavours. More broadly, Islamic social science primarily encompassed considerations of economic and political arrangements. Vibrant and productive Arabic scholarship during the medieval period looked set to continue to lead in the development of the social as well as the natural sciences, but the general economic and political decline of Islamic civilization inhibited further innovation. If the mainstream clerical interpretation of Islam was probably the primary reason for the marked decline of progressive Arabic scholarship. Islam was more than a religion in that it also determined political arrangements and the reaction of noted Islam clerics, not least the theologian Abu Hamid al-Ghazali (died 1111 CE), was to denigrate the value of rationalism. Al-Ghazali's, book 'The Incoherence of the Philosophers', was a thoroughgoing reaction against reason, claiming it to be a cause of the decline in religious piety. More broadly, for Islamic (Arabic) governance, the questioning, analytical, approach of much 'scientific' scholarship mitigated the tight control felt to be necessary for societies under threat from external enemies. This narrow theological outlook also inhibited natural scientific advance in that, the Islamic world was only rarely able to translate scientific discoveries into practical forms of technology; in itself another, if perhaps relatively minor factor in the decline of Arabic civilization.

The impact of the clerical suppression of Islamic science was to some extent limited, especially in the social sciences; with more effective suppression at the civil centers of the faith and weaker at the peripheral. The North African born Muslim Ibn Khaldun (1332-1406) stands out. In his work 'Muqaddimah', he comments on social change and conflict (specifically that between town and desert dwellers) and introduces the notion of generational differences in the context of social change. He also considered social cohesion and the features of an underlying bond (asabiyyah) which holds communities together.

In northern Europe during the mediaeval period, western intellectual debate was focused on clerics (the Church), the so named mediaeval schoolmen. The most notable of these (scholastics) being Thomas Aquinas (1227- 74) whose book 'Summa Theologica', if mostly an extended set of theological considerations, much of which attempting to reconcile some of Aristotle's views with a relatively 'liberal' interpretation of the teachings of the Christian Church, also included ideas about man and society.

The next stage of intellectual development in relation to man (sic) and society would include a determined separation of the theological and the philosophical. The latter in the broad sense of encompassing natural and social philosophies; what would later be termed the natural and the social sciences.

Conventionally, and with some justification, Francis Bacon (1561-1626) is taken to be a key prophet of modern science. His collected works offer a wide-ranging assessment of the accumulated 'western' human knowledge of his time, and also include a set of prescient interpretations of how this process would develop. He (especially in his 'The Advancement of Learning' 1605) set out his ideas of how best to unlock the mysteries (unknowns) of the natural world. His 'key' for this being a particular methodological approach based on obtaining data by observation and experiment and using inductive logic to progress from accumulated facts to general laws. A progression of rational enquiry that would need to avoid various, more irrational, tendencies that human thinking is prone too.

These tendencies are embodied in the 'Idols' of tribe, cave, market-place, and theatre. Each of which has its own form of irrationalism - of natural human weaknesses shared with all men (tribe), of individual character and more generally of subjectivity (cave), of those due to social influences which include the problematic aspects of language (market-place), and philosophical issues such as an unreflective acceptance of ideas based on the inherited assumptions of past philosophers and the inappropriate intermixing of theology and natural philosophy (the theatre). Basically, Bacon endeavoured to outline a systematic, thoroughly rational, methodology with which to progress the accumulation of sound theoretical and practical knowledge. If often assumed to be an empiricist, we need to accept that he also offered a metaphysical basis for the source of all knowledge being in God as well as the human rational soul.

Bacon identified the main branches of knowledge but emphasized the connectedness of these as if the spreading branches of a tree. His optimistic and fundamentally positive, if critical, interpretation of humankind's intellectual achievements, and more so the potential for this to advance, ran counter to some more pessimistic views being expressed at the time. But it was in tune with many of those other thinkers who came to the fore during the period of Renaissance for which it was an early marker of the changing 'western' intellectual outlook. A time when the conception of man was reconceived as being intellectually and artistically admirable, progressive and entitled to, among other freedoms, a measure of religious agency; to make their own interpretation of biblical theology rather than being conceived as inevitably mired in sinfulness.

The more humanistic outlook of the Renaissance was expressed in the works of thinkers such a Bacon, Machiavelli, and Erasmus and for the later Enlightenment in the works of Hobbs, Descartes, and Spinoza. Writers who began to legitimize the rational consideration of aspects of human life in ways that can be identified as the subject matter for the modern social sciences.

Amongst the ground conditions necessary for European pre-industrial development of the social sciences were: the availability and ever decreasing cost of printing and publishing; the growth of an educated leisure class becoming increasingly connected (by printed works as well as in person); the reform of the university curriculum to better reflect intellectual change; the stimulus of expanding global trade; and the inspirational influence of the French and American revolutions as events that were expressions of a wider intellectual realignment of ideas about the relationship between man and governance (and society). The substance of this realignment being epitomized by writers such as Tom Paine, Voltaire (1694-1778), Charles-Louis Montesquieu (1689-1755), Jean-Jacques Rousseau (1712-1778) and John Locke (1632-1704), as well as the philosophers David Hume and Immanuel Kant.

Eriksen and Nielsen (sec. ed. 2013 pp17/18) Highlight the role of Immanuel Kant (1724-1804), their...'.....greatest philosopher of the time', in providing a descriptive analysis of the scope and limitations for human knowledge and how 'judgments' are the active step that transforms experience into knowledge; so experiential knowledge being relative rather than absolute. They suggest that Kant overcame the subjective/objective dichotomy by making the former the basis of a thinking mind and the latter the basis of universal mental faculties. That Kant's reasoned insights clarified the epistemological grounds for the social sciences to progress.

Benjamin Franklin and Thomas Jefferson also visited Europe during this period and were exposed to and actively engaged within its intellectual milieu; the humanistic influence of which would be carried back to the US and feed directly into the US independence movement and influence the form of its first written constitution. For social science more directly, it was writers such as Adam Ferguson

(1723-1816), James Burnett (1714-1799), John Miller (1735-1801) and William Robertson (1721-1793) who took a more 'scientific' (more systematic and mostly reductionist) approach to the historic and comparative study of societies.

Giovanni Battista Vico (1668-1744) with his 1725 book 'The New Science' ('Scienza nouva') being perhaps the first clear ('modern') exposition of a distinct science of society rooted in 'fact's, and seeking the principles of human nature by careful study of the origins of the language, customs, activities, and the institutions, that can be observed in any society. Vico was of the view that as societies were created by men therefore it was possible, given the correct method, for men to understand the ways in which they worked, he suggested that: '....*in the night of this darkness enveloping the earliest antiquity, so remote from ourselves, there shines the eternal and never failing light of truth beyond all questions: that the world of civil society has certainly been made by men, and its principles are therefore to be found within the modifications of our own mind.*'

During the late 18th and early 19th centuries the industrial revolution led to the growth of cities, reflecting the significant movement and intermixing of peoples, and the creation of increasingly obvious class divisions and interest groups. The rapid growth and presence of varied groups within cities involved in the early period of industrialization brought the social consequences of these changes into stark focus. Governments of the time wished to raise tax revenue, to count and control populations, and also they began to recognize the need for a more educated population to serve the needs of expanding industry and growth in the size of civil administration. The increasing need for nation-states to understand demographic aspects of populations, to identify the economic interests of ruling elite groups, and more generally to gain some control over the impact of the rapidly increasing rate of social change, would provide additional stimuli for the social sciences, and would progressively generate a significant dynamic influencing the pace and the direction of the development of these during the 19th and 20th centuries.

The social location of the individual was changing as traditional social roles, with long-standing obligations and normative expectations, were giving way to more contractual (instrumental) relationships within a wider society increasingly structured according to income (and fixed wealth). These developments operated as both drivers of study and also factors that helped to make society more interesting to would be social scientists. In addition, we have a background context of humanistic Enlightenment-inspired ideas of progress and more generally the rising status of enquiry and learning. The growth in literacy, along with cheaper printing costs, providing the means of promoting debate on social and political issues; accessible in newspapers, books, and pamphlets.

Another significant driver for developing the social sciences was the social consequences of industrial work and of city life. Not least the poverty caused by low pay, uncertain work, and high density housing. In the cities and larger towns, poverty was obvious and unattractive. The poverty of cities was loud, upfront, and obvious – the very smell of the poor mingled easily with the smells of industry as evidence of the crowded, fetid, conditions in which people worked and lived. Even the growing middle-classes could not avoid, and so more easily ignore, the physical effects for some of life in industrializing cities.

Early 'social scientists' of the industrial period included the natural scientist Joseph Priestley who wrote on government and in 'Some Considerations on the State of the poor in London' 1782, on social conditions, as did Adam Ferguson in his book 'History of Civil Society' 1767. Two books that contain much in the way of early modern sociological discussion.

But perhaps the most contained expression of the intellectual 'mood/tenor' of the enlightenment period was the 35 volume literary edifice termed the Encyclopedia (Encyclopédistes). This text, edited by Denis Diderot and Jean le Rond d'Alambert, had 150 contributors from a range of political, philosophical, as well as natural and social scientific backgrounds; the aim being to collect together an extensive representation of human knowledge.

The Enlightenment period, covering most of the 17th and 18th centuries, had consolidated and advanced the intellectual progress made during the Renaissance, not least in freeing the emerging sciences from the distorting and constraining influence of theology and of medieval interpretations of some ancient Greek philosophers. As the eighteenth merged into the nineteenth the spread of printing and both formal and informal gatherings of amateur and professional academics, in all cities and most large towns, were facilitating the diffusion of new ideas to a much wider cohort of people. Constituting a growing and participatory intellectual audience, mostly male but with a number of notable female intellectuals who had been able to overcome the socially innate patriarchy, and the institutional barriers redolent of European civil society of the time. Prominent amongst these women were Germaine (Madame) de Staël, Harriet Martineau, and Mary Wollstonecraft who each made a significant contribution to the development of the social sciences.

Wollstonecraft (1759-1797) expressed her outrage at the social and political structures bearing down on women, leading her to offer a lucid, if polemical, analysis of key aspects of British society. Not least on governance, the education system, and the competing tensions faced by women in relation to their complex feelings towards motherhood and their wish for personal independence.

The conventional tracing of the post enlightenment development of the study of humankind and the forms taken by different societies, would highlight the role of Claude Henri Rouvroy Comte de Saint-Simon (1760-1825). Here was an original if unsystematic thinker, appalled by the upheaval of the French revolutionary period and strongly influenced by the advances in scientific outlook made during the Enlightenment. Saint-Simon progressively developed ideas on how advances made in science and industry (as these relate to production) could be brought to bear to facilitate how best civil society can be organized. He was advocating some unification of Christian ethics - as expressed by the teachings of Jesus, especially in the 'Sermon on the Mount' - and science, embodied in the concept of 'socialism'.

Just prior to his most productive period Saint-Simon had met Germaime de Staël who in her book 'On Literature Considered in Relation to Social Institutions' (*De la littérature dans ses rapports avec les institutions sociales'* 1799) had considered the possibility of outlining a science of society. It does seem that Saint-Simon's own thinking was influenced during what became a close (possibly intimate) friendship with de Staël. Some of Saint-Simon's socialist political ideas were taken up by later thinkers such as Owen, Fourier, Proudhon, Marx, and Engels, but here I want to focus more on his contribution to the developing social sciences.

For Saint-Simon, the central task was to seek an understanding of how society come to be organized (or for him, in the case of revolutionary France, disorganized) by the application of a positivist approach to the study of civil history. The aim being to gain information that could contribute to a synthesis of the research undertaken by the various branches of knowledge, out of which would emerge the 'laws of social organization'. An understanding of these 'laws' would provide the theoretical means to design the best possible (most rational) way in which to organize society for the well-being of all; well-being as assessed by both material and ethical conditions. It is easy to see why Saint-Simon was accused of utopianism given his confidence in the possibility that the combined expertise of science and industry - aided by knowledge of the 'laws' of social organization - could offer the informed and enlightened leadership required to construct a productive and cohesive society. Saint-Simon went so far as to call not only for 'scientific government' (composed of scientists and others of the industrial class - such as businessmen, bankers, managers, and workers) but also for science to replace organized religion; that would be for him a 'Religion of Newton!' Beyond this form of government he also advocated an association of European states as a mean of reducing the likelihood of wars between them.

When, in 1817, Auguste Comte (1798-1857) became Saint-Simon's secretarial assistant they soon formed a collaborative relationship as they developed initially shared ideas on society, ethics, and how an impoverished working class might advance its economic and political interests. Saint-Simon's work tended towards the unsystematic and his ideas were at times vague and it would be Comte, following an acrimonious split from Saint-Simon, who would attempt to provide a more systematic and clear exposition of a positivist approach to the study of man and society. Comte was a reclusive but productive (in terms of ideas) philosopher and social thinker, whose central aims were to outline a systematic overview of humankind's intellectual development and to outline the ways in which a positivist approach, as pioneered in the natural sciences, can also be usefully applied to the study of humankind. That 'social scientists' using a positivist approach involving: observation, experiment, comparison, and theorizing from the empirical information this approach made available, would enable them to understand and describe the fundamental nature of human society. An understanding that would identify 'social laws'; laws of social statics and social dynamics. His most famous law involved three stages in the historical development of human knowledge; these being: Theological, Metaphysical, and Positivist. The first two being the simple (theological) and the more sophisticated (metaphysical) forms of understanding, each characterized by supernatural foundations.

Whilst, for Comte, the positivist stage would be one characterized by the application a scientific approach to the world of human experience, with subject-specific positivist methods being appropriate for each science. Most obviously expressed in the accumulating knowledge gained by all of the sciences especially: mathematics, biology, geology, chemistry, astronomy, physics, history, physiology, medicine, and of course sociology, anthropology, and psychology; each of which would became more autonomous scientific disciples in the second half of the nineteenth century.

Comte's main published works were the 6 volume 'Course in Positive Philosophy', completed over 12 years between 1830-1842, and the 4 volume 'System of Positive Polity, or Treatise on Sociology, Instituting of the Religion of Humanity', completed between 1851-1854. He sought the conceptual identification of key aspects of society, the two most prominent being 'social statics' and 'social dynamics'. These two together, along with a more general positivist methodology drawing data as 'facts' derived directly from experience, were to have had an enduring influence on the way in which social science developed during the nineteenth century. In terms of the heuristic description of society, social statics sought to understand how features such as religion, language, family, the division of labour, and other social institutions, operate to maintain social order (a synchronic perspective). Whereas social dynamics sought to understand how society has become what it is, the essential processes of change (a diachronic perspective). Another key aspect of social dynamics was the idea that human intelligence was evolving in a progressive way, that people were (on average) becoming more intelligent. Leading towards a time when altruism would displace the common outlook of selfish egoism and so enable society to operate more harmoniously - which links back to his three stages of the historical development of knowledge. He also used the concept of social class as a fairly neutral way of identifying social difference; an early attempt to identify group interests that would be taken up and developed (in more antagonistic frameworks) by later social thinkers such as Owen, Fourier, Marx, and to some extent Weber.

Positivism was made more easily available to the English-speaking world by Harriet Martineau (1802-1876), primarily with her translation of Comte's 'Course in Positive Philosophy'; followed up with a 2 volume 'The Positive Philosophy of Auguste Comte' (1853). Martineau was herself a noted early sociologist, social reformer, passionate anti-slaver and determined campaigner for women's rights. She identified and articulated the numerous conditions for inequality - education, occupation, marriage, religious, legal and political - facing girls and women. She was not only a prolific sociological author in her own right (50 books, plus numerous papers/essays) but her approach was novel in its insistence that to understand any society one must study all aspects of it including the lives of women and the socialization of children. She visited the United States and published her study 'Society in America' (1837), in which she set out and applied her more 'holistic' approach to the study of society.

The intellectually brilliant husband and wife pair, John Stuart Mill and Harriet Taylor Mill, collaborated in writing a number of books related to the social sciences and to social philosophy. Both were leading proponents of positivism; of the application of the methods used in the natural sciences to the study of the social world. Harriet was a prominent advocate of women's rights and wrote a pioneering study on domestic violence.

Comte had introduced the term 'sociology' to represent what could be both a realist science of society (social relationships and social institutions) and also a form of meta-science able to co-ordinate and offer a socially relevant interpretation of the ways in which all human knowledge has advanced. It is for his ideas on the latter that he is known as the first philosopher of science and for his ideas on the former that he is known as the founder of sociology. Interestingly, Comte also introduced the term 'altruism' as a concept used to express the interconnectedness and interdependency of all life on Earth.

Whilst Comte allowed a place for mathematics in the natural sciences, he did consider this aspect of method to be inappropriate to biology and the social sciences. But in this he was, especially in France, swimming against a strong intellectual tide favouring measurement and quantification. A view promoted by Nicolas de Condorcet (1743-1794 - permanent secretary to the French Academy of Science) himself an articulate and gifted mathematician. Condorcet suggested that positivistic science should form the core of a reformed education curriculum and, like some others at the time, he considered that society would be better (more rationally) run if scientists were directly involved with its administration. And that the efficiency of this rational administration would be dependent on its being informed by a wide range of statistical information.

Commitment to the value of identifying quantitative measures and of assessments related to demographic characteristics of populations and various other economic and social issues, gained a widening audience amongst an educated public as well as the interest of politicians, social reformers, and academics. From early in the nineteenth century we can see politicians peppering speeches with statistics - of prostitutes on the streets of London or Manchester, of populations in cities, of the miles of neglected roads, of the cost of this or that proposal - hard statistics, quantified projections, and assessments of mathematical probability; and, especially in France, the use of the social survey and of inductive probability introduced by Pierre-Simon Laplace. Statistics increasingly fed into the public discourse on a widening range of social issues. As the century turned, the USA and a number of European states followed Prussia's (1719) lead in introducing what were initially fairly basic modern censuses - Sweden 1749, Spain 1768, Denmark 1771, Netherlands 1795, France and United Kingdom in 1801, Belgium in 1846, with the United States introducing its first in 1790. Some of these countries established offices of census along with specific bodies to collect and collate statistical information in areas such as industry, crime, trade, and public health.

Amongst the leading thinkers promoting statistics was the Belgian Adolphe Quetelet (1796-1874), a statistician and astronomer who, in his 1835 book 'A Treatise of Man and the Development of his Faculties', applied statistics to social phenomena and in doing so conceptualized the 'average man' in terms of both physical and mental characteristics; an idea of a normal type by which any individual or group can be compared, and by the use of which predictions can be made. His aim was to use statistical methods, and the insights potentially made accessible using statistical analysis, to create a 'social physics'. 'The London Statistical Society' (LSS) had been established in 1834 and Quetelet organized the first international statistical conference held in Brussels in 1853, out of which 'The Statistical Society of Paris' was established. Both of these following the 'American Statistical Society' which had been established in 1839. Then in1885 the International Statistical Institute (ISI) was founded at a meeting of the LSS. The ISI would go on to provide the principle international setting for statistical information with its bi-annual conference series continuing down to today; the 63rd conference is scheduled to be held at The Hague, Netherlands, in 2021.

A significant impetus given to the categorization and quantification of social phenomena was provided by the need of industrializing nations to gain a sense of having more control over their populations. Even if need was mostly claimed to be in terms of more efficient administration, arguably it was also a means of 'surveillance' of a population; as a body it was the working classes that were overwhelmingly the focus of surveys and statistical accounting. Industrializing states sought statistical data on manufacturing industry, agricultural production, military capability, international trade, criminal activity, along with a range of demographic characteristics of their populations.

As a leading example: in Britain a number of government departments established statistical sections, the stated aim being to inform decision-making. Between 1832 and 1846 about 100 royal commissions of enquiry were carried out by inspectors tasked with assessing living conditions in towns and cities, and the working conditions in various industries, especially those involving factories and mines. Each of these commissions made liberal use of statistical information and their reports were used by many social scientists during the nineteenth century, not least Marx and Engels. Statistical information, as social data, became an essential aspect of the social sciences, if a suggested over-reliance on this approach has been continually contested down to today.

The use of statistical data appeared to offer a more objective way of assessing social conditions and relationships. But some questioned just how 'objective' any survey might be when data collection can be so dependent on the choice and wording of questions. In addition, statistical categorization put synthetic boundaries around what were generally continuous differences and what are often quite indeterminate identities; in effect, the social construction of validity. Problems around the issues of defining employment and unemployment, poverty, adequate housing conditions, intelligence, 'safe' levels of air and water quality, were at times glossed over. For example, surveys of prostitution and sexually transmitted disease allowed some commentators to claim a seemingly authoritative 'measure' of the moral weakness of women and of a community's increasing sinfulness. But these particular surveys did not generally go on to consider the social vulnerability of a women without any means of support other than her body and of men's willingness to pay to gain access to it or, on a more philosophical level, some consideration of a women's right to use her body as she wishes. With any survey, understanding the delineation of categorization and wider social context is crucial. J.D.Bernal highlighted the danger of relying on statistics (giving Francis Galton's work on inheritance - eugenics - as an example) given the '...complex and self-involved nature of human society' and suggests that 'The use of statistics has often given a delusional appearance of accuracy to social data.' (Bernal, 1969 ed.,Vol.4, p1085)

I think (or would like to think) that most social scientists working today, whilst allowing a pragmatic value to statistical information also subject it to close contextual scrutiny and try to avoid making assumptions that go beyond the 'facts'; however much hypothesis-confirming calculations of experimental or correlational significance, numerical trends, and measures of statistical probability, might tempt them. Economics is an, if not the most notable, example of a science that is both essentially dependent on statistical information but also a science historically most liable to claim dubious causative 'laws', and currently to offering assumptions, probabilities, and predictions without the invariably necessary caveats; tendencies accentuated perhaps due to the subject's closeness to governance and profit-seeking and indeed, its tendancy towards ideological bias more generally.

It is often the case that those: governments, businesses, social activists, speculative as well as more enduring investors, and other interest groups who pay professional economists are often seeking just such predictive information and hope for an at least acceptable degree of accuracy. But this does not serve as an adequate apology for 'sloppy science', especially when being promoted by academic economists - not least given the potentially significant social and political implications.

There has been an alternative approach to social science that has a methodological opposition (or at least resistance) to applying statistical information to the study of humankind, one that is not simply a return to 18th and early 19th century romanticism. But rather an approach that considers humankind, psychologically and socially, is just too complex an entity to be usefully accessed via quantification. The German Wilhelm Dilthey (1833-1911), is probably the most notable example of an early advocate for a thoroughgoing 'qualitative' methodological approach to the social sciences. Not least due to his taking the view that the use of the methods of the natural sciences, especially quantification and reductionism, tend to highlight synthetic separation rather than accepting the invariable interconnectedness of the subject-matter of the social sciences (echoes of von Humboldt and the natural sciences - see above). That there is just 'social science', not a collection of autonomous social sciences. Dilthey argued for a hermeneutic approach that sought to translate psychological and social phenomena in terms of meaning rather than in terms of determinate laws informed by quantitative data.

According to H.P.Rickman (1979, p147) for Dilthey: 'The subject-matter, therefore influences the methods suitable for its investigation and this makes distinctive methods for the social sciences necessary'. Dilthey was an early advocate of the need for an interdisciplinary approach in order to overcome the somewhat arbitrary categorization of the various branches of the social sciences: for example, if we wish to understand what a certain person's identity is we would need to bring to bear insights from psychology, sociology, and history, in order to overcome the partial focus of adopting a single disciplinary approach.

Herbert Spencer stands out as an individual - philosopher, social commentator, and sociologist - who made a significant contribution to setting the conceptual framework for the continuing development of the social sciences, especially sociology, during the nineteenth century. Of pervasive influence was his idea of 'society evolving' (later this would become better known, if misnamed, as Social Darwinism); of a sense of human evolution beyond the merely biological. His original ideas, his 'Social Statics', (pace Comte's 'social statics'/'social dynamics') were developed in, at times discursive, detail over the publication of the essays and books encompassed within his 'Synthetic Philosophy' 1862-93. These ideas of social change mostly preceded Darwin's theory of evolution and were stimulated by Spencer's reading of works such as Charles Lyell's 'Principles of Geology' (three vols. 1830-33) and Thomas Malthus's 'An Essay on the Principle of Population' (1798), and as well as his exposure to some ideas of William Godwin, Jean Baptiste Lamarck, and T.H.Huxley. Indeed, it was Spencer who introduced the idea of the 'survival of the fittest', a phrase later to be associated with the concept of Social Darwinism, which became a social/political philosophy often deployed to support a laissez-faire approach to economic activity and to opposing social reforms.

A more nuanced consideration of Spencer's views would, yes accept that he did prioritize individuality, but would also note that he suggested that 'man' had evolved a sense of altruism towards others beyond that of close family. In consequence, evolved ('modern') societies offer a basis for mutual support, with society being constituted by the sum of the individuals of which it is composed.

When Darwin in his 'Origin of Species' (1859), in which he took up Spencer's 'survival of the fittest' phrase, went beyond just asserting the idea of evolution in setting out evidence and in offering an explanation for a possible mechanism driving evolution ('natural selection'), Spencer felt that one of his principle ideas had been vindicated. For Spencer (1851): 'Evolution is a change from a state of relatively indefinite, incoherent, homogeneity, to a state of relatively definite, coherent, heterogeneity.'

The substantial evidential support offered by Darwin's book contributed to the positive reception of Spencer's 'The Study of Sociology' in 1873. A book he was encouraged to publish by his America friend Edward L. Youmans, a writer on science who in 1872 founded the magazine 'Popular Science' (still in print in 2020).

Spencer's own interpretation of Comte's positivism included a view of the sciences as interrelated, with advance in one stimulating advance in others; even contributing to new forms of theoretical frameworks - the theory of evolution being a prime example, arising from biology and geology, but with potentially fundamental implications for psychology, as well as anthropology and sociology.

The central theoretical framework for Spencer's sociology was the comparison of society with individual organisms. For Spencer's 'Social Organism' analogy, the similarities between societies and living bodies are: 'That they [each] gradually increase in mass; that they become little by little more complex; that at the same time their parts grow more mutually dependent; and that they continue to live and grow as wholes; while successive generations of their units appear and disappear; are broad peculiarities which bodies-politic display in common with all living bodies; and in which they and living bodies differ from everything else.' (taken from the final paragraph of Spencer's essay 'The Social Organism' 1860, in 'The Man Versus the State' 1969 p232 penguin edition ed. D Macrae). A key implication is that both society and organisms are subject to what are, in principle, similar 'natural laws'. In order to illustrate a natural law of social evolution Spencer suggests that the division of occupations in society - lawyers, builders, blacksmiths, teachers, watchmakers, butchers, bakers, labourers, etc- progressively arise from the pressure to fulfill human wants and activities rather than from some planned and directed occupational segregation. The wider extrapolation of this principle would be that the constitution of any society is not made as a result of some planned design but rather it has evolved ('organically') into its present state. The seeds of functionalism can be read into this theory as being the underlying dynamic creating social structures and determining the most suitable type of institutions and social relationships. Spencer's three volume: 'The Principles of Sociology' (1876-93) is a fairly detailed analysis of social institutions undertaken from a broadly functionalist perspective.

In terms of Spencer's influence on later social science, we would need to note his significant contribution towards raising public and academic awareness to the wide-ranging implications of evolution. He was also influential in education (especially in the US) with his advocating an overhaul of the curriculum to focus on more practical subjects, from child-rearing to political participation. The numerous debates he stimulated, ranging across a number of issues concerning man and society, helped to raise the profile of sociology as an autonomous science.

The period 1830-60 was for Robert C. Bannister (Cam. History of Science vol.7 - 2003) a time of 'pre-academic sociology', a time when difficulties were being encountered by would-be sociologists with their even just trying to define some precise contour of what is meant by 'society'. To wrench some autonomous common subject-area from more protective - irredentist - adherents in psychology, political science, economics, and anthropology. The German philosopher, become sociologist, Georg Simmel (1858-1918) - influenced by those such as Kant, Weber, and Dilthey - concentrated on establishing the autonomous subject matter for sociology; identifying forms of social interaction between individuals and groups, rather than institutions as such, as the primary sociological terrain.

The progression of statistics continued with the increasing demands to quantify aspects of industrial development (mostly different from the qualitatively human impacts) with its novel forms of manufacturing, urbanization, and international trading patterns characterized by economic and actual colonialism. Those campaigning for social reform to ameliorate living and working conditions of the masses also favoured statistics and surveys to add credibility to the descriptions of conditions set out in official reports and the more dramatic ones of radical journalists as well as authors such as Charles Dickens, Elizabeth Gaskill, and pictured in the engravings of Gustave Doré.

Karl Marx's (1818-1883) standing as an economist, political activist and predictor of revolutionary change has (until relatively recently) somewhat overshadowed the significant contribution he made to the foundation of sociology as a discrete social science. The roots of Marx's sociology are simply stated in his observation that: *'The mode of production of material life conditions the general process of social, political and intellectual life. It is not the consciousness of men that determines their existence, but their social existence that determines their consciousness.'*

(trans. from the preface to Marx's 1859 *'A Contribution to the Critique of Political Economy'*)

The second sentence of this quote highlights the constitutive rootedness of the individual in their social circumstances, whilst the first sentence offers the basis of his analysis of the primary determinant of the elements creating these social circumstances; both being resolutely sociological perspectives. Marx was a meta-theorist of the type that fell out of favour in the late twentieth century, even if the concept of Globalization is suggesting a potential to return to this mode of theorizing. Marx's was a theory of society as rooted in dysfunctional relationships rather than of one where normality was of social cohesion that on occasion has this or that source of specific ('localized') disruption. For Marx, the nature of the relations of capitalist production are a fundamental source of social division and individual alienation. Alienation being a key social phenomena for Marx (although often credited with introducing this important concept Marx himself credits Hegel), this being caused by economic circumstances and the operation of the capitalist state itself that together assume power over individuality, or rather appropriate any self-affirming relationships - especially an individual's relationship to the means of production - that might have been be possible.

Marx felt that in his identification of the importance of class he was only highlighting a social phenomenon that had been noted by some bourgeois commentators; the difference being that for them class had mostly been an acceptable (indeed 'natural' and so cohesive and functional) division, whereas for Marx the relationship between classes was conflictual, being based on irreconcilably different interests.

Marx's problematic perspective on industrializing society represents a more extreme end of a continuum of more leftwing approaches that together stand in contrast to the more conservative and functionalist approaches which have viewed ordered social cohesion as the 'norm' and social hierarchy as a solidifying rather than a divisive feature of social structure; albeit that some degree of social mobility is generally seen as necessary to maintain cohesion. This latter being a 'safety value' for potential frustration; providing formal channels of social mobility along which frustration can be accommodated, and allowing high ability to be deployed to the overall benefit of social and economic systems.

The society as dysfunctional perspective of some nineteenth century social scientists included British socialists (of the type that would become committed to social change on the back of democratic advance) as well as Marxist communists, and some more radical social reformists from Christian and humanistic backgrounds. It would be from within this broad 'left' academic source that the recognition of the need for an academic institution that could pursue enlightened theoretical ideas informed by statistical analysis and combine these in a systematic research programme that led, in 1895, to the establishing of the London School of Economics and Political Science (LSE - made financially possible by a philanthropic bequest of £20,000 from H. H, Hutchinson). With, from 1907, a Chair of Sociology, and a principled commitment to the social sciences as they can contribute to reformist social development. The first professor of sociology at the LSE was Leonard Hobhouse, who had earlier been one of the prime movers in establishing the London Sociological Society (1903).

T.B. Bottomore and M. Rubel (1956) credit Marx with two significant 'discoveries': that of the materialist conception of history (including what Engels referred to as the 'law of development of human history'), and that the basis of capitalist production is the appropriation of surplus value. It is clear that Marx brought a different and politically challenging theoretical perspective to the study of social and economic conditions. But his methodological rigour was at least as thorough as most social scientists of his time and his long-term influence on the development of sociological analysis would easily qualify him to be ranked alongside the founders of sociology as a science. Even allowing that he fairly dismissively eschewed the idea of any 'value free' (objective) social science; consistent with his view of the natural and social sciences as themselves being forms of social activity and so formed in the light of relationships structured according to capitalist production.

Marx's methodological approach included the use of statistical information. Indeed one of the reasons given for his primarily focusing on England rather than France or Germany was the more comprehensive nature of the statistical and other relevant empirical information (especially of living and working conditions) available there. Das Capital, awash with this type of information, is a detailed analysis of social conditions underpinned by empirical information, all within meta-theoretic insights encompassing the primacy of economic arrangements and a labour-theory of value (taken over from Ricardo). Capital is a text taking an historical perspective in sociological, as well as in economic ways.

Whilst not obviously interested in any narrow epistemological issues, other than asserting the primacy of material circumstances and the types of social conditions this generates, Marx did contribute to the sociology of knowledge in his analysis of ideological superstructures operating to create and sustain any politically bounded society. He was innovative in relation to the enduringly important sociology of knowledge, clarifying its production from the predominant ideological perspective and social practices of any society. This more theoretical aspect of the sociological perspective (encompassed by C. Wright-Mill's 'Sociological Imagination' - 1959) was later progressed by those such as M. Scheler (who introduced the term 'sociology of knowledge'), G.Lukács, perhaps most notably by K.Mannheim, and later by Michel Foucault. According to Peter L. Berger: :.......the sociology of knowledge attempts to draw a line from the thought to the thinker to his social world. This can be seen most easily in those instances when thought serves to legitimate a particular social situation, that is, when it explains, justifies and sanctifies it.' (Berger, 1963, p129). The 'line' noted here is the generative link that Marx had made earlier. For him this being that the class position of those producing and sanctifying any knowledge (usually as part of a wider ideological knowledge system) strongly influences the actual content of it; authoritative knowledge in any society being an intellectual expression of the predominant class interest.

Amongst the most substantial sociologists at the turn of the century

- Emile Durkheim and Max Weber (in Europe), Frederic Tönnies (in the US), and Georg Simmel (German but working in the US) - stand out but, given his impact on social science, it would be misleading to exclude Marx as being one of the foundational figures in twentieth century sociology.

For Emile Durkheim (1858-1917)[8] the study of society could be based on a scientific approach using methods similar to those used in the natural sciences; he posited the idea of 'social facts',[9] these being particular phenomena that within any social context shape the behaviour of individuals – marriage, suicide, customs, freedom, god, etc could be, for Durkheim, social facts (B3 Vol.16, 1974, p994) '…..he [Durkheim] argued that there can arise from various kinds of interaction among individuals certain new properties –'social facts''. A central task for social scientists is to identify the characteristics and social implications of social facts – for Anthony Giddens: '…social facts are ways of thinking or feeling that are external to individuals and have their own reality outside of the lives and perceptions of individual people.' (Giddens, 2009, p14). Social facts can constrain individuals but we tend to easily comply and even assume that we are in fact making choices for ourselves. Durkheim was interested in social change and the implication-rich concept of 'social facts' provided him with information in a form that could be used to enable description and analysis of any specific development; particular 'social facts' could assist in the identification of general 'social laws'. For Durkheim social facts, although independent of any individual, are produced within and by social environments. His work ranged fairly widely but shows a particular interest in the impact of social change (especially as seen during the process of industrialization) on any society's institutions and on social cohesion, religion, work and economic life, deviance, crime and cultural diversity. A wider context for these was a socio-evolutionary element seeking to identify how societies have developed. More specifically due to the pressures of modernity, such as the division of labour, and increasing population size, especially in cities, causing the breakdown of consensual

---

[8] Given the importance of Marx, Durkheim, and Weber, to 20th century social science as a discipline, I will be covering each of these in bit more detail in the 20th sociology section in Chapt. 8 below.
[9] Similar ideas to 'social facts' and their social construction has been significantly extended by the philosopher John R. Searle in his 1995 book 'The Construction of Social Reality'.

morality and norms, along with the decline of religious practice and traditional forms of authority.

Durkheim posited two forms of solidarity holding society together – mechanical and organic – mechanical solidarity was based upon generally low division of occupations and by local communities sharing beliefs that have developed during a history of shared experience – creating a strong, and strongly constraining, sense of the normal. Whereas organic solidarity characterizes societies that are based upon relationships founded more on economic ('instrumental') commitments and on occupational specialization.

Unlike Marx, Durkheim was more of a conservative, academic, social scientist, observing and commenting on social behaviour rather than being directly involved with the social conditions being analyzed; if arguably, the insertion of certain values were assumed by his functionalist approach. He produced polemical analyses critical of other social scientists, such as Marx; criticism more related to methodology than ideology. Up to about the beginning of WWI he had himself expressed a general sympathy with moderate forms of socialism, if not ones fundamental critical of the then current social systems. A reasonable case could be made for Durkheim being identified with taking a similar approach to the study of society as Saint-Simon and August Comte (both, like Durkheim, French), and building on foundations laid by them. In line with his belief that the study of society was a scientific enterprise he considered that a positivist approach could be applied to social problems; problems seen as dysfunctional behaviours impacting on the structural integrity of society. He was also closely involved in the publication of 'L' Annee Sociologique' in 1896, an academic journal which, along with the 'American Journal of Sociology' (pub. 1894), was a significant marker of a science beginning to 'come-of-age'.

Durkheim was generally critical of the biological metaphors for social behaviour that were popular at the time but he did accept Herbert Spencer's analogy of any society being like a living organism so having an organic unity that, for Durkheim, was more than the sum of its constitutive parts. He insisted that society is bound together by ideas rather than material relationships and he was sympathetic to the view of Albert Schaffle in his distinguishing between an individual consciousness and a collective conscious.

In his classic study of suicide (1897) Durkheim drew attention to an ongoing concern with the impact of industrialization on the individual. How the rapid changes characteristic of industrialization broke down the 'organic unity' upon which social cohesion depended. The suicide study was pioneering in the sense that it made use of statistical methods in order to understand a sociological problem.

The functionalist approach of Durkheim was taken further by many twentieth century sociologists notably Talcott Parsons and Robert K. Merton, and the structuralist aspects of this approach was taken further by social scientists such as Ferdinand de Saussure, Michel Foucault, Roland Bathes, and Louis Althusser.

Max Weber (1864-1920), for the most part thought that there was a distinction between the natural and the social sciences and that this would imply the need for different methodological approaches for each. Weber had wide ranging interests – politics, law, economics and sociology, philosophy. His approach to methodology differed from both that of the positivism and of the historicism that were the two prominent approaches of the time. Weber recognized the value of identifying factual truths but also the need to progress the search for understanding any social phenomenon to be guided by values. The Stanford Encyclopedia of Philosophy quotes Weber as noting that: 'The capacity to distinguish between empirical knowledge and value-judgments, and the fulfillment of the scientific duty to see factual truth as well as the practical duty to stand up for our own ideals constitute the program to which we wish to adhere with ever-increasing firmness.' (on-line Sept.2012).

Weber accords a certain primacy to individuals and their role in social change. Given this, his wish to take an approach to the study of social phenomenon that incorporates subjective meaning is understandable, indeed necessary. His work in sociology reflects a keen interest in the process of industrialization - the economic and social relationships that were key features of a maturing stage of industrialization - and the impact of this on the individual. In order to understand the outcomes of industrialization he also examined the roots of the process pertaining in parts of Europe in the seventeenth century highlighting: technological innovation, potential markets, trading links, and the presence of individuals prepared to undertake risky investment for the prospect of rich rewards. He considered how the capitalist dynamic that initiated and sustained industrialization came along only at a certain time in certain parts of western Europe. Weber identified a particular mindset arising from underlying religious beliefs that were novel to civil life and which for him provided a further necessary condition for 'capitalist' industrialization.

Industrialization required the investment of capital, and in the past the leading religions had tended to be antagonistic to the accumulation of capital by individual believers (if not by the Churches and religious leaders themselves) and also, when the above conditions were present any excess capital tended to be spent on conspicuous consumption (or warring) including prestigious monumental buildings, or bequeathed to the Church on death. In his book 'The Protestant Ethic and the Spirit of Capitalism' (1904-5), Weber related the accumulation of capital, and the use of this to build businesses, to central aspects of the belief system of Protestant (Calvinistic) religion. Of relevance to the sociological method, he identified a statistical correlation between entrepreneurialship and certain religious beliefs. Calvinism included a belief in predestination, of the fate of a sinner being determined, with eternal hell and damnation awaiting most individuals. Weber suggested that this unbearable spiritual burden led to groups of Protestants adopting an aesthetic approach to life in an attempt to at least mitigate the fate awaiting their mortal souls. To live lives of material moderation and religious devotion in the hope of gaining spiritual salvation. So with this religious - based upon a personal relationship with God, not one mediated by clerical interpretation but directed mainly by Biblical injunction - motivational background, Protestants in England, Holland, and parts of Germany and France, were able to accumulate capital.

Quite extensive parts of Weber's work were reactions to Marx; most obviously, on class where he rejected a class definition based on relationships to the means of production (capital) and the conflictual polarization this was said by Marx to give rise too. For Weber, class is a broader concept based on three central elements: Social class, the economic determination of whether a person is an employee, owner, rentier, etc. – Status class, which is related to the social esteem in which a person is held (primarily based on role position) – and Party class, the affiliation to groups; political parties, TUs, clubs, etc. a person has access to. This broader definition of class is one that has had most influence throughout the first half of the twentieth century (accepting a close call with Marxist interpretations) until 'class-based' categorizations came to include patterns of personal consumption ('embourgeoisment') as primary determinants of identity and so a need to recalibrate the basis of socio/economic division.

The driving force of social change was for Weber the ideas and motivation of individuals. For Weber the process of modernity, involving increasing bureaucratization, alienation from work, and positivistic science, was an inevitable movement of change expressing the increasing rationalization of our experience. Of fundamental concern with this process was the impact on traditional (unifying) cultural values and authority and on the individual as a free agent – this rule-generating rationalization operated to contain individuals within an 'iron cage'.

Ferdinand Tönnies (1855-1936), another scholar working to establish sociology as an autonomous (and intellectually legitimate) social science, attempted a theoretical integration of the nineteenth-century organic and the eighteenth-century social contract views of a basic structure for civil society. His 1887 book *'Geminschaft and Gesellschaft'* ('Community and Society') traced the ways in which society changes. With Geminschaft (community society) encompassing how the maintenance of instinctive traditional rules and a shared sense of community solidarity undergoes progressive change during the process of modernization. A change made towards a Gesellschaft (associational society) where the shared sense of community is gradually transformed into a more individual (if reasoned) self-seeking. A stage in which the traditional 'normality' is no longer suitable for the maintenance of social cohesion, and so the need for more formal rules (laws) and for functional institutions

During the second half of the nineteenth century positivism and more generally the methods of the natural sciences formed the primary methodological approach taken in the social sciences as they developed across Europe; if less so in Germany where the earlier idealistic ('romantic') tradition remained influential up to the 1870s. University reform in France during the 1880s marked a key stage in the institutional division of the social sciences.

For the United States, the end of the civil war has been taken as a key time from which the social sciences developed. The US had experienced an 'industrial war' (perhaps the first in history) and emerged from it with business and finance organizations geared to increase the pace of industrial development. In addition, the constant stream of European migrants, the novelty of native American cultures, and the mass movement of freed slaves and poor whites from the southern plantation economy to the expanding northern cities, all stimulated an academic (and political) interest in social change; and the application of the methods of social scientific investigation seemed to offer the intellectual tools to understand these, often interlocking, processes.

Lester Frank Ward (1841-1913) who, although with a background in paleontology, has been credited with being the 'Father of American sociology'. Ward was an admirer of Comte and so an advocate of the application of the methods of the natural sciences to the study of society, prioritizing the value of experiment and of careful observation. He attempted to modernize Comte's positivism in line with advances in scientific methodology, even if the later work of Durkheim is more often given the credit for this.

In 1905 Ward became the first president of the American Sociological Association (ASA - later became the American Sociological Society) and in 1906 took up the Chair of Sociology at Browns University. He was firmly of the belief that sociology could provide the 'tools' to provide information that would be of practical benefit to society. He considered that society was a natural object constituted by 'social forces' which were themselves a particular type of natural force and so amenable to study by the application of a scientific sociological methodology.

'I regard society and the social forces as constituting just as much a legitimate field for the exercise of human ingenuity as do the various material substances and physical forces' (Ward, 1893, p35)

Ward's form of social liberalism provided academic authority for an interventionist role for government in relation to social issues, and his ideas influenced a number of mainly, but not only, Democrat presidents. His books including: 'Dynamic Sociology' 1893 – 'Outlines of Sociology' 1898 - 'Pure Sociology' 1903 - 'Applied Sociology' - made a significant contribution to the direction that American sociology would take. But early American sociology, although sharing a commitment to the methods of the natural sciences, did not represent a consensus in terms of analytical perspective. An alternative perspective was that of William G. Sumner (1840-1910) who held the Chair in Political and Social Science' at Yale University where he worked from 1872-1909; teaching the first US course specifically identified as sociology (said to have used Spencer's 'The Study of Sociology' as the main textbook). In 1908 he became the second president of the ASA.

Rather than Comte, Sumner considered that the ideas of Spencer were more appropriate for the study of society and were especially suitable for the experience of the industrializing United States. He was a political conservative and considered 'Social Darwinism' a potentially fruitful interpretive framework in that it offered a reassuring (for conservatives) analysis for economic inequality and other hierarchical social differences. An analysis that suggested that these were due to innate differences between people; their 'fitness' to compete in life's competitive settings. Society would continue to evolve naturally, with the 'fittest' driving the process.

In his book 'Folkways' (1906) Sumner suggested an important role for social mores and how these can influence behaviour; he compared a culture to an individual in that for him both exhibit a '.....more or less consistent pattern of thought and action'. And that the wider cultural network of a taken-for-granted pattern of thought and action, have a determining affect on shaping those of any individual. Unsurprisingly, and contrary to Ward's view, Sumner favoured a laissez-faire approach to the role of government and in this approach conveniently conformed to the dominant capitalist business and financial ethos to which most members of the (east coast) ruling elite subscribed.

Although simplistic, we can gain some idea of the way in which sociology (indeed the social sciences more generally - especially marked post WWII) developed in the United States if we identify the approaches established by Ward (traditional liberalism) and Sumner (neo-liberalism) as being the two main ideological perspectives. But if we take a more critical view we can frame both of these as being but variations of a more expansive pragmatic conservative ideology which has driven sociology to limit its ambitions to more practical work, it being mostly circumscribed by discrete (single) issues. One possible exception to these approaches, with their more circumscribed studies, was arguably, 'race-related' issues; encompassing poverty, intelligence testing, crime, as well as employment and educational discrimination. These have been considered as interlinked to a more fundamental phenomenon i.e. systemic racism. But if this is an exception to the general pattern of sociological pragmatism operating within a conservation ideological setting, then this would be due mainly to the extent of increasing public outrage at its links to obvious socio/political injustice.

A little later on, a significant contribution to the 'racism' debate was made by another outstanding social scientist working during the formative decades of sociology in the United States. W.E.B. Du Bois (1868-1963) who, during a long and academically productive life, used his sociological expertise to dispel false popular and academic beliefs about the history of African civilization and the assumed cultural and intellectual inferiority of black people. Du Bois was the first black American to gain a PhD at Harvard. His 1896 (pub, 1899) book 'The Philadelphia Negro: A Social Study' was an early attempt to combine extensive research (based on 2,500 interviews) with census data in order to highlight the reality of racism experienced by the members of the black minority. In a series of books including: 'The Souls of Black Folk' 1903 - 'The Negro' 1915. 'Black Reconstruction in America 1860-80' 1935, Du Bois undertook a systematic, predominately research-based, analysis of how race and racism shape a person's outlook and how this impacts on interpersonal relationships. Unsurprisingly, Du Bois was an articulate and forceful campaigner for civil rights, including rights for those in poverty, and for all women, as well as black people. He was also co-founder, and director of research, for the 'National Association for the Advancement of Coloured People' (NAACP), and the first editor of its magazine *'The Crisis'*.

The first graduate dept. of sociology was established as Chicago University in 1892 with Albion Small as its head and the setting up of the Social Science Group soon followed. Columbia College first established a School of Political Science in 1880 (and its own Department of Sociology in 1894) offering the first comprehensive programme of social science studies. Small took the lead in establishing the American Journal of Sociology in 1895, and this would become the primary publication of the American Sociological Society following its establishment in 1905

A more modern approach to sociology was taken by Robert E. Park (1864-1944) - Influenced by the writing of Ferdinand Tönnies, especially his book 'Geminschaft and Gesellschaft' 1887 - Park's own more original work focused on direct ('street-level') research in mainly urban settings; his work covered ethnicity, sub-cultures, urban gangs, and included pioneering studies of African Americans. Park, in a book co-authored with Ernest W. Burgess ('Introduction to the Science of Society' -1921), 'introduced the term 'human ecology' as a means of suggesting a wider, more interactional, social context. Park would become one of the most influential sociologists in the US for most of the first half of the twentieth century - in 1925 he became the 15th President of the American Sociological Society.

In his first presidential address, published in Papers and Proceedings of the Twentieth Annual Meeting, Vol. XX, as "The Concept of Position in Sociology", Park noted that: *'In fine, the sociologist's interest in human ecology is in man's relation to other men as found in definite and typical patterns. Insofar as social structure can be defined in terms of position, and social changes in terms of movement of the population, social phenomena are subject to mathematical measurement. The growth of a city is more than a mere aggregation of people, but involves many changes which are measurable. Not all social phenomena can be measured in terms of location, position and mobility, for the true unit of social inter-action is a changing attitude. Nevertheless social relations are often correlated with special relations and hence are measurable in a certain degree'*

Sociology is a science particularly suited to understanding (making sense of the structural features and developments implicitly suggested by Park) the ethnically diverse and relatively socially mobile society that was the nineteenth century United States. By the end of the century sociology was part of the curriculum of many US universities, and (as noted above) the American Sociological Society and the American Journal of Sociology had been established. But even more so than the natural sciences, those who progress the social sciences have had to accept that, such is the complexity of the subject-matter it deals with that the insights of perceptive novelists and wise social observers (whether politicians, social philosophers, or others) can sometimes provide as much if not more illumination on aspects of the human condition than those who applied the reductionist (and therefore limited) procedures generally adopted by nineteenth century social scientists. But in areas such as: welfare planning, prison reform, education, transportation, in fact all aspects of running a complex economy and managing a complex society no government would now (21st cent) fail to consult advisors informed by the knowledge of social sciences; even if most advice would tend to be politically legitimized if in-line with any government's ideology.

I have included a relatively extended section on the development of sociology in the United States, this due mainly to it being the country where sociology, along with most other social sciences, gained its widest academic popularity.

The best work in sociology contributes to reflecting key aspects of our social condition and the twentieth century was to see this condition subjected to considered observation, examination, and analysis. If, when lacking some admitted ethical (ideological) framework, it has been analysis directed according to wider power relationships; only occasionally has sociology offered some more profound challenges to this (systemically camouflaged) source of elite-interest bias.

Psychology

In the period immediately preceding 1800 consideration of the nature of human psychology tended to be but aspects of philosophy - Spinoza 1632-1677 and Hume 1711-1776) - or politics - Machiavelli 1469-1527 and Hobbs 1588-1679. Towards the end of the 18th and during the early 19th century, psychology very slowly began to assume a more autonomous place within the nascent social sciences; with a definite focus on the impact of experience to forming the mind (sensationalism). In particularly, the work of John Locke (1630-1704) and Etienne Bonnet de Condillac (1714-1780) initiated a more enduring trend in psychology by highlighting the role of experience in forming the mind that went beyond the more simple associationism of Hume and the naturalism (if materialistic) of Hobbs.

Locke and Condillac led the way in this 'empirical' approach, a more novel aspect of which was their outline of human psychological development. For each of these, the infant mind at birth was empty of content - Locke's infamous 'tabula rasa' (blank slate) - with the 'mental impressions' being gained during experience forming single ideas and combinations of these in the mind. For the most part they both rejected the idea of any innate faculties and dispositions as had been suggested by Descartes even if, at least for Locke, the human-being was considered to be innately curious. For Locke and Condillac, a human mind is malleable and during their development children in particular are susceptible to the influence of social learning. Unsurprisingly, both Locke and Condillac highlighted the importance of education, a cause also taken up with some enthusiasm by Jean-Jacques Rousseau (1712-1778). Locke and Rousseau both enjoyed publishing success with a book more specifically about education, for Locke it was 'Some Thoughts on Education' (1693), for Rousseau it was 'Emile' (1762).

Locke, Rousseau, and Condillac, together made a significant contribution to emphasizing the psychic processes impacting on the developing child, not just in the popular bourgeoisie circles of the time but also in laying intellectual markers that would act as both a stimulus and a challenge to the future course of developmental psychology, and to the narrower field of pedagogy.

The eighteenth century saw three theories related to the operation of the human mind - mesmerism, eclecticism (cousinism), and phrenology - that, although fairly soon shown to be scientifically spurious, did feed into the widening interest in human psychology as a discrete science. And their enthusiastic public reception illustrated the susceptibility of human-beings to seemingly authoritative ideas of how the mind works.

Mesmerism was an idea suggested by the German physician Franz Mesmer (1734-1815). Mesmer considered that he had discovered a magnetic 'energy system' flowing, as a gaseous fluid, from the planets to Earth and throughout a human body ('animal magnetism'). And that if in any individual this flow is disturbed in some way then mental or physical ill-health would result. His treatment involved using 'suggestion' induced by intense one-to-one physical manipulation and (his) lengthy staring into a patient's eyes. An alternative 'treatment' was to convince individuals in a group of patients that their illness was being eased by tapping into magnetic energy being drawn from a large covered tank of water, with iron bars sticking out from its side at a variety of angles and heights (a 'baquet'). Patients were seated around the tank in close physical contact with each other - with Mesmer 'orchestrating' the flow of energy that reached each patient via a rope connected to one of them. The 'cure' was achieved by inducing a beneficial crisis as the disturbed and curative energies interacted; this crisis would eventually be resolved by restoring the patient's energy to a balanced state of flow. What success Mesmer had with his treatment was more the outcome of the hypnotic suggestion ('mesmersim') rather that any actual curative link between 'magnetic fluids' and physical and mental illness.

Mesmerism enjoyed some popular interest but little official scientific recognition, unlike the 'eclecticism' and 'phrenology' which for a time were legitimized by a level of official (academic and political) approval.

Eclecticism was a theory of psychology developed by the Frenchman Victor Cousin (1792-1867), taking an approach that echoed some philosophers of the later classical period in Greece. Major representatives being Panaetius (185-110 BCE), Posidonius (135-51 BCE), Carnaedes (214-129 BCE), and Philo of Larissa (145-79 BCE) who selected what they considered to be the most valuable ideas and systems from the store of wisdom on any issue offered by many of the philosophers that had preceded them. Similarly, at least in his basic 'eclectic' method, Cousin drew on German philosophical Idealism, Scottish Commonsense psychological philosophy (as in the work of Thomas Reid 1710-1796) and French psychology, in outlining his own system. A system that was more a method than a theory of how the mind works; although it did make certain implicit theoretical assumptions about this. Cousins advocated a means of accessing human psychology via an inductive process that progressed from personal psychology to more ontological foundations.

His method for understanding human psychology operated in two stages. Firstly, the student of the subject would be empowered by gaining a clear sense of themselves - an introspective investigation of the 'me'. And so also a strong consciousness of personal moral responsibility and of right and wrong; these for Cousin, reflecting a conventionally conservative moral normality. This would then provide the student with the intellectual tools to look outward towards the world now able to recognize such human-related attributes as authentic truth, the good, and the beautiful (the title of one of his major works was 'On the True the Beautiful and the Good' 1836). For Cousin, this morally infused sense of engagement, allied to a systematic process of clear observation, would open up the student to understanding the world. In relation to human development, Cousin opposed the idea of the mind as a passive receptacle of experience (as suggested by Locke and Condillac) he, following the ideas of Maine de Biran (1766-1824) and Destutt de Tracy (1754-1836), suggested an active role for the faculties of the mind. This being for de Biran, centered on the 'I that wills' and for de Tracy, taking a more phenomenological analysis than de Biran, this being initiated by a consideration of immediate experience and so feelings, memory, judgment, and willing. For both de Tracy and de Biran our knowledge of the world cannot arise from some form of passive accumulation of information - as in Locke, and the reductive approach of Condillac - but must come from an immediate and active engagement with the world. Frederick Copleston (1975) went so far as to suggest that for de Biran, Descartes's foundational awareness of 'I think, therefore I am' became instead 'I will, therefore I am'. Ideas of these earlier theorists influenced Cousin's own conception of a reflexive self-consciousness as being perceptive and affective, so suggesting an active (constituting) role for the mind. Cousin's ideas gained official support in France to such an extent that what was very much his version of eclecticism was offered as a course in many universities and, by order of a National Decree of 1832, to be taught in all Lycée.

The third ('popular') approach to understanding the mind was Phrenology. First suggested by the German physician Franz Joseph Gall (1758-1828) it assumed a relationship between what are claimed to be discrete mental faculties and character traits and fairly detailed physical characteristics of the brain as indicated by 'bumps and shallows' ranged across the surface of the skull. And that, although the actual faculties expressed by these features on the surface of the skull were innate, their relative growth (and so degree of influence on behaviour) was the outcome of a person's experience. The theoretical basis for Phrenology was Gall's 'organology' and his diagnostic technique was 'cranioscopy'. Gall identified 27 functionally different brain regions (19 of these being present in some other animal species) most given fairly crude labels such as: mechanical ability, love of poetry, a propensity to theft and murder (some of his early research was undertaken on convicted criminals), etc.

Gall lectured fairly widely on his 'organology',[10] with his principle published work being: *The Anatomy and Physiology of the Nervous System in General, and of the Brain in Particular, with Observations upon the possibility of ascertaining the several Intellectual and Moral Dispositions of Man and Animal, by the configuration of their Head'* (1819s).

In it Gall makes it clear that his novel theoretical system of human psychology was based on a number of key assumptions, here very loosely interpreted as:

- that the physical brain is the sole basis of the mind
- that the brain is an aggregate of 'organs', each with a discrete function
- that the physical location of these 'organs' is topographically fixed.

---

[10] The name Phrenology was later popularized by Gall's anatomist collaborator (colleague) Joseph Gasper Spurzheim 1776-1832.

- that the size of an organ is indicted by the shape of a particular area of the skull, and that the size/shape of this area indicates the relative strength of a mental faculty or personality characteristic.
- that it is possible for a trained physician to physically examine a person's skull and so be able offer a scientifically (empirical) accurate assessment of that person's mental faculties and personality traits.

Gall's colleague, Joseph Gasper Spurzheim, endeavoured to make the naming of the 'organs' somewhat more scientific sounding, reducing the faculties to 21, identifying them with labels such as: linguistic perception, benevolence, acquisition, and secretiveness. With the size/shape of an area indicating the relative strength of a mental faculty or a particular personality characteristic. In a series of lecture tours, phrenology was introduced into Britain and the US, mainly by Spurzheim, and it was enthusiastically promoted by George Combe who, along with his brother, established the 'Edinburgh Phrenological Society' in 1820, and whose book 'On the Constitution of Man and its Relationship to External Objects' sold 200,000 copies over nine editions.

In Britain and most of Europe, the high point of phrenology's scientific credibility was roughly between 1810 and 1840, from when accumulating experimental evidence - in particular research by Pierre Florens - undermined the suggested links between localized regions of the brain and the topography of the skull. The key research focused on dissecting animal brains to see if removing areas of the brain would result in the loss of some discrete faculties, as would be predicted by phrenological assumptions. But the public popularity of phrenology endured, with few physician's consulting rooms being without a model of the human head exhibiting the surface of its skull neatly 'mapped' according to faculties. In the US Phrenology retained a level of academic credibility, and of poplar interest, throughout the 19th century; with the 'American Phrenological Journal' being published from 1838 (and surviving into the first decade of the 20th). Public lectures and demonstrations of phrenological examination played to packed halls; involving touch, measurement and, on occasion, even the use of a 'craniometer'. In the US applicants for some jobs were subjected to phrenological 'measurement', and similar examinations were even used to assess the compatibility of courting couples.

Although phrenology was never universally accepted in the US its basic assumption, that although mental faculties were innate, the extent of their development was dependant on experience (and so amenable to 'training/education'), was compatible with an individualistic narrative, and seemed to offer scientific credibility to explain a person's financial success or failure, whilst also to offer the possibility of self-improvement.

The three discredited sets of ideas - mesmerism, eclecticism and phrenology - did raise the profile of psychology but, similar to pre-Copernican astronomy, also showed how vulnerable the 'big unknowns' of the Universe and the human mind were - to spiritual, mythological, and even mystical ideas.

Given its superficial empirical methodology it is unsurprising that Comte was a supporter of Phrenology, viewing it as a model of positivism. But of more relevance to the development of psychology, it increased interest in the functional physiology of the brain and the nervous system. In the hands (or rather laboratories and operating theatres) of these such as Herman von Helmholtz (1821-1894), Paul Broca (1824-1880), and Carl Wernicke (1848-1905), the physical brain became a primary area of more useful psychological study.

Helmholtz in his time '.....the greatest physiologist in the world', according to G.A.Miller (1962) moved to Heidelberg in 1858 where he undertook a range of investigations into the operation of the nervous system, not least his being the first to attempt to measure the speed of neural communication (electrical conduction). Broca and Wernicke each identified brain areas more involved than others in the production of speech and its understanding (an area of the brain was named after each of them). This type of work, whilst continuing the functional localization (modularity) debate was at least based on making reasonable assumptions arising from careful investigation - and as such can be judged as an advance in method.

A much less useful development of physiological psychology was that undertaken to correlate intelligence with brain size and in turn to link these to racial categorization. The American (Philadelphia) Samuel G. Morton, trained as physician and was at the forefront of this approach. Beginning in the 1820s he built up what became a 1,000 specimen collection of human skulls (known to friends as the American Golgotha). Morton's focus was on cranial capacity measured by filling inverted skulls with, initially mustard seed then later in seeking more reliable measurement, with lead shot. He interpreted the findings of what were voluminous, and what were taken to be meticulously ordered, sets of data to mean that the cranial capacity (and so by inference intelligence) could be arranged in a hierarchy of supposed races. He set out his findings in a number of books including his 'Crania Americana' (1839); perhaps unsurprisingly given how racial differences had already been socially constructed in white-run America, Morton's hierarchy had whites at the apex, and native American Indians between these and the 'blacks' who were at the base. He also suggested a division within the white group; of Anglo-Saxons, American born whites, and Jews, in descending order - with Hindus, and Chinese similar to American Indians. Unsurprisingly for the time, he noted women as having smaller brains than men in all 'races'.

Even without considering the complex and problematic issue of attempting to even define intelligence, we can highlight the mistake of some simplistic linking of cranial capacity with intelligence and arranging these in a hierarchy categorized by crude 'racial' designations. In 1977 Stephen J Gould undertook a more detailed study of Morton's data and concluded that, in addition to the problems noted above, he found that the recorded data had been liberally misrepresented by Morton, and although he excuses Morton of intentional fraud he does note that: 'Morton's summaries are a patchwork of fudging and finagling in the clear interest of controlling a priori convictions.' (Gould, 'The Mismeasure of Man' 1995, p86). In this book Gould offers a quite detailed analysis of this data and also allows us to view some of Morton's own 'a priori convictions'. In relation to the measurement of intelligence more generally, I would recommend Gould's analytic and historical overview of intelligence testing, and related issues, to any student of psychology.

From the 1860s the misinterpretation of the implications of the Darwin-Wallace theory of evolution gave the seekers of racial hierarchy another seemingly authoritative source of justification. A justification that, whilst more often claimed as the findings of scientists undertaking a disinterested study of humankind, was more obviously simply about 'othering' of the (dark-skinned) peoples with which Western (and US) colonialists were engaged in various forms of exploitation, including the widespread theft of their lands.

As a counterbalance to the studies of native (and other) peoples bias towards supposed white western intellectual supremacy, and of their assessment against assumed standards of civilization, we have individuals such as the noted polymath Alexander von Humboldt. Humboldt was opposed to any ranking of peoples' based on psychological 'measurement'. Humboldt emphasized the unity of the human species, and took the view that: 'All [people] in like degree are designed for freedom.' (Humboldt, 'Cosmos', 1849, p368)

The move towards controlled experiments signaled an intention to use a basic methodological approach (gaining of empirical data - generally positivist and reductionist) taken by the natural sciences. The emphasis in the study of human behaviour being on psychology as 'The science of mental life', noted as a definition of psychology in William James's book 'The Principles of Psychology' 1890.

John Locke's 'Essay Concerning Human Understanding' (although philosophical in framework) and David Hartley's 1748 'Observations on Man', had helped to set psychology on a positivistic road that would lead to the mid-late nineteenth century view that the brain and nervous system was but another machine-like structure that either worked properly or malfunctioned, operating on physico-chemical principles; an approach pioneered in psychology by G.T.Fechner and Hermann Ludwig von Helmholtz. From this influential heritage came laboratory-based psychology.

In the hands of one of the first to pursue experimental psychology, William Wundt, there was a marked softening, if not a complete rejection, of the positivism of Locke and Hartley. Wundt was not prepared to have the activities of the 'mind' reduced to physico-chemical processes (in the reductionist way then understood). And, at least to an extent, Wundt was part of the reaction against positivistic psychology in company of those such as William James, Sigmund Freud, and Henri Bergson. Wundt himself went on to undertake a series of psychological experiments in the laboratory he set up in 1879. He was part of the broad movement making the understanding of psychology a respectable scientific pursuit and in taking a more humane approach to the treatment of problems associated with the mind; one assuming mental illness as being potentially treatable.

By 1900, experimental psychology had been established in laboratories at a number of European and US universities – two leading ones being the already noted of Wilhelm Wundt at Leipzig, Germany (1879) and also that of G. Stanley Hall (a student of Wundt) at John Hopkins University, in the US. A psychological laboratory was also established in 1897 at University College, London, by James

Sully, who had by then already written the first English-language text-book for psychology students, 'Outlines of Psychology' (1884). At about the same time another psychological laboratory had been established at Cambridge University. This served as a base for James Ward who was to write an article on 'Psychology' for the Encyclopedia Britannica, alerting a wider public to the current state of the developing subject. One of Ward's students, George Frederick Stout, went on to write 'A Manual of Psychology' (1899), a book that would become a standard English-language textbook of psychology for the first quarter of the twentieth century.

A generation of students (from the US and Britain, as well as other parts of Europe) trained at Wundt's laboratory; three outstanding students being E.B.Titchener who was to move to the US and make a significant contribution to experimental psychology there (he became a professor at Cornell University); Oswald Kulpe who was to develop his own version of Wundt's 'structural psychology' with his more phenomenological 'systematic experimental introspection'; the third being Emil Kraepelin, who was to go on to undertake pioneering work into schizophrenia (a term introduced by the Swiss - Eugen Bleuler (1857-1939) to replace the term 'dementia praecox'), suggesting that a key aspect of the condition involved linkages between cognitive processes and abnormalities of attention. Kraepelin also outlined an extensive system of classification for psychiatric disorders that was still in use into the 1970s.

The main work of Wundt's laboratory was undertaken by students, with each being assigned specific research tasks. Tasks involving the 'elements of consciousness' that Wundt considered to be the basic constitutive parts of the mind. He distinguished between sensations, basic feelings, and the higher mental functions involving memory, language and social products (such as religion, art, morality, and science). According to Hevern (2003) for Wundt '....the mind is a creative, dynamic, volitional force....and must be understood through an analysis of its activity'.

The Liepzig laboratory introduced measurement into the processes involving sensation. Manipulating the type, strength, and duration, of stimuli and observing, measuring, and recording in some detail the resulting responses. Investigating, amongst other things; vision, hearing, reaction times, association, memory, and attention. Wundt's 'Philosophische Studien' of 1881 was in effect, the first journal of experimental psychology.

Along with the more obviously empirical methodologies, Wundt also considered introspection to be a valid means of obtaining information on mental activities, on the 'content' of awareness. His experiments included introspection as a method and they involved obtaining information from a subject's self-observation whilst he/she was being subjected to a range of different types of sensory experience. Although the laboratory-based studies were focused on a reductive or a subjective consideration of psychology, Wundt's focus shifted later in his life to include more social psychology. In his 10 volume 'Folk Psychology' (1916) he suggested the idea of a 'social mind', one that transcends the minds of individuals, and one including sets of social processes involving collective cultural products such as language, art, morality, and religion. The study of these was undertaken by considering historical and cross-cultural information and using this to trace the ways in which the higher mental processes had developed.

Other famous laboratories included one established at the Sorbonne in 1889 and the very well equipped laboratory at the Imperial Institute of Experimental Medicine, St Petersburg. In 1890 Alfred Binet moved from the Salpetriere Hospital in Paris (where he had been working with Jean Charcot) to the Sorbonne. It was here that Binet was to undertake pioneering work in the design of standardized 'intelligence' testing. Pioneering work was also undertaken at the Imperial Institute (St Pertersburg) where Ivan Petrovich Pavlov, to some extent building on the work of Ivan M. Sechenov, was to undertake work on conditioning, and so inadvertently laying the foundations for behaviourism.

In 1892 Theodore Flournoy established a laboratory at the University of Geneva and also, in 1901 he co-founded, with Edouard Claparede, the journal 'Achives de Psychologie', In 1920 Claparede succeeded to Flourney's professorship and went on to set up an institute specifically for the study of children (the Institute Rousseau) and it would be here that Jean Piaget would succeed Clapereade as Director and go on to direct ground-breaking work in the study of the psychological development of children; their moral, logical, abstract, and concrete 'modes of thinking'.

Wundt attempted to integrate the results of the laboratory-based research into sensation and feeling with the higher mental processes, in his 'scientific metaphysics'. Wundt's experimental approach to the study of psychology (he was the first person to be called a 'psychologist') is primarily considered to have made a significant contribution to the foundations of a scientific psychology, and to the spread of this by generations of students. His theoretical psychology (and to a significant extent introspection as a 'scientific' method) did not have much influence in the twentieth century as the main focus became increasingly on cognitive aspects of psychology. Intellectually Wundt's approach reflected a blend of the psychological issues highlighted in empiricist philosophy (J.S.Mill had discussed the possibility of certain psychological experiments that Wundt would go on to design and undertake) and the study of physiology that had become typical of German universities and medical institutes. He was a prolific writer (producing over 50,000 pages) and he meticulously planned a research program extending over six decades up until his death in 1920.

Wundt's laboratory was to serve as a model for most of the psychological laboratories that were establish throughout Europe, and the US, towards the end of the nineteenth century.

Although obviously selective, we have seen that nineteenth century psychology included a number of dubious (even spurious) approaches. But these did at least help to increase public interest in this new science. More useful endeavours are apparent towards the end of the century with the spread of experimental psychology undertaken in the increasing number of laboratories and in hospitals. Then there was the take up of psychology in universities and the foundation of psychological associations, along with a number of journals and books that offer a clear marker of the maturation of a new science. Theoretically, I think that psychoanalysis[11] stands out and, whilst accepting the problems related to method and scientific rigour, it was a theory that opened up conceptions of the mind (especially the influence of unconscious processes) and one that would receive close attention throughout the twentieth century. The range of what became variations of psychoanalytic theories were ideas of how the mind works and also a source of therapeutic techniques for treating (working with) the psychologically distressed.

At the century's end we can see in place the intellectual roots from which would develop the main branches of twentieth century

---

[11] Although Freud's work on psychoanalysis began in the nineteenth century I will be covering this within the section on 20th century psychology below in order to encompass the peiod when it was most influential.

psychology - crudely put: we can see cognitive psychology coming from laboratory-based experimental psychology - psychoanalysis would generate its own diverse interpretations of Freud's basic insights - the physiological and evolutionary focus would lead to biological psychology and as the century progressed the fruitful sub-discipline of neuropsychology - the influence of psychoanalysis and individuals such as William Dilthey and Edmund Husserl, who also emphasized the importance of qualitative frameworks, would lead to an amalgam of psychoanalytic ideas and phenomenology and what would be termed person-centered (humanistic) psychology (Maurice Merleau-Ponty, Abraham Maslow and Carl Rogers) - Social psychology developed out of influences from anthropology and sociology as they offered insights into kin-relationships, other interpersonal relationships, and the dynamics of various types of social groups.

We can trace certain directions taken by psychology to the end of the nineteenth century and how these provided some basis for further development into distinct divisions into the twentieth century. Certain specific developments were important, especially in divisions such as biological and cognitive psychology where technological innovation would be significant. Advances in the pharmaceutical industry would have a dramatic impact on almost all of the divisions of the 'science of the mind'; accepting that we are now aware that human understanding and behaviour has a wider context than that simply encompassed by the concepts of the brain or mind.

Anthropology

During the Renaissance if in more of a romantic way, and continuing into the Enlightenment when the influence of rationalism and positivism were increasingly brought to bear, there was considerable interest in the nature of 'man', as seen in cultural settings. The academic disciple that soon came to further this interest was anthropology. The name was initially used in some Germany universities in the early seventeenth century for a subject area involving the study of 'man' undertaken in a more systematic way. During the eighteenth, and especially nineteenth, centuries its wide (culture-based) subject-area was eroded as early sociology and psychology carved much of their own from it.

A central, if implicit, focus for anthropology has been the

consideration of human nature, and more generally what is it? Or more specifically, to what extent is it formed by ecological and social environments, subsistence conditions, innate abilities, and socialization processes? Does it differ between identifiable groups? If so, what purpose do different social and cultural institutions serve in relation to human needs? These were the primary type of questions asked, if differently formulated and addressed by mainly 'Western European' writers from the sixteenth century onwards. Questions prompted to a considerable extent by the increasing awareness of cultural and physiological differences due to knowledge arising from expanding global trade, voyages of exploration, and a range of traveler's tales.

One non-westerner interested in cultural variation, was the Muslim Ibn Khaldun (1332-1406 – also noted above for sociology) who traveled across North Africa, taking a perceptive and scholarly interest in the peoples he encountered. He was a significant scholar who, in his book-length introduction (Al-Magaddimah) to a much longer work, covered a wide range of subjects, including history (facts, interpretation, and methodology), astronomy, chemistry, and sociology. It also covered what could fairly be described as anthropology in that it included a discussion of tribal societies, in particular the Berber tribes of the Maghreb ('Bedouin'). Ibn Khaldum highlighted the importance of culture and the cohesion fostered within Bedouin societies by 'group feeling' (Asbyiah). He also noted the role of conflict as a key factor in human history, fueled by the ongoing tensions between nomadic and settled peoples and between those living in urban or rural circumstances.

In Europe, the Enlightenment saw philosophers and social commentators debating social and physical differences, with the ideas of the 'noble savage' and man's 'natural condition' at the centre of this. Leading this debate were the French philosophers Jean Bodin and Michel de Montaigne in the 16th cent., the English philosophers Thomas Hobbs and John Locke in the 17th, along with Montesquieu, Voltaire, and Rousseau in the 18th century. All contributing to an increasing interest in human nature and its cultural expression.

Montaigne's (1533-1592) essay 'On Cannibals', introduced the idea of the 'Noble Savage'; he also drew connections between all peoples. Montaigne was precocious in highlighting the importance of the social setting to determining beliefs and practices, so in this sense an early relativist. He illustrated this by suggesting that if he had been brought up amongst cannibals he could imagine that he would find it acceptable to eat human flesh.

Montesquieu (1689-1755) in his book 'The Spirit of Laws', set out the results of a comparative study of the legal systems developed in different cultural settings, aiming to derive universal principles; with the implication that a universality seen as basic principles of legislative systems could be characteristic of a range of other social institutions. Montesquieu was an early functionalist, in that he felt that certain cultural practices such for example as: cannibalism, polygamy, and slavery, could be understood if viewed as having functional roles within a wider social context.

Rousseau drew a romantized picture of the 'noble savage', characterized by a natural innocence, and of having simple needs that are easily satisfied; it did seem that sexuality was one of the needs whose easy satisfaction in particular appealed to Rousseau. He advocated field work in the form of 'philosophical voyages' that would seek to study the diversity of human societies in relation to their differences and similarities ('according to their likenesses and their differences'). In his book 'Emile' (1762), Rousseau suggested that 'True happiness consists in deceasing the distance between our desires and our powers, in establishing a perfect equilibrium between the power and the will' - and that having this satisfying balance is the original condition of the 'natural man.' (1966, Everyman ed. p44).

This interest in man's 'natural state' was further stimulated by experiences being gained during the wide ranging travels that had been undertaken from the fifteenth century. Some more notable of the early voyages of 'discovery' included one sponsored by the Portuguese - King Henry 'The Navigator' for the exploration of the west coast of Africa; Columbus's five trips to the Americas (1492-1506); and Magellan's circumnavigation (1519-22). These and many other less ambitious journeys generated a number of books and pamphlets that, made available by a rapidly expanding printing and publishing industry, proved popular with the general reader, stimulating interest in seemingly exotic and different peoples.

Louis Antonie de Bougainville (1727-1811), French navigator and mathematician, led a naval force on a world voyage in 1766-1769. Spending some time exploring the southern Pacific Ocean and the island groups of Tahiti, Samoa, New Hebrides, Espiritu Santo (Vanuatu) then sailing north, stopping at Buru in the Moluccas and Batavia in Java before returning home. His popular account of the trip: ' A Voyage Round the World' 1772 ('*Voyage autour du monde'*

1771) fed into the debate on the value of 'man' in the natural state.

James Cook (1728-1779) - In a series of three world voyages (sponsored by the Royal Society and the Admiralty - taking in North America, Australia, New Zealand) undertaken from 1768 up to his violent death in Hawaii in 1779. Cook was not merely engaged in the disinterested tasks of map-making and of facilitating scientific endeavour on his voyage to Tahiti. In fact, he carried secret instructions from the Admiralty to undertake a reconnaissance mission of Australasia and to seize land for Britain when opportunity allowed.

During these voyages Cook meticulously carried out a range of navigational and mapmaking projects as well as taking a group of scientists - including botanists, astronomers, cartographers - to carry out scientific work. The (novel) introduction of the practice of including scientists on voyages of exploration was to be adopted as a general norm, with T.H.Huxley's presence on the voyage of 'Rattlesnake' in 1822, and Charles Darwin's presence on the voyage of the Beagle between 1831-1836, being two later examples. Also on Cook's 1772 voyage was the artist William Hodges, who painted colourful pictures depicting physically attractive and scantily clothed native women set within somewhat idealized desert island backdrops.

Harry Liebersohn suggests that, rather than just compiling a body of factual information on distant lands and people, if taken together these early exploratory journeys would be more accurately viewed as: ' .....operating within makeshift networks of knowledge spun around the world,.....'. (Liebersohn, 2003, p101). Networks out of which, when theorized and systematized, the science of anthropology would emerge.

It was from the Enlightenment period that the concept of 'culture' - to represent group-autonomous accretions of artifacts and social practices - was introduced into academic debate.

In Germany, Goethe (1749-1832) noted the holistic idea of a 'Folk' (Volk), and Herder highlighted the importance of a community's shared history in giving rise to a national character, and so a seeming empirical basis for 'national identity', that finds its expression in a language and in a body of folklore. Creating a more romantic view of group heritage rooted in some idealized shared history.

By the late eighteenth century interest was not just in more easily observable cultural behaviours and for some in physiological differences, but a small number of travelers/scholars took a closer interest in languages; their similarities, differences and possible common roots. Friedrich von Schlegel's (1772-1829) book 'On the Language and Wisdom of the Hindus' (1808) was a pioneering book on comparative language studies. He endeavoured to untangle the historical development of some of the languages of Europe and of the Indian sub-continent, and identified their shared sources in earlier Indo-European forms. This quite early indication of the importance of languages in relation to understanding cultural history would offer a fertile ground for anthropology and become the special field of linguistics.

The polymath, Alexander von Humboldt, raised the standard for careful preparation and detailed observation as he gathered and systematically recorded information mostly gained from extensive field-trips. He highlighted the influence of a range of environmental conditions and political arrangements as well as some more essential characteristics of a people's outlook; he combined the study of philology with then contemporary empirical data on native peoples. His book 'On Language' (1836) stimulated an academic interest in human language that would endure. Edward Sapir (1884-1939) progressed Humboldt's suggestion of language diversity in enlarging the range of human expressiveness - of parsing reality in conceptually complex and imaginatively novel ways - and his study of native American languages was a landmark in establishing the importance of linguistics to an overall understanding of human society and to the ways in which reality can be differently experienced (so a linguistic relativist). In his 1929 essay he noted that: 'No two languages are sufficiently similar to be considered as representing the same social reality. The worlds in which different societies live are distinct worlds, not merely the same world with different labels attached' and 'Human beings do not live in the objective world alone, nor alone in the world of social activity as ordinarily understood, but are very much at the mercy of a particular language which has become the medium of expression for their society........ The fact of the matter is that the "real world" is to a large extent unconsciously built up on the language habits of the group....We see and hear and otherwise experience very largely as we do because the language habits of our community predispose certain choices of interpretation.' (Sapir quote taken from an essay by Benjamin Lee Whorf 'The Relation of Habitual Thought and Behaviour To Language' 1939 from 'Thought Language and Reality; Selected Writings of Benjamin Lee Whorf' ed.

John B. Carroll, 1956 p134) .

Another idea associated with the foundational role of language in constructing the conceptual 'reality' experienced within any group, was suggested by Lucian Levy-Bruhl (1857-1939). He assumed that pre-literate groups do not think in the same way as literate groups. That their modes of thinking are qualitatively different in that their thinking is associative and poetical rather than more logically consistent (used as an assumed ideal in the West). If accepted, this type of suggestion opens up a whole series of challenges for 'western' anthropologists to adequately re-present - making field research more of an encounter seeking conceptual connections, rather than some process of positivistic observation. The challenge being to gain access to the experiential world of pre-literate societies in ways that are sensitive and empathic (non-judgmental). Access to the meanings that infuse the frame-works of psychological orientation within which groups experience their worlds.

Throughout the 18th and 19th centuries foreign lands were (enthusiastically) 'trawled through' to gain anthropological materials from surviving pre-literate groups; the Americas, Africa, Australasia, and the Pacific Islands, proving to be rich in such bounty. Materials used to support national and personal collections of artifacts and documentary records (ethnographic collections) on native peoples were built up, especially in France, Germany, Britain, and America.

Nineteenth century anthropology could be characterized by two main tendencies, or rather two perspectives on comparative difference; one being physiological the other cultural.

The physiological can be identified in the work of Johann Casper Levatar (1741-1801) who based his 'science of physiognomy' on facial characteristics and other aspects of physiology. Johann Friedrich Blumenbach (1752-1840) - compiled a significant collection of skulls mainly obtained during his travels. In his book 'On the Natural Variety of Man' (1775) he set out five types: Caucasion, American, Ethiopian, Mongolian, and Malaysian. Blumenbach linked the varying physiological characteristics to differences in environment, especially climate. It does seem that Blumenbach was not intending to identify separate racial classifications, but rather just to explain the reasons for physiological differences within an overall unity of humankind, along with a common ancestor origin. Some of those supporting a physiological approach used evolutionary ideas as justification for categorizing peoples according to 'race', making a consequent assumption that cultural variation reflected racial differences; and a separate biological ancestry. This did not apply to Blumenbach, who actively opposed ideas related to western cultural superiority and emphasized that the 'negro' was as capable and intelligent as any westerner, and that humankind was a single species.

Some primary theoretical ideas that emerged during the nineteenth century were:

- Early on researchers such as Lewis Henry Morgan (1818-1882) focused on kinship as a principle social structure with which to understand any society. Morgan made a distinction between classificatory and descriptive kinship.

- Ideas on social evolution were suggested by Herbert Spencer, and the biological evolutionary theory of Charles Darwin, being taken up by some anthropologists. As well as offering some spurious legitimation for explicit exploitation and the more implicit forms of paternalism. At worst this was the disreputable search for some 'missing link' and of casting primitive societies as sub-human. More usefully, the implications of evolution offered a wide-ranging (diachronic) explanatory framework for human individual and collective behaviour.

- Whilst as early as the eighteenth century, there had been some primacy given to the influence on the means of subsistence of a society being studied (structures and institutions) by writers such as Rousseau and Turgot (1727-78), it was Karl Marx who provided a more determinate (and universal) theoretical framework for this approach. A focus on subsistence was to be an analytic perspective given primacy by many anthropologists not least, Burnett Tyler (1832-1917), who was the first British professor of anthropology (1896 at Oxford). His landmark book 'Primitive Cultures' (1871) was a clear example of combining evolutionary ideas with a more Marxist emphasis on material conditions for understanding any culture.

- The diffusionist approach, such as that taken by Friedrich von Schlegel (1772-1829), offered a challenge to the cultural relativists in that he questioned the 'historical purity' of seemingly autonomous cultures. Instead, von Schlegel suggested that cultural traits (especially those involving technological innovations) could migrate between groups. He especially identified language as a key potential marker of cultural diffusion. It was Schlegel who (as noted above), around 1800, introduced the term 'Indo-European' to encompass a number of Asian and European languages that were suggested to share ancestral roots. His book 'On the Language and Wisdom of the

Hindus' (1808) along with his other work made a significant contribution to establishing 'comparative linguistics' – according to Eriksen and Nielsen (sec. ed. 2013, p27) Schlegel's '.....success in untangling the history of the Indo-European languages was almost as sensational at the time as Darwin's evolutionism'.

- James George Frazer's (1854 - 1941) book 'The Golden Bough: a study in magic and religion' (1890 - a 'final edition' in 1915) with its detailed (if rather drawn out) consideration of pre-literate societies in terms of conceptualized beliefs such as: magic, taboos, divinities, corn-spirits, myths, rituals, along with the identification of some 'eternal soul' inherent in plants, animals, and immaterial things. Frazer suggested a successional 'three-stage' model of cultural evolution: magical - religious - scientific.

Frazer's longish book is a veritable cornucopia of detailed information on primitive societies. His multi-cultural, throughout touching on the spiritual, descriptive anthropological journey from 'Nemi back to Nemi', offers some illuminating insights into the collective primitive psyche. Towards the end of the book he, in effect, issues a challenge to those that follow when he writes: 'We are at the end of our enquiry, but as often happens in the search after truth, if we have answered one question, we have raised many more; if we have followed one track home, we have had to pass by others that opened off it and led, or seemed to lead, to far other goals than the sacred grove at Nemi.'

Frazer's work had considerable influence on stimulating individual students of anthropology rather than on the direction taken by anthropology as a science. Darwin's evolutionary theory offered a biological authority for the idea of progressive developmental stages suggested by a number of social scientists including Frazer and Comte de Gobineau. Gobineau outlined a hierarchy of human races, predictably placing white Europeans at the top and the black races at the bottom.

Ideas about how human groups might have developed in stages

ranging from 'primitive to civilized' had been a central feature of anthropological debate for some time. It was Charles Darwin's evidence-based evolutionary theory that brought the debate about 'group' evolution (and indeed scientific racism) to the fore. A debate provided with more colour by Alfred Russell Wallace, the co-orginator with Darwin of the theory of natural selection, and professional collector of exotic fauna and flora sent back to England from various far flung locations (including Malaysia and South America - he charted the Rio Negro the largest tributary of the Amazon River system) along with sets of lively notes on the peoples he encountered on his travels. His book 'The Malay Archipelago' (1869) was widely read by both general readers and academics.

- Another theoretical perspective that endured well into the twentieth century was that of 'functionalism' - the application to any society of an interpretative framework that considers social institutions and practices in relation to the contribution they were assessed to be making to the overall cohesiveness of any society; an approach that allowed for the labeling of seeming disruptive institutions and practices as 'dysfunctional'. Whilst a number of anthropologists were to some extent applying this type of approach earlier in the nineteenth century it was Emile Durkheim who gave functionalism a much more developed methodology Durkheim (1858-1917), the first social scientist in France to be appointed to an academic position, was the main influence, on French sociology and anthropology, during the later 19th and the first half of the 20th century. His structural functionalism (or versions of this) would serve as a primary theoretical framework applied by some anthropologists to data generated during their fieldwork. The book 'Primitive Classification' (1903), co-written by Durkheim and Marcel Mauss, rejected the idea of primitive societies being 'survivals' from the past, or their being but stages on a developmental path progressing towards civilization; with the implication that each autonomous society should be considered in terms of its own historical and cultural context. Durkheim's, framework for understanding any society was based on considering patterns of relationships, the organization of formal and informal institutions, the knowledge systems, and some other aspects of a culture (cultural 'facts') in terms of their origins and how they operate to maintain social cohesion; in their contribution to how any society functions (to the social force of 'solidarity').

In relation to theory, Thomas Eriksen and Finn Nielsen (sec. ed. 2013) suggest a line of intellectual development extending through ideas provided by: Kant, Hegel, Marx, Durkheim, and Weber, that would offer a conceptually rich and theoretically fertile resource for working anthropologists to draw on. But Durkheim (in varieties of functionalism become structural-functionalism) was probably the most significant theoretical influence on anthropology (and indeed sociology) during the later nineteenth century and continued to have varying degrees of influence well into the twentieth.

It was by the mid nineteenth century that anthropology had matured into an identifiable academic discipline; or rather became more systematic and institutionalized.

The foundations of the Societé Ethnologique de Paris (1839) and the Ethnological Society of London (1843) mark this intellectually more autonomous stage reached by the study of discrete groups of human-beings, with an emphasis on cultural settings.

In Britain Alfred Radcliffe-Brown (1881-1955), along with Bronislaw Malinowski (1884-1942), were at the forefront of establishing anthropology as a leading social science. Radcliffe-Brown's theoretical approach echoed Durkheim's but he placed more of an emphasis on a positivist methodology. He considered how the institutional and cultural framework of any society influences social behaviours. Describing a model of any society in terms of interconnected systems and subsystems operating in social institutions such as the family, arrangements for conflict resolution, and property rights. All having a functional role in maintaining social cohesion.

Edward Burnett Tylor (1832-1917) was appointed the first British professor of anthropology at Oxford in 1896. Like Morgan, Tyler was another 'cultural evolutionist', but rather than focus on kinship (as did Morgan) he emphasized the primacy of material conditions and used certain cultural traits that seem to have no specific social function as markers of development. Suggesting that most of these residual cultural traits would once have had useful social functions, but that the process of evolutionary social development has left them as vestiges of a society's past; but consideration of these can provide useful information on any group's past beliefs and practices. The first edition (1857) of Tylor's 'Notes and Queries on Anthropology', became the primary authoritative British book on fieldwork.

In his later book 'Primitive Culture' (1871) Tylor offered a definition of culture that was used as a 'touchstone' definition for decades to come, it ran: 'Culture, or civilization, taken in its broad, ethnographic sense, is that complex whole which included knowledge, belief, art, morals, law, custom, and any other capabilities and habits acquired by man as a member of society' (Tylor 1871: from Eriksen and Nielsen sec. ed. 2013, p31)

From about mid-nineteenth century it was academics based in America who took to the social sciences, and anthropology in particular, enjoying steady progress with their work. This was a continent whose native peoples were undergoing rapid and disruptive change, as tribal peoples endeavoured to defend their cultural heritage against the impact of the relentless erosion of their traditional lands (and pressure of rapid/disruptive change on cultural beliefs and practices) by the westward expansion of modern European cultures.

Two individual anthropologists, Henry Morgan and Franz Boas, stand out as setting the direction for late 19th and early 20th century American anthropology.

Morgan (1818-1881) was at the forefront of anthropologists who were aware of the urgent need to record societies that were under intense pressure to change. He took a close personal interest in the groups that he studied, showing an unusual level of empathy with their plight; he campaigned for political rights for Native Americans. Methodologically, he pioneered direct field-work (based on participant observation) and, in the 1840s, lived for extended periods with Iroquois tribal groups; he was adopted into a clan and given the name 'Tayadaowuhkuh' ('he who builds bridges').

Morgan systematically documented the cultural beliefs and related patterns of behaviour of these groups, compiling a body of data from which useful theories could be drawn. So making a significant contribution to supplying theoretical frameworks that he considered to be appropriate for understanding the often complex relationships, social behaviours, political institutions (of governance), myths, religious beliefs, and material artifacts, together producing the intricate social matrix connecting people to each other and to their group's cultural heritage.

One methodological innovation was Morgan's drawing a distinction between classification and description; crudely... classification related to biological kinship (e.g. parent-child), and description related to non-biological kinship relationships (e.g. in-laws). In his 'Ancient Society' (1877) he attempted a synthesis of his work, with a focus on kinship networks. Morgan made kinship a central theme of a large-scale comparative study of Native American tribal groups. His academic authority and intellectual integrity was a strong influence on later socials scientists. Karl Marx and Friedrich Engels in particular were impressed by Morgan's theories and his influence can be seen throughout Engel's book 'The Origins of the Family, Private Property and the State' (1884). Indeed the final Chapter ('Barbarism and Civilization') ends with a longish, if rather ideological, quote from Morgan.

Franz Boas (1858-1942) was appointed a professor at Columbia University in 1899, a position held until his death in 1942. Boas is credited with being the founder of American anthropology as a modern science, he was a leading advocate of the cultural relativist school. A school that placed an emphasis on systematic data collection, and throughout his work he highlighted the complexity and creativity of primitive cultures; using Native Americans as a rich source of supporting evidence. He was a determined critic of racism and made a significant contribution to undermining the turn of the century residue of nineteenth century academic racism inherent in a certain imperialist approach. Boas considered that such was the 'width' of the subject-matter of anthropology (the science of 'man') that it would be better managed if divided into four separate but interrelated 'fields', those of: linguistics, physical anthropology, archaeology, and cultural anthropology. Even if at times he himself attempted to progress an overview of all four, if with mostly a cultural bias. Boas had an enduring impact on American anthropology well into the twentieth century, to the extent that the concept of, a 'Boasian approach' became accepted, and respected, terminology within the discipline.

Like the other social sciences, anthropology identified its particular field of study. If a science characterized more by controversy and methodological division than most of the others. Its leading individuals produced a set of theoretical ideas and of data collection methodologies during the nineteenth century that laid down a rich source of information on human groups that would be significantly improved upon during the twentieth.

By the end of the nineteenth century the social sciences of sociology, psychology, and anthropology (along with history and economics) were considered to be respectable academic disciplines and courses in each of them were on offer in universities in the industrialized countries of Europe and in the USA.

If there was to be a genuine science of humankind whose subject matter was at both individual and social levels, it would involve an intermixing of insights gained from all of the social sciences; to what extent of each being determined by the primary purpose of any investigation and the initially perceived nature of any circumscribed social phenomenon. With the recognition of the potential bias of a social scientist especially in acknowledging that the act of circumscription itself straightway introduces a synthetic dividing off; if one useful for gaining knowledge.

I have endeavoured a somewhat more detailed overview of the development of just the three social science disciplines of sociology, psychology, and anthropology, their being leading examples of attempts to apply investigative and analytic methods pioneered in the natural sciences to human individuals, social institutions, culture, as well as kin and interactive social relationships. It is clear that these were but three of a number of social sciences emerging as separate disciplines during the nineteenth century. As a discipline economics preceded the other social sciences in that it had been undertaken using theoretical frameworks, observation and increasingly more statistical information, from the seventeenth century; if by 'nominally amateur' economists. And history had been an intellectual interest from the earliest times of civil life, and the 'recorded' (in texts, oral traditions, surviving buildings and ruins of others, grave-goods, etc.) historical experience of humankind, has been selectively drawn on by many writers, including those covering a range of subject-matter within the social sciences, to support and illustrate arguments and assertions. The extent to which it has been necessary to consider any historical foundations (and indeed how to interpret the relevance of any assumed 'history') of a particular social phenomenon has been hotly contested academic terrain, at least since the Enlightenment. Bearing in mind that today's written 'histories' are invariably massively reduced, very partial, serially edited, interpretations of the past. Fractured slivers of the past torn from lived and invariably complex contexts and re-presented by those undertaking the recording, of selecting materials, introducing emphasis and outlining implications. That's not to diminish the potential of history to inform understanding of current phenomena just some observations on the grounds for necessary circumspection.

Medicine

As well as advances in the sciences and the interactive and progressive coming together of science with technology as applied to the manufacturing, power generation, communication, transport, and warfare, 'industries', advances were also made in the field of medicine.

The difference between a sense of physical and psychological well-being and the causes of its absence - 'ill-health' - has long been a central aspect of humankind's collective life. Evidence from prehistory suggests that early on people were aware of the medicinal qualities of certain herbs, other plants, and aspects of lifestyle. Folk medicine and the accompanying 'magical' incantations, along with other traditional practices, were part of the sorcerer/shaman/medicine 'mans' art, and this became an important aspect of cultural practice as city-life developed (circa 3000 BCE).

If we count childbirth as a medical event - perhaps excusable given the risks involved prior to modern medicine - then 'midwives' have long been applying their experience and traditional treatments to managing birthing.

Common conditions such as colds, constipation, headaches, would have been treated by practitioners with more or less care, no doubt depending on the social status of the patient. A common belief was that serious or long-standing illness (and especially mental health problems) was due to possession by an evil spirit or to having offended the gods – or that some malevolent or even just mischievous spiritual being had stolen, or otherwise interfered with, a person's soul. A range of methods could be employed to seek relief: prayer, incantations, sacrifices, payment to a priestly caste and similar. The primary aim of any treatment being to entice the soul back into the patient's body. The practice of trepanning (drilling a hole in the skull) has been identified in skulls dating back to pre-historic times and is thought to have been an aspect of this 'cure', allowing an easy route for the soul to pass back into a body. From the early written records we know that there has been a general recognition that a nutritious diet, relatively good personal hygiene, and keeping away from infected individuals, are all important in the avoidance of sickness. Any serious illness was understood to be a problem with the whole person (holistic) rather than a condition located here or there in the body.

For the early civilizations of Babylonia and Egypt (circa 3000 BCE) a range of medical practices were recorded – spells, incantations and prayer, and sacrifices, still formed a significant part of the medical 'man's' toolkit but we also have lists of possible remedies often matched to specific conditions, and a number of surgical techniques being practiced. We can even identify one notable Egyptian physician 'Imhotep' (active 2980-2900 BCE). And for Babylonia, there were laws set out in the Code of Hammurabi (1790 BCE) that apply specifically to medical practice.

For Indian civilization, the holy Hindu texts, the Vedas, note a god of medicine 'Dhanvantari'. To whom supplications and payers was thought to contribute to a restoration of a believer's well-being. During the long period 800 BCE – 1000 CE Indian medicine flourished and became fully integrated into cultural practices; there is even some evidence that inoculation against small-pox was practiced. One aspect of Indian medicine that would today be considered a barrier to advance was the Hindu inhibition on the dissection of bodies. Although later on some limited knowledge of anatomy was gained by the practice of immersing a body in water for seven days by which time the state of the body allowed it to be more easily pulled apart and so avoiding the need to cut.

With early Indian and Greek medicine we begin to see bodily functions being understood in terms of ideas about elemental substances. For Indians it was spirit, phlegm and bile, for the Greeks the 'humours'; these substances were required to be in a 'natural' balance in order to maintain health, with any imbalance being the underlying cause of illness.

Towards the end of this long fertile period for medical advance Indian physicians such as Caraka and Susruta could between them identify 1,120 diseases and over 750 medicinal plants. Animal parts (milk, ground bones, and even gallstones) and certain minerals (e.g. gold, copper, sulphate, and arsenic) were also involved in the extensive pharmacological armoury of physicians. At some point the Hindu inhibition to cutting the body was overcome and surgery was practiced for such conditions as tumours, abscesses, amputations, bladder stones, removing foreign bodies, and even some plastic surgery; using healthy tissue to graft in the place of damaged tissue. Susruta lists the surgeon's tools as including 20 sharp (a range of knives, sharp probes, scissors) and 101 blunt instruments (tubes, hooks, blunt probes) – mostly made of steel.

From 800 BCE to at least 1000 CE, Indian physicians were in the vanguard in terms of advance towards the 'medical (science-based) model' of health-care. But the intellectual roots of the western medical model lies more with the Greeks and to some extent the Romans. These in turn had been able to benefit from advances made in Babylon, Egypt and to some extent even from some influences gained from early contacts with India and China. In the early Greek 'heroic' texts, the Iliad and the Odyssey, we see references to military surgeons. Basic surgery and various types of emergency treatment must surely have long been an aspect of the gruesome activity of warfare.

The Greeks had a god of medicine in Asclepius who might have been modeled upon a real man who lived about 1200 BCE. A man reported to have 'performed miracles'. In the early 1st millennium BCE there were hospitals (more spas) in places such as Athens and the island of Cos. Where therapeutic treatment was based on gentle exercise, diet and bathing. There was also a healing ritual to be followed that included sleeping within a dormitory located in a temple so that the patient could be visited by Asclepius (or one of his priests) who would offer advice. In the fifth century BCE Empedocles suggested that the 'universe' was composed of mixtures of four elements: Fire, Water, Earth and Air and that there were four bodily humours: phlegm, blood, choler (yellow bile), melancholy (black bile). Good health being dependent on maintaining harmony between these humours.

A significant advance was made by the renowned Hippocrates where we can note a move away from reliance on many of the magical rituals and incantations with which medicine had been infused. Hippocrates was born in 460 BCE and he is credited with the authorship of a number of medical texts making up the 'Hippocratic Collection'. In these we see a more rational approach being taken, one based on careful observation and learning from experience (a general characteristic of Greek 'science' of this time). Hippocrates rejected the idea that illnesses were caused by some disfavour of the gods being visited on an individual and instead suggested that the causes of diseases were external and related to environmental factors such as a person's occupation, their diet, and even the climate they were exposed too. He applied a reasoned approach to diagnosis, prognosis, and the treatment of illness.

Hippocrates is known for the 'Hippocratic Oath', intended to guide the behaviour of physicians towards patients in terms of ethical standards. The oath includes guidance on such aspects of a physician's work as: patient confidentiality, commitment not to take sexual advantages, and to not assist in procuring abortions. Hippocrates also offered the much used but still relevant epigram on the art of medicine: 'Life is short, and art long, opportunity fleeting, experiment dangerous, judgment difficult'.

As with most areas of humankind's early intellectual advance, we see the involvement of Aristotle in informing the development of medicine. His work on anatomy, embryology, and biology more generally, laid the foundations for a focus on actual living processes. An approach to medicine that continued in the work of Herophilus (anatomy) and Erasistratus (physiology). In 300 BCE there was a renowned school of medicine in the City of Alexandra. A number of books on medical subjects were produced by Roman physicians included 'De Medicine' by Aulus Cornelius Celsus circa 30 CE., a book that was still being used by physicians down to the sixteenth century.

Mental health was not neglected and, once it was accepted that this was not the (deserved) result of possession by demons, or similar simplistic causative ideas held by early pre and many 'civil' peoples, it was included within the general area of medicine. Asclepiades of Bithynia (born 124 BCE) took a relatively enlightened view of mental ill-health. He recommended that the mentally ill be released from the common 'treatment' of imprisonment and instead he advocated a treatment regime that included creating a relaxed environment (involving the use of alcohol as a relaxant), work as therapy, and physical exercise. The latter in the belief that it would improve attention and memory – a view shared today as an aspect of treatment for most degenerative cognitive conditions such as the dementias that a proportion of the elderly are prone to.

An, at least initial, understanding of the history of medicine can be gained by highlighting the contribution made by outstanding individuals. An example being the Roman physician Galen, whose specialism was physiology. He made a number of significant contributions to this branch of medicine, not least in his identifying that blood rather than air flowed in the arteries and he suggested that that the motion involved in this flow was caused by heat. Galen was a keen advocate of the idea of humours (Greeks) and how these related to the maintenance of good-health. He carried out a great deal of investigative work at first hand, overcoming the Roman legal prevention on dissection of humans by working on apes and pigs. Just as the legacy of Aristotle was both a stimulus and later an impediment to advance in the sciences so too Galen gained a level of authority that would make it difficult to challenge his ideas.

As we are now aware, the treatment of illness might save individual lives and indeed wide-spread inoculation and certain medical practices (such as the uses of antibiotics for infection and antiseptics in surgery) can improve the outlook for large numbers – but really significant sources of good health are measures related to personal and communal hygiene and this is an area to which the Romans made a significant contribution, not just in terms of their technical work – heating of houses, bathing, gymnasiums, water and sewerage systems - but also a recognition that government had a responsibility for public works that contributed to the health and comfort of a population. Roman armies were accompanied by medical officers ensuring that a certain basic level of care was available; if perhaps more in recognition of the contribution this would make to its military effectiveness than out of humanitarian concerns

At the time of Roman advance in medical knowledge and practice, China and other parts of the Far East had also been developing Hippocrate's 'art' of medicine. There is a record of a physician, Fu His, working as early as 2953 BCE. And slightly later on Huang Ti complied the definitive book of Chinese medicine 'Nei Ching' and this, plus to a lesser extent the books 'Mo Ching' (written anonymously circa 300 CE) and 'Golden Mirror' (written 1739 CE), would form the collective body of Chinese medical wisdom; still popular in Chinese communities across the world today. The 'Golden Mirror' was an ambitious project, began with the Qianlong Emperor commissioning Wu Qian to lead a team of about 80 medical practitioners to travel across China seeking out as much information on medicine as possible. From what was a massive body of medical knowledge Wu Qian selected what was assessed to be the most useful, then including the most effective treatments in this landmark treatise.

Again, as with the medicine of other civilizations, for China's we have the idea of a balance of abstract substances; with Chinese medicine it is Ying and Yang and the five basic bodily elements – Ying being the passive female principle, Yang the active male principle, both needing to be in balance for good health; the five bodily elements being: wood, water, fire, earth, and metal. As with Indian, so too early Chinese medicine was inhibited by religious objections to cutting the body, mitigating against gaining more direct knowledge of anatomy. The pulse was used as a diagnostic tool (a procedure taking upwards of 10 minutes using all six sites on the body where a pulse can be taken) to identify obstructions to the channels through which the Yin and Yang flow; complimentary to this was the idea of a continuous circular flow of blood. The sources of medicine were a wide range of minerals, plants, and animal body parts. The 52 volumes of 'Great Pharmacopoeia' (complied by Li Shih-chen in 1552-78 CE) refers to the medical properties of over 1000 herbs and is still used down to today.

Traditional Chinese medicine offers an alternative throughout much of the world and is at times used as a complimentary option to the medical model; and some of its long-known treatments have also contributed to modern medical practice. This includes the use of iron to treat anemia, reserpine (from the Ranwolfa plant) for high blood pressure, castor oil for constipation, kaolin for diarrhea, and ginseng and cannabis for a range of complaints. The Chinese practice of acupuncture has a recorded history of use back to 2,500 BCE.

Historically, Japanese medicine has been strongly influenced by the approaches taken by its neighbour and Japanese medical students travelled to China to learn more at first hand. The 30 volume Ishino (complied 984 CE) is the oldest Japanese medical book and although there is a traditional Japanese focus on the organs of the body the book also shows the extent of the influence of Chinese medicine. And the later (1570 CE) 15 volume work by Menase Dosan, a series of further works by this author, along with the books of Nagata Tokuhun (written circa. 1585-1611 CE), form the body of the Japanese derivation of Chinese medicine. A deeper study than I have been able to undertake of the interconnection between Chinese and Japanese medicine would I suspect show much more of a two-way flow of ideas. For both we also have a conception of natural forces operating within the body, forces that require support by the trained physician.

Similar to India and China, Japan would also from about mid sixteenth century begin to be influenced by western medicine. The Portuguese established a hospital (for the treatment of 'lepers and the poor') in Funai, Japan, and a few Japanese physicians travelled to Europe to exchange knowledge with European physicians. The Dutch, who had established a trading colony in Japan from the early seventeenth century, also taught European medical practices to the Japanese, with some European medical works being translated into Japanese.

European medical ideas and practices continued to influence Chinese and Japanese medicine, as also in other parts of the Far-East, including India and to a lesser extent Indonesia. Throughout the nineteenth century, accepting periods of anti-western reaction, western medicine was being absorbed into Japanese medical practice. In 1857 a medical centre was established in Edo by a small group of physicians that had been trained in Europe. Three years later this centre was taken over by the government and became attached to the Imperial University of Tokyo. Western medicine only had a relatively modest influence on Chinese practices but the Japanese found a more easy accommodation with foreign ideas. Indeed, towards the end of the nineteenth century, Japanese medical researchers made a number of original contributions to the advance of medicine including: – 1894 discovery of the plague bacillus, 1897 discovery of the dysentery bacillus, 1901 isolation of a crystalline form of adrenaline.

Coming back to the Mediterranean region, at its peak the Muslim Empire ruled over lands from Spain in the west across to Persia and northern India in the east. And although no notable achievements were recorded down to the early medieval period it is clear that the art of medicine was being practiced and knowledge gained by Arabic physicians.[12] There are a number of Arabic physicians who stand out, including the Persians Razes (al-Razi – 865-925 CE) and Avicenna (Ibn sina – 980-1037 CE). Rhazes wrote a wide-ranging medical text-book 'A Treatise on the Smallpox and the Measles'; he also wrote a landmark medical monograph on these two diseases. About 100 years later the polymath Avicenna wrote 'The Canon of Medicine' which was a five volume encyclopedia outlining an extensive overview of Arabic medical knowledge, a text still on the curriculum of Montpelier medical school as late as 1650 CE. Arabic physicians benefited from a body of knowledge of chemistry available within the Arab world – including distillation and sublimation and how these, and other, processes could be used to extract and prepare healing constituents of plants and minerals. A medical first for the Muslim world was the writing by Abu al-Qasim of Cordoba, Spain, of the first

---

[12] These would have included Christians and Jewish physicians at times when religions other than Islam were tolerated – which was most of the time.

book on surgery to contain illustrations. Within the Muslim Empire the Jewish Maimonides (c 12th century), philosopher and one time physician to the Saracen leader Saladin, made useful contributions to the debate on ethics in relation to medical practice.

Officially the Christian Church interpreted sickness as punishment for sin and looked to the miraculous intervention of various saints who were each identified with particular conditions: St. Apollonia (teeth) St Lucia (eyes) St Roch (plague) etc. But in practice there were centres where the needs of the sick were carefully administered too. Perhaps the most significant contribution was made by the Nestorians (followers of a form of Christianity, based in Persia) whose scholars translated a range of important Greek medical texts into Arabic.

By the thirteenth century physicians as a body were becoming more respectable and the training more organized and formalized. The famous medical school of Salerno (the first in Europe) was, in 1221, given the monopoly by the Holy Roman Emperor Fredrick II on approving those who wished to practice medicine within the Empire.

As the medieval period was giving way to the Renaissance (12/13th century) western medicine was still very much based on the foundation of a Greek/Roman inheritance. But a focus on observation and experiment had been overlaid on this by Arabic, Jewish, and European scholars; constituting a body of knowledge and practices that would strongly influence the next stage in the development of medical science.

During the time of the Renaissance the advance of European medicine benefited from the degree of intellectual freedom enjoyed more generally in science, the arts, and for religious beliefs. Roger Bacon in England helped to prepare the ground for change with his enthusiastic and well-presented support for systematic observation and for experimental methods. In 1316 Mondino du Luzzi published the first manual of anatomy, a work informed by his own hands-on approach to dissection and examination. Around the same time Guy de Chauliac published 'Great Surgery'. Both of these works would serve as manuals to guide the practice of Western medicine during the Renaissance. This was a time when a more practical, experimental, approach to advancing understanding achieved numerous relatively small additions to the accumulating body of medical knowledge. But of perhaps more longer-term importance, medical schools and hospitals (most connected to various religious groups), were being established across much of 'civil' Europe, and in parts of the Middle and Far East where Western influence was spreading.

One, perhaps the, outstanding figure of sixteenth century medicine was Andreas Vesalis who, as Professor of Anatomy at Padua University, in 1543 published 'On the Fabric of the Human Body', a work in which he systematically challenged many of the views of Galen; a process of the modernization of medicine followed up by a number of Vesalis's contemporaries. In 1604 Hieronymus Fabricius ab Aquapendente carried out a detailed study of the valves in the veins of the body. He taught students by dissecting bodies in his anatomical theatre in Padua. Another significant advance in the understanding of how the body functions was made by William Harvey in his book 'An Anatomical Experiment Concerning the Movement of the Heart and Blood in Animals' pub. 1628. Harvey (who had studied in England and Italy), with the support of evidence derived from a series of experiments, was able to show that instead of the blood moving in an ebb and flow manner as suggested by Galen it did in fact circulate round the body. From this time Galen became more a respected figure in the history of medicine rather than a voice of contemporary authority.

The administration of 'drugs' began to be based on raw chemicals rather than plant materials as the former were being extracted from the latter, soon to be synthesized in early medical 'laboratories'. The somewhat enigmatic Phillipus Aureolus Paracelsus made a number of improvements in the prescribing of drugs and the use of chemicals as drugs replacing traditional 'remedies', in doing so allowing much better control of more refined dosages.

The sixteenth century saw a change in European medicine as many of what had mostly been schools of general medicine became schools (or separate departments within schools) based upon medical specialisms. In 1518 'The College of Physicians of London' gained a Royal charter and the right to license physicians to work in the London area; a marker of the institutional advance towards 'modern' medicine.

In Britain the barber-surgeon was giving way to the profession of physician-surgeon with the fear of the former being gradually replaced by respect for the latter. This transition can be marked by the change in the name of the 'Barber Surgeons Company' - that had been granted a Royal Charter (Henry VIII) in 1540 to - as British surgery caught up with surgical advances made in France, Germany, and Italy

- become in 1745 the 'Company of Surgeons', and then in 1800 the 'Royal College of Surgeons'. During the 200 years between the change of name incremental progress had been made in the training and practice of surgery, and in an understanding of the 'mechanisms' of the physical body. The positivistic approach this fostered was a strong influence on the way surgery, and indeed western medicine, developed across most of Europe and the United States during the nineteenth century.

In the eighteenth century medical training continued to become more formal, with major cities in Europe opening schools of medicine offering a curriculum based on a study of botany, chemistry, and a more systematic approach applied to anatomy, surgery and patient care. This approach was pioneered in continental Europe and gradually taken up in Britain by individuals such as John Munro (ex-army surgeon), William Cheselden (surgery), Percivall Pott (obsectrics). Amongst a group of outstanding practitioners were John Hunter, a researcher who made a significant contribution to the study of physiology and to the status of surgery and William Smellie whose book 'Treatise on the Theory and Practice of Midwifery' (three vols. pub 1752-64) outlined the views, gained from practical experience, of an individual who had established obstetrics as a scientific discipline similar to other branches of medicine. Smellie, who trained at Edinburgh in surgery and pharmacy (and had also studied midwifery in France), favoured natural birth methods and saw surgical interventions as a last resort, to be used only in circumstances where the mother's life was at serious risk. He provided his services free to poor women on condition that they allowed Smellie's students to be present at the birth – thus advancing the practical aspects of training for obstetricians. I understand that there is a birth method (used for 'breach' i.e. head last, births) still used down to today named after him.

Another area of medical advance, informing others, was the application of a more scientific approach to military medicine. Sir John Pringle who, as one time Physician-General to the British Army, had done a great deal to understand, alleviate, and make public, a range of diseases common to military service – his book 'Treatise on Diseases of the Army', along with scientific papers on such subjects as antiseptics and hospital fevers, was presented to the Royal Society. At the Battle of Deltingen 1743 (during the war of Austrian Succession) Pringle suggested that each side should have military hospitals and that these should be regarded as safe sanctuaries. An originating idea of what was, about 100 years later, to be institutionalized in the International Committee of the Red Cross. The formation of the actual organization must be credited to Henry Dunant who, horrified by the slaughter, and later the deaths of the wounded, on the Battle-field of Solferino in 1859, proposed the setting up of a humanitarian organization which was established at Geneva in 1863 as the International Committee of the Red Cross. The recognition of a special (non-combatant) status for medical personnel and victims of conflict was incorporated into the first Geneva Convention in 1864.

Anton van Leeuwenhoek (Delft, 1632-1723) was a skilled maker of lenses and an observant user of the microscopes he constructed. He presented a description of microscopic organisms ('animalcules' – what we now know as bacteria) that he observed in a prepared sample of plaque scrapped from his own teeth, to The Royal Society of London. The power of the microscope could obviously be seen in Robert Hooke's book 'Micrographica' (1665). A collection of remarkably clear diagrams of tiny organisms, including the troublesome flea; a book in which the word 'cell' is first used as a biological term. The discovery in the eighteenth century that tiny organisms carried diseases and could cause infection in open wounds, was a landmark advance; one that changed the focus of pathology and influenced how surgery was to be carried out. This original work helped to provide knowledge that would later lead to the development of 'germ theory'.

In 1847 the Viennese Doctor Ignaz Semmelweis observed that a colleague had died from puerperal sepsis following his dissecting the body of a woman who had died from fever; a procedure during which he had inadvertently cut his finger. Semmelweis realized that doctors, nurses, and medical students, were carrying infection from one patient to others and he recommended the simple measure of hand washing between attending to patients. A measure that led to a marked reduction in deaths by puerperal sepsis in his hospital.

The understanding of 'germ theory' was developed further during the nineteenth century by Joseph Lister, Professor of Surgery at Glasgow University, who suggested that it was microscopic organisms ('microbes' rather than Leeuwenhoek's 'animalcules'), carried in the air, that caused infections to spread throughout hospitals. He introduced an antiseptic carbolic acid solution to be used in the dressing of wounds, in the washing of surgeons' hands, and in the preparation of surgical instruments. He even devised a machine that would release a fine mist of dilute carbolic acid into the air where an operation was being performed. As Semmelweis had earlier found when introducing fairly simple hygiene measures, infections such as puerperal sepsis, were reduced. Lister also noted a significant reduction in deaths in hospitals from infections such as gangrene.

Governments in the industrializing countries were increasingly taking a more active role in at least some aspects of the provision of a healthier environment in terms of water supply, and sewerage and other waste disposal. As well as more obvious motivators such as preventing the spread of diseases that debilitated populations, there was also urging from the more enlightened sections of the medical profession. In 1779 Johann Frank published his 'System of a Complete Medical Policy'; Frank was one of a growing number of physicians arguing for government responsibilities for public health. In the eighteenth century we also see the medical profession taking a closer interest in occupational diseases. Early in the same century Bernardino Ramazzini had written the book 'On the Diseases of Artificers' in which he suggested headaches as an occupational condition and also described the condition of 'writers cramp'; along with the more obvious lead poisoning being suffered by potters and painters.

The practice of vaccination (inducing a mild form of a disease in order to stimulate a defensive response from an individual's own immune system) had been used for some time in parts of the Middle-East. The unconventional traveler, Mary Wortley Montague (1689-1762), is credited with introducing the technique into England on her return from a trip to Turkey in 1721. A trip during which she had observed the practice of Turkish women providing some protection from smallpox for their children by using large needles to inject them with pus taken from someone with a mild form of the disease. Small-pox was an infection which, if it did not kill the infected person, could leave them with horrible disfigurements, with children being especially vulnerable. In England Edward Jenner, observed that milkmaids who became infected with cow-pox seemed to be immune from the considerably more serious, but biologically closely related, condition of small-pox. In 1796 Jenner vaccinated a James Phipps, the son of a landless laborer, with a small amount of pus taken from a cowpox sore on the hand of milkmaid Sarah Nelmes. As a result, the boy did suffer a mild fever but, when later exposed by Jenner to small-pox he remained healthy, having gained immunity to the disease. When he first announced his discovery Jenner was subjected to strong professional criticism, and even to ridicule by the popular press. But he doggedly continued to experiment in vaccinating children and in 1798 his results were published and the value of vaccination (a word coined by Jenner) began to be accepted by the medical profession.

In France, Louis Pasteur undertook a number of experiments involving the process of fermentation, mainly in order to find an explanation for liquids such as beer, milk, vinegar, going 'off'. Again, use of the improved microscopes (achromatic microscopes) allowed Pasteur to see that liquids that had gone bad contained different cellular organisms than did the same liquids when fresh. Pasteur had already suggested that the process of fermentation itself involved the activity of living organisms rather than only simple chemical reactions. In a series of experiments he had found that heating could kill some bacteria and gentle heating or cooling could weaken a virus. Following a similar idea to inoculation, he also found that an injected, weakened, form of a virus could treat viral infections. And the practical success of his 'bacteriology' in treating infections such as anthrax in cattle, rabies in dogs, and cholera in chicken, led to the establishment of the 'Pasteur Institutes', dedicated to research and teaching, of which there are 60 throughout the world today (2021). Pasteur's work led to successful techniques of preserving food (including the pasteurization of milk) and he was able to gain sponsorship from the food industry sufficient to allow his work to be continued by research 'teams'.

Nursing – the close/intimate care given to the sick on a daily basis was of course practiced since the earliest times, and hospices and hospitals had been places where the sick were sent for treatment or to convalescence, from the foundation of civil life (Egyptian, Chinese, Indian, Aztec, Babylonia, and Greek). Caring for the sick became an important aspect of Christianity, especially focused on monastic orders. This was similar with other religions but was prominent in Europe due to the leading part played by 'Christian' Europe in the development of civil life during the medieval period. In the early part of the seventeenth century, St Vincent de Paul was among a number of individuals who undertook a more systematic, 'planned', approach to the organization of nursing and he helped to found the 'Daughters of Charity' (1633) where sisters (nuns) would receive education and training appropriate to the task of patient care. In the $18^{th}/19^{th}$ centuries this role and the training to undertake it came to be more formalized. For Britain, in 1840 Elizabeth Fry helped to found an institute of nursing (on a Prussian model) with a focus on quality training. And experience gained during the Crimean War 1854 (50% death rate for wounded soldiers) convinced Florence Nightingale (asked to go to the war zone by the British Government) of the need to improve basic hygiene and nursing care for the military. The official status and popular interest she gained contributed significantly to the development of nursing as a respectable profession. Like Nightingale, Mary Seacole also travelled to the Crimea but she did not initially benefit from the support of the British Government; even having to pay her own fare to get to Turkey. But she was active in tending wounded on the battle-field and set up her own hospital in Balaclava where sick officers could recuperate. Her activities and book 'The Wonderful Adventures of Mrs Seacole in Many Lands' stimulated public interest and her varied experience in the Crimea gave a more colourful perspective on the issue of care for soldiers and more generally on the value of nursing.

Following the war, Florence Nightingale's reputation grew whilst Mary's gradually faded. Florence was a prime mover in the establishment of a school of nursing at St Thomas's Hospital, London; and in the progressive spread of similar schools attached too, but separate from, hospitals (the 'Royal College of Nursing' would be founded 1916). Across Europe, and beyond, nursing became a respectable career option for (initially only single) women; if low paid and low status, compared with male doctors. One marked feature of the medical profession during the extended period of its becoming formalized and institutionalized was the gender separation of the roles – basically nursing became female work and doctoring male. As the rare exceptions to this, and the development of the medical profession in the second half of the twentieth century showed, this was a difference based on nothing more than male (supported by an implicit female cultural consensus) patriarchal prejudice, unrelated to ability if not to the inhibiting affects of socialization.

Later in the century Robert Koch, building on the work of pioneers such as Jenner Pasteur, Lister, Semmelweis, and others, devised a way of separating different strains of bacteria and of staining them so that individual bacteria could be studied more easily and so enable the identification of the link between an infection and a specific strain of bacteria. This led to a range of discoveries (and identified a methodological tool for many more) including in 1882 the tubercle bacillus (tuberculosis) and in 1883 the 'vibrio' of cholera (cholerae).

Up until the later part of the nineteenth century, the internal working (constitution) of the body could only be studied by dissection of the dead, or during surgery on the living, and to a very limited extent by making conjectural suggestions based on observation of a body's external reaction to various types of medical treatment. But the discovery of X-rays by Wilhelm Rontgen in 1895, then of radium by Pierre and Marie Curie in 1898, was to progressively reveal the more solid (bones and dense tissue) structures of the human body and, by comparing images of healthy patients with those of the sick, the location and nature of a problem, could be shown. Especially in relation to bone disease and disease caused by the abnormal growth of the dense tissue characteristic of cancerous tumors and the shadows on lungs infected with tuberculosis.

The nineteenth century saw medicine and its practitioners firmly established as a respected profession, with professional bodies (often with Royal Patronage) and a range of institutions including laboratories, hospitals, university-based schools of medicine, in which to locate their work (and with 'general practitioners' located in the community). As well as governing bodies to control those entering the professions (and for some time endeavouring ensure the exclusion of women from being Doctors), licensing practitioners, and maintaining ethical and professional standards. The British Medical Association (BMA) was established in 1854, with legislation in 1858 to become the general council of medical education and registration for the UK. A body with the power to regulate training and employment, one that approached its field of interest in a 'scientific' way. So based on a medical model that assumed the body as machine-like; in theory, if not always in more enlightened practice; separating the physical condition from the psychological and social aspects of ill-health.

Another landmark in the development of practice medicine came with the invention in early nineteenth century by Rene Laennec of the stethoscope (an enduring and iconic symbol of the medical practitioner) and his book 'On Indirect Auscultation' pub. 1819 contained descriptions of the sounds of the internal organs of heart and lungs and the implication of these for health.

Johannes Muller, Professor at the University of Berlin, published the results of his own experimental approach to understanding the operation of the human body in 'The Manual of Human Physiology' and Muller's work did much to establish the study of physiology as a subject in its own right. Francis Magendie in France and Sir Charles Bell in Britain advanced the understanding of how nerves and the nervous system operates; in 1811 Bell set out his findings in the landmark work 'Idea of the New Anatomy of the Brain'.

Matthias Schleiden and Theodor Swann in 1839 made the suggestion that the whole body was in fact a colony of cells that had been generated by the original coming together of the germ cells (egg and sperm). The process of growth from germ cells to a baby was followed up by von Beer in the 1840s as he established the branch of science known as embryology. A great deal of work was focused on cell theory, the role of the constituent parts and the function that each type of cell performed. Rudolf Virchow as professor of Anatomy at the Pathological Institute in Berlin suggested, in 1856, that cells reproduce themselves and that they can be healthy or sick (normal or malignant). He is generally considered to be the 'father of cell pathology'.

The scientific approach to health-care led, throughout the century, to one advance following another, with a significant improvement for surgical intervention being the gradual development of anesthesia. It was in the USA that modern anesthetics were first established for use in surgery when in 1846 William Thomas Morton, working at the Massachusetts General Hospital, demonstrated the use of diethyl ether as a general anesthetic. News of Morton's work spread to Europe and a year later James Young Simpson was experimenting with a range of different 'vapours'. Settling on chloroform, which had been discovered in 1831, as the most suitable and this became the preferred choice for a general anesthetic.

The spread of scientific medicine, on the back of trading links and colonization, provided the opportunity and motivation to find cures or preventive methods for tropical diseases and the carriers of diseases such as elephantiasis in 1877 (Filaria worm) and malaria in 1897 (Anopheles mosquito). Carlos Findley (working in Cuba) suggested that yellow fever was carried by the Stegomyia mosquito and the confirmation of this led to steps being taken to eradicate this host during the continuing construction of the Panama Canal – where for workers the death rate from yellow fever subsequently dropped from 176 in a 1000 per annum to 6 per 1000. Inoculation against typhoid fever (a debilitating and sometime fatal disease caused by the bacterium Salmonella typhi) was introduced by Almoth Wright. Out of these early successes the new field of tropical medicine developed.

Dentistry also benefited from the advance of general medicine. A landmark in the practice of dentistry being recognized as part of the scientific advance in health-care was the publication in 1723 of Pierre Fauchard's book 'Surgical Dentistry: A Treatise on Teeth', in which he outlined the anatomy of the mouth, and the function and care of natural teeth as well as the modeling of false teeth. The emblematic individual from the campaign for American Independence, Paul Revere, worked as a dentist between 1768-1770 and in fact was able to used dental work to confirm the identity of a dead ex-patient. It was America that was at the forefront of developments in dentistry, with its first book on dentistry, published in 1801, being Richard C. Skinner's 'Treatise on Human Teeth'. A specific dentist's adjustable chair was made by Josiah Flagg in 1790, improved with the reclining chair made by James Snell in 1832, and improved further in 1877 with the Wilkerson hydraulic chair. The manufacture of porcelain 'false' teeth began in 1825 by the SS White Dental Manufacturing Company, and in 1871 James B. Morris made the foot-treadle dental engine used to power a drilling instrument.

The training of dentists became more organized, signified by the setting up in the US (Baltimore - 1840) of the world's first school specifically for the training of dentists. This was just a year after the launch of the 'American Journal of Dental Science', the world's first journal for dentistry. The American Dental Association was founded in 1859 and six years later it adopted a special code of ethics related to the practice of dentistry – the same year in which Lucy Beaman Hobbs became the first female dentist. Dentistry was also pioneering in the use of anesthetics, with nitrous oxide being used by the dentist Horace Wells one year before Morton's surgical demonstration of its effectiveness. By the end of the nineteenth century 'modern' dentistry was being practiced across the civil world by trained professionals (there were 28 dental schools across the civil world by 1880s) using precision-made surgical equipment, local and general anesthetics, and from about 1896, X-rays. From the 1880s dentists were working on patients who were increasingly using tooth brushes coated in tooth-paste squeezed from metal tubes.

As noted above, as early the first century BCE Asclepiades had been recommending a holistic and humane approach to managing individuals suffering from mental illnesses, rather than imprisonment. But during the early industrial period the approach to the mentally unwell was to view sufferers as 'mad' with most forms of treatment being based on physical constraint. Individuals were often imprisoned and even chained up, giving physical embodiment to their also being 'imprisoned' by the debilitating limitations of their illness – in places even being viewed as subjects for public amusement. There were at least some signs of change during the nineteenth century, illustrated by the approach taken by Phillipe Pinel who, during the French revolution was appointed Chief Physician of the institution in Paris (the 'Bicetre Hospital for the Insane') that housed those considered as 'mad'. Pinel proposed to release the inmates from their chains and suggested that a regime of limited freedom and fresh air would make them more amenable to treatment. As the century progressed, a growing number of psychiatrists began to systematically categorize symptoms into named conditions such as dementia praecox (become schizophrenia), catatonia, depression, etc. This process was brought together in a classification system devised by Emil Kraepelin towards the end of the century.

For a small number of practitioners there was a strong belief, stemming from the understanding of the mind as an electro-chemical mechanism, that mental illness was linked to some underlying physical condition. A view challenged by the ideas of Sigmund Freud, who pioneered a view framing much of mental illness in terms of emotional disturbances (upset of the dynamic balance of mental 'forces'). By the end of the century both approaches were fertile sources for the development of ways to manage and treat mental illness/dysfunction.

From now incremental advances were rapidly accumulating as research became more systematized and the professional status of medical practitioners rose across the world, and of course the chance to make financial gains (especially through pharmaceuticals and later on medical insurance). Medical researchers and practitioners pursuing a positivist medical model, working in Europe, USA and Japan, made a range of contributions to the overall advance in understanding and practice as medicine became increasingly enmeshed in the development of industrialization.

Throughout the history of medicine we see humankind's intelligence and imagination applied to diagnosis, prognosis, and treatment, and later on to systematic research, all motivated to understand and seek relief for a fundamentally problematic area of our experience – to make the sick well or at least to make their sickness more bearable.

***

My outline of some main developments in the sciences down to the end of the nineteenth century is framed within a narrative of their progressive developed into specialisms. I have tended to treat each of the sciences being considered as autonomous generators of knowledge (of 'novel' information) but this, whilst generally valid, can be misleading, in that to a significant extent the sciences have continued to have overlapping boundaries in terms of subject areas and there has been ongoing inter-communication between them. An advance in one scientific specialism has often been of benefit to others, especially in relation to technological innovation. And at a fundamental level there has been a degree of shared consensus on the range of methods that would be appropriate for the 'sciences' (to usefully pursue the 'scientific endeavour'). There were, and still are, differences of view in relation to which, if any, methods of the social sciences should mirror the natural sciences and for both there is the issue of objectivity, and the influence of what would today be termed the social construction of knowledge. This last would, incorporate social factors such as: funding, career advancement, profit-seeking, morality, as well as the related issues of scientific: 'Fashion, Faith and Fantasy', as clearly noted by Roger Penrose (2016) in relation to physics.

The nineteenth century had seen observation, recording and theorizing on a range of aspects of the natural and social worlds being undertaken mainly by interested (if many very able) amateurs to become an activity pursued by a rapidly expanding body of individuals named by mid century as 'scientists'.

Around mid eighteenth century the forums for scientific endeavour had included quite basic laboratories and lecture theatres of a few (mainly European) universities, some still more recognizably alchemical laboratories, some artisan workshops, and a number of clubs and regular private gatherings. In the nineteenth century governments of the world's industrializing nations came to recognize the relation to national status, and the potential military advantages, of scientific discovery and technological innovation. Private industry became increasingly aware of the potential profits to be gained from products and processes that can accrue from a co-operative partnership between science and technology and the production of various commodities. Consequently science (especially the natural sciences) was given a much more significant place in university curricula and was being progressed in numerous private industrial and state-sponsored laboratories. Specialist and generalist scientific societies proliferated, each of the sciences (and even sub-branches of these) had their own journals and these were never short of contributors submitting research and theory based papers; scientific books poured from the presses. In 1800 we can identify about 100 (and these mostly Western European) scientific journals, by 1850 about 1,000, and by 1900 more than 10,000 being published in civil societies across the globe.

The hundreds of scientific institutions (separate from national university systems), supported by government and private industry, were in place across the industrialized world serving to illustrate more formal recognition for the stage reached by what had become a dominant source of world-views. World-views sharing some essential commonality on 'how' to reason in order to gain a continuously improving, in descriptive and explanatory power, understanding of the world. The development of sciences throughout the twentieth century was yes, generated by humankind's quest for secure knowledge in itself, but it was determinedly shaped by the motivation of those funding the activity.

Just one more obvious aspect of this direction of development could be seen in the world-wide arms industry. Massive resources were to be poured into research and development of weaponry by industrialized nations and, whatever slick but disingenuous arguments could be presented to highlighting 'spinoff ' discoveries made during weapons production and their use during conflicts (most directly related to mending the wounds caused by the weapons themselves) of benefit to humankind; the central aim of the industry being to devise ever-better ways in which to destroy property, degrade land, and annihilate human beings.

As the nineteenth progressed evermore 'scientific expeditions' crisscrossed the world's landmasses and oceans, observatories sprouted on hill tops, the experiment[13] became the ubiquitous and the

---

[13] In numerous forms; for example: from particle physics using vacuum tubes, to reaction times in psychology, to cohort studies of medical treatments.

accepted primary means of testing hypotheses, and other theoretical predictions, and of seeking to verify previous experimental findings.

Science was popularized in wide circulation newspapers almost always with enthusiasm, and scientific advance (especially as 'discovery') was offered as evidential proof to support the mechanistic ideas of progress so characteristic of the justificatory narrative of nineteenth century industrialization and colonial imperialism.

Philosophy

It was a combination of philosophical ideas, and indeed the underlying intellectual freedom that was fostered by the spirit, if not always the local circumstances of the Enlightenment, that encouraged philosophers to at least attempt to progress beyond the justifiably respected but intellectually limiting (not limited in itself but limiting in the effect it came to have on medieval philosophy) Platonic and Aristotelian philosophies.

If we accept that the more eminent pre-Socratic and later Greek philosophers endured as an influence into nineteenth century philosophy, we also need to step back to the seventeenth and eighteenth centuries to identify what were arguably even more influential sources of ideas. In returning to these I will progress through aspects of the philosophy of individuals rather than undertake the more challenging task of tracing the often quite subtle intellectual evolution of enduring themes. This is partly due to my own academic limitations but I also consider that linking ideas to names does allow the development of philosophy to be more accessible for a general reader. Given various limitations I can only here offer a selective and so very partial sense of any philosopher's ideas.

It has been conventional to credit Rene Descartes (1596-1650) with being both a brilliant mathematician[14] and as initiating the beginning of modern philosophy.

Impressed by what he felt was the certainty of mathematics, he attempted to consider whether a similar level of certainty could be found in the ways in which we understand the world. If requiring a co-operative God in order to guarantee the certainty in any aspect of life that is beyond the simple certainty of mere human awareness.

---

[14] As the inventor of the graph - the vertical and horizontal lines on a standard graph are named Cartesian co-ordinates after the adjectival sense of his name.

Descartes posited quantity as a fundamental aspect of all matter, and this matter he distinguishes from 'mind'. A dichotomy between the physical and the mental and so a dualistic representation of the world as being composed of both material substance (extended) and thinking substance (unextended). And for Descartes, by implication at least, a God 'substance', whose presence is at least felt in the world; or rather, in the way that it is presented to us.

Descartes undertook a self-reflective search for knowledge about the world that could be established with confidence. He sought certainly and applied a method based initially on doubting everything that he thought he knew and he concluded that the one thing that he could believe with certainty is that he 'thinks' ('ergo cogito sum' - usually translated as 'I think therefore I am').

He then proceeded to make the claim that God would not deceive his creation, so there must be a physical world, the certain knowledge of which could be established by applying the evaluative tests of clarity, distinctness, and freedom from contradiction, to our ideas about it. Variations of this type of 'rationalist' approach to understanding the world was considered by many as successful and this, along with advances in the natural sciences, fostered a confidence in 'mans' intellectual progress. The existence of a helpful God seems the be the single foundation of Cartesian metaphysics, and the ontological justification for this God's existence is based upon a line of reason tracing the view that Descartes can imagine a perfect, infinite and immortal being and, due to his own human imperfection, he could only create something greater than himself if such a being does actually exist!

Two leading philosophical approaches developed from the time of Descartes would be described as empiricism (taken to extreme forms as materialism) and rationalism; for some philosophers in the Cartesian tradition it would more often be a conjunction of these two conceptual strands. Empiricism drew justification from the advance of the natural sciences with rationalism drawing justification from the intellectual freedom wrought during the Enlightenment.

Baruch Spinoza (1632-1677) stands out as an individual sincerely seeking to progress the search for some clear, logically coherent, foundation to our thinking. Bertrand Russell considered Spinoza '....the noblest and most lovable of the great philosophers' that 'Intellectually some have surpassed him, but ethically he is supreme'. Spinoza was a religious man (born a Jew).... and was a Christian in the sense that the teachings of Jesus (also born a Jew) are Christian. He felt that sin was due to ignorance, to not understanding the wider context of one's life; so not dissimilar to Plato's view of ignorance. For Spinoza, a person can live a good life (in an ethical sense) only when they are aware that the trials and tribulations they face can be placed in the perspective of a Universe that is essentially good. He was not advocating a detachment from taking responsibility for others and suggested that a love for others is an aspect of promoting the virtuous life, including an understanding of the 'healing' power of love in the face of evil.

With a love of God being central to this – although, according to T.S. Gregory, for Spinoza the concept of God is presented as a verb rather than a the more conventional noun of religious convention, and so conveying a sense of God as an 'activity', rather than of just a passive presence.

The most significant weakness is his attempt to offer truths by setting out a series of definitions and axioms; which, although offering clarity (valuable in itself), amount only to assertions (epistemologically). At more length he deploys propositions, the proofs of which are but his own views on what it takes to justify each proposition. The proofs form the substance of his philosophical 'system'. A system that, whilst at base subjective, is genuinely rational, at least in so far as it is the literary outcome of the intellect intensely, reflectively, and sincerely applied to understanding human experience.

In Germany, Gottfried Wilhelm Leibniz (1646-1716): probably made his greatest contribution to philosophy in his work on logic. But he also outlined a metaphysical system. He identified two aspects of the world which can be put into 'necessary propositions' which it would be illogical to contradict. These would include mathematics and logic, and also 'contingent propositions' which would be true if they represented conditions that were 'sufficient' – this would include scientific facts and discoveries. Metaphysically, Leibniz suggested an 'atomic' theory of the world with a multitude (infinitude) of substances, each an individual 'monad' (his principle book was titled 'The Monadology'). These monads were un-extended entities, each with a soul and from which the whole of the world was composed; so the depiction of a reality that is not material in the sense of Cartesian matter. The monads do not interact with each other (they are 'windowless') – monads seem to operate 'as if' causal and other relationships exist between them, but this is only an appearance due to a pre-established harmony in the operation of the whole world (the work of God). Each monad is immortal, each has a soul, and human beings (and all other objects) are composed of many monads. All monads 'mirror' the universe but some do this more clearly than others.

Leibniz's attempt to provide an explanation for evil seems to be quite fantastical and pushes the idea of rational explanation to the limits of what this approach would mean. He accepts that there is evil in the world but suggests that God could have created any possible world (that did not contradict the 'laws' of logic) but he did in fact create the one we know because it has the greatest possible amount of good, even after taking into account all of the evil. So therefore, this world must be the best of all possible worlds! (Voltaire's fictional character Dr Pangloss, is said to be modeled on Leibniz). There is the obvious weakness in how this good/evil calculation could be made, not least in being able to clearly define what each of these concepts mean and how they could be 'quantified' (so making a more/less calculation possible). But for Leibniz it does allow a God to exist who cannot easily be held responsible for evil – this 'best of all possible worlds' rationale for evil (and with it a blameless God) bears obvious similarities to similar ideas produced more recently on the existence of evil in a world created by God – Alvin Plantinga - and his idea of 'trans-world depravity' - linking the 'best of all possible worlds' to allowing the capacity of freewill for humans. (Plantinga, 1979)

Descartes, Spinoza, and Leibniz, were leading philosophers in the broad rationalist tradition; each aspiring to explanations that are composed of ideas that are clear and distinct. They outlined epistemologies in terms of abstract concepts mainly considered without recourse to the lived world. This is a general feature of rationalist epistemologies; one that allows for potentially interesting speculations.

John Locke (1632-1704) set a new direction in philosophy. Not radically new as in Descartes, but new in the sense that it was focused on man's psychological constitution, or rather that aspect of it that we now term 'cognitive', and on the process of reasoning and thinking..... to in fact discover the origins of our knowledge rather than their certainty. He makes a distinction between ideas of sensation and ideas of reflection; although the two are connected. For Locke the mind at birth was a 'blank slate' (a 'tabula rasa'), a passive receptor of sensory impressions that were generated externally. The sensory impressions could include simple ideas such as single colours and complex ideas such as space, extension, and motion. The sensory impressions constitute the entities that combine to form more complex ideas (the building blocks) from which man's psychological constitution is constructed. So Locke was clearly an empiricist and indeed, for some later scholars, is noted as the founder of empiricism. Locke had a significant influence on eighteenth century philosophy.

In terms of a theory of knowledge (epistemology), the mind as posited by Locke is one that discovers rather than one that creates. Locke was a prolific writer whose work encompassed theoretical philosophy, education, and politics. His political writing helped to lay the foundation of a liberal political ideology that continues down to today to contribute to political ideas. An ideology of the 'reasonable' on both the role of government and the role of citizens. An arrangement between the two being based on a implicit social contract - or rather the recognition by both of an interlinked set of responsibilities and rights - that aims to 'fairly' balance the responsibilities of government and the rights of citizens within a civil society. 'Fairly' being linked to what is taken as the common good; a rather vague concept for Locke but one that the specific policies he advocated linked the common good primarily to the political interests of the rising middle-class. A key aspect of Locke's political view was that government can only have authority if it is based on the consent of citizens; a view that would have a significant influence in the nineteenth century debates on extending the franchise and reforming government.

The Scottish philosopher David Hume (1711-76) introduced a significant challenge to the $17^{th}/18^{th}$ century consensual agreement on the value of a rationalist methodology. Hume applied his forensic analytic skills to the confidence in knowledge that rational philosophers considered that they had established. Similar to some rationalists, he also took a skeptical approach but he took this to a level of analysis beyond which they were prepared to go. Hume applied his skeptical approach to a range of both theoretical and moral philosophy (he was also a respected historian and economist – if liable to a bias towards most things Scottish) but he would claim that his main work in philosophy was understanding morality; if he was an apologist of slavery. Hume was firmly in the tradition - Bacon, Hobbes, Locke, Berkeley, Bentham, Reid, J.S.Mill - of British empiricism. Hume's classic book 'Treatise of Human Nature' (in Hume's own words a book that '......fell stillborn from the press') was an over 600 page attempt to apply, if rather loosely, an experimental method of reasoning, modeled on Newton's experimental method applied to the natural world, to morality as subject-matter. His empiricism was clear in that he saw all of the basic material of thought and of our beliefs as coming from our experience; if he seems to view experience to include both sensory and introspective material. For Hume perceptions are of two kinds, impressions and ideas, each type of which can be composed of simple or complex forms of perception; there does not seem to be a clear distinction between these, they differ in terms of the force (liveliness) with which they come before the mind. Impressions have more force and are conceptualized as 'sensations, passions, and emotions'. Ideas are initially but faint versions (images) of these and seem to form the material for the more reflective, reasoned, mode of thinking.

For Hume, ideas that come before the mind divide into those that can be presented as propositions (relations of ideas) that can only be true as in geometry, algebra, arithmetic, and those facts about the world that can be true or untrue. He writes of the relations that link impressions and ideas to constitute the 'natural' process of thinking. We become aware of relations and acquire an understanding of these as we compare ideas. This, the relations between ideas, come in seven basic forms: resemblance, identity, quantity, quality, contrariety, cause and effect, and those related to space and time. Hume considers that knowledge can only be based on expectations and probabilities rather than certainties, there also being an influential role for emotions on our behaviour and our thinking.

For Hume we gain a certain kind of confidence in observing repeated 'relations' between certain ideas being confirmed; but the confidence is an outcome of habit rather that representing a consistency of reasoning. He used the relation ('association') of causation, a basic feature of human thinking, to illustrate a relation flawed in terms of its truth value. Hume reasoned that we form the habit early in life of assigning cause and effect connections between events, the constant conjunction between certain events encourages this e.g. a ball travelling at speed when striking another ball – we infer that the first ball 'causes' the second ball to rapidly accelerate in the same direction in which that the first ball was travelling, the effects being the acceleration of the second ball and the rapid deceleration of the first ball. The two events of one ball moving at speed then halting on impact and another accelerating from rest, are for Hume logically separate from each other but reflection 'conjoins' them in a causal relationship. For Hume, we cannot prove the causal (or any other) relationship. Assigning causation is for Hume a step beyond what we can prove rationally and we can see the dramatic 'causal' affect this would have on the confidence of the rationalist philosophers of the time; when his originally, by his own judgment, still-born book was 'reborn' later on following a period of post-birth gestation in the philosophical saloons of western Europe.

Attempts to address Hume's incisive skepticism gave much European philosophy a new impetus and its negative analysis - although there were also aspects of Hume's own work that were not just critical - gave rise to a positive reaction.

In his posthumously published book 'Dialogues concerning Natural Religion' (1779) Hume offers a persuasive challenge to the basis of the arguments for God's existence offered by rationalists such as Descartes, Spinoza, and Berkeley. Hume introduced a timely, if bitter, dose of logical (and common) sense to the overconfident assumptions characteristic of forms of rationalism rooted in a belief in a world sustained by a personal God and accessible to reason.

The great philosopher Immanuel Kant (1724-1804) considered that Hume had '.......awoken him from his dogmatic slumbers', with the challenge that Hume's views had put to rationalism. But that Hume's attack on metaphysics also had a positive aspect, as Kant wrote towards the beginning of his book 'Prolegomena to any Future Metaphysics that will be able to Present itself as a Science' (1783): 'He [Hume] brought no light into this kind of knowledge [metaphysics], but he struck a spark at which a light could have been kindled, if it had found a receptive tinder and if the glow had been carefully kept up and increased.'

Kant's philosophy, which spans the turn of the seventeenth century, can be seen as an attempt to lay down a new direction to the philosophic enterprise that could incorporate Hume's critique of previous philosophy and, of more importance, sought to lay the foundations for a complete understanding of the basis of how human knowledge is formed; to blow light into Hume's spark. Kant's personal disposition was modest but his philosophizing was magnificent in both method and ambition. Not a man of action but a man possessed of a mind given to a tendency to intense and productive introspection from which subsequent philosophy was to benefit.

Kant outlined a complex conceptual architectonic that

endeavoured to focus on explaining human knowledge, one that could take into account both sensory experience and the a'priori elements of the framework we as humans bring to understanding experience, including a sense of time/space and intuitions underlying mathematics and geometry. The type of questions that Kant addressed were related to establishing the reasons why we consider any knowledge to be valid and what are the limits of our reason. With a relatively new approach (certainly in terms of extent and clarity) to the pre-conscious conditions for experience – not pre-conscious in the sense of human personal psychology but in identifying the experiential pre-conditions that make any knowledge possible. An attempt to delimit the fundamental basis of human reason in a practical way, following a procedure that proceeded from analytic, to dialectic, to method. This 'transcendental method' developed from a critical analysis but was also constructive in re-defining the interaction between the external world of objects and the internal world of human knowledge. He suggested three modes of reason – as thinking (sense) as willing (ethics) and as feeling (aesthetic).

An aspect of his reasoning that was mostly ignored by philosophers, such as Fichte and Hegel, who sought to develop his ideas, was Kant's distinguishing between a phenomenal realm we can experience and a noumenal realm that we cannot experience in any sense of its possible 'objects' having any intelligibility (articulated as understanding). This unknowable realm is constituted by the 'things-in-themselves' that are linked to the phenomenon of experience; at times in his writing Kant seems to refer to noumena as being accessible to a mode of transcendental intuition beyond such a'priori categories as space and time. At other times he writes of them as if they were knowable only as an idea of there being a limit to what we can know; a realm beyond the known. This allows Kant to posit some intellectual constitution for 'God'. For Fredrick Copleston, Kant writes of God as being within the realm of noumena:'…as possessing noumenal reality ….of God as a thing-in-itself.' (Copleston, 1960, vol. VI. p271). Kant's positing of a noumenal realm adds the possibility of movement to an otherwise quite static exposition of experience; and also a realm that 'transcends' the subjectivism that his phenomenal system could be liable too. In his occasional linking of the noumenal to 'freedom' he allows a potential place for our making autonomous moral choices; intersecting with the mode of transcendental intuition noted above.

If Kant was simply (at times inconsistently) suggesting that we humans can never expect to understand all that can be known about any phenomenon, that there is always something, some 'thing-in-itself', that will invariably elude our understanding - then this is obvious and of little value. If he is suggesting some realm beyond the phenomenal that gives rise to it, then this too seems to be of little value; more so if he (knowingly) introduced the concept to allow a place for God, an immortal soul, and a space for moral freedom.

But if he is endeavouring to express an aspect of being human that we can know by an intuitive sense but can't use language to describe, we might be seeing a clear-headed thinker positing something quite profound; some aspect of being human that can be 'glimpsed' but not understood – a mode of being that can be 'known of', but which is (constitutionally) unknowable. Kant's own, (generally uncharacteristic) inconsistencies in seeking to explain noumena suggests an intellect 'grasping' for something elusive, but the fact that he repeatedly returns to it in his writing suggests it was of some importance for him.

I just want to offer the reader a quite mundane (but I believe important) suggestion related to the psychology underlying Kant's noting of a noumenal realm. I offer a scenario Kant could not possibly have been aware of. Think back to life on Earth about 200,000 y.b.p, picture some African (savanna-like) terrain occupied by small groups of Homo erectus types. Can we imagine that on occasion an individual might sit 'reflecting' (pre-linguistically, and more emotionally than cognitively) on her life and having a intuitive sense of something more than her experiences; she might just have been glimpsing (feeling a sense of) a realm of consciousness that her descendants (about another 150,000 years later) would attain – in Kantian terms she might have been 'aware' of an inaccessible (noumenal) realm out there but for her being one that was cognitively inaccessible.

Is the idea of noumena but the conceptual expression for the prospect of evolving consciousness? Of course I have moved beyond Kant's own speculations; but can his own 'reflection' have been motivated by his having an intuitive sense of something more than self-conscious human experience? Our (Kant's) realm of experience is existentially equivalent to the ape-like individual's emotionally intuited 'noumena'. Kant's (and our own versions of this) noumena being the realm to be experienced by a future type of evolved consciousness beyond ourselves.

Kant's description of human thinking is one that presents an ideal type (pattern-process) of human thinking – one has a sense of his outlining a complex 'blueprint' but, as with a blueprint, the presentation is rather static and the different parts fixed relative to one another, whereas human thinking is throughout dynamic and relative. His philosophy (perhaps purposely) lacks the personal density of existence and indeed represents the height of objectified rationality.

To highlight two contrasting approaches to philosophy, the more rationalist and the more existentialist, that continue in different guises down to today, let's move into the nineteenth century with the philosophy of Henri Bergson. Bergson criticized Kant's conception of time as being 'measured and quantified' and of its gaining this measurability at the cost of it neglecting the reality of time lived as an authentic sensory experience, as 'duration'.

Kant introduced a form of Idealism into German philosophy; in his transcendental idealism (he preferred the term critical idealism) he posited two worlds; the phenomenal and the noumenal. Kant was not suggesting that all that exists is the content of mind (as would some later Idealists) but only that this is all we, as human beings, can gain understanding of. And that if this limitation is the case then it is rational to consider that there is likely to be more (in reality) than what can be known to human-beings. His more substantial work was presented in three 'Critiques'; those of 'Pure Reason', of 'Practical Reason', and of 'Judgement'. Each Critique in turn having three parts: 1) An Analytic 2) A dialectic 3) A Methodology. Although at times a difficult and challenging body of work I would still recommend any student of philosophy to endeavour to gain some understanding of Kant's critical philosophy. The product of an intensely thoughtful and intelligent man who offered interesting ideas on phenomena, psychology (the structure of thinking), ethics, and even on international politics. On this last subject, I would suggest that his more modest essay 'To Perpetual Peace' (1795) made a precocious contribution to understanding international politics, including relations between nation-states and the process of colonization, which includes perceptive insights directly relevant to today's (political) world.

Kant's work for me (although I can't claim to fully understand it all) offered a standard (a useful base) against which to compare the ideas of later philosophers and, as such, a useful base for understanding philosophy. In some ways Kant redefined philosophy and offered a new method for progressing it.

A notable admirer of Kant's work was Arthur Schopenhauer (lived 1788-1860) who, similar to Kant, considered that there was a noumenal reality inaccessible to our senses. One outside of space and time but not a Kantian alternative reality constituted by 'things-in-themselves'. Rather, Schopenhauer posited this as an undifferentiated, purposeless, 'will'. Although this 'will' for Schopenhauer is impersonal, more like the idea of a type of 'energy' pervading the universe; and is manifest in the world we experience. Simplistically put, we might suggest that the universal timeless 'will' of Schopenhauer is akin to some innate psychological force that drives individuals to action.

What Kant managed, apart from creating a complex system 'about' the formation, validity, and limitations of human knowledge, was his setting up a philosophic framework, created out of a formidable process of reasoning, that would stand as a challenge to future philosophers. He lit an intellectual rocket that still serves to inspire and stimulate philosophers but rather than address the challenge to improve on what Kant felt to be the foundation of reasoning German (and other) philosophy in the nineteenth century was to develop, sometimes quite rarefied, forms of Idealism – Fichte, Schelling – and perhaps the most extensive form being expressed in the work of Hegel.

The foundations for this later development of Idealism in philosophy can easily be traced back to ideas of Plato, and indeed to those of other early Greek thinkers.

George Berkeley (1685-1753) has been noted as the 'father of Idealism', asserting that our perception is the source of all that we can know. This was similar to John Locke's view but Berkeley rejected Locke's derived assumption that if we have perception there must be an objective world that gives rise to these perceptions as going beyond the limit – content of our minds – of what we can actually know. In something of a logically irrational leap Berkeley posits a God (Christian), the content of whose mind encompasses all of reality.

More pure forms of Idealism were set out by a number of philosophers in early nineteenth century Germany: primarily Johann G. Fichte (1762-1814), Friedrich W.J. von Schelling (1775-1854), and Georg W.F. Hegel (1770-1831). Each of which held that the primary focus of philosophy should be self-consciousness. With Johann Fichte we have the denial of some inaccessible, noumenal, world and instead we see a more thorough-going form of the transcendental. For Fichte, we can have knowledge of nothing outside of thinking itself – consciousness is reality – the mind creates the empirical world that we experience. The centre of this reality being established by our moral choices and actions; consciousness and morality being for Fichte synonymous.

Schelling also rejected any materialist conception of matter and posited 'spirit' as the essence of reality. A reality sustained by a single absolute 'mind; the Absolute Spirit. Humans are but parts (as is the whole cosmos) of this larger sense of reality, nothing is outside of it. This conception of absolute sprit encompasses a reality involving change in the form of progress. Schelling suggested that the natural world had developed from a world of lifeless matter and with the insertion (emergence of) of life - plants, then animals, then humans - we have two aspects of the same evolving creativity of nature. Within the creativity of nature was the creativity of human beings – most obviously manifested in their artistic achievements.

Hegel was critical of both Kant and Fichte, as maintaining the existence of a material world, even if versions of this were created, or only known, by mind. In Hegel we have the premier philosopher of modern Idealism, offering a logical dynamism through which progress to the Absolute can be fulfilled. His 'dialectical method' was a process of unfolding advance – he begins his text 'The Phenomenology of Mind/Spirit' (alternative translations of 'Geist'), with the thesis of 'being' then opposes this by its antithesis 'non-being', he then resolves this seeming antagonism in a synthesis of 'becoming'. The two initial movements (the antagonistic relationship) of the dialectic 'being' and 'non-being' become sublated (meaning that there is a sense in which they are still contained) within the higher synthesis of becoming.

From this beginning Hegel sets out on the development of the triadic dialectical process of advancing conceptual understanding leading towards the Absolute. Each synthesising element (concept), lacks wholeness so is flawed. It 'needs' (an 'inner necessity') - this is the basis for the central 'dynamic' driving logical development - to be further developed and so a new antithesis is posited to expose the limitation of the initial concept and these two, as thesis/antithesis, require a higher level synthesis and so on and so on......developing towards a self aware 'oneness' in the Absolute. Echoing Plato, Hegel suggested that reasoning allows us to access a certain type of reality that takes us beyond the idea of a material world; only the rational is the real and the most real is the Absolute. There is an Absolute (mind/spirit) and human reasoning allows us to be part of this; history is an unfolding of this Absolute 'Geist'. With each historical period having its own 'spirit of the age'. The movement of history, as well as the passage of our own conceptual understanding of the movement of 'spirit', can be traced according to the dialectic process.

Hegel seems to have had a clear idea of the final reality, the 'Absolute', and then in subsequent writing he endeavoured to 'fit' the facts of areas such as geography, history, politics, the arts, the sciences, and religion, in line with the idea of showing an advance towards this higher Absolute. The incomplete nature of each of these areas of human life is the source of the dynamic which we see (manifested) as change in each as they advance towards their fulfilment. The core of Hegel's philosophy is that only the whole, the Absolute, is truly real, each fact (even space and time) is illusory taken on its own (or in collections of other facts as in ideas), is flawed in that it can at best only be a part of the whole. Whereas we might say that Kant took the view that the world of our understanding conforms to the structure of human reason, Hegel considered that reason (for him this included human reason but was more than this) was itself the central constituent of the world. The development of reason was evident in the ultra-complex process of advance towards the Absolute, and for the mind this unfolding is discovered in the 'world', not imposed on it. For Hegel: 'The rational is the real and the truth is the whole'. A sense of the steps in the advance toward the Absolute can be seen in the triadic aspects of the developing Spirit:

Subject Spirit – man as personal consciousness

Objective Spirit – civil society, 'the world', the state, etc

Absolute Spirit – art, religion, philosophy

Idealism was an approach that took rationalism to a level of abstraction such that it emerges as determinedly different from types of empirical rationalism considering that we initially gain knowledge from direct experience. For model forms of Idealism, the world designated as physical only has an existence as it manifests in thought. A counter metaphysical approach to this being realism; the view that the physical 'world' is the only basic reality, even if 'physical' has been interpreted in significantly different ways.

For Hegel, all previous philosophies can be contained (absorbed) within the Hegelian system and each has an element of truth, if early Greek Idealism and the critical philosophy of Kant contain a greater element of truth than the other previous philosophies. Hegel's conceptual ambition knew no bounds; even the Absolute Idea is itself unbounded. For him, we think in terms of time due to our inability to understand the whole; the ultimate reality is timeless. Every aspect of human endeavour could in principle be subsumed into the Hegelian system – the whole history of humankind was for Hegel but the diachronic working out (unfolding, but logically so) of the 'Absolute Spirit' as it worked toward fulfilling the Absolute Idea. For example, on a more mundane level of actual outcomes, according to Hegel after passing through stages that included magic, religions of nature, and a range of other religious beliefs, Christianity had now come to represent the form of religion which was closest to the Absolute Idea (most developed expression of). In politics it was (fortuitously) the Prussian state which was the form of government closest to the Absolute Idea. Hegel had begun with the view that Napoleonic France held this place, expressing his admiration for Napoleon (as the 'World-Soul') – following his decisive victory at Jena in 1806 - in a letter to his friend Niethammer, after seeing the triumphant Emperor riding through the town, noting that it was a: '…..wonderful sensation to see such an individual'. He also suggested that the period of German ascendancy would give way to that of America. Unsurprisingly, given his admiration of Napoleon and indeed of Alexander the Great before him, Hegel's view was that the dialectical movement generating the self-development of the Absolute Sprit in history was warfare. But the common dynamic driving the dialectical process more generally was the inherent 'logical contradiction' contained in the second, the thesis/antithesis, element of the triadic dialectic. Nothing in the Hegelian system is wholly true (except the Absolute Idea) or wholly false; ideas should not be self-contradictory, but truth or falsity would be assigned on the basis of the extent to which the Absolute Idea is inherent in any particular idea. Which means of course that only the Absolute idea (and to some extent a philosopher with the acumen claimed by Hegel) can know this – and this will only be when the Absolute Idea has realized itself or, for Hegel's adaptation of the poet Schiller's lines:

'The chalice of this realm of spirits

Foams forth to God His own Infinitude'

(Phenomenology of Mind' – J.Ballies trans. 1931 sec. ed. p808)

Hegel's own mode of logical progression (the dialectic) was also deployed to overcome the potential division of what we know of something (some entity – the aspect of it which we can know) and what it is as a thing-in-itself. The unfolding of the Hegel's Absolute Spirit is a progression of revealing higher levels of abstractions; with the logically preceding levels of abstraction and all associated particulars sublated within the higher levels. When this progression become manifest in the Absolute Idea it will reach its final form – the wholeness of ultimate reality will reveal itself to itself – the Subjective and the Objective in their most developed forms as Ideas will be united.

The influence of Hegelian Idealism was significant, spreading west to Britain: F.H.Bradley, perhaps the smoothest writer of philosophy ever, B.Bosenquet, and the influential teacher T.H.Green, and to the US with J.E. Creighton and Josiah Royce. Hegel was also a significant influence on Marx (he was associated with a group known as the Young Hegelians), famously so in relation to the process of dialectical reasoning and the relation of alienation. The primary differences arising from Marx's criticism of Hegel, and by implication, most other German philosophers of the time, being his passively seeking to 'understand the world' whereas for Marx the point was to actively seek to 'change it'!

As well as providing a conducive academic environment for Idealism in some of its universities, America also saw the development of a more 'home-grown' philosophy termed Pragmatism; basically, a philosophical method aimed at 'determining meaning'. This was the approach initially taken by Charles Sanders Pierce (see 'The Fixation of Belief' pub. 1877 probably first presented in the 1870s to the 'Metaphysical Club' in Cambridge Massachusetts - and the 'How to Make Our Ideas Clear' paper pub. 1878).

The role of the concept of 'sign' represented an important idea in Pierce's philosophy, as: '...a socially standardized way by which something (a thought, word, object) refers man (the community of sign users) to something else (the interpretant) which, in turn, is itself another sign', and so on. 'Pierce's Pragmatism is thus a method for translating certain kinds of signs into clearer signs in order to surmount linguistic or conceptual confusion' – in fact a theory of meaning – if signs are not amenable to interpretation (translation) in this way they are 'meaningless' or vacuous, so not real problems. Clarity comes from making 'signs' connect one to another by practical (pragmatic) considerations: '...thought is purposive but meaning carries a reference to the future' (B3 1974, Vol. 14 p940).

In Pierce we have an intellectual echo of Kant's use of

'Pragmatisch'; the type of thought that is purposeful, and gains empirical knowledge through direct experience. Pierce renamed his Pragmatism as 'Pragmaticism' in order to distinguish it from the Pragmatism of William James and others, much of which he disagreed with. For Pierce, meaning arises from the outcome of thinking through the implications of an idea; from an idea's effects, or rather from the effect that we consider any idea will have. In order to avoid possible nonsensical outcomes being credited as meaningful, Pierce inserted the word rational in relation to outcomes. Pragmaticism was a novel approach to philosophical analysis, one which would allow the easy dismissal of strong forms of intellectual abstraction that were often a feature of Idealism's (and indeed Realism's) grounds for metaphysical justification. Pragmatism more generally, was a forward-looking approach involving: implications, possibilities, and potentials.......in experience, rather than the closed off metaphysics of idealism, the teleology of which was for pragmatists, ambiguously 'post hoc'. Pragmatism also seemed to offer a system of analysis with the potential to overcome the problem of meaning that was inherent in most approaches to metaphysical disputes.

Early in the twentieth century pragmatism would be influential in areas such as the arts, law, and education. Pragmatism was developed (or rather reinterpreted and developed) by the very accessible writer William James (1842-1910). Pierce himself was mostly unhappy with the version that James developed and felt that it was biased towards the 'unscientific', that he was guilty of the oversimplification of the most important issues. As noted above, Pierce purposely termed his philosophy 'pragmaticism' in order to distinguish it from the 'pragmatism' of James and other philosophers.

Taking his own original approach, James brought together the analytical 'tool' designed by Pierce and insights offered by the French philosopher Henry Bergson (born, Paris. 1859).[15] Perhaps because his work is difficult to categorize in terms of traditional philosophy, Bergson's approach has been characterized as 'irrational'. Generally meaning that his method was based on intuition and of taking quite a personal approach to 'existence', and that he eschewed what would

---

[15] One of those philosophical outliers – including Schopenhauer, Nietsche, and Wittgensten, and perhaps James himself - who tended to favour provocation over system in relation to ideas.

normally be accepted as rational analysis – as in a logical thread of meanings that coherently hold any explanation/analysis together (giving them 'sense') following 'rules' such as non-contradiction, necessary implication, and those involving standard linguistic conventions.

For Bergson there are two basic types of entity in the Universe 'Life' and 'Matter' (see 'Time and Free Will' originally pub. 1889 Eng. translation 1910 – and his later book 'Matter and Memory', 1896); the kernel aspect of life being its characteristic as a 'force'. Life being essentially a dynamic movement 'upwards', with upwards meaning movement in 'time'(time as duration, not as quantitatively measured passing), conversely the movement involved in matter is downward. The Life-force (élan vital) evolves but can only do so in ways that cope with the various means by which the opposing force of matter confronts it, it adjusts to these and the outcome is the actual development of evolution. This is a creative process that exhibits (manifests) free-will, and so any attempt to describe reality in deterministic terms would be ill-judged. Bergson suggested that the human tendency to think in terms of 'sameness', 'identity', 'causality' and so on, is misleading. This type of thinking can be an aspect of intellectual thinking but we can only know the world in terms of its underlying life-force by intuition; which is related to instinct rather than intellect. For Bergson, all matter has some element of 'life' in it, even a stone (see 'Time and Free Will').

Unsurprisingly, Bergson rebelled against the rationalist tendency to isolate sensory experience, this red, this hot, this square, and of time constituted by measurable 'bits' of experience. For Bergson experiences run into each other, consciousness 'flows', and time is experienced as 'duration', not as a succession of measurable units. His philosophy attempts to describe and stimulate rather than analyze and intellectually satisfy; certainly if we view 'intellectual' in conventional rationalist terms.

William James offered a perspective on time similar to Bergson but one that could more easily be understood, with his idea of the 'stream of consciousness'. James had a better understanding of more common human psychology whereas Bergson sought to project his own very personal psychology into his ideas. James endeavoured to outline an approach that could combine the epistemological strengths of empiricism with some of the metaphysical insights offered by Bergson, and to do so in an assessable way. An accessibility that was gained at the cost of the criticism, as being academically 'loose', he received from some professional philosophers, including Pierce.

For James there was only 'pure experience' ('Essay in Radical Empiricism' pub 1912), and thought 'holds' aspects of this experience; yes we can think in terms of subject and object and of a distinction between objects and relationships between them, but our experience is of something pure in which these dualisms are but aspects of the one experience; I have a sense of pre-Husserlian phenomenological insight here. For James, pure experience is not 'mind-stuff' or 'matter-stuff', but rather it is something that comes prior to these derivative distinctions; and any experiential situation or viewpoint can best be assessed against possible outcomes.

James was drawn into a traditional philosophic task of identifying Truth. A concept more commonly applied when a statement agrees with our observations i.e. that truth 'copies' (corresponds too) empirical experience, but for James (with his instrumentalist foundations) truth is in fact, or rather in experience, a type ('species') of goodness; that which is true is that which is most good for us in terms of outcomes. So a simple example would be…….If the idea of God is good for humankind then it is true and belief in this God should be encouraged.

But truth can also be relevant in a more practical context such as would for example be appropriate for scientific verification. For James, meaning as well as truth was also linked to outcomes rather than just an immediate context, logical coherence, or to the intentionality of the agents involved. Meaning was linked to the consequences of holding any belief or the consequences of accepting any proposition or idea. In short, for philosophical pragmatists, how we understand the world is based on a methodology that accepts the reality of continual change (of reality as a process) and which assesses experience according to a form of functional efficiency. This methodological approach highlights the contrast between pragmatism and the mid to late nineteenth century versions of Idealism that were to a significant extent what its development was a reaction too.

As the nineteenth century developed advances were made in logic - a branch of the discipline of philosophy that Kant had earlier suggested had reached its completion in the work of Plato and Aristotle - by those such as R.Whately *'Elements of Logic'* 1826 According to the historian of philosophy, John Passmore (1957, p120), Whately's book 'shone brightly'. W. Hamilton, a publicist of the value of logic and a promoter, if not the originator, of the 'quantification of the predicate', a technical innovation that suggested a new area of logic offering fruitful development, A.De Morgan's *'Formal Logic'* of 1849 offered an original way of considering the relations (in particular the copula 'is') in logical propositions There was also a significant turn towards a mathematical logic inaugurated by George Boole, especially in his book *'The mathematical Analysis of Logic, Being an Essay towards a calculus of Deductive Reasoning'*. Although in his later works he suggested that this, especially an algebraic form of logic, was misplaced and in his book *'Studies in Logic and Probability'* 1847 (a collection of writing covering 1847-62) he sought to address this. There was also W.S Jevons's *'Pure Logic'* 1864, J.Venn's *'The Logic of Chance'* 1866 and *'The Principles of Empirical or Inductive Logic'* 1889, that along with J.N.Keynes *'Studies and Exercises in Formal Logic'* 1884, books that attempted to bring together a range of nineteenth century innovations within the framework of more traditional logic. W.E. Johnson's *'The Logical Calculus'* 1892 was a reductionist approach upon which A.North-Whitehead and B.Russell were to draw for their own later and more significant contributions to mathematical logic.

In a series of papers published in the philosophical journal *Monist,* C.S. Peirce suggested innovations, including that of the 'illative relation' (*'The Regenerated Logic' Monist, 1867*) later called the 'material implication', an idea that focused on the role of the relations contained in any proposition, on copulas such as 'is' 'or' 'for'. Refreshingly, Peirce saw logic not as simply about formal relations that pertain between the elements contained within propositions and between them but also as a form of enquiry into 'events' that take place in the real world. For Peirce's 'signs' (see above) – whilst these can be words they can also be any thought or event in the real world that has the logical potential to generate further signs, for example: a cloud is a sign of possible rain and people look for their raincoats – the initial sign, a cloud, has generated a further sign of possible rain.

On the European mainland the Italian G.Peano and his collaborators for *'Formulaire de Mathematiques'* 1895-1908 and the German G.Frege *'The Foundations of Arithmetic'* 1884 and *'Fundamental laws of Arithmetic'* 1893-1903 made significant advances in linking mathematics to certain types of logical ideas; undermining the foundations of logic that had not progressed much beyond Aristotle's formulations. Frege's identification of logical problems (if not so much his suggested solutions) identified areas of logic that would be followed-up by a number of twentieth century logicians.

At the end of the nineteenth century logic was a vibrant field of philosophical endeavour that would bear further fruit during the early part of the twentieth century, especially in the work of Bertrand Russell and Alfred NorthWhitehead, who together strove to identify a logical foundation for mathematics.

In complete contrast to the approach of the formal logicians were the more 'irrational' existence-based perspectives as seen in the novel and mostly original approaches to philosophy taken by individuals such as: Arthur Schopenhauer (briefly noted above), Soren Kierkegaard, Friedrich Nietzsche, and Henri Bergson (also noted above).

Arthur Schopenhauer (1788-1860) lived an easy material life but his later years a rather bitter academic one. For Schopenhauer, we have the view that the 'irrational is the real' as a provocative contrast to Hegel's 'the real is the rational'! He accepted Kant's view that there is a world of experience that appears to us in space and time, containing events linked by the idea of causality and which can be understood in terms of the 'principle of sufficient reason'. But he suggested that this was but a superficial understanding and that this Kantian ground of experience, and indeed the scientific approach that can arise from it, had only limited value in philosophical terms because it could not penetrate to the real world underlying the world of appearances. He maintained a keen interest in the philosophy of the East (Buddhism and Hinduism, especially the Vedas) and this contributed to the formation of his own metaphysics.

Schopenhauer considered that the actual world of 'ultimate reality' was one dominated by a strong, blind, universal cosmic 'Will',[16] a will that expressed itself in the instinctive drives that characterized the behaviour of both animals and men. He picked up on the Kantian idea of an unknown aspect of reality in the 'thing-in-itself' (noumena), but translated this into the will underlying reality. This idea of a cosmic will is metaphysically fundamental but it is imbued with and is the source of evil; the source of human suffering. Only the will is real and all nature (including the human body) both inanimate and animate is

---

[16] Although he used a capital W in the subheading at the start of a relevant section, he used the lower-case w throughout the book 'World as Will and Idea'.

but appearance. Although human reason, in giving rise to phenomenal experience, seems as initially presented to be something superficial it is after-all but a reflection of the World will. Schopenhauer's philosophy was immersed in pessimism, if one made endurable by the attitude of fatalistic acceptance of the evils that are expressed in human life. Individuals can find some consolation in this worst of all possible worlds (in direct contrast with Leibniz's view) in philosophical contemplation, and to some extent in the arts, especially music.

Schopenhauer was impatient with both the philosophy of rationalism with its abstract reasoning, and also of religious beliefs (including Christianity) these being mere allegories of the truth; their shared problem was their timidity. For him 'Either believe or philosophize!' whichever you choose, choose wholeheartedly. But to believe up to a certain point and no further, and to philosophize up to a certain point and no further – this is the half-heartedness which constitutes the fundamental trait of Rationalism.' ('Essays and Aphorisms', Penguin edition 1978, p196). To overcome, or at least bear the impact of the will, a person has the consolation of philosophy and can adopt the Buddhist approach of accepting that the phenomenal world is but one of illusion. The good man will live an aesthetic life practicing, chastity, poverty, fasting, and self-torture, which are all ways of passively confronting the will; there is little evidence that Schopenhauer himself practiced any of these. His most important writing is contained in his book 'World as Will and Idea', published in 1818 but not really noticed in intellectual circles until later in the century.

There was little if any religious timidity in the beliefs of Soren Kierkegaard (1813-1855). His became a rather extreme case of God worship (or rather, the glorification and reveling in a 'blind' faith in God), of a wish to absorb yourself as an individual into the sense of a Godhead. A mode of worship that was an act of abject self-abasement, undertaken as a free act. Existence and freewill are for Kierkegaard inextricably linked. Although mostly critical of their systems, he conditionally admired the intellectual brilliance of individual philosophers such as Kant and Hegel. Seeing some use-value in abstract, objective thinking (including even mathematics) but he railed against using this approach to understand the fundamental nature of being human. These more impersonal abstractions deal in but 'essences', but for Kierkegaard essence is preceded by 'existenz'.

Those aspects of human nature which lay beyond the scope of the level of essence. Essence being a mode of existence that includes the sciences which should only be applied to understanding plants, animal life, and the stars.

We can mark part of the modern foundations of existentialism in the work of Kierkegaard, with his emphasis on free-will, authenticity, and the priority of the personal. But his was an overly introverted version of each of these, with his greatest concern seeming to have been his own personal salvation. The titles of two major essays, 'Fear and Trembling' and 'The Sickness Unto Death', reflect his narrow personal, bordering on the personally (not religiously) timorous, outlook. If there could be a psychology of man's spiritual life then Kierkegaard plumbs to its depths but only draws up knowledge of this spiritual life that is narrowly subjective and based more on fearfulness rather than a bolder form of personal authenticity. Kierkegaard eschews an authenticity with more personal autonomy, one prepared to accept some individual responsibility for a life lived on Earth rather than one lived in the expectation of a life in eternity. For Kierkegaard, our earthly life is temporal and limited but we belong to eternity, and the framework for eternity is designed and sustained by the God of Christianity. 'Truth' for Kierkegaard is religious belief and the true religion is Christianity.

Up to the age of twenty three Kierkegaard saw himself as a bit of a rebel, rejecting his father's Christianity, and taking a rather cynical approach to life. He then experienced a prolonged period of moral questioning that led within two years to a return to Christianity and to his formally taking up the study of theology. Kierkegaard seems to have let this 'choosing' as an act of religious conversion, a choice that allowed him to experience what he felt as being a joyous event, to be identified as the characteristic feature of personal free-will. Not just free-will in terms of choosing between mundane everyday alternatives influenced by social pressures, including the pressure to conform, but the choices in life that leads an individual towards God. He outlined three stages in a person's life – the aesthetic, the ethical, and the religious; a passage that he felt he himself had progressed through.

In the first, the aesthetic, a person lives an impulsive, emotional life of self-indulgence including sexual licentiousness. Religion at this stage is unquestioned (an accidental outcome of birth-place and family) and experienced more as mundane social routine than an authentic personal relationship to God. Morality is based on a narrow perspective reflecting a man's understanding of his own self-interest. If even during this first stage a man can feel an uneasy sense of spiritual dissatisfaction. The second stage, the ethical, is when a man accepts universal moral standards (as defined by the Christian Church) and so a life of moderation which would include sexual impulses being expressed only within marriage. But again, a sensitive man would feel uneasy with this life, there would still be a sense of sinfulness and the feelings of guilt that would accompany this. Once this stage of unease has been reached the individual is in touch with a more personal relationship with God. He is then confronted by the choice of whether or not to make the 'leap' towards God.

In order to achieve this next stage – the truly religious – the individual has to try to overcome his finitude, to escape his human alienation (the alienating nature of human individuality), and move closer to the infinite nature of God. If the 'leap' towards God is made then the individual's morality becomes spiritual, it is the outcome of a personal relationship to God. It seems as if Kierkegaard felt that the closeness, the intimacy with God (as Absolute), invokes a sense of understanding of God's moral will – awareness of which forms a person's conscience.

Life for individuals at home in the stages of aesthetic or ethical is a life lived in uncertainty, lacking in truth, conditioned by the ever-present possibility of sin and so guilt. Whereas a life lived in the third stage – at one with God - was one rooted in certainty, truth, and authenticity. What drives the development through the stages is for Kierkegaard mainly due to a sense of unease (dissatisfaction) and of sinfulness which can generate the feeling of dread – dread is not fear (fear is something more specific.... fear of this snake or of that man, and similar), dread is a mixture of concern about the unknown aspects of what might happen if a person embraces change, or of losing the security of the known, but this can also suggest the exciting prospect of what one might become. Experienced as an adventure that draws one towards the unknown dread, offering the possibility of freedom.

I would speculate that Kierkegaard's intellectual and personal life was one lived in the search for a certainty he felt was attainable in some intermixed human and spiritual oneness with God. And, although there is some attempt to provide a rational case for working toward God, the essential act, the 'leap', the commitment required for the completion of the relationship, could for Kierkegaard only be an act of faith.

I think this is the sense of certainty that in fact eludes authentic reasoning. The projection of reasoned certainty is surely problematic, any patterned process of thinking sincerely progressed would involve the recognition of the possibility of more or less significant alternatives (appearing) in the logical, conceptual, and factual, links along any chain of reasoning, therefore any authentic reasoning process could not involve realized certainty, only relative truths. Are not even our most assured authentic judgments but out-comes of balanced reasoning; at its simplest taking the form of '....on the one hand this...and.... on the other hand that......but on balance, if a judgment is necessary, I conclude therefore that...... .' A balance of the knowledge held at the point in time that any judgment is being made. Any reasoning on serious issues taking place in the temporal world does require a form of provisionalism, there is always the potential for a lacuna between what is known and what could potentially be considered. It does seem that Kierkegaard was aware of this but felt that an act of 'faith' rather than any rational judgment was necessary to gain the freedom lying beyond dread. An intellectual can perhaps only arrive at any conclusion claiming certainty by an act of intellectual 'bad-faith', or by an act of religious 'faith'. I think that there is an implicit recognition apparent throughout Kierkegaard's works, the formed expression of his own intellectual journey towards an epistemologically unknown God realized in faith. For Kierkegaard's God read 'certainty'...... his (existential) journey has been completed – as for the rest of the world: the thousands of children who die of sickness and illness before reaching adulthood, the millions of adults denied the (social and political) freedom to follow Kierkegaard's intellectual route to personal salvation........ we have but silence. Can any personal search for meaning (as was Kierkegaard's) that excludes questions about the material circumstances of others, and more essentially the existence of evil, be cast in a mold shaped by moral requirements and constructed by an intellectual craftsman claiming authenticity?

As I read Kierkegaard (of the 'Concluding Unscientific Postscript' 'Fear and Trembling' and 'The Sickness unto Death') I have a sense of a cowardly, essentially self-centered man – feverishly reaching for some explanation, some rationale, that can provide spiritual solidity (and solace) in his life. Of an emotionally drowning man grasping for a life-raft, and the chance to wash up on some shore of certainty that could include personal salvation. The descriptive character of

Kierkegaard's God made him very similar to the mundane God of the Lutheran Church (in which he had grown up), even if in later life it seems that his distraction with sin and the richer sacral texture and iconic symbolism of Catholicism was drawing him. But the intensity of his personal journey, the very intense focus on personal 'existence', did offer a different form of philosophy to that of mainstream European academia. His focus on personal existence was to be taken up (without the religious elements) by twentieth century existentialists such as Martian Heidegger and John-Paul Sartre. Kierkegaard did not lay the coherent foundations for twentieth century existentialist philosophy but there are parallel ideas in relation to a focus on existence, free-will, authenticity, and the personal – so his approach served to stimulate its development. If the inhuman eruptions of evil in the first half of the twentieth century in world wars, the exploitation and alienation of capitalism and of communist dictatorships, perhaps did more to provide the generative motivation for later existentialists.

I have spent a bit longer on Kierkegaard than on other philosophers due my feeling that the very intensity of his philosophizing is a model of how each of us should approach reflection on our own existence; even if such reflection should move from the merely self-reflective limitations of Kierkegaard's the 'I' in individual existence to encompass the 'We' of humanity in the world.

Another, if more romantically inclined, thinker was Friedrich Nietzsche (1844-1900), who brought a vibrant dynamism to his philosophy that was generally missing from his life. But it was a vibrancy focused on the promotion of a philosophy that challenged almost all philosophy that stood between him and some of the pre-Socratic Greeks. His, at times cruel at times witty (poetic), criticisms were applied to philosophers including Plato, Descartes, Spinoza, Locke (Nietzsche called Locke a 'Blockhead'). Kant and Hegel in particular drew scathing criticism, as did anything tainted with the approach of rationalism, in either its empiricist or idealist forms. There was also a set of implications arising from his philosophy that directly challenged some of the political and ethical views of his time, especially the French revolutionary (Enlightenment) belief of the equality of mankind and the similar views underlying socialism and communism, and indeed a Christ-centered interpretation of Christianity.

Any view that promoted democratic politics, even in less radical liberal utilitarian forms, was to be condemned. Democratic politics would only promote rule by inferior men and even of women!

For Nietzsche, the idea of deciding any issue on the basis of communal interests was an anathema, unless that is, the communal interest was one shared by some elite group of aristocratic 'hero' figures......'Supermen'. Nietzsche valued the rebel, the individual who would boldly refuse to follow the herd, who rejected the invariably mediocre normative values of the 'crowd', in favour of some more eternal values; so we can see some echo of a heritage rooted in German Romanticism. But the values that Nietzsche's hero lived in accordance with were those wrought in conflict and warfare, values that could allow a man to stoically accept pain as part of life and also to be prepared to inflict pain on others. The model for the heroic society was that of ancient Sparta. Even if this society was un- if not anti-intellectual and Nietzsche's own hero was, if not himself a great artist or intellectual, at least recognized their value and would therefore seek to protect them; a model for the heroic individual was Imperial Napoleon Bonaparte. For the hero (superman) normal human morality should not apply. The 'Christian' imperative (promoted as universals by such as I.Kant and J.S.Mill) that we should not do to others that which we would not wish to be done to ourselves, was rejected out of hand as reflecting the morality of the weak, of the cowardly. The superman who tramples over normative morality should not feel guilt nor be expected to have a bad conscience over any outcomes.

The more interesting aspect of Nietzsche's analytical work was the analysis of ideas of some Kantian 'thing-in-itself', or some innate faculty such as Descartes 'I' (ego) or Locke's receptive 'blank slate'. Although his language of analysis is intermixed with the language of emotion and invective and the style is often aphoristic, here we do have an interesting contrast to these earlier types of philosophizing. But I don't think that Nietzsche productively followed through on his initial critical insights.

One commentator R.J.Hollingdale (translator into English of 'Beyond Good and Evil', 1972) suggests that to understand Nietzsche's ideas we should not be tempted into judging him by this aphorism or that fragment but should instead take his work as a whole which he claims '...decisively modified our attitudes towards the nature of truth as such'. I find this to be an exaggerated claim made in support of an odd suggestion about a philosopher who was avowedly unsystematic. To gain an appreciation of a systematic philosopher, such as Kant or Hegel, I can see that an overall understanding of the system would be the approach to take but for Nietzsche, his style invites assessment at the very least at the end of each book......what can for example allow us to better understand what are a series of unsupportable aphorisms and strange assertions about women?

In any case, his towering assertion-based promotion of some idealized 'superman' – the worship of the heroic and strong by a sickly and weak man - would make the appreciation of any aspect of his philosophy difficult for most of us. Nietzsche himself suggested a creative link between a philosopher's 'innate' perspective and their approach to philosophy. The temptation is to see his own obvious limitations as a man creating in imagination, and expounded in a series of books, the literary reflection of his wish to be personally linked to the heroic.

Both Kierkegaard and Nietzsche show an intensity of thinking that is turned inward, rooted in and sustained by drawing upon deep emotional resources, albeit at times expressed with literary brilliance, rather than undertaking a more analytic personal intellectual journey. I think that I should add that a number of philosophers into the twentieth century hold both Kiekegaard, and more so Nietzsche, in high regard.

During the nineteenth century there emerges again in philosophy - in particular for, Kant, Hegel, Schopenhauer, and Bergson - the duality of an accessible reality that we can have direct knowledge of, and an inaccessible aspect of reality that we can be aware exists but of which we cannot gain direct knowledge. Kant's things-in-themselves' is perhaps the most obvious but there is also the type of unknown represented in Hegel's Absolute Idea (out there in some the logical future), Bergson's 'Life-force' (élan vital), Schopenhauer's 'Ultimate Reality' (embodied in the will) – All suggestions of some one underlying reality that we can only know by their 'manifestations' in the range of phenomenal experience accessible to humans.

Ludwig Wittgenstein would also later on make a contribution to expressing this duality in his early book 'Tractatus Logico-Philosophical' (TLP - 1921) – the last proposition (7) of the book being: 'Whereof one cannot speak, thereof one must be silent'. In Max Black's commentary on the TLP he suggests the implication of Wittgenstein's remark is that there 'is' something about which we cannot speak - and he goes on to note the connection P.T.Geach makes to Schopenhauer's Will: 'The silence with which Wittgenstein ends recalls how Schopenhauer refused to give any appearance of positive description to that which is chosen when the Will turns round on its tracks; for us who are full of will, it is nothing; but for those who chose it, "this so real world of ours, with all its suns and galaxies - is nothing." ' (Geach is quoting Schopenhauer here from 'World as Will and Idea' p262 (1995 Everyman ed.) where the passage is translated as: '.....this world of ours, real as it is, with all its suns and galaxies, is - nothing'. (p160) He also notes a distinction between an 'absolute nothingness' and the conditions under which it can appear as 'relative nothing'.

I have only given a quite superficial 'flavour' of the more notable Western philosophers that were most influential during the nineteenth century, including just a handful of individuals. It was a century that began in Germany with the rationalism of Kant and the idealism of Hegel with varieties of each approach being developed by others. British empiricism increased its connection with the sciences, whilst French and German romantics increased their distance from the sciences. In the US pragmatism emerged alongside interpretations of an idealism inherited from Europe.

An approach to philosophizing originating during the nineteenth century that I have not mentioned is the very important approach known as phenomenology. I have omitted any consideration of this here due to my thinking that, although its modern roots lie in the nineteenth century with Immanuel Kant, Bernard Bolzano,, Franz Brentano, and the early work of Edmund Husserl, its much richer expression lies in the twentieth, so will be covered in some depth in Chapter 9 below.

Just as with the natural and social sciences, the number of individuals engaged in philosophy also grew tremendously between 1800-1900 and as the subject matured, like the sciences, it too became a profession; one with all the academic accoutrements reflecting its growing social status. By 1900 we can note thousands of men, and a few determined women, involved in the philosophical quest. Women such as: Catherine Cockburn 1679-1750, Mary Wollstonecraft 1759-97, Harriet Martineau 1802-76, Victoria Lady Wellby 1837-1912 and Mary Whiton Calkins 1863-1930 – women who had managed to overcome the economic and social barriers they faced, to produce high quality philosophy, as well as the insightful analysis of a range of social issues. By the end of the nineteenth century philosophy, whilst continuing to be an area of interest to a fairly narrow elite, offered a reservoir of intellectual information available to assist us in the interpretation of reality and the more essential aspects of lives lived within it.

As the century came to an end the primary 'western' philosophical approaches were in various forms of: Idealism, Empiricism, Romanticism/Existentialism, Rationalism, Phenomenology (see note above), and in the US, Pragmatism. Certainty the foundations of knowledge, and indeed considerations of the very nature of reality, continued to be pursued with intellectual vigor. Logic had been given a radical post Aristotelian revaluation by those such as Frege and Peano and would be developed further during the twentieth century. Thousands of books, journals, pamphlets, and other materials, served as evidence of both a growing interest in philosophical issues and of the advancing accumulation of 'novel information'. If we add this to the even more information-productive natural and social sciences we can see that the 'boundary' of accessible Reality was significantly extended during the century and now the concept of exponential seems appropriate to express the rate of growth of novel information in the form of knowledge.

For the most part, the productive development (in terms of ideas) of philosophy in the nineteenth century – if we allow for some exceptions such as Marx, Nietzsche, and J.S.Mill – was an academic discipline confined to universities and a quite narrow intellectual elite; it had its philosophical debating societies, its journals (e.g. 'Mind'), and its national associations (in Britain the BPA, and in USA. the APA). More widely the first 'International Congress of Philosophy' (Paris 1900) indicated the international ambitions of the subject's practitioners; meetings of which are still taking place in the twenty-first century. Philosophy at the end of the nineteenth century had a range of identifiable approaches, descriptive, explanatory, and analytic, contributing to understanding humankind's reflective presence in the world that would serve as foundations for the discipline to develop quite remarkably during the twentieth.

Summary of 19th century

Politically Europe in the nineteenth century had seen a gradual, if not a complete, change from rule by kings, princes, emperors, their families and coteries of aristocratic elites to forms of democracy – with populations of 'citizens' rather than 'subjects'[17] albeit often limiting the franchise to certain categories of a population. The 'democracies' were still significantly ruled by elite groups of various types, most from backgrounds of the landed aristocracy, financiers, and a rising 'big business' class. Invariably, beyond the form of classical polis-based Greek democracies in which all franchised citizens could voice their views, mass societies within democracies have to elect constitutional bodies to give voice to their interests. So these representative democracies commonly have power structures that are based on hierarchies of order – even if this can be power structures designed to more or less empower citizens, with governance incorporating such mechanisms as referenda, petitions, demonstrations, etc.

The legitimacy of any representative democracy primarily depends upon the willingness of those elected to legislate according to the 'will of the people'; even if this can be difficult to identify. There is also the issue of to what extent the interest of minority groups can be represented and how to protect some basic rights of minorities and of individuals – written constitutions interpreted by an impartial judiciary could offer this. A fundamental aspect related to legitimacy is the issue of the information available to citizens (and how this is presented to them) in all of the areas for which governments have responsibility.

Democracy in-itself is fatally flawed if the population involved is not adequately 'informed'. Accepting that 'informed' needs to clarified – a complex and sometimes subtle understanding of the amount of distracting white/grey 'noise' rained on any population and the ease of access to the type of knowledge that is more specifically relevant to making political decisions – but also relates to how any population is made politically aware during its education (the faculty of critical evaluation). The Nobel prize winning novelist Saul Bellow

---

[17] Although constitutional monarchies like Britain, Spain, Thailand, Norway, the Netherlands and at about a dozen others, still retained 'subjects' as a nominal status for its people.

noted to the effect that…in terms of the news, we only know the small waves and eddies that ripple across the surface we never (rarely) get to know about the deeper currents that move beneath the surface. Those contextual aspects of the 'news' which coalesce to form the more important determinants of how human history develops.

In 1690 John Locke's 'Civil Government' had been published and its focus on the tensions between the natural law and the social contract were to form an important element of political theorizing during the following two centuries. But by the end of the nineteenth century European and US -based writers such as John Stuart Mill (1806-1873), and Jeremy Bentham (1746 -1832) (in England), Montesquieu (1690-1755) and Marquis d'Argenson (1694-1757) (France), Alexander Hamilton (c.1756-1804) and James Wilson (1742-98) (both US based if Scotish born), were analyzing the political possibilities of governance by 'representative democracy', either as constitutional monarchies or as republics in various forms. In the US, a written constitution, as amended by politicians and interpreted by judges, had allowed the nation to develop politically into a two-party state, if each of these being committed to a 'free-market' capitalist economic system.[18] One in which big business - manufacturing, agricultural, media, mineral extraction, transportation - politicians, and an emerging military elite, took the lead. In most industrialized nations this triumvirate would become ever more entwined in terms of personnel and of collective interests. During the century a ruling elite had emerged that included leading members of the triumvirate – big business (including finance), military, and political - and a second layer made up of prominent members of, the legal profession, the Church, agriculture, academic institutions, middle-sized business (including finance), scientific communities, a mass media, and some leading local politicians.

A state-sanctioned upper-class, enabling rule by broader-based elite groups structured to represent, balance and further the interests of the components that make up the elites in each country; this pattern of rule was not conspiratorial, at least when taken as a whole. It was an implicit direction formed by the result of the unplanned balancing

---

[18] More in theory than in fact – from early on the US economy was driven by Government investment and concessions (e.g. land for railways, and from mid. 20th century a massive investment in the military) to private companies – a version of state capitalism, the only form that has been in use down to today.

of interests of the more powerful, outcomes which then operated top-down on all classes in society. Even accepting the dispersed origins (regionally and socially) of the elite minorities in industrial societies, these elite interests had usually experienced a commonality of political socialization (exposure to an elitist, if broad political ideology that assumed entitlement), that gave rise to a primarily consensual approach to economic and political management.

International politics was characterized by a group of leading industrialized nation states that had throughout the century worked to increasingly (US, England, Russia, Japan and France), or newly (Germany and Italy), unite, often diverse, peoples under one flag by creating a national 'ego-identity'. That conceptual core entity of nationhood whose particular form is elusive and changing in nature but which can operate as a powerful 'force'… something that can have a determinant hold on populations. One that can drive a nation to engage in terrible conflict. A force that can be manipulated by leaders to justify exploitation and gross inequality of its own citizens and well as those who live elsewhere. An entity – nationhood - made up of the imaginatively constructed content of a collective consciousness constituted by ideas of shared history, shared language, shared economic interests, if possible a shared religion, based within a geographic boundary. With a similarly simplistic sensitivity to ego-centric national slights as do touchy ego-centric individuals.

Civil nations now had standing armies (and most were able to introduce conscription when required), and whose economic development had provided the incentive to reach out and project their power to South America, Africa, and throughout the Middle and Far East. Nation-states armed by an industry in the hands of individuals prepared to let business interests overcome any moral qualms that they might have felt. Encouraged by politicians inveigled into the national egoism as part of their mindset. Nation-states looked suspiciously at each other's actions as they determinedly sought to advance their own interests. Aggressive economic measures, the threat of military action, and at times actual conflict, were regular features of international relations. The scramble for overseas dominions encouraged international relations to be more about competition than co-operation. Peaceful periods were exceptions and war, in defense of some elusive but conceptually powerful entity called the 'national-interest', was easily turned to. A concept that epitomizes the successfull process of solidifying the world geographically into historically synthetic entities called nations – when the idea of some 'national interest' could be successfully appealed to, without more than some superficial examination of just what this can actually mean. Deployed in a discourse to justify gross economic exploitation, killing and maiming, and the spending of vast amounts of money on the military.

The legacy of exploitation-based colonialism became entrenched across the world – primarily a legacy of slave economic regimes in the Americas and various types of often equally oppressive colonial regimes in Africa, and the Middle and Far East. The leading colonial powers at this time were Britain and France. By 1900 Britain's overseas investment amounted to over 160% of its annual national income, France 120%, and Germany 40% of theirs (each returning approx 5% per annum). The institutionalization of various processes of economic extraction that survived the abolition of slavery; and indeed would to a significant extent survive post colonialism itself from the 1950s. A relentless form of economic exploitation and hegemonic dictatorial political control infused with racism, as 'Western' nations often claimed to be driven by a missionary intent of bringing the benefits of enlightened civilization to the 'backward' peoples of the world.

Elite-group individuals and families gained fortunes during this time, but of more relevance to today, the trade, finance, and political structures that have set the conditions for the world's people in the 20th/21st centuries were constructed and firmly embedded during the 19th. These mostly unquestioned arrangements based on nation-statehood, property rights, and the ability to wield economic, military, and political power.

Financially, industrializing nations-states had further developed banking systems whose roots lay in 15th century Italy and 16th century Holland (the 'United Provinces of the Netherlands'). Many refinements had been added during the eighteenth and nineteenth centuries including: the spread of the use of paper money, more central banks, the systematic investing in the future prices of products, food, commodities, gold and precious stone, and a range of raw materials such as oil, wood, rubber. By the end of this period, giant companies had been created in steel, chemicals, transport, big agricultural, and armaments. Joint-stock companies also grew in number and mergers created larger holdings during this time. A time when British companies such as Distillers, Imperial Tobacco, Tate and Lyle, J.P. Coates, and Lever Brothers were formed. If most businesses were quite small, and many (Cadburys, Boots, Roundtrees, Wedgewood, in the UK) remained family owned.

Across industrializing Europe and the Americas, a similar process of business change and expansion was taking place. Stock markets had been established as early as 1530s (Antwerp) and 1611 (Amsterdam) and later in London (1773), New York (1792), Frankfurt (1879) and Chicago (1882); but by 1900 there many large cities having trading centres/bourses. By the century's end fortunes were being made by financial speculators able to access a series of loosely regulated (or rather substantially unregulated) 'markets'. Markets that could provide a legitimate source for businesses to raise funds for expansion and for investors to gain a reasonable return on their investments. Or markets that could operate as rigged 'casinos' for activities aiming to maximize speculators income with a dynamism expressed by individual greed disconnected from any aspiration to contribute to the common good. Government borrowing (guilts, bonds, debentures) increased, mostly funded by the application of quite complex taxation systems usually based on land values rather than wealth in itself. The fourth quarter of the century was also a time of the further development of ever-larger joint-stock companies and of large corporations.

For most of the nineteenth century there was a nation-based banking system geared more to supporting small business, personal banking, and lending to governments, rather than offering the large sums for industrial development. Industry mostly raised its funds from partners and relatively small groups of shareholders. It was more towards the end of the century that the increasing size of companies and technological developments - chemicals, armaments, paper, coal, steel, glass, transport, etc.- requiring large sums for investment, that the bigger banks were turned too. Bank lending to governments offered the millions required to fund the military, leaving significant debts to be financed from government incomes and increasingly from borrowing (in effect deferred taxation). A military that by the end of the century was, in many countries, making significant demands on a nation's GNP e.g. Germany 3%, France 4.8%, US 1.5% and Britain 6% - all being a steady increase on the 1800 figures and identifying a funding trend that would be carried into the twentieth century.

Many businesses grew in size to the point where managers rather than owners organized their operation and both national and local government developed as hierarchically 'managed' bureaucracies operating in similar ways. The practice of management itself became a subject, a skill, to be learnt with courses in management being offered in technical colleges of Germany, France, Russia, and the US (Britain was late into this qualified manager approach).

In Britain, and most other industrialized states, the displacement of 'royal' power (prerogatives) was in favour of large landowners and big business at the top with, at first the grudging acceptance, of the increasing power and influence of the expanding middle-classes influencing political, economic and social reform policy. Life for many industrial workers was even grimmer than those of their grandparents but as the century progressed their economic function as essential cogs in the profit-making machine[19] allowed them (as a class) to become more aware of the possibility of being able to exercise some power; albeit of the most dilute variety. The working classes made some economic and political progress as the consolidation of trades unionism became a common feature of British, Western European and by the end of the century US, industry – if more to the benefit of skilled rather than unskilled workers. In Britain there was a slow transformation of the political ideologies underlying Conservatives (Tory) and the aristocratic Liberals (Whigs up to 1859) as, with varying degrees of resignation and very little sincere enthusiasm, they adapted to the rising power of the middle class and, towards the end of the century, and to a limited extent, of the organized industrial workers.

Across the globe, an increasing proportion of national populations had been drawn into city-life. By the end of the century the world's largest cites included: London (6.5m), Paris (3.3m) Berlin (2.4m), New York (4.2m), St Petersburg (1.4m) Moscow (1.1m) Peking (1.2m), Tokyo (1.5m), Calcutta (1.0m). A continuing demographic process, with mega-cities such as Manila, Mexico City, and Mumbai, having populations from 16-22 million in 2021. The living conditions in cities during most of the nineteenth century was generally quite poor and in places awful; similar conditions continue to be experienced by many living in the 21th century mega-cities just noted. Life for the lower classes was characterized by overcrowding, noisy

---

[19] Engels suggested that the nuclear family of nineteenth century capitalism was the social institution required to produce and socialize the ongoing generations of workers.

neighbourhoods, unsanitary living conditions, risk of diseases such as cholera and tuberculosis, the health-related outcomes of malnutrition, often dangerous working situations, along with the ever-present threat of decline from relative, into abject, poverty.

Towards the end of the nineteenth century, the influence of both religious and secular social reformers, Trades Unions, and some politicians 'enlightened' by moral conscience or by self-interest (the need for 'fit' workers and soldiers) led to improvements in living conditions in some areas for some people. In Europe and the US, an aspect of civil life best described as 'municipal' was being constructed, as national and local government grew to take responsibility for rubbish and sewage disposal, urban development, public health, policing, education, and to some extent waterways, roads, and for some public utilities. State run police forces, first established in Britain (London) in 1829 were, by the end of the century, features of civil life throughout the world.

The development of a municipal civil life, with the acceptance that certain standards of living and working conditions should be maintained, were important correctives to the conditions that had prevailed. But it was from the groups mentioned – big landowners - business – finance – military – the legal profession - politics - that composed the elite in control of the nation-state, and it was their collective interests that were being primarily advanced. Not as explicit national conspiracies but as thousands of individual decisions made by people in positions of influence and power that, taken as a whole, inclined towards advancing the 'class interests' of these well-placed people. The combined influence of this elite created the social, economic, military, and political structures that so favoured the class interests of those at the 'top' of society. The social milieu within which decisions were taken expressed patterns of decision-making favouring the better-off without considering the need for any revaluation of values and principles.

Individuals making up this relatively homogenous (using simple economic class characteristics) grouping had for the most part, experienced socialization processes within upper - and middle-class families, friendship and extended social groups, clubs and sporting groups, business and social clubs, in schools, in the mass media (re-interpreting events within narratives of elite self-interest) and much of the literature to which they were most likely to be exposed. These factors forming the mindset of individuals making their contribution to economic, political and social life with the certainty of view that their choices and actions might coincide with their own interests but also for the greater good of the nation.

Throughout Britain in the nineteenth century, representatives of the ruling class conceded a series of parliamentary reforms (1832, 1867, 1884) if for many this was more as measures introduced to avoid rebellion than from a sincere commitment to advancing democracy – similar incremental measures to widen the franchise were also taking place across much of industrializing Europe. By the end of the century, in countries with constitutional arrangements that includes some forms of democratic representation, elites could not generally wield power in ways that were overtly aimed at furthering their interests....the intention was by then to have convinced a sufficient proportion of any country's population that the polices being pursued were in the interest of all; were in the 'national interest'. Taking Britain as an example, the colonial enterprise was usually presented as providing work for the British working class (offering markets for British goods and so work and raw materials for British industry), or that a war was required to advance British interests or defend British pride (see passage on captured German submariners in H.G.Wells 'The Undying Fire', 1931, pp 135-148 - some of which is reproduced in Chapter 7 below)

More radical political ideologies – a continuing undercurrent with the range of British social/political ideologies - increasingly offered alternatives to mainstream politics. For most people today, the nineteenth century revolutionary theory is considered to have been dominated by Marxism. But long before Marx in the mid-century, socialists-type ideas had been percolating through sections of the working and middle classes. Ideas that produced more useful action at the community-based level whilst also, if much more slowly, helping to progress the economic and political advance of the majority population.

What might broadly be termed 'socialist' ideas[20] came to the fore in debating and corresponding groups, and no doubt at times in pubs and workplaces and, as the century progressed, this would include considerations more specifically related to trade unionism.

For J.D.Bernal (1969, vol. 4, p1066), men like John Gray 1799-1850 and Francis Bray 1809-95 '.....carried the arguments of the

---

[20] The words socialist and socialism were used from the 1830s.

Utilitarians and of Owen to the logical conclusion of a socialist state in which all will be producers of wealth.' If, for much of the century these ideas only reached a relatively few.

Although very limited, higher education was also becoming available for small numbers of the lower middle and the working classes notably with the London Mechanics Institute (later to become Birkbeck College, London) by Thomas Hodgskin (1783-1869), who also called for the abolition of capitalism. Gray, Bray, and Hodgskin, were just three men amongst many individual thinkers who wanted to go further than parliamentary and modest social reform.

The co-operative movement became a powerful means for working people to gain some sense of consumer agency and, in a range of connected activities, to reinforce community empowerment and social cohesion. Co-operatives can be noted as early as 1498 (The Shore Porters Society of Aberdeen), a weavers co-operative in Ayrshire in 1769 (The Fenwick Weavers Society), with dozens more forming in the eighteenth century in Britain and across Europe (in Russia village-based co-operatives – obshchina - were popular), and in the US where they were known as Credit Unions. The modern co-operative movement in Britain is marked by the founding in 1844 of the Rochdale Pioneers Co-operative Society that would grow to become the wide-ranging retail and banking organization still operating today.

Apart from allowing consumer agency and reinforcing community values, the co-operative initiatives also allowed profits to be shared and/or reinvested – thousands of co-operative type associations provide alternatives to private business (including banking and private loans companies) across the world today (in countries such as Bolivia, Mexico, Spain, and India) and they still serve as a model of what could be built on. Promoting both localism and economic fairness. (see Chapt. 10 below, for more on co-operative-type alternatives to private business)

The developments in communication, the factory system, urban life and available 'ideas' saw the increasingly more effective organization of workers as the century progressed. The ideas were more-often related to economic justice and the advance of basic material conditions but some were fired but more inspirational ideas that had emerged from the French revolution of – equality, liberty, and fraternity –, even if the revolution itself had failed to realize any of these. In the 30 years from 1880 to 1910 a number of socialist/communist political parties were also formed (as in Britain) in Germany, Poland, Russia, and other parts of Europe. Two areas of division that fractured the European left was a sincere difference of view of 'revolution or reform', with a third grouping mendaciously maintaining the rhetoric of revolution whilst implementing the practice of compromise and constitutional politics. Questions of national self-determination (e.g. the campaign for an independent Poland) or internationalism were hotly debated. These differences would be clearly seen in the intellectual relationships between leaders such as August Bebel (Germany), Eduard Bernstein (Germany), Rosa Luxemburg (Germany and Poland), Jean Juares (France), Karl Liebknecht (Germany) Lenin (Russia), Karl Kautsky (Germany), Alexander Kerensky (Russia), Leon Trotsky (Russia). These would-be leaders launched often quite virulent attacks on each other in print and at conferences, focused more on ideological and tactical differences than on the underlying unity of sharing the aspiration for governments based on the representation of the proletariat. The divisive primacy given to national interest at the outbreak of the First World War would effectively crush hopes of an international socialist unity.

In Britain, most other European countries and the US, government become increasingly centralized, with more effective revenue raising arrangements. The industrializing nations of Europe had become mass societies – the influence and control of localism and the traditions based on this had, to a significant extent, given way to a population taking regional, national, (and even on some matters, international) perspectives on a range of issues. This perspective was being created by a national press of newspapers and magazines, by novels, mass education, large populations concentrated in cities, national organizations such as trades unions, production companies, large retail outlets, charities, sports clubs, and the sense of overseas dominions – all of which also contributed to fostering (indeed constructing) national identities.

Mass societies had the potential for mass 'bottom-up' action of the type seen in Britain during the Chartist movement, across much of Europe in 1848, and more locally in the Paris Commune of 1871. But history shows that mass societies are also more liable to be influenced by 'top-down' planning and direction and to persuasion and manipulation (overt and covert) in the interests of controlling elites.[21] The ideal conditions being a population that in Foucaultian terms has 'brought itself to order'; inculcating obedience to the extent that the status quo is felt, at least sufficiently, to be in-line with one's own view – a 'closing down' of possible alternative courses of action, to the point where they cease to be considered (e.g. see 'socialism' in the early 21st century). All of the tools used to order mass populations, honed in the advertising industry, have been developed by governments\politicians (and in the 20th/21st centuries by corporations) to persuade populations to certain views and more generally to manage public opinion.

As the nineteenth century progressed a mass production society became progressively a mass consumption society – even if most economists advocated variations on a supply-side approach for governments overseeing industrializing countries. It would take a global economic crisis in the 1930s, and the obvious failure of supply-side economics for J.M.Keynes case for a demand-led approach to be accepted, with the demand being created by direct government intervention – even if industrialists, included famously Henry Ford, had early on realized that the market potential market for goods could include their own workers.

The expansion of our possible information horizon (Reality) included masses of factual information gleaned from the systematic study of the natural world and from human social life by the newly emerging natural and social sciences and the advance of a range of technologies - agricultural, transport, manufacturing, health-care, communication, warfare, construction. It also included masses of relational information based on assessments made of this or that event, or collection of related events. These being mainly collected in books and academic journals encompassing history, geography, religion, politics, finance, and philosophy. Together representing but the more obvious elements composing the stream of new information that expanded the knowledge boundaries of humankind during the nineteenth century; from now the concept of the 'specialist' or the 'expert' - the curators of circumscribed intellectual phenomena - of this or that subject, and the limitations on individual intellectual horizons that this implies, was firmly established.

---

[21] Control rather than ruling can be an important in terms of ability to dissipate the force of revolutionary ideas.

In the European intellectual milieu both the natural and the social sciences had risen on a tide of enthusiasm generated by the success of those progressing scientific endeavours and of the sense of intellectual freedom of some leading thinkers of the Enlightenment. Up to the end of the eighteenth century, science had, for the most part, been a broad-based activity undertaken by an fairly eclectic mix of individuals, generally working alone (if in communication with others pursuing similar interests) and all following methods similar to those outlined by Francis Bacon focusing on 'facts', based on observations, and using the identification of regularities to formulate 'laws'. With individuals such as Isaac Newton, applying these methods, and also contributing, along with others including Leibniz and Rene Descartes, to a body of mathematics that would significantly enhance the ability of science to quantify its observations and its experimental predictions. The nineteenth century saw the consolidation of this endeavour, with the natural sciences emerging as professions for 'scientists' whose work was primarily based in universities and in the research departments of progressive industries.

The century saw the transformation of science from an activity generally pursued by the financially independent gentleman to a professional role undertaken as paid employment. The national institutionalization of the sciences can be illustrated by the founding of such broad-based scientific organizations as the Royal Society in Britain, the Academy of Science in France, and Royal Academy in Germany. More specialist scientific organizations such as the Linnean Society founded 1788, Geological Society founded 1807, Chemical Society 1841 plus many more, and their equivalent specialist scientific bodies founded in countries such as France, Germany and the US. With their work being expressed in a burgeoning series of specialist scientific journals. An institutionalization reinforced by the progressive inclusion of the sciences in the curricula of education systems.

The most significant intellectual achievement was probably the culmination of the observations and theories that led to humankind having access to knowledge about the age of the Earth and of the evolutionary development of life on it. Numerous specialisms developed in the natural sciences and by the end of the century most could be studied in schools, technical colleges and universities, as well as research departments of industries such as armaments, chemicals, drugs, textiles, food, construction, etc.

For the social sciences, thinkers such as Thomas Hobbs had led the way in advocating the application of the methods of the physical sciences (mechanistic materialism) to individual psychology and to the social world. These sciences that would follow similar paths to intellectual respectability and social recognition as had the natural sciences.

It was August Comte (1798-1857) who gave the name 'sociology' to the study of social life and had argued for, but in his own more speculative approach did not himself follow, a positivist approach to social life. He suggested three 'stages of humankind's historical development – theological, metaphysical, and scientific. He even went so far as to advocate a Positivist State in which sociologists would direct how it should be run. Broadly speaking, Britain led the way in economics, Germany in history, France in sociology, Germany and France in geography

Herbert Spencer's book 'Programme of a System of Synthetic Philosophy' pub. 1860 was an ambitious attempt to apply a simplistic interpretation of evolutionary theory to areas of human knowledge such as society and ethics. This type of work was misapplied to provide some sort of rationale for a competitive society and a capitalist economic system – the argument that competition was 'natural' and that those who 'survived' (were successful) were so due to their superior traits; it also served as spurious support to racist attitudes.

Economics and political theory were the earliest of the modern social sciences to achieve some sort of professional status then in the nineteenth century sociology and psychology were established as professions. Developments due, to some extent, to the social complexities of city-life and a middle-class interest in personal psychology in the context of the intellectual attraction of applying the methods of positivist science to human social and mental life.

In terms of more obvious evils: millions of people died of famines in India (8.5 million 1866, 1879, 1897, 1900), China (20m during the period of the T'ai-ip'ing Rebellion 1850-73, and between 9-13 million 1876-79), Brazil (500,000 in 1879), and 1m had perished in Ireland in the 1850s and another million in Ethiopia 1888/9. These being just some of the more noted. Each of these being caused, or significantly exacerbated, by the action of, usually foreign, governments.

Mechanized, or rather 'industrialized',[22] warfare was developed, producing the slaughter of millions of mostly young men but also of civilians. Conflicts highlighted by the Napoleonic campaigns, towards the beginning of the century, the Crimea in 1850s and the US civil war in the 1860s. Wars of independence such as the series of Italian wars in 1849, 1859, and 1866, and that of Cuba 1895-8. Wars suppressing the many nations being ruled over by empire-building invaders such as the long drawn out US/Apaches campaign and the Anglo/Zulu (1879) and Anglo/Sino wars (the 'Opium Wars - 1856-60). With nearly 300 wars recorded for the nineteenth century, 70 of these being in the last decade; reflecting the increasingly bitter colonial experience and the more conflictual wider international context.

The primary beneficiaries of the preparation and expression of industrialized warfare were private companies such as Krupp (Germany), Armstrong (Britain), Creouset (France), Nobel (Norway), Smith and Wesson (US). Since the first appearance of civil life we can identify competition between groups in the development of more powerful weapons – bronze to iron, iron to steel, foot-soldier to horse/camel/elephant rider, spear to short stabbing sword, crossbow to longbow to musket, musket to rifle, rifle to maxim gun, and this to cannon - was a defining feature of developing civil life. But the industrialized acceleration of this competition, and the related resource implications, began to see government financing, and international relationships, determined on the basis of superior weaponry. A danger being that a country would see its own superiority, its military 'preparedness', as but a temporary ascendancy....another pressure to fight during this time.[23] In countries such as Russia, Germany, France, Austria, Turkey, and Britain, military planning was increasingly influencing political decision-making.

In relation to a central focus for this text: The nineteenth century had seen an exponential growth in the amount of information that had become inserted into human Reality. The century was characterized

---

[22] 'Mechanized' being a concept missing the point of the profit motive driving powerful individuals to favour conflict and the development of ever-more 'superior' weaponry.

[23] The well know 'Thucydides Trap' - currently, if foolishly, considered by some to be a consideration of the US in the face of the military advance of China.

by a significant extension of the information and knowledge (and the more systematic arrangement of the information) potentially available to humankind. But such is its quantity and complexity, and in the sciences especially liable to continual change, that fully informed decisions on anything other than the most simple of political, economic, or academic areas, can to some extent only be aspired too rather than realized. By 1900 the vast majority of the world's population could only encounter and understand issues not from first-hand experience (characteristic of local events) but as events and issues interpreted by others (scientists, politicians, the mass media) – and this allied to each person's background leading to a further filtering and so narrowing of perspective, from amongst all possible interpretations.

The mass of new information that had entered, and shaped, the Reality of humankind's existence had increased exponentially in one hundred years but it was the rate of acceleration of this store of information which had gained a momentum that would continue to rise during the next 120 years. But…..but...... humankind's ability to manage the information was still based on a self-conscious level of consciousness – machines were increasing the productivity of manufacturing, the natural sciences and technology were increasing our understanding and ability to manipulate (control) the material world, and the implications of the advances in the social sciences allowed some understanding of humankind's social and psychological lives and of our economic and political arrangements. The information available could now more easily be disseminated via such mechanisms as a growing mass media, books, scientific journals, political pamphlets.

In terms of understanding the world and interacting with others – of social living - self-consciousness means a narrow view, linked to personal interests. Self-consciousness tends towards seeing the other as friend or foe, and foe was usually the unknown other. Self-consciousness tends towards the stereotypic categorization of others, tends to notice difference rather than underlying sameness, self-consciousness at home in an industrializing society tends towards a focus on self rather than common interests. Tends towards reductionist forms of thinking (not the reductionist analysis of the sciences) rather than more holistic forms. Generally a tendency towards essentialist and stereotypic thinking, of reducing issues to simplistic explanations (and so more easily managed) and, in a mass society, of accepting the interpretations of experts and other influential individuals whose views have a more general coherence with an individual's own; basically a tendency towards intellectual laziness and therefore a milieu that mitigates against the personal clarification of moral implications. Note my use of the word 'tends' this indicates that the characteristics I am describing express core aspects of self-consciousness, but that at anytime aspects of our next evolutionary stage 'world-consciousness' can intrude, we can if motivated 'rise above' (transcend) the limitation of a narrow self-consciousness.

I am positing a conceptual understanding of humankind's psychology; I am not claiming that self-consciousness is easily amentable to categorize, to fix. From its very first appearance on Earth, self-consciousness would have been expressed in kind acts towards others, in taking decisions in the collective (small-group) interests. But I would suggest that these acts were for the individual not outcomes of considered reflection but rather were unreflective responses that follow from socialization processes experienced within small groups. An interactional repertoire that had developed over thousands of years tailored to meet the basic requirements of small-group types of adaptation.

At the end of the nineteenth-century industrial developments: financial systems, property relations, legal systems, the scientific methods, the social world of mass societies, the selection and presentation of 'news' in a mass society, structural patterns of economic inequality, and in the terms of political decision-making and international relations, we see the strands that would grow to influence the structure of the dramatic intensification of inter-connectedness that would define 20th/21st century Globalization.

By 1900 the world had the productive capacity to allow its whole population to enjoy a standard of living where all of their basic needs could easily be met – what would happen to this potential will be seen as I move beyond the century's end.

PART THREE

The modern period

'Human reason has this peculiar fate that in one species of its knowledge it is burdened by questions which, as prescribed by the very nature of reason itself, it is not able to ignore, but which, as transcending all its powers, it is also not able to answer'

Immanuel Kant (preface to first ed. of his 'Critique of Pure Reason' – N. Kemp Smith translation 1929)

Chapter 7 The 20th Century to 1945

'If I could enclose all the evil of our time in one image, I would chose this image that is familiar to me: an emaciate man, with head dropped and shoulders curved, on whose face and in whose eyes not a trace of a thought is to be seen.'

Primo Levi ('If This is a Man')

World pop: 1,671 million (1900)

From the perspective of the central aims of this book I need to note my continuing elongated meander through the accumulation of novel information whose rate of acceleration has been increasingly exposing the individual to a life lived within invariably fractured, so partial and functionally uncertain, deeply contextualized slivers of the wider expanding Reality. These slivers so constituting our own personal sections, our lived reality within Reality.

In a more social context this evolutionary become civil process of Reality-accumulation has encompassed such areas as: complex finance systems, industrialized and post industrial work and leisure activities, the natural and social sciences, history, religion and philosophy. Then there is the daily exposure to an insistent flow of 'news'. News selectively presented and only nominally connected to any measured consideration of the evils being perpetrated across the world – tending to favour info-tainment rather than the impartial presentation of events and issues of more importance to the future of humankind.

Individuals in today's civil societies also have to process an insidious torrent of advertising offering but shallow sources of primarily consumption-based identity. Creating information soaked social environments that can overwhelm any individual and so offer sources of potential psychological dislocation as human-beings endeavoured more or less successfully to adapt to forms of civil life as this developed during the nineteenth and twentieth centuries. A civil life presenting existential challenges to populations as they negotiated their way through the shifting boundaries of individual and collective experience.

The psychological defence mechanisms necessary for survival in such circumstances can include endeavouring to live psychologically within a narrowed world of localized, more predictable, relationships and acquiring some (if sub-conscious) filtering mechanism to insulate oneself from guilt at the miserable experience of others. Seeking to nurture an emotional and cognitive world-view more comfortably circumscribed to mitigate the impact of a wider context redolent of potentially threatening uncertainties.

I want to persuade you, the reader, that, whilst an understandable reaction to 'Reality', attempts to disengage from the more threatening aspects of the juggernaut of accumulating information can only ever be partially successful, aspects of Reality invariably intrude. To the extent that people are successful in, in effect, denying the facts of the world, they do so at the cost of exposing themsevs to the change of inauthenticity; if that is, what we mean by 'personal authenticity' includes a willingness to face the harsh blast of Reality and to accept the consequences of this for ourselves and others. In the face of this to maintain a thought-through ethical consistency – the actual expression of which can be conventionally judged as 'good' or 'evil'. What determines authenticity in this context is the willingness to be open to all types of information, to hold a self-determined set of personal ethics and to endeavour to consistently reflect these in one's life.

From what has been publically known of his life we might judge Albert Camus to be a good example of an advocate of this type of authenticity – he thought quite deeply about the 'world' and concluded that, life has many vicissitudes and unknowns, and that each human-being is faced with: '…..the probability of suffering and the certainty of death'. And this in, for many of us, a godless world and consequently one without any hope for any appeal to a higher authority for justice. Given this, life can only be considered to be absurd, but the fact that even being fully aware of this fearful reality one can still eschew suicide as being a seemingly sensible reaction and instead one can strive to live; a willingness to confront the existential ennui (see especially Camus's small book 'The Myth of Sisyphus' -1942). The recognition and acceptance of the absurd grants my liberation as an individual, for Camus: 'Being aware of one's life, one's revolt, one's freedom…..[the consequence that can be drawn from thinking through the absurd]…... ' By the mere activity of consciousness I transform into a rule of life what was an invitation to death – and I refuse suicide.' The mythical Sisyphus was condemned to forever repeat the absurd cycle of pushing a rock up the hill just to see it roll back down again – wasted effort - an eternal cycle of misery. If we can equate this with the cycle of misery (evil) expressed throughout human history, continuing into today's reality to become our own self-willed burden of assuming the implications of authenticity – the expression of evil hardly diminishes but we can take up the challenge of confronting its source in self-conscious humankind as we seek to promote a world-conscious humanity.

Any even thought-through ethical system, being unable to encompass all possible situations we might encounter, lacks a clear conceptual boundary. So too authenticity has fuzzy experiential implications, and requires regular negotiation set within changing conditions; but I would tentatively suggest that it is the highest form of personal life – to go forth with a willingness to authentically engage within our experience.

Whether or not you consider reaching for authenticity is a better existential strategy than striving for the state of 'happiness' based upon a decided ignorance is probably the most deeply personal question that hangs over each of our lives; the mostly unspoken presence of authentic possibility. How we engage with the world we encounter is the basic, if seemingly general, ethical question. If we have no interest in, no taste for engagement with, the evils of the world beyond those with a more immediate impact on our own lives - engagement which would mean facing the challenge of complexity, uncertainty, and of making choices - then I suggest a person would have lived but a partial life. Forgoing the life affirming potential of being human for the life denying actuality of living defensively. In evolutionary terms, forgoing the potential we have to achieve the transcendental mode of world-consciousness as we determinedly isolate ourselves within the evolutionary mode of self-consciousness. A solemn matter to consider and one that I wanted to place before you as my exposition of central aspects of the development of civil life (overlying and linked to the evolutionary process) continues.

So, let's defer further debate on the question of authenticity for now as we consider an outline of humankind's civil experience during the increasingly information saturated twentieth century; focusing on the accumulation of novel information, and the expression of evil.

The twentieth century civil world begun with some exciting scientific developments but international political relations maintained the same dismally competitive and conflictual patterns of the nineteenth.

Throughout the previous century the initially quite loosely governed nation-states of Europe had each coalesced into more integrated, cohesive, centralized political units, than had been the case at the beginning of the century. Indeed, the second half of the century saw two 'new' significant nation-states, Italy and Germany, being formed. Much of the world was experiencing the colonial domination of European nations set on a strategy of maximising the extraction of resources from their colonies. The United States has been significantly enlarged and consolidated, and South America being (by 1900) separated into a collection of nation-states, if ones mostly run as oligarchies dominated by the owners of huge tracts of land, increasingly led by *'caudillos'* supported by the military. If some ideas of utopian socialism were imported into the continent, along with European immigrants, this most obviously in some of the industrializing cities of Brazil and Mexico.

The development of industrial production, with its transport and communication infrastructure, having the power to produce and distribute a vast amount of 'goods', was increasingly utilising the power potential of fossil fuels and the growing of food that sustained the human work-force being employed on turning raw materials into manufactured products. In the early years of the twentieth century a significant amount of this industrial resource was deployed in an 'arms race' between the leading European nations, swelling the material means for the great evil that would find expression in WW1. 'The war to defend civilization' were the words that would be stamped on the British campaign medals, but it would be a war that in 'defending' civilization did in fact leave vast stretches of territory across which the battles were fought as but wastelands of cratered mud, strewn with unexploded ordinance (one in every three shells failed to explode) and dotted with the skeletal remnants of scorched trees. Invariably, the war also left personal despair all across the continent in the millions of homes grieving sons that had died.

So how could the civil nations of Europe have gotten to the point of throwing themselves at each other at such great material and human cost? War – a time when the best of civil life is put to one side and the historically ever-present evil underbelly of civil life is exposed to unleash itself in an inhuman (but paradoxically all too human) paroxysm of violence.

Seeking for the more fundamental causes of a single historical conflict such as WW1 would takes us into the biological constitution, the underlying psychological characteristics (certainly of the leading individuals), the effect of collective behaviours (tainted by the phenomenon of in-group/out-group antagonisms as a source of separation), and a range of economic, historical, and social factors that would have developed in complex systems of interaction operating over long periods of time. In a limited text such as this I am only going to offer a superficial (this does not mean untrue) level of analysis. One that echoes most standard 'histories' covering the period from the end of the nineteenth century up to the outbreak of war. But if we wish to identify the fundamental cause of war, lying in the depths of humankind's collective psyche, then we need to step back and gain a more evolutionary perspective......war is a characteristic of the 'self-conscious' stage of humankind's evolutionary development (as is evil itself) and creating the conditions that foster progress to the next stage (world-consciousness and a post war world) continues as a possible future. If one dependent on our species being able to design out conflict from international relations; with peace rather than war as a default mode for disagreements unresolved by diplomacy, and a willingness of nation-states to accept decisions on any issue made by a legitimate international body. More than this, the very idea of nation-states should be under scrutiny and we should be asking if can we advance civil organization beyond the 'othering' tendency inherent in the notion of nation states.

The process of the Industrial Revolution, with its mechanization of production, had an underlying dynamic of continual change, involving sets of multi-complex and interlinked developmental processes. Amongst the European industrial (and increasingly political) elites progress became a byword for 'good'. Pretty much anything seen by traditional (or those aspiring to be) members of national elites as obstacles to progress, be they, class relationships, traditional craft skills, local practices, humane conditions for workers and their families, resources held in common, or measures for environment protection, needed to be removed, reduced, or avoided; for industry this meant the externalisation of as much of the production cost as possible in the drive to maximise private profit.

The production and consumption of goods, transportation, communication, and the human power to drive these, were all features of the nations that were increasingly well-placed to fund and take advantage of technological developments to improve industrial processes. And the natural sciences: chemistry, biology, physics, electrodynamics, metallurgy, etc. offered a stream of theoretical and empirical information that would make possible, and so further stimulate, a range of technological innovations involving new inventions and new processes.

Industrializing nations were driven by the determinants of industrial progress to seek out sources of raw materials and expanding markets for their manufactured goods. More and more products, economic development at almost any cost, ever-increasing profits for businesses and so dividends for investors. With even only modest working-class aspirations being satisfied with the prospect of work at almost any cost; work for most being linked closely with self-worth and for many even survival. But the nations in the first wave of industrialization (Britain and the Low Countries) had been able to gain a significant advantage and, in effect had dominated large areas of the globe, in the form of direct colonization or of control over markets. The idea of relentless progress, as a mostly unexamined 'good', was accepted throughout industrial society. Its intellectual form being circumscribed by terms such as positivism in science and liberalism in politics can be seen in the more optimistic books of H.G. Wells and the plays of G.B.Shaw. Some believed that this materialist form of progress could make for a better society, that wealth creation could benefit all. But most of those in the ruling elites were more inclined to see progress as providing opportunities to gain fortunes for themselves; and for the more politically minded, to provide the means to further control of mass populations.

Production itself was a primary process within late nineteenth century industrialization and competition promoted ways of improving efficiency. A novel type of 'scientific' management of productivity being adopted first in the US with Fredrick Taylor's 'Scientific management' characterised by production inspectors deploying notepads and stop watches to inform a 'time and motion' type of analysis used to calculate expected norms of production. In larger factories the workplace came under a level of surveillance undertaken by managers trained to eliminate any digression from what had been 'objectively' defined as the most efficient production systems - incentivised to seek out evermore opportunities for even greater efficiency – the outcome being that the worker became but an adjunct to the machine being operated, or to the production line being serviced. The resulting alienation between worker and product being predicted/identified by Karl Marx, and graphically illustrated (if simplistically caricatured) by Charlie Chaplin in the movie 'Modern Times'.

As the new century began the nation that had been the midwife to the industrial revolution, and which had accumulated the largest Empire, was paying the price of colonization.

Britain was at odds with the settlers of Dutch origin who resisted British control in South Africa. Since Britain had displaced the Dutch from the Cape in 1806 it had served them as a key provisioning point on the long journey to more important imperial interests in India and the Far East. A hardy collection of mainly Dutch and some British settlers enabled the spread of settlements northwards. When, from 1833, Britain ended slavery in its colonies (even if it would introduce racial segregation in South Africa in 1828) Dutch farmers, the Afrikaners (Boers), wanting more freedom from British control, a freedom that included the right to keep slaves, embarked on the 'Great Trek' taking them further into the heart of southern Africa. Fighting Zulus (of the Nguni tribe) along the way, as they ruthlessly occupied native lands. These 'Voortrekkers' founded the political entities of the Orange Free State and the Transvaal. Given that the whole colony was a cost to the British exchequer, British interest in the colony was low and initially they accepted the establishment of the Afrikaans Republics to the north.

The British view changed markedly when the discovery in the late 1860s of commercially viable deposits of gold and diamonds significantly altered the financial prospects for the colony. The productive diamond mines at Kimberly were within the Afrikaner's Orange Free State (OFS), a region that was annexed by Britain in 1871, with the OFS 'government' reluctantly having to accept £90,000 in compensation. The labour intensive activity of mining, along with shortages of white workers, led to a high level of native employment. Although having to live away from their families, and being paid less than white workers, they were able to earn sufficient to purchase modern rifles and gain a certain status within their home communities. The 1870s and 80s had seen the rise of a number of mining magnates working for companies such as De-Beers and Wernher, Beit & Co. One of these magnates being Cecil Rhodes (others were Alfred Beit and Julius Wernher) who by 1890 had already made a personal fortune and was a rising politician. Rhodes allied a sharp business brain and a generally acute political understand to overarching personal ambition. A combination of factors that led him, in 1890, to organize (he did not actually take part) a second Great Trek, one intent on extending white occupation even further north into Mashonaland. This trek was much more an invading force made up of a ragbag collection of white adventurers, prospectors, tradesmen (bakers, butchers, engineers) some wanting to settle, most seeking an easy fortune… unlike the Boer trek which had been undertaken by a more homogenous group of farmers along with wives and children – seeking land and freedom.

The core of Rhodes's group were the 200 'pioneers', lured north by the offer of 3,000 acre farms and the opportunity to prospect for gold; 15 gold claim-plots were to be given to each pioneer. The pioneers were protected by a force of 500 strong police employed by Rhodes's British South Africa Company (enjoying a Royal Charter). The adventure was successful due to a mix of clever negotiations, and lies about their intentions told to local tribes led by the dominant King Lobengula of the Ndebele. This new country that Rhodes had established in the name of Britain he modestly named 'Rhodesia'. Soon after this Rhodes was persuaded by Dr Jameson, the administrator of Rhodesia, to fund an expeditionary force to attack the Ndebele and gain Matabeleland. The militaristic socialization of the Ndebele culture was their downfall. The impis of young men had been sating their bloodlust (a key aspect of gaining status within their tribal groups) by raiding into the lands of more peaceful peoples north of the Zambezi. But they came to view their main enemy as being land-hungry white men and were eager to test themselves and their protective 'magic' against this threat.

The incident that was to precipitate the defeat of the Ndebele occurred when a Shona raiding party from Mashonaland (part of Rhodesia) crossed the border into Matabeleland and stole some Ndebele cattle. They were chased back into Mashonaland by a large group of Ndebele - who still had the right, at least theoretically, to punish this type of lawbreaking - and the Shona group was caught and then massacred within sight of the town of Fort Victoria. This act in itself caused a wave of shock to run through the white community…..a shock made worse when the excited Ndebele then killed or carried off a number of black servants from white homes, and also stole some white-owned livestock. This raid into Mashonaland formed the basis of a stream of propaganda casting the Ndebele as a threat that was linked to unfounded ambitions attributed to Lobengula. This manufactured threat of a 'native uprising' caused Sir Henry Lock, the British High Commissioner in the Cape (misled by the propaganda and by the duplicity of Rhodes) to prepare an official British force to be used to prevent Ndebele aggression.

But by the time this force mobilized and had reached Lubengula's capital of Bulawayo Jameson's force had already invaded (Oct. 1893) Matabeleland and, armed with superior weapons, had defeated the foolishly 'brave' Ndebele impis. It had then moved on to occupy a Bulawayo from which Lubengula and most of its population had fled. A few weeks later the King, by then convinced of the comprehensive defeat inflicted on his people, committed suicide. It had cost Rhodes the lives of 50 of his men and just £50,000 to double the size of Rhodesia.

The history of more or less British controlled South Africa from this time was characterized by a white population for the most part prospering in a social structure that was designed to significantly favour whites; being 'fearful' of a black population outnumbering them by about 10 to 1. An imbalance of economic advantages to whites, with the potential political strength of blacks being contained by a social milieu that fostered ideas of racial superiority, with a clever manipulation of antagonisms between black (then later also 'coloured') groups, along with oppressive laws applied with determination and when required the use of force. On the streets the 'jambok' was liberally wielded to encourage compliance and to discourage protest.

In Rhodesia, the victorious Company (Rhodes's chartered British South Africa Company) interpreted international law to mean that it now 'owned' the whole of the conquered lands over which Lobengula had ruled as king. Jameson's men set about extracting their personal due (under the Victoria agreement), many taking 6,000 acre land-holdings incorporating the most fertile faming land. The Ndebele (when not warriors were farmers and herders) were in effect dispossessed of their most valued properties; their land and cattle. Estimates suggest about 300,000 head of Ndebele cattle were taken possession of by the Company, rustled by whites raiding from the Transvaal, or stolen by traditional enemies such as the Shona. The Ndebele had lost their status as proud warriors and to a significant degree their ability to maintain themselves and their families. They were forced to labour for the white-man, a role that would be the fate of most blacks in Southern Africa for the next 100 years, during which justifiable resentment bubbled under the surface. The Shona, although freed from the power of the Ndebele, also felt the pressures of the white government. In particular a 'hut tax' was introduced and some of their own prize cattle taken by the company on the crude pretext that they might just have been some of those stolen from the Ndebele.

The strength of the Rhodesian police force, based in Bulawayo, was reduced to just 50 men, owing to Jameson taking the main body in an ill-advised opportunistic raid into the Transvaal. A raid for which is believed that the British Colonial Secretary Joseph Chamberlain, possibly with the knowledge of some other members of the British Cabinet, colluded with Rhodes to over-throw an independent state (Transvaal). An action that would for Jameson end with his humiliating surrender following his force engaging with the Boers, first at Krugersdorp and then Doornkop.

In late March 1896 two policemen were killed by Ndebele tribesmen in Bulawayo, an event that was taken as a signal by a section of the embittered native population that resistance and retribution were possible; some with hopes of a return to a previous way of life. Within a week 200 white men, women, some children, and possibly as many of their servants who remained loyal, had been killed, and thousands of head of cattle had been driven from white-owned farms. The remaining whites grouped together in the main towns, dug in, and held the insurgents at bay while they waited for the relief that they were confident would be sent.

Although the natives had access to about 2000 modern rifles that had previously been traded or sold to them by white traders, and many of the traditional leaders (the indunas) were prepared to get involved, the uprising was poorly planned and the actions but mostly disorganized outbursts of crude violence. Some supply-lines to the town were left open and the vital telegraph lines kept intact. After the initial shock and drawing together for defense, the whites raided out from the towns. Then followed a period of quite merciless engagements, with the mobile mounted whites inflicting serious casualties on the natives (mostly Ndebele). By May a force of about 200 defenders riding east from Bulawayo met a relief column of about 600 men, paid by the Company, from Salisbury (led by Rhodes) and together they rode into the town. Just one week later a Matabeleland Relief Force of about 700 volunteers sent north by the British Government arrived and now the uprising was in effect at an end, somewhat to the disappointment of Colonel Robert Baden-Powel (later to found the Boy Scout youth movement) who was with the British relief column and who felt that he had missed a chance of killing natives. But he was not to be too disappointed as now the Shona of Mashonaland – believing their tribal spirits had given them immunity to bullets – launched their own uprising. The British relief column returned to Salisbury and, with the aid of reinforcements from the Cape, were soon able to quell this second revolt. Meanwhile, in the wider context of British involvement in South Africa, the Government was becoming concerned with the increasing Boer wealth and their military power.[1]

In the last decade of the century Rhodes and representatives of other business interests were pressuring Britain to extend its control in SA but of more significance to Britain was the threat of the rising European power of a Germany engaged in extending its influence to the north west of Britain's South African colony.

The antagonism between Britain and the Boers festered – the former being uneasy about the rising strength of the Boers and frustrated at their unwillingness to become part of the British Empire the latter, united by their religion, ethnic identity (including a shared Dutch language) and recent shared community history. This, along with a fiercely independent collective temperament contributed to their being unwilling to give up their independence. In addition, the British High Commission and The Colonial Office (especially Joeseph Chamberlain) were continually being badgered, misled and lied to, by Rhodes as he pursued his long-term ambition of a Federation of the whole of South Africa under British rule (and Rhodes's control). Other SA business men were concerned about Boer control over some trade routes, along with their also wanting easier access to the increasing mineral wealth (gold and precious stones) of the Boer Republics.

In 1848 Britain had made a successful attempt to annex a large part of the Orange River Sovereignty and while at first the financial plight of the Boers made them quite co-operative they increasingly raised objections. The cost of administering this fractious state had led to the British handing the administration back to the Boers in 1854. To become the Boer Republic of the Orange Free State. In the early

---

[1] And about the tacit support of Germany – William II had sent a telegram in support of the Boers at the time they repelled Jameson's (Rhodes) attempted invasion of the Transvaal in 1896.

1880s Britain attempted to annex the Transvaal but Paul Kruger (President of the Republic) led a determined defense that culminated in defeat for the British at the Battle of Majuba Hill in 1881. The ill-fated Jameson raid in 1896 reflected the determination of the British (or at least Rhodes's South Africa Company) to refuse to accept fully independent Boer republics.

Towards the century's end tensions increased, with British public opinion being fed exaggerated information on how British immigrants (Uitlanders) within the Boer republics were being badly treated; one key issue was their being denied the right to vote.

An attempt at negotiations on areas of disagreement was started in May1899, with Sir Alfred Milner (British High Commissioner) leading for the British and Paul Kruger leading for the Boers. These negotiations soon stalled, not least due to the Boers being sensitive to the British Government's attempt of stir up British public opinion against them; framing the dispute as both the victimization of British citizens (the Uitlanders) and a challenge to the imperial right of Britain to rule southern Africa. The obduracy of the Boers, as perceived by the British cabinet, some newspapers, and a section of the British population, gave the British government an excuse to begin sending troop reinforcements to the Cape; most of the first 10,000 coming from India.

The British High Commission, Rhodes, and most of the powerful British business and financial interests in SA, wanted to ensure British domination over the Boers. The British military establishment wanted war, not least as an opportunity to keep the army on its mettle but also to avenge the earlier military humiliation suffered at the hands of the Boers. This, along with a jingoistic mood of the British population, (stirred by a section of the right-wing press) combined to pressure the British Government towards decisive action. The Liberal and Labour parties, and a significant proportion of the population, shared the view that the Government's actions in SA amounted to imperial bullying and argued that conflict could and should be avoided.

By early autumn the Boer leadership felt that war was inevitable and when they learned that a second wave of 47,000 troops were to follow the first 10,000 they decided to act. Jan Smuts drafted an ultimatum that accused the British of breaking the London Convention of 1884 and he set a number of conditions that were unlikely to be agreed by the British, not least the condition not to send any more troops. In the absence of British agreement to accept the conditions set out in the document within 48 hours then the Boers would consider a declaration of war to have been made.

The war began on 12th October when a large well-armed Boer force advanced into northern Natal and by early 1900, following a series of successful skirmishes, the Boers, led by Louis Botha and Jan Smuts, laid siege to the British garrison towns of Mafekin, Kimberly, and Ladysmith. A Christian god was called upon to bless and protect the Boers as they set out to invade Natal just as the same Christian god was called upon to bless and protect the British troops that departed from Southampton in order to progress the war.

As reinforcements arrived to strengthen the British side, the tide of war steadily flowed against the Boers. By mid 1900 the British had relieved the besieged garrisons and had occupied the Boer capital of Pretoria. At the Battle of Bergendal on 27th August the Boers suffered a significant defeat; with Kruger fleeing to Portuguese controlled Mozambique. For this and his other military actions in SA Lord Roberts, in charge of the British force, was awarded a gift of £100,000 and raised in social prestige with his promotion to an earldom. On the other hand when, at the war's end, the ordinary troops returned to Britain many encountered unemployment and poverty, if somewhat alleviated by demeaning charitable support.

In the face of the obvious strength of their enemy in conventional warfare the Boers changed tactics, avoiding mass battles and turning instead to guerrilla 'hit and run' warfare. This phase of the conflict illustrates how a determined force adopting tactics of harassment could, with some measure of success, hold off a significantly superior military force. British frustration at being unable to make significant military progress led to Lord Kitchener (Chief of Staff) ordering the adoption of a brutal 'scorched earth' policy. This meant that whilst the Boer men-folk were away fighting, their homes and crops would be destroyed, their animals killed and their families - the elderly, the wives and the children along with servants and their families - turned out to survive as best they could in the inhospitable veldt. Later on, displaced families were increasingly confined in concentration camps – an inglorious act of revenge. It was in these camps that most of the Afrikaans people died. The camps were overcrowded, disease-ridden, enclosures populated with semi-starving victims, able to access only very limited medical aid. The plight of the Boer women and children was brought to the public's attention by Emily Hobhouse when she highlighted the high mortality rate among civilian Boers. In a somewhat shamefaced response to public outrage in both Britain and mainland Europe the government set up a 'Ladies Commission' headed by Dame Millicent Fawcett. Her report on the situation was a systematic outline confirming Hobhouses's accusations. The Fawcett Report recorded in some detail the grim conditions that pertained in the camps. At their peak they held 111,619 whites, and 43,780 'coloured' people, imprisoned in unsanitary, disease-ridden conditions.

In the British tradition of rewarding its military leaders, Kitchener was given the then small fortune of £50,000 (most of which he used to buy shares in South African gold mining) and made a viscount for his part in the war.

British military strength gradually wore down the Boers and towards the end of the conflict about 5,000 Boers were in fact fighting on the British side. Peace was agreed, by Great Britain on one side and the South African Republic (Transvaal) and The Orange Free State on the other, at Vereeniging at the end of May 1902; with the 'Treaty of Vereeniging' being signed later on in Pretoria. This settlement still left blacks without a vote in the two republics, unlike the by then franchised blacks in Cape Colony. After a period of British military rule, both of the Boer republics were granted conditional self-government as colonies of Great Britain; with South Africa being united into one country in 1910.

The Anglo/Boer war cost Britain 22,000 lives, £200 million, and a large measure of international humiliation. On the Boer side 7,000 fighting men were lost, 28,000 women and children died in the concentration camps, and 14,000 native South Africans also died. In historical terms just another small war but its significance lay in its being an imperial war fought at the century's beginning by the nation that led the world into the industrial revolution at the start of the previous century. A war, the worst aspect of which was that it was a conflict fought primarily to advance the business interests of a small clique of men, and to defend the 'national ego' of Britain. The background to the war illustrates layers of evil being expressed during the nineteenth century as the British fought the Boers who held their lands owing to their killing and taking land from the Zulus who had in turn taken the land from and killed other less aggressive native peoples.

For nations in the later nineteenth century wave of industrial development – nations such as the US, Germany, Japan, Italy, and Russia - the division of interests in the world were regarded as unfair and unjustified. This was not such an issue (for capitalists) in the US and Russia, their extensive land-masses offered opportunities for expansion and their geographic proximity to more remote areas of the world (especially China for Russia and South America for the US) also offered opportunities for investment and trade. For Japan, its relative isolation from most industrial nations (and a more insular national mindset) meant that competition with European nations for markets and raw materials was not much of an issue.

But for Italy, and even more so for Germany, the lack of colonial opportunities - unsatisfied even by the 'gift' of relatively small regions in North Africa for Italy and Cameroon and parts of West Africa for Germany - and the historical antipathy between these and some of their European neighbours (France, Russia, and Britain) contributed to the resentment of their own ruling elites.

Germany, partly due to the relative lack of pre-unification integration of political, industry and finance, adopted industriali-sation later than its major western European neighbours. But once began, and with the benefit of unification (taking place between 1866-71 out of the German Confederation), it experienced the quite rapid expansion of its industries. In the 1880s Germany's economy was performing at about 35-50% of Britain's, on most accepted measures of industrialization such as: iron/steel production, use of power, share of world manufactures etc. But progressively up to around 1910, it reached similar levels and by some measures exceeded that of Britain; including percentage of world manufacturing with output 14.8% Germany to 13.6% Britain by 1913. During this thirty year period the population of Germany increased from 48m to 67m, and the country had advanced to become the leading industrial power in Europe. Its leaders tended to interpret (and in most cases this was a fair assessment) any diplomatic initiative taken by it European neighbours as a potential threat, or at least as an attempt to reinforce existing unfairness. If one man can be said to have guided Germany's industrial development in it would have been Otto von Bismarck (a Prussian), a clever if devious politician. Bismarck was a pragmatic individual and, following the significant part he played in achieving German unification under Hohenzollern rule, he used his diplomatic skills to maintain fairly good relations with most other European nations. His Triple Alliance of 1882 helping to control the antagonisms between Austria and Italy.

Due to tensions between Bismarck and the new Emperor (Kaiser) William II, and with an influential section of the German political right-wing wanting to re-consider relationships with neighbouring countries (especially Russia), Bismarck was dismissed in 1890. Evidence for this change of diplomatic approach, being Germany's refusal to renew the Reinsurance Treaty with Russia; amongst other things, causing Russia to seek French rather than German loans to support its national debt. Relations with Britain, having been based mainly on mutual toleration during the Bismarck era, turned sour when Joseph Chamberlain's repeated attempt (1899-1901) to form an alliance with Germany were unsuccessful due to what were seen by Britain as excessive demands of the German Chancellor Bernhard Furst von Bulow.

The strong influence of Prussian militarism tended towards the build-up of the German military. From about 1898 the country embarked on the modernization and serious expansion of its navy; a project overseen by Admiral Alfred von Tirpitz the 'Father of the German navy'. Between1874-1896 German military expenditure increased by about 50% (as did that of most other European nations), but its GNP was also increasing. It was during the next nearly two decades (to 1914) that military spending would increase significantly beyond the rise in GNP. Between 1880-1914, German military expenditure increased by 400%, compared with Britain and Russia 200%, and France 100%. A national mood was being fostered in these countries of admiration for the military and suspicion of the motives of other nations.

An indirect outcome of the nineteenth century consolidation of old, and the formation of new, nation-states was the uneasy inclusion of minority group within some of these – Irish (Fenians), Basque (Carlists), Spain (Catalans), France (Bretons), Belgium (Flemish), and some of the German speaking minorities of the Russian controlled Baltic provinces. There were Polish speaking minorities in eastern Germany, and a mix of misplaced peoples, principally: Kosovans, Serbs, Albanians, in the Balkans, and further east the Kurds in Turkey. These had a geographic location connected with their minority status; so a sense of identity connected to place that would later provide a focus for campaigning for autonomy. Other, more dispersed minority groups included Gypsies (Sinta and

Romany) and Jews. The former seem to have been prepared to find subsistence, to exist as a group, within the 'interstices' of civil life – to live on the social and economic margins of any national society; earning a living by adapting their traditional occupations to changing economic circumstances occupied as 'outcasts/excluded' – their collective identity being reinforced by their excluded otherness.

Whilst religiously relatively homogenous, the Jews were a significantly more socially heterogeneous minority – ranging from a preparedness to integrate within any national society to those drawing identity as part of a narrative of Diaspora, set in motion when many Jews (Semitic peoples) were excluded (the Galut) from the Middle East in a number of anti-Jewish actions. A Diaspora beginning in recorded history in 721 BCE when Assyrian conquerors exiled a large number to northern Iraq, then around 300 BCE the Egyptian Pharaoh Ptolemy ordered Jews to move from Jerusalem to Egypt (many settled to establish a Jewish quarter in the port of Alexandria) and finally the Romans, following the crushing, in 136 CE of Bar Kochbal (a Jewish uprising) when many Jews were exiled from Judea/Palestine. Times of exile are imaginatively woven into Jewish historical narratives, highlighting their persecution and emphasizing their religious unity as a 'chosen' people.

The Talmud offered a religious text, written over generations by a series of Rabbis and other respected teachers, in which the Jews are advised on ways (laws, moral guidance, and traditional observances) which would later assist their collective survival in exile and in maintaining their Jewish identity. Whilst basically a book of laws the Talmud can also serve as a record of a thousand years of Jewish history. Thought to have been complied over a period of 300 years, it brought together a eclectic mixture of logical precepts, common sense wisdom, moral guidance, along with poetry and at times (in the Haggadah) quite silly imaginative fancies.

There is no doubt that many Jews suffered discrimination and by the medieval period European Jews were subject to a range of regulations and discriminations. Limited to only certain types of occupation, subject to special taxes, and usually denied the right to become citizens. In many of the larger European cities they were confined to ghettos or chose to live in defined Jewish quarters. Jews who were dispersed too (or who had chosen to settle in) Arab regions often fared better than their European counterparts, even if they were still generally treated as second class citizens. In some places complete assimilation or fairly close social integration was possible, in others Jews were reluctantly tolerated, whilst in a few they were actively persecuted. But in most of Europe they were treated as social inferiors and the butt of insults, pictured as caricatures of themselves, and blamed for all manner of economic ills. During the nineteenth century 'pogroms' had been carried out, the most well-known of which were the three pogroms that took place in Odessa 1821, 1849, 1859.

Sections of European Jewry had a prominent role in advancing working class economic and political interests exemplified in the public lives of individuals such a Karl Marx, Rosa Luxemburg, Karl Kausky, in Britain and Germany, and Leon Trotsky, Lev Kamenev, and Grigory Zinoviev in Russia; indeed Jews were over-represented (as an ethnic group) in the Menshevik and Bolshevik parties at the time of the Russian revolution. And a specifically Jewish socialist party/trade union, the 'Jewish Labour Bund', was active in challenging economic exploitation and social oppression. This group mainly operated within Russia, Lithuania, and Poland, between 1897 and the 1920s It was internationalist in outlook, and actively opposed the creation of a single Jewish State (Zionism).

The idea of a return to a mythical, in terms of defined territory, 'Judea' had been a part of the narrative of Diaspora, and in the early nineteenth century we see clear Zionist aspirations being expressed by individuals such as Rabbi Alcalay and Rabbi Kalischer in the 1840s. Indeed, the first Jewish (Zionist) settlements outside of Jerusalem were established at Mishenoit Sha'anaim in 1860.

The first Zionist Congress was held in Basle, Switzerland, in 1897, where the term 'Zionist' was introduced by the Austrian Nathan Birnbaum to describe those seeking a single Jewish homeland. The movement towards this first congress was to a significant extent the work of Theodor Herzl (born Budapest 1860) who chaired the proceedings. This event was an organized call for political action – the first of six congresses held up to 1902. These established the Jewish Colonial Trust, the Jewish National Fund, and also the newspaper 'Die Welt'. The congress adopted the anthem 'Hatikvah', which would become the national anthem of the State of Israel. But there were also some, mainly secular, mostly socialist, groupings (including the 'Bund' noted above) critical of Zionism, instead favouring solidarity with the non-Jewish working class.

Another organization 'The Universal Israelite Alliance'

encouraged Jews to seek their futures in the USA and the fact that there are today (2021) almost as many Jews living in the USA as there are living in Israel, suggests that in the late nineteenth century and the first half of the twentieth many Jews followed this advice.

Herzl was a 'secular Jew', a writer, playwright and journalist. His conviction that the Jews needed a state of their own was formed by personal experience of anti-Semitism while he was a student in Vienna. A conviction reinforced by events such as the notorious 'Dreyfus Affair'; Herzl was at that time working as a journalist in Paris. Alfred Dreyfus was a young Jewish officer court-martialled in 1894 after being falsely accused of treason. During and just following the trail the popular press exhibited its deep-rooted anti-Semitism and mobs paraded in the centre of Paris calling for 'Death to Jews'. Dreyfus was found guilty of passing military secrets to Germany and was sentenced to life imprisonment. A bit later the true culprit, the army major Ferdinand Esterhazy, was revealed along with damning proof that evidence which could have exonerated Dreyfus had been suppressed by senior military officers. In 1906 Dreyfus was released from prison and granted a full pardon.

In his 1896 pamphlet, 'Jewish State', Herzl argued the case for a Jewish homeland in Palestine, a return to 'Zion'. His conception was of a Jewish national homeland established by agreement with the leading nations and one in which the rights of indigenous Arabs would be respected – a country in which Jews and Arabs would have equal rights. His novel 'Altneuland' (Hebrew translation being 'Tel Aviv') was a story based around a utopian blueprint for a Jewish state; a model society with a mixed economy including the public ownership of land and other natural resources. Herzl's first attempt at gaining land for such a state was to try to raise money and to use this to negotiate with the Ottoman Sultan Abdul Hamid II to, in effect, buy Ottoman ruled land in Palestine; to offer to pay off some of the Ottoman Empire's international debt in exchange for this land. A debt due primarily to offset Abdul's spending an average of 60% of annual state revenue on the army and on his cumbersome administration.

Initially Herzl's aspirations had more appeal to many Jews in Russia and parts of Eastern Europe than for the relatively more integrated Jews of Western Europe. He enjoyed the support of some Eastern European political organizations and from smaller Zionist groups. We will return to the Jewish story later on.

In the Far East at this time, Japanese interests, more specifically its wish to control Manchuria and Korea, were aggressively pursued when Japan declared war on China in 1894. A war that had been fermenting for some time, with the main disagreement being over Korea, at that time an autonomous state, nominally a co-protectorate of the Japanese and the Chinese but in fact more closely linked to China. In the background was Japanese suspicion of Russian intentions over northern China and the Korean Peninsula.

A rebellion – the Tonghak Rebellion – was used by the Japanese as an excuse to declare war.

The Japanese won a decisive victory, with significant battles taking place around Seoul and Pyongyang, and surprising defeats of the Chinese navy. The naval battle of the Yalu was both a humiliation for the Chinese and a landmark in naval warfare; being one of the first naval battles in which ironclad ships and torpedoes were used. When they reached Lushun (Port Arthur) the Japanese found evidence that Japanese prisoners had been murdered and their bodies mutilated, with Japanese reaction being to slaughter almost all of the inhabitants of the port.

The Treaty of Shimonoseki (April. 1895) gave Japan control of Taiwan, part of the Pescadores (Peny Hu) Islands, and the strategically placed Liaodong Peninsular (sometimes called the 'Regent's Sword'); Korea becoming in effect a Japanese protectorate. But perhaps the most humiliating and economically damaging aspect of the settlement was the large Chinese indemnity payment, equivalent to about 150m US dollars.

European powers - as if a pack of jackals circling as they prepare to attack an already wounded beast - sought to take advantage of the Qing dynasty's weakness in order to gain more trading opportunities for themselves. In 1897 Germany annexed large parts of Shantang province. In 1898 Britain annexed the Wei-hai-wei Peninsula and gained control of the 'New Territories'. The Russians moved into the Liatung Peninsula which also allowed them control of the port of Lushun. Even the French were active, annexing the region of Kuang-chou-wan and symbolically gaining a stronger hold in the area of Indochina that would see both them and the US suffer military humiliation in the Vietnam War in the second half of the twentieth century. The increasing global ambitions of the US led them to also declare an interest in China towards the end of the nineteenth century.

China's reaction to these encroachments was a degree of internal dissatisfaction from students and others and a call for faster modernisation of its industry and its military. A nationalistic backlash was targeted at European interests, among the victims of which were Christian missionaries with about 30,000 Chinese Christian converts being killed, mostly by marauding mobs. The mobs were composed of members of the new anti-westerner 'Boxer' ('Righteous and Harmonious Fists') movement; a secret society into which members were initiated in a series of rituals and with certain physical exercises ('callisthenics') that they believed would give them protection against bullets. European punitive attempts to defeat the movement in fact stimulated it to spread and by 1900 the Boxers controlled large areas of China, including Peking where they besieged the European compound (Legation Quarter) home to foreign diplomats and businessmen. The western powers (and Britain's Japanese ally) saw in the Boxers a significant threat to their financial (trading) interests so they put aside their own differences and in August 1900 an 'expeditionary' force (Austria-Hungary, Russian, British, French, Italian, American, but the majority of the 20,000 - some sources note 45,000 - troops were Japanese) marched on Peking (Beijing). This 'civil' force destroyed many villages on their way to Peking as they waged war on the local population, and then on arrival proceeded to sack and loot the City (stealing a number of important Chinese historical artefacts), with thousands of Chinese civilians being killed. The subsequently signed Xinchou Treaty (its international status was in fact more 'protocol' than 'treaty') was felt as a complete humiliation by the Chinese and one of a number of unequal treaties, with China having to pay a large sum in indemnity to each of the European nations and to agree to having European troops based in Peking. Taken overall, the impact of this period of turmoil was to significantly weaken the power of the Chinese government over some of the provinces and creating social conditions that would contribute to the revolution that took place in 1911. A revolution led by Sun Yet-sen who had founded a republican movement, which would later become the Kuomintang; taking power when it deposed the boy Emperor.

Late dynastic China was hardy a country that could be respected for its social and economic conditions, but during the final years of the nineteenth century we can see a clear example of opportunistic bullying of one nation by a group of others, as China fell victim to the trading and territorial ambitions of more powerful nations. An alliance of industrialised nations combining to open up China to their trade as naked economic ambitions were being played out in the Far East.

The Japan-Russian competition over Korea and Manchuria came to a head in February. 1904 when the Japanese destroyed a Russian navel squadron moored in Port Arthur. In response Russia declared war on Japan. Given that Russia was an ally of France and Japan an ally of Britain this could have further tested the Anglo-French alliance but a sense of greater common interests (the background reality of increasing German power) allowed the conflict to remain localised to the Far East. Indeed the French and British responded to this potential clash of strategic political interests by resolving some of their own colonial disagreements. The Japanese reinforced its land forces and Russia endeavoured to reinforce its far eastern army. Then, following a number of smaller clashes, a Russian force of 330,000 men fought a Japanese force of 270,000 men at Mukden over two weeks in early 1905. Casualties were high, with 90,000 Russians and 70,000 Japanese being killed.

Japanese success in this conflict was due partly to their own military skills and their modern equipment but also due to the significant logistical problems facing a Russia with its undoubted military might mostly in the west and a lack of the means to easily deploy a sufficient amount of troops and equipment to the far east. The extension of the Tran-Siberian railway (1901-04), through Manchuria to the Russian Port of Vladivostok, was built with agreement from China and but on completion there was insufficient rolling stock for substantial supplies to reach the far eastern army. The lumbering Baltic Fleet did eventually arrive in the region, only to be defeated by the Japanese in the Battle of Tsushima Strait (May 27th 1905).

An offer of mediation by US President Theodore Roosevelt was accepted and the subsequent Treaty of Portsmouth (Sept. 1905) settled control of Manchuria in favour of China with Japanese control of Korea being accepted. Russian expansionist moves to advance its ambitions in the Far East had been halted and the humiliation of this conflict contributed to the fermenting anti-tsarist/revolutionary activity in its major cities. Relatively few Russians cared about a war being waged 7,500 miles from St. Petersburg but many were incensed by the military humiliation.

By 1900 the industrialization of the means of warfare including:

conscript armies[2] officer training in military colleges, and the means to turn a nation's peacetime economy into a wartime economy. The basic element for the national mobilization for total warfare had taken place; military preparedness changed from being seen as a burden on the taxpayers, so one on which expenses were to be kept to a minimum to, by the end of the century, armed forces being accepted as necessary to protect trading interests and to enhance national pride. Even accepting that the 'Concert of Europe', a regulatory system established in the nineteenth century that pertained from 1815-1848 and then from 1871-1914. Initially known as the Vienna Settlement, this was a series of treaties that would reinforce the position of the five 'Great Powers' - Britain, France, Germany, Russia, and Austria. Allowing a certain level of security and independence and was intended to reduce the potential for their fighting each other. This 'Concert' formed the basic political framework for much of Europe in the nineteenth century. As the century progressed there was at least some acceptance of the value of diplomacy for sharing national perspectives on issues and as a process of identifying and negotiating the means of resolving these.

A cynic might suggest that the underlying rationale of holding this agreement together was at least the perception, by the leading nations, of a rough balance of military power (that the Crimean and Franco-Prussian wars proved to be mistaken), so encouraging them to accept a certain if uneasy peace over the uncertain outcomes of war. But militarism was perhaps the most prominent feature of the industrially developed nations during the last quarter of the nineteenth and early years of the twentieth centuries. An incessant determination to develop and deploy ever more powerful weaponry saw soldiers by 1900 armed with modern bolt-action/magazine-fed rifles (Lea Enfield and Mauzers) able to kill at 1400 meters, and infantry with steel field-guns able to fire shells up to 5,000 metres, along with machine guns, dynamite, and barbed wire.

These developments on their own making the close-range battles characteristic of earlier nineteenth century wars no longer viable, now the military advantage shifted towards the well-prepared defender. Navies were becoming equipped with enormous Dreadnought battleships (first built 1905) protected by armour plating from 4-24

---

[2] By 1900 Russia conscripted 335,000 men annually, Germany 280,000, France 250,000, Austria-Hungary and Italy about 100,000 each.

inches thick and able to fire shells of up to 12 inch calibre (they would be even bigger later in WWI). Driving these behemoth's through the seas were the considerably more efficient rotary 'turbine' engines. Their being preferred to the up/down motion of reciprocating engines which were less suitable for moving heavy loads at higher speeds. Rotary engines, increasingly powered by oil instead of coal, were able to power the heavy Dreadnoughts through the water at speeds up to 21 knots. Wireless telegraphy, introduced from 1900, made for a significant improvement in communication between ships at sea and their shore bases. The industrially developed nation-states of Europe were in a position to organise, militarily, politically, economically, and now also socially, for total war.

In recognition of a bristling military and the risk of war, the first Hague Peace Conference (1898) was called to '.....consider disarmament and to promote judicial arbitration of international disputes'. The Second Hague Peace Conference 1907 '.....drafted rules to limit the horrors of modern warfare' (Best et al 2004).

The historian Robert Gildea (1st pub. 1986 3rd ed. 2003) suggests an interesting factor (almost counterfactual) in the late 19th early 20th century militarization of the leading industrializing nations. In the nineteenth century women had been very much second-class citizens, most denied secondary education, professional careers, and even property rights (until in Britain, the 1870 'Act of Parliament'). Victorian patriarchy saw most middle-class men (and indeed most middle-class women) viewing a women's place as being in the home, protected and cared for by the 'breadwinner' husband. This image of the self-satisfied man with bristling mustachios and sense of benign patriarchy towards all that was modestly 'feminine', was a hypocritical contrast when, during the same period, working class women were often endeavouring to bear and raise children whilst working long hours in low paid, low status, work in factories, agriculture, and making up the most significant section of the vast army of domestic labour. Women were economically and socially vulnerable to being pressured into prostitution; harassed by the police, forced to register as prostitutes and regularly subjected to humiliating medical checks – all aspects of state 'control'. Women were often forced by the vulnerability induced by reduced economic circumstances to service the sexual 'needs' of men from all classes of Victorian society.

Across Europe, the working classes were pretty much exploited economically and disadvantaged socially as well as many being denied political rights, but women of all classes faced a series of additional gender-related disadvantages. Earlier, in 1792, Mary Wollstonecraft in her book 'Vindication of the Rights of Women' had highlighted the confining nature of the limited expectations placed by men on women. She also linked the lack of women's aspirations to the lack of educational opportunity. This had already been noted in 1790 as a factor in holding women back by Catherine Macaulay. The repression of women became increasingly less acceptable during the nineteenth century, with (a vanguard of) mainly middle-class women demanding more rights and seeking more opportunities. For Gildea, we see the sign of what he termed the beginnings of the modern feminist movement. 'The British, Continental, and General Federation for the Abolition of the State Regulation of Vice' was founded in 1875 by Josephine Butler to campaign for less state involvement and for a more reasonable approach to prostitution. In Europe similar feminist pressure groups were established including the Russian 'Society for the Protection of Women' and the German 'Frauenwohl Association'. Women in both Britain and across continental Europe led campaigns for property rights and for access to higher education. This rumbling discontent was expressed in journals and with organizations such as: the 'English Women's Journal' 1858, the 'National Society for Promoting the Education of Women' 1859, the 'German Women's Association' 1865, France's 'Society for the Amelioration of the Condition of Women' 1875 that became the 'League of Women's Rights' from 1882, the 'International Council of Women' was founded in Washington US 1888 – 'League of German Women's Association' 1894 'National Council of French Women' 1901. (Gildea, third ed. 2003)

These organizations were generally moderate in approach and were able to gain some legislative success in relation to property rights, divorce laws and gradually (and perhaps more grudgingly) access to universities. Emma Davis had campaigned for access to higher education, publishing 'The Higher Education of Women' in 1858, and she was instrumental, along with Leigh Smith, in the founding of Girton College Cambridge 1873. This was followed by Lady Margaret Hall Oxford 1879, and similar ladies higher educational institutions at Zurich 1865 and London 1878. Then universities in Scotland1889, Russia 1905, and in almost all German universities from 1908. Prior to these a very few, including Queens

College 1848 and Bedford College 1849 in London, had already been offering some education to women. But of course the right to access does not mean the means to access, in terms of funding and of social acceptance.

J.S. Mill's book 'On the subjection of Women' pub. 1869, was a rare example of a man arguing the case for more rights for women. Mill identified three aspects of women's lives that contributed to a denial of rights: social interpretations of a women's role, lack of educational opportunity, and the legal framework for marriage. Mill (supported by his wife Harriet Taylor who herself had published 'Enfranchisement' in 1851, two years before she married Mill) argued for equality between the sexes and opposed the then prevalent assumption that women were 'naturally' inferior to men in a number of socially valued ways. Mill himself made the fairly obvious observation that '…..how can we know what women might be able to achieve when they are denied the opportunity to try'.

Across the civil world, the reading of novels had increased markedly during the nineteenth century. In Britain it was writers such as Charlotte Bronte, Elizabeth Gaskell, George Elliot, and George Gissing, more or less subtly drawing attention to the plight of women and in America writers such as Ruth Hall and Louisa May Alcott also raised feminist issues. The Scottish writer Marion Reid published 'A plea for women' (1843), which was influential in Europe and the US and argued for women's suffrage. In Britain, national figures such as Caroline Norton called for legal changes in marriage laws and Florence Nightingale noted that women had the potential of men but were denied the same opportunities. Women journalists such as Frances Cobbe in Britain and Margaret Fuller in the US had the platform from which to influence the cause in favour of women's rights. But what might be termed the late nineteenth century rise of feminism mostly focused on rights on behalf of middle class women; these campaigns were not calling for equality of opportunity more generally i.e. across classes for both genders.

A groundswell of campaigning seeking equal rights for women and more opportunity in professions such as medicine and law was generated by an increasing number of articulate and determined women. But the demand for political rights was strongly resisted. There were also organizations campaigning via more constitutional means, including mainly peaceful rallies and demonstrations (such as Hyde Park in the summer of 1908 when 500,000 people attended).

Such organiszation included: the 'International Women's Suffrage Alliance' with women such as Millicent Garret Fawcett (and also Christabel Pankhurst, Flora Drummond, Tessa Billington and many other leading women of the movement) in the 'National Union of Women's Suffrage Societies' 1897. On the continent there was Anita Auspurg's 'German Union for Women's Suffrage' 1902 and Jeanne Schmel's 'French Union for Women's Suffrage' 1909. A rather more militant approach to campaigning was taken by Christable's sister Emmeline's 'Women's Social and Political Union'. (the suffragettes)

The first decade of the twentieth century saw the opening up of some opportunities and a relaxation of some of the more restrictive Victorian social codes. The American Elizabeth Blackwell and the British Elizabeth Garret Anderson campaigned for woman's right to enter the medical profession. Taken as a whole, the late nineteenth and early twentieth century feminist movement had cut its campaigning teeth in the anti-slavery, temperance, reform of property and marriage laws campaigns, and in a range of social issues such as rights for prostitutes, and the exploitation of women workers. A primary focus of the movement in the early twentieth century was on the right to vote in national elections. It was the Isle of Man, a small island off the west coast of mainland Britain that was the first self-governed political authority to concede the right to vote to women (1881) followed later by: New Zealand 1893 – Australia (the federal vote) 1902 – Finland 1906 – Norway by 1913.

Gildea's suggested that the combination of these pressures for women's rights and the gradual movement of women into higher education and some of the professions, along with a relatively few working class women gaining semi-skilled positions in factories, was felt as a threat by males. Working class men, fearing loss of jobs or an opportunity taken by employers to lower wages; middle and upper class men fearing the threat to their own social status, including control of the family; and men from all classes reacting to the possibility of their relative advantages being undermined. With, for Gildea, support for militarization (an interpretation of masculinity) being an outcome, he suggested that by early twentieth century: '....Militarism was developed as an anti-dote to feminism just as it was designed to fight socialism.' (Gildea, third ed. 2003)

But surely for most men, certainly most of those in leading political, financial, military and social prominence – those who made the decisions leading to the 'arms race', the range of women's campaigning prior to WW1 would have been pretty much on the peripheral of their, taken for granted, patriarchal outlook. Within the complexity of motivational factors involved in the military build-up and the 'militarization of national perspective', I am sure that Gilda's suggestion of the rise of a feminist movement could have at least some validity. It would be interesting to learn if the biographies of the 'great' men of the period made much reference to the feminist campaign (beyond discussion of the franchise). Perhaps the immediacy of feminist campaigning, as interpreted by the popular newspapers of the time, made the 'man-in-street' (or on the 'Clapham omnibus') fearing his undeserved social status threatened, more amenable to accepting the militarization programmes as being an assertion of characteristic masculine values and behaviour.

What was brought to the forefront of public attention by the early feminist movement was the range of inequalities that together combined to emphasise the repressed position of most women in the industrialized countries. The range of feminist campaigns taking place across Europe (and in the US) was but one of the 'pressures for change' that are a characteristic of societies with inequalities and with marked social, ethnic, and economic divisions. Especially in the modernising societies with the potential for improved communication, and so the identification of common interests between groups of the 'oppressed'; the basis for the forms of solidarity and organization necessary for successful reform.

The rise of an organised working class was a (another) source of 'pressure for change' viewed by many with even more suspicion and fear, than feminism – the shadows of the French revolution, the 1848 European and 1871 French revolutions – and the immediate influence of Marxism, International communists and in southern Europe the anarchists and syndicalists, were causing more immediate concern. It is one thing for a national elite/state to use military force to 'put down' more spontaneous working class and peasant rebellions that, even if well organised at first soon dissipated as state-controlled forces were mobilised to suppress them; as was seen in 1848 across much of Europe, and again in France in 1871. These outbursts of unrest (if quite effective in Germany) were unlikely to succeed given that their aims were over-ambitious in relation to their available resources. In reaction, their enemies were able to become better organised which, along with recourse to trained military forces, meant that 'historical circumstances' were against would-be revolutionaries. But the organized labour movement of late nineteenth century Europe, whilst having a revolutionary element (Marxist, Anarchist, Syndicalist, various forms of Socialism – especially active in Germany, Poland, Italy and Russia), had been developing within broader mainstream movements increasingly aware of their industrial (economic rather than revolutionary) strength. A movement led by people, most of whom were prepared to seek improvement in the circumstances of working people by 'constitutional' means - reform rather than revolution. Leaders such as the German social democrat Eduard Bernstein, and throughout the twentieth century a long list of similar European apologists for an aspiration towards modestly reformist versions of capitalism - wielding the democratic power of the masses. In the 1880s most working people were prepared to put their trust in TU leaders and political elites that offered some form of, even only marginal, improvement.

In Britain, the mainstream of the organised working class sought improvement through moderate Trades Unionism (at times 'radical' in tone but almost always moderate in action) and a general support for the Liberals that would initially translate into political support as the working-class males gained the vote. If a small minority of more radical leaders of the working class did argue for a militant form of Trades Unionism and for the formation of a working class political organization.

Following a period of seriously depressed economic activity from 1873-1896 the period of 1896-1914 saw the pace of industrialization accelerate in the older industrialized countries, with a number of other countries being drawn into the process. Increasingly, the reach of industrialization was impacting on much of the rest of the world. The older industrial countries being: Britain, Belgium, the Netherlands, France, Germany, and the US, newer ones being Russia, Denmark, Sweden, Japan. Most of the rest being those countries that provided primary products such as rubber, oil, cotton, hemp, metals, and minerals, along with foodstuffs such as wheat, meat, sugar, tea and coffee; to be exported to the industrialized nations. The masses in the economically undeveloped countries also provided potential markets for cheaper manufactured goods produced by industrial production methods – and the foreign elites (often maintained in place by the colonial powers and collective obedience to tradition) provided markets for luxury goods. The raw-material producing countries also provided profits for foreign direct investments (FDIs); by 1913 the value of FDI had reached \$150 billion world-wide, with profits being mostly repatriated to (wealthy) investors based in Europe and the US. Large sums were invested in South America railways, along with agriculture, and mineral extraction in both South America and Africa. Investments were made across the increasingly economically colonized world, primarily in such products as: mining, timber, farming, grains, meats and plantations producing rubber, tea, coffee, cocoa, sugar, as well as a variety of fruits. By 1913 25% of Britain's total known wealth was based on overseas investments.

Towards the end of the nineteenth century and in the first decade of the twentieth, the dynamics of industrial development and the associated drive to trade saw a continued growth in overall world trade. But it was growth much to the advantage of the industrially developed countries, with developing countries in southern Europe, south American, and Asia, being at a significant disadvantage, and for the undeveloped countries the actual (or economic) colonies being little more than sources of raw materials and to some extent markets for the goods of the colonial masters. America was able to grow by expansion of trade and with a steady flow of innovative and ambitious young immigrants along with the proximity of countries to the south endeavouring to develop economically; so rich in investment opportunities.

For Roger Osbourne: 'Late nineteenth-century colonization.......... brought the whole world into one trading system, whose rules and conditions were dictated by the industrialists and bankers of Europe and the United States. The introduction of rational economic systems, based on open trade and a money economy, had a devastating effect on societies whose trading systems were deeply embedded in their social relations.' (Osbourne, 2006, p415)

International trade was facilitated by confidence in the value of certain currencies, especially the pound sterling; providing a sense of fixed value. As did the fact that the leading currencies were freely convertible into gold. Even though Britain only held $1/5^{th}$ of the world's gold, sterling was the most accepted currency for international trade at least up to the First World War. But most Latin American countries, China, and some others, continued to use silver as a standard against which to stabilise their own currencies. A gold (or silver) standard 'convertibility' and/or a reserve currency (in effect sterling prior to WW1) offered some stability in providing the liquidity and the confidence for world trade. The ability to adjust the value of individual currencies, in relation to these more stable values, allowed governments to use a flexible monetary policy to control their balance of payments and so serve as a means of regulating their overall financial stability.

Due to more goldmines being opened in the Urals, California, and from 1886 the Transvaal in South Africa, more gold became available, both for circulation and as bullion. The use of gold to support currencies and their relation to trade ran from 1878-1914. From 1914 the US dollar, in effect, displaced the pound sterling as the international reserve currency. Then, following a return to the gold standard by a few countries (including Britain), this form of convertibility came to an end during the world-wide depression of the early 1930s

The role of governments was perceived to be primarily in protecting trade, generally irrespective of the interests of those being traded with. A clear example being the British Governments willingness to defend its merchants 'rights' to trade opium to the Chinese from1839. A reluctant Lord Melbourne (British P.M.) allowed himself to be 'blackmailed' by Captain Charles Elliot (British trade supervisor at Guangzhou) and supported by the lobbying of British big businessmen, into paying the then vast sum of £2m as compensation to British drug dealers whose goods (1700 tons of opium) had been confiscated by a Chinese Government concerned about the debilitating effect the drug trade was having on the increasing number of Chinese people smoking opium. The British then sent a naval force to China to enforce its request for reimbursing the funds paid to the 'respectable' British drug runners. The outcome being China having to agree to humiliating treaty terms, which included it being forced to open up to foreign traders, including those trading in opium. And the British invasion of Egypt in 1882 seems to have been due to the Egyptian Government's threat to refuse payments for British holders of Egyptian Government Bonds - in which Prime Minster Gladstone was himself an investor. Just two examples of the many times that Britain, similar to other western European nations, and the US used, or threatened to use, military action to open markets or to otherwise protect the interests of wealthy investors.

According to J.A.Frieden (2007, p16) 'The opening years of the twentieth century were the closest thing the world had ever seen to a free world market for goods, capital, and labour.' Frieden termed the period 1896-1914 as being progressively '.......the highpoint of international economic integration.' Although, focusing more on communication systems such as faster transport on land (railways) and at sea (steam), and on the overland and ocean-bed telegraph systems, Eric Hobsbawm suggested the period of 1848-75 one in which: '......industrial capitalism became a genuine world economy and the globe was therefore transformed from a geographical expression into a constant operational reality. History from now on became world history.' (Hobsbawm, 1975, p83)

I would note in passing (as preparation for what's to come) that the grossly asymmetric relations of global trade, in addition to western corporate-led attempts to impede industrialization (and so self-sufficiency) in 'third world' countries, was a key factor influencing the process of independence later in the twentieth century. The core strategy promoting international economic efficiency was the specialization of production; in terms of such things as productivity of land, accessibility of minerals, base and precious metals, and labour costs and skills. Wherever in the world (or within a country) a product could be 'best' produced (the 'comparative advantage' - in terms of quality and cost of bringing to the market) that is where investment will 'naturally' flow, at least in terms of narrow economic theory.

For Frieden (2007, p23) 'Global markets led to global specialization........The international division of labour of the decade before World War One transformed whole continents.' Not least in clearing forests, displacing native peoples, and ploughing up vast-horizoned landscapes to graze or grow cheap food destined for Europe.

Frieden (ibid, p24) judged that: 'Specialization was neither easy nor costless. It remade economies and societies and often destroyed traditional ways of life.....The international division of labour divided families, villages, and countries, forcing tight-knit traditional societies apart.'

The heritage of this approach left much of the world (especially India, Malaysia, the Philippines, Africa, and most of South America) reliant on what the western powers felt was to be their specialised role in the global economy - providing raw materials for the industrialized nations and markets for the consumer goods and services these produced. The 'western powers' being in effect, the power elites embodied in corporations, international banking, and groups of large scale investors, whose interests primarily determined any nation's economic strategy. During the twentieth century this economic heritage (based on asymmetric trade dependencies) was to be just one factor militating against successful post-colonial nation building, but one of fundamental importance.

Contrary to standard interpretations, and in contradiction of the assumed 'naturalness' of comparative advantage, certain counties such as China and India, were in effect de-industrialized. In the first half of the nineteenth century, China and India were on a par with the US and Germany in relation to industrial production. Even by 1860 China's industrial output had matched that of Britain. But European Imperial powers increasingly operated to reduce both the market position and the productive capacity of these (politically and economically) vulnerable nations. One example being Britain's protectionist approach to its control over Indian cotton and shipbuilding industries where indigenous manufacturing was undermined, by high import tariffs and subsidised home production, to suit the interests of the colonizing power.

During the period being considered (1896-1914) certain countries, in particular the US, were vulnerable to agricultural depression and shortages in skilled workers. But, taken overall, this was a time of significant world economic growth and of increasing global interconnectedness. Iron and steel were key materials for this phase of industrialisation and their production can serve as proxy indicators of economic development – in 1850 Britain, France, Germany and the US together produced 4.09 million tons of pig iron and this had increased to 50.28 million tons by 1914......steel production in these four leading industrial countries was 11.56 million tons in 1850 and by 1910 this figure had increased to 53.76 million tons; the most significant increases being due to the increased rate of US and German industrial development. In basic power generation, coal was increasingly being replaced by oil, and in terms of activating this power steam was being replaced by electricity. Between 1880 and 1913 World production of all goods increased by over 300% (26.9 - 100 using 1913 as a standard) and world trade by over 200% (38 - 100 using 1913 as a standard).

Facilitating the administration of this industrial advance were technological innovations such as the typewriter, telegraph (overland and trans-ocean), and the telephone. For the most part Europe imported raw materials and foods (US agricultural exports - most going to western Europe - was worth $334m in 1860 rose to $1,896m in 1914) with a range of manufactured goods and 'invisible' financial services going the other way.

World Output of Principal Tropical Commodities, 1880-1910

	1880		1910	000s tonnes
Rubber	11		87	
Coffee	550		1,090	
Raw cotton	950		1,770	
Jute	600		1,560	
Oil seed	Nil		2,700	
Tea	175		360	
Raw sugar cane	1,850		6,320	

Source, E.Hobsbawm 1987, p348 (originally taken from P.Bairoch 1975 p.15)

'The Armaments Race' was a significant factor in driving early twentieth century economic growth. Military expenses of the 'Great Powers' (Russia, Britain, France, Germany Austria-Hungary, Italy) rose from £132m in 1880 to £205m in 1900 and to £397 on the eve of WWI (E.Hobsbawm 1987, p350, original source 'The Times Atlas of the World' 1978, p250). A rise whose material presence can be seen in the building of warships.

The number of battleships launched annually between 1900-1914 being:

Britain:	49-1900	to	64-1914
Germany:	14-1900	to	40-1914
Russia:	16-1900	to	23-1914
France:	23-1900	to	28-1914
Austria-Hungary:	6-1900	to	16-1914

The movement of people and goods caused existing lines of transportation to intensify and new ones to be formed. Movement that took advantage of innovations in shipping[3] the continuing spread of railways then, towards the end of the period, with motorized vehicles just beginning to trundle along the improving highways. In capital

---

[3] Innovations such as steam turbines and the screw propeller – this was a halcyon time for the great passenger liners...... including the impressive but ill-fated Titanic launched 1912.

cities the motor omnibus and modern transit systems moved workers from homes in suburbs to downtown (city-centred) offices now lit by electric lighting.

The expanding network of global trading, being a primary feature of industrialization, was influenced by the inter-nation tensions between a few nations supporting free-trade and most imposing tariffs (or other protectionist trade barriers). But even the most enthusiastic 'free-trader' nation, in Britain, had itself operated a range of protectionist measures during the earlier phase of its own industrialization. Progressing this change from the mid nineteenth century, with the repeal of the Corn Laws (1846) and of the Navigation Acts (1849), as the international trading context became more favourable to Britain. This is a similar pattern of development that most industrialized countries went through; early on as protectionist then, once market conditions suited, a transformation to become often quite ardent advocates of free-trade. Free-trade became a general 'good' when the economically advanced nations held the market advantages. Incidentally, this process of progressive incorporation into the global trade networks was denied to most economically developing countries in the latter half of the twentieth century when the economically powerful nations demanded free-trade conditions from them. Not least in the 'structural adjustment programmes' (SAPs) that would be imposed by the IMF and the World Bank as a condition for financial support.

The nineteenth century had seen a progression in the development of private companies. The older chartered companies (such as British and Dutch joint-stock EICs) continued as a popular form of trading but, in terms of capitalisation, were being displaced by companies with limited liability status. General incorporation with limited liability status was introduced: US (New York State) 1811, Britain 1855, France 1867, Spain 1869, Germany 1870, Belgium 1873, Italy 1883, Japan from the late 1870s. One significant aspect of this being that, whilst the reformed chartered companies had to offer at least some justification (in term of progressing a wider 'public interest') for their activities, limited liability status did not require this more proactive justification. In Britain alone, between 1884 -1899, limited liability companies doubled in capital value from £475 million to £1.1 billion. With many of these seeking to raise capital funding on the equity markets.

Another significant change involving the status of private

companies came in 1886, when the US Supreme Court ruled that a corporation should, in constitutional terms, have the same legal status as an individual 'person'. So would, in future, have the protection of the Fourteenth Amendment to the US Constitution (only adopted as an amendment to the Constitution in July 1868). This move gave US corporations an extraordinary level of freedom to pursue their shareholder interests, with any attempt at regulation being inhibited by the due process of the constitutional laws intended to protect individual freedoms. A further contentious implication of the change was the right of companies to provide electoral funding to favoured candidates. A remarkably anti-democratic aspect of US elections which have been and are overwhelmingly funded by multinational companies and wealthy individuals; a source of reactionary bias compounded by the concentration of media ownership within multinational corporations.

The period 1880-1890 saw the consolidation in the US of a number of very big companies (many taking the form of trusts), by which individuals such as John D. Rockefeller (oil), Andrew Carnegie (steel), J.P. Morgan (finance) (all three having laid the foundations of their fortunes as war-profiteers in the 1860s), the Rothschilds and Barings (banking), H.J,Heinz (food processing) and Cornelius Vanderbilt (shipping) were able to amass large family fortunes during this 'golden age' of capitalist development. An age symbolised by massive investment in industries such as steel, mining, railroads, shipping, chemicals, and oil. In the US. in the year 1900, there were 185 significant company amalgamations worth a total value of $3 billion, and between 1898 and 1902 there were 2,600 company mergers. US Steel was itself valued at $1.4 billion in 1901, and by 1900 there were 300 industrial groupings each with a value of $1 billion or more. This time of multiple company mergers was one in which the big investment banks grew as they served as agents to facilitate these deals. Some very big US companies that would be influential beyond US borders included: US Steel, America Can, Standard Oil, US Rubber, United Fruit Company, Coca Cola, Del Monte, American Telephone and Telegraph Company (AT&T), International Harvester, Dow Chemicals, Dupont, and Monsanto. Similar types of company can also be identified in Europe at this time including BASF, Bayer, Nestles, Sygenta. By 1904, seven of every ten production workers in the US were employed by incorporated businesses. Most of the big companies created in the late nineteenth early twentieth century were to play a significant role in determining national employment conditions and in setting the pattern of international trade (and, by association, influencing global politics). The expansion of these companies, and the fortunes made by many individuals, was due to a significant extent by the availability of finance sourced from the growing equity markets.

The main platforms for equity funding were the chain of 'stock markets' established across the world. At the turn of the century the London exchange was the largest (in terms of turnover), with the New York exchange being a close second. During the nineteenth century the number of exchanges had been growing apace and by 1900 there were 40 stocks exchanges operating in what was increasingly becoming a series of connected global equity markets; even if only seven of these were facilitating a significant amount of business. Thomas Picketty (2013) notes 1870-1914 as the period of the 'first globalization' of finance and trade; he also notes it as being a period of 'prodigious inequality'.

Markets in company shares were now becoming established as were markets in commodities, currencies, and in bonds issued by governments. Markets that, as well as providing liquidity for efficient trading, the capital for company expansion, and credit for governments, also offered the opportunity for 'speculation'; for the trading in financial instruments themselves (including currencies). Speculators seeking to gain a profit by the movement of the value of these instruments, rather than making a direct contribution to the primary activity of the agents issuing this or that equity or currency. Arguably, this activity might be judged as contributing in a socially useful way to the operation of stock markets, but the dominance of speculation over genuine investment that would pertain towards the end of the twentieth century would serve as but another source of financial instability, as well as the accumulation of vast private wealth for a relatively few.

Attempts were made to regulate and to reform these markets but, especially in the US and Britain, powerful financial interests often persuaded governments to drop or dilute any regulatory proposals and clever speculators could generally finds ways to circumvent any controls that were introduced. It was clear that by the end of the nineteenth century the interconnectedness of corporate industry, banking, and finance, characterised the structure of international capitalism. If a form of capitalism heavily supported by taxpayers in such areas as primary investment (infrastructure and research), education and health of workers, and in bailing out the system during the regular periods of crisis. And this, not just in times of repeated crises but also in the funding of a capitalist benefit system of subsidies, trade guarantees, and direct government investment.

Government finance ministers, senior treasury civil servants as well as leading financiers, bankers, and speculators, could (and still can) be identified as forming a 'community' of quite close-knit interacting national and international elite groupings. Grouping that anthropologically we can pretty much identify as self-perpetuating intra and inter-breeding groups, sharing genes, social ambitions, and exhibiting a strong propensity towards nepotism. Sharing an economic mindset of similar career ambitions and a commitment to an economic orthodoxy closely (verging on the wilfully) linked to the narrow interests of the finance industry; with a bias towards the interest of the rentier groupings.

Concerned about the growing influence of the finance industry, a 1912 congressional sub-committee set out to investigate its operation, especially the role of banks and big business trusts. A number of the leading financiers and businessmen that the sub-committee wanted to question managed to be abroad, or otherwise unavailable, during the time of the hearings, and the sub-committee experienced considerable difficulty gaining access to detailed information. But one revealing detail to be noted was that the financier J.P.Morgan had created a network of control that extended across the 32 corporations in which he or his close associates held a total of 2,450 directorships. At the end of their investigation the sub-committee concluded that ' "The facilities of the New York Stock Exchange are employed largely for transactions producing moral and economic waste and corruption" '(Mark Smith, 2003, p100). The recommendations made by the sub-committee to manage this were not progressed by Congress.

By the early twentieth century central banks had become a key feature of government financial strategy – not least in their role in protecting the value of a country's currency. The US had long been reluctant to create a formal central bank. But in 1913 Congress established the Federal Reserve System, a measure taken party in response to a 1907 crisis in the US banking system, but also conceding to the increasing need for the government to gain easy access to funds, and to have some means of smoothing the perturbations of economic cycles; controlling equity, and stabilizing currency, markets. A key change had been made to the banking system when from 1858 the restrictions that applied to joint-stock banking were eased, opening the way for expansion of commercial banking activities. Even Russia, that had been operating state-controlled rather than private banks, introduced commercial banking from the 1860s.

In the second half of the nineteenth century a series of technological innovations promoted the growth of business – telegraph (and the 'ticker tape' innovation in stock markets), typewriter, telephone, high rise office building, and with business 'schools' heralding the beginnings of management as a profession. In terms of industrialisation more widely, the economies of leading Western European countries had attained similar levels of industrial activity as had Britain.

Most European governments oversaw a steady increase in military spending during this period, but there was also an increase in spending on welfare provision. The franchise widened but still only 30-40% of the adult population were entitled to vote and the non-democratic presence of hereditary second houses, controlled by reactionary aristocrats, and/or monarchies opposed to almost any significant change, continued in many states. Against this background of governance there was the increasing organization of the working class and seemingly viable revolutionary alternatives. The more astute leaders of the traditional political parties realised the need to offer concessions if they were to maintain their advantageous (privileged) position. Hobsbawm noted that during the period 1880-1914: 'Democratic politics could no longer be postponed. Henceforth the problem was how to manage them [the masses]' (Hobsbawm 1987, p86). In the US, the power of big business, and its antipathy to worker organization, ensured that any more radical forms of trades unionism and welfare reform would struggle to make much progress.

In Germany, Otto von Bismarck intentionally set out to foster the 'conservative state of mind' in a population. As Reich Chancellor in the 1880s he oversaw the introduction of a landmark social insurance scheme for the provision of medical treatment and retirement pensions. From the 1890s, France introduced a series of welfare measures including: free medical assistance (1893), the setting up of a Dept. of Child Affairs charged with reducing the harsh treatment of children (1904), support for the old and infirm (1905), and compulsory insurance to cover workplace injuries (1910).

In Britain, surveys such as those undertaken by Seebohm Rountree (York 1901) and Charles Booth (London 1886-1903), mapped the life in cities, revealing the extent of the segregation of 'classes' within cities, and living conditions for the poorest that shocked much of the wider population. In an attempt to ease these, often appalling, conditions, and aware of the increasing organization of the working class, the Liberal government (following a landslide victory in 1906) led by Henry Campbell-Bannerman, and with David Lloyd George as Chancellor of the Exchequer from 1908-15, began to legislate for some welfare provision. Free school meals for the poorest were introduced in 1906, and two years later a non-contributory means-tested pension for the over 70s. An age that relatively few of the working class ever reached, when average male life expectancy was 48 years. The liberal government also established Labour Exchanges throughout the country and then in 1911 enacted the National Insurance Act. A contributory scheme to provide funding for certain types of medical treatment, and the provision of a time-limited amount of sick-pay. Following pressure for the Cooperative Women's Guild, a modest level of maternity benefit was also included.

It was the South American country of Uruguay that was at the forefront of government support for the mass of its population. Here the government led by José Batlle y Ordóñez (president 1903-1913), as well as taking important steps to improve the rights of women, also introduced what seem to have been quite radical employment and wider social measures. Measures including, a maximum eight-hour working day and compensation for workplace injuries, free education for all children, a public health system, and some state pension provision. Even though the means to introduce these human rights and welfare reforms was based on successful economic performance - with a strong export income coming mainly from agricultural products (farming and livestock), it also required social pressure and the political will to progress them.

US governments, strongly influenced by big business, were reluctant to provide for its population. The poorest having to rely on charities and a state-based provision similar to the humiliating English Poor Law system. The position with the ex-military was somewhat easier, with some modest support being provided for veterans and their families.

For the industrialising nations, taken as a whole, this was a period of government expansion in size and of their involvement in the practices and institutions of industry, public health, education, and more generally in the administration of growing economies. From 1885-1910, the number of government employees increased in Britain by a factor of 8 (67,000-535,000), France by a factor of 2 (300,000-583,000), Prussia-Germany by a factor of 20 (55,000-1,000,000) with the US (complicated by the federal/state division of administrative responsibility) by a factor of about 8.

Governments of European countries were by the start of the twentieth century involved in the provision and management/regulation of a range of local and national services including: education, transportation, utilities, the police and legal/judicial system, and to some extent public health (as well as the traditional 'defence'). Financing these activities mainly through taxation and by borrowing against future income. The period of 'industrial capitalism' was transforming, if only slowly, into more or less extensive types of 'state supported capitalism'. Including support for private property rights, with a relatively free-market private economic sector heavily subsidised by a range of state support - including contracts for public works, significant government spending on armed forces equipment, and a range of government sponsored research initiatives benefiting the private sectors. An arrangement that was to characterise a balance of private and public involvement in the economic affairs of industrialised countries throughout the twentieth century

The early years of the twentieth century saw a significant reduction in demand for manufactured goods; unemployment increased and real wage-rates in most industrialized countries fell. Sections of the organised working classes were becoming impatient with the 'Liberal-type' (as in British Liberals) politicians in whom they had invested their expectations for democratic change, and were frustrated with moderate trades union leaders too ready to accede to the views of employers. A wave of strikes broke out across industrialised Europe but perhaps of greater longer-term significance working class dissatisfaction with representation by 'moderate' politicians, was the move to support or even form more 'socialist' political parities; including the older SDP in Germany, the newly formed Labour Party in Britain, and socialist parties in most other Scandinavian and mainland European countries. This more robust, even for some revolutionary, approach to advancing their own interest was an expression of a rising class consciousness realising the unjust distribution of the benefits of economic progress.

For Hobsbawm (1987, p117) at this time: '…..labour and socialist parties were almost everywhere growing at a rate which, depending on one's point of view, was extremely alarming or marvellous.'

In the US many of the big companies routinely employed armed thugs (the Pinkertons were specialist 'for-hire', for anti-union activity) to intimidate and physically attack workers striking to gain generally quite modest improvements in their conditions; a practice that would continue well into the twentieth century. The growing dissatisfaction of American workers found organizational expression with the formation of 'The Industrial Workers of the World'.[4] But was more directly expressed in a wave of strikes in major industries, along with some attempts to draw black people, women, and unskilled whites within the working class movement.

When groups of workers (often joined by more radical middle-class intellectuals) gathered to discuss their plight in more general terms (rather than to discuss strategy towards any particular issue/dispute) the discussion would often be intermixed with explanatory frameworks for identifying the causes of ills and to include ideological theories for change that echoed the views of leading anarchists, syndicalists, socialists, communists, as well as more cautious social democrats.

Europe during the period 1910-14 saw widespread, if mainly localized, industrial action taken by workers as they were realizing their industrial and political potential, aware that they were the primary contributors to the wealth creation from which they benefited but relatively little. In Britain the year 1911 stood out as one of particular unrest, with over 900,000 workers being involved in strikes. Action was taken by railway workers, dockers, merchant-seaman, and those working in most of the heavy industries. In south London 15,000 women, working in 20 food processing factories,

---

[4] Known as the 'Wobblies' - 1905 - still in existence and based in Chicago – has members in the US, Australia, Canada, UK, Germany, South Africa, Sierra Leone, Uganda, Switzerland, Austria, Luxemburg - but all of these together only involve very modest membership numbers if these have included some notable individuals - such as Helen Keller, Noam Chomsky, Judi Bari, Eugene O'Neill, Lucy Parsons, Elizabeth Gurley Flynn and Mary Harris ('Mother') Jones – And of course, many unnamed workers at shop-floor level have been endeavouring to protect the interests of their fellow workers.

walked out in protest at low pay. In the forefront of organising this action were syndicalist leaders, mainly operating within trades unions.

Across Europe, in the first decade of the twentieth century, there was a wave of strikes and demonstrations. Elements of a narrative of working-class led revolution was gaining some, if mostly muted, traction on the factory floor, in the docks, in the mines, and in transport industries.

This unparalleled level of industrial unrest caused considerable concern within ruling groups. A concern noted in the US as well as most western European countries. One shared by some South America governments as they also experienced quite widespread working-class action; mainly led by syndicalist leaders committed to revolutionary political change.

For Fernand Braudel (1993, p397) '....it could be argued that in 1914 the west was not only on the brink of war, but was also on the brink of Socialism'

There were some significant if traditional fault-lines mitigating against working class solidarity. Within trade unionism there were antagonisms between skill and unskilled workers in many industries, and between males and females in all of them. Beyond this most in the working classes identified more with nation than with their class brothers and sisters across international boundaries. In terms of ideology, the motivation of the majority of TU and political party leaders (and no doubt most members) was more focused on gaining incremental improvements in wages and working conditions than on the creation of some socialist-type nirvana. If anything united the working class it was a general hatred of the very rich, but they lacked a solid commitment to a system that might eradictate the political and economic conditions that created them.

It would be the nationalist drums of war that would suppress any even only nascent attempts to organize international working class solidarity - evidence for the organization of which was appearing in the Second International, the IWW, May Days holidays, and in the rhetoric of most leaders of the more socialist social democratic political parties formed over the three decades from 1880 - the draw of patriotism depressingly quite easily displaced the more inspirational ideas of a shared working class global identity.

As the First World War approached, the ruling elites in the opposing nations mobilized a patriotic propaganda campaign - one redolent with flags, military show, Royal families re-presented as kindly hallowed national parent-figures, shared romanticized histories, and various other ways cleverly deployed to manipulate a population towards a sense of shared national identity and a generalised suspicion of the 'other' (the foreigner).

In sum: a mendacious preparedness for yet another unnecessary war.

The hate-filled ramparts formed by xenophobic national mythologies were artfully constructed; if mostly produced by an informal collusion involving politicians, the populist mass media, as well as schools, the churches, and even many trades union leaders. It was against these patriotic ramparts that the emerging if tentative links of international working-class solidarity were torn apart, never to be effectively rebuilt and developed into what might have been. This informal conspiracy of patriotic propagandizing was offered to largely receptive audiences within the populations of European nations. As C.A.Bayly (2004, p280) rightly pointed out: 'In fact nationalism and patriotism also drew on more profound desires and aspirations, outside the purview of the state, which had in earlier times often been attached to family, clan or religious groups'. I would add 'tribe' 'club' and 'class' to this list - indeed any of the many identity-based groupings characterised by in-group solidarity and out-group antipathy.

The frayed threads of internationalism were partially reconnected after the war, indeed there was a Third International - but the impact of the primacy given to nationalism over internationalism and to patriotism over global working class solidarity, had undermined the aspiration for any significant global organization of workers. When the threads were picked up again in the 1920s it would be under the guidance of the Soviet Union and so became an internationalism tainted by direct association with a type of dictatorial communism.

The wider political context for war.

In July 1908 a group of disaffected young Ottoman army officers based in the garrison at Thessaloniki rebelled. Amongst these officers was Mustapha Kemal, a future leader of what was to become the Turkish Republic. One of the reforms that these 'Young Turks' campaigned for was to allow more autonomy for all national groups within the Ottoman Empire. Taking advantage of the disruption in the south-east of the Empire a number of these national groups took action – Cretans sought union with Greece - Bulgaria proclaimed independence – Austria-Hungary annexed Bosnia-Hercegovina causing the Serbs (supported by Russia) to reacted angrily. German pressure forced Russia to accept the annexation and in turn the Serbs had, if very reluctantly, to yield to the new political reality. These regional upheavals – in effect leaving the 1878 Treaty of Berlin in tatters - in the context of already heightened level of tension across Europe, would bring the whole continent to the brink of war.

A period of uneasy peace with occasional outbreaks of guerrilla activity was maintained up to 1912. In the two years leading up to the First World War, Turkey (regions of Thrace and Macedonia) was attacked, initially by Montenegrin troops who were within days joined by troops from Greece, Serbia and Bulgaria; driving the Turks out of Albania, Macedonia and Kosovo; which then declared themselves independent. But then Bulgaria was attacked by its former ally Serbia, supported by Greece and Romania; with Serbia then moving to occupy Kosovo and Macedonia. These conflicts, in the First Balkan War, were characterised by revenge killing, widespread rape, and the process that came to be termed 'ethnic cleansing', as different ethnic groups fought to avenge what were perceived as past injustices or to obtain more territory. Inter-group hatred, suspicion, and fear, was fermented by those seeking political control and/or economic advance.

But behind these regional tensions were the Great Powers operating in support of this or that favoured Balkan client state; adopted mostly in line with wider European alliances. This period of conflict substantially brought an end to the Ottoman rule in Europe. The two most significant outbursts of conflict were temporarily controlled by the Treaty of London (Dec.1912) and then the Treaty of Bucharest (Aug. 1913) but the level of inter-ethnic tension, with no real attempts by leaders to resolve divisive issues, was palpable. Written histories assessing the political relationship between ethnic groups in the region at the time use phrases such as 'tinderbox box' 'explosive cocktail' 'hotbed of tensions'… I will add another 'a cauldron of ethnic-based nationalist discontents'…… to capture a sense of the pent up hatred that would be released and expressed in the descent into civil madness that would take place from 1914.

Between 1912-13 the Balkan Albanians had sided with the Turks and fought with them against the Serbs. But the Serbs proved to be the superior force and they managed to expel the Turks and as the Turkish army retreated from Kosovo the advancing Serbs massacred about 25,000 Albanians.

The Armenian peoples of the region abutting eastern Turkey have a history interlinked with the history of civil life in the Middle-East. Their lands were criss-crossed by trade routes between Eastern Europe and the Middle East. As long as 3000 years ago they have been identified as traders and agriculturalists. In response to the Seljuk Turk (Sunni Muslims) invasions in the eleventh century many Armenians fled to settle in southern Turkey and it was here that the Ruberian Dynasty established their new kingdom, with its capital in Tarsus. During this period (1078-1375) Armenian art and literature flourished. Throughout the time of the Crusades Christian Armenians supported the European Crusaders in their campaigns against the Moslems. The break-up of the Cilician Kingdom saw the first significant Diaspora of Armenians when, following Tamberlaine's invasion of Cilicia, 30,000 of the wealthiest Armenians fled to Cyprus. By the nineteenth century most Armenians were living within the Ottoman Empire with the majority Christians among them being subject to the Moslem dhimmi system that allowed non-Moslems to practice their faiths but having fewer political and civil rights; including the right to bear arms or even to ride horses. The Armenians as Christians, and more so as Christians strategically positioned in relation to the politically unsettled Southern European region, enjoyed some support from France, Great Britain, and Russia, who all supported the Armenian campaign for political reform.

The Ottoman Empire had made some concessions in 1839. A move that only encouraged calls, in the 1860s and 1870s, for further reforms and for action to be taken against Kurdish and Circassian tribesmen who had repeatedly attacked Armenian villages; committing numerous acts of looting, rape, and murder. Following the 1877-1878 Russo-Turkish war the Russians agreed to withdraw from Ottoman lands gained during the conflict on condition that the persecution of the Armenians ceased and civic reforms enacted. It was during thse treaty negotiations that the Armenians began to campaign for the status of an autonomous region within the Ottoman Empire.

The uneasy relationship between Armenians and Ottoman Turks increased once the 'Treaty of Berlin' had been agreed, with the ruling Sultan Abdul Hamid II endeavouring to obstruct the implementation of reforms set out in Article 61 of the Treaty. In 1890 Hamid II created the para-military unit 'Hamidge', composed mostly of Kurds. And between 1894-96 this unit engaged in the officially sanctioned persecution of Armenians. Persecution to the extent of looting property, murder and on occasion rape – it has been estimated that as many as 300,000 Armenians were killed in what became known as the Hamidian massacres. Although the Great Powers, previously supporters of the Armenians, were well aware of what was going on (western newspapers carried headlines calling Hamid 'The Bloody Sultan' and 'The Great Assassin') they now decided that their political interests would be best served by non-intervention.

Another massacre took place following an unsuccessful attempt to launch a counter revolution in 1909 when the Armenians were taken to have sided with those wishing to overthrow the regime set up during the 1908 Young Turk revolution. Reprisals against the Armenians saw up to 30,000 being killed in what became known as the Adana Massacre. These events did little to suppress the aspirations of the Armenians and a group in the north rose in rebellion; requiring the deployment of 20,000 Ottoman troops to regain control.

The first Balkan war in 1912 changed the map of the region. Greece, Bulgaria, Montenegro and Serbia had all gained land and most of this at the expense of Ottoman Turkey, and of the Albanians who had just established their own state. 'The Congress of Ambassadors' held in London had resulted in the Balkan nations reluctant recognition of the newly established Albanian state but their own gains from the Congress led to what was in effect the partition of the Albanian peoples. About half of Albanians lived within the new Albania and the other half lived in lands now controlled by other Balkan states. States that, whilst pleased to gain the land, did not want the Albanians.

From 1912-15 Serbia, Montenegro, and Greece, in effect, carried out policies that would amount to 'ethnic cleansing'. The Serbian and Montenegrin armies burnt villages, chased thousands of inhabitants from their farms, villages, and towns, imprisoned many in concentration camps and, in October 1912 the Serbs killed 5,000 Albanians at Pristine. As the Albanians were expelled the Montenegrin and Serbian settlers were moved in to occupy the 'cleansed' farmlands and villages. This steady 'tit for tat 'of genocidal activity – in fact political policy – would continue with periods of more or less violence up to the outbreak of WW2. To be ferociously reignited in the final decades of the twentieth century.

The Balkan region of south-eastern Europe was further unsettled following two local wars; the first involving Serbia, Bulgaria and Greece – the Balkan League - combining to drive the Ottoman Turks out of south Europe and the second, an unhappy Bulgaria at war with its two former allies to progress its demand for more territory. Few if any of the leading nations of this region – Serbia, Bulgaria, Greece, Albania, Croatia, Montenegro, Macedonia, Romania, Slovenia (and indeed the Ottoman Turks) - were at ease with the then existing territorial arrangements. It is hardly an understatement to suggest that for the leaders (and much of the populations) of these groups, the Balkans seethed with ethnicity-based territorial discontent.

It was a matter of when rather than if discontent would be expressed in armed conflict, and the when turned out to be triggered by the assassination on 28th July 1914 of the heir to the Habsburg crown Archduke Franz Ferdinand (and his wife) by a couple of young Serbian nationalists. Franz Ferdinand had been dispatched to assist in the negotiation of a peace that would allow for the Slavic peoples on the southern part of the region to have greater political voice, especially in Serbia itself. Considered in the wider political context of mutual distrust, of nations bristling with modern armaments, led by politicians operating at the nation equivalent level of 'self-consciousness' (so imbued with national egoism), a relatively trivial act of some sort was almost bound to trigger warfare.

Following the assassination (and encouraged by Germany) Austria then declared war on Serbia and began shelling Belgrade; such was the ethnic diversity of the Austria-Hungarian Empire that the mobilization orders had to be issued in twenty different languages. Russia mobilized its army to support Serbia then, on 1st August Germany declared war on Russia, The conflict spread when, on 3rd August Germany declared war on France and informed Belgium that it would have to accept invasion as part of Germany's strategy to attack the French. Great Britain then declared war on Germany and Austro-Hungary, claiming to defend, as newspapers put it, 'little Belgium' from German aggression. So it took but a week or so to launch a war that had been fomenting for at least ten years, but the context for which had been created in the nationalism, industrialism, military technological development, and a competitive capitalist economic system developing in the second half of the nineteenth century.

A characteristic of nationhood was the bringing together of groups prepared to acknowledge and commit to a collective identity. The ethnic divisions between and within nations in the Balkans (south east Europe) continues to be the most obvious way of framing the causes underlying the series of bloody, if regionally contained, Balkan wars. But there were more 'banal' reasons for WW1 related to the intentions of the Great Powers (Austria, Russia, Germany, France, Britain, and Italy) to advance their own strategic trading interests. This, along with the belief of some of the leading military high command that modern supply systems, military tactics (e.g. Germany's Schlieffen Plan), and modern weaponry, would allow short sharp wars favouring those sufficiently bold to commit adequate resources and to strike first.

Nation-statehood was not of course a requirement for conflict between peoples but it is a powerful form for marking out ('constructing') collective identities that facilitate the mobilization of populations for war. There is the underlying difference of 'them and us' that a range of research has suggested the simple recognition of difference can, in itself, foster inter-group conditions for conflict. Consequently nation-statehood, a mode of understanding and magnified difference, can facilitate warfare in ways that would be quite difficult for small 'groups' for whom conflict tends to be limited in casualties and geographically localised. A.C.Grayling in his book of popular philosophy 'The Meaning of Things' (2001 page 78), wrote about nationalism: *'The idea of nationalism turns on that of 'nation'. The word is meaningless: all 'nations' are mongrel, a mixture of so many immigrations and mixings of peoples over time that the idea of ethnicity is largely comical except in places where the boast has to be either that the community there remained so remote and disengaged, or so conquered, for the greater part of history, that it succeeded in keeping its gene pool 'pure' (a cynic might say 'inbred')............Nations are artificial constructs, their boundaries drawn in the blood of past years........Cultural heritage is not the same thing as national identity'*

Eric Hobsbawm (1987, p105) noted for 1890-1914: 'Political life thus found itself increasingly ritualized and filled with symbols and publicity appeals, both overt and subliminal. As the ancient ways - mainly religious - of ensuring subordination, obedience and loyalty were eroded, the patent need for something to replace them was met by the *invention* of tradition, using both old and tried evokers of emotion such as crown and military glory and, ..., new ones such as empire and colonial conquest.'

On the whole a successful strategy, one expressed in patriotic enthusiasm when a generation of young men from different nations were so easily persuaded to kill and maim each other by politicians (backed by industrialists) at the start of the First World War, was to show.

Nation state-hood is not the cause of inter-group conflict but it does provide yet another factor (along with religion, ethnicity, tribe, caste, class, etc) that allows the form of differentiation inherent in collective identities and can foster the perception of a group's 'imagined' shared interests. Due to industrialized nations being able to deploy massive financial, administrative, and propaganda resources to justify conflict, the outcomes, apart from a divided world, has been mass killing of soldiers and civilians; if, in terms of numbers, the latter has been more significant in the twentieth century.

If unnecessary killing is evil then it was evil indeed that was the redolent characteristic reflected in events that took place from 1914 across what would soon become the tree denuded, shell cratered landscapes strewn with glinting threads of barbed wire, and the stench-ridden and rat-infested, more often water-logged, trenches. Landscapes torn by the ear splitting noise of cannonade, the phosphorous flash of bursting shells, the zinging sniper's bullet, a steady stream of lead pouring from machine guns, the poison gas-induced choking as the delicate lining of gasping lungs were perforated, the pitiful cries of wounded and dying men, the very wretchedness of warfare. All contributing to inducing the collective fear that must have gripped the bellies of thousands of soldiers in the eerily quiet moments leading up to the eruptions of live conflict. With images of home forming in their minds as they unready, hoped to live, but necessarily prepared to die.

A multiplicity of more significant and less significant decisions brought the military forces of Axis ('Central Powers') and Allied ('Entente Powers') nations together, each bristling with newly produced weaponry.

Europe's 'civilized' countries, collectively hypnotized with their gaze fixed on their nationalistic ambitions, were prepared to aggressively advance or aggressively defend the ambitions of their military/political leadership. But to claim that they must have been collectively hypnotised, entranced, is to deny the element of human agency that must have been enacted throughout the whole decision-making processes leading to conflict.

But from 28th July 1914 the spark that began the process of actual warfare had been struck. What might be judged as a certain level of rational endeavour had long been building – the clanking choreography of military preparation, generals and government ministers planning for 'what if' scenarios, planning according to knowledge of the potential enemy's military strengths, and according to narrow interpretations of the enemy's intentions. The recruitment and mobilization of hundreds of thousands of young men and the rain of propaganda directed towards populations in order to persuade them of the justification of war was but the culmination of such preparations.

The events that were to be played out on the world's oceans and on the death-blasted fields, heaths, and woodland landscapes across Europe, can surely only be defined as irrationality in its most distilled form. Not just the irrationality of this or that ill-thought out choice, of this or that stupid action, but four years of collective irrationality bordering on the profound; teetering on the incomprehensible to anyone who approaches the world with a humanistic sense of values.

What could justify millions of young men that historical circumstances, economic greed, and political limitations, have caused to form up on two opposed sides whose artillery then engaged in hurling thousands[5] of tons of shells whistling across the divide.

These massive bombardments then being followed by wave after wave of troops, tramping resignedly towards defenders, to meet, then pour tons and tons of bullets, grenades, and at times clouds of poison gas, onto each other. If we add the relentless toll taken by diseases of the trenches we have a death-toll of 10 million.

The suicidal stupidity of Passendale, the heroic stupidity of Gallipoli, the string of murderous confrontations along the eastern front. One can call up a gallery of images symbolising the depressing folly of war – the central weakness of the self-consciousness level of human thinking: selfishness (individual and group), narrowness of focus, the tendency to irrationality (misjudging outcomes and refusing to calculate/assess longer-term interests), the cognitively soothing decisions to decide on a course of action; action itself eases

---

[5] At start of the war the French alone had a stock of 5,000,000 artillery shells, by 1916 they were using this amount of shells every month, and by 1918 it reached 10,000,000 per month – noted in Best et al 2004.

cognitive dissonance for individuals, groups and governments, on any issue. The various forms of human thinking focused on but narrow conceptions of self-interests.

The war at sea also developed, with the German and British fleets manoeuvring around each other, engaging at times – as ponderous Dreadnought battleships hurled 12 inch calibre shells, each weighing half a ton, across miles of water, most landing in the sea (as with most loosed munitions, an expensive waste, if a satisfactory outcome). But with those relatively few, but still too many, finding their intended targets tangling, melting, and distorting metal. Killing and mutilating soft-fleshed bodies, a torrid scene engulfed in red-hot fire until the wounded ship slid, hissing streams of steam, beneath the surface of the sea; to leak extended wisps of thick black oil down to today.

A new type of sea warfare was introduced during WW1, with the submarine. Submarines had been deployed to a minimal extent as far back as the US civil war. But WW1 saw the submarine become an effective weapon when deployed against both military and merchant naval targets – extending warfare to beneath the oceans. In a little known novel 'The Undying Fire', published in 1931, H.G. Wells wrote a section based on submarine warfare, describing outcomes and lucidly suggesting some underlying threads/sinews making up the nationalist structures that lead to man taking up arms against man.

I think it is worth quoting this at length:

On submarine warfare: '…..*I will not recall to you the stories that fill our newspapers of men drowning in the night, of crowded boatloads of sailors and passengers shelled and sunken…… I want you to think of the submarine itself……They are miracles of short-sighted ingenuity for the common unprofitable reasonless destruction of Germans [submariners] and their enemies. They are almost quintessential examples of the elaborate futility and horror into which partial ideas of life, combative and competitive ideas of life, thrust mankind'*

Wells takes up his story… **"Take some poor German boy with an ordinary sort of intelligence, and ordinary human disposition to kindliness, and some gallantry, who becomes finally a sailor in one of these craft. Consider his case and what we do to him. You will find in him a sample of what we are doing for mankind. As a child he is ingenuous, teachable, plastic. He is also egotistical, greedy, and suspicious. He is easily led and easily frightened. He likes making things if he knows how to make them; he is capable of** *affection and capable of resentment. He is a sheet of white paper upon which anything may be written. His parents teach him, his companions, his school. Do they teach him anything of the great history of mankind? Do they teach him of his blood brotherhood with all men? Do they tell him anything of discovery, of exploration, of human effort and achievement? No. They teach him that he belongs to a blonde and wonderful race, the only race that matters on this planet. ....And these teachers incite him to suspicion and hatred and contempt of all other races. They fill his mind with fears and hostilities. Everything German they tell him is good and splendid. Everything not German is dangerous and wicked.*

The boy grows up a mental cripple; his capacity for devotion and self-sacrifice is run into a mould of fanatical loyalty for the Kaiser and hatred for foreign things. Comes this war, and the youngster is only too eager to give himself where he is most needed. He is told that the submarine war is the sure way of striking the enemies of his country a conclusive blow.

'.......This youngster sees himself a hero, fighting for his half-divine Kaiser, for dear Germany, against the cold and evil barbarians who resist and would destroy her. He passes through the drill and training. He goes down into the submarine for the first time, clambers down the narrow hatchway. It is a little cold, but wonderful; a marvellous machine. How can such as nest of inventions, ingenuities, beautiful metalwork, wonderful craftsmanship, be anything but right? His mind is full of dreams of proud enemy battleships smitten and heeling over into the waters, while he watches his handiwork with a stern pride, a restrained exultation, a sense of Germany vindicated...........That is how his mind has been made for him. That is the sort of mind that has been made and is being made in boys all over the world.........Because there is no common plan for the world, because each person in the making of this boy, just as each in the making of the submarine, had 'been himself' and 'done his bit,' followed his own impulses and interests without regard to the whole, regardless of any plan or purpose in human affairs, ignorant of the spirit of God [sic] who would unify us to a common use of all our gifts and energies.

"Let me go on with the story of the youngster...... "Comes a day when he realises the reality of the work he is doing for his kind. He stands by one of the guns of the submarine in an attack upon some wretched ocean tramp. He realises that the war he wages is no

heroic attack on pride or pre-dominance, but a mere murdering of traffic. He sees the little ship shelled, the luckless men killed and wounded, no tyrants of the seas but sailor-men like himself; he sees their boats smashed to pieces……... These little black things, he realises incredulously, that struggle and disappear amidst the wreckage are the heads of men brothers to himself…."

"For hundreds of thousands of men who have come into the war expecting bright and romantic and tremendous experiences their first killing must have been a hideous disillusionment. For none so much as the men of submarines. All that sense of being right and fine that carries men into battle, that caries most of us through the world, must have vanished completely at this first vision of reality. Our man must have asked himself, 'What am I doing?'

"In the night he must have lain awake and stared at that question in horrible doubt……

"We scold too much at the German submarine crews in this country. Most of us in their places would be impelled to go on as they go on. The work they do has been reached step by step, logically, inevitably, because our world has been content to drift along on false premises and haphazard assumptions and nationality and race and the order of things. These things have happened because the technical education of men has been better than their historical and social education. Once men have lost touch with, or failed to apprehend that idea of a single human community.

Wells goes on to give a report of two actual U-Boat sailors who died in a Harwich hospital following their capture after their craft was hit by a mine, whose fate was similar, if their end was no less uncomfortable, than many of fellow submariners.

"Think of those poor creatures dying in the hospital. They were worn out by fits of coughing and haemorrhage, but there must have been moments of exhausted quiet before the end, when our youngster lay and stared at the bleak walls of the ward and thought; when he asked himself, 'What have I been doing? What have I done? What has this world done for me? It has made me a murderer. It has tortured me and wasted me……. And I meant well by it……

So it was with the German youngster who dreamt dreams, who had ambitions, who wished to serve and do brave and honourable things, died.

….Is not this story of youth and hope misled, marched step by

step into a world misconceived, thrust into evil, and driven down to ugliness and death, only a more vivid rendering of what is now the common fate of great multitudes? Is there any one of us who is not in some fashion aboard a submarine, doing evil and driving towards an evil end?....'.

Wells ends this section with an allusion to the place of God (for God read conscience) in our hearts.

'You asked what the Spirit of God in Man was against. It is against those mental confusions, these ignorances, that thrust life into a frightful cul-de-sac, that the God in our Hearts urges us to fight.....He is crying out in our hearts to save us from these blind alleys of selfishness, darkness, cruelty, and pain in which our race must die; he is crying for the high road which is salvation, he is commanding the organised unity of mankind'

I have quoted Wells at length because his outline seems to capture key aspects of the intermixing of the individual, the national, and some of the psychological processes involved in warfare. The use of the submarine in conflict was specifically banned by both the Hague convention and by international law, so both Germany and Britain defied these agreements that they had cynically signed up too; cynically, not least, because they had been undertaking research into submarine warfare years before the war started.

Once the war had begun the German plan was for a rapid advance through then neutral Belgium, to sweep into Northern France (as per General Alfred von Schlieffen's plan) – By the sixth week of the war the Germans were held by the French, and the residue of Belgium, forces about 20/30 miles from Paris. Then British mobilisation steadily reinforced the Allies and within a few months lines of fortifications had been drawn up from Flanders in the north-west, to the Swiss border in the south, and the 'Western Front' was established as delimiting the relatively narrow strip of countryside that, as the war continued, provided the landscapes for the slaughter and crippling of millions of young men. The gory scenes played out here, and with equal ferocity on the eastern front, were choreographed by an unimaginative, uncaring, military leadership (generals – supported by equally uncaring politicians) whose approach to war, for the most part, expressed the retention of a mindset of glamourous cavalry officers schooled in the battlefield strategies of the nineteenth century who could only adapt to industrial warfare by marching droves of young men into the fire of cannonades and machine guns over and over again.

The young men, drawn by the siren sound of marching bands towards what they were led to believe (on both sides) would be a short war, were for the most part neither more nor less brave than their enemy. They were stirred to volunteer or accept conscription by the mass media, politicians, and sections of populations excited with a patriotic fervour that was pervading the lands. Many European communists, socialists and some social democratic politicians despaired at how easily class consciousness and international solidarity between working people could be swept aside. In Germany, Rosa Luxemburg eloquently expressed her anguish at seeing nationalism given priority over the working class solidarity that she and socialist colleagues had determinedly endeavoured to foster.

Across Europe local communities beguiled by propaganda, and fired by a type of optimistic patriotism assuming their forces as being superior to the enemy's, felt the war would be settled in their favour by Christmas 1914. Across the continent local dignitaries including magistrates, teachers, churchmen, and elected representatives contributed to an upswell of community mood impacting on thousands of young men driven by mixtures of patriotic enthusiasm, goading, and guilt, to join-up. At a national level, the elite groups of politicians, business men, newspaper owners and journalists, novelists and populist philosophers, all contributed to creating the national mind-set that underpinned the drive towards war. Newspapers outlined gory details of 'enemy atrocities', most of which never actually occurred and those that did have some element of truth were embroidered by the excited imagination of editorial writer's intent on influencing public mood and to impressing their war-mongering proprietors.

Leading politicians and bellicose sections of the media contributed in their own ways to a narrative presenting their own nation as victim of the 'other's' aggression – of the need for a war for national survival against unprovoked, and so unjustified, aggression.

No balanced historical context, no reasoned admission of perhaps at least some justification for Germany's action.

There were some dissenting voices, mainly on the political left, and the elements of the organised working class (T.U.s), not taken in by the misleading press (the duplicity of which they and their members would have gained direct experience of during recent industrial disputes) and holding to a more internationalist perspective. Peace rallies were organised in London, Paris, and Berlin. But once the conflict had broken out, such was the pressure of a jingoistic national mood that most leaders from these groups swung from opposition to support for the war – German Social Democrats, British Labour Party and the British T.U.C., as well as many French and Russian socialists, anarchists and syndicalists deciding to go with the populist flow.

Any remaining voices of reason (urging restraint and negotiation) were drowned out by the rising tide of war-willingness. In Britain whole battalions were formed by volunteers from the same districts, brothers, cousins and friends that had grown up together, these were the 'Pals' battalions; Liverpool alone formed four 'Pals' battalions. Biographic information notes the excitement felt by thousands of young men heading to the front. 'Your country needs YOU' was for some a stirring call to arms but the generally grim conditions of working class life in all European nations must also have made the chance of regular army pay and 'all found' conditions, along with the imagined image of returning as a 'hero', quite attractive.

The reality intruded on the imagined glory when the Pals regiments first saw action in the Battle of the Somme. Where an ineffective Allied bombardment of German positions left the enemy relatively unscathed and, when the Allied soldiers were ordered to advance into waves of withering machine-gun fire, wholesale slaughter ensued. With many of the battalions losing over half their numbers. When the news got back to Britain whole towns and cities went into mourning as the doleful tolling of church bells signalled the stark, fatal, reality of warfare.

At some point after the war began the balance of power shifted from politicians to the military – by 1916 Germany was in effect, led by the bellicose Generals Ludendorff and Hindenburg, France by Marshal Joffre, Britain by Lord Kitchener (Secretary of State for War) and Russia by a militarily wholly incompetent Tsar – In Austria, the Reichsrat was dissolved in early 1916 and for the remainder of the war the military took the lead.

One million soldiers died and four million were wounded in some ferocious engagements (including the Marne and at Gallipoli) during the first year of the war. Then, from 1915, the land-war settled into ritualised periods of sniper action, artillery bombardment, and bored troops hunkered down in winding rows of cold, wet, rat infested, trenches. With 'advances' being ordered when supplies (of men, munitions, food, medical equipment as well as shrouds and coffins) had been rebuilt to a sufficient level to allow an attack to be launched. Then, following hours during which the artillery sent tons and tons of shells whistling towards the enemy defences, wave after wave of troops were ordered to advance through the smoky no-mans-land. To march in undulating lines across swaths of tree-denuded wastelands bridging the distance between the opposing combatants' lines. This last walk, this tramp towards summary execution for many of these young men, was across muddy, crater-pocked terrains, threaded with a matrix of glinting barbed-wire that by the end of each day's battle would be draped with stiffening, blood-drained, corpses from which had flown the memories of home – of mothers, lovers, and children – along with but glimpsed outlines of future lives never to be lived.

As suggested by Roger Osborne (2007, p423): 'War became a living nightmare of murderous industrial force inflicting anonymous carnage on millions of human lives'

Yes, within most nations lives could meanwhile be lived in relatively untrammeled circumstances, untouched by the War, and still to a significant extent matched to the changing seasons. But the change from the occasional young man leaving a rural region for adventure in a national army would become from 1914 a stream of young men conscripted or volunteered off to war never to return, their blood seemingly spilled to nourish the production of stone-cold war memorials that were later to spread across the country like mushrooms fruiting in woodland glades during the crisp autumnal days that these men would never again see. A vibrant body of clear-eyed young men replaced, in market towns and outlying villages, by a series of inert obelisks on which is recorded each mans premature non-existence in parallel lists of neatly chiseled names.

The rise in populations of most European countries had made millions of young men available for military service and the easy acceptance of the legitimacy of state power allowed conscription, and the propaganda 'machine' of a popular press persuaded many to march with the drum-beat towards their deaths and the killing of their own kind i.e. other young human-beings. The seeming inevitable pull for young men of the imagined 'fields of glory' (of 'glorious honour') that lay in distant lands or in defending one's nation, one's own people, drew them towards the gory battlefields of Europe. Glorious fields that today present as the neatly tended setting for the rows of thousands upon thousands of pale-aged white tablets etched with names and ages identifying just how young they were; around which grow the enduring red-flowered poppies that poignantly symbolise the red blood drained of so many young men so long ago. Fields redolent with glory only in its bitterly-heroic form of glorious futility.

In the five month-long battle of Verdun, during which 23 million shells were fired, over 300,000 men were killed (of the 700,000 casualties) during the relentless German assault on the French held fortress of Verdun - in the four month battle of the Somme 1,300,000 men in total (both sides) being wounded, posted missing, or killed (the British and Commonwealth forces lost 20,000 men killed and 40,000 wounded on the first day of this battle -1ˢᵗ July 1916). And in a 10 day period in the lead-up to the first big 'push' that began the third battle of the strategically situated city of Ypres the Allies fired 4,250,00 shells from 3,000 cannon.

It has been estimated that 300 million artillery shells were fired during the war – one in three failing to explode, with most of these 'duds' still not having been recovered.

The toll is long, with:

1.8m German military killed
1.7m Russian military killed
1.4m French military killed
1.3m Austro-Hungarian military killed
740,000 British military killed (and about 220,000 troops from the Commonwealth)
615,000 Italian military killed
US 116,000 military killed

Estimated 10m fatalities and another 22m wounded, many of these to die from their wounds within a few years of the War's ending.

Just as many civilians (10m) were killed during this conflict as were members of the military.

Throughout 1915 the Germans, experiencing a grisly stand-off in the west, attacked the militarily weaker Russians. They initially launched a major offensive in the south (Gorlice), a move that rolled the Russians back 200 miles within the first two weeks; the momentum gained took the Central Power forces north to capture Warsaw in August. In September 1915 the German 12ᵗʰ Army advanced toward

Riga and, as they had in the south, the Russians fell back in disarray. The better led Germans carved their way through Lithuania, Poland, and Galicia, and made further progress in the Balkans.

The Russians, under General Brusilov, at least partially overcame supply line problems to regroup and push back the Austro-Hungarian army. The Germans were prepared to settle for stalemate in the west to enable them to deploy more forces to the east where they had been able to make progress. But what the Russians did have were numbers of men, along with generals that were prepared to see them mown down in droves by German artillery and machine guns. Russian industry made significant improvement in war-materials production, if long lines of supply and the general inefficient deployment of supplies, led to considerable waste. The incompetent Tsarist regime attempted to fund this production by issuing loans and by the reckless printing of paper money, with consequent high rates of inflation and the political instability that usually goes with it; causing mounting unrest across the population.

As news of rising numbers of casualties and evermore loss of territory became known in Russian cities the (urban) population grew dissatisfied with the leadership, and a significant section even rebellious. In Russian forward positions by late 1916 a number of localised mutinies occurred and by March 1917 some units were defiantly ignoring orders. News of these mutinies, usually exaggerated in their extent, was spread by committed groups of, increasingly more organised, communists.

In 1917 the international socialist movement attempted to hold a peace conference in Stockholm but this was stopped by the allies.

A new technological feature of warfare used during this conflict was the use of the airplanes. Pre-Socratic Greeks had imagined flight (the legend of Icarus and Deadelus) - an 11th century monk, Eilmer of Malmesbury, is said to have built the first 'glider' – Leonardo de Vinci designed a man-powered aircraft – in the eighteenth century two Frenchmen pioneered balloon flight – and the science of aerodynamics was in effect initiated by Sir George Cayley as he identified the forces operating to 'lift' a bird into fight – power, uplift, and drag –; from 1803 he built and flew fixed-winged model aircraft. The German Count Ferdinand von Zeppelin had launched a rigid 'airship' in 1900, and by 1914 Germany had eight of these in operation; although they were difficult to control, especially in poor weather conditions.

The first engine-powered flight was reputedly (unconfirmed) undertaken at Connecticut in Aug 1901 by Gustave Whitehead, who was said to have flown his engine-powered aircraft for 800 metres. But the official credit for the first engine-powered flight has been given to the Wright brothers for a flight undertaken by Wilbur Wright in December 1903 at Kitty Hawk in North Carolina. In 1909, Louis Bleriot flew across the Channel to claim a £500 prize offered by the Daily Mail. For most people powered flight seemed in the early days to be more just a novelty form of transport. But during one of its pre-WWI conflicts, the Italian military had dropped grenades from airplanes onto civilians in Libya, indicating who would be the primary targets of future aerial warfare. During the First World War it was the French in 1914 that first used airplanes (and indeed airships) to bomb civilians in German towns. By the end of the war the strategy of targeting civilian populations was being used by both sides, each of which had by then developed large-load carrying airplanes, capable of long-range flights, that were specifically designed as a weapon with which to kill and terrorise civilians.

In the battlefields airplanes were at first used more for reconnaissance missions over enemy lines. Only later becoming machines for direct killing, including the dropping of munitions on trenches and for the aerial 'dog-fights' that created the first dare-devil pilots in the German 'Ace' Manfred Von Richthofan (the 'Red Baron') and the French 'Ace'. Rene Fronk, each being credited with shooting down about 80 enemy airplanes. The Canadian Billy Bishop (the 'Lone Wolf'), and the English Major Edward 'Mick' Mannock, were also credited with a high number of 'kills'. Aerial warfare, an innovation in WW1, was to become a significant element of warfare for the rest of the century as it spread conflagration from the battlefields to the towns and cities – a development seeing its horrific nadir in the bombing of places such as London, Dresden, Hamburg, Hiroshima and Nagasaki, and across Cambodia during the Vietnam, war - by when civilians had become in effect, taken for granted 'legitimate' targets of warfare.

By 1916 it was becoming clear just how costly was the toll of the conflict being accounted in human lives lost. The futility of the task was seeping into the consciousness and conversation of the troops. Many of the individuals who refused to fight on, or were caught attempting to desert, faced a summary tribunal followed for most by the firing squad – even if they were clearly suffering from accumulative 'fear' or 'shell-shock' – they were sacrificed due partly to the instinctive dislike of any challenge to military discipline but also as a warning to their fellows.

The industrial processes applied to the manufacture of weaponry continued, with the invention of the armoured 'tank'. Similar to airplanes, this was another weapon made possible mainly by the previous twenty year development of the internal combustion engine. But, although they made a considerable contribution to the financial cost of the war, they contributed little to deciding the outcome - being unreliable and slow – of battles.

The introduction of 'gases' caused considerable alarm and in some battles thousands of gas shells were used. The use of poison gas was due partly to the frustration of generals at the stalemate of trench warfare.[6] When released, clouds of gas could kill men taking cover from bullets as it drifted over the sandbagged, redoubts and salient's, and seeped along the trenches. Unlike artillery, machine guns, and rifles, it did not have solid metallic velocity that could take it straight to the heart of the enemy – instead its effectiveness as a weapon was dependant on wind direction and on occasion it would be blown back onto the lines of those who released it. One example being the British release of chlorine gas during an engagement at Loos in September. 1915, the wind changed and the returning gas caused 2000 British casualties. In battles such as that of Ypes in April 1915 the Germans released clouds of yellow-greenish chlorine gas towards the opposing force and, such was the fear and confusion created as the gas wafted toward the French lines, that the French and the Algerian troops alongside them fled, allowing the Germans to move easily forward to occupy the vacated positions.

On both sides scientists increasingly played a central role in the war, and most were as nationalistic as the masses – Scientists in each of the leading nations were conducting research into the use of various chemical gases.

For Jon Ager (2012, p116): 'In general, however, the Great War was seen as a catastrophe for Western civilization, and some, citing

---

[6] The French first used 'tear gas' grenades to delay rather than kill the advancing Germans in Aug 1914 and the Germans initially used a similar non-lethal gas. Poisonous chlorine gas was first used by the Germans against Russian troops and then soon used by British and French.

gas and other technologies, blamed science for contributing to the horrific character of modern industrial warfare.'

Scientists operating as the handmaidens of the military-industrial complex is probably a central factor in undermining any claims to both ethical neutrality and scientific objectivity – especially if, that is, we step back from the immediacy of the research situation to encompass the subjectivity of research directed decision-making.

As the war progressed, even more lethal gases such as phosgene and mustard were brought into use.

For Tim Cook; 'Soldiers exposed to lethal doses of lung gasses like chlorine and phosgene died badly on the Western Front. The afflicted flopped and writhed in agony, coughing up green bile from ashen faces as ravaged lungs struggled for breath before suffocation or heart failure ended their misery' (Cook – 'Journal of Military History', vol. 73 nos. 2 April 2009 672-673)

The Germans first used the more lethal mustard gas (Yperite) against the Russians at Riga in September 1917, delivered by means of artillery shells. By the war's end the Germans had used 68,000 tons of gas, the French 36,000 tons, the British 25,000 tons and if the war had continued beyond 1918 then each side had been planning a significant increase in gas usage…of between 30-50% of all artillery shells. About 100,000 soldiers were killed by gas (including 56,000 Russians, 8,000 French, 8,000 British, 9,000 Germans, 4,500 Italians, 3,000 Austro-Hungary, 1,450 US) and over 1,000,000 were injured. Victims of gas attacks who survived the war were usually quite painfully crippled; 'burnt out' lungs leaving an inability to breath properly and for many permanent blindness. To be injured with gas would be to suffer permanent disablement and for many a painful death in the months or years following the war's end.

The two gases, phosgene and chlorine, made up most of the 124,500 tons (190,000 tons were actually produced) of poisonous gas used in roughly equal amounts by each side in the conflict.

Two of the leading researchers developing poisonous gas for warfare were the Frenchman Francois Grignad and the German Fritz Haber, both Nobel prize winning chemists. The industrial production was undertaken, by workers employed by companies such as BASF, Hoechst, Bayer (these combined in 1925 to become IG Farben). The Allies being supplied by companies such as the US Du Pont and the Dow Chemical Company, and the French Hercules Power Company. The US had a specific military unit, the Chemical Warfare Service, to oversee the production of chemical weaponry, much of which was developed by the up to 1,200 chemists working at the American University Experimental Station in Washington D.C. And for Britain, gas production was overseen by the National Research Council.

The shear futility of trench warfare gradually eroded any confidence that soldiers had in their generals, but an attitude of deference instilled into working-class boys growing up in the class-conscious European states, mostly held the line on discipline; by men exhibiting a passive, almost bovine, willingness to advance when ordered. On occasion, some individuals refused to advance (often owing to the terror induced by 'shell-shock') and these young men (some as young as 16) were usually taken out and shot following a cursory 'court-martial' convened at short order. Most foot-soldiers grumbled amongst themselves and endeavoured to 'keep their heads down' and focus on personal survival. But at times such as: April 1917 when, following a disastrous action killing 250,000 French (and Algerians), almost half of the French army (68 divisions) refused to advance. Possibly as many as 100,000 British soldiers rebelled at Staples. In August 1917 a rebellion by German sailors at Wilhelmshaven sparked a series of similar acts. These, and other similar acts of disobedience, were mostly overcome by a mixture of relatively minor concessions and blunt brutality, along with the imprisonment or execution of those identified as leaders. Newspapers conspired to keep their readers ignorant of such outbreaks of the humanitarian expression of man's common sense.

Populations in the conflict nations were by 1917 becoming increasingly disillusioned with the war – the shortages, for many the hunger, and for almost all a growing awareness of the stark reality of war and of the continuous stream of returning coffins containing the curdled human cream of a nation's future.

In France, along with mutinies in the army, there was public unrest including strikes, bread riots, and a series of protests at the many shortages and at the runway inflation that had seen prices rise by 80% in little more than three years. Dissatisfaction with the war had been building throughout 1916 and in Russia it came to a head with a rising in February1917 in the City of Petrograd. Across Russia most cities saw bitter anger expressed at the war, and at the appalling living conditions that many people were experiencing. Nicholas II (Tsar) and his group of mostly arrogant aristocratic advisors were aware that their position was becoming untenable. The Tsar had only ever shown but little concern for the well-being of the overwhelming mass of Russian people and so could expect little sympathy from them; he abdicated in early March.

The provisional government that replaced the Tsarist leadership was led by Alexander Kerensky but his attempt to continue to support the allies came to an end when General Brusilov's offence run out of steam as it attempted to hold a determined German counterattack. Now the Russian army, in retreat and demoralised, was falling apart – only adding to the rebellious conditions that was by now sweeping through villages, towns and cities. By 1917, what had become a political vacuum allowed the well-organised (or rather least disorganised) grouping of the communists to take power, with Lenin as their leader. Lenin's Bolshevik Party was able to establish a level of control within the confusion of what was a popular, if mainly urban-based, revolution.

In conditions of civil war the Germans at first offered military aid to the White Russian forces ranged against the revolution. But pressures on the western front, and the fact that Russia was steadily coming under the control of the Bolsheviks (the White Russians were being pushed back and looked unlikely to succeed), meant that the Germans faced the choice of continuing an obviously un-winnable war on two fronts or of agreeing a peace, under the favourable circumstances of the then military reality on the ground, with a defeated if not entirely cowed Russia. The treaty of Brest-Litovsk was agreed between German and Bolshevik negotiators and signed on 3rd March 1918 allowing the German military to deploy more forces to the west and the new Russian government to turn towards the task of securing the revolution across the vast territory it sought to control.

A build-up of military supplies and the ability to deploy troops from the east convinced the German High Command that it had the means to launch a last-ditch offensive in the spring of 1918, before the arrival of US forces would inevitably tip the military balance decisively in the Allies favour. The advance initially carried the Germans quite far into France, but the casualties of the initial push and a second attempt in late summer left the German army short of both supplies and reinforcements. It was literally running out of young men to put before the Allied machine guns and artillery! And even given the tactical military skills that allowed the Germans to make some progress they were unable to make the decisive breakthrough required, and the allied counterattacks gradually began to tell. With a disillusioned and angry population at home, mutinies[7] and general ill-discipline in the military, and a political leadership in disarray, Germany was facing defeat. Large anti-war, anti-government, demonstrations took place in Hamburg, Bremen, Cologne, Leipzig, and Dresden, and in Munich socialists led an attempt to set up a Bavarian Free State. In Berlin in early November the City was in turmoil and Karl Liebnecht announced a 'socialist revolution' from the Imperial Palace itself. But elements of the old regime countered, with the pro-war Scheidemann later announcing a republic from the same location. The Kaiser fled the country which was by mid November, at least in appearance, in the hands of workers and soldiers and the opportunity for revolutionary change seemed to be on offer. But it would be an opportunity which slowly dissipated, mainly due to the survival of pre-war conservative institutions and a new leadership intent on reform rather than revolution.

The US had been supporting the Allies for some time (its industry had been boosted by Allied orders for military materials) prior to its direct entry into the war but it is considered that the revelations such as the 'Zimmerman telegraph' indicating Germany's offer of an Alliance with Mexico and Germany's plan for unrestricted attacks on Atlantic shipping that finally convinced the President, supported by Congress, to join the war on the Allied side from April 1917. Best et al 2004, does suggests that the German deployment of U-Boats to disrupt Atlantic shipping was in response to the British\French blockade of the Central Powers; it was in effect a counter blockade.

Now the industrial strength of the US (approx. 2½ times that of Germany) could be mobilised in the war effort and shiploads more food, along with enormous amount of military hardware and thousands of troops, began to cross the Atlantic to replenish, and then increase, the strength of the forces facing the Germans; 800,000 men by October 1917 and about 2,000,000 by the war's end. Actual military defeat happened swiftly as the Central Powers in effect collapsed in the Balkans, Palestine, Syria, and were in retreat along the Western Front.

This war was not some international conflict that had an inevitability due to 'human nature', nor was it the outcome of one side's wish to dominate the other; clearly inappropriate are the

---

[7] Sailors in Kiel, refused to set sail to face near-certain defeat at the hands of the British navy.

simplistic narratives of heroes and villains, good and evil. This war was more the outcome of: the fatal expression of a burgeoning military machine, the draw that battle has for many young men, a series of diplomatic miscalculations and indeed some crude mistakes, along with the tacit encouragement of financiers with fortunes to make. Prominent agents being politicians with their level of consciousness firmly fixed in the self-conscious mode; attempting to assess national interests in terms of short-term economic prospects and territorial control (determined mainly by elite group interests), and the dumb sensitivities of national egoism. And these set in a wider chronological context of the global ambitions of Germany, France, and Britain. All elements of the perverse logic of war, whose operation relies on the thought patterns identified with the hegemonic utilisation of military threat, economic inducements, and political posturing.

What took these nations to war were the relatively small number of elite groups whose members occupied a range of key decision-making positions in each nation – although significant proportions of the masses of each county should bear some greater or lesser degree of responsibility, even accepting that their understanding of issues had been shaped by carefully deployed propaganda.

The war came to an end in November 1918 – as the Germans succumbed to a crumbling political situation in Berlin and Vienna, and the High Command's final acceptance of the inevitability of defeat due to the overwhelming military odds that US intervention had realised. In October 1918 the military government resigned and by early November a Social Democratic government came to power. But it was a power that extended little further than Berlin as beyond the capital workers were organising and military units mutinying – revolution seemed to be a real possibility. But most of the leaders of the many workers and soldiers' councils, formed with a spontaneous enthusiasm for revolution, were moderate SPD men. They had a tradition rooted in the organised working class and could bring collective strength for a shared ideology based on social democracy rather than having the critical weaknesses of the determinedly revolutionary but split-prone communists, anarchists, and other left-wing groupings. Revolutionary zeal was gradually eroded - due in part to much of the population being exhausted and lacking enthusiasm for the politically unknown – giving way to resigned acceptance as the socially and economically structured society of pre-war Germany was incrementally re-established. With similar political and social institutions (political, legal, civil service, landownership, etc) providing the framework of governance for a return to leadership by elite groupings.

The Paris Peace Conference began in January 1919 with a formal peace treaty being signed by the allies and Germany in June 1919 (the 'Treaty of Versailles'). Then, between 1919-23, additional treaties were signed by the Allies and Austria, Hungary, Bulgaria and Turkey. The Treaty of Versailles could have been designed with the foresight to offer a peace with at least some honour for the defeated but instead it imposed conditions intended to humiliate Germany and her allies – a Germany that had not in fact surrendered but had 'concluded an armistice' (a distinction that Adolf Hitler would later take advantage of).

Included in the main treaty were provisions for crippling financial reparations to France and, when disputes over payments came to a head in 1923, French troops occupied the industrial heartland of the Ruhr and, in lieu of missed reparation payments, removed most of the modern machinery and equipment. A measure – indeed a 'looting' - that had a significant impact on Germany's economic well-being, making a contribution to the decision by a government having lost a significant amount of its productive capacity to print money (in order to maintain demand) which in turn was to add to the pressure towards runaway inflation and a period of political instability that offered an opportunity for the rise of National Socialism and Adolf Hitler. The post war negotiations also brought modern Poland, Czechoslovakia, and the pre-Yugoslavian 'Kingdom of Serbs, Croats, and Slovenes' into existence. In addition, by including territories that were formally part of Germany in the settlement, the Allies made another contribution to its sense of injustice and its motivation for the invasion of Poland in 1939 that would trigger British entry into WWII.

In January 1918 US President Woodrow Wilson had suggested a list of 14 points that were intended to offer a more balanced post-war settlement, one based upon collective security and the right to national self-determination, the points included: freedom of the high-sea – more realistic reparations repayments related to actual damage and destruction caused rather than to Germany paying the full cost to the Allies of the war - arms reduction and the setting up of a League of Nations (LoN) and also some more reasonable re-drawing of the more contentious European national borders than favoured by the other

Allied Powers.

Wilson sought a peace that allowed the Germans some sense of being involved in a 'settlement' rather than their being subjected to a totally humiliating defeat. Wilson's points were effectively ignored and the US Senate rejected the Treaty of Versailles in Nov, 1919 then again in 1921 – exacerbating a rift between the US and its European Allies – in effect also rejecting the Wilson inspired idea of a League of Nations. The outcomes being that the US would remain outside of the LoN when one was eventually set up and would also agree a separate peace with Germany. To some extent withdrawing into an isolationist policy, even accepting that its power within the international financial system and its trade interests kept it engaged.

The war has cost the Allies 57 billion dollars (at 1913 prices) and the Central Powers 24.7 billion dollars, and it is in this difference that victories are almost always decided in industrialised warfare – it is economic advantage (which in turn relates directly to the industrial capacity of any nation), not any measure of the relative bravery of each nation's soldiers that decided the outcome of the first (and indeed the second) twentieth-century world war. Military deeds only provided the narratives of self-sacrifice, heroism and national pride that allowed an illusionary gloss (of assumed military skills) to be attached to such grisly enterprises – perhaps a type of defence mechanism of a national consciousness realised to manage the ultimate human stupidity that is warfare.

The distraction of the First World War had been taken as an opportunity by the Turks to progress their ambitions for direct control of the fertile highlands of central and eastern Anatolia; the traditional homeland of the Armenians. This action was a specific policy decided on to cleanse the Ottoman Empire of Armenians in a process known as Turkification. It is important to note that this action – what became a genocide killing over 1.5m men, women, and children – was official Ottoman 'Young Turk' Government policy. In the period leading up to WW1 the Armenians had been very much second-class citizens, with a range of legal restrictions and special taxes being imposed specifically on them. In 1915 the Turkish government, in effect, declared war on the Armenians – the first twentieth century government attempt at 'genocide', an action that would be replicated as official government policy in other countries (Stalinist Russia, Nazi Germany, Maoist China, Pol Pot's Cambodia, and General

Suharto in Indonesia)

This set in train a period of the relentless persecution of Armenians, that would only come to an end when, in 1923, the Ottoman Empire ceased to exist and the Republic of Turkey was established. The Turkish government then instigated the demobilization of Armenian units that had been part of the Ottoman army; they were then reformed as unarmed 'labour battalions' as a prelude to these 4,000 men then being murdered.

It is important to highlight that this period of genocide was a premeditated strategy adopted by a government that was endeavouring to modernise - to become more 'civil' in a western European sense. During the course of the war the thundering throb emanating from the smoke-swept battlefields of Europe were used to cover the cries of a number of Balkan minority groups being subjected to killing or being displaced by their neighbours while most of civil humanity was looking elsewhere.

I have touched on just some examples of inter-ethnic conflict in the Balkan region during the first half of the twentieth century; I would note that every massacre-rape-displacement attributed by one side or the other is either vociferously denied or just as vociferously defended on the grounds of justifiable revenge for outrages against them (or mostly their long dead ancestors). But three things are clear: a) The inter-ethnic violence has been going on at least throughout the 19th and 20th centuries - b) That atrocities (crimes against humanity) were committed by individuals from all of the predominate ethnic groups; but importantly, not by all members of each group - c) That no amount of violence had resolved the underlying issues for the longer-term. The collective memories of each group is only of the injustices and atrocities that they have suffered in the land they shared - I might have added a forth point to the more local ones already noted - d) That prominent European powers, and the US from 1945, have played a disgraceful part in supporting groups who were clearly engaging in the murder and displacement of men, women, and children, and in a 'political policy' of the rape of women. As recently as the 1990s most of the mainstream media were complicit in ignoring evidence, or promoting evidence that was obviously fabricated, in justifying military action to encourage the groups favoured by NATO – the most notorious being the excuse found for the bombing of the Serbs in 1999, killing over 500 civilians in an action that had not been approved by the UN Security Council; the first such non-approved

NATO military action.

Paddy Ashdown – (a UN representative to the Balkans in the 1990s) ex-SBS officer and then ex-leader of the UK's Liberal-Democratic political party, said on a BBC Radio 4 programme (2/4/2010) "I saw Bosniacs drive out Croats, Croats drive out Serbs, and Serbs drive out Bosniacs – and what I saw brought tears to my eyes"

During this period of conflict an elderly Serbian peasant is credited with having pithily observed that these warring groups were: "The same piece of shit divided by the cartwheel of history."

In the history of the Balkans we can see a number of factors contributing to suspicion and fear of neighbours – historical separation mainly due to differences in: religion, culture, mating arrangements, as well as in places separation by difficult to negotiate local terrain, all reinforced throughout the years as grounds for inter-group suspicion and fear become ever more polarized and group identity became evermore entrenched. Difference is reinforced when historically rooted animosities seep into each new generation, with children being socialized into the powerful narratives of past injustices (along with a collusive collective amnesia of the murderous acts of its own people); with leaders mulling over possible opportunities for future retribution. But the basis of these differences are socially constructed, they are but relational differences which overlie the underlying commonality of being human. If taken together they have led to the coalescence into the most powerful basis for inter human conflict. Social psychologists such as Henri Tajfel and John Turner (1979 – Social Identity Theory) have offered theoretical frameworks within which to understand the power of group membership and others such as Muzafer Sherif (1950s and 60s) have offered experimental evidence – which suggests just how powerful simply being in one group rather than another can have in how any individual sees his own group (emphasising the positives and minimising the negatives characteristics), and how he perceives another group, (minimising the positives and maximising the negatives, stereotyping….. to prejudice). If Tajfal and Turner were pioneers on group-related identity and solidarity their findings have been supported by a range of subsequent studies. It is this 'instinctive' solidarity in mere group difference that is grossly exacerbated by the interweaving of the differential embroidery of religion, ethnicity, and nationality. If we can also add the individual motivation of the covetousness of a neighbour's material goods (historically primarily land) and the political ambitions of leadership, then out of this toxic mix - of difference, material greed, and ambition - invariable comes fractured communities and inter-group conflict.

Nationalism (and in the Balkans religion) shows itself as a projection of the in-group/out-group dichotomy writ large. With a complex framework of structural factors formed from, history and culture, to which clings accretions of narratives fostering national self-esteem, collectively acknowledged grandiose images, and the various means that an organised society can deploy to promote elite-group self-interests and to make these appear to be the self-interests of all citizens.

The 'civil' world that emerged from the First World War had seen the demise of dictatorial European monarchies and, while constitutional monarchies were retained in some countries (including Britain, Greece, Holland, Sweden, and also in China, Japan's emperors) and more dictatorial monarchs in some others (mainly central and south-eastern Europe) the mythical idea of some supreme being entitled to rule due to some special state passed into history – and so a 5,000 year long feature of civil life had undergone significant change. Although the need for populations to want to believe that some humans, by right of birth, had a set of 'special qualities' and the willingness of some individuals themselves to collude in this pretence, and so to accept the financial and social privileges and nationalistic 'civil worship' that was offered, were to continue to show some support for supreme unelected (and even elected) leadership during the rest of the twentieth century and beyond.

One country did see the violent disposal of its monarchy - The Russian revolution introduced, on a large scale, an alternative form of civil government and an economic system (seemingly) different to any seen up to that point in human history.

There was an underlying ideology of, at its simplest, communism in its loosely Marxist historical determinist framework which provided an historical rationale for change. With Vladimir Ilyich Ulyanov (Lenin) taking the lead in offering an adaptation of Marxism to Russia tailored to its historical circumstances and to explain the then current crisis situation in the country. But a political ideology only really offers a theoretical framework to locate and interpret circumstances and events, the actual causes of change are the power relations that pertain between completing groups in any society such as: the power of finance, accepted tradition, military strength, the organizational ability of competing groups, media power, and the force of civil will. This latter is, I suggest, usually the most significant single factor in determining outcomes. The 'civil will' of any population experiencing crisis is usually fairly diffuse in the early stages of change. Characterised by an apprehensive apathy of the majority – or at least the majority that have some level of engagement or at least awareness of any crisis. The Russian revolution in its making between 1917 and 1920 probably had little impact on the vast majority of peasants in central, southern, and eastern Russia. Even during the time of Lenin's 'New Economic Plan' from 1921 82% of the population were still employed in agriculture and were mostly warily obedient, rather than enthusiastic, about the revolution.

The element of civil will that was the primary factor in the revolution was mainly expressed in the cities and larger towns, being focused on dissatisfaction with the autocratic government's (Tsars) conduct of WWI. It was the leaders of the Bolsheviks who were able to garner this dissent and lead it towards a statist form of communism. The Bolsheviks also benefitted from the presence of organised groups (cadres) composed of almost fanatically dedicated men and women; activists 'armed' with an ideology that purported to explain the causes of the plight of working people. One that also offered an idealised view of an attractive possible future. An ideology with a set of basic messages that could quite easily be translated into resonant slogans and inspiring graphic images. In theory it would be a revolution by 'workers' in order that their interests, rather than those of an aristocratic elite along with the businessmen and bankers that supported them, that would determine post revolutionary outcomes.

In terms of human history and of lessons to be learned, the Russian revolution was a reaction to social and economic oppression and an obdurate elitist leadership. Compared to Germany, where the mismanagement (loss) of the war had an even more significant effect on the country, but with revolution being averted due mainly to it having institutions that allowed it at least some recognised legitimacy based upon tradition and perceived continuing value. Germany also had the constitutional means to change governments – the Kaiser fled, the military leadership slunk away, most business people and leading civil servants (including those in the legal system) were keeping a low profile. The SDP (led by Friedrich Ebert – became Chancellor of the new Weimar Republic - as well as Karl Kautsky, Eduard Bernstein, and August Babel) was sufficiently organized and ready to fill the power-vacuum.

The Tsarist government of Russia collapsed as in the major cities workers protested about the progress of the war and the lack of basic foodstuffs – in Petrograd 400,000 people (almost half of the City's population) marched through the main streets calling for bread and an end to the war. They were attacked by armed police but as the days of protest continued large sections of the soldiers deployed to break up the demonstrations mutinied and joined the workers, it was then that the police and officials that remained loyal to the government were 'arrested'. Similar insurrectionary activities took place in Moscow and other Russian cities, and it was clear even to obdurate generals and the Tsar that his abdication was a last chance possibility to appease the 'civil will' and to at least to avoid outright revolution.

With the Tsar gone the Duma (parliament) was the constitutionally legitimate body able to take control, a body that had been pretty much treated with distain by the Tsar and his aristocratic coterie. Due to a class-based electoral system this body was overwhelmingly representative of the propertied and the owners of industry, and so lacked a wider legitimacy; even numerically its support was relatively small. Opposed to any political remnants of the old regime were the groups of organised workers, taking the form of representative workers councils. In Feb 1917 a reformist provisional government was established by the Duma, led by Prince L'vov, initially with the tacit acceptance of the workers. It continued to be dominated by landowners and industrialists if with a small element of moderate socialist parties led by Alexander Kerensky.

More time and a willingness on the part of the Duma to make concessions might have saved the government. There was considerable scope for agrarian reform with half of all the land – and this mostly the best farmland – being owned by a small propertied elite, owning vast estates from which they rung as much profit as possible by the sweat of the labour of millions of badly treated peasants. In a country with more efficient civic institutions order might slowly have been restored and perhaps some form of multi-party democracy could have emerged; as in Germany where it did slowly emerge in a country, broken, battered, and itself facing possible revolution, from the war. But bitterness with the war, the rise of regional independence movements (the Fins, Ukrainians, and in the

Baltic states), and deep resentment at the layers of injustice characteristic of Tsarist rule, provided an internal momentum that created a level of disorganisation and dissolution favourable to revolutionary opportunity. It was the Bolsheviks who had the basic organizational structure and the determination to seize the moment. When it was clear that large sections of the military would support them, they also had the means of taking power.

Rumbling discontent with the provisional government increased during the late summer as costs of actively progressing the war led to higher prices for basics foodstuffs and increased hunger for the mass of the populations in the cities. A failed attempt in August 1917 by General Kornilov to march on Petrograd and impose military control contributed to fear, anger, and uncertainty, amongst the workers.

The Bolsheviks had over the preceding years built a workers-based organization that was numerically small but was especially strong in the industrial cities – and in their original and continuing opposition to the war they also had credibility with significant numbers of the population; in particular, with the conscripted, mainly peasant, army and navy. Throughout the summer of 1917, led by the bold Lenin and Leon Trotsky, along with the more cautious Zinoviev and Kamenev, and fuelled by their own self-belief, the core membership of the Bolshevik party dedicated themselves to the overthrow of the provisional government. They took advantage of every opportunity presented to support workers strikes and protests, encouraged soldiers and sailors to challenge orders and called on peasants to demand land reform.

When, on 25th of October, the revolution actually came to fruition the transition of power was relatively low-key. The Bolshevik-led 'Military Revolutionary Committee' in Petrograd had access to an organisational structure of workers that could implement their orders and so impose control and some level of efficiency in the distribution of food and in the selective presentation of the news. The provisional government's own total ineffectiveness was the primary cause of its collapse, with ministers fleeing from the City. Bolshevik control spread from Petrograd to other major cities and more of the countryside seemed prepared to accept, if not socialist revolution, at least the ending of Tsarism and the possibility of significant reform of land ownership; hoping for at least some alleviation of their desperately poor living conditions. After ending its part in the war (Brest-Litovsk Treaty) the two most pressing challenges for the new, 'communist', government was how to motivate peasants and small farmers to provide food for the cities and their having to confront the counter-revolutionary forces of 'The White Russian Army'. This last being a vicious counter-revolutionary force supported by some western European powers.

In Russia a civil war raged across swaths of the county between 1917-22 as the western-backed 'White' army – led by reactionary military men such as Admiral Kolchak and General Denikin along with some others dedicated to the restoration of Tsarism - fought the Bolshevik-led Red Army headed by the brilliant organiser Leon Trotsky (an army 4 million strong by the time it won victory). It was, claimed Lenin, in reaction to the need for the young revolution's survival that an iron fist should brought to bear. To impose a revolutionary terror, with the ruthless suppression of dissent similar to the approach of the previous Tsarist regime. To what extent the need for survival against hostile foreign governments funding a reactionary, counter-revolutionary force, can be accepted as some justification for the ruthless application of terror during the revolution's early years – in the form of: secret police (an institution inherited from Tsarism), sham courts and, at times, politically authorised brutality and murder and, later on the gulags - can be best left to more even-handed historians to assess. To some extent the revolution gave itself a breathing space from one source of potential opposition (and a degree of co-operation) by giving a vast number of peasant's peace, land, and the hope for a better future. By 1923 over 500 million acres of land had been transferred to peasants, thereby allowing millions of citizens to at least consider that they had a stake in the future of the revolution.

The Russian revolution occurred in historical and material conditions somewhat at odds with the predictions of Marx, who had suggested that the internal contradictions inherent in advancing capitalism (and the associated industrialisation), would provide the economic conditions for communist revolution. So Germany and Britain were seen by Marx as the countries that were leading the way toward the communist millennium. But it was to be the mainly agricultural (80% of the pop. still employed in agriculture -1920), industrially backward, Russia that the first glimpse of Marx's historically inevitable communist era first showed itself.

In the early years of the revolutionary government, Lenin and many in Russia and elsewhere, did feel to some extent in the advance guard of the spread of communism throughout the world – at the Third Socialist International in 1919, the 'Comintern', called on representatives of other countries to spread the revolution – and Lenin demanded allegiance to the Comintern[8] as a requirement for 'true socialists'. But internal problems, external hostility, and the seeming lack of any productive revolutionary activity abroad, led Russia during the interwar years to become a necessarily inward looking country. It was however, to serve as an example of what determined revolutionaries could achieve, to many non-industrialised countries – including China, Vietnam, some countries of central Europe, as well as parts of Latin America, and Africa – inspiring a number of the 'freedom fighters' to throw off their colonial masters and gain independence.

Less contentiously, we can see that once the authority of the Soviet Government relied on systems constructed to suppress dissent and to terrorise possible as well as any actual opposition, and once the Government claimed an inextricable link to embodying the expression of the 'will of the people' then any dissent, however modest, could be liable to interpreted as opposition to the people's government.... to the workers of Russia. This enabled the continuation of government by a system of control based on coercion and if necessary domination (as a bureaucratic system of ordering spread across the country) that would continue during the drive for industrialization and agricultural reform.

Between the two World Wars Russia became an insular society as the originally felt commitment to world revolution – 'workers of the world uniting' - became subsumed within the nation's attempt to consolidate its economic and military power in the content of running an industrially backward country that had suffered heavily in the war. Having to make progress in a world where it faced extensive trade boycotts and open hostility from abroad – countries such as Germany, England, France, US, and Japan etc. Britain, France and the US sent troops to attack Russia even after the League of Nations had been established. According to Winston Churchill (then British Minister of War) the intention was to strangle a communist Russia at its birth. A great deal was made in the western mass media of the murder of the Romanov Royal family by the Bolsheviks but very little was made

---

[8] Set up by Lenin, this was a series of congresses, with seven of these being held in Moscow between 1919-1935.

about this privileged family's taken for granted self-indulgence and indifference to the suffering of countless numbers of Russian peasants and indeed the slaughter on the 'Bloody Sunday' of 22nd January 1905 when over 150,000 peaceful, unarmed workers marched to the Winter Place to petition their beloved Tzar; some carried religious icons and most sang hymns and patriotic songs as they marched along. One of the main organisers of this demonstration was Father Gapon, a priest in the Russian Orthodox Church. He had previously assisted the workers in drawing up a petition which called for the ending of the Russo-Japanese War, for universal suffrage, fair wages, and for some improvement in what were generally appalling living and working conditions of the masses.

The Tsar's (who had himself fled the City) Imperial Guard were strategically placed towards the end of the route and they opened fire, killing or seriously wounding possibly as many as 1,000 of the demonstrators. It has been fairly suggested that Father Gapon's seeming support for the workers and his encouragement to demonstrate was an aspect of his work as an agent provocateur employed by the Okhrana, the Tsarist secret police. He was later killed by his socialist friend Pinhas Rutenberg when the priest endeavoured to recruit him to the Tsarist side. For the Tsar the massacre was 'painful and sad' but no concessions were made to workers, and the event had a political impact that contributed to the 1905 and 1917 revolutions.

Governments in most other industrialized countries feared that the Russian revolution, if successful, could serve as a model to be aspired too by large sections of their own working classes: and even perhaps some members of the more idealistically minded middle classes. First World War national economies saw the state taking more control of industrial, and agriculture production, and the Russian Soviet government extended this war-time control as it pursued modernization with a resolutely pragmatic determination. Lenin's attempt in 1921 (the 'New Economic Policy') tried to re-introduce some characteristics of a market economy, a form of state controlled capitalism.[9] State planning took a further step in 1921 with the

---

[9] It's perhaps of interest that as a young left-winger in 1970s Britain I, and my contemporaries, even then spoke of Russia as a state-capitalist country, this due mainly to it being controlled by privileged elites, characterised by nepotism, and with close control over the information being made available to its people – a situation finding dramatic if simplistic expression in George Orwell's 'Animal

introduction of 'Gosplan', the state's determined attempt to drive forward the modernization of Russian industry. On Lenin's death in 1922 five men were ready to lead Russia: Lev Borisovich Kamerew, Joseph Stalin, Grigory Zinaviev and the more intellectual Nikolai Bukharin and Leon Trosky.

The global economy had emerged from the First World War in quite a fragile condition, made brittle due to lack of any real determination of national governments to create a financial system that would transcend limited, short-term, nation-state interests.

The negotiations at Versailles, clearly illustrate the operation, and so the inherent tendency of claimed outcomes to fail, of the promotion of the national self-interest approach noted above. The material costs of the war added significantly to government debt. In Britain, a national debt of £700 million in 1913 rose to £7,100 million by 1919, and the US government used bonds to raise about 65% of its $33 billion war expenses; what were then vast amounts of money provided a massive boon to the shareholders of industries necessary for the prosecution of conflict and to a level of government debt which would be an underlying factor eroding resilience to economic fluctuations, so contributing to the impact of economic depression during the early/mid 1920s. Although Britain retained substantial investments overseas, its level of international debt had changed dramatically in relation to the US., as had that of Europe.[10] In 1914 Europe had been owed $6,000m by the US but in 1918 the US was owed $16,000m by Europe..... a $22,000m change!

The factors that make war extremely profitable for some also make it extremely costly for governments having to raise large amounts of financial (as well as human) capital to sustain conflict. In addition to taxation, another primary source of funding was generated by the sale of government-issued bonds. In issuing countries, especially Britain

---

farm' – and of more historical interest, Lenin himself in the pamphlet 'On left-infantilism and the Petty-Bourgeois Spirit' vociferously addressed critics amongst fellow communists led by Bukharin, and suggested that state capitalism was a necessary stage on the road to socialism - he accused individuals such as Bukharin as being guilty of petty-bourgeois utopianism.

[10] In effect, most of the crippling burden of war debt – reparation – forced upon Germany was money paid to Britain and France who then transferred this to the United States.

and the US, these war bonds ('Liberty Loans' in the US) drew in millions of new, mainly middle-class investors – it has been estimated that the number of individual investors in Britain numbered 1 million in 1914 had become 13 million by 1918. There were possibly as many as 200,000 first time equity investors in the US. By 1929 this would reach 1 million, many of whom had responded to the encouragement of the salesmanship of representatives of the banks.

As they diversified their investments into a range of non-government equities American middle-class small investors also used a mechanism termed American Depository Receipts (ADR) to buy shares in British companies. Britain's rejoining the gold standard in 1926 provided the more stable equity markets that many US investors sought. The growth of these, and other markets, being another sign of main-street Americans being attracted to shares in the second half of the 1920s as but part of an risk-determined investment perspective that became a key aspect of American civil life. An aspect of a gradual change to portfolio investment in shares, rather than only holding bonds. In his influential book 'Common Stocks as Long Term Investments' Edgar Lawrence Smith (1924) focused on viewing the longer-term increasing value of stocks rather than just the dividend income, so a subtle shift towards viewing equities from a more speculative perspective.

At this time there was a general sense of the United States as progressive, entrepreneurial, and of providing economic and social conditions conducive for business development. The portfolio approach to investing in equities (with its potentially more manageable level of overall risk) was to be the financial mechanism that would begin to draw in more insurance companies and pension funds. The increasing involvement of both types of institution being a significant step towards a popular acceptability for equity markets. Up until about the 1880s, stock markets had been considered too risky for pension funds and insurance companies, but these would progressively come to play an important role in markets. The proportion of insurance company assets invested via the London Stock Market increased from 24% in 1870 to 50% and rising in 1930. What had been seen by most as a personal finance activity for the rich had become the experience of many more; the idea of investing in equity markets was becoming normalised behaviour for many of the middle-classes.

Stock markets (by now 90 of these across the world) had ended the war generally depressed and being quite closely monitored by governments. In Britain most private investors had historically held only a few shares, and even by 1914 only 3.2% of the population had significant wealth in shares or other forms of equity. During the war more middle-class people in Britain and the US considered that it was patriotic to buy government bonds as support for the war effort. This experience legitimised involvement in equity investment for many who in the past had tended to be wary of these - people who had previously considered excess income as potential 'savings' rather than as a means of 'investment'. What was a socially significant development in Britain and the US was not seen, to anything like the same extent in most mainland Europeans countries. Most, especially in France and Italy, tended to avoid stocks and shares partly due to their having what were still very much 'cash economies'. In Russia the Bolsheviks had closed down its stock markets in 1917, and those that had operated within the defunct Austro-Hungarian Empire were now moribund. The chaos in the German economy mean that most people were endeavouring to get by on a day to day basis. Whilst the very type of middle class individuals that were being attracted to equity markets in Britain and the US were in Germany (and other central European countries) watching their savings being swallowed up in the hyperinflation of the currency (Deutschmark).

The productive capacity built during the war became overcapacity in the post-war world. With mostly low growth rates and rising unemployment across the industrialized world. Commodity prices were experiencing unsettling levels of fluctuations - impacting on those economically more developed countries (Canada, Australia, Argentina) significantly reliant on export income, as well as the many more less developed countries with an even greater dependence on exports. The 20s and 30s were overall a period of countries endeavouring to promote trade but in a global situation of trade-inhibiting protectionism.

The situation for the US was mixed; emerging from the war as the strongest national economy, with the dollar replacing sterling as the de-facto reserve global currency. But due to it also experiencing the same post-war industrial over-capacity as European countries unemployment was quite high there too. Southern, and some mid-western, states were also affected by low world commodity prices - with the poorest unskilled (disproportionately blacks) being amongst the hardest hit.

For most of the 1920s, parts of the world experienced some if modest economic growth, with manufacturing returning to about pre-war levels. Most countries had returned to gold convertibility, providing a further stabilizing factor for international trade. The US had displaced Britain as the predominant trading and financial nation. With American foreign direct investments and lending rising to over one billion dollars per year. This was the time when the bigger American companies (including many banks – and oil companies such as Texaco, Standard Oil, and Gulf Oil, and automobile companies such as Ford and General Motors, became Trans National Corporations - TNCs) were expanding across much of the world as they opened overseas branches and sought to establish partnerships with foreign companies. The foundations for the insidious 'Coca Cola culture', more usually associated with the 1950s, were being established.

But this was a US still moulded by a generally isolationist past. An isolationism reflected in Congress's refusals to allow President Woodrow Wilson his wish for the US to, in 1920, join the newly established League of Nations. The government was prevented by Congress from becoming directly involved in most international economic discussions, a role unofficially undertaken by leading US bankers such as J.P.Morgan; men who had a determinedly capitalist (rentier) view of economics and a similar limited view of the role of government in economic affairs.

In Britain, unemployment continued as a contentious social and so political issue. The prime minister, Lloyd George, had spoken of post-war Britain as being '…a land fit for heroes'. But the reality for many of the demobilized troops was low paid work or unemployment and either way poverty. This group constituted a body of men and their families less prepared to respect authority than the pre-war generation. This, and the spectre of 'communist revolution', invoked a tangible fear for those in government. Interestingly, most of the right-wing press, conservative political leaders, and aristocracy, were less concerned about the rise of Fascism in the 1920s/30s than the possibility of socialist change. Across Europe, the unemployed and other victims of poverty engaged in numerous ('hunger') marches, petitioning of governments, and mass demonstrations. In Britain many of the returning 'heroes' joined the National Unemployed Workers Movement led by determined trades unionists such as Wal Hannington. One poignant and rather imaginative demonstration of how ex-servicemen were treated took place on November 11th 1922 – Armistice Day.... When a state ceremony involving the 'great and the good' of the British state engaged in the annual 'Remembrance' ceremony at the Cenotaph in Whitehall; then the primary UK memorial for those who gave their lives in WW1. Twenty five thousand members of the London unemployed movement, mostly ex-servicemen, gathered on the day to march past and lay a memorial wreath at the Cenotaph. The police (no doubt following ministerial instructions) had refused a request from the leaders of the marchers to be allowed to march as part of the official ceremony and instead they had to wait, exposed to a bitterly cold wind, in Northumberland Avenue (a wide road adjacent to Whitehall) – the unemployed ex-servicemen had pinned their war medals onto their banners and on the lapels of their mostly threadbare coats and jackets. But on their chests, where their medals would normally be worn, they had pinned pawn tickets – a potent and demeaning symbol of the extent of their poverty. Once the 'official party' (including leading politicians, various royals, and the heads of the armed forces) had completed their ceremony and moved on, in the words of Hannington: 'Then out of the grey mist came the wail of fifes from the unemployed bands and the measured tread of tramping men. Into Whitehall came the long trail of drab humanity, with their medals hanging from the red banners and the pawn-tickets pinned to their coats, as an indictment of the system which praises the dead and condemns the living to starvation' (Hannington, 1936, p78).

The words on the wreath laid on behalf of the marchers read 'From the living victims – the unemployed – to their dead comrades, those who died in vain'.

The decades just prior to 1914 had seen most European governments taking some responsibility for public health, education, and latterly welfare, but in terms of international finance the approach of governments had been more hands-off. Even what attempts had been made to regulate international markets and the banks had mostly proved to be ineffective. During WWI this changed significantly, if not in terms of effective regulation, as the central banks accepted more responsibility for maintaining the stability of the financial system, and this would continue after the war.

The extension of suffrage, expansion of the popular press and increasingly more politically organised working classes, meant that governments were under pressure to respond to social issues such as unemployment and to some extent the general alleviation of poverty. But in actual effect the response was little more than political hand-wringing and yet more promises being made.

Whilst the working classes in the economically developed countries were, as a whole, prepared to accept significant inequalities in both economic rewards as well as educational and employment opportunities, they were becoming more organised. The threat of a revolutionary minority rarely seemed to be offering a viable alternative, expect perhaps in post-war Germany and Italy. The working classes that emerged from the war had valued political stability over more muscular action for significant social and economic changes. On the whole they were prepared to believe the bland promises made by government ministers. Revolution was 'in the air' of most western democratic countries but on the firmer ground of actual national politics the reality was working class support for conservative and nationalistic forms of social democratic, rather than of democratic socialist, political parties. In Britain, the leadership of the Labour Party, and most trade union leaders, were prepared to separate industrial disputes from political ambitions; for the latter this working class leadership was moderately reformist rather than radically revolutionary. A leadership prepared to accept a variety of capitalism that, if reluctantly, enabled gains in productivity to be shared just a little more bit more. Satisfied with some incremental improvement in working conditions, along with a progressive system of taxation and a national insurance system used to fund some, at least basic, forms of welfare.

The British state was embodied in a reactionary House of Lords, a still Conservative/Liberal dominated House of Commons, a self-preserving, if always cleverly cautious, monarchy, an authoritarian legal system narrowly interpreting laws in the interest of the 'state', and a determinedly right-wing national press. With all of these being dominated by middle and upper-class men.

Across Western Europe, working class pressure for change was channelled into 'left' and 'centre-left' political parties. In post-war Germany the short-lived Independent Social Democratic Party (USPD) (formed following a split from the centre-left SDP led by Kurt Eisner) gained more support from workers than the more radical left-wing breakaway movement led by Rosa Luxemburg, Hugo Haase, and Karl Liebknecht, in their Spartacus League; which would become the Communist Party of Germany (KPD). In Italy the Italian

Socialist Party, in Britain the Parliamentary Labour Party, in France the Radical Socialists were ostensibly the primary 'workers' political parties. Progressively, the uncertainty (caused by) of hyperinflation in countries across central and southern Europe polarized politics between communists and fascists each bitterly, sometimes violently, opposed to each other. The constitutional liberal governments of 17 of 27 Europe countries, and also Japan and Turkey, would soon be neutralised or swept aside by more dictatorial or military elements.

In the major European countries the political turmoil experienced during WWI settled during the 1920s into a pattern of fairly moderate conservative-type of mainstream politics with some working class reformist aspirations (focused on working conditions and welfare) but generally accepting a continuation of substantially unreformed state-subsidised forms of capitalism.

Governments, political ideologies and indeed nations, come and go but one enduring idea given substance as an outcome of the war was the recognition of universal interests (shared interests) of all humankind, the most obvious common interest being the maintenance of peace between nation-states. An aspiration that would founder on a lack of international agreement on the type of effective arrangements that might achieve such an outcome.

Leading politicians such as Woodrow Wilson, Jan Smuts, and Roger Cecil, did come to advocate the setting up of some sort of international body to facilitate negotiations between nations in dispute. One of Wilson's 14 points that had been offered to the 1918 peace negotiations was the setting up of a 'League of Nations'. An organization that the US itself was not to join as Congress refused to ratify the treaty of Versailles that had contained the provision for setting up the League.

As long ago as 1784 Immanuel Kant had written: *'The greatest problem for the human species, whose solution nature compels it to seek, is to achieve a universal* **civil society** *administered in accord with the right.* ....Thus must there be a society in which one will find the highest possible degree of *freedom under external laws* combined with irresistible power i.e. a perfectly *rightful civil constitution,* whose attainment is the supreme task nature has set for the human species;.....etc' (Fifth Thesis of essay 'Idea for a Universal history with a Cosmopolitan Intent') and '*The problem of establishing a perfect civil constitution depends on the problem of law-governed* **external relations among nations** *and cannot be solved unless the* *latter is'* (Sixth Thesis) and he urged nations: '..........to leave the lawless state of savagery and enter into a federation of peoples. In such a league, every nation, even the smallest, can expect to have security and rights, not by virtue of its own might or its declarations of what is right, but from this great federation of peoples alone form a united might, and from decisions made by the united will in accord with laws.'

Kant then notes that similar ideas had already been suggested by Abbe St. Pierre and J.J.Rousseau

It was to take more than a hundred years of continuing conflictual international relations before Kant's prescient (but in fact common sense) suggestion was taken up; probably the most moral concept, 'universal peace', being relevant to the morality of human relationships.

It took the terror of WW1 to make leaders (especially Woodrow Wilson) see the need for some supra-national body, with the moral authority and some practical powers, to settle disputes between nations. No member nation was expected to cede sovereignty but all were expected to respond positively to the majority will of the League and, more generally, seek to avoid war. The League of Nations (LoN) was established in 1919 based in Geneva (in politically neutral Switzerland) and incorporated in the Versailles Conference 1919 Treaty with Germany.

The Assembly of the League, supported by a secretariat, had permanent representatives from the principle allied powers with a rotating membership of representatives drawn from the other nations. The League also worked in conjunction with an international Court of Justice based in The Hague (Netherlands).

The primary aim involving: 'Any threat of war is a matter of concern for the whole League and the League shall take any action that may safeguard peace.'

The principle mission of the League was to promote international co-operation and to ensure that nations did not resort to war as a means of settling disputes. At this time (1919 – The Paris Conference) another international organization which was affiliated to the League was also formed: 'The International Labour Organization'. The charter under which the ILO was to operate included measures intended to ensure that workers in all nations that were members of the League had certain basic rights and working conditions and that women and children would be protected; plus the 'free association of workers' was to be a basic right. It was felt that the application of these universal conditions would result in similar costs of employing workers and so would, by reducing labour-cost competition, also contribute to peaceful coexistence between nations.

The Assembly of the LoN had recourse to three central 'sanctions':

1. It could call upon nation-states in dispute to discuss this in a reasonable manner (within the Assembly).

2. If in the collective view of the Assembly one nation could be identified as the 'offender' then it could be called upon to desist from any aggressive or otherwise provocative action.

3. If the view (expressed as a 'ruling') of the League was ignored then it could order economic sanctions to be imposed, even including trade isolation if necessary. In addition, sanctions could be enforced by military action.

Article 8 of the Covenant of the League of Nations: '….committed the signatories to the lowest level of armament consistent with national security and the fulfilment of international obligations'.

It called for a Preparatory Commission to meet in Geneva in order to draft a disarmament convention. The Preparatory Commission did not meet until 1926 and disarmament talks did not begin until 1932. Amongst other issues, Britain, France, and Germany, argued over the status that should be accorded to Germany at the talks. The rise of Hitler (with a resurgence of German nationalism) would ensure that agreement on designing a security system based on disarmament was unlikely. After much pointless wrangling, the Geneva talks on disarmament were formally suspended in 1934.

Apart from having to deal with the daunting task of managing the national self-interests of its members, the League was weakened by the fact that the US refused to join, Germany was not allowed to join, and nor was a Bolshevik-led Russia. So three of the most powerful nations in the world - who had significant potential for conflicts arising from internal 'nationalist' problems, territorial disputes with neighbouring states, or potential conflicts that could arise from their trading ambitions – were not members.

The LoNs had a mixture of successes and failures, with the balance being significantly towards the latter, with this being the cause of its being overall judged an over-optimistic failure:

Some successes:

Aland Islands – 1921 dispute between Sweden and Finland,…both sides accepted the Leagues suggested compromise.

Upper Silesia – 1921 dispute between Germany and Poland…both sides accepted the League's suggested compromise.

Turkey   – 1923 the League was unable to prevent a war but it was able to intervene to ease the humanitarian crises involving 1,400,000 refugees, mostly women and children.

Prevention of war between Turkey and Iraq in 1925/26, and between Poland and Lithuania 1929

When Greece invaded Bulgaria in 1925 Bulgaria appealed to the League and Greece was ordered to withdraw and also pay a fine - Greece accepted the ruling and withdrew.

Some failures:

Italy 1919 – Dispute between Italy and Yugoslavia - The League did try to intervene but to little effect.

Teschen 1919 – Dispute between Poland and Czechoslovakia over control of the coal-bearing land around the town of Teschen – The League's suggested compromise was rejected by both countries and the dispute continued until WWII

Vilna 1920 – Dispute between Lithuania and Poland – Lithuania appealed to the League but Poland refused to consider losing control of Vilna

The Polish invasion of land controlled by Russia in 1920 – no intervention by the League and in 1921 Russia, accepting the reality on the ground, conceded to Poland's demands and signed the Treaty of Riga. At a stroke doubling the size of Poland, but creating an enduring source of bitterness.

When Britain, the US and France continued to send troops to fight in Russia – even after the setting up of the League – The League took no action even though two of its leading members were involved as aggressors on foreign soil.

When Italy and Greece were in dispute over part of Albania the League actually took the side of Italy, the aggressor.

Following Germany's default on a payment of the unrealistically heavy war reparations, France and Belgium invaded Germany's most important industrial region of the Ruhr – thus making it even more difficult for Germany to pay reparations – here were two of the Leagues' leading members in direct contravention of the Leagues rules. The League took no action – and its credibility suffered accordingly.

In 1931 Japan invaded the Chinese province of Manchuria – China appealed to the League under Article 11 of the League's Charter – after some equivocation and a delayed report that on balance judged Japan to be in the wrong, the League ruled in China's favour.....the Japanese response being simply to resign its membership of the League.

In 1935 Mussolini's sent 400,000 Italian troops into Ethiopia in direct contravention of the leagues rules and although the League's Assembly did condemn the invasion some of its leading members (including Britain and Frances) offered tacit support to Italy, again undermining the League's credibility.

During the Second World War the Assembly did not meet and in 1946 its work was superseded by the establishment of the United Nations.

According to Micheline R.Ishay (2004): 'The League's and the ILO's efforts to counter conflict between nations and ease economic inequality, feeble from the outset, would quickly collapse under the pressure of nationalism and war' – and the absence of the US '.....weakened the organization's credibility.'

The position of the League was fatally undermined by the increasing unwillingness of nation-states to accede to its authority –

as the memories of the First World War faded the self-interests of nation-states once again came increasingly to determine international relations. Never very strong in practice, the League was at least a glimpse of an idea of what might be possible…the collectivisation of international security. It was bold if timely in its establishment and ambitious in its aims, but sadly if predictably, disappointing in its implementation.

Although the League of Nations was but a failed attempt at international co-operation it was a sign that nation-states were, at least in theory, prepared to accept some higher (transnational) 'morality-based' authority. It did establish some important actions – child labour, rights of women, anti-drug smuggling – that moved these issues onto the international agenda. In a more practical way the League's humanitarian work included some work in developing countries to improve agriculture (in seeds, clean water, tools, and scientific advice) as well as medical care.

The story of the League of Nations shows the fairly obvious point that the extent to which it would be successful would be the extent to which it included all of the world's nations as members and the extent to which each of these was committed to peaceful co-existence. Fundamentally, the willingness of nations to cede sovereignty over the right to unilaterally engage in armed conflict.

In terms of global finance, in April/May 1922 a conference was arranged to meet in Genoa, Italy, as an attempt to agree measures intended to stabilise the global economy and to boost trade. Delegates of 29 nations attended, these coming mainly from Europe and Scandinavia but also including Japan; with five British dominion states: India, Canada, New Zealand, the Union of South Africa, and Australia, sending representatives. The USA, with an isolationist Congress, declined to take a direct part but it did have observer status. A central focus for the reconstruction of the international financial system was to negotiate conditions that would allow the Soviet Union to engage more closely in trade with western nations. The Soviet delegation offered concessions involving payment of pre-war debts and ownership of (confiscated) property, in return they demanded full international recognition of the Soviet Union, cancelling of war debt, and the acceptance of a proposal for general disarmament. Little of any substance came of this part of the conference - but Germany and the Soviet Union did soon after sign the Treaty of Reppalo, so establishing normal relations between the two nations and committing them to improving economic ties, military co-operation, and ending disputes over territorial claims.

One outcome of the conference that did have general agreement was to return to some form of Gold Standard (a policy favoured by Britain). But some economists, notably J.M.Keynes, argued against this move. Keynes termed it (the gold standard) 'a barbarous relic'. He favoured flexibility for currencies - within a more regulated global system – allowing flexibility in terms of trade and so also more likely to foster currency stability. The convertibility of currencies to gold had been common up to 1914, offering a significant stabilizing factor (constraint), facilitated foreign direct investment, and supported wide-ranging international trade. Most countries engaged in the war had given up convertibility mainly in order to be able to print money to finance their role in the conflict. A surge in the inflation rate at the War's end had initially inhibited Britain and other European countries from committing to a return to gold convertibility. Inflation was raised to hyper-levels in some other European countries: notably Germany but also others such as Austria, Hungary Finland, Czechoslovakia, Yugoslavia, Poland, and Russia. The United States (with a strong export led economy) did maintain gold/dollar convertibility. Its (Fed) index of industrial production rose from 67 in 1921 to 126 in June 1929. This was a good time economically for many in the US – production of consumer goods, including automobiles, was rising steadily in response to strong domestic and overseas demand.

Fears of inflation led many large investors to deposit capital in the relative safety of Swiss currency. The expanding Swiss banking (and investment) system, including banks such as the Union Bank of Switzerland and Swiss Credit Bank, also benefited from the decision taken by the government in the early 1930s to allow anonymity for deposit-holders. Supposedly neutral Switzerland, in effect, acted as a deposit bank for the German Nazi regime, and indeed would later on facilitate the 'laundering' of the gold taken from victims of Nazi death-camps.

The early 1920s was a period of floating exchange rates for currencies and also a time of tariffs and other protectionist trade measures. The US especially used tariffs as a barrier to European exporters. But from 1923 most European countries did revert back to convertibility as they sought to stabilize exchange rates – Austria

1923, Germany and Poland 1924, Hungary 1925, Belgium 1925, France 1926, Italy 1927 – Britain, Netherlands, Switzerland, Australia, South Africa, all in 1925 and Canada, Czechoslovakia, Finland, Chile, in 1926 (B.Eichengreen, 2008). By 1926 there were thirty nine countries back on the Gold Standard (would be forty seven by 1931). For the British Chancellor, Winston Churchill, adherence to the gold standard would allow a wonderfully flexible exchange rate system. His speech on this in April 1925 was to become an infamous example of political error....not least because Britain had set the rate of Sterling against gold at the pre-war parity level (123.37 grains of fine gold to one pound sterling and this equivalent to $4.87) making British exports uncompetitive. This miscalculation was identified by some economists as the primary reason why Britain experienced only low growth rates and double-digit unemployment for the whole of the decade. Other European countries, such as France and Germany, enjoyed stronger export-led economic growth. With convertibility arrangements meaning that gold flowed to countries with undervalued currencies; by 1931 France and Germany had displaced Britain in terms of being the primary holders of gold.

The middle years of the 1920s was a period of general, if slow, economic growth and, as an associated characteristic, there was a world-wide demand for both direct investment capital and for credit. But this demand, in the context of insufficient gold available to central banks, led to a mismatch between money issued and convertible reserves. In 1913 the ratio of gold held by central banks to money issued and deposits held was 48% dropping to 40% by 1927. Instability in international finance was due to the inherent complexity of macroeconomic affairs exacerbated by the action of speculators and of governments unprepared to take decisive co-ordinated action to impose more organization, and so potentially more stability, into the international financial system.

The slow process of recovering from the seismic scale of economic problems caused by WW1 seemed to show some signs of progress (at least in industry rather than agriculture) during the 1925-28 economic recovery.

Towards the decade's end the financial mechanisms intended to adjust the international currency system, designed to take into account fluctuating balance-of-payment differentials, proved to be inadequate to maintain the relative value of currencies. Increasingly, countries moved to protect their currencies by using interest rates and to tighten the availability of credit. These, together with tariffs and other barriers, acted as a brake inhibiting global trade. But by the early 1930s most countries realised that the social effects of this deflationary approach were politically unacceptable and so came off the Gold Standard; Britain in 1931, immediately followed by its devaluation of the pound. In 1929 the British Government had set up a committee to consider what might be done to boost trade and to reduce unemployment levels. This committee was advised by Keynes and in its conclusions (published in 1931) it recommended the lowering of interest rates to encourage consumer spending and business investment, and markedly increased government spending on public works. In an attempt to replace the stabilizing function of convertibility the British government, in 1932, introduced the Exchange Equalization Account to facilitate government intervention, with the US creating a similar body in 1934 with its Exchange Stabilization Fund.

By now the US held 45% of the world's gold reserves, with Britain falling to 20% of world reserves (50% of its pre-war level). European debt to the US, and the shift in holding gold reserves, were but the more obvious signs of a significant shift in the balance of financial power that had now crossed the Atlantic; others indicating the rising economic power of the US would include its industrial output, and GDP/GNP growth-rates. America had emerged from the war changed from being the world's largest debtor to become its biggest lender. US manufacturing output tripled in value during the war years ($23 billion to $60 billion) and between 1914 - 1917 US exports doubled, with munitions sales alone rising from $40 million to $1.4 billion; agriculture 'boomed', especially with food sales to Britain. For its recovery most of Europe depended on American capital, markets, technology, and to some extent its political leadership.

During the 1920s the US had enjoyed a period of steady growth in most industries, with growing confidence and a sense of economic prosperity fostering an amount of recklessness. Many individuals took on large mortgages, personal and company loans, and invested in the heavily promoted and steadily over-valued equity markets. Many in the middle and upper classes did not want to miss-out on what seemed to be easy money. The abstraction of wealth based on debt, along with the overvaluation of assets, inflated the economy and created a critically unstable financial structure vulnerable to adverse changes in real world conditions.

The progressive electrification of industry, innovations in the plastics and chemical industries, along with developments in transport; with bigger better airplanes, faster more affordable automobiles, and steam whistling trains rushing through the countryside, were drivers of economic development. In addition, there were the many technological and scientific innovations read about in the expanding glossy magazine market and seen on cinema screens (in Britain there was the pacey MovieTone News). All of these developments contributing to creating a sense of accelerating movement, of progress, projecting attractive images of 'modernity'.

Taken overall, the 1920s were a time of economic growth during which any considered investment in a balanced portfolio of equities would have seen fairly steady annual returns. The general mood of economic progress, with rising share prices and a housing boom, encouraged a bullish approach to share-dealing. It was the activity of the large numbers of new to share buying middle-class investors whose enthusiasm and optimism increasingly overcame more traditional prudence, even to the extent of many borrowing to invest, that gave additional impetus to stock markets. By 1929 300 million shares had been brought by individuals using money borrowed from banks. From now the condition of the various equity markets would have a central place in the middle and upper-class national psyche. Between 1921-29 the Dow Jones Industrial Average rose by 400%, and in1928 alone the US stock market rose in value by 40%. For B. Mark Smith (2003, p122): '.....accepted wisdom in the last years of the 1920s bull markets blur together into one long, exuberant binge.'

This was a time of a rapidly inflating US property market. A rise that took off in Florida in the early 1920s, spreading north as the decade elapsed. With a rate of rise that was shown to be unsustainable from about 1927 as the prices levelled off then began to fall. A number of banks were by then overexposed to what, in a falling property market, were risky loans. This created another factor eroding the resilience of many US banks, making them more vulnerable to the financial storm gathering in the stock markets.

Contrary to what most mainstream economists and financial journalists claimed post the crash, there were some individual observers who had been urging caution, suggesting that the market was becoming grossly overvalued. Even a congressional committee investigating banking and currency had, in 1928, expressed concern about the impact of intense speculation. Keynes, early on, had noted the similarity between stock markets and gambling casinos. It is difficult to accept that at least some central bankers would not have been privately concerned at the extent of overvaluation - not least due to the way a conventional, if crude, means of assessing the value of a stock by its price to earnings ratio, with its emphasis on current earnings, was being ignored in favour of a valuation that based earnings on predicted future income. A lapse due primarily to lobbying pressure from big business seeking to inflate the value of its shares.

Aware of what would happen if market confidence waned dramatically, central bankers would surely also have felt an uneasy sense of looking into an 'abyss'; knowing that a possible meltdown in equity values would have a wide-ranging impact on the US (and so the Global) economy. One respected economist, Paul M. Warburg (one of the founders of the Fed.), did urge action, suggesting that if action were not taken immediately then the impact on the wider US economy would cause a relatively buoyant underlying economy to sink rapidly into economic depression.

In March 1929 there had been some initial tremors in the market suggesting possible problems. Banks and some leading financiers (with J.P.Morgan taking the lead) moved to absorb the selling, so allowing the markets to stabilize throughout the summer. A similar scare began in September with a similar reaction to halt the decline being taken by financial institutions. But it seems that confidence had reached a critical low and a short pause in the rate of selling ended on 24th October (Black Thursday) with a day that saw increasingly more nervous shareholders and brokers engage in panic selling. Due to intervention by a group of leading bankers there was a rally during the day that steadied share values over the weekend. But the following Tuesday the panic seen the previous week turned to chaos, with the markets being overwhelmed by the rate of selling - by the day's end $40 billion had been wiped off the value of the shares quoted on US markets. Unmanageable chaos settled back into more or less managed panic and a year of quite frenzied selling saw the value of shares being reduced to 90% of their value at the peak of the market.

The government stood back, nervously hoping that groups of leading financiers and at least some element of conventional market correctives, would together resolve the problems. Perversely, it could even have been that the low interest rates set by the Fed, in making share-buying on credit (buying on 'margin') easier, had been a factor contributing to the unsustainable rise in share prices. The government could have limited money supply, the Federal Reserve could have raised interest rates and used other ways of limiting credit, but either action would certainly have adversely affected industry in the US economy beyond the stock market, an outcome the government was desperate to avoid.

But even as late as 1928, when the national mood in the US was still fairly upbeat, most workers (especially blacks) were poorly paid, with only a small proportion, and these the more skilled, benefiting from at least some degree of trades union protection. Many small farmers struggled with a combination of near drought and falling prices for their products; 1 in 20 US farmers lost their farms as mortgages were foreclosed. The 1920s lead up to the Wall-Street crash had been a very good time for some but not for all.

When the 'crash' came no financiers actually jumped from the windows of their Wall Street offices but a number of notable players in the market did eventually face trial for financial misdemeanours and a couple, including Ivar Kreuger (credited with having introduced the 'junk' bond), committed suicide by shooting themselves. Attempts made in October 1929 by leading US bankers to reassure investors did no more than temporarily pause the fall in stock prices. Rumours abounded of banks in financial trouble (exposed to loans taken out by over-leveraged investors) and of banks and other major investors dumping stock as they endeavoured to limit their exposure to the market. In some cases the rumours had substance but for the most part they were based on suspicions rather than fact, but once abroad they only added to the sense of panic gripping the market; 25 million individual Americans owned shares at the time of the crash. As noted above, a grossly overvalued and so flimsy equity market was blown to pieces as confidence in share values drained from investors.

Although the tumbling of the prices of shares listed on the US stock market spread to stock markets across the world (if a more steady selling of shares and reduction in prices than US panic selling) this 'event' did not in itself cause the Great Depression of the following decade. Some more structural economic conditions related to international trading conditions had already created a 'depression-prone' economic environment.

The US economy was so powerful that its (self-inflicted) economic depression – so lack of demand for raw materials and manufactured goods, reduction of capital flows to other countries, and its imposition of import tariffs – did have a significant knock-on impact on a global scale. The initial cause of the slide into world depression might be sourced to the US, but this only exacerbated problems already inherent in the economic arrangements of most other leading nations. The dramatic fall in the price of stock on the US markets had spread a contagion of investor doubt across the world but problems were compounded by underlying fundamentals linked to lack of international co-ordination on exchange rates and also a range of protectionist measures inhibiting international trade, that had 'predisposed' the world's economy to a period of depression.

America banks desperate for liquidity called in foreign loans, an action having a significant further impact on debtor countries. An awareness of the need to find some basis for international agreement on both financial and political matters had been reflected in two conferences undertaken at around this time, including:

-   1927 Geneva (World economic) Conference at which some modest steps were taken to bring down trade barriers.
-   1928 'International Treaty for the Renunciation of War as an Instrument of National Policy' (the Kellogg-Briand Pact) was signed by sixty-five nation states, but it was more aspirational than realistic given the cynical underlying motives and perspectives of the leading nations involved.

In this idealistic spirit of international co-operation the French Prime Minister Aristide Briand proposed a United States of Europe when he addressed the League of Nations in September 1929. Even these only tentative signs of possible international movement towards co-operation and security were relegated to the blurred background of international relations when economic depression engulfed the world. The structural means of co-ordinating international action to ease the financial crisis was disregarded as each nation focused more on its own internal problems.

From 1930 the US entered a period of serious economic difficulties. Across America 85,000 businesses failed, and unemployment peaked at 30% - In 1933 nearly half of mortgage holders were in arrears and repossessions were running at about a 1000 per day. The rate of construction of new homes fell by 95%, 2 million people were made homeless, farm prices had fallen by 60%;

200,000 farms were foreclosed in 1933 alone. National income reduced from a high of $87 billion in 1929, to $42 billion by 1932, and falling even further to $39 billion by 1933. During this time exports fell by 50%, reflecting the impact of spreading global economic recession.

The US government, with a republican president in Hubert Hoover, at first declined to intervene, assuming (hoping) that conventional market corrective mechanisms and direct intervention of the leading financiers would salvage some sort of viable economic system (recovery) from the debris of equity markets reduced to financial rubble. When these mechanisms failed to alleviate the situation even Hoover, with his long-standing commitment to some idealised 'rugged individualism', did reluctantly offer some relief to the growing mass of the unemployed. He established a $300 million Emergency Relief and Reconstruction Aid Fund, made available to the states; but, due mainly to its being spurned by republican run states, only 10% of the fund was actual used. Some relatively modest government investment was also made in public works, most notably in 1932 with the Hoover Dam.

Beyond the US, the global situation was at its worst by the end of 1933, with international trade at about 35% of its 1929 level (all the industrialized countries were maintaining strong tariff trade regimes), unemployment was at high levels with wages being depressed for most of those in work. Industrial and global manufacturing production reduced by as much as 40% - 50% in some of the larger national economies and was significantly reduced in all. Agricultural prices were depressed, with record rates of mortgage foreclosure. Global GDP from 1929-1933 fell by between 20% and 30% as the world sunk into economic depression, and it became clear that conventional market correctives were failing to promote recovery.

Equity and currency speculation was not itself the cause of the global depression of 1929-1933 but it was another factor adding to instability. Even in the early 1930s, when governments were taking some action to promote recovery, speculators sought any and every opportunity for personal gain irrespective of the impact of their action on a fragile recovery; 'hot money' moved about in the search for short term profit rather than contributing towards longer-term stability. Even the US Congress was concerned about this activity as well as the more risky behaviour of banks. The latter was addressed in part by the Glass-Steagall Act (late 1932) and the former partly eased by coming off the gold standard (a measure long advocated by Keynes), and both by rather vague threats of more decisive action.

It was in this economic situation that Franklin.D.Roosevelt swept into office on a wave of popular expectation that a democratic president would take decisive action to alleviate the financial problems, problems that public opinion felt sure were due to irresponsible investors and greedy bankers. The indefatigable FDR did not disappoint his supporters and within a short time of taking power he managed to increase his popularity even further by repealing the prohibition legislation and making the production and sale of alcohol legal activities.

Within 100 days of taking office Roosevelt acted with the support of a Congress that was generally in favour of firm action against banks and of compassionate steps to ease the very difficult conditions being experienced by many Americans. So began the process of introducing the '....New Deal for the American people' that the President had promised; 'We have nothing to fear but fear itself' was a mantra deployed by Roosevelt to ease more immediate social tensions. Within this period all banks were closed for four days under the 'Emergency Banking Act', mainly in order to allow respite from the panic that threatened to overwhelm the banking system. In the period preceding the Crash of 1929 banks had to hold only 10% deposit against any loan offered, so 90% of loans were based on 'abstract' value (in effect unsecured) and when the stock market began to fall, and speculator and investor confidence weaken, loans were called in. If unable to support these with a sufficient level of deposits a bank would fail or be taken over. The strategy of allowing risky high rates of leverage was one that would recur and cause problems throughout the twentieth century and would (return to) make a significant contribution to the financial debacle experienced across the world in 2007/8, when the US government had to step in yet again and save the banking system (not just individual banks) by transferring substantial sums to banks and underwriting $23.7 trillion of debt.

Action, including the passing of the important 1933 'Banking Act' and some other measures, were undertaken in order to restore some confidence in the financial system. FDR took the US off the Gold Standard in 1934, allowing the dollar to float on foreign exchange markets, which in turn allowed a useful devaluation of the dollar against European currencies. The New Deal included a series of fifteen significant legislative measures that were presented to Congress. These were based on what historians have named the '3Rs'.... Recovery: in banking, railways/transport, industry and agriculture), Reform: of Labour rights and the promotion of trades unions (Wagner Act) and in finance – stock markets, banks and transportation - an attempt intended to prevent a repeat of what had taken place in 1928, Relief: focused on government investment in public works.

Between 1933-1936 a series of economic measures were taken including those setting up institutions such as 'US Housing Authority' (1937) and the 'Farm Security Administration' (1937) and passing legislation such as the 'Fair Labour Standing Act' (1938), and the 'Agricultural Adjustment Act' (1938).

Perhaps the most significant longer-term legislation was the 'Social Security Act' of 1935, an act intended to provide some measure of financial security for the poor, elderly and the sick. The cost of the provisions of this Act would increase steadily to become in 2004 $500 billion per annum and as such, the largest (non-military) government spending program in the world. Measures to alleviate conditions of the masses by increased government spending drew criticism from most traditional conservatives. In the face of strong opposition Roosevelt's administration also sought to balance the US budget, reducing the wages of government employees, reducing benefits to veterans and widows, and cutting back spending on the military and on education. Keynes highlighted this fiscally conservative approach as being one that, by reducing demand in the economy, would hold the country in the grip of depression for longer than would have been the case without the cut-backs.

Given that they now had to take social factors (including organised labour) into some account, twentieth century governments had less commitment to maintaining the value of a currency than had governments of the nineteenth century. This currency instability provided an additional source of uncertainty; because investors could no longer rely on governments to support exchange-rates to the extent to which they had prior to WW1. And governments, as well as populations, of 'capitalist' (broadly social democratic) countries had the example of what appeared to be a succession of seemingly successful Russian five year economic plans, operating as what could be perceived as a worker-centred political alternative.

The significant overall drop in demand for the goods and services produced in the industrially developed countries inevitably impacted on those developing countries and regions from where primary products and raw materials were sourced. This included most of Central and South America, Canada, the Middle East (especially Egypt) India, Australia, New Zealand and countries in Europe such as Finland and Hungary.....in fact few of the World's countries were not drawn into the wider world depression that had begun in the industrialised regions. A veritable 'wave' of economic recession reverberated around the globe, impacting on the poorest peoples who had only meagre 'stored' resources (wealth), little power in the market-place, and were generally unable to rely on much in the way of state support.

A range of quantitative indicators reflect the extent of the economic downturn 1929-32 – Over these three years: Industrial production fell by 46% in the US, 23% in Britain and France and 41% in Germany – Wholesale prices fell by 32% in the US, 33% in Britain and France and 29% in Germany – Foreign trade fell by 70% in the US (exports declined from $5.2 billion in 1929 to $1.7 billion in 1933), 60% in Britain and Germany and 54% in France. In the US unemployment increased to 27% of the workforce, Britain up to 23%, Sweden 24%, Denmark 32%, and in Germany it reached 44%; with significant numbers of those who still had jobs experiencing short-time working and reduced incomes.

As the social impact of the financial 'Crash' spread across the World governments, yielding to internal pressures and overall lacking much willingness to engage in international co-operation, introduced a range of measures to maintain their own internal markets by protection and to gain competitiveness in external markets by currency devaluation. These combined to make a significant contribution to further depressing the state of international trade.

It is considered by some economists that it was the US implementation of the Smoot-Hawley Tariff Act in June 1930, introducing protectionist trade measures raising tariffs on over 20,000 imported goods, that set off a chain reaction in which most other countries also introduced retaliatory tariffs; so a primary factor in depressing global economic activity. But the financial discipline necessary to maintain gold convertibility was perhaps an even more significant factor affecting currency exchange rates in ways that also inhibited trade. It was countries coming off the gold standard (especially the US in 1932) that would be a significant factor in beginning the process of promoting economic recovery. In general, the floating of currencies allowed some countries, primarily those in balance of payments deficit, to devalue their currencies which in turn assisted recovery.

The Glass-Steagall Act (noted above) was first presented to Congress in 1932 during the political hiatus between the election of November 1932 which ended the Republican Herbert Hoover's term in office and the inauguration of the democratic Roosevelt in March 1933. Democrat Senator Carter Glass and Democratic Congressman Henry Steagall sponsored the 'The Banking Act', which became law in 1933. This being generally included within the range of government action termed the 'New Deal'. This Act that, amongst other changes involving the US banking system, also introduced a separation between commercial and investment banking activities. Making it illegal for commercial banks to continue the practise of trading in and underwriting corporate stock. Taken as a whole, the Act was very much an attempt to restore public confidence in the banking system following the Stock Market Crash of 1929 and the Great Depression.[11] As well providing help to alleviate conditions of those hundreds of thousands of southern small farmers having to migrate when their land had become unworkable due to the combination of drought and soil erosion that created a 'Dustbowl' in the mid-west.

The New Deal is generally taken to have made a significant contribution to improving the economic situation. Its aim of restoring public confidence was arguable more successful than in significantly reducing risk in the banking system. This ambiguity of outcomes allowed those inclined toward neo-liberalism to successfully lobby to have the Glass-Steagall Act repealed in 1990. With the complex financial products on offer to banks following its repeal, clearly leading to just the type of excessive risk-taking that the Act, if it had been kept in place, should have been able to prevent.

Attempts were made to co-ordinate international action, including the World Economic Conference of 1933 involving 66 countries. A conference initiated by a US that had reluctantly conceded to the need to seek at least some international cohesion on measures to encourage

---

[11] More than 4000 US banks had been closed down or allowed to be taken over by larger banks.

trade, stabilize currencies, and more generally to ease the economic depression. The conference made little progress prior to its being brought to a premature close. National self-interest served as an ever-present inbuilt structural weakness militating against the likelihood of grounds for agreement being identified. But this motivational difference of interests was compounded by lack of international agreement on what were the actual causes of the Depression. International finance fractured as thirty-odd countries retained high tariffs and low quotas on imports. Groups of countries did sign regional trade deals. Including: the Oslo group (Scandinavian countries and Holland, Luxemburg, Belgium), the Danube group (Hungary, Romania, Yugoslavia, Bulgaria), the 1934 Rome Agreement (Austria, Italy, Hungary), and the Ottawa Group which included most of the countries of the British Empire. Groups of countries – crossing over those within trade advantage groups - also formed round different currencies of the Dollar, Yen, Pound.

According to Larry Allen (2001, p227) 'The overall effect of the Depression was to weaken the credibility of free markets as socially responsible instruments for allocating resources'. This was a lack of popular credibility that would have a significant influence on the economic memory and social policy post WWII in Britain and much of mainland Europe. And, for J.A.S. Granville (2005, p163): ' The social consequences of the depression, the despair of the unemployed, the failure to provide adequately for the poor and the sick, the undernourishment of millions of children, unhealthy slum housing and many other ills in the early 1930s turned the mass of people on the continent towards a search for new solutions.'

The seemingly 'ideal' conditions for the masses in the Soviet Union served as a model for the working classes of what could be done and conversely, it provided the threat of what might happen for the middle and ruling classes. The determination to avoid a return to the conditions of the 1920s and early 30s formed the childhood experience of many of the politicians and their supporters that would undertake the more radical social democratic inspired post-war reforms in late 1940s Britain, and in some other of the advanced industrial nations.

The action taken to promote economic recovery meant that at the time of WWII the period of state subsidised 'free' market economics was at an end and for the future governments would continue to play a more direct role in areas that they had previously endeavoured to avoid. This combination of government involvement, and an even more subsidised form of capitalist market economics, would be further reinforced during the coming war.

The economic depression improved only slowly up until the mobilization of industry for war and even this was interrupted when the world slipped back into recession 1937/38. By the end of the 1930s overall economic conditions in the industrially developed countries had improved considerably; even if international trade remained quite stilted due to a mixture of tariffs and import quotas. But now the world was poised to enter yet another period of collective civil madness and 50 million lives (40% of them civilians) would be lost before any sort of international normality would be restored.

The countries that slowly recovered from at least the worst of the depression had governments ideologically committed to communism, fascism, or some version of social democratic capitalism. But they shared one key factor; that their governments had become more directly involved with economic affairs. Germany perhaps being the most obvious with, from 1932, the Nazi government introducing a strategy designed by the economist Hjalmar Schacht who, although never a member of the Nazi party, did feel that its level of control offered the best route to economic recovery.

With an emphasis on reducing unemployment, the German government increased investment from 2 billion marks in 1932 to 8 billion marks by 1934. Funding was directed toward work-intensive projects, mainly improving and developing transport infrastructure including: roads, bridges, port facilities, which all conveniently, would also enable the swift movement of munitions and troops. This, along with subsidies to some employers, military conscription, and a rearmament programme, meant that by 1937 unemployment was about as low as could be expected in a modern economy. A down-side of this direct government involvement was the effective eradication of any useful worker organizations or workplace representation, and very tight control on wages. Private companies, whilst they might expect to benefit from having a compliant workforce, had their prices controlled, and were increasingly directed as to what and how much to produce. If workers or directors raised concerns they would soon draw the attention of Nazi 'thugs'. If we add controls on capital movements and currency trading to the above, we can see that the German economy was by the end of the 1930s basically in autarkic lock-down. The only significant area of cross-border trading was with a few countries to the east, and this on a relatively small scale.

Germany was probably the more extreme form of centralized government involvement but a range of countries, including Italy, Poland, Brazil, Japan, Mexico, and Columbia, adopted similar autarkic economic strategies. Most of the countries that were reliant on primary products for export, and those in the very early stages of industrial development, raised tariffs, encouraged import substitution for manufacturing industry and agriculture, and tightened capital controls.

The 1930s saw the Soviet Union continue to pursue industrial development in relative isolation partly forced on it by antagonistic western countries favouring economic sanctions rather than co-operation with the communist pariah. Early on Lenin's Bolshevik government had taken control of the largest industrial concerns including the public utilities. Then, from the first five year plan (1928-33), Stalin's determination to pursue rapid industrialization saw the government relentlessly pursuing its ideological aims as they related to private property and private business. Business received close direction on production but it was in agriculture that the more significant social change happened. In 1928 97% of agricultural land was still in private (mostly family – such as Kulak) hands, but by the final year of the plan (1933) 87% had been collectivized. The basis of a massive social change in the countryside and one with a dire impact on productivity. Contributing to the famine of 1932-33, a time when about 15% of the wheat crop was being exported. The soviet leadership's (in effect Stalin's) focus on industrial development was successful in terms of standard proxy quantifiers such as coal and steel production - coal 1928 3m tons by 1937 13m tons - steel 36m tons 1928 to 128m tons in 1937.....and per capita GDP was increased by 50% between 1928-1937.

Most of the world's countries with democratic constitutions tentatively endeavored to find a balance between the obvious need for action beyond the failed (laissez-faire) market economics within systems that still countenanced gross inequalities (of wealth, remuneration, and opportunity), privileged private property, and continued to maximize the freedom of 'free-markets'. The latter being a narrow perspective of freedom, the access to which was correlated with economic and social power relations.

The vast country of China was, during the 1920s, only fairly loosely connected to rather than integrated into the wider world economy. But, being a predominantly regionally-focused agrarian economy, life for most of its population was lived within a predictable cycle of basic material satisfaction and rich cultural continuity. But by the early 1930s civil war, invasion of Manchuria by Japan, and extensive flooding in the agriculturally important Yangzi valley, saw the disruption of life across much of the land. By 1932 the effect of the world depression reached China, causing a marked reduction in demand for the key exports of silk and tea. Then, during 1934, the outflow of silver and the steady decline in manufacturing output compounded economic difficulties. A reduction of farm prices hit tenant-farmers hard. The cause of this being suggested as insufficient take-up of agricultural innovation, along with farmers being unwilling to invest savings and labour in their farms when any increase in their productivity would be taken by their landlords via increases in rents. In areas where the Nationalist (Guomindang) Government of Jiang Jieshi (Chiang Kai-shek) was in control it took little action to alleviate the adverse conditions being experienced by much of the population. Throughout the 1930s the masses were left to gain what living they could from whatever family and other local resources they could access.

To the west, Sweden (already left the gold standard in 1931) with the Social Democratic Party and the Agrarian ('Farmers') Party forming a centre-left coalition enjoying strong support from organized labour. Faced with the prevalent global problems of high unemployment (25% in Sweden) and a depressed economy, the government initiated a program combining public works and modernization (1933-35). At the 1936 election the Social Democratic Party consolidated its position and would go on to govern Sweden up to the 1970s. In France a centre-left government (elected in 1936) initiated a similar program of public works, offered support for the struggling agricultural sector, and legislated for a series of social reforms. Wages in the public sector were raised and employment rights introduced, along with a limitation (maximum) of 40hrs on the working week and a minimum of two weeks paid holiday per year.

Governments like these two, whose political ideology would come to be labeled 'social democratic' - a broad ideological descriptor for a generally quite politically pragmatic approach - attempted to find some balance between liberal social norms, laissez-faire free-market economics, and government action to enable economies to operate more efficiently. Efficient being related to their operation beyond the direct interests of the active agents operating directly in the market.

During the 1930s the national variations of social democratic systems were to some extent constructed from a motivational substructure intended to provide forms of governance that would lead populations between the extremes of communism and fascism. Regimes run by political leaders who had during the period of economic crisis become aware of the need to at times support capitalism as well as attempting to contain its own intrinsic inefficiencies. But politicians (and more so wider ruling elites) were conscious that a narrow economic strategy alone would not in itself be sufficient to contain the aspirations of increasingly organized workers who sought security beyond the work-place and improved systems of welfare support. Most forms of social democratic governance sought to offer various rhetoric's of freedom, fairness, and commonality. Whilst unspoken was an assumed prioritizing of private property rights and the continued acceptance of gross levels of economic and social inequality of opportunity and of outcomes; as if these were but some 'natural' conditions of civil life.

The same broad intellectual conditions that contributed to the construction of social democratic governance, taking various local forms in relation to differing national circumstances, also produced a type of economic theory aligned to the types of mixed economy favoured in the social democracies. This economic theory was exemplified in the ideas of John Maynard Keynes. Keynes, who since the early 1920s, had been advocating appropriate ways that governments could and should become active in modern capitalist economies in order to smooth the fluctuations inherent in 'free-markets', and more generally to improve their efficiency. Keynes considered that high levels of unemployment were socially unacceptable and economically unnecessary, and could be significantly reduced given the correct economic strategy. A strategy that, crudely put, prioritized 'demand' rather than 'supply'. This would need a change from the 1920s, if inconsistent, generally supply-side approach of reducing government spending in times of economic depression, lowering interest rates, and of taking steps to control money supply in order to mitigate inflationary pressures. An approach that assumed unemployment would reduce when economic circumstances had driven down wages to levels that would stimulate investment and so create jobs. This conventional mind-set also tended to view welfare support as a discouragement for workers to take lower-paid work so should only be maintained at a minimum level.

The tension between Keynes (supported by his Cambridge colleague the economist R.H.Robertson) and conventional economists was primarily due to his direct challenge to the accepted view that advanced economies were self-correcting at the macro-level. That both capital and labour were sufficiently flexible to adapt to changing patterns of consumption and new technological innovations. Full employment (in line with Say's Law noting that supply creates its own demand) had been considered to be the norm. Deviations from this being corrected following a period when average wage rates and prices both fell. Government could help the situation by keeping interest rates low but other than this governments were expected to take a hands-off approach. The convention being that, however well-meaning, governments should also resist pressures to increase welfare spending during these periods as this would tend to mitigate the impact of lower wages (an incentive for people to take work) and could also increase government deficits; and deficit budgets were only conventionally acceptable during times of war.

Keynes responded to accusations of his ideas lacking a theoretical base when in 1936 his book 'General Theory of Employment, Interest and Money' was published: this was a landmark book on modern economic theory. In it Keynes set out a theoretical justification for the approach he had been advocating over the previous fifteen years. He highlighted action that could be taken by government to stimulate economic activity (create 'demand') by making significant investment in public works. If this gave rise to a deficit budget then this would be a necessary aspect of a wider legitimate economic strategy. Over time increased employment would lead to a higher tax base and so funding for services and the paying down of deficits; a virtuous economic progression, smoothing the economic cycles.

For Keynes, a model economy would be a mix of free-market capitalism regulated by a government having its own public works investment programme. A programme low during times of full employment and high when an economy slides into depression. This approach was one that would prove suited to the bourgeoisie mindset of the cohort of social democratic politicians and liberal intellectuals who rose to prominence during and just after WWII.

In the 1920s and 30s successive British governments were wary of Keynes's views. Treasury advisers, and mainstream academic economists, sought to explain the persistency of high unemployment as being due mainly to the high wage levels reached during and just after WWI (between 1913 and 1920 wage rates trebled) and also to the more powerful position of trades unions during this time.

In 1931 the Labour government set up a 'Committee on National Expenditure', and its subsequent report forecast a budget deficit of £120 million (1931-32) and recommended increases in taxation and a reduction in government expenditure, to address this. Keynes's reaction was to dismiss this, in effect, continuing form of deflationary strategy, calling the report's recommendations 'foolish'. A view supported by the persistence of high levels of unemployment, and an alarming rate of the outflow of gold, as foreign investors reacted to Britain's economic circumstances. The conventional explanation for the causes and cures of unemployment were proving inadequate and the Committee's suggesting yet more of the same seemed to Keynes perverse, being based more on desperation than sound economic sense.

In the US, as we have seen, the New Deal was in practice (if not specifically by design) a Keynesian approach, being based upon a massive federal government spending programme on a range of public works: roads, bridges, dams, irrigation and land reclamation schemes, docks, public building, and new housing estates.

In Britain, the US, and other industrialized countries, it would be economic mobilization for war with its increased industrial and manufacturing output, plus military conscription, that would significantly reduce unemployment; US unemployment would be down to 10% of a larger than 1929 workforce by 1941 and would finally help to pull the world out of the Great Depression. A significant government involvement across much of the industrialized world in stimulating economic activity, the very 'demand-led' economic approach that Keynes had been advocating. But now it would be investment in the means of killing rather than for building bridges, roads, ports, schools, hospitals and housing, suggested by Keynes.

Within but twenty years of the First World War (the 'war to end wars') ending, another major bout of the expression of evil was to begin.[12] History shows that the roots of organized warfare are

---

[12] Bear in mind that I define evil as the cause of suffering that could have been avoided and surely all wars in the history of humankind align with this definition – wars are the outcome of human decision-making, not as an outcome of some fatalistic destiny.

embedded within the very nature of civil humankind - as individuals, groups, and nations. This being primarily due to individuals and leaders interpreting reality on the level of self-consciousness, translating political into national self-interest in international affairs. But for my limited purpose here I will just follow a fairly conventional historical analysis of the causative progression towards WWII. This, analytically superficial but descriptively useful, approach will focus on an admixture of national aspirations and social relations, as well as international economic and political factors.

If we accept that decisions taken by a Nazi-led Germany during the later 1930s made war inevitable given the then nationalist dynamics of international affairs, we can begin to trace some origins of these decisions to the settlement made at Versailles in 1919. Whereas Germany had in November 1918 signed an armistice to end hostilities, the outcome of the conference was to present them with a series of conditions that amounted to more of a humiliating defeat.

Amongst the more contentious of the conditions set out in the Versailles Treaty were: loss of territory, including Alsace Lorraine to France; recognition of the independence of Austria; the re-constitution of Poland, with the German city of Danzig and north-western Prussia isolated along a narrow corridor through Polish territory; the loss of German colonies and other overseas interests. In addition, German negotiators also had to accept de-militarization of German lands west of the Rhine, an army limited to 100,000 men, a very small navy, and no air-force.

Germany was to make repatriation payments (Article 231 - the contentious 'war-guilt' clause) set provisionally at 20,000 million gold marks then finally, in April 1921, this was raised to 132,000 million gold marks, to be paid to the 'victors'. This was a figure set by the Allied Reparation Commission calculated on the basis of Germany paying the cost of the war in terms of the loss and damage estimated to have been suffered by the Allies. These, and a number of other conditions, were felt by the Germans (and to some extent viewed by the US Congress which refused to ratify the final Treaty) to amount to a punitive treaty; their being more about punishment and revenge rather than a justifiable settlement. The conditions of the Treaty gave substance to a simmering criticism by conservative elements of the Weimar government focused on the accusation that the German Army did not lose WW1 on the battlefield but that the war was lost by weak politicians at the Château of Versailles.

The German National Assembly met at Weimar on 6th January 1919. The Assembly being a central democratic element of a new republican constitution that also included a president (initially the Social Democratic Party's Fritz Ebert then the conservative Field Marshall Paul von Hindenburg from 1925-1934) who would serve a seven year term of office, with no limit to the number of terms an individual could serve. There was a division of powers between the Assembly and the President, with the President having the constitutional right (article 48 of the constitution) to suspend civil liberty in the event of a national emergency - a power that would later on be used by Hitler to consolidate Nazi control.

The new German government was a coalition led by the left of centre Social Democratic Party, with Phillip Scheidemann (leader of the Social Democratic Party) as Chancellor. At the conclusion of the negotiations of Versailles Scheidemann resigned having concluded that the Treaty conditions were unfair and the reparation payments unrealistic. If principled, this act was more a token gesture unlikely to affect the outcome when the Assembly met on 23rd June and, faced with the alternatives of either agreeing to the treaty or suffering the military occupation of Germany, (with Gustav Bauer as new Chancellor), it voted to accept the Treaty. The Treaty was finally ratified by Germany on 9th July 1919, to take effect from 10th of January 1920.

The early 1920s was a very difficult time for Germany (indeed for all of Europe with manufacturing output in 1920 only about 75% of its pre-war levels) as its people endeavoured to recover from the general dislocation of war as well as the destruction of manufacturing and agricultural production. Violence between left and right wing groups was common on the streets of Germany's major cities. The socialist leaders, Karl Liebknecht and Rosa Luxemburg, were arrested then brutally murdered by right-wing officers of the Guards Cavalry Rifle Division. The Chancellor Fritz Ebert refused the Independent Socialist's request for an independent investigation into the murders and instead left it to the military to investigate the actions of its own officers. The more radical left-wing newspapers were closed down as communists and more militant socialists became increasingly marginalized. During 1920/21 there were a series of strikes and, when a right-wing coup d'état led by Wolfgang Kapp was attempted in March 1920, it was the workers who rushed to the government's defense.

The reparation debt repayment and the limitations imposed on German manufacturing critically exacerbated an already very difficult economic situation. Although the government attempted to improve trade by negotiating an agreement with the Soviet Union (The Treaty of Rapallo - included German military training on Soviet weapons, especially airplanes), debt default led to the Ruhr being occupied by the Allied powers in Jan 1923, so cutting off an important source of income. As the wider economic situation deteriorated people in the street faced shortages in most goods; inflation rose, in response to which the government printed more banknotes, leading to an inflationary spiral. A trend obvious in the changing dollar/mark exchange rate which, pre-WW1 was just over 4 marks to one dollar - at the start of 1922 this had risen to 162 marks to one dollar, by end of the year it was 7,000 to one dollar and by July 1923 it was 160,000 to the dollar, eventually peaking that year at the astronomical 4,000,000,000,000 marks to one dollar!

Many of the largest German businesses made high profits out of this situation, due mainly to the rising internal value of the foreign currency gained from their exports, and from having their debts dramatically de-valued, but most middle-class individuals saw their savings wiped out. Even given continuous increases, the purchasing power of wages was dramatically reduced.

Unsurprisingly, large sections of the population lost confidence in the government, with many increasingly turning to far right political parties such as: The German Racist Freedom Party, The Catholic Bavarian People's Party, and The National Socialist German Workers Party. The last, becoming better known as the Nazi Party, had been formed as the German Workers Party in 1918 by Anton Drexler - opposed to capitalism and Marxism, anti-Semitic, crudely nationalistic ('Germanic'), it was composed of a motley bunch of misfits and was a party born angry and overflowing with hatred; if one lacking a clear ideological focus. Adolf Hitler, with a record of military service, an assumed ability to identify the causes of Germany's problems (articulated by his improving oratorical skills), and a strong sense of personal destiny, rapidly rose within the Party: becoming leader (Fuhrer) in 1921. In late 1923, seeking to take advantage of the chaotic political situation in Bavaria, he led a putsch attempt in the state city of Munich, his intention being to take control of the state of Bavaria - although at one point the rarely modest Hitler announced that 'The National Revolution has begun!'

This shambles of a coup attempt was over within two days when the, mainly loyal to the government, army moved against the National Socialists. Hitler's own role in the actual fighting failed to match his fiery rhetoric; witness reports suggest that he was nimble and early in retreat. Hitler was arrested, tried, and on 1st April 1924 sentenced to 5 years imprisonment - of which he was only to serve 9 months.

Hitler began serving his sentence in the fortress of Landsberg, where he was treated as a special guest, given his own comfortable room, and allowed a regular stream of visitors. It was during this time that he dictated his 'thoughts' to Rudolf Hess for what was to become his book 'Mein Kampf' ('My Struggle'). The final text - even though edited and much improved in grammar and presentation by Hess and at least two others - remained a rambling, crudely overwritten, outline of Hitler's ideas. It presented a blueprint for a new Germany, a Third Reich. One that would allow a Greater Germany to rise, as a dictatorship, from the ashes of a country humiliated at Versailles in 1919. A Germany that for Hitler had been systematically ruined by a democratic republic controlled by communists, Jews, and a series of weak leaders.

The book also attempted to re-set Germany's genetic heritage. And to do so by inventing some pure Aryan racial identity that would be maintained by a eugenics policy which precluded interbreeding with types of racial 'chaff' that included Jews and Slavic peoples. For Hitler, the Aryan race was responsible for all that was good in German art and science. Ominously, the book also introduced the concept of 'Lebensraum' (living space) to justify a demand for more territory in which to allow the German nation to grow. The heroes of Mein Kampf were the world-historical figures of Alexander the Great, Julius Caesar, and Napoleon Bonaparte. Unsurprising given that Hitler viewed life as an eternal struggle, the book also presented a form of cod-Darwinism, with victory going to the strong and the determined.

For intellectual support Hitler highlighted ideas of individuals such as Johann Fichte, Friedrich Nietzsche, and Richard Wagner. Especially appealing were Fichte's anti-Semitism and his belief in a regenerated Germany (from the defeats of Prussian forces by Napoleon) that had been led by a select elite; Nietzsche (ignoring his disparaging view of the average German) for his idea of a super-race that would be headed by a superman (a race of 'blond Germanic beasts') - to whom any variation of Christian morality was unsuitable and should not apply; and Wagner for his virulent anti-Semitism, claiming that the Jews were out to dominate the world.

The Nazis were gaining an understanding of the value of propaganda, and their newspapers and dozens of widely available pamphlets eulogized Hitler as the leader of a bold attempt to rid Germany of poor leadership. Whilst in prison, Hitler was positioned as a brave patriot who had sacrificed his personal freedom in order to unify and save Germany. Nazi propagandists sought to turn an operational fiasco into a noble project. The Nazi talent for using the media to influence public opinion was cleverly exploited to their benefit. In 1930 the ex-journalist Joseph Goebbels was made head of the Party's propaganda program, a role enhanced once the Nazis were in political power by his elevation to become 'Minister of Public Enlightenment and Propaganda'. The Nazi Party's propaganda strategy took on Hitler's observation in Mein Kampf that: 'The receptive power of the masses are very restricted, and their understanding is feeble.' Just the target public/audience that would later respond warmly to the striking poster images projecting Hitler, the Nazi Party, and their ambitions for Germany, as healthily youthful, heroically militaristic, and decidedly Aryan in racial form - and fueling anti-Semitism by depicting Jews as sickly, shady characters, skulking suspiciously in the shadows.

Following his release from prison at the end of 1924, Hitler led the National Socialist Workers Party in a drive to gain political support beyond the Bavarian state. He toured the country and in speech after speech vitriolically condemned the Weimar government, using Jews and communists as scapegoats for Germany's plight. During this time attempts were made by the Party to garner support from big-business and from most of the smaller right-wing political groupings. The paramilitary SA[13] attacked Jewish owned shops and other businesses; they attempted to break up anti-fascist public meetings and fought in the streets with communist and other left-wing groups. By the early 1930s the SA had 100,000 members, so comparable in size to the whole German army. But even in the 1928 election the National Socialists had still only managed to gain 2% of the national vote.

The economic situation improved somewhat from about the mid.1920s. Aided by international loans, some foreign investment,

---

[13] Formed by Hitler in 1921 as the 'Sturmabteilung' - the 'assault division' that became better known as the Storm Troopers or Brownshirts

and the easing of the reparation payments in the Dawes Plan of 1924. Payments were further eased by The Young Plan of 1929 (an example of some US engagement in European affairs even during a time of its 'isolationist' tendency) that further modified the payments. The Young Plan also set up the Bank of International Settlement, a precursor of the post-war institutions that would be established to allow some international co-operation in finance; if of a clearly ideological type.

In addition to steady economic improvement, another politically stabilizing factor operating up to about 1932 was the republican constitution itself which protected the fundamental rights of citizens, with a supreme court that was prepared to uphold these. Internationally, the Allied occupation forces in the Rhineland and the Ruhr were withdrawn and Germany was made a full member of the League of Nations as part of the outcome of the Locarno Conference of October 1925. The series of treaties agreed at Locarno, seemed to offer the beginning of more hopeful international prospects for Europe.

Gustav Stresemann, with the support from centre parties, became Chancellor of Germany in 1923 but soon resigned after losing a confidence vote initiated by a combination of right-wing and left-wing parties. In the new cabinet, led by Wilhelm Marx as chancellor, Stresemann then became foreign secretary and, initially as chancellor, and then continuing as foreign secretary, he made a significant contribution to improving Germany's economic situation and its international relations. In 1925 the avowedly right-wing Field Marshall Paul von Hindenburg became President.

We have noted that the Wall Street Crash, beginning with the dramatic fall in values of equities sold on the New York Stock Exchange in late 1928, initiated a rapid decline in the international economic situation. A situation further exacerbated by short-sighted defensive measures introduced by the major nations (including the manipulation of exchange rates and the increase of tariffs on trade) that, together, dramatically inhibited world trade. Given its still fragile economic condition, Germany was even more vulnerable than most other economically developed countries. In the early 1930s there was a crisis in the European banking system and in 1931 one of Germany's biggest banks, Darmstatter und Nationalbank failed. Germany was in effect bankrupt; incidentally creating a public mood of uncertainty, with a growing proportion of the population becoming susceptible to fascistic certainties. Unemployment had risen from 1.5 million in 1929 to 6 million by 1932, with most of the population fearing a return to the hyperinflation of the early 1920s.

Between 1924 and 1928 the Assembly had been controlled by a series of centrist if pragmatic coalition cabinets. But in the 1928 election there was a move to the left with the Social Democratic Party taking control and its leader Hermann Mueller becoming Chancellor. Over the following two years the economic situation deteriorated further and, in March 1930 Mueller and his coalition government resigned. The next Chancellor, the Catholic Centre Party's Heinrich Bruening (a ex-army officer and holder of an Iron Cross, who had the general support of the army leadership), failed to gain the support of the Assembly for his economic programme. In order to push this through he persuaded Hindenberg to invoke Article 48 of the Republican constitution so the he could use these emergency powers to by-pass the Assembly and introduce his economic bill via presidential decree. This resulted in a political crisis and to Hindenburg losing confidence in the personally modest and mostly well-intentioned Bruening. The outcome being that Hindenburg removed Bruening and, on the advice of the influential General Kurt von Schliecher, he then appointed Franz von Papen as chancellor. This made little difference to the political and economic crisis that Germany was experiencing, not least as von Papen proved to be unpopular both in the Assembly and with most of the German people.

As the economic situation deteriorated from the late 1920s, the prospects for the National Socialists improved steadily. Between the election of 1928 and 1930 their share of the vote rose from 2% to 20%, elevating them to become the second largest party in the Reichstag; in the early 1932 election this would rise to a 38% share of the vote. Some of the more conservative groups (military, business, and financial) in the country were becoming sympathetic to Hitler, not least due to their wish for some political stability under a strong, anti-communist, leadership. A demographic bulge in the number of young people reaching voting age offered another source (4 million) of potential support for the National Socialists, as this new generation sought a new start with better prospects for their nation. The core Nazi support remained within the lower middle classes and independent working class (especially ex-servicemen, many of whom were unemployed and had joined the SA) who felt let down by the whole Weimar period of government. The Chaplinesque figure of Hitler was steadily being transformed into a potential national hero for many Germans, if a dark and substantial threat for others.

In the July 1932 election the National Socialists became the largest party in the Assembly, gaining 230 seats. They opposed von Papen who, in response, used the powers of Article 48 to rule by decree. An unsustainable situation with Germany now becoming ungovernable both in parliament and on the streets. Hindenburg, in desperation, sacked von Papen and in December 1932 replaced him as chancellor with General von Schleicher. Schleicher had no real commitment to the Republic or to democracy. His main political tactics included attempts to divide the Nazi party and to placate the organized working class by lifting some wage controls and imposing price limits on some basic goods. He also offered a modest proposal on land reform. The wage and price changes were insufficient to gain useful support from the trades unions and indeed, were opposed by powerful industrialists, with the suggested land reforms resulting in the large landowners condemning him for acting like a Bolshevik. Throughout his short, 57 day, term as Chancellor he failed to gain the confidence of either the Assembly or Hindenburg, who then sacked him on 28th January 1933. In June the following year he would be murdered on his doorstep by an SS execution squad as but a foot-note in a wider purge to remove internal political opposition to Hitler.

During the short period of Schleicher's Chancellorship leading Nazi's had been in secret talks with von Papen - Hitler now had to balance his wish for dictatorial powers with the recognition that his popularity with the German voter was falling (the National Socialist vote in the November 1932 election was 2m down on the July election vote) and that perhaps his window of political opportunity was closing. In late 1932 Hindenburg received a letter from an influential group of industrialists, bankers and right-wing politicians supporting Hitler. Whilst on the streets there were rumours of a possible army putsch. On the 29th January 1933 100,000 workers demonstrated in central Berlin to show their opposition to Hitler's being appointed Chancellor and there was talk of a general strike.

Although Field Marshall Hindenburg had never considered Hitler, being in his view uncouth and a mere ex-corporal, suitable to be Chancellor, he was becoming ever more confused at the way in which the political situation was deteriorating. Hitler had meanwhile promised that if appointed Chancellor he would accept von Papen as vice-Chancellor and would appoint a coalition cabinet with Nazis in the minority; a promise that would soon be reneged on. Under political and family pressures the 86 year old president accepted what seemed to be the inevitable and on 30th January 1933, at the age of 43, Hitler took the oath of office and in doing so became Chancellor of the German Republic. Of a Germany whose time as a democratic republic was coming to an end to make way for a fascist dictatorship and the Third Reich.

Within weeks of becoming Chancellor Hitler had persuaded his cabinet to agree to a new election set for March 1933. In the run up to this SA gangs roamed the streets of the large towns and cities attacking opposition political groups and breaking up anti-Nazi meetings, whilst for the most part the police stood back. Opposition newspapers were suppressed and their journalists harassed, while the Nazis used the national radio service (that they now controlled) to blatantly promote the National Socialist Party and Hitler as the only possible saviour of Germany. A lone communist arson attack on February 27th that destroyed the Reichstag building offered a pretext for Hitler to further consolidate his position as he used this as a justification to assume emergency powers.

Even with these powers, and the determined efforts of the Nazis and their sympathizers to hobble opposition, the election result still failed to give them an overall majority in the Assembly. But Hitler persuaded his cabinet to put an 'Enabling Act' before the Assembly. An act that, if passed by a two-thirds majority of Assembly members, would give Hitler the power to suspend the Assembly and rule Germany as a dictator. The necessary two-thirds majority was facilitated when, prior to the vote, Hitler had the 81 communist deputies arrested or excluded, and by his making commitments to the centre-right parties that he had no intention of keeping.

The passing of the Enabling Act provided the constitutional basis for Hitler's dictatorship, with all decision-making power moving from the Assembly and the President to the Chancellor and a cabal of top Nazis. The ruling Nazi elite now moved to dismantle democratic institutions and to suppress any centers of potential opposition. Whilst at the same time they endeavoured to reassure leading industrialists and financiers that their interests would be protected. Many of these powerful companies and banks had already been providing financial support to the Nazi Party, some since the early 1920s.

Tensions between Ernst Roehm the leader of the SA (now with a membership approach 2m) and senior army officers came to a head when General Werner von Blomberg, Minister of Defense, threatened Hitler with an army takeover to restore order. Roehm was becoming a growing threat to Hitler within the Nazi Party, being prominent in a small group that was urging a more radical approach to the Nazification of the whole country. Herman Goring and Henrich Himmler led the SS against Roehm and other senior SA officers who were captured and summarily executed. This, 'Night of the Long Knives' (30th June 1934), not only enabled old scores to be settled and rid Hitler of a potential threat to his position, it also sent a warning to any others that any opposition would be ruthlessly suppressed.

On the death of Hindenburg in 1934 Hitler now with Roehm gone could be more confident of army support. He summarily combined the offices of President and Chancellor embodied in the title of Fuehrer (leader); a combination confirmed by a plebiscite in August of that year. Shortly after assuming the combined powers of President and Chancellor, Hitler asserted his authority over the military (Riechswehr) by introducing a new oath of allegiance. This oath wasn't just to Germany or even to the holder of the office of President, but it was specifically an oath of allegiance, of unconditional obedience, to Adolf Hitler. An oath sworn by a German soldier, and more so an officer, was no small commitment (for Prussian tradition) and for L.R.Eltscher (2014, p151): 'The oath became the single most important obstacle to effective resistance activity on the part of the army.'

From now Germany would see a steady sinking of the country into the dark night of Nazification; into a police state run by a paranoid dictator. The main means to progress this were: astute, if crude, use of propaganda; the forming of paramilitary youth groups; and the unleashing of two prominent Nazi organizations against any significant opposition to the regime. The two primary organs of state terror were the SS (Schutzstaffel) with their black uniforms and oaths of allegiance to Hitler, and the Gestapo, the secret police section of the SA. These two organizations, each run by ambitious thugs leading a band of obedient thugs, were to become synonymous with the very embodiment of all-powerful terror.

Hitler was a leader with a clear vision of what he thought Germany could become.

In this he differed from most twentieth century national leaders who have usually had at least a notional commitment to some political ideology and when in power endeavored to pragmatically manage changing circumstances and public opinion in ways that are broadly in line with their ideology. This is especially the case with democracies, with their limited terms of office and so their vulnerability to political fortune. But Hitler's vision and his now, as Fuehrer, powerful political position, enabled a more considered approach and for planning a prolonged advance towards the fulfillment of his vision for the nation.

When I note 'considered', this could be misleading if it obscured the often bitter rivalries, positioning for power, degree of corruption, and at times administrative confusion, that were features of the Nazi regime throughout its torrid existence. But for the most part Hitler could rely on the support of a small clique of leading Nazis and his power to have opponents removed or suppressed. This was combined with an ability to flatter and convincingly mislead groups such as the army, big business, the financial sector, and the still influential landed ('Junker') aristocrats, whose co-operation he sought. Such were Hitler's skills at persuasion that many of the leaders in these groups themselves became quite enthusiastic Nazis.

If Hitler's main ambition was for Germany to become the world's leading nation, even empire, then his plan to achieve this focused on his racial-based pseudo-Darwinism and on territorial expansion (Lebensraum). His 'programme' could unfold incrementally, with the first step being to consolidate his power and to stimulate the economy into growth. The German economy had been under a relatively high degree of state control for most of the Weimar period so the ground was prepared for further state involvement. Economic action was focused on undertaking public works to reduce unemployment, stimulate consumer demand, and so enable growth in the economy. The main feature of public funding included a massive construction programme incorporating road building (famously with the Autobahn), slum clearance, and later on monumental buildings. At this time socialist and communist political parties were banned and left-wing newspapers closed down. Wage controls were introduced and independent trade unions suppressed, while workers were expected to join the 'Nazi Labour Front'. These anti-left and anti-labour initiatives were praised by many of the major industrial employers who were willing to accept government controls providing that these improved the prospects for profits.

There was also a rearmament plan that would increase dramatically from 1935 when, in direct contravention of the Treaty of

Versailles, conscription would be reintroduced (to expand the army to 36 divisions). An action that drew only the mildest of international criticism from western governments prepared to accept a Nazi version of capitalism and favouring a strong middle European power to contain any Bolshevik ambitions to expand. It was Herman Goring who, with his four year plan, would oversee the military buildup, based on the expansion of the Wehrmacht, the Luftwaffe, and the German navy.

The Soviet Union seemed to be content with the possibility of the Nazis aggravating the western powers, so easing the international political pressure on them. While to the west, governments looked on complacently, if perhaps somewhat nervously, as Hitler withdrew from the League of Nations and from the disarmament talks (1933), pretending disappointment at the slow pace of disarmament by his European neighbours, as he mendaciously expressed his wish for peaceful co-existence between nations.

It would be the SS led by Himmler that would take the primary role in prosecuting Hitler's (Aryan) racial policy. As the 1930s progressed the Nazis flooded the country with anti-Semitic propaganda. Jews were purged from occupations in the civil service, and progressively from the legal and educational systems and most other professions. In September 1935 the Nürberg Act removed civil rights from Jews, banned Jew/non-Jew marriage, and would lead to the widespread confiscation of Jewish property. For the next couple of years the government had to balance its wish to persecute Jews with risking economic instability if leading Jewish businessmen decided to move abroad. But by the late 1930s the balance was shifting towards the former and when on 7th November 1938, a 17 year old Jew shot dead a relatively low grade diplomat serving at the Paris embassy, the Nazi's reaction was fierce. The government used the killing as an excuse to orchestrate a new wave of anti-Jewish persecution and on the 9th November Jewish individuals and families were attacked in the street, Jewish property ransacked and set on fire; with many synagogues also being destroyed. By the end of this 'Kristallnacht' (night of broken glass, aptly named given that an estimated four million marks worth of glass was smashed) 20,000 Jews had been arrested and up to 400 killed.

Now the SS moved more determinedly to corral German Jews into restricted areas ('ghettos') of cities. An approach that would be replicated from the late1930s as Germany invaded one country after another. Himmler and Heydrick were responsible for setting up four special units of the Einsatzgruppen whose role was initially to follow the army into Poland and round up Jews into the ghettos. But later on their more direct part in the killing began when the army invaded Russia and these units were then ordered to closely follow the advancing front and kill all Jews and Soviet political commissars as they hunted them out. It was estimated that in the City of Kiel alone over 33,000 (mostly Jews) were victims of the Einsatzgruppen - the pressure to increase the killing rate led to mobile gas trucks (made by a Berlin company) being introduced and these accommodated the gassing of 20 or 30 individuals at a time. Such was the orgy of blood curdling murder that when the head of Einsatzgruppe Unit D, Otto Ohlendorf, was interviewed after the war he spoke of the 'great ordeal' suffered by his men, with a German military doctor noting the '...immense psychological injuries and damage to their health...' (Shirer 1973, p960). By 1945 these units had been involved in the murder of 1,400,000 individuals.

The concentration of Jews in city-centre ghettoes would facilitate the plan to transport them – men, women, children, babies - to the concentration camps and so to slavery or death. For Himmler's deputy, Reinhard Heydrich (Head of the SS's Secret Service SD that would become the feared 'GESTAPO' - Geheime Staatspolizei) this procession toward death was his undertaking 'house cleansing'; for Hitler and the leading Nazis it was the 'final solution'. The primary scene for this 'solution' would be the network of concentration (death) camps erected across Germany, Austria, and Poland. In places whose names have become synonymous with evil: Buchenwald, Sachsenhausen, Dachau, Ravensbrueck (a camp for women), then later Auschwitz (where as many as 2 million Jews were slaughtered), Treblinka and Belsen in Poland, and Mauthausen with its numerous sub-camps and Lochau in Austria, being the more notorious.

A group of about a dozen senior Nazis, led by Hitler himself, met at Wannsee, Berlin, in June 1942 to plan the next stage of the expression of their deep-rooted anti-Semitism. The outcome being that the decision was made for a pogrom to be progressed in ways that involved a significant increase in the killing rate. For which an expansion of the death-camp system would be required in order to accelerate the rate of progress to the 'final solution' of the Jewish question.

Britain had pioneered the use of such (extra-legal) 'concentration camps' during the Boer war, which had caused horrible suffering and death for thousands of Boer families. The western nations had themselves supported anti Bolshevik White Russians who had carried out a pogrom killing 100,000 Jews in the 1920s. But however merciless these precursors in evil they were not on the same vast scale of the pogrom run by the SS's Deaths-Head Brigade; a group of blindly loyal Nazi misfits and killers (as well as many of the ordinary but obedient) who were proud of the skull-and-crossbones insignia on their Unit's badge. This was a system organized by administrators proud of the efficiency of the evil processes they facilitated.

The first camp, at Dachau, had been up and running since as early as 1933 and by the year's end held more than 30,000 detainees. This would be the model for the later death camps that would initially kill 100,000 people taken from mental hospitals before moving on to 'process' about 6 million mainly Jewish victims but also many, communists, socialists, Slavs, pacifists, religious resisters to the Nazis (in particular the Christian 'Confessional Church'), the disabled, homosexuals, gypsies, and any others judged by the Gestapo as 'anti-social'. Tens of thousands of Russian prisoners of war would also be exterminated by the end of WWII.

Such was Hitler's commitment to his 'racial purity' ambitions that the pogrom to annihilate the Jewish people of Germany and German-occupied Europe was carried out in spite of its diverting significant resources in order to progress this policy. The transportation required rolling stock and engines that could have been used to transport war materials, and at times these movements clogged the railway system. The killing involved the 'loss' of thousands of skilled and professional Jewish and other workers, and the means to progress the overall exercise diverted thousands of troops that might have made a useful contribution to the war effort.

Of wider interest, it was also the case that 400,000 German citizens, categorized by the Nazi's as 'mentally unfit', that had been murdered prior to the start of WWII, were excluded from charges at the post war Nuremberg trials, as this was deemed as possible interference in the internal affairs of a nation. This decision conveniently meant that it also reduced a possible defense of those appearing before the international court that would involve comparing Nazi treatment of those categorized as mentally unfit with how badly these had also been treated in the victor countries; something the latter wanted to avoid.

A truism of civil history is that where there is suffering there is often also the potential for profits, and some of Germany's biggest companies - including the giant chemical conglomerate I.G.Farben, and the munitions-maker Krupps - benefited from access to the slave labour. German and Austrian businesses competed for contracts to provide the ovens and other crematoria equipment. Companies including, I.G.Farben, Tesch and Stabenow, and Degeschalso, also benefitted from their involvement in the supply of the (Zyklon-B) crystals (or the fuel to produce the alternative killing carbon monoxide gas) that, when released, would form the lethal gas that would silently seep through the perforated air-vents set in the walls of the hermetically sealed 'bath-houses' of the cold bleak (barbed wire enclosed) camps. The death camps sited in isolated wasteland localities across which icy winds carried the grey smoke spiraling from the chimneys venting the charnel-houses; with iron ovens in which bodies were incinerated. If, that is, they weren't amongst the naked bodies just heaped into slave-dug pits to be liberally dusted with flesh and bone melting quick-lime.

By the end of 1941 almost the entire Jewish population of mainland Europe was in countries directly occupied, or at least indirectly controlled, by the Nazis. The extent to which the nominal rulers of these co-operated in Hitler's 'final solution' varied. Vichy France, Poland, Romania, the Netherlands, and Austria, were amongst those prepared to cooperate in the deportation of their Jewish citizens to the labour or death camps. Romanian troops themselves actually conducted a massacre of 60,000 Jews in Odessa in Oct 1941. Bulgaria, and to some extent Italy, lacked much enthusiasm for helping the Nazis in this task. And Denmark stood out as an example of what passive non-cooperation could achieve. Most Danish people refused to assist with rounding up and transporting Jews, and many found quite imaginative ways to frustrate the SS. In all, just 116 Danish Jews were victims of the Nazi terror out of a Jewish population of 7,380. But we need also to bear in mind that many individuals in all of these European countries, including Germany itself, risked their own lives to hide Jewish neighbours, help Jews escape the country, or otherwise frustrate the Nazi progrom.

I wish to pause to draw attention to an aspect of my writing style. Throughout the above section, I have been describing individual Nazis using derogatory psychological traits including: murderous, paranoid, thugs. I have used these to make the outline more conventional, perhaps even a bit more engaging. They add some sense of personal drama to the text. I think this is acceptable but I want to highlight the misleading nature of this style. I am profoundly sure that if we are determined to minimize the expression of evil in the world, we should not view evil as being embodied in this or that particular individual This form of demonology is too easy and seems to absolve society from investigating the deeper roots of evil behaviour. It is the behaviours that we should judge as evil, not the individual - this does not in any way absolve individuals from responsibility for their actions; individuals can still be judged as culpable. But as behaviour operates in a social context analysis can more coherently incorporate social as well as individual psychological factors into any consideration.

A more useful investigation into an evil act - such as the killing of 6m Jews and those in other groups - would take us, yes into attempting to gain an understanding of the immediate perpetrators of the killings, the leading Nazis, camp guards, heads of companies supplying the killing equipment, etc. But we must also consider the socialization processes they had been subjected too, seeking to identify the possible sources of traits (primary motivational factors) that would be expressed in the decision-making processes leading to the killing. This aspect of our investigation would identify the nexus of social structures that might contribute to providing the conditions from which evil behaviours could be expresses. I note 'could be' not 'would be'; in terms of individual socialization because we can only seek to identify conditions of possibility not ones of determination.

To the extent that the generation born from the start of the century to the 1920s shared the experience of growing up in Germany beset by economic problems, an international pariah state, and a nation harbouring a sense of being humiliated by the settlement of Versailles, we can see at least some factors that might explain what we might term the 'Nazi mentality'. This is a crude categorization for individuals whose own reaction to the interactive and interconnected processes of growing up in post war Germany made them psychologically vulnerable to the persuasive analysis Hitler offered of the nation's problems and his proscription for making Germany 'great again'.

For many, Germany during the 1920s could seem like a nation in crisis and it is the case that some people are more prone than others to turn to political extremes, to convincing religious or political 'saviours', when their experience is of continuing uncertainty, resentment, and material deprivation. History suggests that such conditions of political and economic crisis offer fertile ground for religious or political extremes, and Hitler and the National Socialists were well-positioned to take advantage of this.

A genuine, cause-seeking, analysis would involve a detailed study of individual Nazis and their supporters, seeking some common intermix of individual psychology and familial and social experience. As noted in the Introduction, the philosopher Anna Arendt, an observer at the Nuremburg trials, noted how ordinary the Nazi defendants looked - she used the phrase 'the banality of evil' to described her feelings on seeing a succession of very ordinary men shuffling into the dock.

Identifying the social/psychological conditions within which innocent newborns become transformed into adult agents of evil should be a primary concern. But to seek to trace the necessary deep-rooted analysis of the sources of evil that encompasses social structures, as well as individual and social psychology, might possibly reveal that the Nazi regime operated through but a more extreme version of similar national social structures (and within international relationships) that pertain in the world today. When we are facing the probability of a third world war and millions upon millions of human-beings being singed off the face of the Earth in a cataclysmic nuclear holocaust.

This might be the consequential conclusion to the many within and between nation conflicts obvious in a world of hegemonic (a world containing numerous disaffected ethnic and religious groups) nation-states bristling with weaponry; with a politically influential 'war-industry' programmed (indeed seeking) to have them used. A world controlled by groups of individual men and women whose political outlook is infused within a narrative where meaning derives from a very partial understanding of national interest, expressed in a language redolent with concepts such as suspicion, duplicity, conflict, threat, and aggression. Narratives of competition spun by politicians who are but another 'branch' of the same interdependent elite-group system in which another, the industrial-military, repeatedly polishes and rehearses the virtual scenarios replicating how to use their awesomely lethal weaponry. Weaponry provided by an amoral industry whose profits depend on the uses of weapons (their products) and/or the development of evermore sophisticated means of destruction and killing - in essence, the same conflictual determinants/conditions pertain today to those that led to WWI and WWII.

A principle theme of this book is that we can trace the origins of the 'conflictual' social structures back to our hominoid evolutionary stage in order to identify the fundamental psychological characteristic (mode of consciousness) that has continued to operate throughout all of civil life down to today.

In evolutionary terms, what mode of consciousness would we be identifying? I suggest the level of 'self-consciousness'. A broad but identifiable level - in terms of information processing capacity and other primary psychological characteristics - of the evolution of consciousness characterized by any individual identifying with 'influence groups' - my family, my tribe, my interest group, my class, my nation, and similar 'accidental' and limited in-group/out-group determinations. I won't develop this more theoretical theme any further here but will return to a more extensive consideration is in the concluding chapter. But if we are determined on the eradication, of even just the grossest expressions of evil such as perpetrated by the Nazis during WWII, then we will need to eschew the narratives of demonology and face the implications of the 'my's' inherent in self-consciousness and the social structures that have been 'constructed' - nationally and internationally - by people operating within the morally limited parameters of this level of consciousness.

The majority of Germans did not vote for the Nazi Party in 1933. We might blame the German people for passive obedience, for not actively fighting and taking up armed or even passive, resistance. But if we sincerely reflect on how we ourselves might have behaved if subjected to similar socialization and in similar political circumstances could we say that, even if we felt bitterly opposed to the Nazis, would we have done more than resign ourselves to the political circumstances, got on with our daily lives, and hoped for the best?

Some Germans were pacifists and refused conscription into the army; some did join protest or urban guerilla groups, but after the war little was said about these brave individuals (see below). This because the international narrative was intent on heaping blame on (demonizing) the German people; most of whom were themselves terrorized by the Nazi regime. How else could allied actions such as the militarily unnecessary slaughter of thousands of men, women, children and babies, in the blanket bombing creating the firestorms that engulfed residential areas of cities such as Berlin, Hamburg, Cologne and Dresden (100,000 civilians killed in Dresden - compared to 13,000 in London's Blitz) have been justified. The Nuremburg trails were a public reinforcement of an Allied 'conspiracy' to blame a nation for the war and the holocaust rather being but a necessary aspect of trying to understand the wider context for the war's origins.

German resistance to the Nazis included:

- The Beck-Goerdeler group and The Kreisau Circle (for these two see Eltscher 2013 p112)
- The Edelweiss Pirates - A group of young people intent on artistic and the other forms of cultural resistance.
- The White Rose group - Led by university students, including Sophie Scholl and her brother Hans, both beheaded in 1943 following a rigged trial before the 'Peoples Court', and the infamous judge Roland Freisler, where to be in anyway anti-Nazi was itself a marker of guilt.
- The Marwitz Circle - An opposition group active up to their betrayal to the Gestapo in 1935
- The Solf Circle - A group of more profession, middle-class people, a number of whom were executed even though their activities were more about raising humanitarian issues than direct opposition to the regime.
- The Rote Kapelle (Red Orchestra) - an independent Marxist group, active in distributing anti-Nazi leaflets and helping political refugees escape the country.

- There were also sections of the German army that refused to obey orders.

This is just a selection of many Germans that sought to resist Nazi domination by joining clandestine groups, refusing conscription, or undertaking unseen acts of individual sabotage in the workplace - A beating from SA thugs might be the minimum punishment for mild dissent, but a night-time visit from the Gestapo would generally mean death on the spot, or arrest, torture then probably murder, or a trip to a slave-labour camp (itself a death sentence for many). The Gestapo, with their network of spies, operated outside any law and held total power of life or death over each individual German and citizen of the occupied countries.

If the 'final solution' was the means of Hitler progressing his program of a genetically inaccurate and ethnically distorted conception of 'Aryan purity', it would be by invading neighbouring countries that he would gain the *Lebensraum* ('living space') he was seeking for a new Greater Germany. The staged expansionist program that he would progress was not just for territory but also for access to the materials that could underpin military strength and so the means to sustain warfare. Alsace-Lorraine held the iron and steel, Rumania the oil, Poland the coal, and Czechoslovakia the armaments industry; all materials required for the fulfillment of Hitler's military ambitions. By 1938 the German army, navy, and its air-force, were considered, at least by Hitler, to be ready for action.

The German forces had gained some real-life military practice in its support of General Francisco Franco, leader of Spain's military rebels (the fascist Falange) in his attempt (1936-1939) to overthrow the elected republican government. Although German military support never reached the level provided by the fascist Italian government dominated by Benito Mussolini, Germany did send a significant amount of men and materials. Early on both governments gave official recognition to the right-wing Spanish rebels. The historian J.A.S. Grenville noted that at the opening of hostilities in late 1936 the republican government and the fascist rebels each had access to comparable military assets but for Grenville (2005, p217) 'What decisively tipped the balance was the help Hitler and Mussolini gave to Franco...' and this help was especially decisive in the early stages of the war; the two countries taken together carried out well over 5,000 air-raids. Whilst the Italians provided over 70,000 men (mostly from the Italian fascist militia) and massive amounts of military equipment, the German contribution was about 16,000 men, including military advisers, technicians, and instructors, and somewhat less equipment. The actual fighting by the German contingent was undertaken by its Condor Legion. This notorious military unit, commanded by General Hugo von Sperrle, included tank and anti-tank companies, at least two battle cruisers (the Deutschland and the Admiral Scheer) and 8 squadrons of airplanes (about 100 planes - Heinkel 51 and Messerschmidt 109 fighters, and Junkers 52 bombers). It would be the bombers that would cause so much destruction during the siege of Madrid, with at least 1,400 civilians being killed. In the Basque town of Guernica, at about 5 pm on market day 26th April 1937, wave after wave of German bombers flown by German pilots, systematical destroyed the town centre. With groups of busy fighter planes machine gunning civilians trying flee the bombs. An event that was graphically immortalized in Picasso's mural-sized painting.

Possibly as many as three quarters of a million people died in the bitterly fought Spanish Civil War. Russia did provide a significant amount of military material for the legitimate republican government, and indeed about 5,000 (primarily politically left-wing) Germans travelled to Spain independently to join with individuals from many other nations in the pro-government International Brigade, or fought in other pro-republican units - about 2,000 of these anti-fascist German volunteers died during the conflict. But in terms of outcomes, it was the support for the Spanish fascists by the fascist leaders of Italy and Germany that made a more significant difference. In relation to the German preparation for its own military ambitions the Spanish experience was noted by Herman Goring (head of the Luftwaffe), as being a useful training ground for its military. He singled out the destruction of Guernica as being especially useful as a testing ground.

Meanwhile the major western powers looked on, assuming neutrality, but prepared to see democracy crushed and indeed to turn a 'blind eye' to the supply of strategically important military and other goods to the fascists – Italian aircraft/bombers flew on gasoline drilled in Texas.

Apart from their shared military ambitions and fascist political views (oh, and massive sense of self-destiny), their involvement in the Spanish Civil War further cemented the relationship between Mussolini and Hitler. Their two regimes formed an anti-Comintern Rome-Berlin pact (Axis) in November 1936. An international anti-Comintern agreement that Japan would join the following year. A Japan that was itself building a formidable military force and which had colonized Korea and Taiwan and, in 1931, had invaded Manchuria and controlled large parts of Northern China. The Seiyukai Party government (supported by large landlords and big business) that displaced the government of the Minsei Party (drawing support from intellectuals and urban workers) came to power in December 1931. The 1930s saw the military high command take increasingly tighter control of the country, and by the second half of the decade it was considering further expansion into British, Dutch, and French, colonies in S.E. Asia; and even the US colony in the

Philippines.

The increasing militarization of the world also expressed itself in the Far East during 1937-8 with the Sino-Japanese War. This war was but another outburst of active conflict during a period of simmering aggression between the two nations. The ambitions of Japanese high command was a primary reason for its elevating a minor skirmish over a misinterpretation of an incident that happened at Lugouqiao near Beijing in July 1937 into war. With the military, in effect, overruling diplomatic efforts to find a peaceful resolution. Japanese troops advanced further into China, meeting weak resistance from a Chinese army unprepared, poorly led, and ill-equipped to face them. But further south in the region around Shanghai, Chinese elite troops were better able to defend themselves and in turn launch a strategic counter attack aimed at encircling the Japanese held area of Shanghai.[14]

A battle for Shanghai ensued, with the Chinese taking significant casualties (possibly as many as 270,000). After three months of conflict Japanese reinforcements landed to the south of the City made the Chinese defensive positions vulnerable and by mid December the Japanese were in control of the City.

Then followed the 'Rape of Nanking' – so named owing to possibly as many as 20,000 Chinese women being raped by the Japanese occupying troops – along with this atrocity it has been estimated that 200,000 civilians were systematically killed (massacred), essentially an orgy of killing.

Coming back to Europe, by late 1937 Hitler felt that his internal control over the German people and his re-armament programme had reached levels that would enable him to move on to the next stage of his 'plan' for Germany. He was also reassured by lack of any significant international re-action to his and Mussolini's intervention in the Spanish Civil War, the impotence of the League of Nations in relation to the Italian invasion of Abyssinia in spring 1936, and similar lack of response to Germany's March 1936 re-occupation and militarization of the Rhineland (in direct contravention of the Versailles Treaty). Hitler and his close Nazi colleagues judged that the complex and somewhat diplomatically muddled state of European politics, especially the extent of mutual distrust between nations,

---

[14] An air-borne attack on Japanese naval ships went wrong, with bombs being dropped on the international settlement of the City, causing up to 3,000 casualties.

offered international conditions conducive for action.

In response to some senior Wehrmacht generals expressing doubts about the military readiness for action, Hitler demanded the resignation of both the commander-in-chief of the army and the minister of defense. He then moved on to undertake a purge of other senior officers, placing himself in charge of the military high command. Now he was ready to begin the expansion of German 'living space', and also to gain control of sources of important war materials. The German army began its move into Austria on 12th March 1938 and on the 13th the German government issued a proclamation noting the end of Austria as a nation state and its new status as but a province of Germany (the so called Anschluss law). Hitler entered Vienna in a triumphal procession on 14th. The street tramp who had roamed the City earlier in the century had returned as would-be saviour. Following close behind came Himmler and his SS thugs who immediately began to arrest thousands of potential opponents to the new regime and, in general, the Jewish population fared even worse. Wealthy Jews were forced to sell their businesses to the Nazis and most others had to look on while their property was looted or destroyed. But the individual persecution and daily experience of petty humiliation that Jews were subjected to was probably a more vindictive expression of the regime's anti-Semitism.

A plebiscite on the question of the creation of a greater Germany was held in dubious conditions, when many Austrians felt that how they voted might be spied upon. But it was also the case that a significant proportion of the population were fervent Nazi supporters and many more were obediently optimistic that a stronger government might bring improvement in their economic circumstances. In a country where the majority were Catholics, Cardinal Innitzer welcomed the Nazi intervention in Austria.

Once Hitler felt that the absorption of Austria into a greater Germany had been settled he began planning for a move against Czechoslovakia; the decision to invade being made as early as April 1938. Then followed a period of intense international diplomacy, led by Britain and France; but pointedly excluding Russia and indeed Czechoslovakia itself. Attempts as diplomacy culminated in September in a conference in Munich, which also involved Mussolini, during which the Sudetenland region, with its largely ethnic German population, was offered to Hitler in exchange for peace. Neville Chamberlin, Britain's Prime Minister, returned home from the final meeting in Munich famously brandishing a piece of paper signed by Hitler below his written commitment to settle all future Anglo-German differences by diplomatic means.

Hitler had to consider a number of potential difficulties as he prepared his next move: he could not be sure how Britain and France would respond to an invasion of Czechoslovakia, his high command suggested that they might not have the military resources to guarantee a success, and there were also signs that a growing proportion of Germans were becoming concerned about provoking a war with Britain and France.

In accord with the Munich agreement, German forces had moved into the Sudetenland in early October. Thus separating this region from a Czech state that was struggling with its own internal political disagreements. Hitler was ready to take advantage of the growing rift between the Slovaks and Czechs (including Slovak pressure for an independent state) the main cause of making the country difficult to govern. The loss of the Sudeten region meant the dramatic reduction of the key resources - coal, chemicals, lignite, timber, and iron and steel - that had made the nation economically viable. Two Czech presidents - up to 5th Oct was Beneš and then Dr Emil Hácha - were vilified in a series of Hitler's speeches, and in direct talks Hácha was being bullied into accepting German control. Even with this pressure - including the threat from Hitler to 'annihilate' his country - the Czech President (accompanied by his Foreign Minister Chvalkovsky) still refused to surrender his country to the Nazis. But the threats from Hitler were relentless, and were at times expressed in ways verging on the hysterical, culminating in Goring's threat to bomb Prague. In March 1939 the German army crossed the border and within a few days Hitler was taking the salute of a parade of German soldiers marching through the streets of Prague; in the same week Germany had also regained control of Memel in Lithuania.

By spring 1939 the diplomatic deception and hegemonic belligerence shown by the Nazis over Austria and Czechoslovakia had at last made the British and French accept that Hitler could not be diplomatically 'appeased' and that more definite action would be necessary. On 31st May they formed an agreement that they would come to the aid of Rumania or Poland if these were attacked. Grenville (2005, p233) pointed out the irony in Britain offering support to the Polish Dictatorship that it had denied to the Czechoslovakian Democracy.

Such is the complexity (and moral vacuity) of international relationships biased towards the narrow pursuit of national elite-group interests, that at this time, Britain was actually encouraging German military support for the Finns in their border conflict with Russia. As an Axis/Allies polarity begun to take more obvious shape Germany formed a 'Pact of Steel' with Italy, committing the country to follow Germany into warfare; an Italy that had recently (May 1939) invaded Abyssinia and occupied parts of Albania, but was militarily unprepared, and had a population generally lacking much enthusiasm, for a wider industrialized war.

Hitler now turned his attention to the east and Poland. By now German re-armament had advanced at a remarkable rate - in 1930 the country had no combat ready air-planes and an army of less than the 100,000 allowed under the terms of the Versailles Treaty. But by the end of 1939 it had over 8,000 combat ready fighters and bombers, an army of 1,000,000 men; a mix of conscript and professional soldiers - now with mainly Nazi supporting generals at its head. An army quite well equipped with modern Panzer tank and anti-tank groups, along with other highly mobile armoured units, and a navy being steadily strengthened, with one battle-cruiser following another as they eased their way down slipways into the cold gray water of the Baltic Sea. Ready to supplement this military capacity were the nearly 8 million (end 1938) members of the Hitler Youth movement - 14-18 year old youths who had been subjected to years of Nazi indoctrination and who had all been expected to take an oath of allegiance committing them to sacrifice their own lives for their Fuehrer, Adolf Hitler. Reluctant parents were warned that if they did not co-operate in the enrolment of their children into the Nazi youth movement they risked having them taken into the care of the state.

The ease with which he had gained Austria and Czechoslovakia reinforced Hitler's confidence in his assessment of likely international reaction. After a period of his trade-mark disingenuous diplomacy Hitler offered the Polish government a deal that involved their agreeing to join the anti-Comintern Pact (along with Germany, Italy and Japan), the return of the free City of Danzig to the Germans, and ceding of a broad corridor through Polish territory in order to allow more easy access to East Prussia. In January 1939 Hitler added the bonus of a promise of some Czech (Teschen) and some Soviet Ukraine territory that Poland had an historic interest in. Hitler felt that the Polish dictatorship also shared his anti-Semitism and anti-communism, so might concede to his demands, along with a mutually beneficial security arrangement. But the Polish government (with their foreign secretary - Colonel Josef Beck leading the negotiations) was determined against conceding to Hitler's demands, its members had more confidence in the capacity of the Polish army than its subsequent performance would justify.

Aware of British and French diplomatic attempts to form a pact with Russia, Germany offered them (Stalin) a more attractive deal and, in August 1939, the German and Russian foreign secretaries agreed a non-aggression pact (the Ribbentrop/Molotov Pact). Part of which was a secret arrangement that included the Soviets being offered the Baltic States and the parts of Poland that they coveted. Hitler considered that the formation of the pact with Russia would deter Britain and France from going to war in support of Polish independence. Behind all the negotiating too-ing and froo-ing during 1939 it seems that Hitler was already determined on the invasion of Poland and, if necessary, of testing his Reich army in the heat of wider warfare. As early as April 1939 he had issued just five copies of the top secret document code-named the 'White Case', in which the 1st of September was set for the invasion date and noted the task of the German armed forces to be: '.......to destroy the Polish armed forces. To this end a surprise attack is to be aimed at and prepared for.'

By August it was clear that Hitler would not gain his aims involving Poland without military action. He was still of the view that Britain and France would be reluctant to go to war over Poland. He used national radio to accuse Poland of provocative border activities that were in fact actions undertaken by SS soldiers wearing Polish army uniforms. So, using this 'provocation' as an excuse, the German army mobilized and in the early hours of 1st September, with the support of air-power, the first of 50 divisions of the Germany army were ordered to cross the Polish border. By the end of the month the mechanized German army had in effect rolled over the poorly equipped Polish defenders and was in control of Warsaw. Then, from 17th September, the Red Army began attacking Poland's eastern border. By 1945 at least 5.7 million Poles would have been killed, with 3 million of these being Jews.

At the end of August Britain had signed an Anglo/Polish alliance committing Britain to come to its aid in the event of a German invasion. The British government followed through on this commitment, and on 3rd September the German government was informed that the two countries were now at war. France soon followed with a similar declaration.

So, within but 20 years (two decades) of the end of the 'war to end war' the hellish terrain of another world-wide conflict lay open to the immediate future. And why would this not be a reasonable expectation given that the same fractured international political system, with essentially the same structural dynamics prioritizing national (elite) interests, continued to be the predominant mode of global governance. World leaders - leading mostly voluntarily dumb and obedient populations to a considerable extent propagandized into adhering to a form of nationalism determined by elite interests - traced a public narrative of peaceful intentions that in limed reality overlay a hard-edged practice of political hegemony and of preparing for and pursuing competition and on occasion conflict.

As Britain and France stood back waiting to see Germany's next move, control over timing as well as military momentum was with Hitler. In early 1940 the balance of military capacity in Europe favoured Britain and France. The two allied nations having 151 divisions facing Germany's 135 divisions, with France alone having access to 3,254 tanks to Germany's 2,439. Whilst Germany had marginally more aircraft, Britain would soon address this difference. Viewing war as his and Germany's destiny seemed to have been a deep-rooted motivational factor for Hitler. But in the early stages of the war he also retained a pragmatic sense of strategy and his next move was taken to ensure access to Swedish iron-ore. In April the German army attacked lightly defended Denmark then crossed the Baltic to invade Norway. Here the resistance, reinforced with British troops and supported by its navy, was the first real test of the German forces. The German casualties reached 5,000 men and its navy received a serious mauling. But Hitler's main military aim had been achieved and, in addition, Norwegian Fiords would provide suitable bases for the growing German submarine fleet, allowing easier access to the North Atlantic and to the trans-Atlantic convoys of material that Britain's war effort would depend upon.

With the Scandinavian campaign judged a success Hitler was ready to move on to further advance, and from the 10th May 1940 (the same day that Winston Churchill had replaced Chamberlin as prime minister of Britain) the German army began its now well-practiced form of mobile warfare known as 'Blitzkrieg' as it crossed into the Netherlands. The Dutch and Belgium army divisions were easily overwhelmed by the advancing German troops. Next would be France and, strategically at that time, the German military leadership was superior to that of both of the main Allies. Its Panzer tanks, and other mobile armoured units, with air-craft in support, proved effective in outflanking the French and British forces. The defenders were divided (in the Ardennes) and in retreat. The allied armies' were soon in a slow, ordered, retreat west that increasingly became a rout; leaving most of their heavy armour behind as they fled.

Within six weeks of crossing the Dutch border German officers were standing on the tops of the cliffs of Normandy surveying the coast of a Britain now isolated across the Channel, and jackbooted troops were strutting along the Avenue de Champs-Elysees in the centre of Paris. It was a Britain that, although retaining some pride from the rescue of over 338,000 British (BEF), and some French, troops from the port of Dunkirk, was being run by a government with a coalition War Cabinet composed of five members (the Conservatives Churchill, Chamberlin, Halifax, and Labour's Clement Atlee and Arthur Greenwood) gravely considering the alternatives of pressing for peace with Hitler or standing alone against him. Halifax, as Foreign Secretary, reluctantly favoured negotiating with the Germans, and in July Hitler was publically calling for Britain to make peace. But Churchill, supported by Atlee and Greenwood, was determined to resist and felt the British people were with him.

Hitler did have plans for the invasion of Britain but the outcome of the aerial engagements together known as the 'The Battle of Britain', in May/June 1940, suggested to the German high command that massive resources would be need to be deployed if a successful campaign was to be progressed. By October Hitler had decided to put his invasion plans on hold and instead turned his attention towards the east. Here lay the vast expanse of the Soviet territories and as much 'Lebensraum' as even he could wish for. In addition, his army (the Wehrmacht) had proved its capability to sweep all before it when engaged in land-based warfare, so why would it not be easy enough to repeat this against, what Hitler's intelligence services were telling him were, the Soviet Union's poorly equipped Red Army.

By spring 1941 the Germans were effectively in control of most of western and central Europe. This control had been extended to Hungry, Rumania, and Bulgaria, and, following the invasion of Yugoslavia and Greece (including Crete), German military occupation reach south to the Mediterranean.

Stalin and Molotov considered that the Germans were militarily stretched just to maintain control of the land they had occupied and that Hitler continued to be distracted by preparation for the invasion of Britain. This misled them into adopting a more aggressive strategy, as Stalin sought control of the Baltic States and eastern parts of the Balkans. Up to spring 1941 Stalin and Hitler engaged in a diplomatic relationship based on mutual flattery, with German expansion in Europe being coded by them as a series of justified 'defensive measures'.

But Hitler progressively lost patience with Russian military activities, especially its occupation of Lithuania on the Prussian border, and in the background was his long-term aim of turning on the communist Soviet Union. Ambition and impatience (and months of secret military planning) came together and, in the early hours of 22nd June 'Operation Barbarossa' was launched. The army that rumbled across the Russian border on that morning was the largest military force that had ever been assembled - 3.5 million men in 190 divisions, 3,600 tanks, and 2,700 airplanes, with a vast supply system ready to enable the advance to maintain its momentum. Hitler's strategy, based on the highly mobile panzer tank-led Blitzkrieg, involved the army advancing on three separate fronts, each aiming to destroy the Red Army forces prior to the wider occupation of Russian territory. Such was his dislike of communism that Hitler directed his generals to ignore the 'normal' conventions of warfare - in particular the Hague Convention - German officers were directed to be brutal and ruthless and not to let any misplaced 'gentlemanly ideology' inhibit their fighting spirit. Of 5 million Russian soldiers taken prisoner during the whole campaign (to 1945) 3 million died and many of these had been brutally shot down when trying to surrender.

By early autumn each of the three German fighting groups had advanced deep into Russian territory, with Leningrad in the north, Moscow in the centre, and Kiev in the south, each under threat. Massive casualties suffered by the Red Army were of little concern to Stalin and most Soviet generals and, in terms of a wider strategy; the retreat had made a useful contribution to absorbing the German momentum. The 60,000 German casualties (announced in German newspapers) within the first six weeks did have a significant impact on public morale in Germany.

Hitler's invasion plans were deficient, due in part to the poor quality of intelligence reports in their gross underestimation of

Russian military resources; the estimate was for about 5,000 tanks when the actual number was 20,000. Hitler also believed that Stalin and the Bolshevik regime had but a tenuous hold on the country and so could not withstand the pressure of a successful invasion. But, as autumn drew on, the Germans faced two key factors which first slowed then halted their advance. These were the steady reinforcement of Russian positions and the beginning of the 'Russian' winter weather; the same two factors that made such a crucial difference to Napoleon's 'Grand Army' in 1812. The rains began in October, turning unpaved roads into muddy tracks and so conditions unsuitable for mechanized units. The temperature dropped to well below zero, causing fuel and water to freeze; with frosts so hard that even just starting tanks and other vehicles became a problem. The freezing cold and blizzard conditions impacted on troop morale, and frostbite would kill 112,000 German soldiers by the campaign's end.

By late 1941, the Germans, their Axis partners, and in the north the Finns, had advanced on all three fronts, with Leningrad almost surrounded in the north and the central army group less than 40 miles (fighting in the forests abutting the western suburbs) from central Moscow. But the Russians had been gradually building their military capacity; consolidating their forces in preparation for a counterattack on the Moscow front. It was a counteroffensive led by General Georgi Zhukov, with 100 Red Army divisions trained and equipped to fight in cold weather at his disposal, being launched along a 200 mile long front. The German resistance was determined, but their supply lines were over-extended and they were steadily pushed back, losing 200,000 men killed and as many as 700,000 wounded. In addition to the actual losses, this action was a bitter blow for Hitler and the German High Command as, for the first time, an army of the Third Reich had suffered a significant setback on the battlefield. The strategy of Blitzkrieg and the notion of an invincible Wehrmacht had been shown to be at least an exaggeration.

In the north, the Germans and Finns had been more successful with the City of Leningrad being almost completely surrounded by September; so began a siege that was to last for 872 days. A period during which 641,000 civilians died from disease, starvation, or from exposure to the bitterly cold winters of 1941, 42, and 43. The 200,000 Red Army defenders held out against 750,000 soldiers of the German and Finnish forces until June 1944 when the siege was lifted.

During 1940/41 Hitler's action against Britain had continued but with little significant impact. On balance, even the mass bombing of British cities (the 'Blitz') had little/no effect on industrial output, and in general made the population more determined to resist. And up to about early 1942 the German navy was unable to sink a sufficient amount of British shipping to make supplies an issue. Indeed in most naval engagements with the British - the flagship German battleships Admiral Graff Spee sunk in 1939 the Bismarck sunk in 1941 and with the Tirpitz badly damaged in 1944 – the German navy suffered the heavier losses. Until the British were able to devise ways of dealing with them, the 200 odd German 'U-boat' submarines active in the Atlantic would pose the most serious threat; sinking 1,664 ships in 1942 alone.

Throughout 1941, Hitler and Ribbentrop had been urging the Japanese leaders to launch an attack on Allied interests in South East Asia. The Germans considered that a threat to US and British interests in the Far East would divert US resources away from supporting Britain; the lease-led scheme, and food and fuel supplies sent across the Atlantic, were providing a lifeline in supporting Britain's and later Russia's resistance. Japan had for at least a decade been frustrated, mainly by US and Britain (extending to an economic blockade), in its attempt to gain access to south Asian raw materials and markets for its manufactured goods. By October 1941 the new government, led by General Töjö Hideki, felt it had no alternative but to go to war. Hitler's success in Europe, based on fast moving mechanized forces, encouraged the Japanese government to think that they could replicate this success in the Far East.

The Japanese attacked the important US naval base at Pearl Harbour (in Hawaii) on 7th December. Within days of the first attack Japanese bombers had also attacked the US Cavite naval base in the Philippines and a number of important US airfields, also in the Philippines (including Clark and Iba airfields). Taken together, these raids inflicted considerable damage to US warships and their air-force, with about half of the US aircraft capability being put out of action.

What has been presented by US and western media and most historians as a 'surprise attack' (by the 'typically' cruel and devious Japanese) is misleading; true in terms of day and place but quite predictable given the way in which a militarized Japan was been treated. If fact, prior to the Pearl Habour action, Henry Stimson, the US Secretary for War, aware of the economic and diplomatic pressure they were putting on Japan (specifically in relation to its occupation of China and the economic blockade), noted in his diary that they, the US, should be seeking a way to 'maneuver' Japan into firing the first shot.

The week following the attack on Pearl Harbour saw extensive Japanese military action elsewhere in the region. On 8th December the Japanese were bombing Hong Kong, which surrendered to a land force on 25th. On 9th December Bangkok in Thailand had fallen; enabling the rear-guard protection of Japanese forces as these moved down the Malaya peninsula, taking Singapore at its southern tip in early February. It was at Singapore that the British suffered the humiliation of having 90,000 troops surrender to a smaller Japanese force. On 10th December the Japanese landed at Luzon in the Philippines and had taken Manila by the 2nd January 1942. With its modern navy, supported by a range of air cover, and a familiarity with the waters of the South China Sea and the western Pacific, the Japanese invasion fleet easily beat off an Allied attempt to intercept it in the Battle of the Java Sea on February 27th.

By March 1942, the Japanese were occupying or otherwise in control of an extensive region. One extending from Burma and Sumatra in the west to the Marshall Islands in the east - south as far as the Solomon Islands and north to part of the large Sakhalin Island and northern Manchuria. Within but five months the Japanese had erupted out of their homeland and inflicted military defeats on the US, China, Britain, and on the other Europeans nations that had been in possession of colonies in south-east Asia. In doing so they gained access to sources of the valuable industrial materials they had been seeking.

When, in early spring 1942, the US General Douglas MacArthur was made supreme commander of the Allied forces in the south-west Pacific region (Admiral Chester Nimitz had a similar role in the south Pacific area). His task at that time was more about containing the Japanese military rather than launching any significant counter-offensive.

To the west, more German military resources had to be deployed to assist the generally militarily inept Italian land forces in southern Europe and North Africa. The Italian government had declared war on Britain and France in May 1940. With Mussolini intent on emulating Hitler's success in both gaining territory, as well as military glory. The Italian people mostly lacked much enthusiasm for war and the military hierarchy cautioned on the lack of preparedness for progressing any lengthy campaign. Italian forces did initially defeat the British forces in Somaliland and occupied most of East Africa. But an attempt to invade Greece ended in humiliating defeat at the hands of brave and tenacious Greek resistance fighters.

The main theatre of war for the Italians was North Africa. Where they began their campaign in early September 1940, using their base in occupied Libya from which to launch an invasion of Egypt. Here the poor quality of the Italian military leadership was clearly exposed as their troops were fairly easily defeated by British and Australian defenders, with 130,000 being taken prisoner. Mussolini had depleted his supreme command of some of the more able officers and promoted a number of inexperienced officers. Men whose loyalty to Il Duce was the primary qualification for their gaining a high command.

In February 1941 the German General Erwin Rommel, with two divisions of German troops (soon be known as the Afrika Korps) and two divisions of Italian troops, landed at Tripoli (Libya). From where they regrouped and, with fast-moving mechanized divisions in the vanguard, they pushed eastwards. Rommel's advance made swift progress, pushing the British and Dominion forces back as far as Tobruk. But here he was unable to dislodge the 14,000 Australian (9th Division) defenders; losing momentum, due in part to his supply-lines becoming overstretched.

Rommel managed to push on to Benghazi (in what had become an Allied rout) by 4th April but he was unable to take Tobruk. A strategically important port that could have been a key supply base for the Axis forces; without it supply was from Tripoli 1500 km behind their lines. The British made two unsuccessful attempts to lift the siege but they were at least able to supply and reinforce Tobruk from the sea. After the initial attempt to capture the town had been beaten off most of the Australians were replaced by British and Polish troops as the port settled into a siege that would last for 241 days, until November 1941.

In addition to supporting the Italian ambitions in North Africa, Hitler had his own more strategic motives for German involvement. If the Suez Canal could be taken then British access to the Far East would be disrupted and from Egypt the Germans could work their way north-east to take control of vital middle-east oilfields.

After a lull in the fighting, during which the Allied army regrouped before launching a well-supplied counteroffensive (Nov. 1941 - Operation Crusader - which also lifted the siege of Tobruk). Then, following a series of fiercely fought tank battles, the outnumbered (in tanks) Axis force was pushed west as far as El Aghelia by the year's end. Here, the Axis force rested, re-grouped, were resupplied and, by early January 1942, Rommel was again ready to launch his force eastward. This time he did manage to capture Tobruk (gaining a useful amount of military supplies and taking 35,000 prisoners), taking Benghazi by end January, and reaching Alexandra (Gazala) by early February. Within but six weeks of the start of Rommel's offensive the Allied forces were desperately trying to hold a defensive position at el Alamein within 50 miles of the outskirts of Alexandra. The first battle of el-Alamein (1-27 July) halted Rommel's advance, partly due to his troops being exhausted. Now the soldiers of both armies were at a stand-off, with their supplies running low and, apart from occasional skirmishes and some probing, the next four months was a period of rebuilding military capacity.

In the spring it had seemed that Hitler's ambition to gain control of the Suez Canal would be achieved within weeks. But Rommel's force had been depleted by the withdrawal of some troops back to Europe and, due partly to effective British naval action against German shipping, his reserves of fuel and ammunition were low. The allied leadership was aware of the implications of losing control of the canal and northern Egypt so sent sufficient reinforcements to allow the Allied forces to prepare for a counteroffensive. By this time very few Axis supply ships – carrying tanks, fuel, and ammunition - were able to avoid the attention of British warships.

In contrast to Rommel's force being poorly re-supplied at the time that fighting restarted, the newly appointed commander of the 8th Army, General Bernard Montgomery, was in a much better position. He had almost six times as many tanks (1230 to 210), nearly three times the number of troops (230,000 to 80,000), as well as overwhelming air superiority, than Rommel. And, due to ill-health, Rommel at this time was recuperating in Austria.

The fighting started again in October (the Allies Operation 'Torch') and it was the 2nd Battle of el Alamein (23 Oct - 4 Nov.) that began to turn the tide of the campaign decisively in favour of the Allies. Their tanks and other armoured units broke through the Axis lines and Rommel (who had been ordered to return to Africa), running short of fuel and ammunition, planned for an ordered retreat that would allow him to preserve his force for a later offensive. But Hitler ordered him to hold the line; a militarily inept order that resulted in avoidable losses. When even Hitler saw this was a mistake, the delayed retreat was less well-ordered than it might have been. A retreat that forced Rommel all the way back to the Libya's western border with Tunisia.

Meanwhile, more British and US forces had been gathered in Gibraltar in preparation for an invasion (a wider, strategic, element of Operation 'Torch') to the west of Tripoli. In overall command was the US General Dwight D. Eisenhower. In November 1942 this invasion fleet cruised east into the Mediterranean and landed troops in a number of locations in Algeria and Morocco. This region of North Africa was controlled by France and although the invasion force initially encountered some resistance from troops still loyal to the Vichy regime this was soon overcome. After re-grouping and consolidating their position, the allied troops advanced eastwards towards Rommel's force.

Now trapped between two armies, and with the Allies having superiority in air and naval support, defeat for the Axis force was now a matter of when rather than if; and the when was completed, after much hard fighting, in May 1943. Rommel had by then resigned his command and on the Axis surrender 250,000 German and Italian soldiers were taken prisoner. The North African campaign had tied down 1,000,000 Allied service personal and their support (often under fire) had been a massive logistical operation, but now these experienced military units and the supply line organization could be directed towards southern Europe.

Nationalism can be one of a number of primary 'contexts' that foster the expression of evil; elements of this context include the construction of some national mythology claiming estimable characteristics for one's own nation, and assigning derogatory characteristics to others. It's interesting to consider the veracity of one of the latter that emerged on the Allied side during the war, and that endured well beyond it.

Italian servicemen have often been subject to superficial assessment as to their fighting ability but, in addition to poor quality leadership and poor training, they also, during most WWII engagements with the allies were armed with markedly inferior weaponry. Even so, there were many examples of Italian bravery and of their fighting skills. Probably the most well-known being the soldiers that were sent to fight with the Germans on the eastern front. Here the mountain troops of the three 'Alpina' divisions (Tridentina, Julia, Cuneense) stand out, especially for their role in the bitterly fought Battle of Stalingrad. Two whole divisions (Julia and Cuneense) were destroyed, and the third badly mauled, as they fought a determined rear-guard action against a much larger Russian force. And, following a number of fiercely fought engagements in Northern Africa, both the British commander General Alexander and the German commander General Rommel praised the fighting qualities of Italian soldiers. National identity does not define degree of bravery, but self-serving nationalist mythologies do. The potential coward and the potential hero lies within each of us, if mostly we just share a self-protective ordinariness - 19th and 20th century industrial wars have invariably been won by the best equipped, largest forces; bravery and cowardice can be features of both the 'victors' and of the 'defeated' equally.

In relation to evil, bravery as an attribute might just make the killing, the expression of evil, worse - just take the 'brave' crews of the German Luftwaffe and British Bomber Command - yes, young men knowingly risking their lives each time they set off on a mission - young men hailed by their own side as brave, be-medaled if they live or die - and yet these missions would flatten city streets and kill hundreds, possibly thousands, of old men, women, children, and babies - what price bravery, paid for in a currency of burnt and twisted flesh?

In North Africa it was the ability to reinforce and sustain an army i.e. 'logistics' that made a fundamental difference to the outcome, not any asymmetric indicator of bravery between combatants.

When the Africa campaign was over, and with the Allies holding the naval superiority across the Mediterranean, military planning turned attention to Italy with its access to southern Germany. The Italian campaign began with the invasion of the large island of Sicily. A seaborne landing saw the first units, of what would be a force of nearly half a million men, landed on the island. The bulk of this force was made up of the British 8th Army under Montgomery's command, and the US 7th Army under the command of Maj. Gen. George S. Patton. The German defenses were relatively weak, with the main resistance coming from panzer tank units. Once he could assess his military vulnerability the German commander, Field Marshall Albert Kesselring, decided to evacuate his surviving force back to the Italian mainland.

The Italian government had lost confidence in Mussolini and he was forced to resign at the end of the month, with the King appointing Marshall Pietro Badoglio as the new head of government. By early April the Allies followed close behind the German withdrawal, crossing the Straits of Messina to establish a bridgehead on the 'toe' of southern Italy. The state of the roads and stiff German resistance made progress difficult. but a second landing further north at Salerno stretched the defenders resources and Naples was taken by the 1st October. Further reinforcements came with another landing on the south-eastern coast that advanced north, capturing Brindisi within two weeks. The Italian King and his government fled south to the safety of Allied hands and then on 29th September Italy surrendered and itself declared war on Germany. Now the German strategy in Italy was to do as much as possible to defend Germany's southern flank. Given this, Kesselring determined on a strategy of military deployment that would make the Allied advance as costly as possibly. A key aspect of this was a defensive line - the Gustav Line - with Monte Cassino at its south-western end. Initially this line of defense held the allied advance and it took a number of combined assaults by the attacking forces to enable a break-through, allowing Rome to be taken by 5th June.

This advance had left the town of Monte Cassino as a smoking monument to the destructive power of the shelling and mass bombing the town had endured. Continued Allied progress was hard-fought, as the German troops put up stiff resistance, buying time for another line of defense to be established across the Italian peninsular - the Gothic Line - just to the south of La Spezia crossing the Apennine mountain range to the Adriatic coast north of Ravenna in the east. Due partly to continuing well organized resistance and the loss of troops redeployed to the newly opened western front in France, the US and British forces made only slow progress. From August the Allies did launch a number of, mostly localized, offensives including the 8th Army's Operation 'Olive' on the Adriatic side of the line on 25th of the month. On the western side, a mainly US force broke through to the City of Bologna, with Forli, Ravenna, San Marino and Rimini, being under Allied control by early November - The Allied force facing the Germans was composed of units of Indian, Canadian, Greek, and New Zealand troops, along with the US, British, and a Free Italian unit. Now the winter set in and this, along with the mountainous terrain, halted any significant further Allied progress. It would be after a spring offensive mounted the following year that the Germans and remnants of Fascist Italy's forces (RSI) finally surrendered on 2nd May.

During this period, Italian Partisans had been harrying the German communication lines and the on the 27th April they captured Mussolini and some fellow fascists as they fled north. Il Duce and his fascist companions were shot by firing squad two days later with his body being hung upside down from a lamppost in the Piazza Loreto in the centre of Milan; an ignominious end to a vainglorious man.

On the Russian front, the government had the ability to mobilize far more military manpower than Germans military strategists had planned for and its expanding Red Army was being supplied by an effective armaments industry, mostly located to the east of the Urals. At the Tehran Conference of late November 1943, Stalin, Churchill, and Roosevelt, had agreed a broad coordinated strategy, intent on defeating the Nazis. Two key aspects of this being that the Russians would aim to push the Germans back from the east and that the US and Britain (and some 'Free' units of nationals from occupied countries) would plan for a landing in France during 1944, so pushing against the Germans from the west.

The German offensive on Kursk in summer 1943 was the last offensive on a similar scale to those of 1940 and 1942 - and here they were fought to a standstill, losing a large amount of men and equipment. The tide of war in Eastern Europe was turning and from January 1944 the Red Army slowly began to take the overall military initiative. The Germans and their Allies initially proved resilient and for the first half of 1944 they managed some successful localized counter-offensives. But only in a few places did these actions temporarily delay the Red Army's progressive advance west. When the western allies landed on French beaches in June 1944, some German divisions were transferred from the eastern front to reinforce their western forces. A change that really only accelerated the inevitable as Russian forces gained momentum on a broad front - they reached Warsaw by January 1945, occupied the Baltic States, reached Budapest by February, Vienna by March, and in early April were pouring into Konigsberg in East Prussia.

Throughout the early months of 1944, the Allies had been building troop numbers and stores of military equipment in locations across southern England - this was facilitated by the Allied navy having gained the ability to significantly reduce the effectiveness of what had been a serious U-Boat threat to Atlantic supply convoys. On 6th June 1944 an Allied army embarked on the task of opening a western front on the mainland of Europe in 'Operation Overlord'. This force was composed of British, US, Canadian, and the 'free' units of countries occupied by the Nazis; French, Polish, Norwegian, Czech, and others. The initial landing, of about 175,000 troops, took place on five beaches along the Normandy Coast. Once the beach-heads had been established, and the port of Cherbourg (and later the large port of Antwerp) captured, 1.5 million men and millions of tons of military equipment would follow within a short time. Before the war's end 3 million Allied military personal would be deployed to the western front. US General Eisenhower was in overall command, with Britain's General Montgomery as operational commander. Operation Overlord was, taken overall, a text book invasion - the defenders were unsure where the landings would take place, so had to spread their resources to cover most of the north-west coast of France. Heavy Allied bombing degraded German transport and supply lines, with fighter aircraft ensuring air superiority for the invading force. In addition, from 1943, the Allies had had access to a stream of intelligence reports based on code machines (British 'Ultra', was especially useful in 'listening in' to U-Boat and command communications, and the US had their own 'Magic' code braker), and code braking experts who been able to break the en-coded forms of German (and Japanese) communications. This allowed the Allied High Command reasonably accurate information of German troop deployments. Even so, the coastal defenses, organized by the now Field Marshall Rommel, provided a major challenge to the invading forces.

The first six weeks following the initial landing saw hard fighting along the new front. With a decisive breakthrough coming in late July early August, when the US army reached Avranches - the Free French were allowed the honour of advancing into Paris on 25th August - a series of German counterattacks failed to hold the progressive, if uneven, advance of the main British force to the north and the US forces through the centre and to the south. In October, the Germans had to surrender a large number of troops and an amount of war materials at Aachen.

As the winter approached the pace of advance slowed and on 16th December. the Germans launched a massive surprise offensive.

Hitler's plan was to force a way through the allied lines, intending to capture the extensive port facilities of Antwerp. Gaining this would enable the Germans to cut the main supply route for the allies and so reduce their capacity to advance, allowing time for the German forces to regroup. The two factors of surprise, and low cloud forcing USAF and RAF planes to remain on the ground, assisted the large highly mobile force that the Germans had mustered. Following a two hour bombardment with heavy artillery, units of tanks and armoured vehicles led the assault, against the US front line. During the first two days of fierce fighting the Germans advanced, gaining a 60 mile 'bulge' in the Allied front. But the Allies had taken up fairly strong defensive positions and, having been fighting for months, were psychologically prepared to absorb the German onslaught. After the first two days the cloud base lifted allowing the Allies to exploit their air superiority. Another critical factor in halting the German offensive was their running out of the fuel vital to maintain their mechanized momentum; a shortage due in part to allied bombing of the German supply lines. This offensive in the Ardennes, the 'Battle of the Bulge' (as it became known), was to be the final action in which any German advance would be made and from now they would be fighting whilst in continuous retreat. The action had cost the Germans 100,000 men killed or wounded and the loss of a massive amount of material, including many panzer tanks being abandoned as they run out of fuel; experienced troops and munitions that they were unable to replace. This action also resulted in 81,000 US soldiers being killed. From early 1945 the Allied advance was renewed and the last major military objective, the River Rhine, was reached by April 1945, with the first crossing being made at the Remagen (Ludendorff) Bridge in March.

The Allies now knew that they were approaching the final stages of the war, and the US/British forces advancing steadily from the west and the Russians from the east, were each determined to overrun as much territory as possible. This, in order to strengthen their position for what they knew would be difficult negotiations, on borders and political influence, once the war had ended.

Since the initial landings in June 1944 there had been a sense of urgency on the allied side as intelligence suggested the possibility of the Germans having the capacity to develop an 'Atomic bomb'. In 1938 the German physicists, Otto Hahn and Fritz Strassmann, had discovered that the bombardment of uranium with neutrons caused the uranium atoms to split, and that a product of this 'nuclear fission' being the release of energy - it would be the release of this energy in an uncontrolled chain reaction that would provide the enormous destructive power of the Atomic Bomb. There was also the more immediate concern with the introduction of the pilotless V1 then V2 rockets, carrying high explosive cargos, mainly targeting London from early June 1944 to end of March 1945. These were the first long-range guided ballistic missiles, capable of speeds over 3,000 miles per hr, carrying 2,000lbs of high explosives; on impact they would cause a huge blast-wave capable of destroying whole rows of London's tightly packed terraced houses. A new weapon had been introduced into the world's military killing capability. One with implications for future weapon delivery systems.

At the end of April Red Army soldiers were fighting on the outskirts of Berlin and by 2nd May the City, now mostly reduced to rubble by Russian shelling and allied blanket bombing, was surrounded. By which time Adolf Hitler and his (then wife) Eva Braun had committed suicide (as had Goebbels and Himmler) and it was left to the German Chief-of-Staff, General Alfred Jodl, to sign the document of unconditional surrender and so both symbolically and actually bring an end to the Third Reich. When the fighting in Europe ceased Russian forces had met their western Allies just east of the River Elbe.

The series of conferences involving the leaders and foreign secretaries of the three leading Allied countries (United States, Britain, and the Soviet Union) held at Tehran, Yalta, and Potsdam, saw each party endeavouring to persuade, cajole, or bully, the others into a post-war redrawing of national borders, and to define areas of control and influence, in line with the leaders' perspective of their own national interests. Little interest was taken of the views of the mass of people whose political future was being 'negotiated'. Soon after the war's end the outcome of the conferences was seen to impact adversely on the people of the Baltic States and on those of Greece and Italy, and with a significant portion of the world's nations being divided into two antagonistic political and military groupings.

In the south-east Asian theatre of conflict the Japanese expansionist strategy had been contained by a combination of national forces, but predominantly with the US taking the lead. The Allied command began to formulate a plan to roll back the Japanese occupation of islands in the western Pacific and South China Sea (island by island);

beginning with the Solomon Islands the Bismarck Archipelago, and the large island of New Guinea.

The initiative on where to begin was taken out of US hands when, in early July 1942, the Japanese occupied the island of Guadalcanal at the southern end of the Solomons where they soon began to construct what would have been a strategically important air-base. The US response was to land the 1st Marine Corps on the island. The Japanese resistance was determined and over the next few weeks each side sent reinforcements. In late August the Japanese launched an attack on the marine's beach-head and so began a period of intense fighting. Initially, each side was able to deploy about an equivalent number of troops (roughly 22,000 each).

At sea, in a series of minor engagements the Imperial navy lost more ships than the US navy. Then, in the Battle of Tassafaronga, the Japanese suffered very heavy losses, including eight destroyers sunk. The US naval superiority in the region resulted in Japan not being able to land significant reinforcements of men and materials on Guadalcanal. Only 4,000 of the 12,500 Japanese troops sent were actually landed. Whereas the US was able to land a substantially greater number of troops. By January 1943 the Allies had double the number of troops than the Japanese and, accepting the reality on the ground, the remaining Japanese force evacuated the island. By this time a force of US and Australians had also staged and consolidated landings on the east coast of Papua (the eastern side of the strategically important New Guinea). These two successful engagements secured the Allied supply lines from Australia and New Zealand.

By mid 1942, the Allies had moved on to open a new front on the Aleutian Island group located about 1,500 miles to the north-east of Japan; on the southern limits of the Bering Sea. On gaining the islands by late spring 1943, the US was able to construct air-bases that enabled bombers to reach targets in Japanese occupied islands in the Kuril chain further south; lying between the Aleutians and mainland Japan.

During the summer the US had continued to advance through the Solomon Islands, often meeting fierce resistance as they progressed. The Japanese fought hard over the island of Vela Lavella but by October they were facing defeat and so evacuated their surviving force from the island. Defending the Solomon Islands had cost the Japanese 10,000 killed with the US losing 1,150 men. The US moved on to the large island of New Britain with the town of Talasea being taken by March 1944. During this period there had been a number of intense naval engagements in the area and although both sides suffered losses the numerical balance favoured the Allies. At this stage of the war the Allies could more easily replace their lost shipping than could the Japanese.

From now the Japanese high command accepted that they would be waging a defensive war and so adopted a broad strategy of strengthening their strategic positions and counterattacking when opportunity allowed. From late 1943 to spring 1944 they endeavoured to reinforce their bases in a line running from western New Guinea to the Caroline Island chain about 1000 miles to the north east. The US command were now aware of the military limitations of the Japanese and were more confident in the fighting abilities of their own navy, air-force, and marine units, in the tropical conditions they were encountering.

Invasion of the Gilbert Islands began in late November 1943 and by Feb 1944 the Allies were attacking the Marshall Islands and bombing air-bases on the Caroline Islands. The impact of the latter being the destruction of 200 air-craft, an outcome that in effect nullified the strategic value of these islands to the Japanese. The next objective would be the strategically important island chain of the Marianas, beyond which would be mainland Japan with little but sea between them. Keenly aware of the need to retain the Marianas, the Japanese poured reinforcements into the area. They now had over 1000 land-based aircraft, with another 450 based on nine aircraft carriers, and all of this within a theater of conflict taking in the Marianas, the Carolines, and western New Guinea. The US offensive began in June, involving 500 ships and over 125,000 troops. They landed two marine divisions on Saipan Island (Marianas) on the 15th, a force facing 30,000 Japanese defenders determined to resist. The US force was able to significantly reinforce its marine units and by mid July, after very heavy fighting, Japanese resistance had been overcome. From the 19th June a significant naval engagement had began between the Japanese Combined Fleet and the larger US 5th Fleet, in what became known as the Battle of the Philippine Sea. An engagement in which the Japanese lost 400 planes and 2 air-craft carriers (the US lost 130 planes). Taking the Marianas had cost the US force 4,750 men killed but the Japanese lost 46,000 killed or taken prisoner. From the Marianas, the long range B-29 Super-fortress bombers could strike at the Japanese homeland. Such was the seriousness of these defeats that the Japanese cabinet led by Admiral Tōjō resigned, to be replaced by a new government led by General Koiso Kuniaki.

On July 27th/28th the US high command, including MacArthur and Nimitz, met with President Roosevelt in Honolulu to consider their position. The most significant outcome being that they decided that the next major US objective would be to expel the Japanese from the Philippine Islands; so, edging steadily closer to Japan proper.

The US chose the relatively small Philippine island of Leyte to begin this new campaign and on the 20th October they landed four divisions, in support of which they had also deployed a large surface fleet (under the command of Nimitz) to the area. As expected, the Japanese defenders had established strong defensive positions and the fighting across the island was fierce. At the time of this land-based conflict there was also an intense navel engagement, the 'Battle of Leyte Gulf'. The outcome of this being a massive defeat for the Japanese Imperial navy, establishing a dominance for the US that would be maintained throughout the rest of the war.

Leyte was taken by December1944 and by early January 1945 the US forces had taken the neighbouring island of Mindoro and had landed marines on the west coast of the most important Philippine island of Luzan. Once again, the Japanese troops put up stiff resistance but the capital, Manila, fell to the US force on 3d March. The US take-over of the Philippines was aided by an indigenous resistance movement that had been harassing the Japanese. The loss of the Philippines was a significant blow to the Japanese, a loss compounded in July when a mainly Australian force landed on the large island of Borneo that, working its way south, was able to cut off Japanese access to the very important oil-fields on the southern tip of the island.

It was during the Battle of Leyte Gulf that the Japanese launched their first concerted 'Kamikaze' mission undertaken by the newly formed 'Special Attack Unit'. The first attack using planes to be flown on purpose into military targets had been against an Australian ship (NMSA 'Australia') when 30 sailors had been killed. From October 1944 there would be over 2,500 planes piloted to destruction on these suicide missions. The (Kamikaze -'divine wind') pilots were between the ages of 19-23, most of whom had volunteered to die on behalf of the 'divine' emperor, but many others had come under significant pressure to volunteer. The use of this type of weapon included speed boats, gliders, and even submarines, all laden with high explosives. The most extreme form that these suicide missions took was the use of the then heaviest battleship in the world armed with the largest guns ever mounted on a warship. This, the flagship 'Yamato', set off in early April 1944, on a suicide mission to Okinawa with only sufficient fuel for the outward journey. Its orders were to run aground on the island and then keep fighting until destroyed. But the US was able to detect the ship on route and it was sunk on 7th April by carrier-based air-craft before it reached Okinawa, with the loss of almost all of the crew. This act reflected the desperation of the Japanese high command, most of whom had by now realized the parlous situation their country was in.

Up to the spring 1943 the British led forces to the west had made little progress in Burma. Then, in May, they reorganized their Far East command structure, with vice Admiral Louis Mountbatten being appointed supreme commander of the British and Dominion force in south-east Asia. The most significant set-back suffered by the Japanese in this theatre of conflict was the outcome of their attempt to invade north-east India; began in March 1944 and named 'Operation U-Go'. Here a series of connected engagements have been recorded as the Battle of Imphal and the Battle of Kohima. The Allied forces had the advantage in terms of air-support and tank numbers and, following a period of at times heavy fighting, by July the Japanese (commanded by Lieutenant General Kawabe) were forced to withdraw. They had lost 30,500 men killed (many by starvation and disease) and 30,000 wounded. In addition to their suffering the biggest defeat in the war up to that this time, these engagements also significantly reduced their ability to defend their occupation of Burma.

In an offensive the following year a force composed of Chinese, US, and British Commonwealth soldiers, led by General Slim, advanced south from northern Burma. Crossing the Irrawaddy River, these units made steady progress against the Japanese. They attacked the strategically important (a centre of Japanese communications) town of Meiktila, overcoming the defenders by 3rd March 1945. Mandalay was taken by the 13th as this disparate military force advanced towards Rangoon. There was a short pause in the fighting due to seasonal rain, with the Allies able to benefit from their more secure supply lines. As the rains eased in late April the Allied advance began again with Rangoon being taken by an Indian division on 1st. May. At this time the Allies had been advancing on three broad fronts. There were the British and Commonwealth (Indian and African) force on the western flank/side. In the centre there was the X-Force led by US General Joseph S. Stilwell (Chief-of-Staff to the Chinese nationalist Army). Due to disagreements with the Chinese nationalist leader Chiang Kai-Shek, Stilwell was recalled in October 1944, to be replaced by Lieutenant General Daniel Sultan. Sultan's force was mainly composed of US troops, supplemented with three Chinese Nationalist divisions (trained and equipped by the US) and a unit, 'Merrill's Marauders', trained by the British (on the model of General Orde Wingate's 'Chindits') in jungle fighting techniques. This group advanced south through the centre of the country with its main objective being to gain control of the strategically important Burma Road. Then, following pressure from the US, Chiang reluctantly agreed to deploy a substantial proportion of his Yunnan Army group (15 divisions of 175,000 men) to the Burma campaign. This, the Y-Force, advanced south on the eastern flank of Sultan's central force. During what had overall been a four month retreat south the two Japanese armies involved had suffered heavy casualties, each losing over 30% of their fighting strength. These losses would be compounded with another 10,000 troops killed as the fighting continued into June and early July, by when the Japanese were confined to the Tenasserim province on the eastern costal strip at the northern end of the Malay Peninsula.

The dropping of the Atomic bombs on Hiroshima and Nagasaki and the surrender that followed would make the final stages of the Burma campaign a mopping up operation rather than seeing any further significant military action.

In the main theatre of the Far-Eastern war the US, at the same time as it was consolidating its hold on the Philippines, had advanced north to the island of Iwo-Jima. Here the 20,000 Japanese defenders, commanded by Lieutenant General Kuribayashi Tadamichi were well-dug in and prepared to offer strong resistance to an attempted invasion. An invasion that began on 19th February 1945 with the landing of US marines. The island was overrun by mid March, following fighting during which 6,000 marines were killed, and at sea some US ships were lost to Kamikaze missions.

It was about this time that the US high command took a decision to bomb Japan into submission. In order to progress this they increased the intensity of the air-raid missions from bases in the Marianas, and began to use napalm fire-bombs alongside the high explosives and to switch to night-time raids in order to accentuate the terror.

The next island target, and on one plan the last prior to an invasion of the Japanese homeland, would be Okinawa. This, the largest of the Ryukyu Island chain is located just 350 miles from Japan. After taking a couple of the small outlying islands in late March, the marines invaded the main island on the 1st April. This was a major action, with 60,000 marines taking part in the initial landing. It would take nearly four months of grueling fighting to take Okinawa; with 12,000 US and 100,000 Japanese troops killed.

Now air bases in Okinawa could add to the capacity of the US to reach Japanese cities. One of the most deadly raids targeted Tokyo on the night of 10th/11th March when a quarter of the City's (wooden) housing was destroyed, with 80,000 civilians killed and about 1,000,000 made homeless. This short period of the intentional mass bombing of civilian populations saw similarly destructive air-raids on 60 other cities and large towns - including Osaka, Kobe, Nagoya, Yokohama, and Toyoma. In effect the ordinary Japanese people were specifically targeted to be murdered and terrorized as they paid the price of having an increasingly militarized leadership. One whose rise to power was in large part due to the unfair economic treatment of Japan by western colonial powers in the 1930s.

Given the parlous state of Japan in June/July - with a beaten military, and a land of smashed and smoking cities- it was clear that surrender was the only reasonable option. But the decision taken at Potsdam, for unconditional surrender caused consternation within the Japanese leadership; with some of the senior military still seeking to prolong the conflict rather than surrender; some arguing for surrender, and the rest being undecided. It was this time of Japanese vacillation and US determination to finish the war, that sealed the fate of the people of Hiroshima and Nagasaki. It was two 'Atomic devises' released (ignited 1,000ft) above these two cities by the crews of B-29s based on the Marianas that would bring a hellish end to Japanese resistance.

This war had seen a culturally obedient nation led to destruction by a deluded military in the service of some fantastical view of the Emperor's divinity. But, as with Germany, the Allied nations (official and populist) post-war demonization of the Japanese nation was an attempt to erase the bravery of many Japanese people who had opposed the war. The main organized opposition to militarism, the Trades Unions and the Communist Party, had been suppressed in the lead up to conflict but their ex-members (those not in prison) were amongst those who were prepared to offer some, if mainly passive, resistance. Resistance that took the form of such activities as strikes (over 400 in 1943), industrial sabotage (especially noted for aircraft manufacturing), and mass absenteeism. In terms of specific organizations, there was the 'Japanese People's Anti-War League' formed in 1942, and even within the military there was the 'League to Raise the Consciousness of Japanese Troops' founded 1939. Diary entries and letters home from troops (especially those conscripted - the 'tokkatai') offer more evidence of opposition to war. A significant number of Japanese Buddhists, perhaps unsurprisingly given its (humanistic) ethical stance, also opposed the war. As we saw with Germany, the Allied propaganda sought to frame the Japanese as being a nation of 'evil villains', and so deserving of the blanket bombing and other indignities that its ordinary people were subjected too.

In the greater Balkan region of Europe, similar to what happened in the First World War, conflict was used to cover an opportunity for some groups to progress their own ethnic-based agendas; primarily in terms of seeking revenge for real and assumed past atrocities, or to progress nationalistic aims, at times with the active collusion of the Nazis.

One more notorious action was that undertaken by groups of Albanians who had sided with the Axis countries. Supported by Germany and Italy, they themselves turned into the perpetrators of genocide in order to progress the aim of a greater Albania, which would include most of Kosovo. Between 1941-43, a Kosovan-Albanian 'police force' (the Vulnetara) established by the Germans, progressed the 'cleansing' of the region of Serbs, Jews, Gypsies, in fact any non-Albanians were liable to be interned, deported, or murdered. Then in April 1944 an Albanian Waffen SS unit – the 21st Waffen SS Mountain Division (Skanderberg Division), mostly composed of Albanian Moslems and some Albanian Roman Catholics; an unruly bunch of misfits, criminals and ultra-nationalists. Within a few months about half had deserted, reducing the force from just over 6,000 to about 3,500. This unit made its own merciless contribution to the ethnic cleansing and genocide of Serbian Orthodox Christian, Jewish, and Gypsy peoples living in Kosovo. One incident in particular illustrates their approach – On 28th July 1944 a unit of the Skanderberg Division arrived at the 1000 year old village of Velika, situated at the bottom of a steep-sided valley. They then proceeded to loot the village (including the churches), set fire to about 300 homes and massacred 428 Serbian villagers, 120 of whom were children. In 1947 one of the Unit's commanders, August Schmidthuber, was put before a tribunal on the charge of participating in a range of atrocities including the massacre and deportation of civilians – he was found guilty and executed. Nearly 500,000 Serbs died in WWII and after the War President Tito expelled 175,000 Moslems from Yugoslavia to Turkey. As parts of Kosovo were 'cleansed' of Serbs Albanians settlers moved in just as Serbs had previously moved into Albanian lands – same ambitions, same techniques, same levels of cruelty, similar results.

So what were the wider outcomes of this, the second 20th century, World War?

The war was fought at a terrible cost in lives and widespread human dislocation and misery, along with extensive environmental damage; with the economic costs being debilitating for all of the European countries involved. But the economic costs bordered on the catastrophic for countries such as France, Britain, the USSR and of course Germany, Italy and Japan. This was a war fought until 'unconditional surrender', as a strategic aim of the allies, had been achieved and as such the economies that fought each other mobilized for a 'total-war' approach and in the process exhausted themselves economically. Populations, especially those of Germany and Russia, had to manage on meager living conditions, as shortages, rationing, loss of citizen's rights (including freedom of expression, of association, of movement, and for most 'aliens' even liberty), and for some the effects of mass bombing, had to be stoically borne as manpower and material resources were diverted to the business of war – a business that in its progressing many private companies made fortunes. Propaganda, disinformation, and censorship, played their respective roles as they were artfully brought to bear on populations in order to progress the anti-democratic 'art' of manipulating public opinion – an art that would now come of age in the science of psychology - along with more practical tactics of persuasion gleaned from the blossoming advertising industry.

If it was not for the vast resources of the US – initially made available via lend-lease[15] prior to their committing even greater resources (men and materials) to the actual fighting – then it is doubtful that the war could have been 'won' by the allies (that's not to say that it could have been won by the Axis powers). More probably, if Russia had not been able to defend a sufficiency of it resource-rich regions from the Germans, some negotiated stalemate in Europe would have been a more likely outcome, leaving Germany in control of substantial parts of northern, central and Western Europe.

In 1940 Germany, Japan, and Italy, were producing $7.75 billions worth of arms compared to the $10 billion of the USSR, Britain and the US – by 1943 the figs were $18.3 and $62.5 respectively. During the 1944 D-Day landings Germany could draw on 320 aircraft to face 12,837 aircraft of the Allies.

It is overwhelming the case that financial power, applied to the operation of economies on war footings, has won 'conventional' (non-guerilla) wars in the 19th and 20th centuries and not some mystical 'national spirit' – many individual Germans, Japanese and Italians were as brave and others as cowardly as many British, Americans, Russians, and their allies.

Statistical 'cost' of WWII.

Killed - 85 million - four times as many as WWI (including 35 million Russians - 13m soldiers and 23m civilians – and 5.7m European Jews)[16]
Refugees - 23 million
British civilians killed by German bombing 50,000
German civilians killed by Allied bombing 600,000
Japanese civilians killed by allied bombing 900,000
Total of 100 million soldiers mobilized, 20 million killed, as were

---

[15] Lend-Lease Act of March 1941 gave power to the President to either lease or lend munitions and supplies to any county considered to be defending itself in a way that is important to the security interest of the US – by the end of the war 38 countries were drawing on US resources via this scheme.

[16] Three million people also that died during the Bengal famine of 1943 – a situation exacerbated by Churchill's refusal to divert allied shipping to transport food.

over 50 million civilians.

Main combatants had: 286,000 tanks – 557,000 combat aircraft - 11,000 naval vessels – 40 million rifles...a massive waste of technological resources.

In term of today's money trillions and trillions of dollars (equivalent to 10 years of total world production)

Massive and wider-ranging environment degradation - from producing and use of the millions of tons of bombs, artillery shells, bullets, miles and miles of steel amour, millions of engines, etc. etc. and even today, the thousands of wrecked shipping rusting on our ocean floors continuing to leak heavily polluting diesel fuel into the seas.

The immeasurable streams of tears and the intensity of heartache and despair that produced them - tears of mothers, fathers, grandparents, brothers, sisters, wives and girlfriends - the children whose fathers never came home and the children never born because of this.

Most tellingly.......... the practices and prejudices of international politics had not been changed - national interest (as defined by ruling elites) continued to determine a narrow range of priorities - and the institutions put in place to contain the potential failings in nation to nation disagreements had lacked the means to enforce even pre-agreed principles.

Prior to picking up world history post WWII (from 1945) I would like to consider a generally more positive aspect of humankind's evolutionary journey and a source of masses of novel information' that has markedly expanded the Reality available for each of us to experience.

Chapter 8 'Twentieth Century Natural and Social Sciences'

'Science calls a world into being, not through some magic force, immanent in reality, but through a rational force immanent in the mind.....Scientific work makes rational entities real, in the full sense of word.'

(*New Scientific Spirit [6.54]*).

The activity of science had, during the 17th-19th centuries, become increasingly involved as a driver of advancing civil life. An activity producing a body of what would generally be termed scientific knowledge had by 1900 seen the accumulation of information that on the one hand allowed progress in the understanding of the natural and of the social worlds ('worlds' in the sense of conceptually circumscribed areas of collective human experience) and on the other hand, through its practical expression in technology, brought about a significant change in aspects of civil life. More obviously in: transport, medicine, agriculture, communication, warfare, and other economic and industrial applications; along with a wider understanding of our personal and social selves, and of our social institutions. These would be central aspects of civil life that would see a significant increase in the rate of accumulation (of knowledge) during the 20th and 21st centuries.

This chapter will continue to trace the intricate and interconnected threads of that accumulation by adhering to the traditional synthetic categories of, for the natural world: physics, astronomy, chemistry, biochemistry, biology, and geology, and in the social sciences, sociology, medicine, psychology.

As the twentieth century progressed, the branches of science incorporating the natural and the social worlds became increasingly interactional, with advances in one branch of scientific endeavour often stimulating advances in others –'science' came to represent a certain method of engaging with the world of experience. My intention here is not to offer a detailed, comprehensive outline of the progression of scientific advance; I am not in any case qualified to undertake such a study. There are numerous texts covering this including The Cambridge History of Science vols. 5, 6, 7, offers a reasonably comprehensive and readable outline of this period, and for an accessible book on how advances in the physical sciences link to industrial development, see Jon Agar's 'Science in the 20th Century and Beyond'.

In a relatively short chapter I can only offer some very limited sense of how some of the sciences have developed and these within one of the principle themes of this book – increasing the amount of information available to human reality (consciousness). The notion of the accumulation of 'novel' information, infusing and expanding accessible Reality, should be at the forefront of the reader's mind.

The expansion of scientific knowledge has probably advanced human understanding of Reality more than any of the other endeavors such as religion, politics, and philosophy. Even if understanding remains partial and tends toward a positivistic and reductionist bias - so limited in perspective, but generally arguably justified given its explanatory success and wide ranging technological innovations. Although each of the other human endeavors noted can be informed by and adapt to scientific developments, science differs from these in that its approach collects and collates information as it identifies regularities, significant patterns, and generates related theories in ways that open up our understanding of phenomena and in doing so enlarges our world-view in terms of expanding the horizons of knowledge.

A simple example of advance might be that Isaac Newton's theory of gravity took into account and sought to explain the observations and calculations of earlier astronomers.[1] But as the collection of data and the theoretical circumscription of astronomy, mathematics, and physics progressed, the accumulation of knowledge and related ideas revealed explanatory weaknesses in Newton's theory. Specifically that the orbit of Mercury is the one planet in the Solar System that did not fit his formula, and there is also an inconsistency between Newton's laws and the laws of electricity and magnetism as formulated in Maxwell's equations. Weaknesses overcome to a significant extent by Einstein's special theory of relativity, with its limiting of the constancy of the speed of light and to the relativity of time and motion. Initially Newton's 'revolutionary' explanation had been absorbed with wonder by the scientific community and

---

[1] Indeed, Newton in completing the Copernican revolution – and the acceptance of an Earth moving through space – had a significant impact on religious and secular world-views beyond the relatively small community of science of the time.

gradually extended to the wider civil world, but this was then superseded by a theoretical perspective with greater explanatory power; allowing the infusion of a new 'higher level' understanding, contributing to a new civil world-view.

Although quite a simple ideal example, the Newton-to-Einstein development does illustrate the way science advances, not just in accumulating data (and generating theories) but also in offering advances on our world-view in terms of its greater explanatory power.

Stephen Pinker (2017, p392) casts doubt on the idea of some universal 'scientific method'. For Pinker: 'Scientists use whatever methods help them to understand the world: drug-like tabulation of data, experimental derring-do, flights of theoretical fancy, elegant mathematical modeling, kludgy computer simulations, sweeping verbal narrative.' Pinker views scientific endeavour as more a medley of 'reasoned' methods. I would add, as guided by parameters of intelligibility and allowing intra-disciplinary experience itself to influence choice of appropriate method.

But, whilst acknowledging this methodological eclecticism, there are similarities in terms of methods and underlying values[2] allowing us to infer that there is such a unified entity as 'science', with the consequence that we can discuss science, in broad terms (not denied by Pinker), as covering the seeking of facts and theoretical information in all of its various traditional branches. We might find it easier – in relation to identifying subject-matter and how to draw data from it – by separating the 'natural' from the 'social' sciences.

As the twentieth-century progressed, the tension rose between social scientists seeking to closely follow the positivistic/reductionist approach characteristic of the physical sciences and those valuing a more qualitative/phenomenological approach. And for all of the sciences there has been a thoroughgoing tension between the notions of 'objectivity' and 'social construction' in relation to knowledge. By the end of the century most social scientists considered that the context appropriate collection of qualitative, as well as quantitative, data can generate potentially rich evidence, of the types most suitable to understand the complexity and relative unpredictability of the subject-matter. Relative unpredictability being a defining characteristic of human behaviour, whereas natural scientists have

---

[2] Plus how subject-matter is circumscribed – and given some level of 'authority' by such processes as peer-review.

considered that their subject-matter as being similarly complex as the social but with patterns of behavior that are relatively - not a pun but perhaps an interesting stimulus for more epistemological considerations - predictable.

The commonality of epistemological, methodological, and organizational perspectives deployed in seeking to understand and explain a range of phenomena allows the use of the concept science to be applied to the various branches of the sciences; natural and social.

All of the sciences are closely associated with the needs of civil society in terms of administration, healthcare, communication, education, warfare, civil infrastructure, transport, and general economic circumstances. In this last area, the nineteenth century had seen an increasing development of a process whereby scientific advance is rapidly transformed into saleable 'products'. The study of electricity, thermodynamics, of the properties of light, and of various chemical substances, are just some areas that proved suitable for economic exploitation. A model example of this translation of discovery into product being the discovery of X-rays that, within ten years they were being used by doctors to peer into the skeletal structure of humans and animals. And also for scientists to exploit their use in crystallography to study a wide range of materials that would soon find industrial application. A model institution for the interrelation of pure science, technology, and industry, was the German Physikalisch-Technische Reichsanstalt. Germany led the way in establishing scientific institutions primarily with the large number of German Kaiser Whilhelm Institutes, examples being the Institutes of: Biology (1912), Chemistry and Electro-Chemistry (1911), Brain Research (1914), and Physics (1917) (the latter with Albert Einstein as Director).

Similar scientific institutions were soon being established across the civil world to serve as research centres positioned to undertake their own original work, and also to exploit the stream of discoveries coming from business, university and other primarily state funded, laboratories. The twentieth century saw the professionalization of the sciences, with the nineteenth century categorization of the sciences usefully fracturing into multiple sub-branches. There was an exponential increase in the number of individuals earning a living as scientists, more directly as: researchers, practitioners, teachers, scientific journalists, philosophers of science, advisers to industry and government, etc.

Key features of science in the late nineteenth and throughout the twentieth century, included the steadily improving quality of laboratory-based and other observational equipment and instruments, along with a range of new units of measurement.

Jon Agar (2012) has written quite extensively on the interplay of pure science and technology, and their economic exploitation (driving innovation and discovery as this circumscribed the context of research) operating within what he terms 'working world concerns'. A world in which scientists worked to solve problems presented by the economic and social systems. For Agar: 'Working worlds are arenas of human projects that generate problems.'(Agar, 2012, p3) and: 'I am arguing that science is the making, manipulation and contest of abstracted, simplified representative of working world problems.' (Agar 2012, p5).

Science as an activity has developed a particular way of approaching the world that it studies (its 'subject-matter') – it differs to a significant extent from religion, philosophy, and other intellectual modes of considering and explaining the phenomena of our experience, in that science has a particular (if broad-based) method, one agreed by its practitioners and one that allows authority for scientific activity within wider society. Science also gains authority due to its practical application; via technology (the natural sciences) and social policy (the social sciences).

As the twentieth century advanced this authority became increasingly recognized and supported by the most powerful institutions in civil society. An authority underpinned by facilitating advances in theoretical understanding and more practically in being able to control (and offer predictions about) natural and social phenomena. Science came to impact, for good and for evil, on almost all of the World's people. The accrual of authority for science was increasingly due to its political influence as it contributed to the 'war industry'. This was especially apparent during the Second World War and the 'cold war' period that followed, by when governments had become the major funding source for most of the sciences, especially physics, astronomy, computing, cybernetics, and chemistry. Investments more-often presented to the public as progressing the peaceful pursuit of useful knowledge (to the benefit of humanity) but often having an underlying military rational. Where these latter could involve: nuclear weaponry, rocketry, robotics, drones, spy and GPS

1017

satellites and other forms of provocative surveillance, and biological/chemical weapons.

Authority was also gained by the ability of industry to rapidly assimilate advancing scientific knowledge and translate this into usable consumer-type 'products' – transistors, plastics, nylon and lazers, as well as transport and communication technologies, along with a wide range of medical advances such as in drugs, surgical techniques, prosthetics, and body scanning equipment.

One contentious aspect of the scientific method - central to questions over epistemological credibility and social legitimacy – involves the concept of 'objectivity'. Based on the notion that it is possible to design scientific studies (the processes involved in the production of knowledge) intended to gain observational and/or experimentally derived data that has not been influenced by immediately confounding factors, by any personal prejudices, by other tacit subjective bias of the scientific practitioners, or by aspects of the wider social context in which knowledge is produced. I will come back to this important aspect of the scientific enterprise at the end of the section on the sciences.

Today, science has become a veritable industry for the production of knowledge and the generation of technological development – one aspect being the 'expertism' that rose to influence during the post-war period but which is now experiencing a crisis as some disillusionment with expert interpretation and prediction has become a feature of twenty-first century civil life.

Scientists working in the natural sciences have approached phenomena with the underlying working assumption that there is a natural world independent of human beings (if also including them) – within which can be observed: patterns, regularities, and causal relationships operating according to determinate 'laws'. This positivist perspective had been a primary assumption underlying the development of science in the 18th/19th centuries.

Paul Feyerabend offered an interesting, if provocative, nuanced challenge to the assumption that progress made in the sciences as being due to the application of rationality (Feyerabend, 1975, and 1978). But, for my more discursive level of consideration, I think it is reasonable to assume that forms of intellectually rigorous analysis, subsumed under the general concept of rationality, has characterized the theorizing and interpretation of data that has, at least ideally, driven the activity.

Some social scientists considered a positivist approach inadequate to understand the complexity of human behaviour. In reaction to positivism, other approaches, taking a more 'phenomenal approach', developed and indeed, by the latter part of the twentieth century most social scientists approached their subject-matter using a range of methods that reflected a pragmatic mixture of both quantitative positivism and the qualitative sensitivity of phenomenalism.

I now go on to offer a brief overview of 20th/21st century science by considering developments in some of the more traditionally categorized sciences - Physics, Astronomy, Chemistry, Biology, Geology, then moving on to Sociology, Medicine, and Psychology – the intention being to offer just some if more general 'sense' of the accelerating rate of the accumulation of knowledge. And this more especially in relation to a central purpose of this book, to dip into the increasing rate of increase in 'novel information' (the undying dynamic generating evolutionary progress, its complexification) that we have access too; expanding the horizons of the Reality within which we experience existence.

Physics

By 1900 the energy emitted by elements were increasingly becoming a focus for physicists. Their primary interests had turned towards the mirco-level of the material world and the outcome would be a fundamental challenge to what we mean by material.

Ernest Rutherford had identified that the radiation emitted from a cathode ray tube as alpha waves were doubly ionized helium atoms with a positive charge and that beta waves were electrons and as such carried a negative charge. In 1902 Rutherford and his colleague Fredrick Soddy, whilst considering the radiation emitted by thorium, noticed that over time the rate of emission declined and that a new form of thorium appeared. They were able to graphically describe this 'radioactive decay' as a fundamental property of matter, the identification of which would enable advances in a range of areas; including geological dating methods. In 1905 Rutherford used the rate of radioactive decay, and the associated accumulation of helium gas in rock, to offer an estimate of the age of the Earth at 500 million years. So, although significantly below the Earth's true age, it was a useful step towards more accurate geological dating methods.

Having the property of electrical charge meant that the passage of radiation through the vacuum tube could be controlled and amplified and so made more amenable to study. The study of electrons was improved further with C.T.R. Wilson's invention of the 'Cloud Chamber', used by J.J.Thomson to measure the charge and so be able to calculate the mass of the electron. A much improved version of the cloud chamber was made available by 1911 and this made it possible to photograph the trail of water droplets indicating the passage of an electron. An advance enhanced when Paul Villard discovered a different type of energy and named it gamma radiation. This being a form of radiant energy that would much later be exploited in medical imaging techniques.

A suggestion made in December 1900 by Max Planck that radiated energy is emitted (from atoms) in discrete packages or 'quanta' would signal a profound advance in the understanding of the material world (would in effect de-materialize as it was 'energized'). Quantum physics had arrived! Planck was seeking to explain black body radiation - a phenomenon that had puzzled physicists for some decades, in which bodies that are heated emit radiation of a type dependent on temperature rather than on the material being used.

The assumption of this radiant energy being emitted as 'quanta' allowed Planck to very closely match the mathematical calculations to the experimentally derived data. In 1883 Ludwig Boltzmann had already offered a mathematical description of black body radiation and a theoretical link between radiation and heat. Planck's own calculations required a 'constant' which was based on a relationship between the energy of a photon and the frequency of its own electromagnetic wave. Formulated as $E = hv$, and described by Bernal (1965, p737) as '....a constant amount of action, Planck's constant, that controlled the quantity of all energy exchanges of atomic systems'.[3]

This constant was later adjusted by Albert Einstein to incorporate

---

[3] Planck scales: Planck's constant, was arrived at by the manipulation of the two constants:
of the speed of light and the gravitational constant. And whilst considering this, Planck constructed three very tiny measurements:
- Of mass, as 21 millionths of a gram, so 21 micrograms. Planck mass.
- Of length, as 16 millionths of a billionth of a billionth of a billionth of a millimetre. Planck length.
- Of time, as a millionth of a billionth of a billionth of a billionth of a billionth second. Planck time

the speed of light and wavelength (formulated as $E = h\nu$ over λ). It would be five years on from Planck's 'kinetic' (and fruitful) insight that would lead to a marked change in the understanding of the material world when Einstein began the process of drawing out some implications of the quantum model.

Einstein was to use Maxwell's differential equations, especially the constant speed of the electromagnetic 'light' waves that they suggested (minus Maxwell's 'molecular vortices'), as the initial point of reference for his theory of special relativity. But Einstein focused on the fact that the then (1905) understanding of the speed of light was based on some notional fixed point of measurement and so did not take into account the position ('relative' movement) of the observer.

Amongst a series of theoretical papers that Einstein produced during 1905 was one that mathematically demonstrated that electromagnetic radiation followed a quantum pattern. Indeed, his general theory of relativity also included mathematical innovation, in particular with the tensor calculus. In this landmark paper, he also suggested that the photo-electric effect (the phenomena that when light is shone onto a metal surface it emits electrons) was due to electromagnetic radiation (light) displacing electrons from the metal object. Light had, from towards the second half of the nineteenth century (classical mechanics), been considered to travel in waves; although Newton himself thought that light travelled in particles – through an aether. Einstein suggested that light travels in discrete units of radiant energy, 'photons', a suggestion that was able to explain some of the experimental findings. Einstein's view also gained experimental verification in the work of Robert Millikan who in fact set out with the expectation of being able to show that Einstein's interpretation of the photo-electric effect was wrong, but by 1915 had to concede he had been right. In 1909 Millikan had already set out an experimental method that would enable the precise measurement of the negative charge of an electron. He went on to offer a theoretical justification for a wave-particle duality in the behaviour of light.

The year 1905 was a prolific year for Einstein, during which he also stated the equivalence of mass and energy – expressed in his famous formula $e = mc^2$, where c represents the constant value of the speed of light.

A scientist on whose work Einstein built was Hendrick Lorentz who had in 1904 conducted what was then considered to be a failed experiment seeking to measure the motion of the Earth relative to the space through which it moved. Lorentz noted that as the speed of objects approached that of light then some of their properties – their length, mass, and the time within which they moved – changed, the implication being that these properties were relative to motion. Also relevant were the Michelson-Morley experiments (1880s), showing that the speed at which light itself traveled was always constant irrespective of the direction of travel relative to the Earth – confirming Maxwell's equations. It would take until 1926, and advances in measuring techniques, for Michelson to be able to measure the speed of light at 299,796 km/s, close to the speed accepted today.

The brilliant insight of Einstein had brought together these and more recent discoveries to provide a new (mathematical) description of matter. His 'Special theory of relativity' (1905) lent support to the quantum-related suggestions of Planck, in effect, establishing the quantum physics that would be a central theme of twentieth century physics.

At aound the same time, two other physicists working with the New Zealander Ernest Rutherford in Manchester, Hans Geiger and Ernest Marsden, were able to show that if alpha particles travelled through thin metallic sheets then very occasionally one would appear to hit something which, given the speed and density of the stream of particles, had to be very small and very 'solid'; to bounce off, or rather, be deflected. An event that Rutherford himself found to be incredible. The nucleus of the atom had been discovered and, given that electrons were known to have a negative charge, the integrity of the atom could only be maintained if the nucleus had an overall positive charge equal to the total electron charge (negative) of the atom. Now the basis – nucleus and electrons – of the structure (how the electrons were arranged in relation to the nucleus) was available. It was Rutherford who first used this new understanding of the atom to suggest how its structure might be described. In 1910 he proposed a structure in which the electron was suggested to be 10,000 times smaller than the overall atom in which it was held, consequently suggesting that the atom, in terms of mass, was composed mainly of a central nucleus with electrons moving around in 'empty space'; moving in shell-like bands named as orbitals – 'mazy orbits'.

Rutherford's laboratory in Manchester attracted some outstanding physicists, one of whom was Niels Bohr who, in 1912, combined a number of recent developments in the understanding of the atom (including Planck's theory of quanta) to propose that the interior space of atoms was such that electrons orbit the nucleus at different 'levels' and that it would take energy from outside of the atom to displace an electron from one orbit (energy level) to another; to undergo a quantum 'leap' from one level of orbit to another. It was the overall balance of charge that gave the atom stability. Emissions such as light (photons) and X-rays occurred as electrons moved from higher to lower energy orbits, enabling the release of energy from an atom. Bohr's work on the atom gave an adequate if pretty bold explanation for the phenomenon of differences in the characteristics of radiation emission.

Rutherford's scientific genius was his ability in 1912 to interpret the experimental results of Geiger and Marsden and so to combine these with Bohr's insight and other already known properties of atoms into a new 'model'.

The new, Rutherford-Bohr model, of the tiniest constituent parts of the physical world, was useful for physicists[4] in enabling the prediction of atomic properties simply by knowing the number of electrons any atom contained. It was a model - a form of miniscule 'solar' system - with the main mass being concentrated at a central nucleus. It was also a model that made advances in physics available to a wide range of non-scientists, if in a graphic and general way, rather than in its complex mathematical formulation. This model was also able to account for the fact that each element had its own unique spectral identification pattern. In 1914 Rutherford's continuing research into radioactivity bore more sub-atomic fruit when he identified the proton – the particle that contributed the positive charge to the nucleus of an atom.

The emerging 'model' of the atom was enlarged further when in 1913 Francis Aston discovered that atoms of elements can come in different forms – isotopes.

Rutherford and others had shown the unstable nature of the radioactive elements, that they were liable to change and decay, and in 1919 he went further. By bombarding the atoms of the stable (non-radioactive) elements with his favoured alpha particles Rutherford was able to demonstrate that these can also undergo disintegration

---

[4] And for chemists – not least in providing a quantitative explanation for the arrangement of elements in the periodic Table.

(e.g. transforming nitrogen into oxygen). The whole 'world' of elemental matter was shown to be relatively contingent and potentially transformable – if there was an 'elemental substance' it was perhaps energy itself.

One aspect of the work of Rutherford's team was to bear poisoned fruit over two decades later. In 1919 they managed to break up ('split') the nucleus of an atom of nitrogen by a direct hit with an alpha particle. Humankind had now released the energy locked within an atom (Prometheus was unbound!) – just one seemingly 'neutral' (objective) outcome of scientific endeavour that would be technically exploited by the 'war' industry.

For physicists, the work of Rutherford and his team using the method of 'firing' subatomic particles at atoms in order to create collision events - with outcomes that could be used to better understand the constitution of atoms and their sub-atomic phenomena - was to provide the incentive to the development of particle accelerators as a research tool.

Rolf Widerase had shown how electromagnetic induction could be used to accelerate electrons, a process that would come to be used in the 'betatron', a type of particle accelerator that used a combination of electrical field and varying magnetic fields to drive beta particles (electrons) up to high speed within a circular orbit prior to their being smashed into the material being studied. The first successful betatron accelerator would be operating from 1940 in the US.

The earliest particle accelerator had been devised by J. Cockcroft and E. Walton who, in 1930, designed a 200,000 volt transformer that was able to accelerate protons along a straight path, their purpose being to test for a phenomenon known as Gamow's Tunnelling. A marked improvement in high-energy physics research came in 1931 with Ernest Lawrence's invention of the cyclotron. Then in 1932, Cockcroft, Walton, and Rutherford designed an accelerator (of 400,000 volts) that could bombard lithium with protons, so managing to split an atom of lithium into two atoms of helium. They went on to split the atoms of more than a dozen other elements and in doing so demonstrated the research potential of the 'atom-smasher'; built with the assistance of the electrical industry. For the following four decades, accelerator technology continued to improve, with a debate between preferences for circular or linear pathways.

The early accelerators had been relatively primitive machines compared to high energy particle accelerators such as the Stanford

Linear Accelerator (SLAC 1960s), Fermilab's Tevatron (from 1983), the Large Electron Positron (LEP 1989 CERN) in operation during the 1990s. With the latter being replaced, in terms of leading edge research, in 2005, by the Large Hadron Collider (LHC 2005) also situated at CERN – near Geneva. The LHC is buried deep underground and is sufficiently powerful to accelerate particles (protons and antiprotons) along a 26 kilometre circuit at seven times the speed of the Fermilab's Tevatron. The Tevatron (U.S. Illinois) had cost $120 million to build in 1983 and another $290 million to upgrade in 1994 with its useful research life being in effect ended when the LHC (initial cost over 3 billion Euros.) became available to researchers. Indeed, such were the costs of building an accelerator twice as long as CERNs – the Superconducting Supercollider - in the US (Texas), was abandoned due to the projected cost.

The commitment to construct the LHC reflected a preference for circular over linear accelerators. The principle example of the latter being the SLAC, operating along a two mile long tunnel in California. The progressive development of the particle accelerators illustrates the way high energy physics became, as the century progressed, far less an activity that could be funded by any university-based or private research unit operating on relatively modest budgets, to an activity only affordable by governments – from WWII the unlocking of the mystery of high energy physics became an aspect of 'Big Science'. As to particle accelerators: they have been adapted for a range of medical and research applications, and there are now about 30,000 such machines operating across the world.

Earlier in the century, another physicist working alongside Bohr and Rutherford, Harry Moseley (subsequently killed at Gallipoli during WW I), was using spectroscopic analysis to show that the behaviour of electrons was determined by the charge rather than the mass of an atom; giving rise to two standard ways of categorising atoms, by charge (the atom number) and by mass (the atom weight). The use of atomic weight did pose a problem related to the periodic table but this was resolved when in 1913 Soddy suggested that, given that elements can occur in isotopic forms (so having different atomic weights), it was possible that isotopes of one atom could 'overlap' into another atom and thus affect the assessment of atomic weight.

In 1912 knowledge of the atom was increased by Theodore Richard who was able to provide an accurate way to determine atomic weight. With the techniques of investigating the structure of atoms being advanced further with the demonstration in 1913 by Johannes Stark that spectral lines (emitted by elements under experimental conditions) were affected by electric fields.

Stepping back somewhat from the immediacy of scientific advance – the process that leads from the initial late nineteenth century (focus on radiation) indication that atoms might not be the smallest package of matter to the design of the Rutherford-Bohr atom, we can see the application by a number of scientists of both theoretical insight and experimental investigation and observation. As each contribution led towards a clear stage of major advance in understanding an aspect of the world (in interpreting observations and predicting behaviours); interlinked processes exhibiting the incremental and collective nature of scientific advance.

The phenomenon of radiation and the subatomic 'world' more generally held an unsettling but exciting fascination for physicists in the early decades of the twentieth century that would continue down to today. According to Eric Hobsbawm (1994, page 534) 'The twentieth century was to be the century of the theoreticians telling the practitioners what they were to look for and should find in the light of their theories; in other words the century of the mathematicians'. One notable mathematical prediction was that of Rutherford's suggesting the immense power 'locked' up in the nucleus of an atom.

The use of X-rays (a technique employing the diffraction of the X-rays by the relatively solid structure of crystals) in 1912 by Max von Laue to study crystals was able to go beyond the then traditional optically observed properties to identify their wave-like property. The development of X-ray crystallography also enabled the structure of molecules (collections/colonies of atoms) to be revealed. This work allowed the scientific community to realize the further potential of X-ray diffraction for research into crystals and molecules. A potential enhanced when in 1916 William Coolidge improved on his own version of a vacuum tube to more accurately direct the X-rays – an improvement, supplemented by contributions of William and Lawrence Bragg (including 'Braggs Law'), that would provide an effective research tool for physicists (solid state physics) and later for the molecular biologists, including Linus Pauling's study of crystals and other aspects of organic chemistry in the second half of the century. It would also be deployed in the medical use of X-rays.

In 1916 Karl Siegbohn made some technical improvements to X-ray spectroscopy and was able to significantly advance understanding of the way in which electrons filled the 'shells' (bands) around the nucleus and in doing so also enhanced the understanding of the elements. Bernal compared the importance of crystallography as a research tool to that of the microscope, the latter giving optical access to the very tiny but with the newer technique being able to reveal the fine structure of crystals and molecules to the point of identifying the position of individual atoms.

The 10-15 year period following the presentation of the Rutherford-Bohr model of the atom was to be fruitful for physics. Whereas the Newtonian - Galiliean framework remained useful for understanding the behaviour of matter within a circumscribe range of 'conditions', quantum mechanics now offered a valid framework for a wider range of material reality, if at the cost of a certain uneasiness in the unsettling form of the framework. At the sub-atomic level it described causation and outcomes as probabilistic rather than the deterministic relationship upon which the classical models were based. A theoretical framework causing particular problems for physicists in the Soviet Union having to reconcile quantum uncertainty with the deterministic dialectical materialism that was the basic assumption they were 'encouraged' to assume – a clear case of political ideology inhibiting scientific progress.

Another theory of Einstein's was, in 1915, to direct physicists to a consideration of, not just the electrical and magnetic forces focused upon in his early theories, but one which had significant implications for phenomena related to the very large – gravity. Einstein's General Theory of Relativity suggested that the force of gravity (like motion in the Special Theory) could affect distance and time – that what they measured was 'relative' to the force of gravity operating on an 'object' – be this light rays or planetary motion - that was being measured.[5] In 1923 Louis de Brogile was able to show how Plank's constant could be generalized and so applied to any sub-atomic particle, and in 1924 he suggested that 'matter' (all electromagnetic radiation) can be shown to exist in the form of waves as well as particles. A suggestion supported by Einstein himself and confirmed experimentally (along lines suggested by de Brogile) by the physicist

---

[5] In 1915 Einstein also suggested that the photon (radiation that travels at the speed of light, with rest mass of zero) was also another elementary particle – the existence of the photon was demonstrated experimentally by Arthur Compton in the early 1920s.

Clinton Davisson in the electron diffraction experiment – showing that electrons targeted at a crystal of nickel would be diffracted; experimental proof that particles of matter also had wave-like properties.

De Broglie's central mathematical proposition (equation) was that all phenomena of the sub-atomic level, including electrons, exhibit behaviour that has wave-particle properties. According to Bernal (1954, p748) for de Broglie 'There appeared indeed to be a general correspondence between particles and waves; every particle could be deemed to be accompanied by a wave and every wave to consist of particles lined up on wave fronts'. Now we had the somewhat confusing situation of sub-atomic particles behaving 'as if' particles and 'as if' waves.

The concept of 'quantum field' was introduced to overcome some problems of the wave/particle duality of photons. For Jon Butterworth: 'This quantum field spreads and travels like a wave, it has a frequency and a wavelength, and can exhibit interference and other wave-like effects, but it is telling us the probability of a particle (photon) being present at any given place.' (Butterworth, 2017) This idea became more fully developed as 'quantum electrodynamics' (QED) during the 1940s; becoming a key component of the Standard Model.

Whereas features of quantum theory can seem puzzling (in some contexts counter intuitive, not to say contradictory) it worked as a predictive theory in relation to experimental outcomes; allowing a level of confidence in its offering some useful understanding of the basic constitution of matter. As the century progressed, with more of the subatomic level of matter being revealed, quantum theory was adjusted and revised in ingenious ways to accommodate the new information. Although offering quite powerful predictive theories these revisions (see next paragraph) were never sufficient to be able to satisfactorily explain all of the phenomena that were being observed.

The anomalies apparent in the initial quantum theory of Bohr's (basically, its overly simplistic description of the behaviour of subatomic entities) were addressed during the 1920s when quantum theory underwent significant revisions in the work of a number of outstanding physicists. Erwin Schrodinger (1926 – picking up on the work of de Broglie, attributing the wave-like behaviour to various types of vibrations of electrons) suggested that waves were not 'flowing' but behaved more as 'localised vibrations', forming patterns of electrons the identification of which could allow significant predictive and explanatory power – quantum harmonic oscillation. Werner Heisenberg contributed to the revision of quantum theory with a complex mathematical description of the behaviour of electrons when, operating as particles, they 'quantum leap' from one band of sub-atomic energy levels to the next. Heisenberg and his co-workers constructed a complex mathematical matrix and with it, along with the contributions of Schrodinger and Born (see below), the beginning of quantum mechanics. He also introduced his 'uncertainty principle' to accommodate the seeming impossibility of being able to experimentally determine both the position and the velocity of any particle - the more precisely you endeavour to measure one of these properties the less accurately can the other be determined. Heisenberg's suggestion, whilst potentially useful for allowing certain theoretical anomalies to be explained, was based on the hypothetical role of an observer which he suggested would introduce 'uncertainty' into quantum theory, not merely as a artefact of quantum theory but as a central feature of it and by definition a central feature of the 'material' world, so making a significant contribution to redefining the meaning of matter. The physicist, Paul Dirac, took both Schrodinger's wave-based reformulation of quantum theory and Heisenberg's particle based reformulations and offered a third version suggesting that the first two were mathematically equivalent. Dirac went on to offer a wave-based equation that allowed the behaviour of an electron to meet the implications of the special theory of relativity. By the end of the 1920s, instead of conceptualizing the properties of sub-atomic matter as wave-particle, the expression 'quantum state' was considered to be more appropriate, with 'as if' wave or 'as if' particle being alternative manifestations of this state.

At about this time (1925) the model of the atom was further developed with the work of Wolfgang Pauli, with his 'Exclusion Principle' suggesting that any atom (or rather 'quantum system') can only have one of its electrons (or indeed any of the other fermions) in any particular quantum state (having the same quantum number) at the same time. This contributed to an explanation of the electron limit for each of the bands surrounding the nucleus of an atom – 2, 8, 18, 32, etc. electrons in the bands; 'excluding' any higher number in each. So for any electron to be added to an atom it must either 'eject' one already in place or occupy a space in the outer band where one is available. This was a feature of atomic structure of profound significance to the formation of compounds as will be seen when we consider chemistry (molecular bonding). Max Born completed this stage of revising sub-atomic properties by giving a conceptual explanation that sought to describe how the 'wave' property of a particle was essentially the probability of it being in a particular location.

For Lisa Rezende (2006, p292): 'Taken together, Schrodinger's wave mechanics, Heisenberg's matrix mechanics, and Born's probabilistic interruption, gave rise to modern quantum mechanics.'

One possible implication of Dirac's equation for the electron was the existence of an unknown particle with the mass equivalence of an electron but with a positive rather than a negative charge. The presence of this subatomic entity, this 'antimatter', would later be confirmed experimentally in the early 1930s by Carl Anderson who was able to identify (during the study of cosmic showers) just such a positively charged particle as had been predicted by Dirac in 1928 - initially named the positron. It is now assumed that all subatomic particles have an antimatter equivalent with opposite quantum properties.

This was a fertile period for physics - as early as 1923 Rutherford had modestly suggested it to be '.......the heroic age of physics'.

A seeming anomaly to the then currently favoured model of the atom had been that the combined mass of the protons and of the electrons was less that the total mass of the atom. Pauli had also suggested that the 'decay' of elements seen in beta decay seemed to violate the 'Law of the conservation of energy', and so must be a process involving yet another particle, one that would have to have a neutral charge. And so would enable the overall integrity of the atom to be maintained during decay. The anomaly was partly resolved when, in 1931, James Chadwick discovered (by bombarding beryllium with alpha particles) the presence of a third particle, the 'neutron' that, due to its being of neutral charge did not upset the overall balance of electrical charge between the electrons and the protons but did explain the previously 'missing' mass. The neutral charge of the neutron made it the best candidate for studying the nuclei of atoms. Its neutral electrical charge enabled it to be 'fired' into any nucleus without being repelled as would have been the case with positively charged alpha particles and protons.

In 1933 Enrico Fermi (developing an earlier theoretical suggestion of Pauli) focused on the beta decay process and suggested that the weak nuclear force caused a neutron to decay into three other particles – an electron, a proton, and one new neutrally charged particle that Femi named the 'neutrino'. The strength of Fermi's suggestion being the explanatory power of the mathematical representation of the energy emitted during the decay process and its agreement with experimental observations.

The neutrino was first detected in the midd-1950s – suggested to exist in four forms: each with a mass only slightly (if anything) more than zero (100,000th that of an electron) and an electrically neutral, very weak, interactional force. It is thought that neutrinos (emitted by the Sun and other stars) were present, along with photons, electrons, and some other particles, from one second after the Big Bang event. But unlike most of the electrons that from that time interacted with their antiparticles to annihilated each other and so produce more photons, neutrinos and anti-neutrinos escaped this fate due mainly to the very weak force operating between them and other particles.

John Gribbin takes the view that: 'The identification of the neutrino completes the set of particles and forces that are responsible for the way things behave in the everyday world.' He follows this with a succinct description of the then understood properties of basic matter: 'We are made of atoms. Atoms are made of protons, neutrons and electrons. The nucleus contains protons and neutrons, held together by the strong force, in which beta decay can take place as an effect of the weak force (and from which, in some cases, alpha particles may be ejected as a result of the internal readjustment of the nucleus). The electrons are in a cloud outside the nucleus, held in place by electromagnetic forces but only allowed to occupy certain energy states by the rules of quantum physics. On large scales, gravity is important in holding bigger lumps of matter together.' (Gribbin, 2003, p525)

As the 1930s drew to an end, the accepted model of the atom included the properties of: Four 'particles' – proton, neutron, electron, neutrino, plus their energy equivalent antimatter particles – and the four forces of - electromagnetism, gravity, and the strong and weak nuclear forces.

The concepts of: the sub-atomic, relativity, uncertainty, probability, are ones that soon passed into the discourse of popular imagination and modes of communication. But some developments of science were to have material as well as conceptual impact. The one that is held to be of some significance was the developments leading to nuclear weapons – although in fact this was no more than a continuation of links between science and technological development to improve the 'efficiency' of killing that had already been seen with features of warfare in areas such as: communications, transportation, munitions, and biological and chemical weaponry.

In 1938 Otto Hahn had shown that bombarding uranium with neutrons resulted in nuclear fission. Simply put: the process of bombarding nuclei with neutrons resulted in the release (liberation) of several neutrons from each nucleus and if this process (used on any suitable element) released one more usable neutron than the number of neutrons originally impacting on the nucleus, then a serial reaction could be initiated and the relentless release of energy could be controlled to make usable power or uncontrolled to produce an explosion.

In 1939 Einstein had written to President Roosevelt drawing the President's attention to the fact that recent scientific discoveries – such as those made by Joliot-Curie, Szilard, and Fermi – had made possible a weapon with massive destructive power. This correspondence gave a significant impetus to the setting up of the 'Advisor Committee on Uranium' later that same year and, within a short time, establishing the 'Manhattan Project'.

Following the success of Fermi's initial experiment in the Manhattan Project, the US government was persuaded of the viability of the military use of nuclear power and of the need for a new ($440,000) laboratory in which to progress related research. The focus of the Project would now be moved to the Los Alamos Ranch School set on a hilltop to the north-west of Santa Fe, New Mexico. It was here in the middle years of the war that a number of the world's leading physicists were gathered including Teller, Pauling, Fermi, Bethe, Compton, Chadwick, and others, under the leadership of Robert Oppenheimer – a vast amount of calculating and analytic reasoning power gathered to progress the production of the atomic bomb. The personnel scientific route to nuclear weapons can be traced in the award of Nobel prizes in chemistry and physics throughout the 1920s to early 1940s

Advances made in physics up to 1940s show the energy of highly motivated scientific endeavour operating in a fertile intellectual environment. The many discoveries made during this time offered answers to known questions (resolved problems), but in doing so they also opened up the conceptual and material hinterland of scientific horizons; so expanding the field of potential discovery ever further.

The science of physics emerged from WWII having made significant advance in our understanding of the invisible micro-environment of sub-atomic particles and associated forces and was an activity held in a certain level of fearful esteem by most of the public and was a keen interest of the military and governments of the major industrial powers.

The incentives offered by war also led to advances in the development of computers. In the nineteenth century the idea of mechanical calculation had been suggested by Charles Babbage who designed, but did not build, a calculating machine. Around the same time George Boole showed a way of outlining logical reasoning by the use of algebra, developing the Boolean Logic that came to be used in some modern computer programs. Progressing mechanical calculation was to some extent a minority interest amongst electrical engineers and mathematicians. In the 1930s the Massachusetts Institute of Technology (MIT) had developed the 'Differential Analyzer' to undertake the complex calculations involved in designing interconnected systems for the emerging electronic communication industry.

The motivation to break German military codes during WWII gave urgency to innovation in code-braking. Especially the codes used in the messaging system by which German command centres relayed orders to commanders of the U-Boats that hunted and destroyed thousands of tons of Atlantic shipping employed in transporting vital supplies from the US to Britain.

The mathematician Alan Turing and his colleagues gathered at Bletchley Park by 1943, built the machine aptly named 'Colossus' a machine that dramatically increased the speed at which coded messages could be broken. Colossus was the first electronic computing device. John von Neumann's theory of how information might be stored via a computer program advanced the understanding of how storage capacity could be increased to complement calculating power. In 1946 the military, by now well aware of the military potential of computers, sponsored the development of the ENIAC machine which was 1000 times faster than the first, the Colossus, computer. The same designers also went on (10 years later) to design a computer, UNIVAC, made available for commercial use.

Further, quite dramatic, improvement was made possible by the introduction of the micro-chip, invented by the engineer Jack Kilby (Sept. 1958), offering a significant contribution to reducing the size of computers - these would in turn be superseded by nano-chips which have the capacity to hold individual features 0.000002 of an inch in size; introduced by the start of the 21st century.

Norbert Wiener in his 1948 book 'Cybernetics or Control and Communication in Animal and the Machine', focused on the links between mechanical and biological feedback based control systems and the possible relationship of humans and computers. Claude Shannon at the 1948 Bell Laboratory, was working on the efficiency of communication systems, as 'information theory'. These two were at the forefront of founding the science of cybernetics. Interestingly, Wiener felt that the implications of a 'computer revolution' would be mass unemployment and saw a possible solution to this being: '...to have a society based on human values other than buying and selling.' (see John Naughton, 'A Brief History of the Future', 2000, p65)

Another early (1950s) computer-based system was developed for the SAGE US defense strategy. This involved 23 computers designed to identify and track hostile airplanes – these computers incorporated a relatively simple type of Radom Access Memory (RAM). Housed in a large room, the SAGE computer system weighed in at 250 tons, SAGE cost $10 billion (about $69 billion at 2021 values allowing for inflation) so would probably never have been viewed as a viable commercial proposition, but then US government money is generally readily available for military projects. In terms of practical scientific application, by 1951 Dirk Brouwer was able to use the calculating power of a computer to calculate the planetary orbits (set out in his book 'The Coordinates of the Five Outer Planets'). In doing so, clearly highlighting the potential of computers.

Historically, the most successful computer programming language, FORTRAN, was introduced by IBM in 1956. This was a general purpose programming language especially suited to the computational needs of scientists and engineers. The most recent version of this specialized computing language, now Fortran 2008 (introduced in 2010), follows a long line of improved versions developed in the 50 odd years since it was first introduced. By the 1960s computers of increasing information storage capacity and computing power were being developed for a range of military, government, and commercial purposes. Throughout the 60s, 70s, and

80s, computer science, as both hard and soft-ware, developed at a pace.

ARPNET – sponsored by the US Department of Defense -, the 'blue sky' project under the ARPA from 1966, shut down in 1989 – saw the linking of interacting computers ('packet-switching') thereby allowing operators to draw on a network's combined computing power and for the computers to 'communicate' within the system. The ARPNET system combined computer networks with the protocol suit TCP/IP and this was the technology that underpinned what would become the 'Internet'. It was in 1992 when Tim Berners-Lee made available the first internet web-browser and in doing so, in effect establishing the public space of communication and information storage that is the World Wide Web (WWW). A 'public space' that, by 2020, had been significantly eroded ('enclosed') by the web's monopolistic corporate commercialization (the means to moneterization interactions and platforms) plus copyright and government action to edit/control (see 'Digital Disconnect' McChesney, 2013).

In general, physicists took easily to computers, the internet, and its development in the WWW. Computers, and the linking of these in intranets, gave them access to massive computer power: allowing complex calculation, data collection and analysis, and the modeling of various types of processes. Access to computers and the internet allowed the sharing of information with peers working across the world on similar projects and also an accessible platform for informal peer review. As it grew in content, it revolutionized access to the collective store of 'humankind's' accumulated knowledge; via information made available directly in the public spaces of the WWW and that available by subscription and/or permissions in a range of general and specialist libraries and other types of repositories of knowledge.

The information revolution, made possible by computer-based technology and the internet, has dramatically expanded the content of accessible Reality. And in doing so expanding the potential information horizons of our own slice of lived-within segment (arc') of reality; our personal reality.

As physics settled into the post-war world the 'shell' model of the atom offered an explanation, based on a certain ('magic') number of protons and neutrons – and described how this contributes to maintaining the integrity of stable atoms. A series of discoveries during the 1950s further advanced the understanding of the sub-atomic environment. From 1954 Robert Hofstadter studied the effects that electron scattering has on atomic nuclei and in doing so was able to show the structural characteristics – size, shape, and the electrical charge - of these particles. Then, in October 1955, Erwin Muller became the first person to observe an atom and doing so by utilizing the magnification and resolving power of the field ion microscope. So bringing the previously only theoretically describable and indirectly observable, into the world of direct observation. It would not be until 1972 before another scientist, Hans Dehmelt, was able to isolate a single electron.

In the 1950s the realm of sub-atomic particles was an appealing area of study for some of the best physicists, and generous government funding was contributing to making technological advances in the tools available, especially improving particle accelerators and cloud chambers.

In terms of explanatory scope and predictive power, two theoretical frameworks, (mutually inconsistent) were taken as the 'best yet' descriptions of the physical world – general relativity and quantum mechanics. General relatively focuses on the forces of gravity and on events and properties on the large scale, whereas quantum mechanics focuses on the sub-atomic events and properties on the very small scale. Seeking to reconcile these two theories was a significant ambition of theoretical physicists in the second half of the twentieth and early twenty-first centuries - in some unifying theory encompassing the 'quantization of general relativity'.

The world of particle physics was complex and, if not confusing, at least at a fundamental level still somewhat of a land of mystery. An attempt to bring some (systematic) order to the sub-atomic world had been made in 1962 by Murray Gell-Mann, with his 'The Eightfold Way' system. Gell-Mann used the properties of each type of particle to place them into one of eight categories. He also suggested that underlying the differences was an even more fundamental particle from which the known particles were constituted named 'quarks', and of course their anti-quarks.

The two primary constituents of any atom's nucleus – protons and neutrons – were linked to the concept of quark. The proton was identified as having three quarks (two 'up' one 'down') each of a different 'colour' (red, blue, green) and a neutron also having three quarks (one 'up' and two 'down') each of a different 'colour' (red, blue, green). The strong nuclear force holds the nucleus (proton/neutron) quarks together with a particle named as the gluon (spin-1) facilitating this interaction (S.Hawking would later on suggest that quarks are held together by 'strings' of gluons). Some experimental support was offered to Gell-Mann's theoretical idea of quarks when, between 1967-1973, physicists using the US SLAC particle accelerator (2 miles long) discovered traces of their existence.

In 1974 Burton Richter and Samuel Tring, working independently, discovered the 'charm quark' (a type of quark composed of both the quark and its anti-quark). Then, later on, in 1995, a team of scientists working at the FERMI Lab. in the US were able to show the generation of a 'top quark' from a collision between a proton and an anti-proton.

Fifield (ed. 1992, p9) notes how CERN's ability to re-create the conditions prevailing less than 100th of a second after the Big Bang facilitated the creation of the weak nuclear force carriers, the W- and Z-bosons. It was later, in 1983, discovered at CERN that the W and Z particles are intermediate states in the neutron radioactive decay process, states occurring prior to the generation of an electron and a neutrino.

Bernal suggests that the range of different types of particles, some having only the merest flicker of a flicker of existence (some with 'life' as short as 10^{-27} of a second!) could perhaps be better described as '....different states of the same basic energy concentrations or mathematical singularities of some field deeper than that of the electro-magnetic or the conventional meson fields' (Bernal, 1965, page 764)

Gary Zukav used the concept of 'particle zoo' to highlight the colourful, unpredictable collection of particles that had been shown to inhabit the sub-atomic realm. He suggested that: 'The world view of particle physics is a picture of chaos beneath order. At the fundamental level is a confusion of continual creation, annihilation and transformation.' a realm: '...... without 'stuff' where what is = what happens, and where an unending tumultuous dance of creation, annihilation and transformation runs unabated within a framework of conservation laws and probability.' (Zukav, 1979, p213)

Notions such as particle and wave, and their associated mathematical representations, are ways of conceptualizing the fundamental matter of which the Universe is constituted and by the end of the twentieth century sub-atomic 'events' could be described in terms of a range of properties and forces.

So looking back over the twentieth century, we can see that the foundations of a Standard Model were laid down in the 1930s (if to an extent building on earlier work) and was more or less completed during the 1970s. This, the Standard Model of the 1970s, simply described: is of a subatomic realm composed of 12 fundamental particles and three of the four elementary forces (not gravity). With the particles being divided into two groups, quarks and leptons, each made of six different types of particle, linked together in pairs according to mass (light – heavy). For quarks, these three pairs are: are up/down charm/strange and top/bottom – quarks also come in three 'colours'. For leptons the pairs are: electron-electron neutrino, muon-muon neutrino and tau-tau neutrino. Each of the three forces has its own specific boson and these are involved in energy transfer between particles. Gravity also has its own predicted boson, the 'graviton', but as yet this has not been found.

A key strength of the Standard Model is that it has proved able to successfully explain almost all of the experimental findings – and has successfully predicted a range of phenomena. It was also apparent that general relativity and quantum mechanics could not be reconciled within the Standard Model and so were unlikely to be the deepest level of explanation for the way in which the Universe behaves on the very tiniest and very largest of scales. The Standard Model of the 1970s, slightly modified, was the default descriptive position for particle physics for the rest of the century and is the model that a unified theory (a theory of everything – TOE) seeks to go beyond. A unified theory that would seek to resolve the internal inconsistencies within the standard theory and the incompatibility between relativity and quantum mechanics.

A more recent discovery that - that most physicists are now pretty confident about - would vindicate a theoretical prediction made by Peter Higgs (and the Belgium physicist François Englert) in the 1960s. A prediction based on the assumed presence of an entity named the Higgs Boson. The Higgs Boson is an energy field that is thought to impart mass to matter; suggested to have been around since very close to the Big Bang; possibly much less than 1 second later. It is suggested to operate as a sort of treacle-like (substance) that slows down sub-atomic particles and in doing so allowing them to 'accrue' mass. The evidence, provided by the LHC in December.2011 (as part of the CMS and ATLAS projects), has convinced the world of high energy physics that a lightweight form of the Higgs Boson (and so the presence of the Higgs field) has been confirmed, further underpinning the 'Standard Model' of particle physics.

A potential proposition to supersede the Standard Model was one that came to the forefront of theoretical physics in the later twentieth century seeking to overcome the descriptive weaknesses of the standard model, initially in relation to the strong nuclear force and later of gravity. This, 'string', theory that, according to John Gribbin, is based on the idea that quarks and their behaviour might be better understood as '....manifestations of even deeper layers of activity involving tiny loops [later also non-loops] of vibrating 'string.' (Gribbin, 2003, page 528). We are now considering the behaviour of matter within the atomic nucleus, where each string is so tiny[6] that it would take 10^{20} of them laid end to end to match the diameter of a nucleus.

The notion of string theory had initially been suggested by the work, in 1968, of Gabriele Veneziano (working at CERN), who linked a mathematical description (the Euler beta-function), set out two hundred years previously, to a modern understanding of sub-atomic properties. Then, in 1970 two physicists, Holger Nielson and Yoichiro Nambu, working separately, were able to build on the earlier work and show that if it were assumed that instead of elementary particles being conceived as packages of energy moving in space they are more usefully conceived as one-dimensional (wave-like) vibrating strings. At that stage of development the predictions that arose out of the theory were not supported by experimental observations and by the mid 70s initial versions of string theory were pretty much relegated to the history of science. With more fruitful looking theoretical ideas - such as 'point-particle quantum field theory' and variants of the Standard Model - being progressed by all but a relatively few physicists. These few, perhaps drawn to the theory by the neatness of the related mathematics, kept the faith in string theory.

In 1974 John Schwarz and Joel Scherk (working at the California Institute of Technology) made a link between theoretically vibrating strings and a particle related to gravity – the 'graviton' - and this appeared to offer the potential for fundamental unification. Schwarz

---

[6] Just one unit of one Planck in length, so 16 millionths of a billionth of a billionth of a billionth of a millimetre.

and Scherk's idea differed from initial versions of string theory, not least in assuming a massive increase in the tension within strings. Once again, when exposed to examination, some problems with this link were revealed and the idea of some string-like character of 'matter and energy' at the sub-atomic level, was to remain on the periphery of advancing physics.

Renewed interest in the theory was stimulated when, in 1984 Michael Green and John Schwarz, wrote a paper that resolved problems related to incorporating aspects of quantum theory within string theory; one implication of this being the assumed propagation of 10 instead of 4 dimensions. Theirs was a significant paper, hinting at the potential of string theory, stimulating a number of physicists to embrace the challenge and apply themselves to working on its further development. Within two years of the Green-Schwarz publication research papers poured from physicists - over 1000 according to Brian Greene (1999). By the end of the 1980s, physicists had identified five different versions of string theory, each requiring 10 dimensions. Greene wrote that: 'A number of us consistently worked deep into the night to try to master the vast areas of theoretical physics and abstract mathematics that are required to understand string theory.' (Greene, 1999, p139).

A significant landmark in the development of string theory came in 1995 when, at a conference of physicists held at the University of Southern California, Edward Witten introduced a new, a 'superstring', theory that could link all five of those that had by then

been identified. And to do so partly by incorporating a characteristic known as duality and including one more dimension (so 11 - 10 in space as well as time). The extra dimension replaces the idea of strings with a vibratory pattern based on membranes. This, and some other ideas, led to the progression of string theory into M-theory. Considered by many physicists to be at the frontier of early twenty-first century physics and generally thought to be the most likely source for providing a unifying theoretical framework for string theory. Achieving this unification by a description of the sub-atomic realm that offers a significant (if not complete) increase in explanatory power.

The role of M-theory as a fundamental unifying theory for the five primary versions of string theory has so far not fulfilled the initial more optimistic predictions. Continuing issues include the problem of the cosmological constant and the need to stabilize the multidimensional context for string theory. Lee Smolin (2006 p154) noted that in 1998 a serious problem with string theory emerged when observations of supernovas showed that the Universe was not only expanding (as had long been known) but that the rate of expansion was accelerating, meaning that the cosmological constant had to be a positive number, a phenomenon apparently difficult to reconcile with standard versions of string theory.

Such is the complexity of string theory that adaptations were made when in 2003 a number of physicists (string theorists) felt able, among other things, to introduce 'antibranes' to wrap around the spatial dimensions of strings along with branes. Branes being posited as physical entities with mass – and possibly a charge – that link 'idealized' sub-atomic particles (point particles) to the higher dimensions required for string theories. With the brane/antibrane framework allowing the cosmological constant to be assumed as being very small, so providing stability to the string structure.

Early in the twenty-first century theoretical considerations, focused on being able to accommodate complexity with different versions of string theory, generated ever more imaginative notions. Including the idea of there being an almost infinite number of versions of string theory, each being applicable to an almost infinite number of universes – a multiverse – with 10^{500} versions of the theory; considerably more than the total number of atoms in the known universe!

More recently a 'perturbative' approach has been introduced to explain how strings might interact; although some physicists consider that this – a basically mathematical-innovation - tends to limit the wider potential for string theory. They are looking beyond it and are doing so with the aid of 'supersymmetry'. Supersymmetry relates to the fact that different particles have different 'spin' characteristics and how these might link to the coupling properties suggested by each of the string theories.

Symmetry in physics is the representation of the way in which the fundamental forces behave, highlighting the way in which reversing a process involves the same interactions as the original process. With a similar symmetry being seen with processes involving some, but not all, particle interactions. Supersymmetry is a theory seeking to link gravity to the other three fundamental forces and to make this link by identifying a relationship between the two classes of particles – bosons and fermions.

Supersymmetry could enhance the Standard Model by filling in some of its theoretical gaps. For Jon Butterworth (2017, p264) Supersymmetry if introduced: '…..between bosons which carry the forces, and the fermions which make up the matter' - it could open up the scope for revising the Standard Model. Because as supersymetric particles only decay into other supersymmetric particles they offer stability in the final decay particle (the one with lowest mass named 'the sparticle'), which means that those final decay particles created during the Big Bang period should still exist – And according to Butterworth they are a potential candidate for dark matter (as WIMPS – Weakly Interacting Massive Particles)

For Julian Barbour (1999, pp191-2 this 'superstring' theory, is seeking to combine '……the idea of supersymmetry [allowing the mathematical inclusion of particles not available to the Standard Model – including super-electrons, super-quarks] with the idea that the complete 'zoo' of particles known at present are simply different manifestations of the vibrations of a string…' In superstring theories the idea of particles located in space is replaced with particles located along open or closed 'strings' in ever-changing locations (vibrations). Each string occupying a particular location in space.

The brilliance of the conceptual imagination of some physicists has 'saved', or rather extended string theory as a possibility. If string theory does lead to unification of the three quantum fields and that of gravity this would allow for linking the description of the tiniest entities of matter with ones on the scale of the Universe.

The story of developing string theory has tended to illuminate the futility of pursuing a unification theory to the lay public.......a public (myself included) unable to grasp the mathematics, so unable to properly understand the descriptions offered even by physicists attempting to popularize their subject. It was perhaps ever thus with advances in science but string theory, and its lack of any reasonable prospect of experimental verification, does encourage skepticism.

Stepping back to consider implications, we might question whether the developments in string theory represent a complex mathematics-based conceptual flight away from material reality or a progressive advance towards explaining its interrelated conditions of complexity. There continues to be many physicists who are endeavouring to construct a string, or superstring, theory that can incorporate such aspects of the phenomenal world as: super-symmetry, cosmological constants, some implications of general relativity and quantum mechanics, quantum gravity, gauge theory, branes and anti-branes, duality, and no doubt others that I haven't noted; the theory remains live. With perhaps the most significant problem that string theory needs to resolve being the mismatch between the need for a fixed background (or background-independent version of quantum gravity) in a Universe that seems to be better expressed in term of general relatively with its process-like implications.

As well as popular skepticism (perhaps 'incomprehension'), string theory has also been subjected to critical consideration from within physics. Roger Penrose, during an informal radio interview (BBC Radio.4 20th June 2016) suggested that string theory was more about fashion than serious science, that it did not offer predictions, even if the mathematics was 'beautiful'. Lee Smolin broadened the critical evaluation, not least in relation to career prospects for non-string physicists and of the amount of resources made available for research related to string theory being diverted from other, arguably more promising, GUTs. Smolin is critical of the amount of institutional commitment directed toward this theoretical approach and he suggests that: 'If string theory is right, the world would have more dimensions and many more particles and forces than we have so far observed' (Smolin, 2006, p. xvii)

Greene (1999) has offered a somewhat more optimistic and more accessible description of string theory: '.....String alters this [the Standard Model] picture radically by declaring that the 'stuff' of all matter and all forces is the same. Each elementary particle is composed of a single string (perversely, perhaps even just the vibrations without the strings) - that is, each particle is a single string - and all strings are absolutely identical. Differences between the particles arise because their respective strings undergo different resonant vibrational patterns. What appear to be different elementary particles are actually different 'notes' on a fundamental string. The universe-being composed of an enormous number of these vibrating strings – is akin to a cosmic symphony........string theory provides the promise of a single, all-inclusive, unified description of the physical universe: a theory of everything (T.O.E.).' (Greene, 1999, p146)

Greene's description emphasizes properties such as the mass and force charges of different particles being linked to the vibrational patterns occurring within a string.

The development of string theory has made a significant contribution, not just in developing mathematics (particularly geometry and topography), but also in identifying a range of complex problems that need to be resolved by any unifying theory of matter.

A central theme of this book has been 'information' and its accelerating accumulation as/in the storehouse of humankind's available knowledge, a defining aspect of the Reality within which we live. The super complexity of string theory, and its almost infinite variations in the almost infinite number of universes (multiverse), allows us to realize just how complex – information laden - our potentially accessible Reality has become and how just a relatively small phenomenon within the history-long consideration of the fundamental constitution of the world has generated petabytes of novel information. Thales and his fellow hylozoists had a single substance 'moisture', with space and time taken for granted and similarly with Aristotle's four constituents (fire, earth, air water + 'quintessence') have over but 23 centuries transformed by the scientific method into the complexity of the Standard Model – string theory - M-theory – superstring theory - and a number of much less prominent theories of matter.

One possible fruitful link to what we can observe is that between string theory and black holes. String theories seem to offer useful descriptions (and modeling of) certain atypical types of black holes in relation to entropy, temperature change, and information loss, but for the standard black hole the mobile geometry considered to pertain for these is not one that any multidimensional (background-dependant) version of string theory has yet been able to adequately describe.

Such has been the popularity of string-type theories within the community of physicists that each year a specific conference is arranged to discuss progress. Although string theories probably remain the dominant focus of advancing physics, there are other theoretical perspectives being pursued. Arguably, some of these are much closer to recent experimental data than current string theories.

Some non-string theorists are working on ideas involving such areas as loop quantum gravity, theories linked to causal dynamical triangulations, twister theory (Roger Penrose), and even challenging the more conventional descriptions of time (Julian Barbour 2001) as well as the supposedly fixed constant of the speed of light (Joao Magueijo, 2004). The particle known as 'top quark', with a mass 200 times that of a proton, remains to be clarified and the process of doing this might mean a fundamental revision of the Standard Model, or even its supersession by something entirely new. There remains what could now be justifiable termed the 'perennial problem', of uniting gravity and the rest of particle physics within some Grand Unification Theory. But the exciting prospect offered for humanity as a whole by complex physical theories parallel the growth in the complexity of our collective experience of Reality. The progression of civil life has revealed an intensity in the complexity of Reality that requires uber-sophisticated forms of description and explanation if we are to adequately understand it.

The level of technology currently being used by physicists, not least super-colliders and laser interferometers, with superb quality components, is quite breathtaking for the lay-person. The further development of equipment for observing behaviour at the subatomic level, aided by the data processing and analyzing power of quantum computing, could reveal an entirely new framework for explaining the structure of matter.

From a different perspective, Julian Barbour offered the provocative suggestion that: 'Physics must be recast on a new foundation in which change is the measure of time, not time the measure of change.' and 'It strengthens my belief that all the physics of the universe can be described by a timeless wave equation' (op cit 2001, p2 and p310 - plus see web-site www.julianbabour.com). Lee Smolin is also uncomfortable with current assumptions about time, he suggests '...I have the feeling that quantum theory and general relativity are both deeply wrong about the nature of time. It is not enough to combine them. There is a deeper problem, perhaps going back to the origin of physics.' (Smolin, 2006, p256)

It might be that the basic descriptors (theories) used in twentieth century physics need themselves to be fundamentally revised. Even that some fundamental revision of mathematics is required to cope with the implications of what seems to be an increasingly more 'qualitative' complexity of the subatomic realm.

Physics in the early decades of the twenty-first century is a vibrant field of study – The leading experimental focus continues to be on the use of high speed particle accelerators. The subatomic realm is now described as being occupied by a colourful population of what at least are taken to be the significant entities - mesons, bosons, baryons, muons, - arranged in six groups ('up, down, strange, charm, top, bottom').

Looking back over the past nearly 120 year development of physics, if building on foundations laid mainly in the second half of the nineteenth century, would show how radically altered our understanding of matter has become. To the point that fundamental 'matter' has been transformed from being composed of hard particles with determinate behaviours, into vibrating energy-rich entities with behaviors based on probabilities. A transformation that has facilitated a significant contribution to post-industrial technologies and offering epistemological credibility for the cultural trope of uncertainty.

Nowhere is the Universe entirely 'empty' of this fundamental matter – the Universe is spread with four quantum fields – the fundamental forces of gravity, the weak and strong nuclear forces and the electromagnetic force. Within the quantum field particles and waves of energy, are continuously/spontaneously being created and annihilated as they borrow and return energy to the quantum field. This activity was first discovered in 1997 and is known as the Casmir effect. And it is to the exciting if enigmatic phenomenon – the Universe - that I now turn.

Astronomy

Early on in civil life individuals speculated on the phenomena passing across the night sky. The 5th century BCE Greek philosopher Leucippus is said to have suggested that:

'The whole is infinite… …Worlds unlimited in number are formed from these ['elements'] and dissolved into them. The manner of their formation is this. Many bodies [atoms] of all sorts of shapes are cut off from the infinite and stream into a great void, and these when collected in a mass produce a single vortex, following the motion of which they collide and revolve in all sorts of ways and begin to be sorted out, like to like. But when owing to their numbers that can no longer be carried around in equilibrium, the small atoms pass to the void without, as if through a strainer. The rest hold together, become entangled and move in conjunction with one another, so forming a first spherical complex. From this complex a kind of membrane becomes detached, containing within itself bodies of every kind. These whirl round in proportion to the resistance of the centre, and the membrane becomes thin as the contiguous bodies continually flow together by contact in the vortex. In this way the earth was formed, by the cohesion of the bodies which had moved to the centre. The

enclosing membrane in turn is augmented by the influx of atoms from outside; and as it whirls around, it adds to itself those that come into contact with it. Some of these become interlocked and form a complex that is wet and muddy at first, but drying out as they are carried round in the universal vortex they finally catch fires and form the substance of the stars... ...All stars are ignited by the speed of their motion....just as a cosmos is born, so also it grows, declines and perishes by some sort of necessity, the nature of which he [Leucippus] does not specify. '

W.K.C.Guthrie vol.II, 1965, pps 406/7 on Leucippus circa. 490 BCE (as compiled by Diogene Laertius from a version recorded by Theophrastus)

Not too bad an early imaginative start for the widening understanding of the heavens that was to follow, as speculation informed by observation and imagination gave way to the science of astronomy as the primary descriptor of the cosmos.

Direct access to the invisible world of subatomic phenomena is a closed one for most of us, with our only realistically being able to gain indirect understanding of it from physicists prepared to popularize (make accessible even if the cost is an extent of simplification) advances in their science. Whereas the attraction of the vaulted heavens – the dark mysterious terrain liberally peppered with multiple clusters of mobile bright lights – has been an ever-present since the pre-civil life of humankind. The image of a person, pictured in silhouette, gazing upon the overarching panoply of a starry sky seen on a cloudless night, is one symbolizing the mysteriousness of life, of being, and of eternity. I can feel a shared sense of intense yet uneasy awe with the person stepping clear of their stone-age village (or perhaps minding a flock of goats at night on some dusty hillside) five or more millennia ago. A timelessly shared experience of wonder projected across time and down generations since consciousness crossed a threshold of reflexivity. Humankind's shared encounter with the fate-filled echo of immensity as measured against eternity.

The science of the tiniest phenomena can provide detailed information on how the largest of phenomena came to take the form it has; of the Universe out there beyond the Earth's modest coating of atmosphere. Current thinking seems to be that an understanding in some unified theory, of the very tiniest and the very largest phenomena, could lie within the conditions (especially the implications of the recently detected gravitational waves) that apply deep within the black holes, currently closed to direct observation if not to theorizing.

Humankind's extended civil encounter with the Universe, and the resultant mass of novel information, has contributed to our store of available knowledge, and is yet another element of information-accretion contributing to continuously enlarging the Reality within which we live. But the accrual of factual knowledge is overlaid by the parallel enlarging of the imaginative horizon within this wider realm.

When we confront the Universe our conventional conceptual thinking is challenged – we easily slip into questions such as what happened before the Universe began, what will happen after it ends. The cognition evolved in response to the species-long (genealogical) earthly experience and the language which has sought to explain/describe and conceptually manipulate this experience has to reach for a 'meta-cognitive' level of conceptualization to describe the Universe – fortunately, (as with the sub-atomic realm) we have mathematics to describe the cosmic magnitudes and our imagination can offer images and analogies to allow at least some sense of grasping the cognitive terrain of a cosmos whose actual horizons are only constrained by the power of our probing technologies.

The twentieth century saw the development of technologies that would open up the visible Universe – and continue the work, the foundations of which had been laid by generations of astronomers dedicating themselves to long hours of observation and generally quite meticulous record keeping and cataloguing.

Notable ('western') astronomers included: Galileo Galilei and Tycho Brahe in the sixteenth century - Edmund Halley, Christian Huygens, Ole Romer and John Flamsteed in the seventeenth - Francis Laplace, John Mitchell, Thomas Wright, Caroline and William Herschel in the eighteenth. By the nineteenth century, hundreds of astronomers were working to improve our understanding of the Universe, some of the more notable being: Pierre Pickering, Friedrich Bessel, Pierre Jansen, Norman Lockyer, Norman Pogson, Thomas Henderson. The twentieth century saw thousands more, as a mostly amateur activity was transformed into a professional discipline, including:: Arthur Eddington, Henry Norris Russell, Ejnar Hertzsprung, Milton Humason, Edwin Hubble, Vesto Slipher, Henrrietta Swan Leavitt, Fritz Zwicky, Walter Baade, George Hale, George Ellery, Fred Hoyle, Herman Bondi.....just a few of a long line of committed 'star gazers' whose work has widened the actual and imagined horizons way beyond the limits of our planet Earth.

These 16th - 20th century astronomers had in turn built on the work of observation and recording undertaken since the dawn of civil life. Especially in the 'catalogues', of celestial bodies that had begun to be compiled by Babylonian astronomers from about mid 1500 BCE; one of the earliest noting 36 stars, carved onto clay tablets. The Chinese, during the Shang Dynasty (1600-1050) BCE, recorded their observations on 'oracle bones'. In Greece by 370 BCE, Eudoxus had listed all of the classical constellations. With the first actually known star catalogue, and this only known indirectly via Ptolemy, being that of Timocharis of Alexandra (320-260 BCE); a record of 18 stars noted by their declination. This was followed by that of Hipparchus in 130 BCE, and Ptolemy's own 'Almagest' in 120 CE (1022 stars visible from Alexandra). The quality of cataloging was improved with the 'The Book of Fixed Stars' circa 964 CE by the Persian astronomer Abd al-Rahman al Sufie. He was also the first astronomer to record the massive Andromeda galaxy – but of course was not aware of its status as a galaxy.

Cataloging, as did astronomy generally, enjoyed an marked impetus with the invention of the telescope in 1608 and notable amongst these were John Flamstead's listing of 3000 stars in 1712, James Bradley's 1762 'Star Catalog', William Herschel's 'Catalogue of Nebulae' (1786) expanded by his son John as the 'General Catalogue of Nebulae and Clusters of Starts' (1864), and even further expanded as 'New General Catalogue' (1880s) by J.L.Dreyer. The publishing history as well as the increasing amount of content nicely illustrating the accumulative nature of astronomical data.

We now have access to various types of catalogues, perhaps better described as 'celestial mapping' in which are recorded and located a range of different of types of celestial object; alphabetically running from George Abell's catalogue of star rich galaxies (includes 4,072 galaxies) to Fritz Zwicky's 6 vol. 'Catalogue of galaxies and clusters of galaxies' (complied 1961-68). The Guide Star Catalogue II (GSC II) complied using the resources of the Hubble Space Telescope launched in 1990 (with a life expectancy into the 2030s) notes 500 million stars. This replacing the original 'Guide Star I Catalogue' (GSC I) created by the Photometric Sky Survey (1983), that contains information on over 10 million stars; increased to 19 million by 1989.

The technology that became available in the new millennium allowed a significant increase in the rate of compilation, an example being the US Naval Observatory's 'Robotic Astrometric Telescope Star Catalogue'; with quite detailed information on 228 million stars. The largest catalogue currently available, the meta-catalogue NOMAD, has positional and magnitude information on 1.1 billion stars. On a even greater cosmic scale, the 'Sloan Digital Sky Survey' is set to measure the red-shift of over one million galaxies, further enhancing our understanding of the structure of the Universe.

Currently, we understand that we live on a planet rotating within in a solar system mainly composed of eight planets orbiting a star at its centre, as but one of about 300 billion other stars in our (Milky Way) galaxy which in turn is but one of possibly as many as 2,000 billion galaxies in the Universe; a figure revised up from 100-200 billion in 2016 following work by the Hubble Space Probe.

Usefully, given the sheer number and complexity of types of celestial bodies, the naming conventions for new stars is overseen and regulated by the 'International Astronomical Union' (IAU), an organization founded in 1919, with the primary aim of promoting international cooperation in astronomy, an aspect of this being to standardize the naming of celestial objects. Currently the IAU, based in Paris, has over 12,500 individual members, almost all working as professional astronomers in 101 countries

Technological advances in the understanding of light made in the 18th-19th century had laid the foundations for advances that followed. By then Isaac Newton had already coined the word 'spectra' for the patterns of coloured light that could be identified if the light rays from the Sun were defused by being passed through a prism. And Thomas Young and Augustin Fresnal, working separately, had between them established that light travels in waves (contrary to Newton's light as 'particles')

William Wollaston passed light from the Sun through a prism and noticed some dark lines crossing the spectra (identifying 7 dark lines in 1802). Between 1814-17, the instrument-maker Joseph von Fraunhofer, building on the work of Newton and Wollaston as well as Young and Fresnal, constructed a crude prism 'spectrometer', which was built to study the phenomenon of the thin dark lines that could, in suitable conditions, be seen in the spectra of light. He designed a grating with lines of slits through which light could be projected, a mechanism that overcame the problem of standardization inherent in using prisms made of different types of glass. The light emerging through the grating formed a pattern of 'bright and dark fringes' and could be used to measure the wavelengths of spectral lines ('Fraunhofer lines'). Fraunhofer extended the number of dark lines seen between the red and violet ends of the spectrum and he also mapped the wavelength of these 576 lines. He was able to demonstrate that the lines were a property of the light rather than of the prism through which it was passing. Fraunhofer also identified dark lines in the spectra of Venus and of a few stars. In 1848 Leon Foucault gave the first laboratory demonstration of the effect of light being absorbed by a material – of sodium absorbing the yellow light from a strong arc light; the process giving rise to the dark lines – incidentally, he also (1850) calculated the speed of light to within 1% of today's accepted figure.

In the second half of the nineteenth century the study of spectra was taken up by a number of European scientists. In Germany during the 1850s Gustav Kirchhoff and his colleague Robert Bunsen had established that if you hold a sample of a chemical substance in the clear flame (such as that produced by a 'Bunsen' burner) a substance-specific coloured light would be given off (see above). Within the spectrum of this light could be detected a patterning of spectral lines similar to what had previously been detected by Fraunhofer and Foucault. The notions of 'fingerprint' and 'barcode' have been used as analogies for this uniqueness. The bright lines are the result of a substance radiating light (emission) and the dark lines the result of a substance absorbing (absorption) light; with both processes operating at the same wavelength. Kirchhoff and Bunsen were able to relate the phenomenon of spectral lines directly to the properties of substances. The implication being that each chemical element or compound had its own unique spectral pattern and so, once the spectral pattern of a substance had been noted, its specific chemical composition could be identified. In 1859 Krichhoff, with Bunsen's practical help, was able to use this characteristic of light to identify the spectral line pattern for sodium in the light passing through the Sun's atmosphere and hence showing that this element is present there. And then, in 1868, this technique was used to identify an unknown element, Helium (helios = Sun), to be identified – unknown pattern of lines must necessarily be a characteristic of an unknown element - in light from the Sun.

Between 1860 and 1910 the new investigative method of 'spectroscopy' was involved in the identification of 21 of 27 newly identified elements. The continuing development of spectroscopy included the refinement of X-ray spectroscopy (by 1916) and laser-based precision spectroscopy – allowing a significant improvement in accuracy of the measurement of frequencies of each. By 1900 the 100 plus year (over 200 years if we go back to Newton) development of spectroscopy meant that astronomy now had an experimentally established technique to identify the elemental composition of a range of cosmic bodies.

In 1913 H.N.Russell clarified the spectral composition of stars which gave an indication of the way this changes over time, their 'evolution'; as a star ages it becomes cooler. This was building on the earlier work of Angelo Secchi who by 1867 had classified the spectra of 4000 stars into 4 main categories I-IV. By the end of the century Secchi's four types had been extended to ten (O,B,A,F,G,K,M,R,N,S) main divisions, each having subdivisions – Our Sun being G2.

The characteristics of the spectral composition of light also allowed an understanding of the movement of bodies in space. As a cosmic body moves the pattern of its spectral lines changes – towards the blue end as it travels towards an observer and towards the red end as it moves away. This 'Doppler shift 'can give information about the direction and speed of bodies moving in space. With the movement of galaxies relative to each other (a non-Doppler red-shift) allowing us to determine that the whole visible Universe is expanding and so, by implication is its age. The first astronomer to observe the red-shift of galaxies was Vesto Slipher in 1912

As the nineteenth century moved into the twentieth, photography had already become established as a useful aid in the study of cosmic phenomena. The 1851 solar eclipse had been photographed and by 1879 William Huggins was producing usable photographic images of the spectra of stars. Photography was used by astronomers to provide fixed images of the spectra of stars, so allowing a more detailed (time independent) examination and, in relation to their movement, time-lapse photography could be used to identify very small shifts in the wave-lengths (red-shift and blue-shifts) of light from bodies moving through space.

Measurement of distances was another key to extending our knowledge of the Universe. In 1838 Friedrich Bessell was using stellar parallax (using an instrument called a heliometer) to determine the distance to a celestial object by reference to the movement of the Earth, and so the change in position of an observer, to measure distance of a star. But Earth-bound parallax was not a practical means of measuring the distance to far off stars so by 1900 the distance to only a small number of stars (60, all within the our own galaxy) had been determined. The ability to photographically fix images of stars at different times as they moved across the sky allowed better use of stellar parallax and so the distance to more distant stars to be determined.

Another advance in measuring cosmic distances was initiated by Henrietta Leavitt who in 1912 used photographic techniques to study the Small Magellanic Cloud (SMC), focusing on stars whose luminosity varied according to a cyclical pattern over 1-50 days (cepheid stars). The SMC is a cluster of stars; in fact we now know it is a galaxy, relatively close to our own. Leavitt had identified features of the variable luminosity of cepheid stars that could make distance measurement possible. This potential method of distance measurement became actual when, in 1913, Ejnar Hertzsprung was able to use the method of stellar parallax to estimate the distance to the SMC at 30,000 light years. By 1950 stellar parallax had been used to determine the distance of 10,000 stars, and by the end of the century of 120,000 stars, and these with a relatively high degree of precision. The spectral classification of stars and their apparent magnitude (relative to other stars) was being used to measure the distances of even more distant stars using 'spectroscopic parallax'.

Throughout the twentieth century techniques to measure celestial distances improved significantly. The satellite Hipparcos (European Space Agency - ESA) was launched in 1989 to measure the position of stars (and other celestial objects) and this data enabled the position of over 100,000 stars to be determined. All relatively close to the Earth, their 'only' being up to 1,600 light years away. But in the context of the Tycho 2 catalogue, with its 2.5 million recorded stars, there remain large areas of the distant Universe to be more fully mapped. The European Space Agency's 'Cosmic Mission' series of projects – planned to run to 2022 (JUICE) and 2026 (PLATO) - will continue a range of cosmological investigations, including distance measurements.

A range of different types of parallax: Secular parallax, moving cluster parallax, and dynamical parallax, have been designed to measure astronomical distances. But the precise measurement of stellar distance only (in a relative sense) applies to stellar objects up to about 1000 par secs. (1 par sec = 3.26 light years or 30 trillion kilometers); beyond this, distances are estimates based more on astronomically informed assumptions than precise measurement.

Photography and spectroscopy were two key techniques at the beginning of the modern era of astrophysics, as was the use of mathematics. From the 1980s space-based observatories, along with the use of the computing power and the information storage capacity of computers, have significantly enhanced the advance of astronomy. During the past 20 years the internet has made the sharing of information (between professionals and amateur astronomers) much easier. There has been a proliferation of web-sites and phone-based applications offering masses of information on astronomy, and most of the big land-based observatories allow supervised public access. .

In terms of hardware: at the start of the century the 40 inch Yerkes telescope was at the forefront of astronomical research. But this, the largest ever refracting telescope, was to mark the high point in the popularity of these instruments as during the twentieth century significantly improved reflecting telescopes became more popular. Improving a technology that had been introduced as long ago at 1704 when Isaac Newton utilized a curved mirror to gather light prior to it being reflected and focused at a 'focal point'

The first permanently sited telescope constructed in the twentieth century was one constructed on Mt Wilson (California) in 1904. This was the 40inch Solar telescope used to undertake important work on the spectra of sunspots. The initial instrument being supplemented by a new 60inch mirror reflecting telescope, constructed in 1908. The capability of the observatory was further enhanced by the newer telescope being fitted with a 100inch mirror, the Hooker, in 1917. The astronomers working at the Mt Wilson site were at the forefront of the fast developing science of astronomy up to 1949 (it being the world's largest telescope until that time); not least in the use of 'variable stars' (cepheids), whose periodic expanding and contracting makes them suitable for measuring distance. Astronomers based at Mt. Wilson, produced a stream of data throughout this period, especially in relation to the classification of stars according to their light spectrum. The observatory was also involved in an experiment to accurately determine the speed of light. Even more notable advances included the measurement of our galaxy (the Milky Way) and in discovering that our sun was not the centre of it. The Mt Wilson observatory continues to contribute to astronomy as at 2020.

A controversial issue (touching on religion as well as science) was the size of the Universe – at the turn of the century it was thought that the whole Universe was constituted by just one galaxy. Although as early as the eighteenth century the philosopher Immanuel Kant had suggested the possibility of star systems beyond the Milky Way. Evidence of estimated distances of observed bodies beyond the Milky Way galaxy, and more especially of the possibility of stars within nebulae led, in the 1920s, to the 'one galaxy' position being challenged. In 1924 Edwin Hubble identified a cepheid variable star with a high luminosity in the Andromeda spiral nebulae with an estimated distance of 1,000,000 light years (now estimated to be 2,250,000 light years distant) and so way beyond the outer reaches of the our own galaxy. Andromeda is a massive galaxy composed of one trillion stars, vast drifts of dust, and with a giant black hole at its centre. Throughout the 1920s the American Edwin Hubble and the Estonian Ernst Opik increasingly identified cepheid stars within spiral nebulae, and so accumulating evidence of numerous galaxies making up the visible Universe.

It was in 1924 that the mathematician Alexander Friedman first suggested that the Universe is expanding and had had an explosive beginning. Then, in1927, as a result of his solving the equations of Einstein's theory of general relativity, George Lemaître suggested a non-static, indeed expanding, Universe. Lemaître's suggestion was given evidential support by Robert Hubble in 1929 when he oversaw a detailed analysis (by colour) of light being emitted by galaxies and confirmed that galaxies are moving away from Earth. Within but one decade the conception the Universe had changed in terms of its size and the revelation that it was expanding. Both facts having significant implications for the understanding of the Universe.

The Hale Telescope was another significant instrument, built in 1948 (sited at Mt. Palomar) using a 200 inch reflector, was soon making important discoveries about galaxies and pulsars and has made a series of other original contributions to astronomy over its 60 years working life. In eastern-Europe, the Russian 'Special Astrophysical Observatory' (SAO -Russian Academy of Science), based in the Greater Caucasus, was operating from 1974. It is Russia's largest ground-based observatory, running both a 236 inch diameter reflector optical telescope and a radio telescope. The work of the SAO has focused on a range of cosmological areas, including the cosmic background radiation and the early Universe as well as the dynamics of galaxies and their chemical composition.

More recently, the W.M.Keck Observatory, sited on the summit of

Mt Kea in Hawaii, has been operating since 1993 using Keck I twin telescopes, with a Keck II operating from 1996. The Kecks were the world's largest optical and infra-red twinned telescopes, each of them weighing 300 tons and each having a 10m diameter primary mirror, with the novel feature of each of these being mirrors composed of 36 hexagonal segments coordinated to operate together. This precision technology was improved further in 1999 with the introduction of 'adaptive optics', a system that was able to enhance image clarity. With a further improvement in capability being made in 2004 when Keck became the first observatory to use a laser guided star projector. Keck operates with nanometer precision and can offer images of cosmic objects with high sensitivity and impressive clarity. As at 2021 the World's largest terrestrially-located reflecting telescope was the Grand Telescopia Canaria, constructed in 2007 on the Spanish island of La Palma. An instrument that can peer far into the cosmos via its 10.4m mirror; with an advanced OSIRIS spectroscopy system able to provide detailed information on celestial bodies.

Another giant telescope, using similar technology to Keck II, the 'Large Binocular Telescope', began operation in 2005 from a mountain range in eastern Arizona. This utilizes twin mirrors each 8.4 metres in diameter, using adaptive optics, with each mirror having 672 small magnets attached to the back enabling the mirror to be adjusted up to 1000 times per second.

The ability to resolves images from light and infra-red radiation waves was enhanced with the introduction of the radiation gathering technique enabled by radio telescopes. An early version being Karl Jansky's 30m telescope operating from 1931. The basic technique deployed by Jansky was incrementally improved throughout the next 90 years, with innovations such as the introduction of a parabolic reflector by Grote Reber in 1937, and in 1946 the introduction of the use of a linked array of parabolic reflectors (astronomical radio interferometry).

Today, just as with optical and infra red telescopes, radio telescopes are sited across all of the continents (including Antarctica) and also in space (HALCA and Zond 3 being two of these). The most powerful radio telescope has for some time been the Aceribo Observatory in Puerto Rico 305m. But an even more powerful radio telescope was completed at the end 2016, sited in Guizhou Province China 500m; 8,000 people were displaced from their homes to make way for the massive construction site. Taken overall, the increase in observational power made available to the world's thousands of professional astronomers (aided by the commitment of a number of enthusiastic and gifted amateurs) since 1900 has been quite staggering.

Radio telescopes operate via two or more arrays of mirrors or numbers of radio telescope antennas. They are able to pick up radio waves from a range of sources including: pulsars, quasars, standard as well as neutron stars, and various types of dust cloud. It was the use of radio telescopy that provided evidence to support a key, and initially hotly contested, scientific prediction that the Universe began with a 'Big Bang' event.

But before considering this notion let's just consider aspects of the most notable 'celestial objects', those grouped under the category of 'stars' (even at the cost of repeating some of the comments made in Chapt.1 above). Observational study has revealed the evolving nature of stars, from their relatively gentle formation to their, occasional spectacular, demise. Put very simply......the beginning of a star's life can be noted as the time when a cosmic cloud (initially very cold) of sufficient density to generate the required gravitation force, containing mostly hydrogen and some helium, condenses down under the increasing pressure of its own gravitational force. This increased pressure raises the temperature to over 10 million degrees centigrade at which point the process of nuclear fusion begins; a process of changing hydrogen into helium. So generating a massive amount of energy in the form of heat and light as the star begins its brightly shining life. Small stars have temps of about 3000 degrees centigrade at the surface; our own Sun has a surface temperature of 6000 degrees centigrade, and for bigger stars this can go up to 30,000 degrees centigrade. As the hydrogen begins to get used up, and pressure and temperature increase, heavier elements such as carbon and oxygen being formed.

A significant factor in determining the next stage of a star's life is mainly dependent on its mass and, whereas the heaviest stars use up their available hydrogen in a relatively short period, the lightest of stars can shine for one billion years (our Sun has been shining for about 5000 million years and is about halfway through its lifetime as a star). As a star's hydrogen is used up it swells to become a Red Giant with a core composed mostly of helium atoms which then, due to rising temperature and pressure, fuse into heavier elements, firstly carbon then silicon, iron and neon. Currently the star Betelgeuse, located in the constellation Orion, is an example of a Red Giant (sometimes noted as a Supergiant) and as now seen is 100 times its previous size. It has drawn the attention of astronomers as it is predicted that 'fairly soon' (in terms of universe timescales) it will explode in a Supernova explosion

These dying stars, whether as supernovae or as planetary nebula, release massive amounts of elemental material into the space. Providing elements with a suitable atomic structure that would enable the molecular conditions for organic life; and this material continues to be released in enormous amounts, all across the Universe. The conditions (heat and density) within the core of stars have been and are the cauldrons in which the potential for organic 'life' have been forged.

Out of this mix of one body dying but in doing so gifting the Universe with material for complexification (and consciousness – we humans are in effect composed partly of 'star-dust') we see a universe exhibiting entropy, a universe undergoing a protracted process of cooling - but is this a process towards ending or of evolving? Will our universe evolve into something new? And, if so, will any new universe contain the seeds of its progenitor, and does our universe contain any residual information from of its own progenitor? Serious questions posed to the enigmatic emptiness of a starlight space (more dark than light) that stirs our emotions and stimulates our imaginations as we gaze upon the night-sky.

Continuing on the evolution of a star, the outer layers of a Red Giant, created from small to medium stars, dissipate relatively gently (as visually stunning planetary nebulae) into space whilst the core continues to contract and, having used up its nuclear fuel, would slowly cool and fade to become a White Dwarf with a large mass but only about as big as the Earth e.g. the co-star of Sirius, named the Pup Star due to the much brighter Sirius being named the Dog Star. The Red Giants formed out of massive stars have a core composed mostly of helium but due to the mass of these stars the pressure and temperature at their core increases and reaches a point when the atoms of helium fuse to form carbon and then even heavier elements such as neon and iron... processes which release energy to allow the star to continue to shine. These bodies are generally quite unstable and the instability reaches a point where it begins, in seconds, to collapse; a process causing the release of a tremendous amount of energy, resulting in the outer layers of the dying star exploding out to form the brightest of celestial objects – a Supernovae - with an explosion generating 10 to the power 10 times a star's normal energy levels, using up any available nuclear fuel.

Estimates suggest that there have been 200 million exploding stars in our galaxy since its beginning – just gazing into the sky on any night you would see evidence of 2 or 3 exploding stars.

What's left of the core of a supernovae star can continue to collapse until its atomic constitution reduces to leave only neutrons – when a 'Neutron Star' is formed; these being composed of tightly compressed matter but are only about 25 kilometers across. A certain type of these were named pulsars due to the pulsed rhythm of the radio waves that they emitted (the Fermi Gamma-ray Space Telescope, launched in 2009, has identified over 2,000 Pulsars). But if the core of a supernovae is too big to form a Neutron Star the internal forces of its own gravity causes the core to continue to collapse until it is reduced to a point with no measurable size but with infinite density, within a wider region covering minute to massive distances and having a gravitational force that will allow nothing, even light, to be released/escape - to become a 'black hole'. Neutron Stars can also, via a quark star stage, collapse further to become a black hole. Anything being drawn into this gravitational field simply 'disappears' and can never return to the visible Universe. Although Stephen Hawking was able to provide mathematical support for a 'quantum effect' by which some radiation (Hawking Radiation) is emitted by black holes as they slowly shrink in size (evaporate) and heat up. The conditions of black holes seem to very similar – massive density – to the conditions at the time of Big Bang, and a certain stage of each is termed a 'singularity'. Singularities emerge from Plank's era (about 13.7 billion years ago) and also lie deep within black holes. This is why some theoretical physicists consider that the mystery of pre-Big Bang could be revealed (or at least better understood) by a close study of black holes.

Black holes had been theoretically predicted by astronomers in the 1930s but during the 1980s their presence was confirmed. Ranging in size from very very tiny to 'super-massive'. There seem to be black holes all across the Universe, with a large one at the centre of our own Milky Way galaxy (Sagittarious A – with a mass equivalent to 4 million Suns) and another, appropriately named the 'Oldest Monster Black Hole', created about BB + 690m years that, being 800 million times larger than the Sun is pretty big even by cosmic standards. It is thought possible that each galaxy could have a super-massive black hole at its centre. Black holes retain a large mass of material relative to size, and so also energy, but such is its density that it is also able to generate a massive amount of gravitational effect (or a steep 'space-time slope' towards its interior); even light itself cannot escape this effect. It seems that black holes can vary in size from the tiniest phenomena (down to the 21 micrograms of mass on the Planck scales – applicable to conditions in which gravity and quantum physics are unified) to the very largest. The cosmological conditions deep within black holes seem to replicate those of pre-Big Bang, not least in terms of density and also gravity, so investigation of these could offer useful information on the Universe's beginning; such investigation could also progress research into the various types of multi-verse theories (see below).

Other significant cosmological bodies include 'quasars' and 'pulsars'. Quasars are located in the central region of a galaxy (possible a type of galaxy in themselves) that emit an intense output of radiation, generated as a quasar's material is being drawn into a black hole. Such is the intensity of the (synchrotron) radiation emitted that most quasars outshine the galactic material that surrounds them. Quasars can 'shine' more brightly than a hundred billion stars. Pulsars (first discovered in 1967) are compact spherically shaped bodies not much more than 10 kilometers wide, but with a mass many times that of the Sun. Their regular rotation causes their emitted light (radiation) to appear to 'flicker' ('pulse'). The study of pulsars has contributed to increasing the understanding of neutron stars, the group of stars to which they belong. At 2020 about 2,300 pulsars have been detected.

In 1930, as an outcome of his identification of an expanding Universe (see above), Edwin Hubble proposed that a consequence of this was that the Universe had expanded from an infinitesimal point, a 'primitive atom'. This idea was further developed in the 1930s by Ralph Alpher and Robert Herman – informed and guided by their senior colleague George Gamow – who introduced the idea of a massive 'explosion' (sarcastically termed the 'Big Bang' by the alternative 'Steady State' proponent Fred Hoyle).

The idea of an 'explosion'[7] of super hot, super dense, radiation at

---

[7] A 'zone' of very special activities taking place; a very special type of event creating time - space - material – gravity characterized by rapid expansion and cooling.

the beginning of the Universe came into the mainstream of science (at least as a theoretical idea) with a paper presented in the spring 1948 edition of the 'Physical Review'. If the Universe had began with a massive explosion of radiation then, even billions of years later, there should be some residual, if much colder, background radiation still present in the Universe. It was a faint echo of this radiation-fireball that Arno Penzias and Robert Wilson detected in 1965 (by radio-telescope), as a background radiation spread evenly throughout the Universe, by now cooled to a temp of fractionally over 2.73 degrees K. A discovery offering neat confirmation for a theoretical prediction and, as such, strong evidential support for the Big Bang theory. And by implication, greatly weakening the position of the leading alternative theory – Fred Hoyle and Herman Bondi's Steady State theory of the Universe which suggested a Universe that has no beginning and no end, held in a 'steady state' by the continuous creation of new material. In order to take more recent discoveries into account the theory was updated by Hoyle and colleagues in 1990s as the Quasi-Steady State Theory.

Penzias and Wilson were not immediately aware of the implication of this annoying 'interference' to their own work, and it was fellow astronomer Jim Peebles, then at Princeton undertaking research microwave radiation, who was able to explain what they had found.

The detection of background radiation provided very strong evidence that the Universe was created out of some form of 'singularity' – as already noted, singularities are also thought to lie deep within the infinite density environs existing within black holes. In sum: the central evidence for the Big Bang includes: the evidence that the Universe is expanding (moving away from an observer – as discovered by Edwin Hubble – Hubble's law – in 1929)....the 2.73 ° K background radiation, and also the presence (abundance) of so much hydrogen and helium in the Universe.

Interestingly, we say that before the Universe began there was 'nothing' – no material, no space, no time (as the Universe evolves material became more complex, space expands, and time runs, making these last two a unity as space-time) – and yet the creation of something from nothing defies the laws of nature as currently understood, and is also contrary to our own personal experience. In relation to cosmology, the concept of nothing is but an empty proposition applied to ignorance.....what happened in any pre-singularity zone we do not know – when humanity (as a collectivity) encounters any new experience we only have the language that has been used prior to an initial encounter with the novel so we have to adapt this. Accepting that language does, through numerous small scale (micro) adjustments and as the more brilliant 'leaps' made by poets and other writers, change and evolve. The only human analogy for the pre-singularity zone is of 'nothing'– but the exciting idea of some persisting 'no-thing–ness' stimulates the imagination of science fiction writers, and the scientific imperative to seek to explain, induces informed speculation by scientists on what might have been beyond – before and after - the known Universe.

Some cosmologists and theoretical physicists have endeavored to offer plausible (assuming the validity of quantum physics, and the known characteristics of gravity) descriptions of pre Big Bang conditions – one suggestion is of an 'inflation' era. An era of pre space-time conditions, with gravity operating as a repulsive anti-gravity force. Creating the conditions applying to some decaying 'inflation field' that generated sufficient energy to blast the visible Universe, and with it space-time, into existence. An implication of this should be that there would have been some exotic form of particle involved in setting off the Big Bang, and with it the visible Universe. Most of such particles would not have survived but some should have, and the presence of these 'inflatons' (and an associated 'inflaton field') might be detectable in today's Universe. Further informed speculation (see Christopher Galford, 2016) has suggested that around 8 billion years post Big Bang, following a steady expansion of the Universe, this left-over inflaton material had sufficiently dispersed for its anti-gravity properties to quite dramatically influence i.e. increase, the rate of expansion; a change that was detected in 1998.

Currently pre Big Bang conditions are highly speculative, but James Hartle and Steven Hawkin suggested a credible option with their Hartle-Hawkin's 'wave-function' theory of the Universe. Hartle-Hawkin endeavoured to describe the pre-Big Bang period (the Planck era when the laws of nature as currently understood no longer apply) in terms of quantum possibilities translated into mathematical formulations. As we closely approach the initial Big Bang Einstein's relativity breaks down just as it is thought to do deep down within black holes.

The other horizon to the Univerrse is out there.......at the furthermost reaches of the Universe, beyond which there is no light, no time, or even any 'beyond' as we would normally understand the term. Other that is, than the sense we have that the future of the Universe (and perversely the 'past' also started there as expanding space-time bore it away) is beyond the 13.72 billion year old space-time horizon. The conditions in this 'beyond' seem to be even less knowable than those of the pre-Big Bang.

Throughout the 20th and early 21st century the range of technological extensions to our senses enabled the hovering up of observational data drawn from across a mysteriously sparkling Universe. Transforming what had been the realm of imagination and science-fiction into the substance of knowledge (rooted in masses of statistical information) and understanding. Even accepting that there remain only tentative theories and quite imaginative suggestions in relation to aspects of the Universe such as: its evolution, dark matter, dark energy, and black holes.

The dozens of more significant observatories currently operating across the world (with 'sensory' extensions in space) are continually enhancing our knowledge as they receive, record, and interpret the forms of radiation pouring towards the Earth from across the sky, to be added to the informational data-base.

The current cutting edge of astronomical technology would include the Herschel Space Observatory. Launched in May 2009 and operating as a European Space Agency program. With ten countries, including USA, involved. According to its website, two-thirds of its observation time is '…available to the international scientific community'. The observatory is currently in an orbit just over 900,000 miles from Earth, 'facing away' from the Earth and the Sun. It uses three different types of spectrometer, each sensitive to a specific range of wavelength bands. The 'telescope' uses the gravitational force of very special types of galaxy to study the cosmos (only about one in 50,000 galaxies meet the requirements). These, galaxies can serve as giant gravitational lenses that bend, focus, and magnify light from galaxies lying 10 billion light years away. The Herschel-based astronomers can detect and record the infrared light waves being emitted by cosmological objects; this also enables the relatively rare 'gravitational lens' galaxies to be more easily detected. The study of these far distant galaxies is expected to provide valuable information of how stars and galaxies are formed.

In addition to this work, the Herschel Space Observatory is proving to be a valuable tool in the hands of astronomers. Amongst other work it has: shown (2011) that an exploding star (supernova) can expel up to the equivalent of 230,000 Earth mass in the form of cosmic dust (the basic material for star formation), has also been able (2011) to detect oxygen molecules in space, and also, at least potentially, has advanced the understanding of the phenomenon termed dark matter (see below).

During the time of writing this chapter the construction of a new telescope that will be the World's largest terrestrial telescope – appropriately, if not very imaginatively, named the 'European Extremely Large Telescope' – is to be sited in an elevated location in the Atacama Desert in Chile. So being able to take advantage of the clear, dry, atmosphere of the region. Its optics will include a composite mirror made up of 786 hexagonal mirror-elements, each 45 ft across. There are a number of ambitious aims for this new instrument – claimed to be more powerful than any previous terrestrial telescope. Included in the aims are: the investigation of dark matter, looking back into the approx 14 billion years of known time and, perhaps of most popular interest, to scan the skies seeking habitable planets beyond our solar system.

Can there be any of these other than our Earth? It was in 1995 that Michel Mayor and Didier Queloz identified the first planet beyond our solar system (51 Pegasi b – otherwise named Belerophon or Dimidium - about 60 light years distant). The search for such planets has continued, receiving an impetus with the launching in 2009 of NASA's Kepler space telescope. Now about 2,000 planets within solar systems have been noted, with possibly as many as 15 being 'Earth-like', and 3 of these seem to offer the necessary conditions for 'life'. In statistical terms, an event that has only happened once (life on a planet), has an unknown probability of being repeated – but probability can become significant if we view the 'necessary conditions', rather than life itself, as the 'event'. Then it would seem that we could have millions, if not billions, of planets with the 'necessary conditions' for life in the Universe. We can then quite validly extrapolate that necessary conditions are, given the laws of nature (chemical and biological), very likely to generate at least some forms of life. Back in the 1970s the astronomer Frank Drake devised an equation to predict the probability of civil life having been developed on another planet within the Milky Way galaxy – his formula for this was composed of a range of cosmological and biological life-condition factors. Drake concluded that there was a 'high probability' of civil life having evolved elsewhere. Subsequent interpretations of his calculations varied from the optimistic (mainly cosmologists) to the skeptical (mainly biologists).

In some ways this type of speculation is somewhat academic for us (as least for centuries to come) because the distances to any planet likely to be inhabited by conscious life are so great that the possibility of actually making contact (even via radio communication) remain the domain of science fiction rather than plausible reality. And in some way, contact with any conscious life elsewhere would, given the human colonial experience, be conflictual rather than peaceful – the idealized movie world of benign exploration is contrary to the reality of our earthly politico-economic experience. When in the past our civilizations have made new contacts with peoples on Earth their treatment has been characterized by aggressive competition and rapacious exploitation rather than peaceful and cooperative coexistence, so why would this be different for extraterrestrial contact? The history of humankind suggests that if any form of extraterrestrial people wish for peaceful coexistence we would seek to take advantage!

During the 1990s, an evidential gap involving the creation of matter was addressed by NASA's Cosmic Background Explorer (COBE) satellite, that in 1992, was able to identify tiny temperature fluctuations (1 part in 100,000) in the cosmic background radiation (CBR), a finding that provides support for a theory suggesting that the material Universe (baryonic) was produced by the micro-dynamism of these primordial fluctuations. Later, finer-grained, COBE research into these fluctuations highlighted a discrepancy between the known visible matter and the amount suggested by the scale of the fluctuations – hinting at the presence of some invisible ('Dark') matter. The COBE mission was superseded by the Wilkinson Microwave Anisotropy Probe (WMAP) which has produced an improved map of CBR and a new Standard Model of Cosmology.

We have a Universe containing billions and billions of tons of visible matter, but it seems that this represents less than 5% of the mass of the Universe, the rest being labeled as 'Dark Matter' and 'Dark Energy'. The Dark Matter - unable to either absorb or emit light - was predicted by Fritz Zwicky when, in 1933, he extended the astronomer Jan Ort's observations on the Milky Way to other galaxies. Ort had already offered the term 'Dark Matter' for the unexplained mass necessary to generate the rotational movement of the Milky Way at the speed being observed. Zwicky's own estimation of the amount of mass required to allow the predicted movement and actual movement to equate would be nine times more than the visible mass (mainly stars). Suggesting a Universe composed of about 5% visible matter, 23% invisible Dark Matter, with the other 72%, being Dark Energy. .

In 2007 the Cosmic Evolution Survey – combining the observational resources of the Hubble space-based telescope working in conjunction with a number of earth-based observatories - produced a three-dimensional map of dark matter showing that it should be concentrated in specific areas of the Universe, noting how this might serve as a structure supporting the formation of galaxies. It is thought that dark matter could be composed of exotic particles named as 'weakly interacting massive particles' (WIMPS). These particles ('supersymmetric' or 'sparticles') are predicted to collide with 'normal' atomic nuclei and in doing so emitting a tiny amount of energy as a 'flash' of light and this being potentially detectable. Another suggestion is that dark matter is made of ordinary matter – the cooled remnants of long disintegrated cosmological matter that would originally have been neutron stars, white dwarfs, or black holes – but that this matter that is just too faint (in terms of radiant energy) to observe. This material has been named 'massive astronomical compact halo objects' (MACHOS).

Current thinking is that dark matter is going to be detected before the even more enigmatic dark energy. Dark energy is thought to be the source of the energy that powers the accelerating expansion of the Universe, at a rate faster than the speed of light; but this of the whole Universe so not subject to Einstein's suggested limit. Whereas the Hubble constant would predict a decelerating Universe (due to entropy), initial observations made in 1997 of a number of Type 1a Supernovae suggested an expansion rate about 8% faster than expected. This was followed up by a large-scale project, carried out in 2002, by George Efstathiou, leading a team of 27 astronomers and involving the study of 250,000 galaxies. This project confirmed the earlier explanation and gave an estimate of 65-85% of the mass of the Universe as being required to generate the actually measured rate of expansion.

A more recent project is that of the NASA-Europe-Canada James Webb Telescope; an observational study of clusters of galaxies at different distances from each other, probing their radiation emission with infrared light detectors. This study will consider the relationship between 'normal' and 'dark' matter, in the expectation that this could provide useful information on both the nature of dark matter and so on how the Universe has evolved.

Apart from the more simple suggestion of 'wimps' or 'machos' being dark matter there seems to be two more radical views on what dark matter and dark energy might be. For one, they could be aspects of gravity that have not yet been fully understood, or they could be an entirely new, so a fifth, source of mass and energy; named by some as 'quintessence' (reaching back to Aristotle's 5th element).

Two areas of recent interest to astrophysicists relate to the suggestion of more than just one Universe. The background to this being a need to reconcile current theory with the discovery, first made in 2004 (by NASA's WMAP satellite) then confirmed in 2013 (by ESA's Planck mission), of the presence of a 'cold spot' within the cosmic microwave background radiation. If such a phenomenon does exist – and it is not just more evidence of anisotropies, the more natural temperature fluctuations, that operate to 'trigger' star and galaxy formation – then its presence would be contrary to the current 'inflationary' model of the Universe. One explanation has been offered which suggests that the 'cold spot' is a location in space-time where two universes have collided. This fits with a version of 'multiverse' theory. A broad theoretical notion that outlines a cosmos in which there are a multitude, indeed potentially an infinite number, of universes; each of which has its own version of Reality. Think of quantum indeterminacy with all possible outcomes being realized – a superposition of quantum possibilities. The universe we experience directly being the one we observe so, in effect, the state of 'quantum collapse', but with all the possible universes still being 'out there', as yet unobserved!

There is also the idea of universes being created, in a sense, within our universe as 'Bubbles'. Universes arising from quantum fluctuations in the early Universe's vacuum energy. This relates to the notion of a pre Big Bang quantum gravity state and the remnants of this that at about 8 billion years post Big Bang, with its accelerating rate of the Universe's expansion, the creation of bubble universes ceased. These bubble universes are also known as 'pockets' with some suggested to contain their own galaxies and could even have different natural laws from our own universe.

Such is the degree of hypothetical speculation with the notion of a multi-verse that a number of different versions have been suggested. To the extent that we now have 'categories' of different types of multi-verse theories – Max Tegmark notes 4 'levels' and Brian Green has nine 'types', at least one of which, 'Branes', is closely related to string theory of particle physics. The value of multi-verse theory is in how it can account for a range of currently unexplained phenomena.

Turning to more mundane aspects of cosmology....early in the century the possibility of manned (sic) space fights had been suggested by Konstantin Tsiolkovsky who, in 1903 published 'Research into Interplanetary Space by Means of Rocket Power'. He suggested multi-stage rockets running on liquid propellants, and he doggedly continued to develop the basic idea for the next quarter of a century. The Soviet Union built two prototypes rockets (1933 and 1939) each of which was designed to use liquid propellants. The technology facilitating the exploration of space via spacecraft advanced significantly during WWII with intensive research into self-steering rocketry and the use of rockets (e.g. the V2) to deliver explosive materials (so heavy payloads).

The first steps out beyond the Earth's atmosphere (able to gain the velocity, 40,320 kp/h, required to escape the gravitational pull of the Earth) was in 1957 with the USSR's Sputniks 1 and 2 (the second carrying a dog named 'Laika'). In the 'cold war' context the two superpowers vied for some sense of global superiority in terms of international political influence, size of nuclear arsenals, and in the race into space. In progressing this, the USA, in 1958, launched the 'Explorer' craft, and Vanguard 1, the first satellite utilizing a solar battery. The following year it launched Luna 2 and Luna 3, then later in the same year Discovery 13, as the first successful re-entry craft, with in turn the USSR sending two more dogs into space aboard Sputnik 5.

The space rivalry was stimulated further when, late in 1961, the USSR astronaut Yuri Gargarin became the first person to orbit the Earth. His flight in Vostok 1 lasted for 1 hr 48 mins at the end of which he was successfully returned to Earth. In response, the following year the USA astronaut John Glen orbited the Earth in Friendship 7.

The Russians seemed to have gained superiority in manned space flight when in 1963 Valentina Tereshkova became the first women in space, completing 49 orbits of the earth in Vostok 6. The next advance would be the first space walk undertaken in 1965 by Alexei Leonov, making the landmark step from the hatch of Vostok 2 (this flight involved two astronauts but only Leonov went for a walk).

Whilst manned orbiting spaceships provided information on the atmosphere surrounding the Earth (including weather patterns), on conditions in very near space, and at the time brought political kudos, going beyond the more immediate vicinity of the Earth was also being undertaken by unmanned vehicles (space probes). In 1962 Mariner 2 (USA) flew past Venus, sending back information on the planet's rotation and its atmosphere. A number of other unmanned space probes were launched to study the planets and in 1965 Mariner 4 was able to photograph the surface of Mars. Both the USA and the USSR were sending space probes to explore the near planets such as Venus and Mars and in the 1970s to the outer planets of Jupiter, Saturn, Uranus and Neptune. In 1975 the USA undertook a controlled landing of Viking 1 on Mars.

Funding was now being poured into a techno-scientific program via NASA in the US and three different space-craft design teams in the USSR. These projects had industrial and military possibilities, as well as political implications. And even if the USA did very soon manage its own space walk with the Gemini 4 mission, to have the Russians seeming to be in the lead in the space race was unacceptable to the then American president John ('Jack') Kennedy who, in September 1962, promised that America would put a man on the Moon by the end of the decade. The Apollo range of spacecraft was designed with this end in mind. Although set back by the loss of Apollo1 in 1967, costing the lives of all three astronauts, the Apollo program delivered on the President's promise in July 1969 with Apollo 11's successful flight to the Moon and the obviously 'choreographed', but scientifically pretty much pointless, walk and drive across a small area of the Moon's surface.

Manned and unmanned exploration of space has produced a range of information on the Earth's atmosphere and of the planets in our solar system. And space-based telescopes have made a significant contribution to cosmology. But I am not sure that manned flights has added any knowledge that could not have been gained (and at much less cost) by unmanned flights. Even the effect of long-term weightlessness, and of certain drugs, on the human body could presumably have been investigated in an artificially created earth-based 'space environment'. Given advances in computer controlled robotics, I would have thought that experiments requiring fine dexterous control, as well as the requirements of maintaining and repairing craft, could be undertaken without the need for human astronauts.

But the presence of humans captures public interest and creates the next generation of 'heroic figures' that the mass media requires and the promoters of nationalism seek to maintain. Part of the 'frothy news' that the mainstream media tends to focus on – what is abstracted for popular consumption, selected from the range of deeper levels of news in order to distract attention from exposure to information that might challenge the self-serving perspective on world news that is mainstream media; controlled in effect by states, and big corporations.

Since the first privately funded space flight, undertaken in 2004 with SpaceShipOne, the prospect of space tourism became a reality. But the likely extent of this form of venturing into space is comparable to someone putting a toe into the Pacific Ocean from some Californian beach and saying that she had ventured into the Pacific, true but hardy some heroic encounter with the unknown depths! And in reality, the celestial ocean into which any toe goes will be trillions of times bigger than the Pacific.

Given our current understanding of the laws of physics, and for practical human purposes the barrier expressed in the constant of speed of light (and also the impact of prolonged weightlessness on a human body), the exploration of space by 'manned' travel is unrealistic and, I suspect, unnecessary for purely scientific purposes. We can write and film fictionalized stories of space exploration, but the hard limiting reality of time, distances, and speed, in the Universe means that fiction is what manned flight should remain. But that's not to say the investigation of the Universe is not an exciting activity, one filled with the potential for discovery and a sense of scientific adventure.

One potentially more sustainable exploratory project is the 'message to other life-forms' probe, launched into space in the 1970s: Pioneer 10 in 1972 and Pioneer 11 in 1973, each with a metal plaque attached that offered a graphic representation including a line drawing of a naked human couple and a 'solar map' indicating where the spacecraft originated from – these craft and their contents were the first man-made objects to venture beyond our solar system. This theme was continued with Voyagers 1 and 2, their carrying similar graphic plaques to the earlier spacecraft with this supplemented by two phonograph records on which were recorded a range of 'earthly – sounds'. The Pioneer and Voyager missions also carried out a range of observational research as they passed close to planets within the solar system and continuing as they progress beyond it.

A current example of a somewhat more cooperative venture has been the International Space Station (ISS): Construction of which began in 1998, with the station being completed in 2011; having a productive life expectancy to 2028. Led by the US (NASA) as the major financial contributor (about $60 billion – of the estimated $150 billion total cost), with Russia also holding a leading place alongside fifteen other nations, plus the European Space Agency, being involved in this ambitious project. The station's low level Earth orbit offers a microgravity space environment suitable for novel experiments and other types of research into a range of areas including: biology, physics, astronomy, and metrology. The ISS also contains the technically advanced Alpha Magnetic Spectrometer (AMS), a possible means to detect the predicted presence of the Dark Matter calculated to constitute about 23.3% of the mass of the Universe.

To gain some sense of the size of our Universe, think of the Sun whose radiating energy has sustained life on Earth for possibly more than two billion years, a star of average stellar magnitude located on one of the fours bright spiral arms radiating from the Milky Way galaxy's main body, approx 30,000 light years away from the centre. A galaxy containing about 300 million stars in a Universe containing up to two trillion galaxies. Our galaxy is one of almost 50 others clustered together in a Local Group, including the 'relatively' nearby Andromeda, Small Megallanic Cloud (SMC), and Large Megallenic Cloud (LMC) galaxies. All within a hyper-space whose 'visible' horizons extend out in any direction for billions of light years.

Beyond our own local group there are billions of other similar 'Local' clusters composed of stars, their satellites, gas clouds, comets, meteorites, and other cosmic material spreading out through space-time. If you could travel through the Universe at some super-hyper-speed you would note that the cosmos is overwhelmingly 'empty space'; and that the galaxies are but islands of material within what seems to be vast stretches of emptiness. If you travel far enough you would at some point arrive at the outer edge of the observable Universe (where the material is over 13 billion years old).A journey that, if undertaken at the speed of light, would take 46 billion light years to travel from the Earth to the outer limit of the observable Universe. Where you would have arrived at a peculiar type of boundary. One beyond which light is no longer emitted, a light/no-light boundary – 13.4 billion years old. To arrive at what is termed the 'surface of light scattering', from when theory, informed by observation and known laws of physics, gives way to theory stimulated more by informed imagination.

How can we even begin to understand distances and amounts that we (and indeed the whole of humanity) have never encountered in cognitively manageable forms? Or manageable only at the cost of simplification – of reducing the cosmic 'eternities' to the earthy mundane; distances that we can't easily conceptualize. Measures of immense periods of time that allow the chronological 'freedom' to spread to (indeed 'create') distances that cannot be adequately captured by words but only by some sense of what numerical representations of measurement means

Astronomers also use the measure of par sec.; with par sec. being equivalent to 3.26 light years or 30 trillion kilometers. Use of such measures (conversions) can allow us to gain some sense of relative distances.

For most of us we gain a sense of the size of the Universe (and the number of cosmic objects in it) by….. wide-eyed bemusement at the numbers, moving to projected imagination of far off vistas. Free-flowing imagination structures vistas of endless starry clouds spread across vast space-oceans of dark emptiness, silent of all but the cosmic 'hiss' of radio-waves, the residual signal of the Universe's origins. We mostly settle for some intuitive sense of just how awesomely different the Universe is to our general experience.

But then it took humankind 0000s of years to conceptualize 'Gods' with distinct value-systems and behaviours from out of the mysterious sense of something beyond the daily human/primate experience – 90,000-10,000 y. b.p. So perhaps given a few thousands more years of cognitive absorption humankind will have evolved a more intellectually satisfying conceptual form of access to the Universe. Meanwhile we, as but earth-bound observers, experience 'space' (the Universe) as an overarching span composed of a myriad of tiny sparks (points) of luminosity piercing an inky-black sky; far distant glows of the living and dying sparks of suns seen against the solemn darkness. All that we could mean by Infinity passing through

Eternity expressed in the concept of the Universe.

Reflection on this highlights the relative insignificance of our galaxy, as one of possibly as many as 2000 billion galaxies, of our Sun and its own modest planetary system with 300 million other suns in our own galaxy and of each one of us as single points of consciousness amongst the over 7 billion individuals alive on Earth today preceded by the billions that have experienced self-consciousness since human life has existed for but a micro-moment in the life of the Universe.

Reflection on the possible implications of humankind's place within the Universe can stimulate a sense of the profound 'accidental' presence of life, and with a form of life gifted with consciousness. A sense of the insignificance of human life as well as a sense of our developing understanding alongside the evolution of the Universe itself. As individuals we have only limited periods of existence. Its ephemeral nature being expressed in the phrase, thought to originate in rural Ireland, as 'a sigh between two silences' – for some life-spans measured in months or a few years for others 70 odd years – within the time of more complex multi-cellular life on Earth of 470m years and within the Universe aged 13.72 billion years, individual existence can only be the merest flicker of consciousness. But what can collectively endure are discovery, knowledge, and understanding, together contributing to raising consciousness as it both reveals and creates Reality.

The future of astronomy will focus on continuing the 'mapping' of the Universe – more conventional telescopes will be enhanced by new X-ray based technology, and a new generation of CMBR (Cosmic Microwave Background Radiation) satellites, along with new space-based instruments. The study of gravitational waves will intensify. These waves, as ripples in the fabric of space-time, have been detected around very large cosmic objects such as large black holes, supernovae, and neutron stars. Their presence can also be as remnants of the gravitational radiation (perturbations in the CBR) created at the very beginning of the Universe. Ripples set in an otherwise smooth CBR during the early period of rapid expansion.

Invariably, the search for life on other planets will continue, if more likely to find evidence of micro-flora, than any form of fauna (animal life). At a more fundamental level astro-physicists will progress attempts to converge high-energy particles physics with properties seen in the Universe (in string and other GUT theories), not least with: black holes, dark matter, dark energy, and gravitational waves, pre Big Bang conditions and also the conditions that might pertain beyond the horizon at the end of the universe - the cosmological inflation.

Contemplation of the cosmos invokes a type of meta-human reflection and as such expands our imagination and offers challenging horizons over-which lie further discoveries and so potentially fertile terrains of knowledge.

Chemistry

All around and within us a multiplicity of chemical reactions are continually taking place: touching, hearing, smelling, tasting, and the perception of light, all involve complex chemical reactions in the body responding to chemical reactions taking place outside of it – the entire physical development of my body since conception and my thinking about the words and ideas that I am now writing about involve complex chemical reactions in the brain: most obviously the role of potassium, sodium, chlorine in neuronal communication. Life is bathed in an irreducible complexity of chemical actions and reactions that create and sustain it.

From the simplest to the most complex arrangements, along with its inherent (thermo) dynamism, matter can be described in terms familiar to the science of chemistry. Chemical actions and reactions underpin the form, function, and development of what we see around us – the elements (starting with hydrogen), fashioned out of some inherent and changing properties (process properties) have given the Universe substance, form, function, and consciousness.

I noted in the physics section above how the key to the combining of atoms, and so molecular formation, was the 'freedom' (certain properties) electrons have to attach themselves within the orbits of other atoms. Brian Cox and Andrew Cohen note that: '.....electrons can be transferred or shared between atoms of different elements, and this is what drives the formation of molecules. The science of chemistry is fundamentally related to movement of electrons, and the movement of electrons can lead to complexity.'(Cox and Cohen, 2016, p146)

Particle physics allows us to gain knowledge of the most basic constitution of matter but an understanding of the forms that matter actually takes (and can possibly take) is more the field of chemistry.

In a fairly simplistic way it is useful to consider the path to self-organizing organic matter in terms of levels of organization.... one level being the elements themselves, another being the combining of elements into molecules, molecules to compounds, which then make up single cells, and these in turn combining to form multi-cellular organisms (and so species), which collectively form populations. The science of chemistry focuses on the properties of atoms, as constituted by neutrons, protons and electrons (determining the elements and their isotopes), and the properties they exhibit in forming (or not being able to form) molecules and compounds.

As with all of the individual sciences, the approach to gain knowledge of the material forming the focus of chemistry is based on a mixture of intellectual analysis, theorizing, and experimental activity (including observation) according to B3 Vol. 4 p168, in chemistry '...experimental results set the boundaries within which the theoretical approach develops concepts, hypotheses, theories, and models'.

By the early decades of the twenty-first century scientists have identified a generally agreed 92 naturally occurring elements, with 15/16 more having being made by chemists. It was Robert Boyle who is credited with identifying the basic nature of chemical elements. In 1789 Antoine Lavoisier drew up a list of 'elements' (which did mistakenly include some compounds such as silica and lime), 16 more being added by late eighteenth century (including chlorine, bromine, iodine between 1810-26 with 82 more added by 1970.

It had been in 1869 that Dimitry Mendeleyev (then lecturing at St Petersburg University) made known a table of the elements that brought a more coherent arrangement, providing a useful tool for chemists He arranged elements according to their relative mass and in doing so was able to use a 'periodicity' of this property.

According to Thomas Crump (2001, p182) the law of periodicity runs: '...the properties of the elements, and thus the properties of simple or compound bodies of the elements, are dependent in a periodic way on the magnitude of the atomic weight of the elements'.

Mendeleyev outlined his 'periodic' system in his book 'Foundations of Chemistry' (1869), and more accessibly in his later pamphlet 'An Outline of the System of the Elements' (1870). His initial table listed 61 elements arranged by mass, allowing the grouping together of elements with similar properties. The value of his systematization was confirmed when, soon after his book was published, three of the elements predicted by his method of systematization were found – aluminum 1875, boron 1879, silicon 1879. Then in 1888 neon, krypton, and xenon, filled more gaps.

The accumulation continued into the twentieth century, starting with radon in 1900. Of the approx. 40 elements discovered since 1879 21 had been predicted by Mendeleyev's system. The system was improved in 1914 by Henry Moseley who first proposed the use of atomic number (the number of protons) rather than mass; he had developed a technique, based on using element-specific wave-lengths generated by X-rays, to measure atomic number.

All naturally occurring elements with atomic numbers greater than 83 are radioactive. Synthetic radioactive elements were first being created in the laboratory by Frederic and Irene Joliot-Curie in 1934. They had used alpha particles to bombard nuclei, and in the same year Enrico Fermi had used neutrons instead of alpha particles to try to create new radioactive elements. Fermi's method was used by others to produce a series of elements including in 1945 Americium (95 protons), 1949 Berkelium (97 protons) and Californium (98 protons), 1955 Fermium (100 protons). In 1958 a linear particle accelerator was used to create Nobelium (102 protons) 1961 Lawrencium (103 protons), 1963 Rutherfordium (104 protons) 1967 Dubnium (105 protons), 1974 Seaborgium (106 protons), 1981 Bohrium (107 protons), 1982 Unnilennium which has a half-life of less than a second (109 protons), Hassium (108 protons), and in 2004 Russian scientists produced an element with 115 protons that rapidly decays to one with 113 protons.

The elements that can't be found on Earth are termed transfermium elements; they usually have a short 'life', soon undergoing decay. In 1952 the element einsteinium (99 protons) was found to have been produced in a thermo-nuclear explosion which alerted scientists to the possibility that the fiery furnace found within the stages of a 'stars' life could also provide the conditions for the production of elements.

Atoms can have 'normal' forms and also 'isotopic' forms – a difference identified experimentally by Francis Aston around 1918/19. The name isotope had earlier been given by Fredrick Soddy in 1913 who had suggested that some different form of elements might explain what seemed to be inexplicable chemical behaviour. Isotopic forms are similar to the standard form of the atom in that they have the same atomic number but they differ due to having a different atomic weight. Most elements have isotopic forms, generally two, but this can go up to ten (tin).

The primary structure of the atoms of which elements are made is based on a central nucleus composed of neutrons and positively charged protons with one or more negatively charged electrons circulating the nucleus in 'orbits'. For chemistry, the term shell is more generally the term used for the orbit within which electrons travel. These shells radiate from the nucleus in a set pattern, one which includes a maximum allowable number of electrons in each shell. It is the arrangement of electrons in the outermost shell that provides the conditions for atoms of one element to join (bond) with those of other elements – forming molecules that in turn can join (bond) to form macromolecules.

If we think of the classic model of a 'quantum' atom we have an image of an entity with a centre composed of (positively charged) protons and (neutrally charged) neutrons around which there are orbital 'cloud-like shells' within which (negatively charged) electrons move in a wave-like manner, even if the actual position of each electron cannot be determined; only predicted in terms of probability. Each shell is spaced at an increasing distance from the central nucleus of the atom and each shell can only contain a maximum number of electrons – the closest shell to the nucleus of all atoms can hold a maximum of 2 electrons, when this has been filled then atoms with more than 2 electrons have these contained within a second shell which can hold a maximum of 8 electrons, then elements with more than 10 electrons have more shells, each further from the nucleus. Atoms with full shells (so e.g. three shells of 2, 8, 18,) are less amenable for linking with other atoms than are the less stable atoms with incomplete shells (1, 3-7, 11-17 etc). Beyond the third shell there are complications to the basic pattern but these are not such that we need to overcomplicate a description of atomic bonding; the property of elements which forms a primary focus for the whole of chemistry.

The patterning of electron-positioning is based upon the overall distribution of energy between electrons, and the arrangement of the electrons tends towards a stability that minimizes the overall energy within the atom.

So atoms that have incomplete shells e.g. hydrogen with only one electron in its inner shell and carbon with 6 electrons (2 to complete the innermost shell and only 4 in the next, which can hold up to 8) are less stable and so more likely to form bonds. As early as 1916 Gilbert Lewis had suggested the idea of atoms being able to form a bond by sharing a pair of electrons. The key to element (atoms and their isotopes) and molecular bonding is the relative instability that is a feature of the outer shell of atoms. And the outcome of the various types of chemical bonding is what we see, smell, and hear, all around us.

Here I will just briefly note the three primary forms of bonding - from the strongest, covalent, via ionic, to the weakest, hydrogen.

If we start at the basic material level for chemistry it would encompass the processes that allow atoms of different (and the same) elements to be held together and the explanation for this can be made in terms of quantum mechanics. As noted, there are three main forms of bonding operating at this level, covalent, ionic, and hydrogen, bonds. The overall bonding pattern of any molecule – the way in which atoms combine and recombine to form different molecules – determines its properties.

Covalent bonding involves the sharing of pairs of electrons (the 'valence electrons'). One possible configuration would be four hydrogen atoms, each sharing its electron with one in the outer shell of an atom of carbon that has room for four more electrons in its outer shell. Incidentally, carbon is amenable to bond in a similar way to a range of elements whose atoms have an incomplete electron shell. It is the combination of atoms held together by the strong covalent bonds of carbon that congregate to form the very large macromolecules that underpin all of life on Earth. It is yet more evidence from biochemistry that links all the myriad types of life as but expressions of similar basic processes. It has even been suggested that biochemistry could be termed the 'science of carbon'.

Another form of chemical bonding, albeit significantly weaker than covalent bonding, is the ionic bond. This form of bonding is due to the operation of the electrostatic force of attraction. The bond is formed when an atom of one element is able to gain an electron from an atom of another element (or rather to gain the charge property of this electron). Owing to the original arrangement of each atom this exchange (bond) results in each of them becoming more stable. The atom giving up an electron becomes a positive 'ion' of the element (a cation) and the atom gaining an electron becomes a negative 'ion' of that element (an anion). This exchange results in the first atom having an overall positive charge (caused by the loss of an electron) and the second atom having an overall negative charge (caused by the presence of the addition electron) and so, as these atoms now carry opposites electrical charges, they are attracted to each other. Most elements can form ionic bonds. Ionic bonds have a tendency to shatter if under stress e.g. atoms (ions) of chlorine and sodium form ionic bonds to become rock salt and its crystalline structure will make it liable to breakdown if even just a light force is applied to it. Whereas compounds formed of molecules held together by covalent bonds can more easily absorb stress e.g. carbon and hydrogen can combine to form rubber which has a strong propensity to absorb force.

A third form of chemical bonding is the hydrogen bond. These are much weaker even than ionic bonds. Atoms of hydrogen (with its single electron) are easily amenable to bond with atoms of elements such as oxygen, nitrogen, and fluorine, when they come into contact. The bonding process is completed when the non-hydrogen atom is able to attract the electron part of the hydrogen 'shell' and so drawing it (the negative charge) away from the hydrogen atom. The result being that the original hydrogen atom is now more positively charged and the non-hydrogen atoms are more negatively charged and so, in a similar but weaker way to ionic bonds, the opposites are attracted and the bond completed. Hydrogen bonds are important in the formation of organic macromolecules such as proteins and nucleic acids, but can also be present in non-organic molecules such as water. Most large organic molecules are formed by a mixture of covalent, ionic bonds and hydrogen bonds. The different elements and various types of bonding allow the formation of a myriad of different substances with a wide range of properties – for organisms this type of arrangement can offer a suitable balance of stability and adaptability.

Rather than just considering some mental image of atoms attached to each other – which I accept can be useful, certainly for building models of the actual or possible atomic arrangement of molecules – it is probably of more value to note that the understanding of molecular bonding in quantum mechanical terms enables the energies involved to be accurately calculated. At its material foundations life is dependent on the electrostatic forces relative to the overall energy levels of atoms in order to form anything beyond single elements. But it is forces, and other properties related to energy, that maintain the atoms themselves and so make them liable to form inter-elemental bonds. The essential flexibility of different types of organic bonding – the balance between strong and weak bonds – is necessary for dynamic living processes to take place; for life… its metabolism, development, and reproduction, to be possible.

Linus Pauling's (a double Noble prize winner, for chemistry and also for peace) focus was on chemical bonding at the fundamental material level and he applied insights – most obviously the exchange of energy 'quanta' involved - gained in quantum mechanics to explain how bonds could be formed.[8]

In the 1930s Pauling brought together chemistry and quantum physics (especially its mathematical representations) to explain chemical bonding. Most obviously the exchange of energy 'quanta' involved in the process. Setting out the basic propositions, the quantum mechanical rules, in his scientific paper 'The Nature of the Chemical Bonds', and expanding on this in six follow-up papers. By 1935 Pauling felt able to note that: 'I felt that I had an essentially complete understanding of the nature of the chemical bond.'

In relation to the stability of both atoms and molecules the most stable arrangements are those that require the least energy. The description of atoms and molecules in terms of energy made a significant contribution to making chemistry a quantifiable branch of science. Quantum mechanical principles can be used, in theory at least, to determine the energy held within atoms and molecules.

Following its introduction earlier in the twentieth century, it was Pauling who would more fully realize the potential of the technique of X-ray diffraction for the study of molecular structures. Many elements (as atoms, ions, or molecules) can form crystalline structures and if these are subjected to X-rays the structure scatters the X-rays according to material-specific wavelengths to form a 'diffraction pattern'. This pattern provides a range of information about a material's molecular structure, especially bonding arrangements and non-covalent interactions.

Physicists and chemists (as well as mathematicians) had been fascinated with crystalline structures since Johan Kepler published his own study of snowflakes in the seventeenth century. Studies of various aspects of crystalline formations were produced throughout the 18th and 19th centuries. Then in 1912 Max von Laue found that X-rays (discovered in 1895 by William von Röntgen) were diffracted by the crystalline structure of elements in a particular way, so offering a method of analysis that could further the understanding of elemental matter. The technique of X-ray crystallography being improved by

---

[8] Schrodinger's wave equation suggested that the 'energy in a system can only change by a definite amount 'quanta'.

William Coolidge's design of a vacuum tube (1913). Then, in the 1920s, William Bragg and his son Lawrence built a much improved X-ray spectrometer with which they were able to more precisely determine the pattern of atoms as arranged in a number of substances.

The Braggs also set out a 'law' to describe the process. According to Thomas Crump Bragg's law: '….related the wavelength of the X-rays to the separation distance of the layers of atoms forming the crystal planes and the angle of incidence of the X-rays' (Crump, 2001, p200).

Initially X-ray crystallography focused on solid state physics and would be used to reveal the relatively simple one-dimensional symmetry of crystals then, as techniques and equipment improved, two and three dimensional arrangements were produced. As the use of this technique spread it would prove to be of immense value to molecular biology.

Especially useful being the more precise identification of the three-dimensional structure of the very large molecules so important for living systems. It was in the 1950s that Rosalind Franklin used a type of X-scattering (fibre diffraction) to reveal the double helix structure of DNA.

Pauling was to note later in his life that: 'Our present understanding of the nature of the world of atoms, molecules, minerals, and human beings, can be attributed in large part to crystallography.'

Whilst studying chemical bonding and the properties and behaviour of molecules, chemists (especially those working in private industry) have also sought ways in which these processes can be combined and otherwise manipulated to create substances that are useful to support civil life. If the pace of the creation of new materials (spurred on by the implication-limited dynamism of profit-seeking) has often outrun knowledge of their long-term impact on the human environment. More notorious examples being: chlorofluorocarbons (CFCs) in aerosol sprays and fridges, asbestos in insulation and fire-retardant materials, microbeads (polyethylene plastics) in a range of cosmetic products, and polychlorinated biphenyls (PCRs) in electrical equipment and lubricants. Just four of very many examples highlighting the need for caution when introducing novel substances into an already complex chemical environment. Of course, the value of a wide range of new materials – pharmaceuticals, coatings, adhesives, textiles, artificial fertilizers, food preservatives, and in medical scanning techniques, to name but a few – has been immense.

If we plan research and production rationally (prioritizing human values over financial gain – so approaching innovation with due caution) then we can perhaps have advances in chemistry that offer benefits without such a large potential for harm as is currently the case with profit-driven innovation.

Chemistry throughout the twentieth century has been very much a laboratory-based activity, one that has seen a focus on developing both observational instruments and experimental methods. Contributing to provide the mass of quantifiable data out of which more theoretical frameworks have been formed. Instruments such as calorimeters, potentiometers, Geiger counters, X-ray spectrometers, and improved mass spectrometers, ever more accurate balances and scales, added to by advanced optical and electron microscopes, centrifuges, and a range of types of electronic scanning methods. More recently computers have aided data processing and the modeling of the behaviour of simple molecules and of chemically more complex materials. As early as 1969 John Pople had designed a computer program (Gaussian), based on the laws of quantum mechanics, to aid the analysis of molecules and of the chemical reactions they undergo. The 1986 Swiss-Prot. Project involved Amos Barioch's development of software for analyzing proteins; with the project using computer files to store composition information on all of the proteins currently known. Today computing is simply an assumed tool of chemistry for analysis, modeling processes, and of course teaching and communication.

Methods of separation and purification such as the more traditional distillation, fermentation, filtration, heating, cooling, sublimation, extraction, and for more complex compounds, dialysis, electro-dialysis, electrophoresis, centrifugation, chromatography, are just some of the techniques that have contributed to the understanding of chemical substances and their action and reaction.

Advances accrued throughout the century as an increasing body of theoretical and research chemists applied themselves, using newly developed research instruments and more traditional equipment, to understanding our material environment.

Just some landmarks in twentieth century chemistry include: the 1909 development by Soren Sorenson of a scale measuring acidity (ph scale) - the discovery in 1920 of superfluidity by Pyotr Kapitsa – in 1923 the explanation of acids and bases – the 1928 synthesize of the ring-shaped compounds of organic molecules.

In 1934 Paul Flory's work focused on large complex macromolecules involved in a range of materials, including polymers and also those involved in living matter. In 1947 chemists devised techniques to study fast chemical reactions. By 1950 Derek Burton was highlighting the importance of the three-dimensional structure of molecules to biological function (his work focused on molecules called steroids). Fukui Kenichi offered an explanation, in 1952, for how some chemical reactions take place. In 1956 John Polanyi pioneered the use of infrared chemiluminesence to study chemical reactions. And in the same year Nicolaas Bloembergen pioneered the use of laser technology to study the structure of atoms and molecules.

Roald Hoffman and Robert Woodward's work on the formation of complex from simpler molecules allowed for a better understanding of how some molecules can combine to form molecules with a ring-structure – many of which are important for biological processes. In 1967, The synthesis of specialist binding molecules important for understanding protein formation was advanced by Charles Pederson's work on the cyclical molecules named crown ethers. Work that was further advanced when, in 1969, Jean-Marie Lehn synthesized crown ether molecules that had properties mimicking those of enzymes.

At the start of the century Germany had led the way in the development of what might termed applied chemistry, and its industry produced a range of applications. By 1913 Germany was exporting 40% of the world's chemical industry products. Leading the way in improving processes in steel production used to make precision instruments including those used in dentistry and surgery (stainless steel), engineering, armaments, transport and in the more efficient exploitation of sources of power such as electricity, oil, coal; all benefited from developments made by the chemical industry. The education system (in Germany the technical colleges and in the US in certain universities and with certain types of philanthropic sponsorship) produced the thousands of skilled chemists required each year as the science developed

Increasingly, as the century progressed, competition between profit-seeking private companies was able to benefit from a large input of government funded research. Not least the Manhattan Project 1939-45; estimated to have cost more than all science research undertaken up to that time (Roberts, 1993, p 414). A project producing a wide range of information on isotopes that would progressively be released to private industry in the second half of the century.

Today across the civil world millions of individuals are working as research chemists, lab technicians in chemistry laboratories and teachers, all working to support and advance the science of chemistry mainly in colleges, universities, government research institutes, and many more in the many private laboratories and sprawling industrial chemical plants sited across the world.

The chemical industry has helped to create products that require a large amount of raw material extraction and processing, much of which has been and is being progressed in relatively unspoilt landscapes and seascapes....mountaintops, deserts, forests, polar regions, tundra, continental shelves, ocean bottoms…all potential sources of usable (so profitable) material are being sought out, dug out, sucked out, cut-out, drilled out, and in many places simply plundered.

Industries at the forefront of the application of the science of chemistry include those involved in dyestuffs and textiles, pharmaceuticals and medicine more generally, food taste enhancing, processing and preservation, in agriculture with fertilizers, herbicides and pesticides, as well as construction with glues, resins and insulation materials. And more specific synthetic materials such as: stainless steel, rayon, carbon-fibre, perspex, teflon, nylon, various forms of plastics, ceramics, detergents, dacron, neoprene, velcro,…. being just some of the new materials created during the twentieth century.

As with other branches of the sciences, the science of chemistry has also been determinedly used by governments in finding ways of killing and maiming human beings and by private companies to made profits from of this – most obviously as gas clouds released across the battlefields of Europe in WWI (90,000 immediately killed, with about 1,000,000 injured, many to linger on, maimed, to die during the following years). And by the Nazi regime in the 1930/40s, using lethal gas to murder Jews, socialists, trade unionists, homosexuals, and the disabled.

In August 1919 Winston Churchill (then Secretary of State for War) planned and ordered the use of fatal chemicals (the M-Device – diphenylaminechloroarsine) to attack Bolsheviks in a number of villages in Russia,[9] possibly ordered their use against Kurds in Iraq,

---

[9] As these weapons proved rather less effective in eroding the moral of the Bolsheviks, all of the shells remaining, after about eight villages had been attacked, were just dumped in the White Sea where, 40 fathoms down, they remain to this day.

and enthusiastically argued for use against rebellious tribes in Northern India.[10] Acts that, for Churchill, were acceptable because they were against 'uncivilized tribes'. The use by Spain of mustard gas in the Rif War in Morocco 1921-27, the use by Italy of mustard gas in large quantities in Ethiopia 1935-36, Japan's use of toxins against China 1937-41, the use by the Egyptians of mustard gas in Yemen 1963-68, the saturation of paddy-fields and farmlands of Vietnam and Cambodia with agent Orange by the USA, the use of large amounts of toxins in Laos by the Vietnamese, and Saddam Hussein's use of mustard gas against the Kurdish people in the north and Shiite Moslem civilians in villages such as Halbjah where 5,000 were killed and again used by the Iraqis (with the support, if not direct collusion of US and some western governments who had supplied the toxic materials during the Iraq/Iran war of 1980-88). More recently the 2016/18 use by the Assad regime in Syria, dropping 'bombs' of lethal chemicals onto Syrian civilian populations in order to terrorize people, including women, children and babies, deemed by the regime to be 'rebels'.

Few of the world's major powers are uncontaminated by some form of association with poisonous chemical attacks on civilian (as well as military) populations and few of the world's largest chemical companies have not profited from supplying the means to pursue this murderous and cowardly practice. This in spite of global agreements that from early in modern history had accepted the inhumanity of chemical weapons. Agreements that can be dated from as early as 1675 when France and Germany agreed not use caustic material as weapons; in 1874 the Brussels Convention extended this agreement. The Hague Peace Conference of 1899 set some basic conditions that would be reflected within the terms of the Geneva Protocol in 1925. More recently, an international ban on the use of chemical weapons was introduced in 1968. And since 1997, there has been the theoretically more substantial Chemical Weapons Convention, banning the 'production, stockpiling and use of chemical weapons'. This latest 'agreement' being ratified (at 2016) by 192 of the world's countries – but not Israel, The State of Palestine, North Korea, South Sudan, and Egypt.

Chemistry is set to be at the forefront of scientific advance during

---

[10] An aim prevented by the intervention of the India Office, suggesting such action to be 'unreasonable'.

the twenty-first century – in particular the industries of: warfare, textiles, big-pharma, energy extraction, construction, corporate agriculture, computing, environmental science, and a range of bio-technologies that will all develop at a pace. I would note just two areas of innovations that could underpin advance in most of the industries noted above: superconductivity and nano-technology.

Superconductivity initially came to the fore in 1911 with the discovery (by Dutch physicist Heike Kamerlingh Onnes and his colleagues) that certain materials, if they can be cooled to a very low temperature (below 4.2 K - so close to absolute zero degree Kelvin or - 273 ° Centigrade), can conduct electricity with minimal resistance. In 1986 it was found that a range of materials could act as superconductors at the higher temperature of 35 degrees Kelvin. Between these two discoveries research into superconductivity drew the increasing interest of chemists. The construction in 1957 of a 'fundamental theory of superconductivity' ('BCS' after John Bardeen, Leon Cooper, and John Schrieffer) opened up the possibility for commercial exploitation of this chemical property. Generally, the twentieth century saw a range of potentially superconductive materials being identified (including 27 metallic elements), most making the transition from normal to a superconductive state at around 20 degrees Kelvin; with tiny changes in energy levels as a material cools to the superconductivity state. By the century's end scientists were able to study materials reduced to a temperature of 0.00000000005 degrees Kelvin!

Devices made from superconductive materials can operate at high speed, with high sensitivity, and can make very efficient use of the energy (power) passing through them.

Superconductivity has been exploited in a range of products (devices) including generators, transformers, computers and other information storage systems, and in medical magnetic imaging equipment. The property of superconducting has been exploited in the design of new super conducting magnets, improving on types already being used in magnetic resonance imaging and for separating minerals. New designs (such as FRESCA2) are intended to replace magnets currently being used in high speed particle accelerators, such as the one at CERN, in order to increase the energy (and so speed) of accelerated particles in circular colliders.

It was in 1957 that the physicist Richard Feynman first suggested the possibility of the direct manipulation of atoms. A possibility that is being realized in the field of nanotechnology; one dealing with entities with at least one dimension of less than 100 nanometres. The use of the scanning tunneling microscope (invented in 1981), with its ability to visualize single atoms and any bonds between them, greatly assisted researchers interested in the very tiny. By 1989 this specialist equipment was able to facilitate the manipulation of single atoms, as had been predicted by Feynman about 30 years earlier.

Interest developed during the 70s and such was the increasing awareness of nanotechnology – nanomedicine, nanoelectronics, and nanotechnology applied to bimetals – that in 1986 Eric Drexler established the 'Foresight Institute' (not-for profit), specifically intended to inform the public on the potential of this new technology.

In 1985 three American chemists found that carbon atoms can form shell-like groups each with 60 atoms (C_{60} – 'Science Magazine's' 1991 'molecule of the year). The shape of these groups (agglomerations) invoke the concept of the geodesic dome and they were named 'Buckminster fullerene' after the designer of these domes (Buckminster Fuller). In 1991, the Japanese scientist Iijima Sumio found carbon in the form of nano-tubes was a by-product of the formation of fullerene; and that these nano-tubes had the property of semi-conductors, offering practical uses in powerful microscopes and a range of other electronic devices. The first practical nano circuit was produced in 2001 and was used as a transistor for a relative small (16-bit) memory circuit.

Nano-technology seeks to exploit the possibilities inherent in tiny agglomerations of atoms (used in the synthesis of complex molecules) – a nanometer is equivalent to a length of one billionth of a metre. One way of utilizing some of the useful properties has been the use of 'nano-whiskers', (ultra-thin strips of atoms each about 10 nanometres in length) in the manufacture of clothing and other fabrics as well as sunscreens and bandages. Nano-engineering can produce materials that are lighter and stronger (and even potentially programmable) than conventional materials

Protective coatings made of films of nano material can be applied to a range of surfaces and make them resistant to corrosion, impact damage, and radiation. Nanotechnology can produce materials of value throughout manufacturing industries including a range of computer-related hardware. Its raw materials tend to be carbon, silicon, and hydrogen, which can be processed in relative small manufacturing/fabrication facilities rather than the more traditional vast chemical plants and factories used in the processing of steel, oil, and a range of conventional synthetic materials. There is a possible downside to the widespread introduction of billions and billions of nano-particles into the environment. A concern highlighted in an early twenty-first century report by the Royal Society which included some quite controversial information, suggesting the need for caution in how nanotechnology is progressed

If the potential benefits of the uses for this technology outweigh the potential for harm (and if any the potential harm is non-critical) then according to Britannica on-line (June 2017). 'The potential impact of nanotechnology processes, machines and products is expected to be far-reaching, affecting nearly every conceivable information technology, energy source, agricultural products medical devices, pharmaceuticals, and material used in manufacturing.'

Chemists have during the twentieth century significantly advanced the understanding of the elemental basis of matter and the forms that compounds of these can take. This increasing understanding has developed in tandem with dramatically improving ability to manipulate atoms and molecules, and to created new substances and materials. A key aspect of this science - allied to the chemo-technology of material, and so product, creation - has been its marked contribution to our understanding of life expressed at the molecular level.

Bio-chemistry

Biochemists study the molecular processes involved within living matter. So obviously the best way to understand this perspective is to focus down from the level of whole organisms to the molecular-based processes that sustain or threaten the biochemical integrity of these. The Mathews and Van Hodle 'Handbook of Biochemistry' (1996, p4) suggests that: 'Biochemistry seeks to describe the structure, organization, and function of living matter in molecular terms.'

In terms of approach, biochemistry is primarily reductionist and functionalist. Reductionist in seeking to understand how the molecules it studies operate according to the basic laws of chemistry, and functionalist in relation to how the living processes contribute to the functioning of a living system or to the maintenance of the organism as a whole. Living processes of central interest to biochemists include: metabolism, respiration, photosynthesis, replication, immunity, fermentation, oxidization, and the information processing of nervous systems.

By 1900 a separate sub-branch of chemistry studying living (bio) processes was quite well established, one set to build on advances that had already been made. Up to 1828 the scientific consensus had included a clear distinction between living and non-living matter, and for many that there was some essence, some 'vital' spark, in living matter. But in this year Friedrich Wohler was able to show that the organic substance urea could be synthesized in a laboratory setting from the inorganic compound ammonium cyanate, and in doing so he had demonstrated a bridge between inorganic and organic matter.

Some level of research, especially in the brewing, dyeing, and cheese-making, industries, had been undertaken during the nineteenth century but vitalism continued to hold a central place in biology. Then, in 1897, the two German brothers Hans and Eduard Buchner (Eduard being professor of chemistry at the Berlin Agricultural College) demonstrated that the fermentation process turning sugar into ethanol could be facilitated by the introduction of dead yeast cells. They had begun the century-long activity of revealing the significance of various enzymes and the metabolic processes they were involved in.

Not only did the Buchner brother's discovery provide an impetus to similar types of research already being progressed in laboratories in Denmark, the US, and some other German cities, but it also significantly undermined the vitalist position. A position which, according to Mathews and Van Holde (1996) took the 'final fall' when in 1926 J.B.Sumner demonstrated that the enzyme urease could be crystallized, as could any organic compound. Instead of vitalism, the difference between living and non-living matter came to be understood in terms of molecular complexity and the process of replication.

In addition to their advancing the economic focus of organic molecular research, improving optical microscopes had also throughout the nineteenth century continued to reveal the realm of micro-organisms living in soils, within plant materials, and in the tissues of organisms. In 1898 the Dutchman Martinus Willem Beijerinck was able to filter the micro-organism ('viruses') causing the tobacco mosaic disease. Later on, in 1935, Wendell M. Stanley would show that these viruses were mostly constituted by similar proteins and nucleic acids (but the latter as RNA rather than DNA) to be found in the chromosomes of organic cells. In doing so further highlighting that the difference between living and non-living material is not simply binary.

The identification of the main blood groups (ABO by Karl Landsteiner 1900) and a bit later of vitamins (1912), highlighted the potential of bio-chemistry for understanding the operation of the human body in terms of well-being and illness. The role of vitamins was identified by Fredrick Hopkins and Casimir Funk, two pioneers in the science of biochemistry, who during the first decade of the twentieth century, working independently, suggested the 'vitamin hypothesis' in 1912. An hypothesis predicated on the view that the deficiency in small amounts of certain substances could lead to disease; by then famously so with scurvy, a condition that a small, regular, amount of vitamin C prevented.

Electron microscopes, as well as high precision light microscopes, also played a central role in revealing the composition of larger molecules within cells and their organelles. As the twentieth century progressed an understanding of how living materials are formed in nature, or can be synthesized in the laboratory, was being progressively advanced. With an understanding of the overall three-dimensional structure molecules (including lipids and proteins) being aided by the use of X-ray diffraction.

Numerous biochemists contributed to this advance in understanding but as already noted Linus Pauling stands out as an individual who brought together a basic understanding of chemistry, insights from quantum mechanics, and the potential value of X-ray crystallography, to bio-chemistry.

For Ager (2012, p246) the description by Pauling, in 1930, of the tetrahedral bonds of carbon was a distinct achievement: 'In Pauling's hands, quantum mechanics had made sense of the chemistry of the basic elements of life, a connection from physics, through chemistry, to biology.' Further work by Pauling, and his colleague Alfred Mirsky, revealed that the molecules of material – as fibrous proteins in polypeptide chains held together by hydrogen bonds - were much larger that had been previously thought possible. The realm of these 'macromolecules' would increasingly become the focus of study for industrial chemistry, medicine, and for more theoretical biochemical research.

Substances important for all life are composed of macromolecules constituting proteins, with each protein having its own unique three-dimensional structure. Pauling, based at Caltech, California, was at the forefront of research into proteins. Utilizing X-ray diffraction he and his colleagues were able to analyze properties of the amino acids of which proteins are composed, enabling a significant advance in the understanding of how a protein operates to fulfill a particular role within a living process.

If we assume one gene codes for one type of protein then we have a minimum of 20,500 different proteins in the human body (its proteome) but I have read estimates suggesting the possibility of the human body being able to generate 2 million different types of protein and an estimate of 10 million for all biological organisms!

In 1937 Max Perutz and John Kendrew (at the Cavendish, Cambridge) also used X-rays to analyze the structure of two proteins vital for animal (including human) life; the proteins myoglobin and hemoglobin - both involved in the transport of gases through the blood stream. A further advance in the understanding of the structure of proteins was made by Frederick Sanger when in 1949 he was able to identify the amino acid sequence of insulin; he soon moved on to sequencing RNA and DNA ('Sequences, Sequences, and Sequences', Sanger, 1988).

Since early in the twentieth century, when research had already shown the impact of yeast in brewing, it became increasingly clear that certain substances acted as 'catalysts', initiating molecular reactions and greatly speeding up their rate of development. The action of these 'enzymes' became easier to study from the 1920s when a suitable purification process had been designed. The role of enzymes was found to be fundamental to the molecular processes that recreate and sustain life. The fermentation process (converting sugars and carbohydrates into alcohol) itself involves 20 different enzymes. Which stimulate and influence the direction of molecular activity as catalysts involved in the chains of actions and reactions. A simple example of enzyme operation can be seen in the decomposition of hydrogen peroxide ($2H_2O_2$) to water and oxygen ($2H_2O$ and H_2) a process that would occur if left to itself but one significantly accelerated (by 1000 fold) if a tiny amount of ferric acid (as $FeCl_3$) was introduced.

Bernal vol 3 p 892 suggests that: '....one molecule of an enzyme like peroxidase can activate a million molecules of hydrogen peroxide per second.'

Enzymes are highly specific in operation, being vital to the living processes taking place within a cell and those between a cell and its local environment; certain forms of RNA can also behave as if enzymes. Biological process, such as fermentation, oxidization, digestion, respiration, photosynthesis, etc. each involve many more than just a single enzyme. The impetus to molecular processes obtained by the involvement of enzymes is quite remarkable. Jim Al-Khalili and Johnjoe MacFadden go so far as to note these as 'the engines of life.' They link this dynamic characteristic with key aspects of quantum mechanics, suggesting that the: 'extraordinary catalytic power is provided by their [enzymes] ability to choreograph the motions of fundamental particles and thereby dip into the quantum world to harness its strange laws.' Also that: 'It seems that life's catalysts [enzymes] are able to reach down into a deeper level of reality than plain old classical chemistry and make use of some neat quantum trickery.' (Al-Khalili and MacFadden, 2015, p140)

They also suggest that: 'Enzymes have made and unmade every single biomolecule inside every living cell that lives or has ever lived. Enzymes are as close as anything to the vital factors of life.' (AL-Khalili and MacFadden, 2014, p137)

In addition to enzymes acting as catalysts there are also substances termed 'co-enzymes' that were identified as early as 1906 as being important in initiating and directing molecular processes. A key difference in the two types of catalysts is that enzymes are mostly made of proteins (if certain forms of RNA can also behave as if enzymes) but co-enzymes are not.

By the 1940s biochemistry had became firmly established as a science with its own range of research methods (added to those of more basic chemistry) and specialist equipment. Biochemists, in industry, medical, and university, laboratories had contributed to an understanding of numerous biological processes – to reveal the role of a range of proteins, enzymes, and co-enzymes. In the field of medicine the advance in drug development made a range of illnesses with previously poor outcomes curable: the sulphanilamide (syphilis and other streptococci infections), penicillin (pneumonia and many other infectious diseases - tetanus, syphilis) and other antibiotics such as actinomycin and streptomycin – a bit later (1950s) there was cortisone to treat inflammatory conditions and in mental health there was lithium to treat manic-depression and chlorpromazine for schizophrenia (R.Porter, 2003).

As the twentieth century progressed biochemists also indentified the elemental composition of living creatures. Noting that they are made primarily from Carbon, Hydrogen, Oxygen, and Nitrogen (C.H.O.N.) each of these four having a strong tendency to form covalent bonds, which make for molecular stability and they also have the potential to form multiple bonds (single, double, triple) which makes them amenable to form complex molecules composed of a wide range of elements.

According to Prim Vevi ('Modern Science Writing', Richard Dawkins (ed), 2008, p385) 'Carbon, in fact, is a singular element: it is the only element that can bind itself in long stable chains without a great expense of energy, and for life on earth.......precisely long chains are required. Therefore carbon is the key element of living substance ...'

Given that the sharing of electrons (in carbon bonds) is taking place relatively close to the nucleus of the atom the bond is strong. Carbon is amenable to bond in a similar way to a range of elements whose atoms have an incomplete electron shell. It is the combination of atoms held together by these strong covalent bonds that congregate to form the very large macromolecules that underpin all life.

Human bodies are composed of a limited collection of elements:

Oxygen 62%
Carbon 20%
Hydrogen 10%
Nitrogen 3%
Calcium 2.5%
Phosphorous 1.14%
Chlorine 0.16%
Sulfur 0.14%
Potassium 0.11%
Sodium 0.10%

A body of about 95% CHON material, with another six elements on this list making up a further 4% so together constituting 99% the human body; the remaining 1% is composed of minute amounts of the elements such as: magnesium, iron, cobalt, boron, zinc, iodine.

Across the whole of organic life the range of shared basic biochemical processes and material composition, functioning according to the same chemical laws, provides powerful evidence that all earth-bound life forms have common origins – in terms of biochemistry, life is a set of unified and interrelated processes.

Biochemistry is a branch of science where different activities are closely interlinked, but even so I think it is broadly of heuristic value to suggest that during the first half of the twentieth century a primary focus was on the cell's structure and its metabolic functions, and in the second half the primary focus was on reproduction (genetics). But of course most advances in understanding each of these advanced the understanding of both.

Cellular material had been of interest to scientists since the 17th/18th centuries when Antoni van Leeuwenhoek and Marcello Malpighi, using the newly invented microscope, first drew attention to the discrete bodies in blood and sperm cells. That all organisms are composed of cells – discrete entities, with a definite structure – was accepted by the middle of the nineteenth century. The use of newly developed achromatic microscopes allowed early biologists to undertake detailed examination of organic tissue. This led to Robet Hooke identifying these discrete units, in a tiny piece of cork, by - as seen through his compound microscope - units that he named 'cells'. Biologists soon learned that the shape of cells differed depending on their function: squarish for liver cells, long cells for muscles, even longer cells for some nerves. The idea of cellular reproduction and of aggregations (colonies) of cells were suggested by Matthias Schleiden and Theodor Schwann in the late 1830s early 1840s. Schwann suggested that all living entities are composed of cells, so establishing similar compositional 'basic units' for plant and animal life. In 1833 Robert Brown was able to describe the 'nucleus' as a specific structure within cells. And in 1844/5 Friedrich Miescher isolated the nuclei of cells (from human white blood cells – leucocytes) and identified that these contained a substance very different from proteins, a substance he termed 'nuclein'; this would later be identified as nucleic acid. He was soon able to confirm the same substance in a range of other cell types.

Improving optical microscopy, along with staining techniques developed by those such as Camillo Gogli, led to productive work on identifying discrete structures (organelles) within the cell. A type of nerve cell (the Purkinje cell) was identified by Jan Purkinje using this method in 1837. The increase in the understanding of organelles within cells by the use of staining techniques can be illustrated by the work of Albrect Kossel who, towards the latter part of the nineteenth century, was able to identify that organelles were composed of both large and small molecules.

By the end of the nineteenth century it was accepted that all organisms are made of different types of cell and knowledge of these discrete bodies included: the identification of organelles (not the understanding of their specific function), the identification of the cell's role as the building block of organisms, and also that the cell's nucleus was directly involved in reproduction (heredity). The discoveries on which increasing knowledge of the cell was based generated a keen interest in the life sciences; an interest that would drive intensive and productive research throughout the twentieth century.

From its invention, in 1931 by Ernest Ruska, the electron microscope allowed biologists to more closely study the inner workings of the cell, including the complex organelles such as mitochondria and chloroplasts In 1945 Albert Claude published the first photographic images of living cells, as seen through the magnifying and resolving power of an electron microscope.

Knowledge of the cell was advanced with research into how cells operate within the extracellular environment, as both producers of essential materials (the protein 'factories') and where necessary in transporting these to the sites required, and also their role in the body's communication network, which includes the body's immune, hormonal, and neuronal - systems.

Understanding of the communication and control systems in the human nervous system steadily accrued, along with more general knowledge of cellular biochemistry, during the first half of the twentieth century. As early in the century as 1914, the first neurotransmitter – acetylcholine – had been identified. And in a series of scientific papers published during 1951/2 Alan Hodgkin and Andrew Huxley (building on experimental work of the neurobiologist Julius Bernstein) identified the flow of sodium and potassium across the membranes of neurons – a key aspect of the 'action potentials' that mediate the propagation of communication within the brain and wider nervous system.

The introduction of computer-based tissue scanning systems markedly improved the accessibility of neurological material. But even prior to these becoming available (from the 1980s) the use of sophisticated optical and electron microscopes, and EEG recording devices, had been able to provide a steady stream of new information on brain structure and function.

Complex internal processes and cell specialization show the amazing (almost mysteriously formed) constitution of bio-material phenomena, as well as the essential unity of life. During the twentieth century the 3 billion year progressive bio-chemical formation of the cellular level of life's chemical organization has become clearer. The human body alone has about 210 different types of cell. In the adult human body about 96 million cells die each minute but fortunately, during the same time, about 96 million other cells divide to reproduce - total number of cells in a human body 3.72×10^{13} in humans most of these being specialized as liver cells, neuronal cells, blood cells, skin cells, stomach wall cells, muscle, connective tissue, hair, skin, etc.

Quantum mechanics and the laws of thermodynamics, as related to the ways living systems arrange intra-cellular energy transformations, the atom-based forms of molecular bonding, as well as molecular action and reaction are linked together. Biochemists have provided a theoretical framework (the 'molecular paradigm') that has enabled some useful understanding of how the primordial cells could have been formed. And for these to have progressively evolved into evermore complex (multi-cellular) organisms, within the changing environmental conditions that advances in such branches of science as physics, chemistry, and geology, have been shown to have pertained since the presence of the most basic organic molecules first offered the potential for living entities to form and to evolve.

Daniel Dennett in a 'New Statesman' article dated 19th December 2011 noted that:

'Cells may be the simplest life forms on the planet – even the simplest possible life-forms but their inner workings, at the molecular level, are breathtakingly complex, composed of thousands of molecular machines, all of them interacting to provide the cell with energy it needs to build offspring and maintain its membrane.'

By the 1970s, generations of biochemists had contributed to what has become a fairly clear understanding of the internal constitution and the bodily functions undertaken by the different types of cell in the human body. With its two hundred odd different types of cell, making up a compliment of just over thirty seven trillion cells in total; over half of which are bacteria!

Crudely put: a cell is a discrete 'body' enclosed by a membrane through which selective material can pass. Within the area bounded by this membrane are about twenty different 'organelles'. Each type of organelle functions in specific ways to maintain the cell's integrity. The major organelles would include the nuclei which, if there were one, would be the 'command and control' centre for the cell. The nuclei is a dark area enclosed by a permeable membrane and it is here that about 90% of the DNA is located, with about another 10% located in the mitochondria; possibly a residue of the time when it was itself a free-living cell. Within the nuclei is an area termed the nucleolus, where RNA is stored ready to be mobilized in the intra-cellular communication system as the molecular medium for transferring genetic information generated from the DNA to a location, such as the ribosomes, where proteins are synthesized from a selection of 20/21 amino acids. Proteins are the primary component of cells; these constitute the structure of the cell as well as being produced by it. Although, as noted above, fairly recent protein sequencing activity suggests there are just over 20,000 different proteins in the human body. With some of the newly formed proteins moving into the cell's Gogli apparatus for further modification.

The many processes being undertaken within a cell require energy and the source of this for animals is the complex molecule adenosinetriphosphate (ATP); synthesised in the mitochondria from material drawn into the cell. According to the 'Biochemistry Handbook' (1996, page 78): 'It is probably no exaggeration to call ATP the single most important substance in biochemistry'. Perhaps so, if we accept that ATP is a 'substance' whereas carbon is an 'element'. The knowledge that the energy is required to power cells was stored in the complex molecule ATP was added too by Peter Mitchell's (1960) proposal on how the ATP was actually formed within the mitochondria.

The energy source of plants (and some algae) derives from the process of photosynthesis operating as the Sun's radiation is processed by the plant-cell's chloroplasts and made available as proteins. A plant's ability to gain energy from sunlight allows it to be self-sustaining (autotrophic), at least in not having to 'consume' material sourced from other forms of life. Plant cells also differ from those of animal cells in their having a tough 'cellulosic' covering over their membrane.

Some other intra-cellular bodies include the ribosomes embedded in the rough endoplasmic reticulum, with the smooth endoplasmic reticulum providing the fats (lipids) required for the cell's metabolism. Other discrete intra-cellular areas include cytoplasm, vacuole, microtubules, microfilaments, lysosome, and centrioles, each making a specialist contribution to a cell's structural integrity and to the overall metabolic processes.

It is the process of cellular and organism reproduction that I will now focus on; beginning by stepping back to consider early discoveries. Advances in understanding reproduction, were made in the late nineteenth century by a number of researchers. In 1882 Walter Flemming used a novel staining technique to distinguish the tiny strings of material within the nucleus of cells and was able to describe the way in which they were seen to divide during cell division (mitosis). At about the same time August Weismann identified these 'chromosomes' as being the carriers of heredity information. They had been isolated as early as 1869, by Friedrich Miescher, but at that time their central role in heredity had not been recognized

The accumulation of discoveries culminated around 1900 in three individuals, working independently, identifying that hereditary could be understood in terms of gene expression. These three, Carl Correns (Germany), Eric Tschermach (Austria), Hugo de Vries (Holland), soon realized that they had in fact 'rediscovered' Mendelian genetics.

It was in 1909 that Wilhelm Johannsen introduced the concept of the 'gene' to cover the hereditary constitution; that which is passed on in reproduction.

Up to about the middle of the nineteenth century the relatively small international scientific community had been composed, in large part, of amateurs beavering away within their own particular area of interest. If the concept of 'community' does rather exaggerate the level of interaction and the sharing of information that was taking place it does express the communality of ambition and increasing agreement on appropriate methods.

One of these 'amateur scientists' was the Moravian monk Gregor Mendel; he had become a priest in 1843. Whilst studying for a teaching diploma at the University of Vienna he was judged by as being not very bright and was unable to complete his teaching course. Mendel was sent back, seemingly a failure, to the monastery at the age of 31 (1853). Fortunately the monastery offered an environment with a strong tradition of horticulture and a library suitable for members of an order with significant teaching responsibilities. On his return to the monastery he embarked on an intensive study of the natural world and also began a well-organized, doggedly relentless, regime of experimental study focused on an understanding of heredity; using the common pea plant as the means of observing this.

Just to remind ourselves of what was noted in Chapt. 4 (above)....Mendel identified seven specific plant characteristics, including colour and shape, and suggested that the expression of any of these in any pea plant involved two 'particles', one gained from each parent. He found that if any pair of particles were different then one would be dominant and so would be expressed, the other recessive and so would not be expressed.

Mendel pursued his experimental programme for a period of eight years and then, in 1866, published his results in a local-circulation natural history journal. His work was effectively ignored or rather, simply went unnoticed. Two years later Mendel was promoted to become the abbot of the monastery and any useful experimental work in heredity effectively came to an end. It is interesting that this 'failed' teaching student, judged to have a poor intellect, would be promoted to this high ecclesiastical position. Perhaps a flair for administration, including planning and record keeping, that led to his ecclesiastical promotion were the same attributes suited to his extended experimental programme. But Mendel also had the insight to see the value of understanding heredity and the ability to interpret his results in relation to how it might operate.

By the early twentieth century the importance of the cell had been noted and that its structure included a number of types of 'free-floating' organelles including a nuclei in which were stored the chromosomes that had already been identified as having a central role in heredity. Molecular biologists were also aware that the cell was mainly composed of proteins but that the chromosomes were composed of both proteins and nucleic acids. This accumulating knowledge culminated in 1902 with William Bateson demonstrating that Mendelian inheritance applied to organisms as well as plants, and his naming the study of cell-based heredity 'genetics'.

Between the 1930s and 1950s there was a period of the bringing together of neo-Darwinian natural selection and the advances made in genetics. This, the 'Modern Synthesis', can be seen in a range of scientific papers and books published during this time. Julian Huxley's 'Evolution: the Modern Synthesis' (1942) offers a fairly clear presentation of this coming together of natural selection and genetics. Huxley's book was dedicated to T.H.Morgan and also acknowledges a debt to Ronald Fisher and J.B.S Haldane, all three prominent in this new wide-ranging biological paradigm.

The mention of at least two of these biological scientists, Huxley and Fisher, raises the spectre of a darker side of genetics; eugenics and the idea of selective breeding. Although influenced by Herbert

Spencer's 'survival of the fittest' interpretation of Darwinism, it was towards end of the nineteenth century that Francis Galton more obviously promoted eugenics. In his will Galton endowed a new seat of eugenics to be established at University College, London. The first Galton Professorship was awarded to Galton's protégé Karl Pearson. Galton and Pearson also applied mathematics to genetics but for the first half of the century this more valuable contribution was overshadowed by their influence on the eugenics movement. A movement involving some leading biologists, such as Huxley and Fisher, until the rise of Nazism with its own murderous 'eugenics' policy cast a dark shadow over the idea of selective breeding. But it was an idea that, somewhat differently presented, did continue as a feature of civil life in the sterilization initiatives introduced in the US, India, and China, after WWII.

A landmark paper authored by Oswald Avery and his junior colleagues Colin Macleod, and Maclyn McCarty, published in 1944, proposed that the basic information carrying substance in a cell was deoxyribonucleic acid (DNA). A number of experiments during the 1940s confirmed this proposal. Around this time it was also confirmed that it is DNA that determines the synthesis of proteins required for an organism's metabolism.

It was known that gene 'mutations' were the means of selecting for increased 'fitness' (within an environment), and that the exposure to X-rays could induce mutation, but ideas on the biochemical mechanism for this were more speculative (theoretical) than research based.

The physicist Erwin Schrodinger's 1944 essay 'What is life', set out an explanation of genetic mutation in terms of quantum mechanics, offering an understanding of biological molecules that makes it assessable for the layman – he explained genetic mutations as being due to '...quantum jumps in the gene molecule.' produced by '....chance fluctuations in vibrational energy' and concludes '...Thus we account, by the very principles of quantum mechanics, for the most amazing fact about mutations, the fact by which they first attracted De Vries's attention, namely, that they are jumping variations, no intermediate forms occurring.'

Schrodinger considered that the number of atoms in a gene (from the square root of 'n' point of view) is too small to '.....entail orderly and lawful behaviour according to statistical physics - and that means according to physics'. Schrodinger's essay, whilst not itself adding much to a direct understanding of molecular biology, inspired others, such as Linus Pauling and Francis Crick, whose work did.

In terms of reproduction, as early as 1858 Robert Virchow (developing a suggestion originally made by John Goodsir) had noted that all the cells that exist have arisen due to their creation from previously existing cells. But what forms of life existed prior to the evolution of cells continued as an active twentieth century research area, one informed by significant progress made in the understanding of micro-biological processes, especially those involving nucleic acids and the proteins.

For the early evolution of life-forms, we can postulate some forms of pre-cellular life - perhaps with reproduction controlled by RNA rather than DNA – that came to form constituent parts of the cell were once thought to be free-living units e.g. the mitochondria and the chloroplasts.

It is possible that some form of self-replicating chains of amino acids 'reproduced' in the sense of growing identical copies on copies, and it as has been suggested (see George Johnson 'Fire in the Mind', 1995) that perhaps some flaw ('mutation') occurred that was advantageous to replication within a certain environment.

Michael Brooks 'New Statesman' 5th March 2012 suggested that: '....we have now answered a fundamental question of evolutionary theory. According to the best hypothesis, a billion and a half years ago there was a bacterium that could turn sunlight into energy. One day it invaded one of the first cells to contain a nucleus. The resulting super-organism was the ancestor of all red and green algae and land plants. Until this past week, this story was just a suggestion. Now, thanks to analysis of the genomes involved, just published in the journal Science, it has moved from hypothesis to fact.'

It is now thought that a number of the cell's organelles originally lived as free-living organisms. With the mitochondrion and chloroplast each retaining a vestigial genetic apparatus, including RNA and DNA ribosomes and other molecules directly related to reproduction. A number of eukaryote cells are suggested to have arisen by the originally symbiotic relationship of separate free-living prokaryote cells. These types of progressive fusion of two organisms into one can be found in about two dozen organisms living today. Gerard Piel notes that Lynn Margulis and her colleagues have suggested that it was the '.....fusion of an Arcaebacterium and a Eubacterium that founded the eukaryotic line' (Piel 'The Age of Science', 2001).

At the start of the 1950s at least three groups of researchers were closing in on being able to accurately describe the molecular structure of DNA – Linus Pauling and his team at Caltech, California; Maurice Wilkins, Raymond Gosling, and Rosalind Franklin at Kings College, London; and Francis Crick and James Watson at the Cavendish in Cambridge. The two British teams were funded by the UK's Medical Research Council.

Pauling had already identified the molecular structure of fiberous proteins and noted how these polypeptide chains wound around each other to form helical shapes based on hydrogen bonds. He used X-ray diffraction to show that DNA must form a helix, recognizing that a helix would be the simplest form of self-organizing that amino acids could take. Pauling's key mistake was to assume a triple helix for DNA, a basic error that he would have been aware of had he been able to access Rosalind Franklin's X-ray generated images.

It was due to Maurice Wilkins complicity, and without his seeking Franklin's permission, that Crick and Watson were able to gain a clear advantage on viewing these important pictures. They were also able to benefit from a visit by Erwin Chargaff who was able to explain his 'rules' on base-pair formation to them,[11] not least to clarify the limitations on possible base-pair arrangements. It was in April 1953 that the journal 'Nature' published Crick and Watson's paper in which they outlined the molecular structure of DNA in the form of a double helix with paired nucleotide bases (from guanine, cytosine, adenine, and thymine, paired as A-T and C-G). So having genetic information recorded twice, once on each helix. Key features in the double helix structure are the strong (covalent) bonds linking the

---

[11] As noted above, As well as Franklin's pictures, also fundamental to understanding the composition of DNA were the 'Chargaff rules'. These rules are based on two descriptions, each aspects of the chemical make-up of the base-pairs of DNA; limiting composition to certain proportions of the sugar (purine) and acid (pyrimidine) nucleotides. Erwin Chargaff and his team devised techniques to measure the amounts of Adenine, Guanine (the purines), Cytosine, Thymine (pyrimine), in samples of DNA. From this two 'rules' (necessary conditions) were identified.

1) That the amounts of purine and pyrimidine in a sample of DNA is always equal.

2) That the amounts of Adenine and of Thymine is always the same and that the amounts of Guanine and Cytosine is always the same.

Although the specific composition of DNA differs between all species, these laws pertain throughout all forms of earth-bound life. They provide rules that helped to make an understanding of the double helix structure of DNA clear.

components of each 'string' (helix) and the weak bonds (hydrogen) linking the helixes in pairs – allowing for strength within each helix but an ease in terms of separating the pair when necessary for reproduction.

Whilst Crick and Watson had been noted by their Cavendish colleague Max Perutz as '....intellectually arrogant young men....' they had revealed the molecular platform for transferring genetic information from one generation to the next.

It had been in 1952 that Rosalind Franklin, a gifted scientist, had been able to provide first-class X-ray crystallography images of a DNA molecule, clearly indicating its helical form. These photographs showed that the DNA in the fibres must have some kind of regular, repetitive three-dimensional structure. Francis Crick and James Watson considered that the diffraction pattern of the fibres would require a helical secondary structure. They suggested that there must be 10 base pairs (of A-T and G-C, in line with Chargaff rules) at each turn. Further, that the density of the fibres shown on the images suggested two DNA strands making up each of the very large helical molecules – so a 'double-helix'. As noted above, without consulting Franklin, her colleague Maurice Wilkins had shown her photographs to Crick and Watson (especially image nos. 51), thus aiding their discovery, in 1953, of the molecular structure of DNA.

Franklin was herself progressing a similar line of model construction as Crick and Watson, one based on the idea of a double helix, with hydrogen bonds holding the base molecules together. She might well have announced the structure of DNA before them if, that is, they had not been given access to her X-ray images. This was a time when the scientific community was pervaded with misogyny.

As Richard Dawkins observed ('Unweaving the Rainbow', 1998, p191): 'It is truly appalling (as well as desperately sad) that Rosalind Franklin, whose X-ray diffraction photographs of DNA crystals were crucial to Watson and Crick's success, was not allowed in the common room of her own institution and was therefore debarred from contributing to, and learning from, what might have been crucial scientific shoptalk'.

Of the individual scientists (and these overwhelmingly women) treated badly by some of their colleagues Rosalind Franklin stands out – deprived of the chance to gain priority in a discovery and at that time denied adequate recognition for the crucial contribution she had made to it.

The elucidation of the structure of DNA is taken as a landmark discovery in twentieth century science, indeed in the advance of the branches of the whole 'scientific enterprise', as focused on understanding the natural world. That heredity – life's continuity in different forms - was fundamentally about the transfer of information and that the chromosomal carriers of this information were chemically arranged in a particular way. A way common to all life forms we know of. Scientific curiosity and an increasing awareness of the commercial potential combined to, in effect, begin an intense focus on 'molecular biology' in general and in particular on the process of reproduction (genetics).

Between the 1940s – 70s the understanding of large bio-molecules was advanced by individuals such as Linus Pauling, Desmond Bernal, Dorothy Hodgkin, Max Perutz, and John Kendrew. It was research groups informed by pre-1952 advances that continued to focus on identifying the molecular structure of DNA in more detail and an understanding of how it operates during the process of replication and protein production.

Proteins are built of chains (peptides) of amino acids. 'Certain properties of the amino acids force the chain to fold in particular places, producing a three-dimensional structure whose shape is critical if the protein is to perform its job properly' (Richard Fifield, 1988 p255). Each amino acid is represented by a code of three bases (a 'codon') e.g. valine = GTG.

The 'transcription' process – DNA to protein - operates by a section of the DNA (containing a string of 'codons') in the nucleus of a cell being copied by an enzyme called ribonucleic acid ploymerase and in this process a molecule called messenger RNA (mRNA) is formed. This molecule then moves out of the cell's nucleus into the cytoplasm where it serves as a template upon which the translation of the mRNA into the codons of the amino acids takes place to form the specific protein required. It is molecules of transfer RNA (tRNA) that transport the 'raw' amino acids to the mRNA. The binding process is enabled by the fact that tRNA is made of triple bases called anticodons that bind with the complementary codons on the strand of mRNA. At the point of a protein being formed, the gene is said to have been 'expressed'.

A primary biochemical source of the variation of organisms is now assumed to originate in genetic mutation; 'errors' made during the DNA replication process. Broadly speaking, these seemingly random errors alter an organism's genetic constitution in ways that can reduce or improve its 'fitness' in relation to the environmental conditions it experiences. Most mutations have a deleterious outcome and organisms with any such mutations tend to reproduce to a lesser extent than the 'normals'. Whereas those organsims with any mutations that allow an adaptive advantage in a particular environment would tend to breed to a greater extent than the normals. So providing a biochemical mechanism that allows any species of organism to evolve toward forms (even new species) better adapted to an environment. This explanation theoretically assumes that an environment remains sufficiently constant - which they rarely do over long-periods; complicating but not fundamentally effecting the overall evolutionary process.

Each gene is composed of up to several thousand nucleotide pairs, or genetic 'letters'. Three nucleotide pairs in a row specify an amino acid. The amino acids in turn are assembled into proteins; proteins are the building blocks of the cells, and the cells are the building blocks of organisms. DNA from one human chromosome pair is contained in 2 enormous molecules each with a molecular weight of $2x10^{10}$ so 20 billion;[12] a much simpler protein molecule would have a molecular weight of about 150,000 so the complexity of DNA can be suggested. The about 20,500 genes in a human-cell are arranged in 46 chromosomes. Apart from the sex cells which have just 23 chromosomes that come together as pairs (so making 46 in the new organism) during the fertilization process. Genes are the portions of the DNA that ultimately contribute to the expression of traits; as simple as the color of wings and as complex as the means of flight.

An obvious area that remains to be understood is the relationship between a mass of seemingly meaningless sections of the chromosomes interspersed with (between) the coded sections. It seems that possibly as much as 98% of human DNA is constituted by lengths of these 'introns', with only 2% being currently sequentiable material, suggesting that our understanding of what constitutes the biochemical information supporting life could be markedly deficient. The presence of these 'introns' was discovered in 1977 by Philip Sharp at MIT and separately by Richard Roberts of Cold Spring Harbor Laboratories.

---

[12] Molecular weight, or atomic weight, is the sum of the atomic weight of each element in a molecule times by the number of atoms of each element.

It is possible that the introns have a role in the coding of proteins such perhaps as in triggering neighbouring genes into action. Or, as some geneticists have suggested, they are but evolutionary remnants of viral infections survived by our long-gone eukaryote ancestors. Introns offer an intriguing puzzle of just the sort that scientists have proven to be so good at solving.

Harry Harris (1970, p1) noted that: 'Four major advances made it possible to begin to understand the nature of genetic diversity in molecular terms. The first was the discovery that the particular chemical substance that endow a gene with its characteristic properties is deoxyribosenucleic acid (DNA). The second was the elucidation of the molecular structure of this substance. The third was the recognition that the primary biochemical role of DNA in the cells of an organism is to direct the synthesis of enzymes and other proteins. The fourth was the unraveling of the genetic code.' This fourth advance being the outcome of a scientific enterprise of some magnitude.

The sequencing of human DNA would amount to creating a molecular-based map from which could be read key aspects of humankind's evolutionary journey (the route and the landmarks) as well as a gene-based map that could offer an understanding of the biological 'blueprint' and its role in the development of all of the cells in the human body. Genes require a suitable physical environment for developing our emotional and cognitive faculties and a social environment for their behavioural expression. It is a complex interactive intermixing of these that form any individual.

From the discovery of the structure of DNA in 1953 there was an intensive focus on the molecular structure and synthesizing processes of proteins and other large organic molecules. Undertaken using a range of modern technologies, including X-ray crystallography, improved optical and electron microscopes and, from about the 1980s, computers and nuclear magnetic resonance imaging equipment.

What might be termed the first very simple gene map had been drawn up in 1911 by Alfred Sturtevant, who located genes of the fruit fly Drosphila melanogaster. But a practical method of genetic sequencing was only realized in work, begun in the 1970s, by Sydney Brenner. Brenner was a model example of a scientist committed to sharing research findings and to developing his colleagues and students. He began by sequencing the genetic code of the transparent nematode roundworm 'Caenorhabditis elegans', this being completed by 1998. Continual improvements in techniques developed for sequencing this relatively simple organism (of 100 million base pairs compared with the human 3.3 billion base pairs) suggested to biologists the possibility of sequencing the human genome.

Some earlier attempts had been made to launch the commercial decoding of DNA, Walter Gilbert's 1986 Genome Corporation being one of the more notable. But the pace and the focus of research increased when in early 1990 the US government committed up to $3 billion to the initial research plan (overseen by the US Dept. of Energy). But this, the 'Human Genome Project' (HGP), was an internationally coordinated endeavour involving, in addition to the US, countries including Japan, UK, France and Germany.

As with almost all large scientific projects, where profit is not a short-term prospect (such as: in most space exploration, astronomy, high energy physics), the HGP was funded by taxpayers. There were attempts made by private interests to get involved, with the most significant of these being the company Celera Genomics (capitalized to the amount of $300 million) set up in 1998 by Craig Venter. Venter was setting out when able to benefit from an amount of progress already made by publicly-funded scientists who, as a matter of principal, made their results publically available.

M.Brooks (2011, p.143) offers a sympathetic assessment of Venter 'All he wanted was the freedom to work (and salaries for his staff), but beyond that it was all about discovery....he made the largest single deposit in GenBank, the publicly accessible database of genetic information. Many biologists working in the public sector rejoiced'. Nigel Calder (2003) lends support to Brooks's views and he suggests that Venter's private involvement stimulated the pace of the publicly funded HGP. He also noted that when he left Celera Venter returned to working in the not-for-profit sector, establishing the 'Centre for the Advancement of Genomics', a think-tank specifically task with considering ethical issues for the new science.

However we might interpret his motivation, Venter's level of showmanship at press conferences and Celera's assertive approach to gene sequence patenting seems to challenge any idea of his company acting solely in the wider public interest. Indeed the parent company behind Celera, Applied Biosystems (with its own parent company PE – later renamed Applera), is not noted for much if any disinterested funding of scientific endeavour. Even if we accept Venter's own motives were balanced towards scientific endeavour in the service of human well-being rather than naked commercial interests, it does seem that for his financial backers the balance would be perhaps have been different. Venter's initial hyped up press releases and over-ambitious claims set a pattern for the way possible advances in genetics would be made by a range of senior geneticists, most often those with a personal financial interest in the private sector. It was Venter's own genome that was the very first to be fully sequenced, with this information being made public in 2007, the second being Francis Watson's – perhaps a reflection of the self-regard of these two talented biochemists.

Celera, with other commercial enterprises poised to follow, had sought to gain patent protection for parts of the human genome; to make human genetic information yet another marketable commodity. When, in March 2000, the US President (Bill Clinton) and UK Prime Minister (Tony Blair) suggested that patenting of the human genome sequence was inappropriate (Clinton later backed down on this), approximately $50 billion of market capitalization was lost by biotechnology companies within just two days.

Governments (and the scientists working within the HGP) have stated a commitment to open access to the results of genetic sequencing. But it is clear 20 years on that the potential for profit from genetic (and indeed biochemistry more generally) research has been significantly directed according to the narrow interests of private industry – led by Big Pharma and some venture capital backers. It has been a science where quite a few individual scientists have become wealthy entrepreneurs, and many aspire to do the same. Where the idealized images of some otherworldly scientists beavering away for the greater benefit of humankind has been exposed for some as a secretive, competitive activity, driven by the search for the profitable.

For Hilary and Steven Rose: '…..money has joined prestige and become entangled with the control of intellectual property, patents, and access to hugely profitable stakes in instrumentation, biotech and pharmaceutical companies. This new hybrid production system of science is radically different from that of the past.' They also note that: '……the hegemonic values of global capitalism, including its Promethean promises, have further woven into the interstices of the technologies of human life……. genomics, stem-cell research, and the neurosciences.' (Rose and Rose, 2013, p31)

The role of the profit-seeking private sector in genetics might, as

Brooks suggested with Venter, offer a dynamic to drive progress. But for sure the extent to which this dynamic would be effective will be reflected in the extent that it will shape the direction of research. If towards areas where it considers the greatest profits lie it could be an approach that could risk neglecting possible research areas that could return significant human (or animal) benefit but with the potential for no or only very low profits.

Aided by improving computer technology, advances in understanding of genomics, and international cooperation, the HGP was able, in February 2001, to offer a rough draft of the human genome. Full sequencing was completed by April 2003 and by May 2006 the last chromosome had been sequenced and made available as a final version ('The International Human Genome Sequencing Consortium'). The HGP sequencing process did not include all human genetic material and approx. 8% of the human genome remained unsequenced. But now the genetic constitution of a humanbeing - biochemical information on over 3 billion base pairs arranged in about 20,500 individual genes, stored in over 700 megabytes of data - lay open to scientists with the potential for both advancing understanding and for genetic manipulation; the later clearly presenting as a double-edged sword. But it is also open to the wider public via databases including Genbank, US-NCBI, and the Human Genome DataBase.

Today the international cooperation involved in Genbank includes its being up-dated on a bi-monthly basis. There are also over a dozen gene-based databases and another dozen or so protein/amino acid databases – all contributing to open access on our genetic and bio-chemical heritage.

I have noted that this genetic information can provide a bio-chemical narrative of the evolutionary journey of humankind; it is a potentially decipherable record of the generations that have gone before as embodied in our genes. The hope is that it can also provide information that, when sufficiently understood, can perhaps offer the possibility for treatment - preventative measures, alleviation, and even cures - of almost any physical disease or life-impairing psychological condition. Although genetic information is only one, if very important, aspect of any individual's development.

But the relatively well funded science of bio-genetics is still at the understanding phase in most areas of healthcare, with conventional epidemiological studies currently offering more utilitarian healthcare outcomes. The story of genetic research is replete with extravagant claims for 'miracle cures', and medical 'holy grails', having been found; made public at carefully orchestrated press conferences. Unsurprisingly, given the complexity involved, most of the claims turn out to be, misleading, overblown, or just plain mistaken. As authors such as R.C. Lewontin (1991) and H.and S. Rose (2013) have pointed out, the role of environment can be at least as significant as the genetic constitution in terms of outcomes. So much of ill-health (especial psychological conditions) can be as much social rather than simply a genetic issue. And any genetic contribution to ill-health is more often confounded by molecular complexity enmeshed in more or less influential environmental conditions; and these both pre- and post birth.

Knowledge of the human genome also implies significant moral (ethical) issues – most obviously issues such as: stem cell research, designer babies, genetic testing for selective education, genetic testing for criminal tendencies, genetic testing for the purpose of life insurance valuation, etc. etc.

In 2002 The Human Genetic Commission stated that: 'Each individual is entitled to lead a life in which genetic characteristics will not be the basis of unjust discrimination or unfair or inhuman treatment'.

Overblown claims of genes being some fundamental causal source of physical or mental health, intelligence, innate abilities and aptitudes, personality traits, etc. etc. are based on an insidious ideology of reductionist causation. Simplistic claims of even well-meaning geneticists can be liable to be selectively deployed by individuals holding political and economic power in order to progress their own ambitions, or exaggerated by journalists lacking the ability to adequately assess the claims being made.

Theodosius Dobzhansky ('Mankind Evolving', 1976 ed., p77) cautioned that: 'What genetic conditioning does mean is that there is no single human nature, only human natures with different requirements for optimal growth and self-realization. The evidence of genetic conditioning of human traits, especially mental traits, must be examined with the greatest care.'

The economically disinterested pursuit of genetics could contribute to the alleviation of a range of life-limiting conditions (especially those of childhood) and in the longer term could ease the personal consequences of such conditions as cancer, congenital heart failure, diabetes, and degenerative neural disease. But we should be very cautious of any claims and consider each condition not just in genetic terms but within its whole social context.

Then there are the profoundly difficult moral and the ethical issues related to the exploitation of genetic knowledge for private profit. With genetics, as with the arms industry, the corporate ethos coded as efficient management includes where possible the externalization of costs, secrecy, maximization of profit, and the avoidance of social responsibility. It encompasses the influencing of academic focus in public as well as private research institutions, viewing data as but a commodity to be determinedly protected rather than shared within the scientific community. Industry has long had a place in directing scientific advance, but up until the second half of the twentieth century this was a more of a role in this rather than having evermore control of it.

The idea of science as open knowledge has always been more an ideal than a reality, but it was at least an aspiration and many individual scientists and most scientific institutions have endeavoured to live up to this ideal. But now neo-liberal values are eroding even the ideal as it deploys its increasing hegemonic economic and political power to 'privatize' and 'marketize', scientific knowledge.

The cost of the HGP was about $3 billion and it has been estimated that by 2011 the HGP-linked information suggested that it had generated $796 billion worth of economic impact. Although the original HGP was funded by public monies,[13] governments are committed to transferring as much information as possible to the private sector and to offer further support by the direct funding of private research projects.

Even as early as 2001 20,000 patents on DNA sequences had been applied for with 800 being issued by the US Patent Office – suggesting the fact that hard-nosed commercial interests have viewed the near certainty of significant fortunes to be made trading, or biochemically exploiting, the very archive of life – its store of diversity. Yet another 'commons' that is being commodified, if not plundered.

There have been a number of attempts to build genetic data-bases. Ones involving whole populations, or supposedly representative

---

[13] And some private – Rockefeller in US and Welcome Trust in UK – funding that was not commercially motivated

sections of these: including in Iceland, the Quebec state in Canada, Sweden and the UK. These have included access to publically held personal medical records. The methodology, the ethics, and not least the financial viability, of each of these attempts to build gene-based Biobanks have been widely criticized. Most of the private companies involved (generally in some form of public-private partnership) have closed, been rebranded, or absorbed into other existing or new companies. Few if any medical benefits can be directly attributed to research accessing these Bio-banks, but the drive to profit from genomics will be a dynamic hard to resist in our increasingly more neo-liberal economic environment. Where the progression from senior biochemical researcher to medical entrepreneur is becoming an assumed career development, if one still realized for only a small minority.

For Rose and Rose (2014, p170): 'In the age of intellectual property rights, genes have become big business.'

The '1000 Genomes Project' (1KGP) launched in January 2008 planned to sequence the genetic constitution of 1000 individuals (it had completed 1,092 by 2012) drawn from a range of ethnic groups including: Japanese, Chinese, Luhay and Masai from Kenya, Gujaratis from Indian, Mexican-Americans, African-Americans – the aim was to include a representative sample of ethnic variation. The data generated by this project will allow potentially useful information on the regions of the chromosomes that are thought to be associated with particular diseases. This multi-disciplinary project involves biologists based in countries including Italy, Peru, Nigeria, Japan, Kenya, China, US and the UK; again, as with the HGP, this further publically funded genome project will make its findings publically available – yet another source of free knowledge for Big-Pharma and venture capital to develop into profitable products.

During the last decade the primary hub leading advances in genomics has been shifting towards China. A change characterized by the work being produced by geneticists based at the Beijing Genomics Institute (BGI) in Shenzen. Generously funded by the China Development Bank, so able to purchase the most up-to-date sequencing technology, the BGI had by 2014 sequenced 57,000 individual genomes. If the application of bio-ethics is questionable in the West, due primarily to its being tainted by too close an association with private companies, then the ethics of genome-based research in China is just as concerning in a country where ethical standards have generally taken third place to political motives and economic outcomes.

Sequencing continues as a focus for bio-chemistry, with a number of ongoing studies based on direct sequencing projects, of both genomes and proteomes. An economic illustration of the rate of advance can be seen in the relative change in cost of sequencing - $100,000,000 for a single genome in 2001 reduced to little more than $1,000 today.

As noted above, biochemical reductionism tends to mask (by default) the body's whole material constitution being expressed within wider material and social environments. And from a more metaphysical (philosophical) perspective any gene-determined idea of human being-ness such as suggested by more radical socio-biologists, evolutionary psychologists, and epitomized in Richard Dawkins's 'Blind Watch-Maker' - even excepting Dawkins's recognition of some space for human agency - would be inadequate. It is important to accept that biochemical processes involving genetic material also includes a range of different types of 'trigger' molecules shaping the timing and direction of development. Perhaps gene expression in humans could be more adequately viewed as a patterning process involving matrices of genes operating in a wider molecular environment and this within a social context.

This tension between the value of either reductionist or more holistic explanatory frameworks would impact on the gene-based treatment of medical conditions. We might accept that some 7,000 illnesses can be linked to single or a small number of genes (estimates are that in the UK about 35% of childhood hospital admissions are due to genetic disease), but the means of 'treating' these by genetic engineering might not simply be about zapping individual genes or even cutting out or adding sections of DNA. The media presentation, to some extent fostered by sections of the pharmaceutical industry, is often of simplicity and 'miracle cures'. Whereas biochemists have to manage public expectations as well as having to deal with the challenges presented by biochemical complexity.

Sidney Brenner noted that: 'In multi-cellular organisms, increased complexity has been achieved not by the invention of new genes but simply by the regulation of gene expression. This reaches its apotheosis in the central nervous system of advanced animals in which the same repertoire of molecular entities is used to generate complex cellular networks.' (Dawkins, 2009, p43)

We need to be aware that the 'molecular paradigm', with its reductionist perspective, does not capture the 'being-ness' of human-beings; it tends to contain humanness in terms of form and function.

Whilst eschewing any sense of spirituality, or indeed of neo-vitalism, we do need to be aware that biochemical reductionism feeds into a wider scientific reductionism and that this offers but one (agreed very important) perspective on the human condition. A perspective that we might be tempted into applying because we feel that it gives both explanatory value and a sense of controllable knowledge. If this ignores the fact that it is based on an epistemologically ratiocinated understanding of the human condition. I am not decrying (reductionist) science - I am in awe of what this approach has accomplished – I am just offering a caution based on its primary flaw, one exposed when set in the context of social settings and a wider humanbeing-ness. And that too often it draws influential individuals and institutions into assuming science, and its practical arm technology, is the primary source of solutions to human problems.

Campbell suggests that 'Molecular and structural biology have been extraordinarily successful'…but he then quotes Woese (2004) on the 'molecular paradigm' and his suggestion that '…..it is no longer a reliable guide - it has run its course.' Woese seems to consider that there is some higher level perspective from which a better understanding of life can be modeled and studied.

Further implications radiate from the idea of genetic engineering being acceptable, not least those many ethical issues directly related to what we mean by the 'normal' (to be engineered) in terms of such aspects of being human as physical shape as well as physical and cognitive performance; indeed, the core issue of human individuality and the validity of difference.

Sydney Brenner noted that for biological systems: '…….in addition to flows of matter and energy, there is also the flow of information. Biological systems are information-processing machines…' Whilst I would challenge the link to machines here, my own ideas about evolution are entirely predicated on the assumption of information-processing as its biological dynamic.

Carl Worse took the information processing model a qualitative step further by rejecting the idea of any linear form of processing to introduce a more dynamic, feedback dependent, systems model – offering a more holistic conception of life.

1114

The most significant discoveries made in the 20th/21st centuries allowed notable advances to be made in the understanding of the molecular processes involved in life itself. Discoveries that clarified the evolutionary mechanisms and some of the other processes that contributes to the unfolding development of each individual animal or plant and to their reproduction 'in their own image'.

And it is to these whole organisms that I now turn.

Biology

To remind ourselves of four clear levels for the organization of life:

- Molecular – The basic chemical and energy transformations related to life, as embodied in molecules and their atomic arrangements.
- Cellular – What have been termed the building blocks of organic structures.
- Organisms – Individual single or multi-cellular forms that are able to maintain, and replicate, themselves.
- Populations – Focus on collectivities of species (groups or populations) for most non-human forms and for some human forms inhabiting a specific area or region – this level became a key aspect of biological study as the 20th century unfolded. With Francs Galton as perhaps the first person to use the concept of population to obtain a mean value of species variability.

This section focuses on the level of organisms, touching on the other three as they contribute to the biological context for this level.

Just as basic chemistry merges easily into bio-chemistry so also the step from single cell biology to the next, the multi-cellular, level, is a scientifically logical progression in the process of attempting to understand the complex, dynamic, now 'thinking', entity termed life.

As we have seen above, even some general familiarity with a single cell would surely invoke a sense of wonder at it structural integrity and functional complexity. The next step is to consider the latent potential inherent in cellular life as expressed in terms of its potential to form multi-cellular groupings which at some level of organization form interdependent co-operative arrangements to become whole organisms.

My own suggestion of the primary driver for organic evolution is the formation of organisms, as individuals and collectives, able to process evermore 'information'. Assuming this source of shaping dynamism then the progression from single cell to multi-cellularity, and so to organisms, is commensurate with an information processing model

Evolution from prokaryotic cell to eukaryotic cell, from single cells to multi-cellularity, then from simple to complex organisms, is dependent on the process of reproduction, and this on the copying of genetic information. The biological mechanism for the development of different forms of life – based on improving the interactive adaptation to environments and underlying this to new forms being shaped by enlarging the information processing capacity - is the entity termed 'genetic mutation'. Not the somatic mutations limited to most single cells that only affect their immediate descendents, but the germ-line mutations occurring in the chromosomes of sex cells - for humans and other animals the egg and sperm cells - to be inherited by future generations.

Since the very first self-replicating strings of molecular material (RNA-like) of 3-4 b.y.b.p directional[14] evolutionary development has depended on genetic mutation; with biological creativity being sourced from copying 'errors'.

Steve Jones (1994, p81) noted: 'The first genes appeared some four thousand million years ago on short strings of molecules, which could make rough copies of themselves. At a reckless guess, the original molecules in life's first course, the primeval soup, has passed through four thousands million ancestors before ending up in you or me (or a chimp or a bacterium). Every one of the untold billions of genes that have existed since then emerged through a process of mutation. A short message has grown to an instruction manual of three thousand billion letters. Everyone is a unique edition of the instruction book that differs in millions of ways from their fellows. **All this comes from the accumulation of errors in the inherited message.'** (emphasis added)

Bear in mind that the option for any organism of the range of variation available for any mutation/environmental interaction is constrained by the structural limitations of the organism involved –

---

[14] Not 'directed' – so 'directional' here is an a'posteri observation rather than some more metaphysical/teleological description.

simply put…..progressive development towards a fifth leg might not be possible for a four-legged creature but longer limbs, a tail, or upright walking, could be.

The philosophically reflective biologist Theodosius Dobzhansky ('Biology of Ultimate Concern', 1967, p41) noted the adaptive flexibility to changing environments that natural selection via genetic mutation has made possible (even if most mutations are harmful), he suggested that: 'The raw material of evolution are the genetic variants which arise by mutation. The astounding property of the mutation process is its adaptive ambiguity……mutations alone, uncontrolled by natural selection, could only result in degeneration, decay, and extinction.' For Dobzhansky a species creating gene (phenotype)-environment mutuality operates as a: '…….cybernetic device which transfers to the living species "information" about the states of its environments. This device also makes the evolutionary changes that follow dependant on those that preceded them. The genetic endowment of a living species contains, therefore, a record of its past environments, as well as the imprint of the present one.' (Dobzhansky, 1967, p42)

A simply outline would be that: at the biochemical level a mutation occurs as a chromosome produces a copy of itself and in this process a codon - a set of triple bases (in human DNA three from guanine, cytosine, adenine, thymine) that would specify an amino acid that in turn would contribute to the composition to a specific protein - copies 'incorrectly'. For example, a codon CAT miss-copies (mutates) as CCT and now specifies a different amino acid and so a different type of protein. Why we don't know, but ideas related to quantum theory have been proposed. That random processes operating at the subatomic level translate into random mutations in the process of genetic copying. In terms of affect, mutations can range in size from a single gene to encompassing a large number of genes located on a length of a chromosome.

A quantum mechanical explanation for genetic mutation is quite a controversial theoretical approach. This conventional (in physics) theory of the behaviour of states of matter at the sub-atomic level becomes ultra-reductionist when applied to higher (cellular) level of life. But given the explanatory power of quantum mechanics the extension does seem is least worth considering. Unlike most applications of reductionism, the involvement of quantum causation would presumably deny determinist interpretation of mutation (and so of evolutionary processes) as it frames mutations in terms of probabilities.

Jim Al-Khalili and Johnjoe MacFadden in their 2014 book 'Life on the Edge: The Coming of Age of Quantum Biology', set out a fairly detailed possible quantum mechanical explanation for genetic mutation. I will offer a very simplified version of this; the interested reader would benefit considerably by referring to this original and quite accessible book.

As noted above, it was in 1944 that the brilliant physicist Erwin Schrodinger published his precocious essay titled 'What is Life' in which he suggested that genetic mutations occur due to quantum 'jumps', altering the molecular form, occurring during the gene copying process. This essay seems to have set the initial challenge for finding a possible quantum mechanical mechanism for this event. The explanation offered by AL-Khahili and MacFadden suggests that: At the level of base pairs, say A-T (Adenine and Thymine), the link holding them together is the hydrogen bond, a form of molecular bonding that directly involves the single proton within each hydrogen atom. In this link one proton (say P1) can be closer to one of the base pairs (say A), and another proton (say P2) can be closer to the other base pair (say T). To note 'closer' does not mean at a fixed location; in quantum terms their actual position is probabilistic; each of the protons would be in a probabilistic quantum state.

For Al-Khalili and MacFadden these two protons, holding what are in effect genetic letters (say A –T) together, could 'jump' (tunnel) to each other's initial (probabilistic) position, with each of them being closer to their opposite base, so P1 is now closer to T and P2 is now closer to A. The outcome of this very rare event being a different form of hydrogen bond known as tautomeric. Perversely, following a second proton 'jump' the bond can revert to its original, 'normal' condition. The tautomeric, condition, with its altered form of bonding, is the basis for a base-pair copying error, a mutation. Al-Khalili and MacFadden note the paucity of evidence for this theoretical explanation but they do highlight the work of a research team based at Duke University Medical Centre (US) which they consider does at least show that tautomeric proton position is a possible source of genetic mutation.

Al-Khalili and MacFadden go on to consider the cause of the 'jump' resulting in changing proton positions. Although they do also admit that there are possible explanations for this phenomenon based on 'classical' (non-quantum) physics. I think that explanations in classical terms would determine a very slow rate of mutation, significantly slower even than one in a billion base pair copying. A quantum explanation would offer 'quantum tunneling' as a mechanism allowing protons to overcome the nuclear forces holding them in position. They note Per-Olov Löwdin's proposal '......that quantum tunneling could provide an alternative way for protons to move across hydrogen bonds to generate the tautomeric, mutagenic form of nucleoitides.' The quantum uncertainty involving protons is resolved during the copying process that, in effect, constitutes a 'quantum measurement' – similar, in terms of outcomes, to what happens when physicists attempt to measure the location of subatomic particles.

Another aspect of mutation (and so of evolutionary development), considered by Al-Khalili and MacFadden, is to what extent are they are random events. Since Lamark's eighteenth century theory of evolutionary development, based on the inheritance of characteristics acquired during a parent's lifetime (e.g. the Giraffe's neck, the blacksmith's muscles), was discredited due to a lack of evidence, along with a viable evidence-based alternative (natural selection), it has been assumed that the environment-led process of natural selection has operated on organisms altered by random mutations occurring during the copying of genes. A randomness supported by research such as that undertaken by Salvador Luria and Max Delbruck in 1943 that for Al-Khalili and MacFadden: '.....established the principle of the randomness of mutation as a cornerstone of modern evolutionary biology.' But in a 1988 paper John Cairns suggested that genetic mutations can be directly caused (invoked) by environmental influences, with the gene-copying process being affected by the feedback of environmental information. This controversial paper generated a significant amount of research into this suggestion of a form of 'adaptive' rather than 'random' mutation. Most of this research has been based on subjecting microorganisms to various forms of environmental stress – complete lack of all necessary nutrients, or lack of single but essential ones such as lactose or yeast.

Although conclusive evidence, of at least a primary role for 'adaptive mutation', is still lacking, the research does indicate some likelihood of environmental feedback affecting gene replication. On a relatively simple level, if nutrients required to progress the replication (such as some essential amino acids) were not available then presumably at least some impact (one would think fatal) would pertain.

In the absence of any molecular feedback mechanism explained in terms of classical biochemistry, then a quantum explanation involving quantum tunneling or even perhaps quantum entanglement should be considered. Perhaps some feedback mechanism coordinated by 'entangled' action-at-a-distance operating between information available in the external environment and suitable receptors within a cell. But as Al-Khalili and MacFadden admit '..... whether quantum mechanics plays an important and direct role in genetic mutations – that *infidelity* in copying of genetic information that is so vital for evolutionary development – remains to be seen.' If adaptive mutation (from whatever cause) does occur, then presumably evolutionary change would be much more efficient than random mutation alone, and could reinforce current understanding of why so much variety of life-forms developed during 'but' 3.7ish billion years.

The continuance of viable life-forms is dependent on highly accurate fidelity of genetic replication and yet responding to changing environments, and being able to exploit environmental opportunities, requires the ability for organisms to adapt. In evolutionary terms genetic mutation has provided the main means to realize this adaptive flexibility. The rate of mutation is thought to be about one for every one billion base pairs; there are 3bn base pairs in the human genome - single genes can be made up of anything between 27,000 and 2 million base pairs.

The evolutionary development of life on Earth seems to be dependent on the accumulation of patterns of adaptive 'mutations', the seemingly random and seemingly simple bio-chemical copying 'errors' occurring deep within the veritable substance of our bodies. The meaning of this mysteriously directional 'adaptive ambiguity' (Dobzhansky) eludes ontological explanation, we can but accept an epistemological explanation based on an understanding, of bio-chemistry become biology, from an a'posterior perspective.

A primary biological theme running through the twentieth century was the question of the origins of life on Earth. How could life emerge from non-living materials? In the middle of the nineteenth century Thomas Henry Huxley had suggested that earthly life could have originated from elsewhere in the Universe. And in the early twentieth century the Swiss physicist Svante Arrhenius suggested that living 'spores' could have drifted through the Universe, propelled by the light-energy generated by stars, to settle on Earth. Incidentally, Arrhenius was also the first person to calculate the impact on global temperatures of the industrial processes releasing carbon dioxide into the atmosphere; he felt that it would be a beneficial to live on a warmer planet. Arrhenius's authority as a noted scientist (he was awarded the Noble Prize for chemistry in 1903) lent credibility to his 'panspermia' theory of early life on Earth and the idea came to be supported by a number of scientists. Notable amongst these were Francis Crick and Fred Hoyle, themselves both Nobel prize-wining scientists. In his 1978 book 'Lifecloud' Hoyle noted a 'cosmic cradle' for life's origins, with living matter being bought to Earth stored within the frozen material of comets.

Although supporters of panspermia can still be found, the primary focus has been on earth-bound ideas of origins. The two scientists, Alexander Oparin and J.B.S. Haldane, working separately, produced a theory now known as the Oparin-Haldane theory of origins (abiogenisis). It was in 1924 that Oparin set out a chemical (become biochemical) explanation for the possible origins of living matter followed in 1929 by a very similar idea of Haldane's (at this time Oparin's paper 'The Origins of Life' had not yet been translated into English). The Oparin-Haldane theory assumed that early on the Earth's atmosphere was mainly composed of water vapour, methane, hydrogen sulfide, ammonia, and carbon dioxide; so a reducing atmosphere with no free oxygen. With no protective ozone layer the Sun's rays could beat directly onto the seas – with about 10% if this light being composed of high energy ultraviolet light (a form of electromagnetic radiation). Over time the chemical mix in the seas, stimulated by the Sun's radiated energy, formed into increasingly more complex chemical compounds. With these developing (probably in more than one place) into accretions of carbon rich monomers and polymers, then some of these progressively becoming enclosed within membranes. In Haldane's Sun-warmed prebiotic mix, in the shallows of primitive seas, touched by a reducing atmosphere (no free-oxygen), non-living matter became replicating molecules, proto-cellular, then cellular life-forms.

Charles Darwin himself, whilst being unaware of the detailed biochemical pathways, had over sixty years earlier shared his own, more speculative, idea of life's beginning with his friend Joseph Hooker (Feb. 1871) writing: 'If (and oh, what a big if) we could conceive in some warm little pond with all sorts of ammonia and phosphoric salts – light, heat, electricity [lightening] present, that a protein compound was chemically formed, ready to undergo still more complex changes......'

Adding, on the final page of his 'The Origin of Species', that: 'There is grandeur in this view of life, with its several powers, having been originally breathed into a few forms or into one: and that, whilst this planet has been cycling on according to the fixed law of gravity, from so a simple beginning endless forms most beautiful and most wonderful, have been, and are being, evolved.' (1859, Pelican Classic ed. 1970, p.459)

Attempts have been made to recreate the same chemical conditions within which life had been thought to form and then to observe the process of chemical reactions. Perhaps the most notable being those conducted by Stanley Miller at the University of Chicago (1953). In a series of experiments Miller mixed hydrogen, ammonia, methane, water vapour, and other chemicals thought to be present at the time of the earliest formation of life. He then passed an electric current through the mixture (stimulating the lighting that would have been common at that earlier atmospherically unsettled time) and was able to produce various types of organic material, including amino acids, the constituents of proteins. Miller's research generated keen interest from chemists and biologists. In 1986 Gunter von Kiedrowski - achieved molecular replication without an enzyme catalyst – so the first successful laboratory chemical replication but, although a significant step towards it, this was not yet 'life'. This type of work has at least demonstrated that pre-biotic self-replicating molecules could be formed in the environmental conditions thought to pertain on the Earth circa 4 b.y.b.p., lending support for the Earthly origins of today's Earth-bound life.

More recently, Andy Pross (sec. ed. 2016, pp16-19) linked basic biochemistry to a consideration of the beginnings of life on Earth and suggested that: '.....the essence of life will be found to lie in the dramatic difference between catalytic and autocatalytic reactions.' Catalytic reactions proceed 'linearly' whereas autocatalytic reactions proceed 'exponentially' – a massive difference in terms of the speed of reactions. Pross highlights the special kind of autocatalytic reaction that characterized early life – one that drives the process of metabolism that, together with replication, provided for Pross, the necessary conditions for '...life to emerge from its simple inanimate beginnings.' (Pross, 2016, p159). For him, the interlinked processes of molecular metabolism, replication, and complexification, provide a dynamic bridge between pre-life chemistry to earliest life-forms (abiogenesis) and on to the increasingly more complex chemistry of higher forms of life. The use of 'higher' here merely applies to gradation in terms of biochemical complexification – and for Pross, it is systems chemistry that '....can lead to the smooth merging of living and non-living systems, thereby offering a unifying framework for chemistry and biology.'

He offers the causal sequence for this process as being: 'replication-mutation-selection-evolution' (Pross, 2016, p128). Each of which is for Pross evident at the chemical as well as the biological level. With pre-life molecular replicators (RNA) '...mimicking biological ones...' (p130). He then adds 'complexification' as the bio-chemical bridge between (chemically) replicating pre-life and (biologically) replicating life so: 'replication-mutation-complexi-fication-selection-evolution'. On the, for me, key feature of mutation Pross has little to say, just noting (p153) that: 'The process is initiated by the emergence of some oligomeric [a relatively simple molecular complex of just a few monomers] replicating entity susceptible to imperfect reproduction.'

Pross offers a summary of his views on the appearance of life: '....life on earth emerged through the enormous kinetic power of the replication reaction acting on unidentified, but simple replicating systems, apparently composed of chain-like oligomeric substances, RNA and RNA-like, capable of mutation and complexification. That process of complexification took place because it resulted in the enhancement of their stability - not their thermodynamic stability, but rather the relevant stability in the world of self-replicating systems.....' which is for Pross their *dynamic kinetic stability* (Pross, 2014, p183).[15]

We can look back over perhaps as much as 4 billion years to a time when it was possible that the most primitive forms of life emerged from inanimate substances, and about 3.4 billion years to a period when the first single-celled organisms evolved from increasingly more complex, self-replicating, self-maintaining, molecular formations ('micro-organisms').

---

[15] In Chapter 1 I set out a theory on the origins of life involving deep oceans vents ('black smokers') and the conditions that pertain there – I won't repeat this here where the focus has been more on the biochemistry.

There is some fossil evidence suggesting early life-forms present in precipitates laid down as early as about 4.29 b.y.b.p., so relatively soon after the formation of the Earth itself. These oldest known organic materials would have been micro-organisms originally living in hydrothermal vents (Nuvvugittug, Canada). More convincing evidence was found in material laid down as biogenic graphite 3.7 b.y.b.p. (South West Greenland). These discoveries set the age of life on Earth further back than had been assumed for some time.

At some point a threshold in the complexification of the constitution of molecules present in the primal environment had been passed when some types of prokaryotic organisms were able to deploy a 'genetic code' able to communicate information that would determine the form of their descendents. This early period, down to about 2.5 b.y.b.p. (the Archaean), has been termed the 'Age of the Prokaryotes'. These are single-cellular life-forms (including certain types of bacteria and cyanobacteria) whose genetic material (probably RNA rather than DNA) did not take the form of discrete chromosomes and was not contained with a membrane-bound nucleus. Similar organisms can today be found in extreme environments such as hot sulfur springs.

A generally accepted line of organic development involves relationships between different types of prokaryotes. It seems that some larger organisms, came to form mutually beneficial relationships with smaller free-living prokaryotes, including the 'mitochondria' and the 'chloroplasts'. These smaller prokaryotes were contained within only thin membranes lacking a more substantial cell wall that would have inhibited exchange of information with the larger host prokaryote. Over eons of time it seems that up to about twenty different types of small prokaryote settled into the larger cell's cytoplasm, establishing a mutually beneficial 'endosymbiotic' relationship. A form of symbiotic relationship that can be seen in some organisms existing today e.g., the giant amoeba Pelomyxa palustris, lacking mitochondria, is able to obtain energy owing to the endosymbiotic relationship it has formed with types of aerobic bacteria which supplies the energy needed by the host cell.

The impact of environmental conditions operating on some of these prokaryote relationships seems to have favoured this type of arrangement, to the extent that the organelles gradually became incorporated into the host cell. It was out of the increasing prokaryote complexity that eukaryotic cells arose perhaps as early as 2.2 b.y.b.p. The earliest evidence interpreted as the first fossil record of eukaryotes appeared in rocks laid down about 2.1 b.y.b.p, in what is now Michigan USA, possibly a species of Grypania; thought to be a type of algae. More definite evidence is of traces of microfossil remains from rocks dated as being formed 1.7 b.y.b.p. (Australia).

The 'eukaryotic' cells, with functioning hereditary material now encoded in the chemically more stable DNA set within a membrane-bound nucleus, evolved within an atmosphere becoming increasingly rich in oxygen, so facilitating the formation of multi-cellular organisms. By size the average eukaryotic cell was up to ten times larger than the average prokaryote.

For the biologist A.Pross, and the paleontologist (and Jesuit priest) P.Teilhard de Chardin, the process of prokaryotic to eukaryotic cells, was increasing the purposeful complexification of life-forms, for myself it was an organic 'means' (entity) of increasing organic information processing capacity. Two closely related concepts with different emphasis, complexification being more of a static observation, information processing expressing more of a dynamic potential.

As cellular life increased, proximity and possible adaptive benefit of collectives led to groups of cells forming layers (nets) and this, about 1.5 b.y.b.p., to forming multi-cellular life-forms. Possibly one of the earliest of these metazoan organisms being *Gryparia spiralis:* taking the form of a flat disc about 5" across, so exhibiting radial symmetry. It has been estimated that about 47 different types of early multi-cellular life-forms evolved out of eukaryotic ancestors, with just six of these serving as the ancestors of the more complex forms of life to come; as in animals, plants, fungi and three types of algae.

Plant-life preceded animal life by some considerable time, making a significant contribution to the formation of a more oxygen rich atmospheric, conditions suitable for animal life. It would be at the Pre-Cambrian/Cambrian boundary (approx 600-580 m.y.b.p) that the many phyla of multi-cellular animal life first appeared.

I have noted in the biochemistry section (above) that reproduction of more complex organisms is dependent on DNA replication based on biologically specialized 'germ cells'. The emergence of DNA replication by meiosis as an alternative to mitosis dramatically opened up the scope for genetic variation (via sexual reproduction), as genetic material is then contributed 50/50 from parents rather than

100% from a single parent.

In mammalian sexual forms of reproduction two germ-cells – 'sperm and egg' - come together to initiate a process of fertilization. The early form of the embryonic life of mammals shows them as morphologically very similar – reflecting their more or less shared ancestry. I will track the more obvious stages of human pre-birth development in order to illustrate this truly wonderful phenomenon. An improved understanding of which twentieth century advances in biology have made possible.

The fertilized egg-cell (zygote) is a relatively large cell containing sufficient nutrients to sustain a number of rounds of division (of 'cleavage') to get to a stage of multi-cellularity when specific bundles of cells can then operate to secure nutrients from the mother's body. The initial single cell divides within 24 hrs and these then divide within 45 hrs, with an 8 cell stage, and then a 16 cell stage being reached by 3-4 days. At this, the morula stage, there is an undifferentiated 16 cell 'mass'. Now the morula opens slightly into a hollow ball of cells, the blastocyst, which soon begins to break down as it implants in the wall of the uterus. At this stage cells in the blastula migrate to locations in its cell-mass where the process involved in cell differentiation will begin. This, the process of gastrulation, sees the cells separate into three main types. The endoderm that will form the gut – the mesoderm that will form the skeletal system, musculature, connective tissue, and some of a body's organs - the ectoderm that will the form the skin and the nervous system. The whole process is 'organized' (orchestrated) by a superbly timed, ultra complex, on\off patterning of the expression of genetic constitution in bio-interaction with the environment (more immediately the mother's body) within which it develops. Up to about the end of the epiblast stage - the stage of the embryo having grown to become a small disc constituted of the cells from which all of a baby will develop - radial symmetry is maintained. Now the epiblast cells begin to produce a 'signaling protein' that attracts surrounding cells towards them, initiating the formation of a 'primitive streak'. It is upon this new structure that radial symmetry begins to be transformed into a bilateral symmetry, with the growing cell-mass elongating as the primitive streak grows from a posterior out to form an anterior end. Processes based on inter-cellular signaling, attraction, adhesion, and ever-continuing multiplication, see the marked progression of cell specialization continuing to be based on the primary separation of endoderm, mesoderm, and ectoderm, noted above.

It is from the ectoderm that the next key stage (for vertebrates) develops as a band of cells along its central line (adjacent to the primitive streak) detach themselves to form a rod of cells known as the 'notocord'. Although there could be a variety of embryonic cell signaling systems involved in coordinating the stages of development, the specialist cells of the notochord will play an important role from this point on – its central position along almost the whole length of the embryo facilitates a communicating and coordinating function.

The possession of an embryonic notochord is a defining characteristic of the classificatory Phylum, Chordata; with most species being in the sub-Phylum, Vertebrata. The notochord will develop into the backbone (vertebra) along which will run the body's primary sensory and signaling highways.

The internal bilateral symmetry has now to change if the location of internal organs are to be arranged efficiently in relation to available space and each of their bodily functions. The positioning of bundles of cells that will form each of the internal organs is achieved by the movement of cells equipped with beating 'cilia' moving within the liquid medium of the growing embryo.

For Jamie A. Davies at this point (15-17 days on from fertilization): '…..there is an elongated body, with clear head-tail, back-belly, and left-right directions, with three distinct tissue types arranged in a definite order, and with a central notochord running along the body. The basic form of an animal is there, and elaboration of internal structure can begin.' (Davis, 2014, p52). As can the continuing differentiation into the 210-odd types of cell constituting the human body.

Davies (2014) posits the concept of 'adaptive self-organization' to express the internal control mechanisms (diffused throughout all cells of a body) that guide the development of a life-form from conception to adulthood. A conceptual mixture encompassing an organism's basic structure, its metabolic processes, along with its ability to determine cellular replication in forms designed to sustain its development, and also the feedback mechanisms involved in all of these. Davis (2014, p13) suggests that: '…..adaptive self-organization is critical to human development, at levels ranging from self-organization of molecules within a single sell to the large-scale construction of complex tissues.'

I will return to the developing embryo a couple of pages on following a short digression into some aspects of the biology of information processing, so involving a primary focus on the evolution of the nervous system. The eminent zoologist Ralph Buchsbaum noted that: 'All but nerve cells were present in the most primitive multi-celled organisms, the sponges. Nerve cells are added by the coelenterates.' (Buchsbaum, Vol.1 p.84 - 1973 reprint). These coelenterates would include organisms such as jelly-fish and sea-anemones, and here we see radial symmetry as the common bodily form. With primitive nervous systems being defined by nets of nerve cells; the evolutionary precursor to the considerably more complex mammalian nervous system within bodies based on bilateral, rather than radial symmetry, and so head and tail 'ends'.

Multi-cellularity, cell differentiation, the presence of nervous systems, along with morphological bi-lateral symmetry, and to some extent physical size, set in the context of 100s of millions of years of evolutionary development enabled the biological pre-conditions for the emergence of nervous systems able to process evermore, and evermore complex, information. With landmark higher (in information-processing terms) animal life-forms being the bony fish, amphibians, reptiles, mammals, primates, and hominids.

A key characteristic of a nervous system is its involvement in 'learning' and the identification of this behaviour has been useful for tracking the system's evolutionary development. The form of cell specialization necessary for learning can be seen in the primitive arthropods which can display learning, by changing their behaviour in response to their own individual experience, as can sea-anemones. Insects and mollusks can also learn, as shown by the ability to return to a home location; suggesting a net composed of nervous tissue within which some 'topographical map' being involved as an internal representation. A representation formed by some subtle but effective combination of learning (processing sensory information and reinforcement) on some genetically based receptivity to form both 'latent' and 'active' memory nets within the nervous system, with latent switching to active or non-active as required.

The biologist Richard Dawkins noted that: 'I believe that every species that has a nervous system uses it to construct a model of its own particular world, constrained by continuous updating through the sense organs' (Dawkins, 1998, p274)

Information processing more generally can be seen in the relatively simple organism, the hydra, in which a nerve net (synaptically connected) can be identified running throughout the body, with a slightly greater concentration of sensory cells around the mouth area. A nerve-net that co-ordinates a range of fairly simple behaviours. At this stage there is no evidence of a central coordinating area (a 'brain') but according to Buchsbaum (Vol. 1, 1973 reprint, op. cit., p94): 'All the essentials of a simple nervous mechanism in a many-celled animal are present in the hydra'.

With an organism such as the hydra (as well as amoebas, sponges, and sea-anemones) we have animals processing a range of sensory information (reacting to: heat, salinity, light, identification and locality of food sources, etc.) and coordinating a range of possible behaviors in response to this information – moving towards a more conducive temperature, salinity, or in seeking to engulf food particles, and exhibiting avoidance behaviour by moving away from adverse environmental conditions.

The 'Cambrian (species) explosion' of about 570 m.y.b.p. saw a marked step in the radiation and complexification in the development of organisms with evermore complex nervous systems emerging, and so progressively increasing information processing capacity. I have covered this development elsewhere (Chapt. 1) so I will just 'jump' straight to humans, the most capable organic processing system so far evolved.

There are about 210 different types of cell in a human body including, red and white blood cells, liver cells, and the different cells involved in the brain and the rest of the nervous system. There are also those of the multitude of types of bacteria which live parasitically or symbiotically upon the human body.

The human body contains about 30 trillion human cells, and with about 39 trillion bacteria (both figures calculated by biologists working at the Weismann Institute 2012), but each of these amounts can vary quite considerably between individuals. Roughly 90 billion of these cells are the neuronal cells of the brain with about another 1 billion operating throughout the full nervous system (including 500m in the enteric nervous system, the gut - and 100m in the spinal cord). A number of different types of cell comprising the central nervous system (CNS) and the peripheral nervous system (PNS) undertake a range of specific and general functions. The highly specialist cells are unusual in the extent to which they connect to each other – each single neuron in the brain can have between 1,000 – 10,000 (dendritic) connections to other neurons. Just reflect on the complexity of a system with a cellular architecture of 90 billion brain-based processing units each connected to thousands of others – trillions and trillions of possible conformation patternings within a dynamic processing environment.

The most common connection made between neurons is via chemical neurotransmitters moving across a narrow channel separating two neurons. It was in 1954 that Ulf von Euler demonstrated that neurotransmitters are stored as 'packages' sited adjacent to a cell's extended axon end, from where they can be mobilized to engage in a communicative link between neurons. Connections which can be excitatory or inhibitory, both modes together generating the informational flows that are characteristic of complex sets of intercommunicating sub-processes.

I would want to suggest, the primary driver of the evolution of life on Earth (perhaps of the Universe itself) has been based on organic information processing (and 'creation') capacity. As a generality, I just want to remind the reader that information is 'difference' – metaphysically put, these are perturbations in the fabric of awareness and that 'awareness' is a common characteristic of organic life – not awareness in the conscious and self-conscious sense which is the preserve of the more recently evolved animals (self awareness) but awareness in the sense of a receptivity to information that informs behaviours. This awareness is the key essential characteristic allowing the flows of information to be assessed (processed) by an organism. It is not the place here to consider any further what I mean by 'awareness' as it refers to both human and non-human animals, for this we move more into deeper philosophical speculation that are as yet unable to meet some more rigorous expectations of science. But I would just caution any assumption of awareness as being some characteristic of evolved nervous systems simply acting to exercise co-ordination and control. Suffice to note that awareness is an integral aspect of any organism's information processing capacity, not some operation apart from it.

Each organism has its own information-rich environment (its 'reality'), and species have similar circumscribed, bounded, range of information that they can process (electro-chemical 'band-widths'). For humans, such is their form of self-conscious awareness that they, as a species, have been able to break through their pre-human species limitations and have developed in ways (initially biologically then culturally) that have markedly expanded the information content of their species 'Reality'.

The human brain is often considered to be an integrated system (Olaf Sporns, 2011),[16] and this can serve as a valid descriptor for the day-to-day functioning of the brain as a discrete organ. Expressing its role in maintaining homeostasis and a range of regular rather than spontaneous behaviours, but for a descriptor of the role of the brain in human evolutionary terms then its underlying 'instability' might (shown by its proneness to psychological instability as well as inventiveness and creativity) provide the ground conditions for further evolution. And indeed, its role in allowing humankind to adapt – as a species - to a wide range of environmental conditions and progressively, in the last 20,000 - 10,000 years, to adapt the environment to suit their own needs.

In describing the development of the human-being, I earlier left the developing embryo at the point of forming its internal organs at 15-17 days post fertilization. It is also about this time that the first physical sign is a slight 'dimple' on outer cell layer of the embryo (ectodermal) appears. Chemical communication passes between cells of the mesodermal to the cells of the ectodermal layer which appears to be the trigger for the ectodermal cells to begin to form the central nervous system (CNS), including the brain. Initially this is based on a neural plate (of about 130,000 cells) – at this point the embryo has an identifiable gut around which are layers of mesodermal cells topped by a neural plate formed from ectodermal cells, all contained within the ectoderm. As the neural plate grows it turns in upon itself, forming a central 'neural' tube which then becomes more detached from the ectoderm (which then forms the skin of the back). From about four-six weeks post-conception, when the embryo has grown from but a single cell into a body composed of thousands, the three areas that will develop into three main brain sub-divisions can begin to be identified. Nerves and neural connections will now accrue within the growing brain and neural tube, along with nerves and muscles in the rest of the embryo. The processes of cell differentiation and functional complexification continues until at birth the brain is

---

[16] Although this has been contested by various types of 'modular' and otherwise 'divided' brain theories.

pretty much formed in terms of specialist areas and the main connections between these. But by no means have all of the intricate neural networks characteristic of the early juvenile to about mid 20s been formed.

When considering the operation of the brain as a functional entity, the phrase 'neural networks' has been used to describe the interconnectedness of neural systems but perhaps the image of a complex weave of enmeshed matrices, better captures the complex processing flexibility of the neural anatomy (its bio-architectural superstructure). Superficially described as a binary coding system - the single on/off 'action potential'. But if extended to a description of the brain's communication this descriptive process miss-interprets what happens within discontinuous waves of reentrant neural communication. No single neuron communicates – dynamic, intricate 'patterns' do.

Complex particulate waves of information flow throughout 'systems-like' neural networks, always novel; in the sense that each wave is in some form original. If at times passing through these system networks along often well rehearsed (reinforced) routes, at times tracing new patterns, mostly both types overlapping and infusing each other. Each with a range of signal strengths, each pattern behaviourally manifested in different levels of consciousness, from unconscious to fully aware.

Another descriptive challenge is how we can describe the brain's processes in a way that will enable us to understand how these can give rise to (underlie) consciousness rather than only identify and describe correlations between the brain's biological processes and consciousness (behaviours) – even accepting that significant correlations can be powerful links between two phenomena.

If we visualize the overall relatively 'fixed' patterning of neural connections in the brain then it is significant that no two individuals have the same patterning (even identical twins) – each person has their own unique neural-system (if the basic functioning brain areas are common). The cellular architecture of the brain is one level of visualizing function, but a fuller understanding can only come from including the continuous interchange of electro-chemical transmission systems, along with neural-transmitter and hormonal influences, within wider bodily conditions.

For Sporns (ibid, p72) 'The key question.....is how cognitive function *emerges* from the specific anatomical and physiological subunits of the brain', and he note (ibid. p206) 'Viewed form a network perspective, cognition is nothing more (and nothing less) than a special kind of pattern formation, the interplay of functional segregation and integration and the continual emergence of dynamic structures that are molded by connectivity and subtly modified by external input and internal state. The shape of cognition, the nature of the information that can be brought together and transformed, is determined by the architecture of brain networks.'

Bear in mind this architecture is, for Sporns, formed by the intricate patterning of neural nets, overlapping net edges and with principle nodes taking on particular coordinating roles, he notes: 'The network perspective differs radically from serial, representational, and symbolic accounts of cognition. Perhaps network thinking will eventually allow us to move beyond neural reductionism and cognitive functionalism and formulate a theoretical framework for cognition that is firmly grounded in the biology of the brain.'[17]

The early twentieth century also saw significant advances in biochemistry informing the wider science of biology, especially in relation to the metabolic and reproductive functions of organisms. Fredrik Hopkins and his colleagues led the way in progressing our understanding of the body's biochemical needs, especially in relation to essential vitamins and amino acids. In 1927 Ernest Munch offered an explanation for the transport of nutritious materials within plants (the 'mass flow' hypothesis), with the process of 'osmosis' playing an essential part.

Further key advances were made in 1932 and 1937 by Hans Kreb, who was the first to explain how bodies excrete urea in order to rid a body of the excess nitrogen that results from the consumption of proteins, so identifying an important metabolic pathway 'the urea cycle'. Then, later in the decade, he identified the metabolic processes involving the body's means of extracting energy from carbohydrates via the 'citric acid', or 'Krebs', cycle. These advances, relating to the basic metabolic pathways of plants and animals, represent but a few of the headline discoveries laying the foundations for hundreds of notable, if incremental, advances that continued. Just a few examples of how productive a reductionist approach to biological research can

---

[17] For a broader consideration of bodily-based consciousness see the psychology section below.

be.

This laboratory-based study of the biochemical processes operating within cells and organisms was a major research area for twentieth century biology – one working at the interface of industrial, medical, and agricultural operations. By the end of the century the understanding of primary bio-chemical mechanisms within cells, internal organs and whole organisms had been significantly advanced including areas such as – respiration, circulation of fluids, thermoregulation, digestion, reproduction, immunity, indeed all of the multi-factoral interrelated aspects of metabolism. In addition, the most obvious communication systems – the hormonal and the peripheral and central nervous systems - had been tracked, and their basic operation and function identified, at least to a considerable extent.

Along with the reductionist approach to laying the foundations for revealing the basic biochemical constitution involved in living processes, the biology of the first half of the twentieth century was also characterized by revealing, recording, and systematizing the diversity of life-forms – extending our factual, classificatory, knowledge of the biosphere.

As the century began optical microscopy had revealed the unitary features of cells and their universal presence as the basic constitution of both animal and plant materials. Accepting that a universalism pertains at the fundamental levels of life-forms, the classification of organisms, according to morphological and/or molecular similarities and differences, has enabled biologists to manage the complex variety and interconnectedness that life on Earth confronts them with.

In terms of the interconnectedness of life-forms, Woese (2004) suggested that the traditional idea of an evolutionary 'tree' is misleading and only of any real relevance once the 'Darwinian threshold' has been reached and the initial phase characterized by 'Horizontal Gene Transfer' (HGT) has been past - HGT is the exchange of genetic material that can occur between species, or early on between self-replicating entities. This highlights weaknesses in the evolutional tree model and complicates the biochemical interrelationships of life-forms, especially when considering early life on Earth. Post the Darwinian Threshold the cells become more organized and 'Vertical Gene Transfer' can take place.

In 1977 Woese and his colleagues had identified a whole new biological Domain, one composed of prokaryotic-celled (unicellular

- no nucleus) micro-organisms living in inhospitable environments (salt lakes, thermal vents, – these extremophile organisms - heat-loving, sulfur-eating, methane-breathing, bacteria) were classified in the new Domain of Archaea. Considered to be a separate group to the true bacteria (Eubacteria) and now assumed to be the earliest forms of life on Earth. Woese also offered a system that arranges all organisms (life-forms) within three Domains and six Kingdoms. The Domains being: Bacteria, Archaea, Eukaryota. The six Kingdoms being: Archaebacteria, Eubacteria. Protista, Fungi, Plantae, Animalia.

The Domain Eukaryota and the Kingdoms Plantae and Animalia encompassing the 'higher' (in crude evolutionary terms) life-forms, including animals and plants. With these macro-divisions being made primarily on the basis of differences in ribosome RNA (specifically 16s rRNA). The task of clarification and of the assignment of organisms to suitable biological classes has also underlined the presence of 'fuzzy edges' at classificatory boundaries.

The basic circumscription of a life-form is the concept of the species – Every single type of eukaryotic-celled organism that has ever lived is unique in terms of the detailed genetic constitution. For multi-cellular creatures this difference has historically focused on morphology (famously illustrated when Darwin observed this during his study of barnacles) and in the twentieth century to include molecular characteristics. A species is generally characterized as a group of organisms (single- or multi- cellular) that share a range of morphological, biochemical, and behavioural characteristics; nowadays extending to the genetic constitution on which these characteristics are based.

In the last quarter of the century protein sequencing was transforming the classification of organisms, a molecular approach to classification refined further with the sequencing of RNA and DNA. Even accepting that the application of these new methods confirmed much of the species evolutionary relationships that had already been suggested. There is now a generally agreed system for arranging relationships between life forms, the hierarchical phylogenetic 'tree' based on inferred (informed) evolutionary relationships.

Life itself: Being all entities (organisms) that can potentially reproduce themselves, can grow, and can maintain bodily metabolism, and can react to stimuli. I accept that high functioning AI systems might achieve these (even including a mechanical form of reproduction) in the future but, if so, then either life can be redefined in a way that excludes these innovations or such systems can perhaps be included within a new Domain.

The current biological classificatory hierarchy runs:

Domain
Kingdom
Phylum
Class
Order
Family
Genus
Species – uses a two-part name. The first for the genus e.g. Homo, the second for the species e.g. sapien. So Homo sapiens for the species category for humans.
Sub-species

No single biological classification system seems to enjoy universal agreement, but I think that Woses's Domain and Kingdom system (of three and six) is the one now generally accepted. In reality, I doubt that many working biologists get hung-up on the precise classification of organisms and are more focused on differences and similarities of molecular, morphological, and behavioural, characteristics of organisms within the specific groups they are working on.

Although we can generally accept the concept of species as a way of discriminating between different types of organisms, facilitating systemization and an understanding of relationships between organisms, including some understanding of their evolutionary relationships, I don't think the concept of species should be considered to be some profound differentiating marker for life-forms. Its use as a systematizing marker has been found to be useful, and to a certain extent theoretically robust, but its use should not mislead us into ignoring the possibility of more 'holistic', 'transcendent', ways of circumscribing living processes. Species is but one, albeit informative and useful, way of viewing the different forms that self-sustaining, self-reproducing, living processes have taken.

There are two primary objections to considering the 'species' concept as a clear-cut marker of similarity and difference. The first is that not all organic life forms can be easily classified by either the ability to successfully breed fertile offspring or by chromosome and nucleotide numbers. There can be quite 'fuzzy' boundaries between very similar organisms, making classification sometimes a matter of reasoned judgment rather than clear-cut fact. Secondly, there is the more profound philosophical objection based upon the idea that viewing life as separated into various 'species', using traditional markers of similarity and difference, could entail obscuring other possible relationships (of alternative forms of similarity, difference or interdependence) that might allow a more profound understanding of life itself.

Edward.O.Wilson notes that: 'The real world, then, consist of species that differ from one another in infinitely varying directions and distances. So far as we know, no way exists to lump or split them into groups except by what the human mind finds practical and aesthetically pleasing' (Wilson, 1992, p.146). Species are part of an evolutionary process of change that is characterized by the fact that one species can evolve into a new species – so at any point in time the fuzziness causing classificatory problems in fact offers some proof of the ineluctable operation of natural selection.

The determined task of classification has been paralleled by the seeking out and identification of new species. Biologists working in the 20th and 21st centuries have built on 19th century foundations, as they continued to collate the diversity of plant and animal life on the world's landmasses and throughout it rivers and oceans. What has become clear is how much, in species terms, we have still to discover. A fairly recent estimate is of possibly as many as 8.7m species of organisms on Earth - 6.5m on land and 2.2m living in marine environments (pub. PLoS Biology - 2011). With the same study estimating that 86% of land-species and 91% of marine species as yet undiscovered and so unrecorded; so a potential treasure-trove of genetic information. Pick up just a gram of soil from the forest floor and you could have about 10 billion individual organisms between your fingers.

Of bird species there are 9,040 surviving (of about 12,000 species circa 10,000 y.b.p.). Of ants there are 9,500 known species, with estimates of up to 20,000 more. Of reptiles 8,240, of amphibians 6,199, of mammals 5,416. Only 1.2m species of invertebrates have been identified (of which 290,000 are species of beetle) out of possibly over twice this number. There are possibly as many as 250,000 species of angiosperm (flowering) plants - 50,000 tropical tree species – 15,000 mosses – 10,000 ferns – and 26,900 species of algae, with most of these living in the seas. Also populating the rivers and seas are 30,000 known species of fish; of sharks alone there are 350 species and sharing some of these watery ecosystems are species of 81,000 mollusks, 40,000 crustaceans, and 2,172 corals. Of the lowly fungi, estimates are of over 3 million species with only about 150,000 of these identified so far. Even of the pervasive bacteria, at least 5,000 species are land-based and another 5,000 inhabit marine environments.

Species-identification is a veritable bio-industry of meticulous collection and classification, with about 10,000 new species being discovered each year – a rate that reflects both the abundance of life-forms and clearly suggests the sheer number of still unknown organisms out there.

A list of statistics, whilst useful, can but offer a partial perspective on variety, perhaps a more prose-like 'glimpse' into nature's finery can at least hint at the rich organic tapestry through which life is woven – let's just pause to consider its wonderful diversity, vibrant colour, and intriguing complexity.

In our own gardens, local parks, and other open spaces we can observe the lowly earth-worms and by using a magnifying lens the numerous types of microbes that prodigiously burrow throughout damp layers of leaf-mould, easing nutrients into the dark-soil, maintaining the rich loess created by the work of generations upon generations of their ancestors. Beyond the local, the numerous species of insects (beetles, ants, wasps, flies), that pick or fly their way across dusty desert, flowing grasslands, and bare tundra; in fact almost any habitat where the simplest of multi-cellular organisms can garner sufficient nutrient to sustain themselves. Everywhere on Earth there are organisms inhabiting their species-suitable ecosystems. The inky-black, shiny-carapaced, scarab beetles tunnel their way through mounds of dung deposited on the arid desert terrain – or the tiny bark beetle tucked comfortably into a cleft in the coarse bark of a conifer tree.

In the darkly blue/green oceans the languid solidity of the sperm whale drifting through the marine depths as it hovers up nutrient-rich waves of plankton. The death for-shadowing outline of the Great White Shark, tiny eyes and tiny brain, fixed on the instinctively magnetic outline of its seal and penguin prey that in turn would have thrived on the clouds of shrimp-like krill swarming as vibrating canopies of marine life in the southern oceans, these in turn grown plump by harvesting the oceanic fields of single-celled phytoplankton.

The slow, regular, flap of the manta-ray's wings as it cruises the sandy ocean floor, high above which dolphins plough through the surface foam from which they leap in seemingly joyous enthusiasm.

An oceanic life-world whose essential fertility was captured by Rachel Carson ('The Sea Around Us' – from Dawkins ed. 'Modern Science Writing' 2008, p137) observing that '……from the grey shapes of cod that have moved, unseen by man, through the cold sea to their spawning places, the glassy globules of eggs are rising into the surface waters. Even in the harsh world of a winter sea, these eggs will begin the swift division by which a granule of protoplasm becomes a living fishlet.'

All along the wave-necklaced strands serving as the abode of shore crabs, mutely blooming anenomies and flashing coloured slivers of tiny fishes seen darting hesitantly within the broad waving fronds of gelatinous browns and greens of the sea-plants. And with the very occasionally seen, exquisite, almost fairy-tale sea-horses moving with the tide's flow and its own gentle tail movements taking it gracefully between the swaying stems of light-green sea-grasses.

At the margins of oceans, whilst shyly seeking the secure comfort of coral crevasses the octopus waits patiently for any passing prey, its skin camouflaged into the background having, as expressed by Richard Dawkins, 'Waves of colour [that] chase across the surface like clouds in a speeded up film; ripples and eddies race over the living screen. The animal signals its changing emotions in quick time: dark brown one second, blanching ghostly white the next, rapidly modulating interwoven patterns of stipples and stripes'

Across steaming salt-pans an array of extremophile bacteria survive, indeed thrive, with many others also adapted to the -20 degree C. temperature of the tiny grooves channeled in the Arctic's frozen ice. An abundance of new species have been discovered in these and other extreme environments including those to be found in the oceans at depths beyond 2,500 meters clustered around the thousands of hydrothermal vents. The still mysterious' black smokers', whose volcanic-like activities steadily expel a stream of warm, gaseous, water into the oceans. Here a range of niche-living species have been found including an array of strange crustations, most bleached white, living at depths where pigment of skin or shell is irrelevant.

On Antarctic ice flows, flatworms and small crustations are sustained by the algae growing there. Even in the relatively hostile *environment of the human gut Escherichia coli survive, whilst further along the digestive system Helicobacter pylori can populate the acidic conditions of the stomach. With a multitude of other types of microbial bacteria found within the digestive system and on the skin surface of almost all living organisms. The rapidly evolving bacteria constitute 50% of the world's total biomass. Their study can inform our knowledge of the early formation of eukaryotic cells with their incredible examples of bio-symbiosis. A bio-relationship seen with a boat-shaped microbe living in the gut of an Australian termite that is able to harnesses the combined power of about 300,000 bacteria attached to its membrane, these (fellow travelers) all 'wiggle' in unison and their doing so provides the otherwise static microbe with the ability of movement and so more effectively searching for its food. With its busy termite host being unaffected by the frenzy of microbial activity being played out within its gut.*

The steaming, buzzing, depths of the tropical forest with streamers of the more ephemeral lianas gracing the gnarled limbs of long-lived hardwoods that arch cathedral-like to frame the activities of the myriads of known and unknown species tumbling over themselves to fulfill their action-packed lives below. A complex range of dense vegetative ecosystems ringing with the eerie echoes of new-world monkeys, parakeets, and as night falls the glowing point-bright signals of fireflies add a sense of magic.

In Indian forests increasingly rare big cats prowl silently along paths crisscrossed by the many small mammals that populate the dense undergrowth. The cats pad uneasily past the powerful Elephant whose bulky shadow also falls on the many species of insect, spiders, lizards, and snakes that live within their tree shadowed habitat. The expansive super-organism that is the Amazon Rain Forest, with its 400 billion trees of 16,000 known species – breathing for humanity - amongst which lives the greatest variety of life on Earth, now threatened by human greed and disinterested ignorance. A greed also impacting on the life-sustaining, water purifying, mangroves fringing delicate swamp-type ecosystems under the threat of erosion by industrial shrimp-farming and ocean pollution.

In semi-protected pockets of African bush the spiky acacia tree offers afternoon shade for the lazily disdainful pride of lions languidly digesting the previous night's kill. Whilst the leftovers still on the skeleton of that same meal continues to be assiduously picked over by a pack of snapping hyenas, a scene being impatiently observed by a group of scrawny–necked vultures hopping awkwardly too and fro between dusty ground and low perch, whilst keeping a safe distance from the hyenas determined to protect their scavenged prize. In the distance, a flight of vast flocks of spindly legged flamingos take to the air from the life-buzzing margins of an east-African lake; a silky pink-feathered cushion of avian life wafting high into the blue sky as it circles over the lake-side nesting sites dotted with their impressive hollow mud-molded nests.

The uniformly proud stands of evergreens line the hills and valleys in the temperate zones of the northern hemisphere. The trees themselves, leaf-shingled, truncated and branched, as they sprawl across familiar landscapes, retaining precious soil and absorbing the Sun's energy, along with the air-bound carbon dioxide choking our world. From the towering Giant Redwoods of California, the majestic oaks and teaks, the rustling beauty of limes, birch, and maples; and the enduring Baobab tree long revered by Buddhists. Spanning North-West America swaths of native conifers in disordered clusters grow along valleys and across hillsides trodden by bears, wolves and the magisterial elk. Whilst in the southern hemisphere grow the cypress, olive, mahogany, palms, eucalyptus, acacias, ginkos, and many, many, other solid-pillared life givers initially seeded long before the dawn of civilization. Immeasurable quantities of densely woody material that has built boats, shelters, bridges, coffins, warmed humanity's hearths and cooked its food; all since time immemorial.

The clustered battalions of 'mundane' - plants grasses, fungi, and bushes, - coating the worlds' landmasses as they directly and indirectly harvest the energy from the Sun's rays. With many species being in turn (due season) harvested by machine or grazed by domesticated animal, to offer essential support for human life. The conversion of solar energy into the means to sustain organic life on Earth. The more aesthetically pleasing flowering plants, ranging from the gorgeously extravagant water lilies to the walls of vegetation intensely punctuated by colourful 'globules' of sweetly scented petals characteristic of the climbing pastel-colored roses and honeysuckle sharing our suburban gardens and the undulating countryside graced with the warm-hued pastel colours of trailing montana's, rambling roses, hibiscus, and rhododendrons. And this but a wafting scent of plant life on Earth, and of its variegated suggestiveness; its mesmeric palette of colour.

The winds that swirl and blow around the world, spreading pollen, seed, and scents, sharing energy with the lands they stir in passing. The wind-blown, heather-spread moorland, the wind-brushed savannahs and pampas grasslands – the same winds blowing though the low-land forests and along the mountain valleys. The warm breezes nudging the fluted stalks of reeds and rushes, generating widening waves of fluffy seed-heads, animating the lonely marshlands with their rustling flows. Wind, with Rain, Sun, Soil – as a generous quartet of energies that nourishes and sustains life on earth.

Darwin's '....entangled bank, clothed with plants of many kinds, with birds singing on the bushes, with various insects flitting about, and with worms crawling through the damp earth.....' caught a sense of life as does the prospect of buzzing, rising fish-plopping, humming miasma, of the Sun-warmed peat-bog, fringing a European lake, on a mid summers day – the brief one-day life of the delicate damselfly born but to breed; a diurnal 'blip' tracing the lightest of existences.

The small clouds of midges drifting across the rippled reed-fringed surface of a lake, the net-winged dragonfly flitting amongst breeze-bent reeds above the tenuous surface on which pond-skaters and water boatman skit over scenes of dramatic encounters below where long-shanked pike cruise and spike-dorsalled perch flash through the murky waters in pursuit of their prey. The green-latticed lacewing settled lightly on an island of floating pink-tinged white-flowered water-lilies, gazed upon by the patient leathery skinned toads and smoother skinned frogs all under the gimlet-eye of the oh so still Heron. A seeming world of mostly gentle nature but as dusk turns into night the hunting creatures emerge, sniffing the dew-moist night air as they scent out their prey; across most of northern Europe the owl, polecat, badger, otter, and fox are abroad, busily seeking out their prey.

As the autumnal sun goes down on Western European days, the pre-roost commune of thousands of anonymous starlings at an 'ungiven signal' rising into the evening sky to weave twisting tunnels, and then shape themselves into funnels of flowing wave-like patterns – the shadow-like 'mermerations' of these avian sky-mobiles.

I have infused this somewhat wistful passage with human values and perspectives mainly to emphasize that animal species in all their rich variety are a store offering food for our sustenance, a genetic heritage for our survival and a richness of colours, textures, and forms for our aesthetic satisfaction. We relate to them as humans described in anthropomorphic terms allowing a sense of ownership, which is fundamentally wrong, but given our destructive power this human-centric perspective would hopefully be one imbued with an awareness of an essential responsibility for their survival.

However we relate to life's diversity – awe at its wonder, pragmatically appreciate its value, or both - we can surely appreciate that its underlying genetic variety is a potential source of biochemical information that could serve to support the survival of human life on Earth.

Many pharmaceutical drugs have been derived from organic materials, aspirin from Willow Bark, medicine for lowering cholesterol levels from a Japanese fungus, penicillin from penicillium mold, and codeine and morphine from the opium poppy, have long been known. Just three of the more recently developed drugs are paclitaxel derived from the Pacific Yew, combretastatin derived from the South African Bush Willow both used in the treatment of cancer, and the Rosy Periwinkle as a source of a substance used to treat Hodgkin's disease and acute Lymphoma.[18]

Its been estimated that about 25% of all prescription drugs are gained either directly, or derived, from plants and that approximately 80% of the world's people still depend on plant-based substances for their primary health needs. According to Botanical Gardens Conservation International; '....almost half the world's species may be threatened with extinction, cures as yet undiscovered may exist in plants as yet undescribed.'

Microorganisms are continuously trying to adapt to changing environments and when an environment includes human and animal bodies is given drugs to combat disease, then it is resistance to these that any threatened micro-organism are striving to gain. So an ongoing challenge for chemists working in human and veterinary pharmacology, and the loss of species could mean loss of some (as yet unknown) source of valuable molecular precursors to more effective drugs.

It might be that within the genetic information stored in the chromosomes of some yet unknown plant surviving deep within a tropical rain forest, or in some parasitic organism living inside the gut of a shy crustation inhabiting an isolated coral atoll, that the source of

---

[18] Steve Jones, 1994, p278 – gives 7 of 25 top global drugs derived from natural products.

some potentially effective medicines lie.

I have used these two examples of where genetic material potentially useful for the survival of humankind (or the animals and plants that we depend upon) might be found because it is species inhabiting the fragile ecosystems of rain-forests and coral reefs that are under imminent threat of extinction as a result of humankind's activities.

Across tropical regions coral reefs are reducing in area and being degraded in terms of the variety of life that can be sustained - pollution, including oil accidentally spilt and intentionally cleaned from bilges, run off from land contaminated by pesticides and sewerage, increasingly the residues of chemically complex prescription drugs passing through humans into the seas, dredging, the collection of coral itself and of the more visually attractive creatures that live upon it – the general degradation of a reef signaled by the loss of pigment as vital algae die off (especially the single-celled zooxanthellae) with the coral taking on a bleached appearance – a degradation resulting from different forms of pollution and exacerbated by the warming of the shallower waters in which the reefs are located.

The tropical forests, especially those of central and south America, India (Western Ghats), Indonesia, Malaysia, the Philippines, New Caledonia, Sri Lanka, and West Central Africa, have been under relentless pressure from the middle of the twentieth century. The plunder of the valuable timber, poisoning of the forests and rivers due to mining (especially gold) activities, slash and burn agriculture, and also in places to unsustainable hunting, fishing, and plant collection. Habitats under pressure from politically powerful national elites, financially powerful international interests, along with indigenous peoples desperately endeavouring to adapt and survive as the economic foundations of their subsistence-based cultures are eroded.

These two eco-systems, coral reefs and tropical forests, are among the more well known ecosystems that are increasing being degraded, including on-going species extinction. From the Arctic to the Antarctic and all around the world, in terms of species survival, there are a range of identifiable habitats being degraded, including: mountain valleys, open heath-land, marshland, mango swamps, semi-arid terrains, shrinking lakes, river systems, and throughout the oceans and seas. Habitats for thousands of species now under threat, and so of rich stores of genetic potential, disappearing each year due to human activities.

A rough estimate of the entire genetic diversity of life on Earth 10^{17} (100 quadrillion) nucleotide pairs containing a vast and valuable reservoir of 'life'. – in which inheres the potential to support the viability of human life. Each single species that becomes extinct, removes a unique package of genetic information

As Gerard Peil ('The Age of Science', 2001, p399) observes: 'In the high diversity of tropical vegetation, the indigenous people distinguish and have use for an apparently endless number of plants. Fruits and tubers in their cuisine are coming on the world market. The typical shaman commands a pharmacopoeia of nerve poisons (for the points of arrows and darts), antibiotics, contraceptives, psychotropics, and apparent cancer-inhibitors. The pharmaceutical industry is making a business of ethno-botany.' An industry seeking to commodify the medicinal wisdom of eons-long cultural heritage.

The extent of the current species loss is so great that we could be experiencing the 6th wave of mass extinctions, with this being the only one due to human activity. The previous and probably the most well-known such event being the mass extinction of 65 m.y.b.p that included the demise of the dinosaurs, this one probably being caused by the impact of a massive meteor (Gulf of Mexico) raising a global dust cloud that accumulated in the environment to a point where it was unable to support most of the larger organisms/animals. Estimates are of 99% of all species (so possible as many as 5 bn) having become extinct since life on Earth began. The 1% that remains still represents a vast store of natural beauty, a vast reservoir of genetic (informational) resources.

Shockingly, the current extinction rate is estimated to be between 1,000 - 10,000 times the natural rate (1-5 species) per year! Estimates are of 30 -50% of all species that were present in 2014 becoming extinct by 2050. The majority of these species having not even been recorded, let alone studied. The 'headline' endangered species (at 2018) included: the Borneo Orangutan, Darwin's Fox, the Giant Otter, the Amur Leopard, the Andean Mountain Cat, and the Sumatran Rhinoceros and for plants: the Texas Wild Rice, Georgia Aster, Quachita Mountain Goldenrod, Raffasia Flower (this last is thought to be the largest flowering plant known). Currently (2021) about 3,000 species of large animal are endangered.

E.O.Wilson (1996, p194) notes that some recent local mass extinctions: '.....include half the freshwater fishes of peninsular

Malaysia, half the 41 tree-snails of Oahu, 44 of the 68 shallow-water mussels of the Tennessee River shoals, as many as 90 plant species growing on the Centinela Ridge in Ecuador, and, in the United States as a whole, about 200 plant species with another 680 species and races now classified as in danger of extinction.'

There have been some attempts to limit species loss. Prominent amongst these has been the International Union for Conservation of Nature, with its 'red-list', a list that increased in terms of endangered species of animals by over 200% from 1998-2012 (1,102 to 3,079 species) and for plants by about 160% over the same period (1,197 to 2,655). Most individual countries are at least trying to limit species loss but for many, especially in economically developing countries, economic realities, spiced with political corruption, undermine much progress. Even in the United States, where an Endangered Species Act has been in place since 1973, species loss has continued – with hundreds of species lost since the passing of the Act and hundreds more currently listed as endangered. Across the world, poaching, deforestation, industrial agriculture, mineral extraction operations, pollution, and global warming, are the primary causes of species loss.

My focus has been on considering species loss more in terms of practical benefit to human-kind but arguably ethically at least as important is the responsibility that humans have to maintain the variety of animal and plant life. A view of humanity as the curator and conserver of the world's life-forms. We need to address questions such as: by what right can we justify the casual elimination of species after species as we degrade habitat after habitat – disrupting the often delicate balance of interconnected ecosystems. Is there a sanctity in life itself that we should be respecting? As we attempt to consider the wholeness of nature........ finding expression for me in a sublime ('oceanic') sense of transcendental wonder at complexity, interdependency, and beauty – a sense that soon develops into one of sadness at loss and of responsibility for what remains.

The genetic constitution of organisms has been formed over thousands of generations living during millions of years, the survival packages that can potentially provide a rich reservoir of 'information' inhabiting a range of environmental conditions available to humanity. Perhaps our ability as a species to adapt to changing conditions (the unforeseen plague, crop disease, pollutant) could depend upon preserving as much of this heritage as possible. Nigel Calder highlights the potential to use nature to mitigate pollution: 'There is probably no kind of man-made pollution, even including oil spills, plastic bags and nuclear waste, which one microbe or another could not help to control' (Calder, 2003, p295)

For E.O.Wilson (2008, p147 'Modern Science Writing')

'About the orchids of that place [Amazon rainforest] we know very little. About flies and beetles almost nothing, fungi nothing, most kinds of organism nothing. Five thousand kinds of bacteria might be found in a pinch of soil and about them we know absolutely nothing'

It is this variety, this storehouse of potentially valuable genetic information that is under threat by the activities of humankind – even as governments and corporations now talk enthusiastically of 'sustainable' development. Publication from government departments and political initiatives are cleverly framed in 'green-sounding' terminology: sustainability, appropriate technology, corporate responsibility, targets and aims and of course the colour 'green' has been insinuated into corporate logos and product packaging - as are processes of corporate re-imaging ('green washing'). And yet the cold fact of relentless species disappearance highlights the marginal reality of the actual sustaining of species-rich ecosystems. A would-be assessment based, not on simple cynicism of the motives of corporations and governments, but rather of a rational analysis of the past and current rates of environmental degradation would suggest that sustainability for these agencies seems to be based on a perspective that in fifty years time there will still be some protected environments in national parks, nature reserves, and some partially protected areas will be 'sustained'. Even this form of 'protection' hardly allows for the continuing increase in global warming and in declining air quality.

Apart from these doubtfully 'protected environments', a range of species living in such ecosystems as: alpine meadows, tropical and rain forests, savanna grasslands, along with different types of native woodlands across the world, mango swamps, mudflats, marshlands, large species-rich lakes and inland seas, grasslands, heath-lands, and coral reefs – are under threat. The rewards being sought involve any ecosystem that has valuable minerals underground (oil, gold, aluminum, water, diamonds, coal, etc.), valuable products on the surface (timber, fauna, flora). Or any environment that can be adapted to generate wealth (even if only in the relatively short-term) including: mango swaps to shrimp farms - rain forest to cattle grazing - tropical woodlands and native grasslands to palm-oil or bio-fuel production. And of course, global warming threatens any species that is unable to adapt to changing weather-patterns.

Less obvious species loss is exacerbated by the ongoing displacement of indigenous farmers, with their variety of traditional crops, of pastoralists seeking grazing land for cattle, sheep, and goats, of nomadic peoples following migrating herds of buffalo, reindeer, and gazelle. Lifestyles (indeed whole cultures) increasingly only available to collective memory, anthropological record, and group mythology.

Acts of institutional land thievery have been established as legally protected fact by property laws made subsequent to land-grabs or by the introduction of laws designed to make, what is in effect theft, 'legally' possible. Native Americans, Australian Aborigines, Scottish and Irish crofters, peasants and serfs as well as indigenous peoples all across the world have had, during the last three centuries, to yield 'common land' to superior military powers and relentless elite controlled economic processes. Displacement continues, with peoples being deprived of land and living today as they are being forced to yield to callously wielded forms of political and economic power in Africa, South America, China, and India.

In terms of a duty to protect the World's store of beauty, of the life-forms with which we share this planet, and in terms for simple human self-interest, we need to maintain species diversity; surely a fundamental moral duty for humankind. A world fit for overall species diversity is also likely to be one more conducive to human survival.

The loss of species from more natural environments is compounded by loss of plant species that humanity has for generations used for domesticated food crops. The increasing understanding of the genetic constitution of crop-plants such as maize, rice, wheat, soya, has allowed genetic manipulation to create varieties that seem to be genetically better-shaped to increase overall crop-yields and ones that also have a greater resistant to disease or drought. Any increased productively is a potential that generally cannot be realized without the creation of growing conditions suited to hybrid seeds – conditions often requiring large amounts of fertilizers, herbicides, and pesticides. Being hybrids they also (unlike traditional seeds) have to be bought new each season.

There is some concern that an intensively engineered-seed approach to crop growing could threaten the long-terms fertility of soils, it might also lead to water that 'runs off' being polluted with a range of complex chemicals; so threatening fauna and flora, and sometimes even human settlements, down-stream. The introduction of genetically engineered seed is relentlessly displacing those varieties selected over generations by hard-won experience and the reflective 'eye' of generations of native agriculturalists, farming across the developing world.

Seed provision, and crop support systems, are becoming increasingly dominated by a small number of multi-national corporations. These have deployed their formidable and well-coordinated political lobby power to ensure that a swath of new trade agreements 'liberalize' (open-up) agriculture in both the economically developed countries and the still more traditional farming countries of Africa, South-East Asia and South America. Small farmers (who still support about 70% of the worlds' people's food supply - 80% in Africa) are struggling against the profit-seeking behemoths and their local political agents. In addition, the government subsidized industrial agricultural farmers of the US and Europe are allowed to 'dump' their overproduction on the economically undeveloped countries, further undermining the financial viability of local producers.

The top ten seed supply corporations currently hold over 70% of the global market.

The largest, Monsanto, on over 20% and the next, Du Pont, on over 15%, with all top ten seed-supply corporations being based in the older economically developed countries – US, Japan, Germany, Denmark, France, and Switzerland. Four of these companies also have 55% of the world market share of agrochemicals, with most being prominent in the production of pesticides, herbicides, and fertilizers.

Unsurprisingly, the diversity of world food-crops has been declining steadily. Estimates suggest that about 75% of crop-plant genetic diversity has been lost since 1900 - with 2% more continuing to disappear each year. This is a trend that had been progressing throughout the twentieth century. Between 1903 and 1983 estimates are that 90% of seed varieties were lost to agriculture, just two examples being: lettuce from 500 varieties to 36, and peas over 400 varieties reduced to but 25. According to New Internationalist (Sept. 2010) 'There are almost half a million known plant species, and still more to be discovered. Yet we now rely on just 15 species to provide

90 per cent of our food crops.'

There has been a stark narrowing of seed dependence involving the world's basic food-crops. Today, 75% of the substantial rice crop grown on the Indian sub-continent is planted with just a dozen varieties, once there were 30,000 - 80% of 'Mexico's maize varieties grown in the 1930s have vanished' - of the 10,000 varieties of rice grown in China a century ago only 10%, and reducing, are still in use - 90% of the fruit and vegetable varieties in the US were lost to agriculture in the twentieth century, with a similar proportionate loss of varieties on all continents.

At the local level there has been some resistance to this trend and 75% of farmers across the world (albeit this is very different from the proportion of agricultural land they farm) continue to rely on traditional seed varieties. Most food is still consumed relatively local to its production. A situation seriously threatened by global agri-business and its influence on designing the agriculture-related conditions of international trade agreements.

Just one example of thousands of other small-scale attempts to resist the global expansion of profit based mono-seed agriculture comes from a group of six Quechua communities in Peru. Here groups of small famers have established a 'Potato Park' in which 1500 varieties of potato are cultivated ('a living gene bank'). This diverse and precious store of genetic memory is the resource that will enable the best variety to be grown for the prevailing conditions.

Some of the world's governments are becoming more aware of the potential risk of species loss and have established a number of 'Noah's Arks' to store seeds of identified plant species. Probably the most significant being the 'Svalbard Global Seed Vault' on the north Atlantic island protectorate of Norway. A number of the economically developed countries also have some seed storage capacity e.g. Kew Gardens in Britain, Navdanya in India (specializing in traditional farming seed), the National Centre for Genetic Resources in the US, the Vavilov Research Institute in Russia. But these only contain 'samples' of seeds and genetic stock, rather than sufficient quantities required if there were to be a catastrophic failure in a globally or locally important food-crop. These seed-banks, valuable as they are, could not possibly offer short or even medium - term alternatives to the steadily reducing range of varieties. In addition, given the vast amount of as yet unrecorded species out there the seed-banks currently only store a proportion of the potentially available, and potentially useful, global genetic variation.

The world's seed-banks and its millions of small farmers and sharecroppers still using traditional varieties of seeds could perhaps together provide the genetic ark that will support human life in the long-term if the application of big-agriculture led genetic modification, with its high energy input agriculture, does turn out to be unsustainable. But these do need to be protected.

A corporate-led determination to dominate global agriculture is a cause for concern especially in relation to the displacing of traditional farming and of the long-term impact of genetically engineered life-forms loosed on our ecosystems. But 'if' suitable checks and balances are in place then genetic modification does offer a technology that could make a positive contribution to agriculture as well as animal husbandry. Unfortunately, the 'if' clause in the previous sentence depends upon very different political and economic decisions being made.

Gene focused research is providing some benefits, just some being: In the Far East (Malaysia, Philippine, Vietnam, Thailand, Indonesia) scientists are working to develop a variety of the regionally important crop papaya with a delayed ripening characteristic; the University of Nottingham and the private company Zeneca are also involved.

Biotechnology applied to cheese production is using enzymes produced by micro-organisms that could provided much cheaper alternatives to animal rennet (as a cheese coagulant). Another example: 85 million tons of wheat used each year in the making of bread....enzyme maltogenic amylase added to the flour prolongs the 'shelf-life' of the bread. Current estimates are that 10-15% of bread is currently thrown away because stale, so if the eatable life can be extended by 5-7 days then 2 million tons of flour could be productively used annually rather than wasted.

Plant variations have been developed to reduce vulnerability to adverse environmental conditions e.g. the use of plant gene At-DBF2 from the weed thale cress has been inserted into a tomato plant to significantly improve resistance to drought, salt, cold and heat. If initial trials do prove successful then this same gene can be used to extend the growing range and the productivity of a number of crops. More generally, biotechnological research has focused on reducing the use of chemical pesticides by giving the plant stronger internal (genetic) protection against pests. Genetic engineering has also produced varieties more tolerant to the herbicides sprayed on fields to reduce weeds (although the use of herbicides can be an issue). Genetic engineering has also been used to create transgenic rice plants resistant to yellow mottle virus. Across Africa, this is a virus that decimates rice crops and makes any surviving plants more vulnerable to fungal infections. It is clear that the bioengineering of food crops can potentially improve taste, texture, and appearance, as well as the more important nutritional qualities and increased crop productivity and viability.

On the obverse side of this issue there are a number of problems with genetic manipulation in agriculture including: the inadvertent 'breeding' of herbicide resistant weeds (as well as health-threatening viruses and bacteria), the possible adverse impact of GM crops on neighbouring non-GM (especially 'organically' grown) crops, run-off of chemically enriched water into waterways, and the economic implications of repeat costs of hybrid seed and the necessary fertilizers, herbicides, and pesticides. Bio-technology does seem better suited to the operation of corporate agro-businesses and the growth of these pose a serious threat to local economies currently based on using traditional farming methods.

In the US, multinational agribusiness, dealing with a series of quite easily persuaded governments, has enthusiastically progressed the introduction of genetically modified organisms (GMO). In terms of food-crops, as at 2020 85% of US corn is grown with GM seeds, 90% of its canola and 50% of its sugar-beet, similar level with soya, alfalfa, zucchini, tomatoes, apples (and indeed cotton) and many other crops – 80% of the ingredients in its processed foods have been subject to genetic modification. Some of these seeds have been modified so that they contain antibiotic-type properties 'engineered' to provide some immunity to disease. Humans ingest this food, along with the many meat products sourced from animals liberally treated with antibiotics as a preventative rather than a curative measure, and so contributing to the significant increase in exposure to residues of over-prescribed antibiotics in the environment. Adding to the already serious issue of antibiotic resistance being gained by some rapidly evolving micro-organisms.

As GM crops have been introduced in the US the levels of childhood food allergies have also dramatically increased; currently only a correlation but one quite suggestive of a potential link. And links have also been found between GMO foodstuffs and childhood gastrointestinal aliments and from these to the dramatic increase in autism seen in US and some European countries. Correlations are of course not proof of casual links but with issues such as human health the ones between genetic modification of foodstuffs and health-related conditions we do need to investigate further and when possible operate according to a precautionary principle.

This launch into GM food has only been happening during the past 30 years so the long-term implications of this bio-technology remain unknown. The advocates of big agriculture claim that GM crops are necessary to maintain the economic viability of the world's small and medium-sized farmers and to provide sufficient amounts of food-crops for the world's (7-8 billion people) population. And yet twenty-first century global hunger is not a product of food shortages but is in fact an outcome of current distribution systems. In essence, the result of exclusion from food markets; so poverty not production, and distribution rather than availability.

With increasingly more elite-controlled land in developing countries being given over to 'cash crops' intended for export, or made available at inflated prices to local markets. Even the pet-owners of the world's economically developed countries can afford pet-food with nutritious ingredients (such as fish-meal) exported from countries in which people suffer from malnutrition and at times even experience starvation; populations of the richer nations can access global and local food-markets denied to the poor.[19]

If issues of the long term impact of GM crops such as on soil fertility, human health, species cross-contamination, and the security of food-supply, can be determined, and these seeds can be appropriately supplied to the world's farmers, then this scientific innovation could serve to improve prospects, especially for those farming at the margins of agricultural viability. But 'appropriate' would include affordable seeds without a heavy dependence on often uncertain water supplies and expensive fertilizer and pesticide inputs; so mitigating against high debt levels for small and medium sized farmers. But for sure, the issues involved in GMO food-crops, and genetic engineering more generally, are at least as much political as they are scientific matters.

Manipulation of the biological basis of life can offer opportunities for improving the human (and by implication the general)

---

[19] It is estimated that about 30% of the world's available food is uneaten each year, most just thrown away.

environmental conditions but doing so involves potential risks, some known and calculable, some certainly unknown and so incalculable. How can we know of unknowns? Well firstly, there is some past experience of the unintended consequences of genetic manipulation. But secondly, and perhaps most relevant, the weight of argument would suggest that, given the relatively crude level of understanding of the complexities and interrelatedness of life-form and the fragile balance of life in some eco-systems, unforeseen consequences seem likely. It does seem to a layperson such as myself that the 'precautionary principle' should be an appropriate approach for GM being applied to food-production.

In sum: Currently the world's genetic heritage seems to be being treated as but a corporate-led global 'gold-rush'........an extensive resource subjected to rapacious corporate plunder, only partially being controlled by governments committed to variations of some form of corporate-led economic neo-liberalism. But set against this is the truly profound potential to manipulate genes (genetic constitutions) in order to produce abundant food-corps with a 'built in' ability to resist pests and adverse environmental conditions (droughts and high soil salt levels) and these without the need for heavy crop spraying.

Clearly there is a need for some international strategy that can optimize the benefits of genetic engineering of foodstuffs whilst ensuring safe, sustainable, food supplies and respect for traditional forms of agriculture and the many communities this sustains. The most obvious issues are: Is there a need for an engineered product? Who controls it?

What would happen if any genetically-engineered seed fails (due to insect pests or plant viruses gaining resistance)? What impact would its introduction have on any local community?

So, as with all profound choices that humankind as a collectivity is faced with, a careful analysis should be made of the issues, and decisions on an adoption strategy of this still relatively new technology should be on the basis of benefit to human life rather than enhancing corporate income.

During the twentieth century biology was advancing rapidly in terms of biochemistry, as well as in understanding the form and function of organisms, but also in widening of the theoretical perspectives used to enhance our understanding of life. In 1935 Arthur Tansley was a pioneer in introducing the idea of 'ecosystems'; how the interdependency of organisms sharing a particular environment can be described as an interrelated system. With the implication being that if one element, say the primary predator, is removed then the system can 'break down', with one or more other species dramatically increasing in numbers and so destabilizing the whole local ecosystem.

In relation to the social behaviour of life-forms, individuals such as Konrad Lorentz, Niko Tinbergen and Karl von Frish intensively (bordering on obsessively) collected information on the behaviour patterns of different species. Although they did investigate some fairly simple learned behaviours, their primary focus was on behaviours they assumed as being instinctive. Behaviors such as imprinting, aggression (Lorentz - geese and tropical fish), and communication (Tinbergen - 3-spined Stickleback, Herring Gull and Honey Bee, and von Frisch - Honey Bees), All three shared a 1973 Nobel Prize (physiology and medicine) for discoveries "...concerning organization and elicitation of individual and social behaviour patterns.'

During the second half of the century two notable primatologists, Dian Fossey (Mountain Gorillas) and Jane Goodall (Chimpanzees), undertook patient, decades-long, observational studies of primates in their natural environments. Studies in which they were able to show the variety of individual primate behaviours and the often subtle complexity of their social relationships.

A third, if wider, approach to understanding life that, due to its comprehensive implications, has created some controversy, is sociobiology. Although the concept and related ideas can be traced back to the coining of the term by John Scott at a conference held in late 1948 this explanatory theory underwent more substantial reconsideration from the publication in 1974 of the US zoologist Edward O. Wilson's book 'Sociobiology: The New Synthesis'.

In this, and subsequent books, Wilson drew on advances in the understanding of genetics, and those made in ethology by individuals such as Tinbergen and Lorenz, to draw a suggestively deterministic link between genetic constitution (as the outcome of natural selection) operating on social behaviour.

Key areas of controversy with sociobiology include those to do with both the substantive biological claims and the social implications. For the latter, sociobiological explanations could be used (or misused) to justify social inequalities by treating them as 'natural'. With echoes of social Darwinism, as interpreted by those such as Herbert Spencer and his 'survival of the fittest' and supporters of laissez-faire economics and individualism such as the American sociologist William Sumner. A strong challenge to sociobiology was launched by a group of Wilson's Harvard University colleagues, encapsulated in the book 'Biology as a Social Weapon' (1977).

On the biological claim Wilson, as well as drawing on ethology more generally, also undertook detailed studies of the social behaviour of ants and a number of other non-human species (only one chapter of his 1974 book is devoted to the human species). He also identified seemingly instinctive human fears, e.g. of snakes, as suggesting the validity of the wider application of genetic links to more complex social behaviours. Apart from the obvious criticism of drawing over-strong parallels between non-human animals and humans, prominent writers on science such as Leon Kamin, Steven Rose, Steven Gould, and Richard Lewontin, are critical of sociobiology's adaptationist (ignoring the influence of contingency and chance) heuristic framework and what they view as its reductionist methodology.

If read sympathetically sociobiology is an approach to understanding animal and human behaviour where the balance of effective influence is strongly, but not entirely, shifted towards the accrued outcome of a species's evolutionary experience. With a significant driver of this experience being the maximization of reproductive opportunities. Wilson himself was at times fairly equivocal in relation to the balance between genetic constitution and social behaviours. In an essay on altruism and aggression (pub. 1996) he rejects Lorenz's claims for a determinate instinct for aggression and admits to some uncertainty regarding any instinct for altruism suggesting that '……the intensity and form of altruistic acts are to a large extent culturally determined'. Although his wider view of cultures does suggest these as being the accrued outcomes of selective evolution.

For Wilson: 'Human social evolution is obviously more cultural that genetic. Nevertheless, the underlying emotion [towards altruism], powerfully manifested in virtually all human societies, is considered by sociobiologists to evolve through genes.' (Wilson, 1996)

Let's consider homosexual behaviour in sociobiological terms: On initial sociobiological consideration, homosexuality would seem to be an aberration (so 'unnatural') in that the reproductive imperative appears not to operate. Further consideration suggests that this could in fact be a form of altruistic behaviour and that homosexuals could be benefiting the whole group to which the homosexuals are related, in ways that increase its overall reproductive capacity – an example of altruism supporting kin selection. So in fact it is a behaviour aligned with the reproductive imperative (so 'natural') afterall.

This is a somewhat dubious conclusion in that homosexual men can impregnate women, so can directly reproduce their own genes rather than just support the 'diluted' version as with kin selection. And also, what role in supporting a group is there that cannot also be filled by heterosexual men? Would not abstention from procreative sex need to carry a substantial kin-selection advantage and so the support required from non-maters would surely be quite obvious to the ethologists? Wilson himself admits that there is no hard evidence to support the view of homosexuality as an altruistic option, but he does suggest that it is consistent with types of kin selection that can be observed in other species. Lack of some contribution favouring kin-selection does not of course make homosexuality 'unnatural', not least due to 'natural' being a socially constructed definition of behaviour; 'natural' being perhaps the most misused biology-related concept.

Given the generality of sociobiological theory e.g. Wilson (1996) notes: *'What the genes prescribe is not necessarily a particular behaviour but the capacity to develop certain behaviours and, more than that, the tendency to develop them in various specified environments.'* And he writes that: 'It is this *pattern* of possibilities and probabilities that is inherited.' (1996, pp89-90). He does suggest a genetic bias when he comments on male/female social roles but here again he is equivocal, advocating '....gender-blind admission [to professions] and free personal choice.' So there seems to be some level of inconsistency in Wilson's approach, if perhaps one that reflects the complexity of human behavior in the context of our inability to unweave the causative balance between gene constitution and environmental conditions.

As an explanatory framework sociobiology can be much more persuasive when applied to non-Hominid species but much less so when applied to Hominids; especially for humans (Hominin) where individual behaviour is played out in conditions of pre-existing social structures and institutions. Conditions which themselves can strongly constrain and shape behaviour. As Karl Marx suggested, we are born into circumstances not of our own making, and that: 'The tradition of all dead generations weigh like a nightmare on the brains of the living.' (The Eighteenth Brumaire of Louis Bonaparte' 1852)

A key epistemological issue (potential weakness), with insights from sociobiology (and perhaps more so with its associated evolutionary psychology) being applied to human beings, is that any human individual or group behaviour can be 'explained' in evolutionary terms. Consequently, its assumed comprehensiveness can dissipate its explanatory value.

Methodologically, research to investigate such explanations is problematic with humans due to the difficulties in isolating genetic influence from the potentially confounding influence of social circumstances and individual psychology. But sociobiology does serve as a necessary corrective in highlighting a potentially important source of influence on behavior to be considered alongside the other, more obviously socially constructed, influences.

Two other, more philosophical, explanatory frameworks have been applied to living processes are biosemiotics and biosemantics. As with sociobiology, I can only give a 'flavour' of these approaches here.

In the view of Kalevi Kull (1998/99) biosemiotics offers: 'A new paradigm for [theoretical] biology'. He defines biosemiotics as '…the science of signs in living systems' and quotes J,Hoffmeyer (1995) that: 'The sign rather than the molecule is the basic unit for studying life'. Kull goes on to quote J.Deeley (1990) that: 'The introduction of symbiosis and reciprocity into the heart of the evolutionary process along with the selection of mutations, makes of these new concepts an extremely fertile ground for further development of semiotic consciousness, and an inevitable frontier that semiotic theory cannot for long delay exploring.'

Biosemiotics was inspired by ideas of the German biologist Jakub von Uexhüll. Writing in the first half of the twentieth century von Uexhüll suggested that each organism creates its own inner 'world', its Unwelt (partly a species-selected interpretation of its external environment), in which it acts purposefully in relation to its level of 'awareness' of the environmental limitations and possibilities it encounters. The purposeful acting is possible due to a process of internal communication characterized by a form of organic (biosemiotic) reflexivity – not the simpler systems-related feedback mechanism as a self-regulating process but something more complex, more directed, than this. An obvious example being the process of epigenesis; in humans the development of a new life from fertilization to birth.

For Hoffmeyer (1996): 'The most pronounced feature of organic evolution is not the creation of a multiplicity of amazing morphological structures, but the general expansion of 'semiotic freedom', that is to say the increase in richness or 'depth' of meaning that can be communicated' and (1995) to repeat the previous quote; 'The sign rather than the molecule is the basic unit for studying life.'

Biosemiotics – considers life in relation to signs and codes by applying a novel theoretical framework as well as insights from the study of linguistics. Drawing parallels between language as written in codes and DNA as written in codes; and indeed parallels with these and communication systems of other organisms e.g. such as that exhibited by bees when communicating the location of food sources to their fellow bees. But I am not sure what form of 'coded' communication processes have been identified by biosemiticians - I assume coded communication systems are ones using 'symbols' as subunits, most obviously letters in human language and nucleotides in DNA. But for any 'symbols' operating at a molecular and/or cellular level biosemioticians seem, at best, vague on this.

The experimental anatomist J.A.Davies ('Life Unfolding', 2014) offers a more tangible, less abstract, means of molecular-level communication. His focus is on the developing embryo and the truly amazing interlinked processes of coordinating cellular growth and differentiation. He suggests this is based on an intricate 'signaling' form of communication written in the '…language of protein biochemistry.' It is a form of communication very much linked to the messages sent and the particular type of cell receptor, for Davies '….The creation of detailed pattern [cell differentiation and positioning] in a previously monotonous embryo [the initially undifferentiated stem cells] is therefore the result of multitude of cellular conversations.' He writes of '…conversations, conducted in the language of proteins….' (Davies, 2014, pp88-90).

Davies has the 'signal' as being an essential property of '…any molecule that carries information about some state of affairs, and that affects the behaviour of a cell that receives it.' So, for Davies, the biosemiotic message is presented in the medium of a molecule's biochemical configuration.

The biochemical language, whose communicative (and organizing) activity Davies highlights, takes advantage of the biochemical sensitivities (actions/reactions) that characterize proteins at the molecular level. There remains the issue of central control and coordination for this highly complex set of interlinked processes, but presumably this can be traced back to a body's, initial and ongoing protein synthesis in response to the genetic code (beginning in the germ cell for embryos).

Biosemiotics offers a novel paradigm which assumes that all living things can be interpreted as semiotic systems – so raising the perspective above (in terms of degree of abstraction) theoretical descriptions based on more mundane molecular and evolutionary interpretive levels.

Whilst this suggests a potentially revealing way of considering living processes, semiotics is associated with perspectives, meanings, and so is perhaps more hermeneutic than explanatory. Given the epistemological implications, I would be cautious about applying semiotics as an explanatory framework applied to life. I can see the relevance of our applying semiotics to our own (human) understanding of biological phenomena but this does not seem to me to equate with the projection of, what would in effect be, anthropomorphism to molecular, organelles, or cellular entities. Organic entities interacting 'as if' in a community rather than more bio-chemically. Biosemiotics seems to have subject matter that inheres in life as expressed in some phenomenal 'language' that overlies the material necessity constituting the subject-matter of the more conventional reductionist approaches. Biosemitoics assumes that there are communication systems inherent in the material necessity of living processes operating most obviously at the molecular, organelle, and cellular levels. And that these coded communication systems can be translated to interpret the properties and behaviors of these living processes, an interpretation that enlarges the horizon of biological knowledge.

Biosemiotics has enjoyed a resurgence of interest in recent decades with the founding of the 'International Society for Biosemiotic Studies' in 2005, and a 'Journal of Semiotics' from 2008.

It was in 1984 that the philosopher of biology Ruth Millikan's book 'Language, Thought and Other Biological Categories' followed by her 1989 paper 'An Evolutionary Theory of Thought', brought to the fore another novel way of considering human thinking in evolutionary terms - biosemantics. An approach focused on how neural states become mental representations as an outcome of processes akin to natural selection.

For Millikan (2017, p3): 'The assumption is that we, along with other animals, are evolved creatures that use cognition as a guide in dealing with the natural world, and that the natural world is, roughly, as natural science has tried to describe it.'

Millikan focused on the cognitive conditions that make knowledge possible by taking a very different approach to that of Immanuel Kant for whom these conditions are outlined from a purely 'rational' perspective. For Millikan, a Kantian approach is insufficient in that it does not take into account the relationship between cognition and the natural world. She outlines this relationship in terms of communication systems based on 'signs' – natural signs, social signs, and individual mental representations. A natural sign system has purpose in relation to function, and purpose also underlines the production of mental representations. Simply put, the natural realm can have a significant impact on how and what we think. Biological constitution (derived from evolutionary development shaped by natural selection) and cognition are interwoven in mental representations.

Donald Favareau of the National University of Singapore offers a simpler if still rather general definition: 'Biosemantics is the study of the myriad forms of communications ....observable both within and between living systems. It is thus the study of representation, meaning, sense, and the biological significance of sign processes – from intracellular signaling processes to animal display behaviour to human.....artifacts such as language and abstract symbolic thought' (New Scientist web-site 2020).

Similar to biosemiotics, biosemantics also seems to be blinkered by its easy recourse to anthropomorphisms. Is this a failure in understanding or more excusably a lack of appropriate conceptual terminology whereby the living (signaling) processes involving organic matter can be adequately represented in non-anthropomorphic ways. The New Scientist article on biosemantics goes on to note the need for biosemantics to go beyond the use of metaphor with the biologist Charbel-El-Hani's suggestion of: 'The importance of going beyond metaphor and really building a theory of information [that] is underlined by the reiterated claim that biology is a science of information'.

There is an uneasy ontological difference between the human realm of mental representations and the natural world of processes. Such that (similarly to biosemiotics), in the absence of identifying a specific code-based communication system - a form of 'symbolic communication' for the natural world that can be translated into the language of human cognition - we are perhaps limited to applying descriptive metaphors drawn from the social realm to be applied to molecular and cellular processes, and to the natural behaviour of organisms. It is difficult to see what form a 'theory of information' would take to allow it to transcend the ontological differences between the natural world and mental representations. But I accept that 'information' does seem to offer at least the possibility of providing the conceptual link required.

As thought provoking and intellectual stimulating as they might be, most working biologists seem to have resisted committing to any of the theoretical explanations set out above.

A more conventional theoretical approach that, even accepting some claims to the contrary, does includes the option of a reductionist methodology, was suggested by Paul Weiss in his essay 'The living system: determinism stratified' which was his contribution to a 'Beyond Reductionism' symposium (1969). Weiss set out a perspective based on the idea of a hierarchically structured general system theory: '.....systems theory would have to be granted primacy for the treatment of organized systems; for the systems concept is the embodiment of the experience that there are patterned processes which owe their typical configuration not to a prearranged, absolutely stereotyped, mosaic of single-tracked component performances, but on the contrary, to the fact that the component activities have many degrees of freedom, but submit to the ordering restraints exerted upon them by the integral activity of the "whole" in its patterned systems dynamics'. ('Beyond Reductionism: The Alpbach Symposium', A. Koestler and J. R. Smythies, eds. 1969, p91)

Biological systems theory assumes that there are clear levels of analysis (the hierarchy noted by Weiss) and that at each level entities (atoms, molecules, cells, bodies, social organization etc.) operate in ways that allow 'emergent properties' to be identified.

Weiss felt that: '....systems are products of our experience with nature, and not mental constructs....' (ibid p10) He suggests that this view of systems is of 'open' systems, similar to that outlined in Ludwig von Bertalanffy's 'General Systems Theory' (1973) - Weiss seems to go on to equate reductionism with 'arrogation' from experience. This claim of systems not being mental constructs is difficult to accept given that these can only be based on conceptualizing observations and surely conceptualizing is the mind engaging in the production of 'mental constructions'. I think it might be more realistic to view systems as mental constructions that provide explanatory (revelatory) frameworks for encapsulating the dynamic interrelationships (including action thresholds and continuous feedback mechanisms) of living processes in a more coherent and comprehensive way than a more limited reductionist framework that arrives with its biological framework constituted by static, sub-units of atoms, molecules, organelles, and cells.

For Weiss (ibid p21): 'The only thing that remains predictable amidst the erratic stirring of the molecular populations of the cytoplasm and its substructures is the overall pattern of dynamics which keeps the component activities in definable bounds of orderly restraints. These bounds again are not to be viewed as mechanically fixed structures, but as "boundary conditions".'

Systems theory interprets living processes as interconnecting systems with properties such as regulatory feedback mechanisms, hierarchical levels, and outcomes that are more than simply the sum of any systems/levels parts - the concept of 'emergent properties' is hard to resist. Emergence can arise as a property of a system operating at any level in the biological hierarchy. If represented as a system then the mind can be viewed as an emergent property of the neurological physiology or, on a much finer-grained level even as an emergent property of the system level of the atoms constituting the human body.

Stephen J. Gould (2003, pp201-2) notes the importance of emergence and contingency in evolutionary biology – emergence as a fundamental property of biological systems and contingency as an important aspect of evolution insufficiently acknowledged by reductionist biologists who have focused on the more continuous bio-mechanism of random variation. Emergence can be viewed as a valid inference of observing biological processes through a systems framework or they can be viewed as conceptual labels attached to phenomena that we don't really understand.

In the twenty-first century, versions of systems theory are probably at the forefront of theoretical biology; an attraction being that it also offers a manageable research tool. One that allows the computational and mathematical modeling of living systems, along with types of detailed feedback mechanisms characteristic of general systems theory. Models, such for example, as those of intra-cellular: signaling, protein synthesis, metabolism etc. and running these models as interactive 'living' processes. Enabling researchers to follow both the process as it unfolds and for them to be able to identify any properties that emerge from a model.

Methodologically, explanations and predictions of systems theory can meet Karl Popper's test of falsifiability (offering the possibility of a certain type of 'scientific' authority), whereas it is difficult to see how sociobiology, biosemitotics, and biosemantics, can meet this requirement. Whilst not of course fatal to any claims for their scientific value (the Popper test is itself contested) this does present a research challenge in terms of empirical verification for researchers, and at least highlights a potential methodological weakness.

Earlier in this chapter I mentioned a theoretical interpretation of a number of biological processes involving quantum mechanics. So in this section on theoretical approaches I merely note it as offering a fundamental and coherent explanatory framework for various aspects of living systems – enzymes, photo-synthesis, genetic mutation, and indeed the passage of 'communication' in nervous systems. It offers an exciting approach to twenty-first century biology. For Jim Al-Khalili and Johnjoe MacFadden (2014), the role of quantum tunneling, quantum superposition, and quantum entanglement, can potentially explain currently puzzling aspects of the behavior of living matter at the molecular level. They suggest that: 'Life appears to have one foot in the classical world of everyday objects and the other planted in the strange and peculiar depths of the quantum world. Life….lives on the quantum edge.' (Al-Khalili and MacFadden, 2014, p46).

In the absence of any authentic ways of determining which approach might be more valid I tend to prefer my own conception of viewing these – sociobiological, biosemiotic, biosemantic, systems theory, and quantum biology - as but different thought-provoking theoretical perspectives on living processes, each offering some useful descriptive value whilst none of them being substantially satisfying. I can't resist the obvious observation that what perhaps emerges as the best theory will be the one that survives the intense scrutiny of working biologists and philosophers of science, the one selected being so on the basis of its being the more 'fit' in terms of explanatory power.

A reductionist, more positivist, approach to the study of the biosphere, with its focus on laboratory and in-the-field research, has served the biological sciences well. During the twentieth century it was an approach operating within a wider theoretical synthesis of genetics and natural selection; a series of modifications to the 'Modern Synthesis' set out in the 1930s. But in the later 20th and early 21st centuries new theoretical ideas such as those noted above have been proposed.

The rich variety of wide-ranging theoretical explanations that have been set out during the twentieth century should be seen more as imaginative complements to the fine-grained, relentlessly revealing, research programmes that have made such a massive contribution to biological knowledge and to improving human life, not least in: agriculture, animal husbandry, food storage and processing, general medicine, pharmacology, education, human physical development and aging processes, and human physiology and neurobiology. The period covering the 20th and early decades of the 21st centuries has seen a dramatic increase in our factual knowledge of the biological realm due to the work of thousands upon thousands of biochemists, ethologists, psychologists, zoologists, physicists, and other branches of what could broadly be included as the 'biological sciences'.

For the purpose of this section on biology I might state that 'crudely put' we could suggest that the twentieth century began with an understanding of some basic biochemistry of living processes (especially the observation of chromosomal reproduction in the nucleus of the cell) that erased (or effectively suppressed) any residual vitalism inherited from the nineteenth century. The focus of biology became - following the wider predominate approach of the natural and to a lesser extent the social sciences - reductionist in paradigm and broadly positivist in theoretical approach. But throughout there have also been a number of attempts to offer alternative interpretative theoretical descriptions and explanations.

Geology

The life on Earth that we have been considering exists within just a relatively thin bio-layer (biosphere) extending but 8.5 km. above sea level and about 11 km down to the deepest part of the oceans. During the twentieth century we have been able to learn a great deal about our planet. This spherical lump of material spinning through space, girdled by its thin and fragile biosphere. In the second half of the century we have been able to learn much more about the impact that human activities have had and are continuing to have upon it. Geology is one of the life sciences which have been making a series of significant contributions to our understanding of both this human impact and also of the material history and current constitution of the Earth.

As with most of the sciences, the intellectual foundations of geology can be traced back to the Greeks. At the forefront of this development was Aristotle (384 - 322 BCE), a genuine polymath whose wide-range of interests included weather patterns and an observation-based consideration of the formation of landscapes. Aristotle's authority did a great deal towards introducing the study of the Earth's physical characteristics into academic consideration. Theophrastus's (c 371 – c 287 BCE), who became head of the Lyceum established by Aristotle, wrote 'On Stones', in which he described different types of minerals and rocks, especially those found during mining activities. He classified different materials according to their relative hardness. And also commented at some length on fossils and the seeming mystery of fossilized marine creatures being found hundreds of miles from the coast. Interest in the formation of topographic features continued into the time of Roman political ascendency; with Pliny the Younger providing a fairly detailed description of the eruption of Mt. Vesuvius (79 CE).

In Chinese texts from as early as 527 CE we see the recording of fossils, and of the origins of mountains being speculated upon. As is well known, the Chinese have long been keenly interested in the cause of earthquakes; understandable given the destructive impact on their lands. Later on the Chinese scholar Shen Kao (1031-1095 CE) offered his theory of 'geomorphology', a theory based on careful observation of land formations and of marine fossils found inland.

During the Arabic scientific efflorescence of the early medieval period scholars keenly debated the creation of the surface of the Earth. In the tenth century two competing theories of geological formation were on offer; theories that would be returned too, in slightly different forms, in the eighteenth century. One idea was formation from processes of sedimentation in watery environments (Neptunism) followed by a drying out of the land. The other (Plutonism) suggested more dramatic origins from volcanic and other subterranean sources and with rivers moving rocks and soils to their, then current, locations. Neptunism was favoured by the 'Brothers of Purity' as set out in their 'Encyclopedia' completed 980 CE. The alternative view, of 'Plutonism', was set out by Ibn Sīnā (Avicenna - 980-1037 CE) who suggested earthquakes and the 'uplift' of the land and the sea floor as being the source of topographic features, primarily in relation to mountain ranges. He considered Aristotle's views on minerals and weather patterns, going on to offer his own ideas on the formation of different types of terrain, the cause of earthquakes, and the role of mountains in the accumulation of clouds.

Interest in geology (as with mathematics and other sciences) continued in the Arabic world. But in the west the threatening influence of a powerful, reactionary, Catholic Church, with its dogmatic commitment to biblical explanations of creation, inhibited consideration of more rational alternatives. A similar anti-scientific turn by Islamic religious leadership, feeling their authority being challenged by rationalism, would later also impact on Arabic science.

It would be the period known as the Renaissance (from about 1400 CE) that saw a modest weakening of the western Church's influence on sections of the middle and upper classes, allowing a renewal of interest in the sciences, to the benefit of geology. A development inadvertently aided by the Protestant challenge to the authority of the Catholic Church (precipitated by Martin Luther in 1519 CE) and its claim of being the only true source of biblical interpretation. During the Reformation some believers asserted their right to certain religious freedoms and of an individual's direct relationship to God. This seemingly dramatic, if intellectually quite narrow, step toward freedom of thought was significantly extended with the later Enlightenment. A much wider extension of non-religious debate, broadly covering the period 1600-1800, focused on politics, the arts, and also underpinned the rise of modern science.

Arguably, the intellectual midwife at the birth of geology as a modern science was Nicolaus Steno (1638 -1686 CE). Initially more interested in anatomy, it was a growing interest in fossils (in particular fossilized sharks teeth) that brought Steno to a closer study of geology. The fossilized remains of organisms were found in strata laid down over eons and Steno suggested that layers of this type of strata were laid down according to age ('superposition' - seemingly obvious to us but an important insight at the time), And that those layers of strata currently seen as perpendicular to the horizon would originally have been parallel to it. The clear implication being of tremendous pressures 'folding' layers of minerals and rock materials deposited at earlier times. Steno's highlighting of stratification, not least the absence of any fossils at the deepest (oldest) levels, established bio-stratigraphy as an important sub-section of geology throughout the following centuries. Providing a focus that would invariably link to how the Earth had aged in terms of geological formations, and when it had originally been formed. For Gabriel Gohau (1991, p66): 'Despite all his limitations, Steno provided a considerable leap forward in methodology for histories of the earth.'

The 17th and 18th centuries saw a relatively small number of individuals progressively laying down the foundations for the 19th century's coming of scientific age for geology. Henry Gautier, Giovanni Arduino, and especially James Hutton, were at the forefront of this progress. It was Hutton who led the challenge to Bishop Usher's claim of the Earth being created by God in 4004 BC – with the final day of creation week being Sunday 24th October that year! Although Hutton's own calculation at least claimed to maintain some biblical credibility, his suggested figure was 75,000 years ago. The ageing of the Earth set a context for determining the stages of the fossil record, deposition patterns of strata, and of the formation and aging of topographical features: mountains, volcanoes, rivers, continents, oceans, etc.

In England, William Smith was able to show that certain types of fossils were unique to particular types of sedimentary rock (17 types initially, later he added 10 more). A discovery that contributed to his being able, by 1815, to compile the first geological map of England and Wales. In France Georges Cuvier used similar biostratigraphic identification by fossil types to compile a geological map of the Paris Basin. Then, in 1812, Cuvier was able to offer conclusive evidence of fossil invertebrates that had no known living counterparts. A significant discovery that would feed into the growing debate about the creation and the evolutionary development of life.

Towards the end of the eighteenth century the earlier (10th century) competing theories of Neptunism and Plutonism were revived. The former by Abraham Gottlob Werner (1749-1817) who proposed that in the past the Earth's landmasses had been covered by shallow seas and that the geological features and more open terrain of the continents were the result of continuous depositions made from materials once suspended within the turbid primeval oceans. He suggested that the differing layers and types of rock were due to different deposition periods. With the terrestrial features being revealed as the seas receded. Contrary to Werner's theory, James Hutton, initially in an essay 'Theory of Earth' (1788), proposed that, 'given sufficient time', the then assumed processes of deposition of sediments and the erosion of land and rocks could account for much of Earth's geological formation, without the need for much oceanic contribution and so no need of a world covered by sea. His Plutonist (Volcanist) theory suggested that the Earth was a dynamic body, whose very hot interior produced the magma and lava that then solidified into the older igneous rocks. Consequently, that it was subterranean heat that caused the uplift forming the more prominent terrestrial features.

The issue for Plutonism was 'given sufficient time' which, for Hutton, would need to be considerably greater than the scriptural 6,000 years. So presenting a direct challenge to the Church's authority. Hutton's theory only slowly gained the acceptance of his peers. But its sense, along with a more general recognition of the 6,000 years being unsatisfactory for geological development, was hard for the rationally minded to resist. The theory came to be more generally accepted when it gained the support, in the early 1830s, of the respected scientist Charles Lyell. Lyell set out his ideas in his substantial 'The Principles of Geology' (three vols. pub 1830 – significantly assisted by his wife Mary) and suggested that the Earth of his time was the outcome of numerous small-scale changes, a multiplicity of drawn-out processes that had created geological features, even the high mountain chains of the world.

Increasingly, the rocks, soils, and prominent geological features of the world were seen as fertile areas for the inquisitive and rationally minded to observe, collect data from, and upon which to offer theoretical explanations as to composition and origins. Nineteenth-century geology went hand in hand with paleo-biology in seeking to understand the curious phenomenon of animal fossils (shark teeth in Steno's case) found in layers of rock set into mountains ranges located far inland. Throughout the century those few with the leisure time and the interest tramped over the foothills of the Alps, the Pyrenees, and other European mountain chains (then later the Appalachian and the Andes in the Americas), along steep-sided river valleys, descending into caves systems, and seeking out locations of high volcanic activity such as the Bay of Naples (Mt. Vesuvius).

In addition, various activities related to the progress of industrialization, especially in nineteenth century Britain, offered rich sources of materials for would-be geologists. The construction of railway lines, canals, and excavations of clay, rock, slate, tin, copper, as well as deep coal mines, provided opportunities to view strata and collect useful rock and fossil materials. Some individuals were becoming closely interested in fossilized materials and rock formations revealed by quarrying, when tunnels were being carved through rocky hillsides, as well as in the channels for canals dug along valley-floors. These were mainly curious, 'scientifically minded', amateurs but also more practical men employed in construction and surveying. Appropriate then that the first geological, indeed the first specialized scientific, society was founded in Britain in 1807.

The navy of Britain, and those of other industrializing nations, had been surveying coasts and landmasses across the world from the early eighteenth century. The three voyages led by the navigator James Cook (1768-1771) saw a range of discoveries of previously unknown territories (if long 'known' to their often numerous indigenous peoples) and the drafting of the first modern map of the Pacific Ocean. A bit later on the voyage of HMS Beagle (1831-39) was a mapping and survey project, as well as providing a seminal experience for the young Charles Darwin. The Beagle was sent to complete a survey of the coastline of South America that had been started (1826-30) by a previous expedition.

But the voyage of HMS Challenger (already noted), beginning in 1872, was a more significant step in the foundation of the sciences of geology and oceanography. The Challenger was launched in 1858 as an 18 gun corvette (it was a sailing ship with auxiliary steam power) and was converted - guns removed - into a state of the art floating scientific expedition ship. It carried biologists, chemists, physicists and surveyors, in one of the first multidisciplinary expeditions. Along with and a range of scientific instruments, a well-equipped chemistry laboratory for the chemists and physicists, and an equally well-equipped natural history laboratory for the dissecting and preserving work of the biologists. For the these and the surveyors there was a range of below surface and sea-floor sampling tools, measuring equipment, trawls nets, along with 144 miles of sounding line with which to plumb, and begin to map, the depths.

Over a four year voyage the Challenger steered a zig-zag course as it circumnavigated the globe, visiting every continent including

Antartica. In March 1875 the Challenger was in the North Pacific Ocean and had let out five miles of sounding line into the Mariana Trench (about 11 km deep) but still without reaching the ocean floor. It would not be until 1960 that August Piccard accompanied by Lt Don Walsh would descend in his bathyscope 'Trieste' to the bottom of the Trench, where they found evidence of marine life (new species of flatfish and shrimp).

Throughout the nineteenth century evidence, both from geologists and biologists, accrued to challenge religious time-scales on the age of rocks and by implication the age of the Earth. It was becoming increasingly difficult for rationally minded people, informed by a growing interest in geology, to allow priority to the religious interpretations. A number of geologists (along with some paleontologists) had progressively suggested that the age of the Earth must be well beyond the bible-based calculation of about 6,000 years And a few of these scientists considered that for a significant part of this time the Earth was devoid of humankind.

The outstanding natural scientist, Georges Buffon had endeavoured to retain some sense of biblical interpretation as he managed to extend the assumed age of the Earth to 75,000 years, Cuvier (1812) had suggested thousands of centuries, Marcel de Serres (1838) noted millions of years, and around the same time William Buckland raised the perspective with 'millions and millions' of years. By the century's end it was clear that the Earth was much older than had been assumed and just how old was still being hotly debated.

The identification of radioactive isotopes, initially by Henri Becquerel in 1896 then in the work of Pierre and Marie Curie, led to more accurate work on ageing the Earth and also offered a means for geologists (geophysicists) to improve the methods used to determine the age of rocks and, as the techniques were refined, the accuracy of this method improved significantly. During the twentieth century a number of isotopic elements including: uranium 238 and 235, potassium 40, thorium 235, rubidium 87, and carbon 14 (this last present in all living organisms), were used to date rocks and fossilized materials laid down at different times. The radiometric method takes advantage of the fact that each of these radioactive isotopes decay to another isotope at a regular rate e.g. uranium 238 decays to lead 207 and carbon 14 decays to the more stable forms of carbon 12 or 13. The decay-rate is measured using a standard of 'half-life'; which is the length of time taken for 50% of an amount of an isotope to decay to a new isotopic form. So, in any sample of material the different amount each of the original and decayed-to isotopes allows its age to be calculated e.g. the half-life of uranium 238 is a very long 4.51 billion years and that of carbon 14 a quite short 5,730 years, with the others noted above falling between these two. These isotopic materials serve as silent radiometric clocks revealing the Earth's geological timeline.

Increasing geological evidence supported an accumulating sense of vast time-scales for the Earth's existence. And a focus on strata obviously laid down in sequence, led to attempts to provide periods of geological time. Between Aruino naming the 'Tertiary' in 1768 to Henry Shaler Williams naming the 'Pennsylvanian' in 1891 over 20 more periods were suggested. It was from a mixture of most of these, with ongoing arguments and adjustments about appropriate boundaries, that today's timescales emerged; even if still today there is a continuing debate about boundaries; understandable given the vast timescales and the nature of the evidence being considered. The relative uncertainty of periods and boundaries between them has at least been partially resolved by the 'International Union of Geological Science' (established 1961) with its 'International Geological Correlation Program' which began in 1967.

A fairly conventional table of geological periods would have four significant periods:

The Precambrian (by far the longest) from about 4.6 b.y.b.p. to 570 m.y.b.p.- the Paleozoic 570 to 225 m.y.b.p – the Mesozoic 225 to 65 m.y.b.p. - the Cenozoic from 65 m.y.b.p to the present. With each of these being sub-divided and sub-sub-divided into shorter periods. Such a scheme of division, when presented graphically, allows an accessible understanding of geological ages and periods.

The work of the geologist Eduard Suess (1831-1914) could fairly be said to span the 19th/20th century. His classic book was first published in separate volumes (3 vols. 1883-88) and translated into English in 1904-24 as 'The Face of the Earth'. It has been considered to be a fair synthesis of nineteenth century geology. Suess was interested in the historically records and in the current movements in the Earth's crust; covering records of ancient earthquakes, of volcanic eruptions, and of biblical floods. Suess suggested that the history of the Earth was a history of its cooling. He identified two main types of movements or tensions: tangential, where the pressure was lateral to the surface, producing such features as mountain chains and the folding beds of rocks, and radial movements, or tensions, that produced pressures perpendicular to surface (vertical in general direction) causing the Earth's crust to collapse. Suess also made suggestions in relation to the materials lying below the Earth's crust, noting that at the center (the 'nife') of which was a thick (5,000 km) core of nickel and iron, and overlying this a layer (the 'sima') made of silica and magnesium (approx 1,500 km thick) and this topped by a thin crust (the 'sal') made up of silica and aluminum.

In 1903 Johan Herman Lie Vogt, in a landmark book 'The Molten Silicate Solution', set out the results of his examination of the chemical composition of igneous rock and it would be via analysis of chemical composition that was to be the main way in which rocks were categorized. At the beginning of the twentieth century rocks had been characterized into three main different types that are still broadly accepted today.

Firstly, there are igneous rocks, making up about 65% of the Earth's rocks, resulting as the molten magma (extruded by volcanic activity) formed within the heat and pressure of active volcanoes cools and solidifies, these include: basalt, obsidian, granite. Then there are sedimentary rocks, about 8% of rocks, usually found in age-related layers derived from consolidation of mineral and organic materials, that has mainly been precipitated from solutions, organic matter, and eroded fragments of older types of rock (sediments) includes: gravels, sands, and types of limestone. Lastly there are metamorphic rocks, 27% of rocks, formed when igneous or sedimentary materials are exposed to quite extreme conditions of heat and\or pressure, examples being: marble, slate, and quartz.

The most fossil-rich of these being the sedimentary rocks e.g. the White Cliffs of Dover in south-east Britain.[20] At any given period in the past the whole surface of the Earth would have been mainly composed of igneous rocks. Progressively overlying areas of this would be sedimentary and metamorphic rocks – the depths, distribution, and exposure, of all three types being determined by local environmental conditions, including uplift, and the various forces of erosion. The surface floor of the ocean would become composed mainly of sedimentary material (now about 5 km deep) and beneath this a much greater depth of igneous (mainly basalt) rock;

---

[20] These cliffs are primarily composed of the skeletal remains of plantonic green algae – coccolithophores.

underlying both of these would be metamorphic rocks. With about 90% of the Earth's crust made up of oxygen, silicon, iron, calcium, aluminum, potassium, magnesium, sodium.

It was quite early in the century that a dramatically new theory was suggested on the movement of landmasses, an idea that was to become one of the century's fundamental theoretical advances. In the early decades of the century it had been assumed by mainstream geologists that the presence of identical species (living and extinct) on continents now separated by oceans could be explained by the presence of narrow strips of land that had once made links between them. This, the 'Landbridge Theory', was supported by authorities such as Lord Kelvin, who also assumed that the material beneath the Earth's crust was solid. Then, in January 1912, Alfred Wegener (a meteorologist) proposed a radically new theory set out in a paper presented at a meeting of the Geological Society of Frankfurt, and published in 1915. The delay in translation into English (1922) and French (1936) being perhaps an indication of the reluctance of the scientific community to take his theory seriously. Wegener suggested that at a long time in the past today's continents formed one large landmass, a super-continent he named Pangea (Greek for 'all lands'). But that around 200 million years ago this supercontinent began to split and form the landmasses that would make up the continents we are now familiar with; these then slowly 'drifted' apart. Gondwana was the name given to the landmass making up the southern hemisphere including: South America, India, Antarctica, Australia, Africa, and most of Middle East. And Laurasia being the name given to the landmass making up the northern hemisphere, including: North America, Europe and north and central Asia including Siberia and China.

It was as early as 1910, according to Wegener himself, that he first began to notice the 'fit' between continental coastlines and was becoming aware of paleontological evidence of a past connection between South America and Africa. The possible matching of these coastlines had been noted by Francis Bacon much earlier and in the mid nineteenth century by Antonio Snider-Pellegrino; and the possibility of moving continents by Frank Taylor in 1908. But it was Wegener (in a number of revised editions of his book 'The Origin of the Continents and Oceans') who more closely identified a shoreline fit, and offered a range of fossil evidence to support his idea. Evidence such as that of that a living species of garden snail to be found in both the Americas and Europe. To explain the drifting apart of continents Wegener made the fairly obvious suggestion that if landmasses can rise and fall (which was a generally accepted view amongst geologists) then the material below the whole surface would surely be viscous and hence could provide a medium upon which drift would have taken place.

Even though there was observational evidence related to the possible fit of the edges of continents, and accumulating evidence of similar types of extinct and living flora and fauna, it was to take nearly fifty years until this theory was accepted. Indeed Michael Brooks (2011) notes a symposium organized by the American Association of Petroleum Geologists in 1929 specifically convened to undertake a critical assessment (in fact to denounce it) of the drift theory. And also Harold Jeffrey's 1936 'mainstream' textbook in which he notes Wegener's theory as '....an impossible hypothesis.'

But drift theory had its supporters, including Alex du Toit, who drew attention to persuasive evidence related to rock formations between continents set out in his 1937 book 'Our Wandering Continents'. Another influential supporter was Arthur Holmes a respected geologist who, in a 1929 address to the Edinburgh Geological Society, outlined his own ideas on continental drift. Holmes suggested a possible source of the force that had the power to generate drift. The inability to identify a convincing source of power had been considered to be a significant weakness with Wegener's suggestion. Holmes suggested that the heat generated by radioactivity within subterranean material caused convection currents to rise to the surface and that, on reaching the Earth's crust, the currents then split to run in opposite directions under the surface. Even in the face of a predominantly unsympathetic geological community Holmes held to his view and in his 'Principles of Physical Geography', first published in 1944, he included a whole chapter on continental drift. The high quality of explanation, along with the obvious excellence of Holmes as a geologist that was apparent throughout the book, prepared readers from a new generation of geology students to be receptive to the final chapter in which they encountered the continental drift theory.

In the late 1960s researchers based at Cambridge University used an early type of computer modeling to compare the coastlines of continents and found that, when they compared the now submerged continental shelves, an even closer fit could be identified. Very similar types of sedimentary material suggest that South America was joined to Africa until about 200 m.y.b.p. The way in which the drift theory was managed by the geological community could be judged to be a model example of Thomas Kuhn's theory of scientific progress in the stage leading up to a 'revolutionary' change (a paradigm-shift) – simply, of initially strong resistance being gradually eroded by increasing evidence to a point where the new theory becomes accepted. If further evidence had been required to support continental drift theory then this was available from the accumulating fossil record.

Sampling bores made into the sedimentary material that has accumulated on the ocean floor shows that the pattern of spread of the fossilized shells of rapidly evolving planktonic organisms (especially the single-celled foraminiferans and radiolarians) is consistent with sea-floor spreading and so continental movement (R.Forty, 2005). Given the range of convincing evidence made available by the mid 1960s, Wegener's theory of continental drift became widely accepted by the scientific community

The theory of the separation of continents by 'drift' was to receive further convincing scientific support by a consideration of the phenomenon of the shifting magnetic polarity of the Earth. It was known by early Greek and Chinese writers that the Earth has a strong magnetic field but it was William Gilbert who in the seventeenth century suggested that the Earth has the characteristics of a very large bar magnet. Then, in the twentieth century, it was suggested that the Earth's magnetic field was subject to changing, to 'reversing'. But it was improvements in measuring instruments (especially the electric magnetometer) that, from the 1950s, allowed detailed patterning of the changing magnetic pole phenomenon to be clearly mapped. Most rocks contain small amounts of iron and during the process of rock formation these tiny particles of iron settle into a position oriented to the Earth's magnetic poles. Careful measurement of the orientation of the magnetic field in any sample of rock can allow the latitude at which the rock was first formed to be determined. The alignment of the patterning of geomagnetism, as outlined for each continent, offered quite conclusive evidence that the continents would once have been joined.

Early explanations for this phenomenon identified differential rotation of the mantle and crust relative to the Earth's core, which then (via impact on electrons) acts as if a natural dynamo, so generating a magnetic field. More recently the focus has been on the suggestion of undulations in the boundary between the Earth's core and its mantle.

An understanding of the phenomenon of changes in the Earth's magnetic field also gave support to the theory of sea-floor spreading (suggested by Harry Hess in 1960) – the process that involves the uplift of new materials from fissures located deep in the world's oceans. The material rises to the ocean floor at ridges located at great depths. One of the most active being the Mid Atlantic Ridge (with similar ridge systems in the other oceans) and geologists sampling rocks at various distances from this ridge found alternating bands of magnetic patterning, suggesting the production of rock settling during periods of different magnetic orientations. In addition, the samples taken from rocks at a similar distance each side of the ridge show the same magnetic orientation. So the sea-floor spreading theory suggests that magma (viscous material) rises from the Earth's mantle and, as it cools, it solidifies into a large section of basalt, with the iron particles becoming aligned according to the then current magnetic polarity of the Earth. Then, as more magma rises, the pressure splits the older solid basalt, with the new magna then cooling and magnetizing in line with the then current magnetic polarity of the Earth. This sea-floor spreading is a process taking place over millions of years and so encompassing numerous changes in the periods of magnetic change. For Richard Forty: 'The rocks pointed their time-frozen finger at the pole as it was at the moment of their magnetization.' (Fortey, 2005, p168).

It was the Cambridge-based geologist John Tuzo Wilson who in 1965 combined the ideas of continental drift and sea-floor spreading in his suggestion that the Earth's crust is made up of large mobile 'plates'. In 1967 this idea was developed by geophysicists who proposed that when plates rub against each other there is some 'under-thrusting' as plates slide alongside each other; making for geologically unstable 'fault-lines' such as the San Andreas Fault in western USA. With the edge of one plate slipping beneath the edge of the other, resulting in a deep trench being formed along the line of contact. This is also suggested as contributing to providing the uplift creating the world's mountain chains, both on the continents and beneath the oceans. The outcome of the new material being produced at ocean ridges (magma extruded from the asthenosphere into the lithosphere) is to an extent balanced by the material that is pushed down beneath the crust by the pressure of plates colliding ('under-thrusting').

As an aspect of anti-submarine warfare the allied nations engaged in the second world-war had undertaken the magnetic mapping of extensive sections of the ocean floor. Providing oceanographers and geologists of the 1960s with some initial information as well as a method by with they could progress this work. This program identified a pattern of huge interlocking tectonic plates, in very slow but constant movement over the semi-molten material on which they rested (M.Brooks, 2011).

By the second half of the twentieth century there was a general consensus accepting the theory of plate tectonics – a theory high in both ecological validity (material evidence) and also wide-ranging in explanatory power. An Earth with a lithosphere (crust) in continuous movement, having tectonic plates moving at a rate of 1-7 centimeters per year away from the ocean ridges. It was the UK's Open University that, in 1971, became the first university in the world to run a science foundation course featuring the theory of plate tectonics.

The Earth is undergoing continuous geological processes generating the powerful forces that have created and shaped landscapes for over 4.5 billion years. Forces that we can see operating, most obviously in earthquake activity, volcanoes, and via satellite-based detection of continental movement, going on beneath our feet. From 1972 the 'Landsat Program, jointly managed by NASA and the US Geological Society, has been generating a series of satellite images providing geologists with a stream of data that has facilitated the detailed mapping of the global geological structure. Including information on possible sources of natural energy, and data that allows the fairly accurate tracking of the movement of the tectonic plates.

It has been known for around 200 years that the strength of gravity can vary according to the geological structure being tested. And over the next century and a half the use of pendulum-based devices gave way to mechanical, then electronic, gravimeters. The material making up the Earth varies in terms of density, and this in turn gives rise to variations in the gravitational force. A section of dense rock such as basalt measures stronger in gravitational force than would a deep pool of oil beneath the surface.

Satellites circling the Earth have produced a range of data on this gravitational variation, from Seasat in 1978 to the later multi-national project Gravity Field and Steady-State Ocean Gravitation Explorer (GOCE - built by the European Space Agency launched March 2009 project ended Nov. 2013). These were equipped with highly sensitive measuring instruments as they orbited the Earth at a distance of about 250 km and similar projects will continue to contribute to refining the gravitational map of the Earth. This data, in addition to other evidence provided by seismic data and laboratory-based research, should be able to confirm the primary driving forces for geological processes. Similar to the landmasses, the ocean floor has also been mapped and shown to be a subterranean 'land' of mountain ranges, deep ridges, undulating plateaus, and vast sea-scapes as topographically interesting as the land itself.

Since the Earth was first formed (about 4.5 b.y.b.p) it has been the site of geological processes generated by high pressure, convection forces, and heat (thermodynamics). If a pressure/temperature measuring instrument could travel towards the centre of the Earth the pressure and temperature would be seen to gradually increase to reach levels of possibly 2000 kilobars of pressure and 3,000c of temperature at the inner metallic core. The forces and processes of geological activities have become evermore amenable to reproduction in laboratory based studies. And laboratory-based study has been a feature of the science of geology throughout the twentieth century, as a supplement to the more field-based and theoretical work - the Geological Laboratory of the Carnegie Institute in Washington D.C. established as early as 1904, being one of the first. Towards the end of the century pressures of about 40 kilobars and temperatures up to 2,000 centigrade had been achieved but, by early in the twenty-first century pressures of 1,000 kilobars plus were been obtained in laboratory settings. Making possible the useful reproduction of conditions that pertain deep below the Earth's surface. Tiny samples of material subjected to these conditions within a laboratory can be 'frozen' in the transformed state and then studied by the use of technically sophisticated spectrometers.

The use of the petrographic microscope and X-ray diffraction equipment, has allowed access to the crystalline structure of minerals held within rocks and the laboratory-based study has been further aided, from about the middle of the century, by the use of the electron microscope.

It had long been noted that shock waves follow earthquakes and, by the end of the nineteenth century, sensitive instruments had been devised for recording these waves - 'seismographs'. Their use soon enabled two main types of shock wave, P (primary) and S (secondary), to be identified. The first seismometer was developed in Italy in 1875, although the Chinese had been using tremor-detecting devises possibly as much as 2,000 years earlier than this. The first 'at-a-distance' recording of an earthquake was made in Germany, detecting shockwaves of an earthquake originating in Japan in 1889. By 1892 forty recording stations had been establish across the world. The value of a wider use for seismology in investigating the material composition below the Earth's surface became clear when, in 1906, Richard Oldham used seismology to discover the Earth's dense central core. Then in 1936 Inge Lehman was to discover an inner core even deeper down.

As well as Oldham and Lehman, notable early twentieth century seismologists also included Beno Gutenberg and Andrija Mohorovcic. Mohorovicic analyzed the data from an earthquake occurring in Croatia in 1909. The varying speed of radiation (propagation) from the source allowed Mohorovicic to detect a significant change in material at a certain depth. This change marked the boundary between the crust and the mantle and has come to be known as the Mohorovicic discontinuity.

Seismology has been a key tool for investigating the constitution of the Earth beneath its surface. Simply put, pressure waves radiating from a source can pass through different materials at different rates. These rates being dependant on any wave's frequency and the: temperature, density, pressure, and the elemental composition of the material being passed through. Consequently, once the seismic characteristics of any material is known (from sets of tests already made) then the passage of a wave through new material can be plotted and the constitution of the materials passed through can, to a useful extent, be revealed.

By the 1950s improved seismometers were highly sensitive to the detection of seismic pressure waves and a number of different types of artificial 'shocks', such as those made using echo sounders, explosives, and other types of percussive signals. The sensitivity of the detection and recording instruments continued to improve during the second half of the twentieth century. In 1935 the 'Richter Scale' (ML) had been introduced to measure the strength of any pressure waves caused by dramatic geological events such as: earthquakes, volcanic eruption, nuclear explosive testing, and the impact of large meteorites. Although continuing to be used in more popular settings, this scale was displaced for most scientific use from the 1970s by the more sophisticated 'Moment Magnitude Scale' (Mw), a scale introduced by Hiro Kanamori (in 1977).

The potential of seismology was clear from the earliest time of its being used to study the Earth's constitution. In about 1959, this potential received a further impetus with the introduction of the 'World-wide Standardized Seismic Network' (now incorporated into IRIS – a consortium of universities funded by the US National Science Foundation) and the establishment of 150 seismic recording sites at locations across the globe. In addition, research groups now have access to portable recording devices and between these and the fixed sites the Earth's 'vibrational' activity is pretty much covered and we have a fairly efficient means to look deep into the Earth.

Data from the global network of recording stations has offered further support for the connected theories of continental drift and plate tectonics. Such data collection, processing, and presentation, has been significantly enhanced by the use of computer-based technology and the ability to significantly amplify the signals associated with the passage of pressure waves. From the 1990s a technique using a number of seismic recording stations, linked but located apart from each other, has allowed three dimensional images of the Earth's interior to be outlined; the technique of 'seismic tomography'. And information from IRIS, and other sources of seismic data, is now streamed continuously to publically accessible internet web-sites.

We now know that the planet is covered with a relatively thin Crust, with this and the Mantle, making up the Lithosphere, Asthenosphere, and Mesosphere. Then, at about 2,900 km down we would find the Outer Core made of molten metal then, just over 5000 km down there is the solid metallic Inner Core. The Inner Core and Outer Core are mainly composed of ion and nickel. These five sections of the Earth's interior make up the five 'layers'. In relation to composition, just three sections are usually noted: Crust, Mantle, and Core.

Seismology can give indirect information of what lies below the Earth's surface and reasonable informed conjectures can be made in interpreting this data. But to obtain direct evidence samples of material need to be examined. The most obvious way to obtain this is to drill into the crust, an activity that has been going on mostly just with commercial drilling, for gas and oil, throughout the century. But this has only been at relatively shallow depths, and in locations identified more by commercial potential rather than by possible scientific value. Somewhat more scientifically motivated initiatives have included the Russian 'Super-deep Borehole on the Kola Peninsula in northern Russia which has been able to sample material 12.5 km down. Another deep borehole sunk on Maui Island in Hawai (for the US Geological Survey) has been able to drill down to 6 km and has retrieved rocky material about 700,000 years old

The sub-ocean drilling 'Ocean Drilling Project', undertaken from 1969 in the purpose-built ship 'Glomar Challenger', has traversed the world's oceans drilling deep into the ocean floor and feeding masses of data to geologists; a new ship, the JOIDES Resolution came into service in the late twentieth century. And in the second decade of the twenty-first century the Japanese are constructing a ship that will allow scientists to obtain samples from a depth of 7 km beneath the ocean floor. Enhancing the means to probe further into the Earth's crust. The conventional map of the ocean floor, designed by Bruce Heezen and Marie Thorp, was loosely informed by the knowledge of the undersea world circa 1967, made more appealing by the exercise of a significant degree of imagination, is being progressively improved upon as it is regularly up-dated.

The ocean terrains are being mapped in evermore detail. Mapping initially made by the use of sounding lines has been developed into a precise approach made possible by the introduction of sonar. Sonar (similar to echolocation) proved itself as a technology when used in 1925 to reveal the mid-Atlantic ridge, it was developed further during WWII for anti-submarine warfare then, from about the 1980s it value was enhanced with the innovation of 'multi-beam' high resolution geosonar. Towards the end of the century digital scanning, aided by computer-based technologies (and of course the now ubiquitous GPS location system), provided another enhancement to the tool-chest available to geologists. Divers have also contributed to an understanding of the geology of continental shelves and the shallower areas of the ocean floor. The development of bathescopes (both manned and remote controlled) and submarines have provided first-hand, observational information on the ocean depths. An early journey into the deep was undertaken by Felix Vening Meinez in 1920, during which he discovered the Java Trench. Two more recent deep dives being those of August Picard who (as noted above), in 1960, descended to the bottom of the Challenger Deep, and of Jeff

Bezos, the founder of 'Amazon', who journeyed down to the Mariana Trench (36,201 BSL) circa March 2012.

A more recent 'Challenger' expedition has led to a significant advance in the understanding what lies beneath the oceans of the Earth. Along with a range of other research activities, this expedition has also been attempting to understand the movements of deep ocean currents and their impact on the flora and fauna with which the seas teem (if much less so than they did 50 years ago).

As the century progressed, the role of the oceans in absorbing CO^2 was studied. As was its capacity to absorb the millions of tons of polluting materials such: as human and animal waste, oil-spills, and oil continuously leaking from thousands of sunken ships, a range of heavy metal waste, plastic waste, a range of toxins, including arsenic and the runoff of of insecticides, herbicides, and fertilizers used in agriculture; all relentlessly being 'disposed' of. Tons and tons of pollutants are poured into the rivers and seas each day, flowing to the seas to degrade the oceans whose limited capacity to absorb this potent mix is increasingly becoming obvious.

Thanks to the investigative and synthesizing work of 20th/21st century geologists, we now know that we live on an Earth formed some 4,550 billion years ago from an accumulation of materials brought together by the forces of gravity and centrifuge, with most of the surface now being composed of rocky materials that can be identified as continuously forming from possibly as early as 4.0 billion years ago. The Earth has a circumference at the equator of 40,075 km, a diameter at the equator of 12,756 km and a diameter taken between the north and south poles of 12,713 km. It has a surface area of 510,072,000 km^2. With the land making up 29% and the oceans making up 71% of this. The deepest point in its oceans is about 11 km. The highest point of land probably being Mt Everest at 8,848 metres above sea level, the lowest on land probably the Dead Sea (Israel/Jordan) at 390 metres below sea level. The total mass of the planet is approximately 5.9736 x 10^{24} kg. (6,600,000,000,000,000,000,000,000 tons).

This blue/green planet spins on its axis at 1000 miles per hour (rotational speed) as it orbits the Sun at an average distance of 150 million km, at a rate of 108,000 km per hr. At its centre is an 1,270 km depth of solid metallic material under immense pressure, at a temperature of about 3000^0 C at the outer core, rising to perhaps as much as $5,000^0$ C at its very center. Pressures and temperatures that decrease as we move towards the surface where the crust temperature is about 375 degrees centigrade. The distance between the surface and the very centre being 6,400 km. These statistics are but the quantitative expression of our planet, circumscribing (signaling) an array of complex data sets that have been, and are being, generated by geologists.

New material is being continuously extruded to the surface via deep ocean ridges, as old material is subducted at continental margins. The continents creep - 'float' - on a series of tectonic plates; possibly as many as 12 (8 large and a number of smaller ones). The motive power causing their movement comes mainly from powerful convection currents involved in a process that keeps millions of tons of material in constant, if generally very very slow, motion.

Along with the broad-based advance of science, geology in the twentieth century has expanded the boundaries of available information and knowledge of the material (geological) aspects of the Earth's constitution and how its current form, - mountains ranges, rift valleys, sweeping plateaus, lakes, rivers, and oceans - came to be shaped. But there is still much to be learned, not least the movement of deep currents and heat within the oceans and the inter-connectedness of the atmosphere with oceans and climate; and also the more recently identified phenomena of hotspots, flood basalts, mantle plumes, and impact events (especially of meteorites). The search for economically exploitable sources of oil, gas, coal, economical valued metals and minerals, continues at a pace, with NGO and publically employed geologists, metrologists, and oceanographers, at the forefront of more disinterested research. The scientific understanding of the material Earth parallels other branches of science as geology also adapts technological innovation to generate ever more information, and so potentially evermore explanatory power.

Twentieth Century Social Science

Throughout the development of civil life – of civilization – a wide range of observations and related reflections on individual and social behaviour have been recorded, if often selectively. Consideration has been given to human behaviour, both in terms of behaviours related to individual and group interaction and also to the design and function of tribal cultural arrangements become civil social institutions – structures of governance, economic arrangements, and the range of other social institutions involved in civil life. These would include those involving: education, healthcare, legal systems, sports, religions, artistic and other cultural practices, warfare, and a wide range of formal and informal organizations - that have been socially constructed, most often being shaped by processes intended to fulfill specific (functional) aims.

How key social institutions are constructed offer constraints on how these institutions can develop but, simply if crudely described, the factors that are most influential in shaping institutions are those designed to primarily protect and further the interests of the more powerful groups in any society. Institutions are socially constructed usually within quite complex social processes. But it is those more able to deploy situationally relevant combinations of political, economic, and social power, who are able to determine both the wider framework within which any social institution operates and more specifically, they can directly shape the ways in which the institutions function. If perhaps the form taken by some social institutions and some wider social outcomes have at times been unpredictable outcomes of more intentional social activity.

The nineteenth century had seen the development of a broad approach to understanding human behaviour (individual and collective) as this became systematized into the social sciences including: economics, anthropology, sociology, psychology, political studies, and also history; as the latter progressed to describing social phenomena beyond idealistic descriptions of the lives and loves of royalty and the aristocracy and the machinations involved in pursuing their egotistic political aspirations.

The intellectual environment within which this systemization took place was created yes, by sharing with the natural sciences a basic curiosity about 'the world' but also by such influences as: the rationalizing impetus provided by the Enlightenment, by the imperatives arising from revolutionary political aspirations, and by progressive changes taking place in the economic and social conditions arising from industrial developments. The social sciences developed throughout subsequent centuries as a 'scientific method' that has been progressively improved. The key element that highlights the value of the application of the scientific method was the link between its application to any phenomenon and the outcome in terms of explanatory power. As information gained from experiment, observation, personal biographies, surveys, documentary evidence, and guided reflection, formed narratives that made sense of the behavior of people and groups engaged in social worlds. More broadly, both the natural and social sciences gained increasing intellectual credibility, and in turn social recognition, as their contributions to knowledge enabled, or at least facilitated, technological developments to be used in such areas as industry, transport, warfare, education, medicine, what became the range of communication and leisure activities; and more specifically for the social sciences in informing social policy.

The social sciences endeavoured to use a method designed during the 16/17/18 centuries, further honed during the nineteenth and improved again and deployed more effectively, with fruitful if at times contested outcomes, during the twentieth.

The debate on the legitimacy of the scientific status of the social sciences has ranged methodologically widely and philosophically at some depth. This subjection to scrutiny, whilst at times resented, whilst at times felt as a distraction, has resulted in practitioners being made acutely aware of the standards required to collect and analyze data if the findings of research and any theorizing are to be of value and able to gain the respect of fellow social scientists.

To what extent (if any) can a reductionist approach, as pioneered in the natural sciences, be applied to social science research? Would this be legitimate providing that the limitations of wrenching some social phenomenon - as a process, interaction or institution - out of its wider social (including historical) context are acknowledged?

The noted sociologist, Max Weber (1864 – 1920), drew an essential difference between the natural and the social sciences by suggesting a distinction due to 'meaning'. The view that the individuals involved in any situation interpret and act according to perspectives infused with meanings. Whilst the variability and personal nature of meaning is of central importance when we consider the claims to objectivity of all the sciences the meaning-context with which the social sciences operate does seem to require particular consideration and careful design of method. The behavior of matter in the material world is more easily characterized in terms of regularities and predictability, rather than meaning, the analysis of its characteristics can produce 'laws' of material behaviours. We, as practitioners, do infer meaning to phenomena of the natural world, whereas meanings emerge from social behavior as outcomes of the interaction between social scientists and those being studied. Glibly, we study the material world from the outside whereas we study human individual and social behaviours from the inside, with meanings emerging when we move from one to the other. We are constituted by the material world but we constitute the social world; in an obvious sense, the material makes us whereas we construct and are constructed by the social. Perhaps it is the case that we 'interpret' the social world and 'discover' the material world, but each of these would be about emphasis rather that exclusivity.

Many of the nineteenth century pioneers of the social sciences were motivated by Enlightenment optimism in the application of reason, and most were imbued with confidence in the idea that knowledge of the social world could be produced by the application of a positivistic scientific methodology. This sense of optimism was to dissipate somewhat in the twentieth century as the complexity involved with understanding both individual and social behaviors became clearer.

The complexity of the subject-matter of social sciences presents as a significant challenge but the importance of understanding our social words is a necessity, not least to help us to understand the impact of the various factors constituting the complexity. As a general observation, the social sciences are almost always theorizing at the boundaries of knowledge where data is characterized by uncertainty, complexity, and where historical context often needs to be taken into account.

The reductionist approach, characteristic of positivism, when applied to subject-matter of the social sciences can be problematic. It can be productive in fairly limited circumstances but such is the continuously changing patterning of social behaviors (its inherent creative dynamism) that any findings gained at the micro level extrapolated to macro level theorizing needs to be carefully managed, and no doubt hedged round with methodological reservations.

Towards the end of the nineteenth century Wilhelm Dilthey attempted to outline the type of methodological approach best suited for the social sciences. He drew attention to key differences in subject-matter between the natural and the social sciences and emphasized the need for the subject-matter of the still newly emerging social sciences to be informed by an awareness of the methods of the natural sciences but to seek to design a methodological approach best suited to interpreting the unique individuality of social experiences. Whilst requiring the social sciences to be precise and to produce systematic knowledge, Dilthey wanted to avoid the restrictive methodological frameworks that types of positivism can impose on social phenomena.

According to H.P.Rickman (1979, p147) for Dilthey 'The subject-matter, therefore influences the methods suitable for its investigation and this makes distinctive methods for the social sciences necessary'. Dilthey was an early advocate of the need for an interdisciplinary approach in order to overcome the somewhat arbitrary categorization of the various branches of the social sciences: for example, if we wish to understand what a certain person's identity is we would need to bring to bear insights from psychology, sociology, and history, in order to overcome the partial focus of adopting a single disciplinary approach.

Sociologists working in the social constructivist tradition assert that there are affective social contexts within which all knowledge is produced and that any particular social context is an outcome of various social processes. That it is more useful to view knowledge as being processes of production rather than acts of discovery. Social scientists can identify patterns of behaviours and can offer predictions on outcomes that have some degree of reliability and are a functionally framed outcome of behavourial complexity. My somewhat artificial separation between natural and social sciences is not meant to mask the fact that at a deeper level of analysis the search for all robust, sound, knowledge, from a wide range of scientific perspectives, is but a central aspect of an on-going world-view based upon a shared commitment to 'truth' and to the progressive accumulation of knowledge that should be the primary motivator of those engaged in the search.

So, to some extent the traditional more positivistic methods of data collection and analysis can be adapted to facilitate access to any of the phenomena focused on as the subject-matter of social sciences. And would significantly contribute to the value (soundness) of the knowledge gained; and of course the 'test' of peer review is a valuable check on the reliability of all types of research project. All of the sciences should also be subject to public scrutiny, not only in relation to the nexus of funding and research selection but also in relation to methods.

In general, it is much easier for the natural sciences to 'control' the experimental situation than for the social sciences. You can more easily design an experiment to test a prediction about the behaviour of subatomic particles, of a newly synthesized material, or the process of a sun's life ending, at least within certain bounded conditions. To the point that one can be reasonably confident that correlations and possible causes can be identified, reliable predictions can be made, and that any such experimental finding would have strong ecological validity. Whereas an experiment to determine the intelligence of various ethnic groups, the causes of delinquency, voting intentions, or the impact of an education policy, is fraught with difficulties of establishing correlations, causes, and so of ecological validity. Not least, we would need to a start with a discussion of what we mean by 'intelligence', by defining 'ethnic group' or 'delinquency', of determining the 'honesty' of potential voters, or of what we accept to indicate 'learning'.

Some natural scientists seeking to claim some pure form (authority of) of 'objectivity' for their endeavours might suggest that their work is about the 'is' of phenomena – just seeking to explain what 'is' – but some might argue that the social sciences lack the possibility of objectivity due to the necessary influence of the 'ought'. The closeness to ethical issues of the subject-matter of the social sciences mean that both the 'is' and the 'ought' are central tensions, but perhaps they should also be so for the natural sciences; at least in as far as the natural sciences are also social practices, and so have social responsibilities; all the sciences are at one level social practices and should not all social practices have concomitant social responsibilities?

The conception is that the natural sciences can generally pursue their activities focusing on sub-atomic particles, chemical compounds, organic molecules, geological strata, genetics, synthetic materials, etc. as if within an arc of ethical neutrality. But when we draw back from a focus on the immediacy of the 'day-to-day' work of the natural sciences the extent of the social construction of these scientific activities can be revealed; when, that is, personal ambition, political ideology, sub-conscious bias, prejudice, economic interests and similar, are drawn into view. Set between the practitioners and institutions of all of the sciences and their subject-matter there is a terrain redolent with the potential for a range of personal and social influences to appear. Ideally, it bears upon the individual scientist as practitioner to strive for 'objectivity' in the collection and analysis of data and it bears upon this individual as an ethical being to choose to investigate phenomena in ways and with objectives that enhance the human condition.

Ernest Nagel considers that it is possible in the social sciences to make a distinction between factual and value judgments – and considers that social scientists need to '...strive to give expression to this distinction in their work'. Steven Lukes goes further, suggesting that the social sciences are redolent of moral and political positions and that different interpretations are made of the same empirical evidence. That there is an underdetermined aspect of theories allowing different (sometimes conflicting) theories to be compatible with the same data. For Lukes '....observations of social phenomena, involving agents', desires, beliefs, and actions, always and ineradicably involves interpretation on the part of the observer.' Both the Nagel and Lukes quotes taken from their essays reproduced in 'Society and the Social Sciences' (1981, ed. David Potter).

Whereas the basic observation-based method of data collection in the natural sciences is overwhelmingly passively descriptive, that of the social sciences is overwhelmingly actively interpretive so more liable to bias.

Nagel, in 1961, noted four possible sources of bias impacting on claims to objectivity in the social sciences:

1) the selection of problems.
2) the determination of the contents of conclusions.
3) the identification of facts, and
4) the assessment of evidence

He goes on to examine each of these in turn, and optimistically concludes that these potential difficulties '.....provide no compelling reasons for the claim that an ethically neutral social science is inherently impossible.' (Potter ed.1981, p406)

I have taught (for the UK's Open University) a broad-based, multi-disciplinary, foundation course in social science and at times throughout any presentation I would initiate a discussion on the concept of 'objectivity', and what this ambition means for science in general and social science in particular. As an aspect of this ongoing debate I would be presenting the case that, as social scientists we should 'ideally' do all that we reasonable can to choose research areas that are socially important to human life. Areas we consider that we could defend on this basis to ourselves and to others. Then go on to collect and analyze data in line with a carefully thought through methodological approach, and present findings in a way that is as free from our own personal interpretations, or those necessarily favouring any institution or interest group, as possible.

A clear value of the peer review process is the role it can play in identifying bias as well as sloppy methods. So, tending towards a pragmatic approach, I am immediately suggesting a selection bias, but that once selected we should endeavour to collect, analyze, and re-present data, as objectively as possible. I think that we do understand what we mean by objective, even if only as an ideal we have discussed in detail, as under-graduate students and post-grad researchers, to be aspired too. I accept that my advice might seem naïve to more radical social scientists but for students I feel we should be highlighting ethical issues, and together discussing possible sources of bias. But as we actually undertaken research to then aspire to the ideal of 'objectivity' – I would argue that this approach would enable research findings to be robust and that, being so, would allow a certain level of authority to any findings. An authority that can underpin any political policy orientated argument for positive change.

Throughout any research process we should include moments of reflection, with a preparedness to revise an approach and adjust methods at appropriate stages. Without inducing some sclerotic impact as an outcome of over-analysis, there should be a process of reflexive scrutiny and flexibility to the extent of the potential for contestation of any aspect of the area/issue being considered. This intermixing of objective method (accepeted only as an 'ideal') and social responsibility would provide the scientific authority and the social legitimacy that I assume both natural and social scientists would aspire to achieve.

There is no disinterested science, there are only sciences as social activities, with all the associated implications. The world is brimming with inequity, unfairness, abuse of human rights and of power; such that it can be difficult to bear. But, as natural and social scientists we do have a commitment to the general idea (ideals) of there being some intellectual terrain of 'scientific truth'. Not as some ultimate determinant/standard of 'what is', or 'how things are'. Rather as a ground for evaluating the production of knowledge that gains truth-value by such features as this being subjected to scrutiny of peers and by deploying various ways of assessing the robustness of any research or and/or experimental findings.

Accepting that for social scientists even basic sociological theoretical approaches - In sociology there are: marxism, critical theory, functionalism, structuralism, and some others. In psychology there are: psychoanalysis, neuropsychology, cognitive psychology, evolutionary psychology, and some others - have foundational assumptions that can influence the chosen field of study and also determine the appropriate method for progressing knowledge production.

I accept that morally my justificatory ground can be open to valid challenge; not least as the justification of a comfortably situated individual reflecting on a world characterized by gross inequalities, exploitations, and for many, circumstances of downright misery. But the challenge of this debate is one I would willingly engage in – and indeed some members of each new cohort of students usually put me to the sword during discussion of the ethical/moral issues and on the subjective/objective ideals debate.

A debate that allows me to gain a level of confidence that we are involved in the training of new generations of mostly scientifically aware and morally concerned practitioners in social science.

Such is the complex dynamics of our world that rational debate and perspective-sharing is invariably mutually beneficial, especially for scientists prepared to consider their work as an improvable social activity. I reach my own view (and use it as advice for students) aware that I cannot claim to be value free as a social scientist, only one who strives to minimize its influence in the actual production of knowledge and to maximize its influence in the wider context of research subject selection and in the social contextualization of any findings. Similar to all scientists, I carry a socially rooted 'arc of intentionality' (Merleau Ponty, trans. 1962) as a pre-condition of my work.

If we step back and consider the vast accumulation of theorizing and of research undertaken by tens of thousands of social scientists, working across the globe, over the twentieth and early decades of the twenty-first centuries, we might have reservations about many theoretical claims and research findings. And be disappointed how many findings have been used (subject to political or corporate distortion) in the design of social policy – especially in more contested areas such as those involving intelligence, social mobility, governance, impact of media, gender issues, deviancy, criminality, etc. – but overall we have seen a significant accumulation of useful knowledge about our social world and also the increasing refinement of the theoretical frameworks and the methodological tools for progressing this work.

How this social knowledge is used – in a context of the truism that governments and corporate business seeks to influence and control populations – is a serious question, one intimately connected to the legitimacy of any government and their commitment to human rights and other freedoms. In order to gain some level of public legitimacy, the social sciences need to ensure that they do not serve as what Franz Fanon noted as another of '......the "bewilderers" separating the exploited from those in power.' (Fanon, 1961, p29)

The focus here will be on twentieth century sociology, medicine, and psychology. Just three branches of the social sciences but, if space had allowed, I could easily have included anthropology, economics, social geography, and history. Whilst it is, at least initially, useful to distinguish each of the natural sciences in terms of levels of analysis, the social sciences are more mutually interdependent. Any individual's psychological constitution is formed and she/he experiences awareness within a social context, with economic structures and cultural practices constructed during historic processes – the individual, the social, the cultural, the economic, and the historical are interwoven. Accepting the limitations, I hope that considering just three branches of the social sciences will at least offer some understanding of how social science has been developing.

One obvious characteristic of this development has been the changing involvement of women. From about the second half of the twentieth century the increasing contribution that women social scientists have been able to make has significantly enhanced the range and depth of the understanding of social behaviors and the role of social institutions. But even given the barriers against women academics (and possibly in the case of George Eliot and Charlotte Bronte, socially perceptive novelists) prior to recent times, some women could be identified as early social scientists.

Sociology (the 'Science of Society')

As we have seen (Chapt.6), the foundations of the twentieth century social sciences had been significantly developed during the nineteenth century and by 1900 sociology could be identified as a specialist branch of these. Apart from the accelerating rate of collection and analysis of statistical information, along with the widening scope of theorizing, there was the symbolism of sociology attaining other conventional academic milestones, including the introduction of sociology courses in higher education, with the USA leading the way and France and Britain close behind, as in:

1876 – John Hopkins University: sociology introduced in courses offered in the dept. of history and politics.

1889 – University of Kansas, new dept of history and sociology and first course, 'Elements of Sociology', offered in 1890.

1890 – Colby College and Bryn Mar College offer courses in sociology

1892 – University of Chicago – Albion Small established the first specifically sociology department in the world – soon followed by similar at Universities of Columbia, Michigan, Yale, Brown and by the end of the century almost all American higher education institutions were offering courses in sociology –

1895 – 'American Journal of Sociology' first published (University of Chicago) about the same time as similar journals began to be published in some other economically developed countries.

1895 – First European Sociology course presented by Emile Durkheim at University of Bordeaux

1896 – 'L' Annee Sociologique' pub. In France

1904 - First British Sociology dept. established at London School of Economics.

1905 – American Sociological Association formed – professional body

As the new century begins we see sociology emerging into an 'institutional age': equipped with a range of basic methods then considered to be appropriate for its subject matter, publications for sharing knowledge and offering a wider forum for 'peer review' the sharing ideas and research findings, a training regime for practitioners, a body of accumulated knowledge, commercial links (of public and private sponsorship guiding research and the utilization of insights gained); indeed all of the formal and informal institutions of a science. As with any social science, sociology generated a range of fairly broad theoretical approaches.

Sociology's central focus is on the institutions and social settings where individuals interact within their social worlds – we each have a self-identity (simplistically, ourselves 'looking out') and a social-identity (simplistically, society 'looking in') and sociology considers the social terrain where these interact.

Amongst the most substantial sociologists at the turn of the century Emile Durkheim (1858-1917) and Max Weber (1864-1920) in Europe stood out but, given his impact on twentieth century social science, it would be misleading to exclude Karl Marx as being one of the foundational figures of twentieth century sociology when considered as a social scientist rather than as a political polemicist.

David Emile Durkheim was born and grew to adulthood in the town of Épinal in north-eastern France. Following a fairly conventional French education, and early employment in teaching, he took a year's leave of absence in 1895/6 to travel to Germany in order to learn more about experimental psychology, especially that being undertaken by Wilhelm Wundt. He also took a keen interest in anthropology, with its focus on the social structures and cultural practices of diverse types of society. He came to the view that we can make a distinction between individual and collective consciousness; each governed by its own 'laws' (regularities).With the laws of one type of consciousness not being applicable to the other. For Durkheim, the study of society could be based on a scientific approach using methods similar to those used in the natural sciences.

Durkheim drew attention to the impact of modernization on the industrializing nations. How increasing population density (in the rapidly growing towns and cities) and ever-increasing occupational specialization were two key factors in disrupting social cohesion. A social cohesion that he assessed to be breaking down, with signs of this being the weakening of moral norms and the loss of any shared objectives. With a key symptom of this being the (increasing) presence of individuals exhibiting an excess of a form of social separation he termed 'anomie'. Characterized by individuals excessively focused on their own self-interests and lacking any sense of social responsibility, disconnected from traditional norms and values.

Just to remind ourselves and develop some key aspects of Durkheim's (and next Weber's) approach already noted in the Chapt. 6 section on social science.

Durkheim introduced the concept of 'social facts' as a collective representation (and probably a result of the influence of his positivism) for particular phenomena occurring within the social world that are external to any individual but which shape, constrain, and generally operate as a coercive form of power on the behaviour of individuals – marriage, laws, customs, religion, etc. could be, for Durkheim, social facts. New social facts can arise during the process of social interaction in which novel ideas emerge. A central task for social scientists was to identify the characteristics and social implications of any social facts – for Anthony Giddens: '...social facts are ways of thinking or feeling that are external to individuals and have their own reality outside of the lives and perceptions of individual people.' (Giddens, 2009, p14) Social facts can constrain individuals but we tend to comply, whilst generally assuming that we are in fact making choices for ourselves.

Durkheim was interested in the processes of social change and the concept of 'social fact' provided him with conceptual information in a form that could be used to enable description and analysis of any specific development – 'social facts' could assist in the identification of 'social laws'. For Durkheim, social facts, although independent of any individual, are produced within and by social environments. These social facts are independent of any individual and are rooted in the antecedent conditions of any particular society, but they do structure the collective consciousness; so are important for constituting the social framework within which all individuals live.

Stepping back, we see that Durkheim's work ranged fairly widely but that it shows a close interest in the impact of modernization on society's formal institutions and on social unity, religion, work and economic life, crime, and cultural diversity. He set out an evolutionary view of social change. With some more primitive societies being characterized by a 'mechanical solidarity', evolving into more complex societies characterized by 'organic unity'. In the former, individuals are mostly self-sustaining in terms of their day to day occupations, but they do maintain close personal ties with family, clan, and tribe. These social collectives have a strong sense of cultural traditions including a collective consciousness with shared cultural practices infused with religious beliefs. More complex societies involve larger populations, with more specialized occupations. Such developments that encourage more instrumental relationships beyond the family and other types of quite narrow groupings. Perhaps rather perversely, these societies have a strong sense of unity fostered by the instrumental interdependency of individuals, if with a more defused sense of collective consciousness. This organic solidarity is characterized by societies that are based upon relationships founded on economic commitments and on occupational specialization, for Anthony Giddens on Durkheim: 'Relationships of economic reciprocity and mutual dependency came to replace shared beliefs in creating social consensus.' (Giddens, 1971, p15)

Although he accepted Hebert Spencer's analogy of any society being like a living organism Durkheim mostly eschewed the many, then popular, biological metaphors being applied to social behaviour. For Durkheim 'organic unity' was more than the sum of its constitutive parts, he suggested that society is bound together by ideas rather than material relationships. He was sympathetic to the view of the German sociologist Albert E. Schaffle, distinguishing between an individual consciousness and a collective conscious made up of shared (normative) values that, for Durkheim, operate as a key aspect of social control. But a control liable to break down during times of significant social change.

In his classic study of suicide (1897) – the suicide rate being a clear 'social fact' - Durkheim drew attention to an ongoing concern with the impact of industrialization on the individual. How the rapid changes characteristic of industrialization degraded the organic unity upon which social cohesion had depended. He identified four different types of suicide: anomie, egoistic, altruistic, fatalistic, each of which in a different way identifies social disconnection. The suicide study was pioneering in the sense that it made use of statistical methods in order to understand a sociological problem. As well as identifying statistical patterns of suicides he also highlighted shared social characteristics – marital status including age at marriage and presence or absence of children, gender, seasonal time of suicide, age, rural/urban setting, religion. His study highlighted the key role of social integration (religious, political, familial) of any society and the relationship of this to suicide rates.

Although Durkheim is generally considered to be an early functionalist – his own version of this would place a greater emphasis on processes of social change and the individual rather than on some more static idea of social unity. The more functionalist aspects of Durkheim's approach was taken further by many twentieth century sociologists including Talcott Parsons, Robert K. Merton, and much later by Anthony Giddens.

Functionalism was going to become a primary approach taken by sociologists, and indeed anthropology in the hands of anthropologists such as A.R.Radcliffe-Brown and Bronislaw Malinowski.

Functionalism can be loosely defined as being: '......based on the recognition of the interrelatedness of the parts of society in bonds so thoroughly interpenetrating that a change in any single element would tend to produce "general disturbance in the whole'"(Encyclopedia Britannica, 14th edition. Vol.16, p995)

In contrast to Marx, Durkheim was more an academic social scientist, observing and commenting on social behaviour rather than being directly involved with the social conditions being analyzed. Up to about the beginning of WWI he expressed a general sympathy with moderate forms of socialism, if not ones (more revolutionary versions) explicitly critical of existing social systems. But the implications of his analysis, especially the social impact of modernization, invariably identified dysfunctional aspects of the industrializing nations. In terms of methodology, a reasonable case could be made for Durkheim being identified with taking a similar empirical/positivist approach to the study of society as Saint-Simon and August Comte (both, like Durkheim, French), building on foundations laid by them.

Durkheim was appointed lecturer at the University of Bordeaux in 1887 and taught the first European-based course in sociology (1895), going on to establish the first university department of sociology. In1913 he was made professor of 'The Science of Education and Sociology' at the Sorbonne. His book 'Rules of the Sociological Method' (1895) was, in effect, a 'manifesto' of what sociology is and how it should be undertaken as a positivist science. He was also closely involved with the publication of 'L' Annee Sociologique' from 1896, an academic journal which, added to the 'American Journal of Sociology' (pub. 1894), were significant institutional markers of a science beginning to 'come-of-age'.

Max Weber (1864-1920) – Born in Erfurt, Germany before moving quite early on to Berlin, where he spent most of his childhood. He grew up in a quite controlling family situation which would probably have made at least some contribution to Weber's generally fragile emotional state. Following a fairly conventional middle class education in which he exhibited remarkable intellectual ability allied to academic application, and a year's compulsory military service, he moved easily into teaching. Becoming professor at Freiburg University, then moving on to a professorship at Heidelberg in 1896. He experienced a serious breakdown in mental health in his mid thirties, taking about five years before he could return to teaching and research. His gaining a generous financial inheritance in 1907, allowed him to become financially independent.

For the most part Weber thought that there was a distinction between the natural and the social sciences and this would imply the need for different methodological approaches for the branches of each. Although, even more so than Durkheim, Weber also placed an emphasis on the need for the social sciences (sociology) to strive for objectivity in method. This shared ambition is a central aspect of their determination to gain a level of intellectual authority similar to that allowed for the natural sciences.

Weber had wide ranging interests – politics, law, religion, economics, and sociology. His approach to methodology differed from both that of the conventional positivism and of the historicism that were the two prominent approaches of the time. He recognized the value of identifying factual truths but also the need to progress the search for understanding any social phenomenon being guided by values. Stanford Encyclopedia (Sept. 2012) quotes Weber as noting that '....the capacity to distinguish between empirical knowledge and value-judgments, and the fulfillment of the scientific duty to see factual truth as well as the practical duty to stand up for our own ideals constitute the program to which we wish to adhere with ever-increasing firmness.'

Weber accords a certain priority to individuals and their role in social change, given this, his wish to take an approach to the study of social phenomenon that incorporates subjective meaning (allied to objectivity of method) is understandable, indeed necessary.

His work in sociology reflected a keen interest in the process of industrialization - the economic and social relationships that were key features of a maturing industrialization process - and the impact of this on individuals. In order to understand the social outcomes of industrialization he also examined the roots of the process as these began to appear in parts of Europe during the seventeenth century. These included: the accumulation of surplus capital, individuals prepared to undertake risky investment for the prospect of rich rewards, technological innovation (especially in transport and agriculture), trading links and expanded market opportunities. Weber had a particular interest in how the capitalist dynamic that initiated and sustained industrialization came along only at a certain time and only in particular parts of Western Europe.

Weber identified a particular mindset arising from underlying religious beliefs that were novel to civil life and for him provided a further necessary condition for 'capitalist' funded industrialization. Industrialization required the investment of capital (the accumulation of surplus value - 'profit') and in the past the leading religions had tended to be antagonistic to the accumulation of capital by individual believers. If the Catholic Church did encourage 'gifts' to the glory of God, as embodied in the Church buildings and lifestyles of senior religious leaders. Traditionally, when capital had been accumulated (such as by merchants and a rentier class mainly composed of aristocrats) then this excess tended to be spent on conspicuous consumption (or military conflict) including prestigious monumental buildings, or bequeathed to the Church on death. Weber took a considerable interest in the world's major religions: Hinduism, Taoism, Buddhism, ancient Judaism and Christianity. In his book 'The Protestant Ethic and the Spirit of Capitalism' Weber related the accumulation of capital, and it use (investment) to build businesses, to central aspects of the belief system of Protestant (Calvinism) religion.

Of relevance to the sociological method, he identified a statistical correlation between entrepreneurial-ship and certain religious beliefs. A Calvinistic belief in predestination, of the fate of the sinner being determined even before birth, suggested that hell and damnation awaited most individuals on death. Weber suggested that this unbearable spiritual burden led to believers adopting an aesthetic approach to life in an attempt to mitigate the fate awaiting their mortal souls. To live lives dedicated to work, thrift, and religious devotion, in the hope of gaining spiritual salvation. So with this religious motivational background groups of Protestants (especially Calvinists) in England, Holland, and a bit later parts of Germany and France, were able to accrue the necessary capital, allied to an applied work ethic, facilitating investment in the technological innovations and adapting to the changing economic conditions that pertained in these countries during the 16th and early 17th centuries. Weber did not consider this 'Protestant ethic' as being the only cause of capitalism's development but did suggest this as being a key aspect of it during the early stages of industrialization.

The driving force of social change was for Weber the ideas and motivation of individuals. For him the process of modernity involving, increasing bureaucratization, alienation from work, and positivistic science, was an inevitable movement of change expressing the increasing rationalization of social institutions. Of fundamental concern with this process was the impact on traditional (unifying) cultural values, traditional forms of authority, and on the individual as a free agent.

Significant aspects of Weber's work were reactions to Marx. He was most obviously critical of Marx's over-emphasis on an historical-materialist interpretation of social change, and the focus on economic class to identify social stratification. Rather than this more deterministic basis for social change, Weber suggested that human motivation, ideas, and values, were more important factors directing transformation; that within certain limits individual are able to act freely. Weber tended to downplay the influence of the social structures external to individuals and highlighted the role of individuals engaged in a complex interplay of actions. So, given the focus on individual behaviours and their wider social implications, the 'meanings' diffused throughout these actions was, for Weber, a central focus for sociological study.

Weber also rejected the deterministic class definition based on relationship to the means of production (capital) and the conflictual polarization that this was said by Marx to give rise too. Whilst accepting that class is rooted in economic relationships ('market position'), for Weber, social stratification is a broader concept based on three central if overlapping elements: -a) *Social class*: the economic determination of whether a person is an employee, owner, rentier, etc. b) *Status*: which is related to social esteem (prestige) in which a person is held, often based on pre-capitalist social roles - so a relatively poorly paid 'vicar/priest' or relatively impoverished aristocrat, can have quite high social status – for modern post-industrial societies social status can be signalled by such things as: managerial-type employment positions, and high status patterns of consumption in housing, cars, clothes etc. – c) *Party*: affiliations to 'groups' such as, political parties, Trades Unions, nationalism, sports clubs, religions, etc. where a person's allegiance can be stronger to other group members than to her/his economic class. This broader, multidimensional, definition of class is one that has had most influence throughout the first half of the twentieth century until narrower class-based' categorizations also came to include patterns of personal consumption as determinants of identity, as in 'embourgeoisement'.

Another of Weber's sociological interests was the sources of power. He used the concept of an 'Ideal Type' in the analysis of power as well as in a range of other social areas. Ideal types rarely if ever actually exist, their being concepts that serve as 'models' with which to understand the social world; methodological 'tools' by which to compare actual types in relations of more or less similarity to the ideal. For his analysis of power he posited three 'ideal types' (categories) of authority: Traditional, Charismatic, and Rational-Legal. It being the last one that has become more common in relation to the sources of power in modern society, as it increasingly displaced more traditional forms of authority. The Rational-legal 'type' is suited to a industrial society characterised by sets of rules, laws, and other forms of regulation associated with central government, large organizations, and various manifestations of bureaucracy. Weber was concerned that this tendency towards evermore bureaucratic domination could reduce human freedom and even crush the human spirit. His borrowed the concept of "disenchantment" from the poet Friedrich Schiller and used it to represent the sense of loss caused by the displacement of religion and other forms of superstition by the rise of rationalism in general and of the sciences in particular – of traditional sources of spiritual sustenance by the processes of 'modernity'. Weber was a central figure in early German (indeed later on international) sociology and helped to establish the German Sociological Society in 1910

Karl Marx (1818-1883): Generally considered to be a polemical political economist is becoming more fairly assessed as also having made a significant contribution to twentieth century sociology. His language was clearer than most theoretical sociologists of the time; perhaps due to his having a wider audience in mind. His works do not contain the word 'sociology' but this is thought to be due more to his antipathy to the positivism that dominated sociology in the second half of the nineteenth century than to any particular wish to distance himself from the social implications of his more specific theories and of the research that he used to support these. Indeed, it was the social impact of economic relationships that became a central theoretical narrative of his (and his colleague Friedrich Engels) life's work.[21] Marx's grew up in Trier, a city in a strongly Catholic region of

---

[21] I would recommend Engel's own book 'The Condition of the Working Class in England', 1846, as an example of an early sociological text – if one reflecting the particular interpretive bias of the 24 years old politically aware author.

Germany. His parents were Jews who converted to Lutheranism, seemingly in his lawyer father Heinrich's professional interests. The Marx household was intellectually stimulating and politically favoured the radical liberal left. By his late teens Marx had lost whatever religious beliefs he might have had, and from early on he held quite radical political views. Leaving home at the age of seventeen he began undergraduate studies as the University of Bonn. Unhappy with his son's drinking, dueling, and general lack of academic application, Heinrich insisted that Karl move to Berlin University one year later.

Following his gaining a doctorate at the age of 23, Marx was soon working as a journalist for the left wing *Rheinische Zeitung* newspaper in Cologne, going on to become its successful editor. On the paper's suppression in March 1843 he moved first to Paris, then Brussels, back to Cologne, then Paris again (during the revolutionary year of 1848) before, in 1849, settling in London where he and his family would be based for the rest of his life.

Moses Hess (1812-75) was an early influence on Marx's intellectual (including political) development. Hess was a committed communist who aspired to the creation of an egalitarian society based on common ownership. Marx was less enthusiastic than Hess about the more limited aspirations of most communist writers of the time who were mostly intent on establishing small-scale utopian communities. He was more interested in mass society and the underlying conditions for, and impact of, industrialization. Coming to outline a theory of social development ('historical materialism') based on the centrality of the means of economic production. He identified four primary types of social conditions constituting an evolutionary series leading to capitalism, these being: primitive communism, ancient slave-based society, feudalism, capitalism. For Marx, each of these stages exhibit a distinct mode of the exploitation of man by man, with each mode being a form of economic adaptation. With the means of economic production, invariably controlled by ruling elites rather than religion or other cultural factors, being the central determinants in the design of social institutions and of any dominant ideologies.

Marx's methodological approach included the determined use of statistical information. Indeed one of the reasons given for his focusing on England rather than France or Germany was the more comprehensive nature of the statistical and other relevant empirical information (especially of living and working conditions) available for it. His most substantial work, *Das Capital,* awash with this type of data, is a detailed analysis of capitalist economics and occupational conditions underpinned by empirical information, all within a meta-theoretic insight encompassing the primacy of economic arrangements and a labour-theory of value (taken over, if modified, from Ricardo).

Capital is a text taking an historical perspective on sociological, as well as economic, developments.

Whilst not obviously interested in epistemological issues, other than assuming the primacy of material circumstances and the type of knowledge this generates, Marx contributed to the sociology of knowledge in his analysis of ideological superstructures operating to create and sustain any politically bounded society.

One fairly novel example of his sociological method was Marx's compilation of a questionnaire/survey (the 'Enquete Ouvriere') containing 101 questions designed to draw useful information from working people on most aspects of their working conditions; seeking direct information, as Marx put it, on '....the evils that endure'. This was a pioneering attempt to capture the direct experience of working-class life. In 1880 25,000 copies of the questionnaire were distributed to working class organizations across France. The questionnaire was in four sections covering: the ownership of their workplace, whether production was based on machine or hand power, working times, and a range of work-place conditions including sanitary arrangement, accidents, meal breaks, contractual arrangements, the extent of child employment, etc. Also included were questions about household income and necessary expenditure, questions about government support for employers, and government backed action against employees taking industrial action.

The two final questions are especially interesting:

Q100 asks *'What is the general physical, intellectual and moral condition of men and women workers employed in your trade?'* Clearly a first order sociological question even accepting the obvious potential for value-judgment.

Q101 the final question, asks for *'General comments'.* So a specific invitation to offer personal (qualitative) perspectives.

Marxist sociology is focused on: class formation and its potential for conflict, on a materialist interpretation of history, and on the primacy of economic arrangements for shaping social institutions and the dominant ideas (ideologies). Although early on he did frame the mode of economic production as a determining factor, towards the end his life he softened his position somewhat. His close colleague (and on-going financial supporter) Friedrich Engels had economic arrangements as being a determining factor, 'in the last instance', in economic and social relationships; as well as being an important formative influence on the very consciousness of individuals. Marx constructed what was in effect a clear intellectual challenge to social scientists – such were the political implications of his (historic-materialist) theoretical interpretation of social change, allied to his egalitarian ethics, that he could hardly be ignored. In terms of sociology as a science, the methodological weaknesses with Marx's theory are problems with empirical verification and the vagueness of much of the terminology, as well as a slight but noticeable shifting of emphasis between the influence of economic and other social factors.

A number of notable later twentieth century social scientists' integrated aspects of Marx's analysis of capitalism into their work. Including Antonio Gramsci, Jürgen Habermas, Louis Althusser, and Michel Foucault; who all contributed to re-interpreting Marxism (for Foucault more critically) in the context of twentieth century social and political developments into what is very broadly known as neo-Marxism; even accepting that this also encompasses political philosophy. Specific areas of interest for these post-modern sociologists and social philosophers have been: consumerism, gender issues, power, knowledge as a social product, crime, deviancy, mass media and communication, personal identity-alienation, and governance.

As a sociologist, Marx's influence extended throughout the twentieth century. His ideas underwent various forms of development in the hands of others, mostly providing a sense of realism to more intellectualist social theories. So clearly serving as a marker of theoretical difference, as a primary point of critical reference, initially to theorists such as Weber and Durkheim, then later on to most sociologists working outside of the critical tradition during the twentieth century. Social scientists associated with the influential Frankfurt School were influenced by some aspects of the work of Hegel, Weber, Freud, and some early existentialists, but even more so by Marxist ideas (see more on critical theorists and the Frankfurt School below).

The breadth of interests of these three foundational social scientists

(Durkheim, Weber and Marx) influenced their ability to assume meta-perspectives out of which came grand narratives infused with insights related to human social behavior and the tangible and intangible products - including processes and institutions - of social relationships. A 1998 survey of International Sociological Association (ISA) members highlighted the continued respect in which Weber, somewhat less so Durkheim and Marx, were held in Britain and the US. These three, whose insights into humankind's social circumstances had been at the forefront at the opening of the twentieth century, continued as a theoretical presence as the twenty-first century began.

During the twentieth century a number of clear, if often overlapping, differences in theoretical approach developed. These can be identified mainly by differences in: theoretical assumptions, research methods, analytic processes, as well as explanatory ambitions and predictions. The more notable of these being: Functionalism, Symbolic Interactionism, Ethnomethodology, Social Constructivism, Discourse Analysis, Marxism/Critical Theory. One more recently developed approach allows primacy to the concept of Globalization as a key factor that has affects and influences impacting at all levels of social life - from transnational corporations, to employment, to the mass media and the new forms of social media, to family life and relationships, and more obviously the phenomenon that is the internet. An approach focusing on the transnational flows of goods, people, and information: as well as on modes of mass communication.

The multiplicity of these approaches (as developed by sociologists), to what is ostensibly the same subject-matter, can fairly be considered as being at least partly due to the nature of the subject-matter itself; with its inherent complexity and being liable to varying interpretations. But common to these differing perspectives has been a shared commitment to seeking knowledge in a rational way, developing theoretical perspectives and employing experimental methods considered appropriate for understanding the social phenomenon being considered.

As with my consideration of the other sciences, here my intention is also modest, trying to offer just a sense of some of the theories available as I attempt to set the wider development of sociology within its 20th/21st century context.

The theoretical approach of Functionalism (or Structural

Functionalism as it came to be termed by the second quarter of the 20th century) came to be the dominant sociological paradigm up to the 1960s, and has continued to have at least a presence within sociology down to today. Comte, Spencer, and Durkheim, are generally credited with setting sociological endeavour within a framework that views society as a functioning whole composed of institutions (political, economic, legal, religious, educational, etc) and the contribution these make to maintaining any society. Spencer made the comparison between society and the human body – both viewed as organic wholes liable to dysfunction; assuming the healthy body and the social status quo as being synonymous. Functionalists view society as being a self-regulating system composed of interrelated sub-systems.

Talcott Parsons was instrumental in enhancing the popularity of a version of functionalism (Structural Functionalism) in the United States. Following undergraduate study in the US, Parsons spent a year at the LSE in England, moving on to gain his PhD at the University of Heidelberg, before returning to the United States and spending the bulk of his academic career at Harvard University; becoming President of the American Sociological Society in 1949. His two most significant books being 'The Structure of Social Action' 1937 and 'The Social System' 1951.

Parsons brought together functionalist ideas derived primarily from Durkheim, but also with insights from Weber and the economist Vilfredo Pareto. He outlined a form of structural functionalism based on interrelated 'action systems'. Action systems are social processes around which a boundary can be identified. They are processes that are composed of interrelated parts – possibly sub-systems - all operating in ways that sustain the whole within a wider social environment lying beyond the boundary. This approach was encapsulated in Parson's AGIL model that included four key functions necessary to maintain the integrity of any social system: Adaptive, Goal Attainment, Integrative, and Latent. With each of these having identifiable subsystems e.g. for Integrative function subsystems would include community level organizations and groups. Any particular action system based on this model could be a whole society or some sub-system within one of the four functions; subsystems such as religious, legal, family, political, economic, etc. Parsons was more a theoretician and a teacher than a researcher, with many of his students going on to become prominent sociologists.

Two of these students, Kingsley Davis and Wilbert E. Moore, made a significant contribution to structural-functional theory. These two being co-authors of the Davis-Moore hypothesis (initially presented in a 1945 paper), that was an attempt to explain social stratification within a structural-functional paradigm. They suggested that the position that a person occupies accrues power and prestige not due to an associated high income, but rather that the high income is due to their fulfilling a functionally important role, one requiring the sort of skills that are in short supply. So theirs is an attempt to rationalize (functionalize) income inequality. This form of justification for economic inequality as functionally necessary for social stability is liable to the same fatal, and obvious, criticism as the 'market value' alternative. In that both effectively ignore issues such as the power of individuals (and also social and occupational groups) in the marketplace; nepotism, corruption, and more generally of differential access to 'social capital', as factors in strongly influencing the form of social stratification in any society.

Although sympathetic to structural functionalism, Robert Merton (also a student of Parsons) endeavored to address what came to be seen as problematic aspects of Parson's theory including the taken for granted functionality of social institutions, suggesting that there could be alternatives ways of meeting social needs than those that have developed in any particular society. Functionalism initially focused mainly on setting out the macro level of social phenomenon, tending to view the individual more as a passive operator fulfilling a wide range of socially defined roles within social structures and processes. Yes, individuals are important in contributing to the collective set of values and norms upon which a society is sustained, but these values and norms are inculcated during the socialization process; again suggesting a high level of passivity for any particular individual. If shared norms and values are the basis of the bonding that holds any society together (facilitating social solidarity), it was also suggested that some level of economic and social inequality (Durkheim's 'natural inequalities', and the Davis-Moore hypothesis noted above) was necessary for any 'healthy' society. Most functionalists view deviance and crime as dysfunctional phenomena, rather than as being inherent aspects of any civil society or signs of deeper structural problems.

Alvin W. Gouldner drew attention to the conservative (indeed bourgeoisie) ideological basis for the academic (and wider political) popularity of functionalism, noting that: 'Functional Sociology is a social theory consistent with the middle class's need for an ideological justification of its own social legitimacy......' (Gouldner, 1970, p126)

Kurt Lewin and other sociologists, contrary to the initial more macro focus of mainstream functionalism, applied the basic functionalist framework to micro level research; investigating social relationships in small groups, families, and military units.

From about the 1940s to the early 1960s functionalism came to dominate US sociology just as US sociology came to dominate the subject internationally by the middle of the twentieth century.

The influence of functionalism – an approach that had also been taken up by some psychologists and anthropologists - declined markedly from about the late 1960s when most forms of traditional authority were being challenged on the US campuses as well as on the city streets. Structural functionalism has been criticized as being mostly about description rather than analysis, and for assuming the 'normality' of prevailing institutions. It was also considered that functionalism lacked a credible defense again the charge of implicitly supporting political and economic conservatism (not least with its systemic patriarchy) and a seeming inability to adequately account for social conflict and radical social change.

More recently there has been something of a renewed, if modest, interest in functionalism, blending aspects of evolutionary theory with a consideration of the functional role of social processes within which cultural phenomenon and social structures are formed and maintained. Given that there is a certain, fairly obvious, value of at least including the function of social institutions that provide the wider context within which any social phenomenon being considered, it is hardly surprising that in some of today's sociology the influence of functionalism can still be quite easily traced.

Another approach to the study of society that developed in the intellectually fertile 'modernist' academic environment of the USA during the first half of the twentieth century was the approach known as 'Symbolic Interactionism' (SI). This approach allows priority to the type of qualitative (meaning-rich) data that had only low relevance for functionalism. A key figure in establishing symbolic interactionism as an approach to understanding human social behaviour was George Herbert Mead (1863-1931) who was based at the University of Chicago. Lenard Broom and Philip Selznick (1968,

4th ed.) apply the term 'social psychology' to Mead's approach, which I think reflects, and usefully highlights, Mead's focus on the individual in society.

Central to Mead's theoretical framework is the question: what comes first, the individual or society? A question of more relevance during a time when the 'contract theories' (such as those originating from Hobbes and Rousseau) still continued to underpin debates about an individual's relationship to society. Mead's answer came to be that individuals were in fact the products of social circumstances, rather than being, at least theoretically, voluntaristic participants. For Mead: 'The self.....is essentially a social structure, and it arises in social experience. After a self has arisen, it in a certain sense provides for itself its own social experiences, and so we can conceive of an absolutely solitary self. But it is impossible to conceive of a self arising outside of social experience' (Broom and Selznick, 1968, p94). Not surprisingly, given Mead's focus, understanding the socialization process of any society was a fundamental requirement for explaining the behaviour of individuals.

Mead suggested that from an early age the individual is exposed to pre-verbal communication, initially with primary carers. This pre-verbal communication is composed of facial and other bodily gestures, tone of voice (rather than syntax), and is based on copying the behaviour of others. For Mead, language develops out of (indeed is dependent on) this pre-verbal communication. The progressive acquisition of language then allows the formation and communication of ideas and so moves beyond more simple behaviours. As children undergo the process of socialization they increasingly become self-conscious (gaining a sense of an autonomous self) and aware of their own developing social selves. They learn to adapt to others, both the significant other and the generalized other as they acquire selfhood. But a self that is to a significant extent the outcome (indeed the product) of having absorbed the attitudes, values, and views of others.

These three concepts: 'significant other', 'generalized other' and 'selfhood', represent key interactive aspects of the socialization process of any society. The significant other is any person with whom the child has regular more meaningful contact and would include parents and other family members, teachers, priests. The generalized other is those involved with interactions beyond the child's family and close social world, allowing her to gain an understanding of how to play certain social roles. Or rather, how it is expected that an individual should behave in certain social situations, including an awareness of the aims of any group. These others whose ideas and attitudes are more likely to be internalized (accepted as credible), a process that seems to work cognitively and in a similar way to the later developed 'Theory of Mind', as seeing the behavior of others from their perspective and identifying oneself in this process.

Mead divided the self into two psychological perspectives, the 'I' and the 'Me. The 'me' being the social self, the internalized social self, the conformist, conventional, aspects - based on the awareness of social expectations, constraints and shared values - of our nature. The 'I' represents the creative, original, aspects of our identity, our unique personality. In any social situation an individual's behaviour is the outcome of an intermixing of the two. For Mead, in any primitive society the 'me' would predominate as the pressures to conform are strong and the punishment for non-conformity serious. But in industrially developed society, although a certain level of conformity is expected, more value is placed on innovation and creativity and so the balance between the 'me' and the 'I' can shift towards the expression of the 'I' (the self-expression).

John Dewey, William James, Charles H Coley, are also noted as being influential on early SI, if more from a psychological perspective, highlighting the internalization of interpersonal relationships and other social processes. With the sense of self being derived from this internalization, expressed in behavior as an individual endeavours to maintain this sense of self, possibly including a projected (desired) self-image.

Herbert Blumer, a student of Mead, in his book 'Symbolic Interactionism: perspectives and methods' (1969) – focused on one-to-one interactions and the meaning individuals derive from these and from other types of social interaction. Blumer attached the label of Symbolic Interaction to Mead's approach and he developed the idea of social interaction being based on interpretations made by participants; on the meaning each individual derives from the linguistic and other forms of symbolic behaviour of those they are interacting with, or more passively observing. The interpretation of meaning is the crucial element influencing behaviour and this meaning can be derived from a wide range of signs and symbols involved in communication. For Blumer (1969), meaning can be defined in terms of the action elicited (or expected) and its consequences, with the combined consequences of individual and collective social engagement being the creation of social reality. Taking outcomes into account to some extent reflects the influence of pragmatists such as John Dewey, William James, and William I. Thomas.

At the time that Blumer was working the behaviourist approach in psychology, an approach that did not feel the need to take meaning into account – only information in and behaviour out - was in the ascendancy in US social science and he directly contrasted symbolic interactionism with behaviourism. Blumer considered that he was working in a tradition established by social scientists/philosophers such as: George Herbert Mead, John Dewey, William James, Robert Park, Charles H. Cooley and Louis Wirth.

As a generalization: for symbolic interactionism people live in a reality redolent of symbols (a symbolic 'domain') and symbols are culturally derived social objects, having shared meanings that are created and maintained in processes of social interaction. The most common expression of this symbolism is in language, and also other more obvious aspects of interpersonal communication. The negotiated, interpretative, and internalizing dynamics of social processes support the notion of social reality as being a social product, with self, mind, social institutions and culture, being dependant on the symbolic interactions for the form (limits and potential) these take.

Both Mead and Blumer highlighted the importance of the inner conversation that people engage in, what Mead termed 'minding', involving the stage prior to responding during an interaction; the time of interpreting, and possibly negotiating, meaning from the communication on offer. The reality that human-beings experience is an internalized social reality – mediating the social and physical worlds beyond. Not surprisingly, the importance of social roles became central to this approach. This aspect of symbolic interactionism was building on Charles H. Cooley's concept of a 'Looking Glass Self', the self-reflexive ability of a person to see themselves as others see them - such a key feature of successful interaction –, of assimilating or adjusting to the perspectives of others and of negotiating shared views during an interaction. Ervine Goffman's 1959 book 'The Presentation of Self in Everyday Life' gives a clear outline of this aspect of symbolic interactionism. In his 'dramatological theory' Goffman introduces the idea of interactions as being about 'performances' within which people 'act out' social roles according to their own understanding (Mead's 'me') of what is expected. But performances that could include some improvisation, some space for original interpretation (Mead's 'I'). Goffman quotes W.James '....We may practically say that he [the anonymous individual] has as many different social selves as there are distinct *groups* of persons about whose opinion he cares. He generally shows a different side of himself to each of these different groups. Many a youth who is demure enough before his parents and teachers, swears and swaggers like a pirate among his 'tough' young friends...' (Goffman, 1959 reprint 1990, p57)

The negotiation and interpretation involved in interactive situations is heavily dependent on the ability of the people involved to take the perspective of others. For Blumer, meaning, as well as being a feature of objects, also inheres in action and the outcomes of this. 'The meaning of a thing resides in the action it elicits' [or the expectation of appropriate action] and '...in practice, the meanings of things are highly variable and depend on processes of interpretation and negotiation of the interactants' (Blumer, 1969). Interactive social processes whose outcomes are also dependant on the extent to which the individuals involved are able to take the perspective of others. For Blumer the 'symbolic' of SI is centered on language, and language is the primary source of meaning; later SI practitioners would also emphasize the meaning-rich symbolism of images. After spending some time reading about symbolic interactionism I want to suggest that for this approach meaning is both an inherent and an emergent property of interactions. But I do find 'meaning' a bit vague, something taken for granted by SI theorists. For Blumer meaning is '....defined in terms of actions and its consequences' (reflecting the influence of pragmatism) so is defined by what it is not and only by what its presence in any setting produces. This might be acceptable given the wider SI metaphysic, but it does suggest a lack of conceptual precision; if over the most difficult of concepts to precisely define.

Blumer offered a summary of SI in two propositions:
1) People act towards things based on the meaning these things have for them, and
2) These meanings are derived from social interactions and [are] modified through interpretation.' (Blumer, 1979)

An early and classic study, pioneering methods later identified with symbolic interactionism, was the William I. Thomas and Florian Znaniecki study *'The Polish Peasant in Europe and America'* (1918-

20) – a study focused on the experience of Polish immigrants to the US and to Germany – people exposed to rapid social change. The method of data collection was mainly qualitative, the core source being 754 letters sent from the home country to migrants and from migrants to the home country (correspondence from a range of social classes), and other personal documentary material. Material was also obtained from some newspapers of the time but in addition, information was also sought from potential immigrants as well as about groups that were formed in the US. A further, and rather novel source of information, was a semi-autobiographical personal history written by a young Pole (Wladek Wisznienski) who was paid by the authors to write his story. A key feature of the methodology was the 80-90 page presentation of their research in which Thomas and Znaeicki set out the theoretical framework for the approach taken by the study.

According to the 'International Encyclopedia of Marriage and Family' (2003), (accessed on-line Sept.2012).

'The study focused on the adjustments and transformations in personality and family patterns in the Polish peasant community, in the course of immigration to the United States during the early 1900s.'

The study shed light on the process of translating different sets of meaning-rich social environments. Of having to adapt to a new social and economic environment, using the understanding of symbolism and conceptual frameworks gained from socialization processes experienced in the old one. This study was a pioneer in showing the value of research focused on the interpretation of qualitative data in a scientific milieu that tended towards the quantifiable.

Studies taking an analytical approach, in line with the theoretical framework of symbolic interactionism, were undertaken throughout the century, especially by the Chicago and Iowa Schools from the 1930s (although the latter did also rely more on quantitative data than the former), and were generators of a wide range on information-rich research; led by Blumer at Chicago 1960s and Manford Kuhn at Iowa 1960s.

Research taking this theoretical approach has, amongst a range of interesting findings, been able to identify the various ways in which individuals seek to present themselves in a 'favourable light' and in defense of a 'valued identity'. Anthony Giddens ('Central Problems in Social Theory', 1979) is critical of this approach, suggesting that it places too much emphasis on normative conceptions of roles and their influence on behaviour. He allows much more scope for individuals themselves contributing to the interpretation of how any role should be played which, in turn, contributes to the evolving social construction of any role.

For Giddens '....*social systems are not constituted by roles but of (reproduced) practices:* and it is practices, not roles, which (via the duality of structure) have to be regarded as 'points of articulation' between actors and structures' (Giddens, 1979, p117).

For symbolic interactionism the 'acts' of interaction are the basic units of study. In social interactions individuals, very much as thinking subjects, are viewed as being active rather than passive participants (agents).

In any interactional situation the power and status of participants (the asymmetric nature of power and status strengths and disparities), relative to the situation itself, are important factors in influencing outcomes including how the central ideas are defined. For Marvin Scott and Stanford Lyman (1968): '...examination of the use of excuses, justifications, and accounts, speak to the intricacies, involved in the situational definitions. When power or status disparities exist, the dominant interactants' definition of the situation is likely to prevail.'

Also important (as initially highlighted by Mead) is the process of socialization pertaining in any society – the complex set of interlinked processes (especially those experienced during childhood) within which any individual understands roles, values, and other normative expectations inherent in any social environment.

During the past century Symbolic Interactionism provided a range of useful insights into human social behaviour – the emphasis placed on the 'mind' of the individual means a significant area of common ground with social psychology – especially fruitful has been the examination of how individuals and groups negotiate their adaptation to social change. Times when the interactional situation involves a range of novel symbols that require translation and adaptation too.

Throughout the 40s 50s and 60s symbolic interactionism served as a counterbalance to the more macro, quantitative, approach of varieties of structural functionalism and also of behavourist psychology. Naturalistic studies were a fundamental requirement for SI researchers (not surprising given the micro-level of its subject-matter) such as the studies undertaken in the 1980s which highlighted the value of positive parenting and reciprocity (acknowledging the child's perspective) during the socialization process.

Apart from Giddens's criticism noted above, there were also doubts about how robust the collecting and interpretation of mainly qualitative data could be and of a somewhat unsystematic approach to theorizing. Key strengths of SI is its focus on the fine-grained micro-world of social interactions, a perspective somewhat neglected prior to the 1950s, a weakness might perhaps be the translation of the implications of the personal interactive conditions to a macro-level of social institutions and relationships. Towards the end of the twentieth century SI (in the work of Sheldon Stryker and Manford H. Kuhn) attempted to apply methodological and theoretical insights of SI to the more structural aspects of society. Research using methods derived from SI has focused on a wide range of social issues including: criminology, sub-cultures, social movements, education, ethnic groups, and computer software design. Is it reasonable to suggest that SI was a theory, at least initially, responding to perceived inadequacies of positivism; especially the lack of attention to meaning-rich social environments.

The 'Society of the Study of Symbolic Interactionism' (SSSI) is the primary US-based professional organization for this approach, with its journal 'Symbolic Interaction'.

Ethno-methodology is generally viewed as an offshoot of symbolic interactionism with Harold Garfinkel as a leading proponent. Originally a student of Talcott Parsons at Harvard's Dept. of Social Relations, Garfinkel came to reject Parson's '....emphasis on conceptual formulation and theoretical generalization'. He moved to Kansas University (via Ohio State University) where one early piece of work was focused of how jurors undertake decision-making when confronted with complex and contested evidence, and the differing points of view of individual jurors. He found that jurors devised their own strategies for managing this, potentially quite tense, social situation. This, and similar studies, stimulated an interest in group-dynamics.

Garfinkel moved to UCLA in 1954 – going on to work with several generations of students and producing his well known book 'Studies in Ethnomethodology' (1967). Garfinkel's 'breaching' experimental methods were a novel way of using the problematic to reveal the normal, highlighting the ways that individuals devise to overcome problems by adopting strategies that have a certain practical sense.

He also undertook a range of studies related to gender, for example: Of Agnes a male-to-female transgender – this was a study rooted in the subject's personal engagement with the process of gender realignment, revealing the overt and covert strategies displayed by Agnes as she negotiated her changing self- and social- identity.

Garfinkel's corroboration with the younger Harvey Sacks produced their 1970 book 'On Formal Structures of Practical Action', in which they set out a more focused consideration of conversation.

Garfinkel developed this focus on discourse in studies of various types of natural scientists (including mathematicians and astronomers), and the ways in which they discuss their work. To reveal the something more that goes beyond the more formal workshop type of discussion to reveal the more creative, the 'embodied', practices that cannot be predicted. His 2002 book offers the central claim of ethnomethodology which is to go beyond the order of '...formal analytic theorizing as it exists in the field of sociology and elsewhere in the human sciences' (Maynard and Karnash, 1991). Garfinkel did not see ethnomethology as replacing more formal methods of analysis but rather of it enriching these. This approach focused on the study of concrete social situations. For ethnomethodology: '....there is a self-generating order in concrete activities, an order whose scientific appreciation depends upon neither prior description, nor empirical generalization, nor formal specification of variable elements and their analytic relations' and 'Members of society achieve this intelligible organization through the actual, coordinated, concerted, procedural behaviours or methods and practices.' (ibid)

Fieldwork plays a central role in this approach, one initially aimed at collecting extensive observation and interview notes along with both still and moving photographic images - moving to audio and video recording by the 1980s. Towards the end of the century the use of computers has enhanced the ability to process and store large amounts of qualitative (as well as quantitative) data. The internet provides access to a range of information considered to be amenable to the ethno-graphic approach, not least the wide range of public forums (dating agencies, hobbyists, and many other single-interest groups as well as social networks) – ethno-methodology combines insights of anthropology and sociology in designing research methods appropriate to study people in social settings. Especially ethnic groups: gypsies, indigenous peoples in North and South America and

Australasia, as well as culturally identifiable groups – punks, goths, triads, and mafias.

Many sociologists (early on Dilthey) have felt that overly positivistic theoretical structures and research methods fail to capture (allow access too) the meaning-rich perspectives and conditions of the finer intricacies of human social behaviour – especially in terms of motivations, as well as interpretative and communicative meanings and understandings – that give rise to the institutions, relationships, and other processes involved in the multiple social networks that constitute any society. The interconnected networks of influences, constraints, and opportunities, within which individuals express their behaviours. Symbolic interactionism and ethnomethodology place a significant value on qualitative data, not that they necessarily deny the value of quantitative data.

I would suppose that the philosophic position that best represents the wider background to these more 'humanistic' approaches would be phenomenology, the view that we should be led into analysis by the ways in which any phenomenon is presented to us; to endeavour to undertake a presuppositionless analysis of what we experience (free of any limiting preconceptions) – An approach echoing elements of philosophical methods taken by Edmund Husserl, Maurice Merleau-Ponty, and Alfred Schultz. Given the 'critical' background of the social scientists influenced by phenomenology, the analysis was hardly 'presuppositionless', but it was novel in many illuminating ways and was prepared to mine the complex depths of meaning; its generation, discovery, and role in communication. The published works show that it did and still does offer productive methodological means of gaining access to the less obvious forms of authority, the social body, culture, and other more structural influences impacting on individuals.

Often the interpretative process begins with the identification of some single social object (cultural artifact) or social process (judicial system, mass media, pedagogical practices) and, via a narrative following the social implications (including for some such as Michel Foucault the outlining of genealogical roots) of the phenomenon, to reveal underlying essences and at times the ideological context.

Amongst the other alternatives to positivist sociology was the approach known as Social Constructionism. This approach shares a number of theoretical assumptions with Symbolic Interactionism, especially with its criticisms of structural functionalists and positivistic sociology more generally. But here we have more of an emphasis on tracing the social roots and normative implications, of institutional as well social, phenomena. Rather than a focus on interpreting social interactions and what these might reveal about any society's socialization processes and more immediate social conditions. Social constructionists highlight a primary role for the forms of knowledge that pervade and shape social understanding (including norms and values) and the form that social institutions: religious, educational, the legal system, governance, etc. take.

A classic mid-century text stating the social constructionist position was the accessible 1966 book 'Social Construction of Reality' written by Peter Berger and Thomas Luckmann.

Social constructionism is based on the view that the social reality we inhabit has been 'constructed' as a result of, often complex, social processes involving human actions and the ways in which language is deployed. The form and function taken by social institutions are the outcome of these processes; 'Social constructs as by-products of countless human choices' (Wikipedia 'Social Constructionism' accessed Oct. 2012). As well as seeking to understand the impact social phenomena have on any social issue social constructivists also endeavor to identify the contributions that people in groups or as individuals make to the formation of their own understanding of the social world they inhabit. A key difference between social construction and the positivistic approaches is suggested by Jennifer Platt (2010) as being, that social construction: '......sees social 'facts' as socially constructed rather than having a real independent existence.'

Although rather vague when presented as a theoretical approach, we can better see the value of the social constructivist approach when we consider the sort of issues focused upon. For example: What do we understand by the concept of 'gender'? Are the characteristics and behaviours associated with men and women preordained (natural), and in some way essential markers of difference, or are they formed by the ways in which individuals and groups have contributed to shape (construct) the way each sex is to be understood in social contexts such a family life, education, the world of work, in art, the media, etc. etc. For social constructionism, the characteristics and behaviours (leading to the ways in which the sexes are 'managed' and expected to behave) are the products of processes that have been social constructed and have become embedded (often simply taken for granted) within any society's shared set of values, expectations, and ways of relating to each other; as reflected in any society's formal and informal institutions.

Obvious evidence to support the social constructivist view would be the ways in which different societies (social settings), and even different groups (and individuals) within any society, understand gender characteristics, social roles and expectations of behaviours differently. Gender-based expectations and behaviours can differ, their being culturally relative and rooted in social process such as those related to work, marriage and child-rearing, media representation and a range of discourses (projecting these) that translate the female and male biological conditions into the feminine and masculine social products. The bourgeoisie western cultures have traditionally framed the female as physically frail, submissive, lacking in intellectual ability, unsuited to the world of business. A set of stereotypic characteristics that have been shown to be perhaps related more to the masculine wish to control the sexuality of women than to any essential characteristics of females. And for the most part, the child-bearing role hovers over the whole debate as an uncomfortable reality; requiring compensatory measures if economic egalitarianism is to become a reality. We can see the wider, more interpretative, approach taken to the consideration of gender roles by social constructivists.

Another social phenomenon suited to social constructionist analysis would be racism, expressed as a set of expectations and behaviours directed at a particular group in any society. Perhaps more usefully conceptualized as 'racialization', highlighting the processes which underline the formation of these expectations and behaviours; as well as their institutional embodiment. Social constructivists would be seeking to identify (and possibly challenge) the social institutions and processes, generally rooted in past processes of construction and reinforcement, that are involved in the identification of the very idea of racially based differences. As well as the linguistic and social practices reinforcing racial stereotyping (and 'othering') and the, overt and covert, types of social discrimination that has been related to this.

'Race' has become (especially from the early nineteenth century) used to separate groups of humanbeings; to create difference due to ignorance (assumed racial superiority) or malign intent such as 'othering' as a strategy adopted by the more powerful when competing for resources. Its more modern justificatory interpretation does usually assume biological difference as well as historically the separate living of groups identified by cultural differences and/or skin colour. But there is no biological evidence to support the idea of racial difference in humans. For biologists, the concept of race would be applied to an interbreeding sub-set of a species - so high rate of gene exchange within the sub-set and no exchange beyond it. The outcome being that members of this sub-set would share a significantly greater proportion of alleles with each other than with members of wider species. An allele is the term for one form of a number of alternative forms of gene; identifying these is a crude way of identifying genetic differences.

There is no evidence that this has happened with any group of humans having the necessary level of genetic difference to qualify as being a biologically defined 'race', separate for other human groups. Indeed, if we think of 'races' as White Anglo-Saxon – Jewish (Semitic) – Oriental – Latino – Nordic – Germanic – Slavic – Bushman - African - Arab etc. or the equally synthetic but broader archaic racial notions of 'Caucasoid' 'Negroid' 'Mongoloid' 'Australoid' peoples – then we can see that the genetic differences within each of these 'races' are on average the same as the difference between 'races'. On average, white Christian people living in England are likely to be just as similar or different genetically from their white Christian neighbours as they are from their Black or Jewish neighbours. Just one implication being that: 'Any attempt to use skin colour as some biological marker of race therefore makes no sense' (F.Toates, ed. 1992, p22). Given the lack of biological support for the idea of human races, to understand the use of race in this or that narrative (group mythology) we would need to focus on the racialization process operating in each social context. This would include such aspects of the process as: historical development, the social positioning of the racialized subject, assumed characteristics and behaviours, and the motivation of those deploying a particular categorization.

In sum: Race is a social construction, an imagined mode of 'difference' but which then draws discriminatory power from the social operation of this separation.

Taken at face value i.e. without ontological assumptions about the relationship of subjectivities to reality, we can perhaps usefully rephrase the social constructionist approach and ask of each (problematic) social issue....... *to what extent* are the social representations, social processes and social institutions as well as any claims being made in various normative discourses....socially constructed? Those sociologists taking a social constructivist approach have tended to frame a range of social issues as being problematic so highlighting inequality, oppression, discrimination, and injustice, by deploying a theoretical framework based on an epistemology of social relativity - of knowledge the status of which is liable to negotiation and interpretation - and a clear emphasis on the fundamental importance of human agency in creating the social world. The complex interconnectedness of the institutions, processes, and relationships forming the social worlds within which we live.

Berger and Luckman suggested there was a need when conceiving a sociology of knowledge, to take into account 'man'(sic) in his history, man as presented in humanistic philosophy as well as the need for empirical considerations to be placed at the forefront of research into the 'object of inquiry' which is man. According to Berger and Luckman (1966, p211 the final paragraph of the book) 'This object is society as part of a human world, made by men, inhabited by men, and, in turn, making men, in an ongoing historical process, It is not the least fruit of humanistic sociology that it reawakens our wonder at this astonishing phenomenon.' They even go as far as closely, formatively, linking psychological status to the idea that '.......the social definitions of reality in general is itself socially defined.' (1966, p196).

Epistemologically, we can link the social constructivist starting point to the Duhem-Quine thesis of there being: '....no single privileged explanatory framework that is closest to the [any?] "things in themselves" – every theory has merit only in proportion to its explanatory power'. The primary assumptions of social constructivism assume that 'socially dysfunctional phenomena', are defined by relative judgments, and are intended and unintended products of human activity – two assumptions hinting at the potentially diffuse explanatory power of social constructionism.

An interesting counter view on the nature of social reality is the 1995 book 'The Construction of Social Reality' by the philosopher John R. Searle, in which he sets out the case for an objective (non-subjective) reality that can be shown to be the case by an analysis of how language is used. A reality that constrains subjective or other types of relative interpretations of social phenomena. Both Searle's and the earlier Berger and Luckman's books fall into the category of 'Sociology of Knowledge'. An area of theoretical meta-sociology injecting reflective stimulation into the science – exemplified by the significant contribution made by Karl Mannheim.

Another (more recent) approach that can be said to focus on meaning-rich data. Drawing on symbolic interactionism and the emerging approach of 'ethno-methodology' as these began to adopt what has been termed the 'narrative turn', with a closer focus on the ways in which language is used by agents involved in social situations. This comes within the theoretical approach known as Discourse Analysis. An approach that harks back to insights in the way language (or rather the 'symbol systems' used in communication) is used of people such as Ferdinand de Saussure, Benjamin Whorf, and Edward Sapir, and also drawing conceptual influences from the pragmaticism of Charles Peirce and the pragmatism of William James and John Dewey – and later those of Erving Goffman, Noam Chomsky, and Michael Foucault. So an eclectic set of influences that cross disciplinary boundaries in the social sciences.

More especially there is a clear overlap with psychology, but for sociology the analytical perspective taken to discourse is in relation to social rather than individual implications. Discourse analysis focuses on the meanings interwoven through and sustaining the ways in which we communicate. It has been defined as '…..a way of finding out how consequential bits of social life are done and [how] this knowledge is relevant to the process of building knowledge and theory in the social sciences' (M.Wetherall, S. Tayor and S.J.Yates, 2001, p2). The 'consequential bits of social life' can be varied encounters, and studies have included the analysis of communication shared in such setting as: internet chat room conversations, GP consultations with patients, political debates, children playing together, analysis of archive records of court proceedings, newspaper coverage of an issue, telephone calls to emergency services, etc. Basically, data can be sourced from any setting in which interpersonal communication is taking place.

The analytic focus is on language as used, the 'discourse'. Clearly, the range of potential interpretations of any set of discourse research data can be open-ended and any potential practical value can dissipate with overmuch application of the fine-grained analysis that this approach is liable to. Fortunately, leading practitioners in discourse analysis have progressively developed a body of methodology that has allowed the ways in which communication can be structured by such elements as: power relations, assumed tropes, shared values, negotiation strategies, motivations, the 'othering' of minorities, conflicting perspectives, etc and these as expressed within, often very influential, cultural settings. The best examples of discourse analysis have revealed often unnoticed threads of intention and implication that runs through communication situations. Methodological insights gained by discourse analysis have been taken up by later developments of the next theoretical approach to sociology that I now move on to.

A wide range of closely related theoretical approaches has been categorized as 'Critical Theory'. The intellectual roots of which were initially developed within the, at times, quite loose grouping of German academics that became known as the Frankfurt School. With philosophical influence of the German Idealism of Georg Hegel reinterpreted, initially by Marx then, from the 1930s, by social scientists such as Max Horkheimer, Theodore Adorno, then later Herbert Marcuse, and as the century past into its final quarter Jürgen Habermas.

The Frankfurt School was initially, 1923 onwards, based at the Institute for Social Research at the University of Frankfurt, then continued from 1933 in the USA by social scientists fleeing the uncomfortable intellectual (and anti-Semitic) environment created by the rise of Nazism. Leading members included Max Horkheimer, Leo Lowenthal, Herbert Marcuse, Walter Benjamin, Friedrich Pollock, Eric Fromm, and Theodore Adorno. A central interest for these was culture (especially mass culture), and the social implications of technological development in areas such as radio, T.V, photography, and cinema. Their approach was one of 'critical analysis'; assessing the impact of mass culture and mass communication on individuals and on social relationships. Highlighting the tendency, becoming apparent during the interwar period, of the uniformity of goods (commodification) and a more general drift towards cultural homogeneity. Classic texts such as Horkheimer and Adorno's 1948 book 'Dialectical Enlightenment' in which, according to Douglas Kellner: 'They argued that the system of cultural production dominated by film, radio broadcasting, newspapers, and magazines was controlled by advertising and commercial imperatives, and served to create subservience to the system of consumer capitalism'.

They noted the '....production of massified cultural products and homogenized subjectivities....' (Kellner, web-site accessed Sept. 2012). The approach taken by the Frankfurt School became known as Critical Theory, and it was an approach that was taken up by sociologists based at universities across much of the world. Continuing to make a useful contribution to the development of sociology into the twenty-first century.

A shared focus of this strand of sociological endeavour is to undertake acts of reflexive theorizing; to construct a hegemonic theory of praxis by combining a meta-theory informed by neo-Marxist ideas, with data gained from the empirical world. And so 'armed' with a practical conceptual framework designed to challenge the range of exploitation and oppression they have identified, related to economic inequality, as well as gender, racism and other forms of discrimination; to consumer society, and the misuse of power more generally. To offer an explanation encompassing historical origins, current economic conditions, elitist motivations, and other elements contributing to forming the conditions for exploitation and oppression.

The process of re-considering Marx's idea of collective consciousness (for Marx as it links to class identity) and its relevance for twentieth century capitalism initially prompted a keen interest in the mass media. But concern about the authenticity of democratic processes and the 'public sphere' has recently done more to shape the primary interest of critical theory. The development of consumer society, with economic and political priority being given to commercial rather than public interest, has for most critical theorists subverted the underlying interests of the public. In the classic text 'One-Dimensional Man' (1964) Marcuse distinguished between real human needs and false ones – and highlights the ways in which the advertising industry has developed various ways of seducing us into valuing (indeed admiring) the 'false' over the 'real'. Degrading human dignity and the scope for personal creativity as it promotes the reduction of humanness to our patterns of material consumption and the types of social identities based on this.

In a 1937 essay, Horkheimer gave a clear outline of critical theory, he noted that the aim of critical theory is '...to liberate human beings from the circumstances that enslave them.' An aim that would I am sure resonate with all critical theorists. With the priority this approach has given to liberation, it's hardly surprising that practitioners in the critical theory tradition have focused on social movements that raise issues, such as those linked to: gender, ethnicity, citizen rights, emancipation, sexuality, power - of oppression, exploitation and inequality.....and for Habermas, a focus on the social and political conditions necessary for genuine democratic governance based on the identification of differences between formal and substantive systems of democracy.

Critical theorists were antagonistic toward much of positivism, accusing it of being a 'new mythology', one that offered tacit support to conservative political perspectives and, by purposeful default, tended to inhibit radical alternatives. A more theoretically fundamental criticism was the objectification of 'social facts', and the lack of attention given to their formulation and interpretation. Although much of critical theory was also critical of Marxist forms of positivism which, whilst accepted as offering a radical alternative to liberal democracy, was seen to take a similarly narrow (orthodox) view compared to possible political arrangements better suited to allow the expression of liberation.

Most critical theorists recognize the value of empirical research but consider that this could only contribute to providing credible information if aligned to a thoroughgoing examination of assumptions underlying the approach taken to the analysis of any social issue. Positivism was criticized for constructing theories and employing methodologies that seek to objectify social facts rather than ones that allows for analysis grounded in actual social experience, and to undertake research that seeks to identify factors that condition this.

Georg Lukács and others endeavoured to identify the factors that inhibited Marx's predictions for revolutionary change - the assumed outcome of the critical conjunction of the contradictions inherent in capitalism. Factors that included: ideological accommodations made (if reluctantly) by ruling groups, populist adjustments to capitalism, 'assumed' democratization of governance, as well as economic concessions; what were in effect a range of collective 'coping mechanisms' (operated by both ruling elites and the masses, if taking different forms for each) serving to defer revolution. These critical theorists developed an interpretation of a Marxism aligned to the realities (including the persistence of inherent, if non-fatal, contradictions) of twentieth century welfare capitalism. Ben Agger focused on the position of workers noting that: '......the Frankfurt theorists believed that Marx underestimated the extent to which workers' (and others) false consciousness could be exploited to keep the social and economic system running smoothly.' That people: '.......internalize certain values and norms that induce them to participate effectively in the division of productive and reproductive labour'. (Agger,1991) So the internalization of hegemonic twentieth century capitalism inhibited workers from accepting the viability of radical alternatives and so (pragmatically) settling for ambitions of but relatively modest personal material betterment and some collective provision of key public services.

A broad aspiration expressed within critical theory was to unify the social sciences into forms of rationality that can best access the human experience via analysis and explanation. Forms of rationality that take into account the perspective of subjects. Critical theory aims to offer an explanatory framework based upon values (normative) for understanding social conditions along with proposals for radical social change.

As a general criticism of a critical analysis that frames social issues as problematic, there is lack of outlining what type of society would be necessary to resolve the problems they highlight; although some critical theorists have stayed true to the neo-Marxist aspirations of a socialist society.

Critical theorists mostly reject the technocratic perspective (specifically termed as 'technocratic' by Habermas 1971, 1973) taken by the positivistic social scientists and they take the view that researchers should not only be reflexive and flexible in relation to theoretical interpretation, but they should also see themselves as participants (not just as observers) in social life; gaining knowledge to be widely shared, not knowledge to be confined to narrow vested interests whether academic, political, or commercial.

For Habermas (1984): '....rationality consists not so much in the possession of particular knowledge, but rather in "how speaking and acting subjects acquire and use knowledge." Crudely put, critical theorists would not just feel an intellectual duty to seek some sort of authentic explanation of any social issue but would consider that it would be a necessary moral requirement. An integral aspect of any explanation must be the identification of outcomes, the identification of 'winners and losses' – as measured against resource allocation and other markers of social advantage and disadvantage.

The variations of critical theory that developed in the second half of the century widened out to become more inclusive, seeking to identify relative strengths and also the weaknesses of some traditional theoretical approaches. Probably no theoretical approach to the study of society has become more personalized, in relation to practioners, than critical theory.

In the fourth quarter of the twentieth century critical theorists made a significant contribution to stimulating a discussion of governance, a discussion that has been able to identify the principles underlying governance based on democratic systems and also the conditions that make a democracy meaningful, highlighting possible forms of 'participatory democracy'. For Habermas (1996), some version of a constitutional state is required in order that necessary constraint (in any pluralistic, economically developed, society) can be under democratic control. He drew attention to the complexity of activities and interests that make the design of any democratic system problematic, a complexity that limits the range of individual and group political participation.

There seems to be some ambiguity amongst critical theorists in relation to Globalization and its implications for governance. A phenomenon accepted as significant by all, but viewed by most critical theorists as constraining democratic institutions and denying the voice of the economically disadvantaged a right to be heard. Globalization is seen as a phenomenon that highlights exclusion for some at the same time as intensifying forms of, mostly superficial, inclusion (entertainment – random access to knowledge – communication) for others.

Prior to considering Globalisation in a bit more depth I want to note, just briefly, the approaches to sociological endeavor that became known as structuralism, post-structuralism, and post-modernism. More so than with most other sociological theories, these three are quite often personalized to individual proponents (theorists) rather than their being more neatly subsumed under a set of shared ideas, so these approaches can arguably be more easily identified with each theorist rather than by shared ideas. These approaches were mostly generated within the intellectually vibrant milieu of post-war France, where a number of prominent social scientists can at least be said to share a general dissatisfaction with structural-functionalism. More especially with its epistemology rooted in positivism and its assumption of the possibility of methodological objectivity.

Structuralism picks up on of aspects of Durkheim's structural functionalism that emphasized the role of institutions as they act to constrain individual actions, to circumscribe the forms that the social could take. Assuming the form of social institutions as being much less the outcome of the activity of individuals. But for most structuralists this was more a matter of a shift of emphasis from institutions *determining* the social to their operating in more of a primary role in *shaping* it. Anthony Giddens offers the term 'structuration' to represent the '......process of active making and remaking of social structure.' (Giddens, 2009, p89). Suggesting an interactive process of individuals in forming the social. But he also notes that any individual's knowledge-base is itself the outcome of experience gained within existing social structures.

Given its broad-based approach, sharing a view of the importance of social structure, structuralism has been found to be useful across the social sciences, especially anthropology, psychology, sociology, and literary criticism.

Structuralism gained prominence in the 1940s/50s and early 1960s, especially with the work of the social anthropologist Claude Levi-Strauss. In his approach to understanding central aspects of culture Levi-Strauss sought to identify the structures in everyday activities that produced the 'meanings' serving to bind individuals together within any society. These meanings being produced by such elements of social life as: mythology, kinship relations, and techniques of food preparation.

Other writers associated with structuralism, taking a more sociological perspective, were Louis Althusser, Roland Bathes, and Jacques Lacan, although arguably they would probably be more liable to be noted as social philosophers or in Barthes's case a literary critic and in Lacan's a psychoanalyst. Althusser (although critical of the French communist party, was a Marxist) emphasized the ideological role of the twentieth century state in perpetuating old and creating new structures that, whilst not overtly repressive did operate more implicitly to gain the consent of any population in service of elite (ruling) group interests. Barthes, developing the original insights of Saussure, focused on the use of language and his 1964 book, 'Elements of Semiology', provided a theoretical impetus to the detailed analysis of language (and other cultural 'artifacts') that came to be associated with structuralism. Barthes was interested in power and highlighted the ways in which language and power are associated, he noted: 'The object in which power is inscribed, for all human eternity, is language *(languge)*, or to be more precise, its necessary expression: the language we speak and write *(langue)*' (Bathes, 1977, in R.Kearny and M.Rainwater eds. 1996, p365).

Structuralism is a somewhat 'portmanteau' concept that can only usefully be applied to those social scientists who support an explanatory paradigm causally linking the parameters of social relationships within the institutional systems of any society. For example, education systems form structures (or settings) for perpetrating norms, values, and expectations. Key (controlling) aspects of any cultural setting that pervade the language as it is learned. And it is the structure of how these processes operate that is the task of sociologists to identify. Although critical of positivism, structuralism in practice has tended to prioritize empirical data. This was a central aspect of its methodology that was criticized by the post-structuralism that emerged from structuralism.

Post-structuralism adhered to the structuralist focus on language, especially what an analysis of it 'in use' (mainly in texts) can reveal about wider cultural institutions, the power relations expressed by these, and the impact this structural nexus can have on individuals and groups. But it also differs from original structuralism in the emphasis it places on the need to contextualize issues; to take into account the wider social context, including the historical origins and subsequent development, of social institutions.

Taking a slightly different approach, Peter Blau (1977), emphasized the importance of identifying the form taken by the social structure, the different social dimensions making up its composition by which individuals can be distinguished – gender, ethnicity, wealth, religion, political affiliation, etc. So the structural components constituting a person's (or a group's) social identity

Noted post-structuralists would include Jacques Derrida and Julia Kristeva. And, although he denied the post-structuralist label, I suggest that Michael Foucault's work spans the two - structuralist/ post-structuralist - approaches. Given this, I think it would useful to consider Foucault's work in just a little more detail. In his own at times eloquent prose he noted structuralism as not being a new method but that: '…it is the awakened and troubled consciousness of modern thought.' (Foucault, 1974, p208)

With the work of Foucault in the 60s and 70s we see an original, if at times conceptually opaque, attempt to highlight the role of language, or rather of discourses (and the wider narratives within which they are deployed) in the ways in which social issues - sexuality, modern medicine, punishment, deviance, mental illness, and power - are produced. Unlike most of his postmodern/critical contemporaries he rejects (see his 'The Order of Things' 1966 English trans. 1973) the fundamental tenants of both phenomenology and Marxism.

His focus is on the social practices that characterize, indeed constitute (along with social institutions), any society. How the individuals in any social setting can only understand (interpret) this through the meanings that are available to them and that these meanings are socially constructed – and this in forms that support the interests of dominant groups; he is particularly scathing about bourgeois values and cultural products. He seeks to identify how the sets of meanings are produced (implicitly and explicitly) to foster 'control'. For Foucault, individuals have little genuine autonomous control over their lives and a combination of historical processes and prevailing power relations operate to constrain individual agency. He suggests that people are not necessarily aware of these constraints; instead he highlights the ways in which people 'internalize' the power relations within which they live. He seeks to highlight the implicit 'rules' '...that operate beneath the consciousness of individual subjects and define a system of conceptual possibilities that determines the boundaries of thought in a given domain or period.' (Stanford Encyclo. article accessed on-line summer 2015).

Foucault suggests that the ways in which social issues are represented influences (and limits) the meanings that can be derived. Consequently, those with the power to represent also have the means to control individuals or populations; discourse can operate as a powerful 'regulatory mechanism'. Part of a wide-ranging interlinked matrix of social processes operating in such ways that (if unchallenged) lead to our, in effect, colluding in our own subordination to the normative values and an economic agenda set by the powerful.

People, in a strong sense, bring themselves to order as they grow in a context of interrelated social processes and respond to the various ways in which their lives are under 'surveillance' – this internalization process operates to bring people to an order aligned to normative, usually bourgeois, values. For Foucault, people endeavour to develop identities and engage in practices that are 'normal' and in doing so cooperate with their own subordination; the non-normal is the deviant, the social outcast!

There are numerous ways in which social issues or behaviors become shaped into objective truths when they are in fact the product of discoursive practices in which various types of expert play leading roles as they deploy 'rational', often 'scientific', interpretations of social conditions. A key aspect of these discourses being the unspoken voices the unseen identities and the ways in which people (and populations) are socialized to foster self-control. For Foucault, when presented with any social issue we should begin our investigation by posing the question whose interests are being served by the ways in which any issue is being presented?

Foucault's research would mainly access information expressed in the form of texts; of documentary evidence rather than field work with subjects' in natural (if for Foucault mostly unnatural) settings.

The third post-war approach, quite closely related to structuralism and post-structuralism, is post-modernism. To an even greater extent than the other two, postmodernism frames conventional society as dysfunctional for many of the individuals and groups of which it is composed of. It focuses on issues of conflict involving inequality, exploitation, and oppression; so on issues such as: racism, gender, and poverty.

Post-modernism is highly critical of the processes of modernity, including the deification of material progress, the forms taken by (homogenization of) mass culture, and more generally the commodification of much of life. As the institutions and processes that support these changes increasing limit the social space for the expression of both individual freedom and social solidarity. These ordering aspects of society are mostly taken for granted and embodied in institutions such as legal systems, economic arrangements and the forms of governance; supported by surveillance and maintained by the threat of punishment. More implicitly, the education system serves to inculcate normative values and the mass media operates in ways that diverts or distracts attention from what are arguably life's more important issues. For post-modernists, the role of education should be to train a child to think critically and to be able to value freedom of thought as an adult. An enlightened, post-modern education system would also be able to more authentically reflect the experience of non-whites, females, and the poor.

The post-modernist Jean-Francois Lyotard was one of a number of social scientists who rejected the overarching theories that had characterised the social sciences and he argued for a realignment of theorizing. An outline of his position was set out in his 1984 text: 'The Postmodern Condition: a Report on Knowledge'. For Lyotard we can gain an understanding of any society if we consider it from a perspective drawn from more personal narratives, peoples' 'subject positions', rather than from the discourse of meta-theories. Lyotard argued for the end of grand meta-narratives (his 'totalizing perspectives') such as Marxism, positivism, functionalism, behaviourism – in this he was echoing the earlier view of Robert K. Merton who in 1957 had highlighted the methodological difficulties in empirically testing grand theories; with their propensity to accommodate almost any evidence.

A considerable amount of postmodern sociology has drawn attention to the impact of developments in economically developed societies on personal identity – how features of identity derived from traditional types of social status have been displaced by features of identity involved in material consumption and display (similar to Weber and Veblem on 'status value'). Identity placed within the hyper-reality created by the interlinked mass communication processes of late capitalism; identities which for Agger are: '..constructed by powerful media and other cultural sources'. (Agger, 1991)

The inclusive grouping of the sociological perspectives that take a critical approach towards much of positivistic science – critical theory, post-structuralism, post-modernism (in a narrow sense) – share a view that events, issues, indeed all knowledge, can only be understood with a wider historical, social, economic, and political context, and it is in exposing this and its implications that is a fundamental sociological task.

For Agger p.121 '...critical theory, postmodernism, and post-structuralism attune working empiricists to the ways in which their own analytical and literary practices encode and conceal value positions that need to be brought to light'

I do have some sympathy with Agger (1991) and his noting that: 'One cannot help but wonder why these theorists [specifically Lyotard and Derrida] do not write more clearly and in ways that show the empirical (political, cultural, existential) relevance of their work more directly'. And I would admit to initially struggling to see much explanatory value in most post-structuralist and much post-modernist sociology (more perhaps social philosophy) with its focus often being on but narrow phenomena. A type of analysis exemplified by Jean Baudrillard's (2005 ed.) book 'The System of Objects', where there is an intense analytico-imaginative concentration on the relatively trivial, finding hermeneutic complexity in the ordinary. And yet, I have come to appreciate that much can be revealed about the wider social and cultural environment of any society by mining the conditions and implications of what mostly passes unnoticed (unseen). The cultural objects in which inhere the conditions of the social circumstances that come to objectify them.

Post-modernism was, to a significant extent, a reaction to aspects of change that came to be associated with globalization – especially the implications of the exponential growth of knowledge, and the relentless spread of commodified (crucially homogenized) media, made available via 20th/21st century electronic communication technology.

Globalization is viewed as a relentless macro-level set of interlinked processes increasing the rate at which the world's fault-lines of economic division, conflict, and social displacement, are growing. An alternative view (Bohman, 2003) from within critical theory accepts the negative aspects of globalization but offers an alternative interpretation of its potential, with the possibility for new forms of political and social engagement, along with the potential to create new institutions that can facilitate new forms of global and local networks of relationships and a new, globally situated, interpretation of citizenship.

The phenomenon of 'Globalization' has become something of a specialism within sociology. A phenomenon characterized by markedly increased 'flows': of goods, finance systems, ideas, information, entertainment, and people. Challenging national identity as power becomes evermore redirected to multinational trading blocs, global communication networks, transnational companies, and facilitating the hegemonic tendencies of the world's more powerful nations.

David Held defined globalization as a '.....set of processes which are reshaping the organization of human activity, stretching political, economic, social and communicative networks across regions and continents. Power is no longer simply articulated in particular geographic sites and locations, but is spread and diffused across the world in such a way that what occurs in one place can have ramifications across many others.' He also suggests that it at least seems like: 'Democracy and globalization pull in different directions.' (Held, 2010, pp. xi/x).

Theories of globalization range from those that view it as but an (if accelerated) continuation of past trends, supporting forms of change that can be identified as emerging from the eighteenth century (or even earlier) to those that view it as exhibiting a qualitatively different set of processes shaping new types of social institutions and new forms of social life itself.

These interpretive polarities and the intellectual ground between them have been encompassed in the categorization of difference arranged by Allan Cochrane and Kathy Pain (Held ed. 2004) as: Globalists (optimists and pessimists) – Internationalists - Transformationalists.

Just briefly: Although they interpret the impact differently, all Globalists share the view that the pace and range of changes in economic, technological, political, and social developments, over the past three decades have been significantly different from anything seen in the past. For optimistic globalists, these changes have been mostly positive, opening up opportunity for individuals, increasing standards of living and lifting millions out of poverty; as well as bringing the world's people together. They argue that a new global order is being developed, leading to a borderless world and creating international agencies that will dramatically reduce the power of nation-states. Optimists accept that the increase in economic activity has raised the issue of sea, air, and land pollution but expect that technology will provide a solution. For pessimistic globalists, this new global order has created stark patterns of 'winners and losers'. And the 'winning' nations have been mostly those in the economically developed countries, whilst losers have been mostly those of the economically developing nations; as well as low skilled workers and women in most of the world's countries. They also draw attention to the ways in which culture is becoming homogenized and how local and regional cultural artifacts – be it reggae or rap music, clothes styles, or the fortunes of European football or US baseball teams – are being commodified on an international scale. The communications technology associated with globalization has facilitated the promotion of a media-based leisure industry dominated by corporate products, displacing the local in favour of the profitable.

For the Internationalists, what have recently been identified as dramatic and significantly different forms of economic and cultural developments are but a continuation of the type of interdependencies that has been going on for hundreds of years. They consider that nation states remain powerful players on the international scene and that they can control the power of global finance and trade. They also highlight the fact that most of the world's trade is between countries on a regional basis rather than globally: with the EU, NAFTA, MERCOSUR and AFTA – being examples of large regional trading groupings. Some Internationalists would even locate the beginnings of global interconnectedness to the 15th/16th century voyages of 'discovery'.

For Transformationalists: there is the acceptance of the significant changes that have been associated with globalization but (similar to pessimistic Globalists) consider that the non-democratic agencies (such as financiers and large corporations) can be controlled by nation-states and international 'public' bodies. Although they do accept that the autonomy/sovereignty of nation-states is limited, at least in certain areas, by the power of agencies driven by private profit rather than the public interest, and that these two can often conflict.

The social scientists, Paul Hirst and Grahame Thompson (1999), also represent a more skeptical interpretation of globalization, as they focus on what they see as the prioritization of international finance. They consider that the promotion of global-wide developments has been based on serving the narrow interests of the international financial community. They go so far as to term globalization a 'necessary myth' required to promote the trend toward international finance. They recognize the increase in the rate of various global activities but are critical of the ways in which these are invariably framed as positive. Highlighting how most of these global developments exclude large sections of the world's people, with the economically developing nations consigned to the margins as locations for resource extraction, foreign investment, and international trade based primarily on low-labour costs. A key aspect of globalization for transformationalists is the complexity of recent changes, the 'numerous intertwined global networks' – the multiplicity of interconnections.

Saskia Sasson has generated a range of theoretical insights into the phenomenon of globalization. She has drawn attention to the role of the world's major cities serving as core 'control centres' for setting the terms of the new global order. At the forefront being London, New York, and Tokyo (today Sasson would probably include Bejing and

Frankfurt in this grouping) with a second group of cities such as Paris, Toronto, Mexico City, Hong Kong, Buenos Aires, Seoul, Kuala Lumpur and about 20-30 other of the worlds' major cities, all for Sasson, interconnected: '....nodes for the international coordination of servicing of firms, markets and even whole economies that are increasingly transnational.' (noted in William I. Robinson, 2009)

'Global cities around the world are the terrain where a multiplicity of globalization processes assume concrete, localized forms. These localized forms are, in good part, what globalization is about.' (Sasson, 2005, p40)

The significant change in the movement of peoples (especially in the developing countries) from country to country, and within countries from rural to urban; driven by similar economic forces that pertained during the period of nineteenth century industrialization; people usually following economic aspirations. A number of sociological studies have focused on the 'push' and the 'pull' factors underlying this mass migration and to what extent different groups are able to adapt to and integrate into new social and cultural settings.

Newer theoretical frameworks have emphasized the need to re-conceptualized notions of time and space. The anthropologist and economic geographer David Harvey suggests that the speed and reach of communication networks have compressed conventional notions of time and space to the point that these can no longer be seen as constrains on the ability of the economically powerful to operate across the globe.

He notes that: '....we have been experiencing......an intense phase of time-space compression that has had a disorienting and disruptive impact upon political-economic practices and the balance of class power, as well as upon cultural and social life.' (Harvey, 2017, p109).

David Held has also drawn attention to the development of a global counter-culture that is using global communication systems to coordinate opposition to the global hegemony of the most powerful elite groups within the world's most powerful nations He notes that: 'The struggle over the accountability of the global economic order has been intense. Violence in Seattle, Prague, Genoa, and elsewhere marked a new level of conflict about globalization, democracy and social justice.' (Held, 2010, p27)

The noted social scientist Anthony Giddens offered an overview of Globalization in relation to theory: 'We are now living through a period of global transformation that is probably just as profound [as some in the past] and yet is much more widely felt across larger areas of the world. We seem to need new theories to help us understand and explain the new developments that are transforming our societies today.' (Giddens, 2009, p103).

Globalization is probably the grandest and most complex of meta-narratives so it is hardly surprising that it has been liable to a wide range of theoretical interpretations.

What has been rapidly expanding 'frontier territory' into which human innovation has been unleashed in a pseudo-neoliberal (the only type that have ever actually been realized) context of but light legal, taxation, and other regulative controls, has created a massive 'informational reservoir' whose depths are serving to draw a range of social scientists into setting (outlining) theoretical frameworks with which to express, contain, and reveal core patterns of activity within a ultra-dynamic terrain of ever-increasing complexity and novelty.

Alongside the vast accumulation of texts emerging from all of these more theoretical approaches noted above has been their on-going application by practicing sociologists undertaking research. Thousands and thousands of research projects into social behaviours related to such as: relationships, group dynamics, identity (individual, group and national), communities, the work-place, crime, governance deviance, sport, sex, social stratification, religions, gender, and a range of social institutions and organizations including those delivering healthcare, education, mass media, governance communication systems, and other types of public and private services.

So in the final quarter of the twentieth century (and into the twenty-first) sociology can be seen as being occupied by two broad camps, each divided by theoretical definitions and methodological approaches. On one 'side' we have the sociological perspectives developing out of the positivist tradition – most notably Functionalism and positivist Marxism – and on the other we have the perspectives that can, if somewhat superficially, be viewed as a reaction to these, indeed for some post-modernists (following Nietzsche and Heidegger) even perhaps a reaction to a central Enlightenment programme of seeking assured knowledge.

Offering a positive perspective we might suggest that traditional approaches laid some foundations for the study of society and post-modernism has significantly widened its scope and potential explanatory power.

Critical and other types of post-modern theory offer a set of fundamental challenges to the assumed authoritativeness of positivism. But across the world today thousands of students study sociology and thousands of graduates go on to become practitioners. Practitioners who have gained skills that can be applied to social situations in ways that can produce 'useful' knowledge, with usefulness being measured against the purpose for which any research is undertaken. Down-playing the influence of theory and attempting to design each research program on the basis of a scientific but pragmatic approach (exposing inequalities or informing social policy-making) they consider will allow the best access to this or that social issue.

I think that most practitioners would draw their methodological 'tools' from a tool-box that has been contributed to from across the range of theoretical perspectives. Even if the framework chosen for any research such as, 'macro structures or micro interaction', or taking a consideration of historical influences into account or with a more narrow focus on the immediate circumstances, might themselves be determined by a practitioner's educational experience and theoretical inclinations.

According to Jennifer Platt (2010, p121), for sociological theory: 'There is no longer a dominant paradigm, but many possible alternatives coexist and are offered to students as possible choices.'

Is my suggestion of researcher eclecticism too optimistic? Is sociology characterized by theoretical fractures and fundamental methodological disagreements to the extent that working sociologists are contributing little to our knowledge of the multiplicity of social worlds that co-exist. Are they limited to acting has but handmaidens of this or that government or commercial interest? It might be the case that theoretical and methodological differences reflect some combination of the complexity of the subject-matter, exposure of practitioners to this or that theoretical tradition, and the stage in the development of the science of sociology.

The enlightened sociologist C.Wright-Mills, in his essay 'On Intellectual Craftsmanship' (originally written April 1952), noted that: 'In brief, "methods" are simply ways of asking and answering questions, with some assurance that the answers are more or less durable. "Theory" is simply paying close attention to the words one uses, especially their degree of generality and their inter-relations. What method and theory properly amount to is clarity of conception and ingenuity of procedure, and most important, in sociology just now, the release rather than the restriction of the sociological imagination.' (Wright-Mills, 1953, 'The Politics of Truth', 2008 edition, p44)

In order to gain some idea of the actual work of twentieth century sociologists it is worth considering a sample of the classical studies that laid the practical foundations for the eclectic mix of theoretical frameworks that sociology has generated. A brief overview of classic studies would begin with late 19th early 20th century examples such as Veblen on the leisured classes, Durkheim on suicide, Weber on the 'Protestant Ethic and the Spirit of Capitalism'. In the US (but also to some extent in some European countries) there were more community-level forms of early types of 'action research', exemplified by innovative work centered on the Hull House settlement house in Chicago (from 1895). Working out of Hull House, sociologists such as Jane Addams, Florence Kelly and Julia Lathrop collected a range of data on the conditions facing some of the most disadvantaged, mostly living in slum conditions. Between 1895-1935 twenty-seven significant books were generated from Hull House. Jane Addams's *'Hull House Maps and Papers'* (1895) and W.E.B. Du Bois *'The Philadelphia Negro: a Social Study (1899)*, were landmark studies on social life at the community-level.

From the 1920s the Chicago studies inspired by the vision of Robert Park and driven forward by Ernest W. Burgess starting with 'The Gold Coast and the Slum' (a 1929 study of a district of central Chicago) set standards in how to conduct the detailed fieldwork that was required to gain the type and amount of data required to understand social behaviour of the neighborhood - 'Middletown' (1929) and the follow-up 'Middletown in Transition', focusing on life at the community level and adding a longitudinal perspective.

Eduard C. Lindeman (Chicago School) text 'Social Discovery' (1924) was one of a number of Chicago School studies heavily reliant on the careful observation of people engaged in social interaction. These types of observational study adopted an approach to gathering data that stimulated a wider discussion on subjectivity/objectivity and so the value of the classification and categorization of observations that still has relevance down to today. William Healy (pioneer of criminology in US) carried out a longitudinal study involving several hundred delinquent boys growing up in pre-WW II Chicago – and Clifford R. Shaw's (Chicago School) 'The Jack-Roller', was a richly qualitative study of a single criminal whose own account is testament to the value of letting a person's experience of social identity speak for itself. Taken together, the early-mid twentieth century (Chicago School) studies deployed a mixture of methods: statistics, interviews, surveys, personal testimony, and both passive and participant observation. In many ways the work of the Chicago School was a testing ground for a more detailed examination of methods appropriate for any particular subject-matter.

Just one outcome of an extensive research programme into business, management and the work-place, run by the Harvard Department of Industrial Research (set up in 1926) was the range of experiments involving the 'Hawthorne' studies including: Elton Mayo's 'The Human Problem of an Industrial Civilization', T.N.Whitehead's – 'The Industrial Worker' 1938 – a '.....statistical examination of the data collected in the Hawthorne Experiment' (Hawthorne Works of the Western Electric Company – outskirts of Chicago), and Roethlisberger and Dickson's 'Management and Worker' (1939). The Hawthorne studies were based on non-directive interviews and observation. A series of studies that, if subject to some criticisms related to 'sinister' manipulation in the workplace and to focusing on a worker more as a unit of production, laid the foundations for the study of the workplace (primarily in terms of productivity and management).

William Foote Whyte's study of 'Street Corner Society' (1943) – a study undertaken on micro-level interactions (highlighting the 'unseen' identity of the less fortunate in society) – a central aspect of Whyte's method was participant (or perhaps better 'involved') observation. Participant observation was pioneered and distinguished from 'objective' observation by Eduard C. Lindeman (in the 1920/30s) on people living within a rundown area of Boston with an emphasis on the people themselves rather than the community more generally. He considered individuals within groups and developed a technique of understanding group dynamics termed 'positional mapping'. Whyte's work revealed a complex range of interaction within sub-cultures that had been pretty much unnoticed by mainstream sociology.

Alfred C. Kinsey - sexual behaviour 'Sexual Behaviour in the Human Male' (1948) and 'Sexual Behaviour in the Human Female' (1953) were revealing studies on the range of human sexual practices. Based on data gained from 12,000 interviews (7,000 of which were administered by Kinsey himself), collected in that late 1930s, which highlighted a considerable difference in the publicly expressed expectation of sexual behaviours (more puritanical) and the actual behaviors that characterized less inhibited private practices.

Gunner Myrdal's 'An American Dilemma' pub.1944 offered a 1,500 page examination of the position of American black people (funded by the Carnegie Corporation) a central aim of which, as stated in Myrdal's initial terms of reference, was: '.......determining the social, political, educational and economic status of the Negro[sic] in the United States as well as defining opinions held by different groups of Negros[sic] and whites as to his "rights"....' An aim that highlights the moral perspective of research that had positioned the social condition of Afro-Americans as problematic. This was a significant research project involving numerous assistants and consultants – some of those involved included notable social scientists such as Ashley Montagu, Edward Shils and Louis Wirth. It was also one of the first social science research projects to receive significant institutional funding. Myrdal was later (in a 1953 address to the British Sociological Association) to claim that the work of sociologists in the area of race relations has made a considerable contribution to changes in race relations legislation that had began (albeit slowly) to happen. Making clear links between sociological research, public awareness, and social policy.

Studies undertaken in the UK during the 1950s/60s, by sociologists such as Young and Willmot of life in the East End of London, also adopted a community-level approach, revealing the socially relevant in 'ordinary' daily life. In follow-ups to this type of city-based research, sociologists studied the break up and dispersal of many from these communities and their resettlement in modern housing estates. This led to an understanding of people coping with change and the depth of commitment to the social as embodied in locality.

Twentieth-century sociology has generated a trickle, become a stream, become a river swelling into a veritable flood of studies undertaken across the civil world. Receiving an impetus with the US economic crisis in the early 1930s and closer involvement of many governments in administrative and social affairs during and following WWII. And of course the advertising and mass media industries have sought to understand human social behavior in order to better manipulate it. These earlier twentieth century studies were increasingly dominated by the more conventional instrumental-positivist (especially structural-functionalist) studies, heavily dependent on quantitative data, for the most part considering unconventional behaviour as 'dysfunctional'. Implicitly accepting the status quo as embodying preferred social arrangements that might just need some modest reform. Contrary to this, at the start of the century pioneers, such as the Hull House project noted above, were undertaking research rooted in the community and heavily dependent on qualitative data, as they sought to offer a 'voice' to the poor, dispossessed, and exploited ('Action Research'). This thread of more radical sociology was maintained throughout the whole century but only really returned to serious acceptance within the mainstream from the late 1960s onwards and is considered in a bit more detail below.

The issues involved in the necessity of methodological objectivity and the rejection of this as a realistic possibility continues. In practice, sociologists working today have issues such as methodological rigor and research ethics as ongoing operational challenges.

Sociology in a sense provides information that enables the characteristics of populations to be 'measured', for social behaviours to be better understood and so predicted, allowing the necessary civil support services to be identified – and perhaps more dubiously for populations to be 'controlled'. So it is understandable that the more efficient administration of countries involved in the type of rapid social change that as characterized modernization (including more recently, globalization) has provided conducive bureaucratic as well as academic conditions for the development and spread of sociology.

By the century's end contributions to the subject's development, and to the accumulating store of knowledge of human social behaviour, spanned the civil world. – aided by computer technology, the internet, SMS communication, the proliferation of academic periodicals and journals, and regular national and international conferences.

As well as being a mainstream academic discipline, primarily focused on university sociology depts., sociologists are working in a range of areas including all levels of national and international governance, advertising, general industry, as well as more specialist areas such as healthcare, the media and the wider communication industry.

If we exempt sociology in 'communist' countries and most French academics, then the two decades following WWI were ones in which the US became generally dominant in terms of conventional sociology world-wide. This due mainly its own political position in the world and its access to financial resources via government, universities, business, and charitable foundations (significant research sponsors being the Carnegie, Fulbright, and Ford foundations) which supported the generation of a mass of experimental and field-based research into a wide range of, mainly US based, social life. In addition, the US dominated academic publishing with its large publishing companies and the international ubiquity of the English language.

Just to gain an overview of increasing interest in the study of the subject in the US during the second half of the twentieth century:

US:1960 – 1st degrees in Sociology	7,600
1966 -	15,203
1974 -	35,915
1980s - reduced to about	15,000 per year
Then rising steadily to reach	24,000 in 1997

The level has settled somewhat in the 21st century, with 26,500 graduates in sociology majors in 2009. In terms of PhDs (US), peaked at about 700 per year in 1970s reducing to about 500 per year in late 1980s with a slight increase to about 550 per year in the late 1990s.

A similar post-war level of expansion had been the experience of countries on all five inhabited continents. We see an increase in the founding of new national sociological associations and the growth in membership of those already established.

From the 1950s there has been a steady increase in the numbers of journals of Sociology: for 2006 there were 93 primary sociological journals listed on ISIs Journal Citation Reports. A 1990/92 study into published sociological articles noted that: 56.9% were from U.S. and the UK second with 7.6%.

At the International level, the modest - Institute International de Sociologie was founded in 1903. But it wasn't until 1949 that the International Sociological Association (ISA) formed (sponsored by UNESCO) with its main office initially in Paris (today in Madrid) and with Louis Firth of Chicago University elected as its first president.

By 2007 56 national sociological associations were affiliated to the ISA (about double the number of the 1950s) – and now hold a global conference every four years. Each of these national associations has sub-groups ('sections' – from 5 - 30 plus sections for each national association) specializing in particular areas of the subject; prominent in these are: criminology, gender-studies, education, stratification, media, religion, the family. The work of each sub-section is usually published in area-specific journals, the number of which has steadily increased from the 1950s to the 1990s. In 1994 the first on-line Electronic Journal of Sociology became available. By the twenty-first century such web-sites as SocioSite (just one of many open-access sociology sites) were making available a wide-ranging and quite comprehensive directory of sociology resources; listing about 150 specialist areas alphabetically from 'Abuse' to 'Youth'. And thousands of university sociology depts. have libraries and data sharing sites available via academic permissions.

Similar to other sciences, sociology has benefitted significantly from on-line communication systems for sharing ideas, including the use of web-sites to post articles and research papers for peer review. Key utilities of the internet also include its facilitation of data sharing and of allowing extensive research cohorts to be constructed. Although there remains the issue of understanding the social context from which internationally available survey and interview type data has been produced. Then there are networks of institutions that facilitate this world-wide data sharing already in place to take advantage of the significant opening up of this sharing activity including:

The International Federation of Data Organizations (founded 1977)
The Council of European Social Science Data Archives (formed 1976)
The Inter-University Consortium for Political and Social Research (established 1962)

Innovations in the means of analyzing statistical data were introduced and developed to suit sociological research including: game theory (Von Neumann and Oskar Morgenstein) – mathematical modeling, enhanced by computers – sociometry (introduced in the 1930s by J.L.Moreno) – Coefficients of Correlation, highlighting a potentially significant relationship between two variables – multi-factor analysis (enhanced by use of computers) which can highlight variables in terms of causality or correlationally, as intertwined in complex ways within large amounts of data.

Sophisticated data managements systems have been introduced, along with a range of computer based data-collating software. There has also been the influence of systems theory; mostly inspired by the work of Ludwig von Bertalanffy (1968) and, in the US, represented by World Systems Theory. In the 1970s Jean-Paul Benzécri developed a mode of data analysis 'correspondence analysis' (a multivariate statistical technique) which was subsequently used by Pierre Bourdieu in his study 'La Distinction' (1979)

There has of course also been the increasingly more sophisticated facility to 'replicate' social systems, and even micro-level interpersonal interactions, using computer modeling.

Another progressive development since the 1960s has been the continuing increase in the proportion of female sociologists (in line with the wider 'feminization' and expansion of higher education) a change that has been considered to have been an important influence on more recent sociology, especially in relation to preferred research methods and areas of interest: ethnicity, women's studies, poverty, domestic and paid work, and deviance, have become primary areas of research interest.

As the new (21st) century began we can still see the ongoing influence of American and European sociology, but studies undertaken by sociologists in each inhabited continent are producing a steady flow of original, high quality, work, with the internet and other forms of international cooperation facilitating the sharing of work by social scientists from across the world.

The difference in preferred types of data - quantitative/qualitative - continued, even accepting that a wide range of research included both. The survey as a source of data collection was favoured, but increasingly interviews, biographies, various types of case studies, participant and experimental observation, and longitudinal studies, were employed to generate masses of qualitative and quantitative data. Made easier to collate, process, and present, by the development of computers.

From the 1970s the focus of research studies shifted (or perhaps widened) – In the US work – organizations – elites – mobility – and community studies continued to be focused on and in Europe (especially Britain and France) education – social mobility - working class life –migration – and governance. The last quarter of the century saw the focus shifting again to include newly accepted forms of inequality and discrimination such as women studies encompassing issues of equal pay and other work conditions, and domestic violence and home-based servitude (e.g. Hannah Gavron 'The Captive Wife', 1966 and Ann Oakley 'The Sociology of Housework' 1974), ethnic groups, and aspects of transnational issues under the general heading of Globalization. In the increasingly more confident sociology depts. of the universities in countries of Africa, Asia, Australasia, and South America, sociologists were contesting forms of sociology they viewed as being founded on western values. Ones not necessarily appropriate to understand the issues facing their own national circumstances, where experiences such as actual colonization and ongoing economic neo-colonization have left an indelible mark on social institutions and where relationships with cultural and economically more powerful countries have influenced the production of a range of 'local' issues.

Sociology has seen advances in agreement on terminology and on more efficient ways of obtaining reliable statistical information. But the issue of inflated claims and over-interpreting research findings, along with the continuing problem of bias, are still present.

It might be idealistic to think that as a social scientist, a sociologist, should be seeking to understand and explain human social behaviour in an academically disinterested way. Designing research to be as objective (in the relative sense of all sciences) as appropriate for any particular social phenomenon. But that as a moral agent conscientiously considering the implications of how the research issue has been selected and how any findings could be misused, and these in a context of having a responsibility to (presupposed) scientific ideals. This open acceptance of the responsibility of some sense of moral autonomy by the agents involved in the production of knowledge within a scientific endeavour could be a way of balancing the tension between scientific rigor and social responsibility – and could have a central place in the training of social scientists. A fundamental condition of this autonomy would be the expectation of researchers being committed to clarifying what they consider to be obvious sources of influence of approach and in the interpretation of results. This would include such aspects of research as: funding sources, theoretical assumptions, selection of method, as well as institutional and personal motivations. Even the act of deciding what aspects of social life are worthy of study - social mobility, gender issues, inequality, crime, ethnicity, governance, sexual behaviour, etc. is, in the act of identification, a judgment. Linked to this are issues of funding and of a researcher's own personal interest. Should a social scientist engage in a research activity - say the study of crime (or a 'deviant' behaviour – when even the categorization of a behavior as criminal or deviant is a social act) and assume that the use of any findings would not be based on narrow ideological considerations. For many types of research there is also the consideration of....to what extent should the direct 'voice' of the subject group be included?

For example, on interpretation of outcomes alone: how would we expect a sociologist to manage a research result that suggests that members of a certain ethnic minority group have on average lower IQs, compared with a general population? A social scientist would be aware of the sensitivities of such a finding and that certain social groups would want to misuse this to reinforce certain types of discrimination; so a moral dilemma to publish as is, rewrite (and fully contextualize results), or just to not submit for publication; given the pressure on academic researchers I doubt that the last is a realistic option.

I think that in this context it would be important for researchers to highlight any methodological limitations of the research – and to highlight the epistemological issues such as circumscribing what is actually meant by 'intelligence', and indeed by the concept of ethnic minority. It would also be pertinent to contextualize outcomes for any sensitive issue (which is probably most) by offering – historical, social, economic – factors relevant to the results and even, if appropriate, suggestions on how prospects for a group deemed disadvantaged can be improved.

In a speech made when seeking (successfully) the presidency of the ASA in 2002, Michael Burawoy, suggested that: 'As mirror and conscience of society, sociology must define, promote and inform public debate about deepening class and racial inequalities, new gender regimes, environmental degradation, market fundamentalism, state and non-state violence...the world needs public sociology – a sociology that transcends the academy.' (Platt, 2010, p118)

The 1960s saw the re-emergence into mainstream of a radical movement challenging the assumed scientific credibility of US sociology – a movement, not only acknowledging sources of bias, but one activity promoting these as they advance the cause of social justice. This community-focused 'action sociology' had been a core element of US social science in the late 19th early 20th century with a number of prominent women and black sociologists at the forefront. This clear alternative to structural functionalist and other types of more conventional theorizing and research based on this, has been largely written out of the history of sociology. A recent 1,000 plus page A-Level introductory text on the subject, whilst allowing some space to Marxism and Critical Theory, offers no acknowledgement of the place of any form of more radical liberation sociology (and its associated 'Participatory Action Research Strategies'); its historical role or on-going contribution. (Giddens, 'Sociology', 6th ed., 2012).[22]

Proponents of liberation sociology have traditionally focused on community-level issues and have endeavoured to allow the lived circumstances of the subject-groups to form a primary element of any research. Research that seeks to combine quantitative and qualitative data in ways that allow the 'voice' of subjects to be expressed within a robust research framework.

Four quotes from the 2001 book 'Liberation Sociology' by Joe R Feagin and Hernán Vera offer a sense of the motivation underlying this significantly more radical approach:

- 'A decision to practice liberation sociology is a decision to take sides with the oppressed. Liberation sociology is committed to the causes of the oppressed.' (page 23)
- 'The point of liberation sociology is not just to research the social world but to change it in the direction of democracy and social justice.' (page 1)
- 'Liberation sociology struggles to disrupt or destroy the causes and realities of oppression, the taken-for-granted, "natural", order that supports it and makes it possible.' (page 17)
- They quote Berch Berbegoglu (1991) as noting a: '....new generation of critical scholars – envisioning a society without exploitation, oppression, and domination of one class, race, sex, or state by another – helped provide the tools for analysis for the critical study of social issues and social problems that confront contemporary capitalist society.' (page 3)

We can mark the renewed interest in types of libration sociology

---

[22] Given Giddens's credibility as a sociologist, I accept that he might take the view that there are sound academic grounds for this exclusion, perhaps in relation to scientific status. And he does include less conventional approaches such as Critical Theory, Marxism, Postmoderism, and similar, but at the very least I would have expected some mention of liberation sociology if just 'in passing'.

(and so 'action research') with the election, in 1974, of the radical Alfred McClung Lee to the presidency of the American Sociological Association. In his active career Lee was involved in the setting up of a number of progressive organizations including the 'Society for the Study of Social Problems' (1951), 'The Association of Black Sociologists' (1960s), 'Sociologist for Women in Society'(1970), and 'The Association of Humanist Sociology' (1976). Lee was important in establishing 'The Insurgent Sociologist', a radical journal that became 'Critical Sociology'. He was also, sometimes in collaboration with his wife Elizabeth, a fairly prolific writer on a range of social issues.

If our own pedagogical influence makes us hesitate to accord a scientific status to such an approach we do need to consider the charge that not taking up an overtly ideological (at times political) position as that of liberation sociology, by default, offers support to current ideologies and the political status quo.

Is it academically possible to separate a 'scientific approach' from any political context? Is it morally right to do so? This approach has been liable to the accusation that sloppy research methodology risks dubious findings and so invites valid criticism and would be of little use in pursuing useful policy change. Fortunately much of the research produced the by the (bottom up) Participatory Action Research Strategies, favoured by most liberation sociologists, combines robust methodologies with high quality analysis; as the same time seeking to offer a means for subjects to express their social experience.

The academic thread of liberation sociology in the US can be traced through a line of active practitioners running from the likes of Harriet Martineau, Jane Addams, Julia Lathorp, W.E.B. Du Bois, Robert Lynd, Gunnar Myrdal, Oliver C. Cox, Saul Alinsky, Alfred Lee, Mary Jo Deegan, C.Wright Mills – and more recently Nancy Mathews, Robert G. Newby, Maxine Baca Zinn, and T.R.Young. Young has pioneered the use of the internet as a platform for his radical approach to sociology.

These and many others working in US sociology helped to spread the practice of liberation sociology abroad, especially in Latin America (where it helped to inform liberation theology) and some of the countries emerging from colonialism during the post war period. Bear in mind these radical sociologists were mostly working against the tide of conventional US sociology. Their various biographies show how many saw their careers held back and experienced an on-going struggle to find research sponsors and publishers. And yet, such was their commitment to forms of participatory sociology focused on the experiences faced by the excluded, the poor, and those being discriminated against, that they continued (and continue) to offer a necessary challenge to the sociological status quo.

Echoing much critical theory, liberation sociologists challenge the view that any social research context can ever be value-free. There are always objectivity-confounding factors such as: the motivation of research sponsors, the selection of an issue to be studied, the presumed validity of isolating one aspect of social life from the social nexus within which it is rooted, and a range of characteristics of the researchers, including career ambitions, personal preferences, and unconscious prejudice. Alvin W. Gouldner in his book 'The Coming Crisis of Western Sociology' (1970) drew attention to the psychological sources of potential bias, noting that: 'What I am saying, then is that the work of sociologists, as of others, is influenced by a sub-theoretical set of *beliefs*, for that is what background assumptions are.........they are often internalized in us long before the intellectual age of consent.' (1970, p32) and on objectivity he notes: 'In its present, historically developed form, as a claim of contemporary professional social sciences "objectivity" is largely the ambivalent ideology of those whose resentment is shackled by their timidity and privilege. Behind objectivity there is a measure of alienation.'

Gouldner (ibid, p441) goes on to castigate this type of professional sociologist, secure in their tenures: 'For tenured faculty, the university is a realm of congenial and leisured servitude. It is a realm in which the academician is esteemed for his learning but castrated as a political being. Indeed it is this trade-off, in which the academician has the right to be a tiger in the classroom but the need to be a pussycat in the Dean's office.' The disingenuous academician as: '...the gelded servant of the very system in which he is, presumably, the vaunted star.'

Although action sociologists tend to favour qualitative data, considering this more suitable for allowing the 'voice' of the subject to be heard, they also consider that appropriate quantitative data can enhance the overall quality of a research project.

For Feagin and Vera (2001, p133): 'The problem is not quantification per se but the too-frequent unreflective use of quantitative methods, including advanced statistical techniques, without consideration of the research's social context, societal relevance, uncritical assumptions, probable uses, moral and ethical implication, and major limitations in regard to probing the deeper social realities of a given society.'

Each practitioner has to *choose* to ignore or consider:

- To what extent must a researcher strive to produce 'objective' 'robust' knowledge of any social issue (or for a natural scientist, a material phenomenon)?
- To what extent should a researcher exercise direct moral autonomy in their work, or can moral action be left to the social scientist's role as a citizen, as separate from their research?
- In sum: to what extent can these issues can separated – simply put, but ferociously difficult, if ferociously necessary, questions to be addressed by researchers.

Outside of determined liberation sociology, research sociologists at the start of the twenty-first century generally take an eclectic approach to theory - although as a mature student in the 1990s I still felt a sense of the shadow of positivism cast across the research in practice. Perhaps in a good way, reminding researchers to consider the rigor and robustness of their work as well as the wider validity (which perhaps represents the light shone on sociology/social studies by some critical theories and post-modern sociological theory), adopting methods that are deemed to be more appropriate for any particular social issue. Even accepting that a more favoured theoretical approach could have a determining effect on identifying and selecting the particular issue to be researched.

It's quite easy for me to end this section on sociology with a positive spin, highlighting the pragmatism of eclectic and subject-situation appropriate methods, as if data could be gained, and neatly labeled and filed, according to unbiased assessments that emerge from initial considerations of the subject-situations, but this would be just too rosy a representation. Sociology faces similar challenges to the other sciences (social and natural) of producing knowledge about our world that is robust in terms of scientific credibility but also reflects broad ethical concerns and personal morality.

A clear contribution made by the more critical range of post-modern theoretical and methodological approaches to the understanding of humankind's social conditions has been as a corrective to overly positivistic sociology, and has provided a stimulus to broaden the conceptual range of perspectives, to highlighting causes/circumstances of the existential rift between individuals and their social conditions (alienation), and to identifying the unidentified. Drawing attention to the hidden, unspoken-about identities.[23] On this last, writers such as Foucault ('practices') and Derrida ('texts') have revealed the presence of the 'unspoken', of the 'concealed' – most obviously in the (institutional and ideological) ways in which some options for social change are hidden (not to be spoken of) and how some views are excluded (just a word in the US 'communist', 'atheist', 'un-American', 'American' is sufficient, no more need be or can be said – words represented as barriers to rational consideration, even more challenging 'pedophile', 'racist', 'terrorist', 'Jew', 'Islamist'). The use of discourse to 'not-mention', to exclude by mostly unnoticed omission; concealed by the smothering power of the normative. As Foucault suggested processes '...that operate beneath the consciousness of individual subjects and define a system of conceptual possibilities that determines the boundaries of thought in a given domain or period'.

This is not an observation of chance happenings as social development continues but rather is a phenomenon arising from the conjunction of vested interests and the consciously or unconsciously motivated outcomes of restricted thinking – and can be present within any individual living within any type of society.

Critical (and 'liberation') social scientists have exposed, and in doing so have challenged, the synthetic boundaries between the normal and the non-normal.[24]

The Australian sociologist Raewyn Connell argues for a Global sociology, one that offers a multitude of perspectives sourced from the world's regions – sociological perspectives that arise from particular regional historical experiences and their contemporary

---

[23] Not just the voices of the overtly oppressed, but also to the life-conditions of those living within the shadows (margins) of industrialized society, drawing their experiences into a more critical light.

[24] See A. Gouldner (1970, p488) on 'Reflexive sociology'. An approach advocating that practitioners relate their work to its wider social implications; a preparedness to challenge theoretical assumptions and actual practices in this context.

relationships to Global economic and cultural power centers including more obviously the USA, Europe, and increasingly China, India, and to a lesser extent Australia and Russia. The duty to make sociology socially relevant (in a humanistic tradition) and to engage with the public has been a call emphasized in the work of Michael Burawoy and his appeal for a 'public sociology', a call that has stimulated much international debate. For Burawoy (echoing views such as those of C. Wright-Mills, Mary Jo Deegan, Franz Fanon, Pierre Bourdieu, Raymond Aron and Maxine Barca Zinn) sociologists should seek to reveal the nature of any society, drawing attention to any disparities between the assumed and the actual conditions – and to ensure this work is undertaken within open public forums. The urgency and importance of a range of social issues have ensured a continuing debate within sociology about its nature and place in the twenty-first century.

But the range of methods - qualitative and quantitative - whose effectiveness has been tested and assessed over the twentieth century (and whose limitations and strengths seem clear), have survived as viable research methods and continue to be available to all practicing sociologists. It is their responsibility to balance academic considerations, the inevitable, even if potentially 'neutral', vested interests (sponsors) and social responsibility towards the subject-matter, the wider 'scientific project' seeking underlying 'truths', and their own conscience. To tread but delicately on the lived experience of people's lives.

C. Wright-Mills, in a letter to his friend Dwight Macdonald, on ways of writing about sociological issues advised that: 'Maybe we could call it sociological poetry: It is a style of experience and expression that reports social facts and at the same time reveals their human meanings......If we tried to make up formal rules for sociological poetry, they would have to do with the ratio of meaning to fact, and maybe success would be a sociological poem which contains the full human meaning in statements of apparent fact.' I suggest that the somewhat 'gilded' nature of the prose can be excused in what was a letter – but even allowing for the hyperbole it does convey a magnificent sense of the possibility of a science that can more adequately encompass our social experience.

The potential of sociology to reveal the lived-in contexts of humans in society (in its contribution to a multi-faceted/ multidisciplinary - underpinned by value-orientations - understanding of the human condition) is significant. I recommend two books that highlight how sociology can illuminate, and in doing so inform, our understanding – Peter L. Berger's 'Invitation to Sociology', and C.Wright-Mills 'The Sociological Imagination'.

The education of sociologists (indeed all social scientists) should be designed to fire the imagination for the study of social conditions and to align this with a sense of scientific rigor underpinned by a commitment to human values.

The Social Science of Medicine

The nineteenth century had seen something of a transformation in medicine – developments during the 20th/21st centuries would see the processes underlying this transformation becoming an integral aspect of its further advance. For Britain (and similar for other industrializing nations) a key influence driving medical progress and the improvements in public healthcare was the need of an advancing capitalist-type economy for an available pool of labour in a sufficient physical condition to carry out repetitive (and often heavy) work over quite long working days whilst living in cramped housing conditions of the town and city slums. A pool of labour also serving as a potential reserve of manpower available to be deployed, as soldiers and sailors, to enforce Britain's international ambitions; including maintaining control over its extensive colonial interests.

Britain's colonial adventures also provided the incentive to find treatments for a range of tropical diseases to which staff (diplomatic, private business, and military) and their families deployed overseas were vulnerable too. There was also the ongoing need for a labouring population of Britain able to reproduce itself, requiring an infant mortality rate low enough to at least ensure a stable population level and so the continuing supply of labour.

Along with these more 'administrative' drivers of healthcare there was also the issue of work-related diseases. Pressure came from increasingly stronger trades unions, religious groups and philanthropic charities, along with the political threat of an emerging Labour Party (formed 1900). Some more enlightened members of all classes, saw Conservative and Liberal governments prepared to take action to mitigate the sources of ill-health.

Michael Foucault ('The Archaeology of Knowledge' 1969, p180) noted that: '......at a period in which industrial capitalism was

1255

beginning to recalculate its manpower requirements, disease took on a social dimension: the maintenance of health, cure, public assistance for the poor and sick, the search for pathological causes and sites, became a collective responsibility that must be assumed by the state. Hence the value placed upon the body as a work tool, the case to rationalize medicine on the basis of the other sciences, the efforts to maintain the level of health of a population, the attention paid to therapy, after-care, and the recording of long-term phenomena.'

The factors contributing to this social dimension were the, mostly understated, primary drivers of the development of scientific medicine, but also involved the advance of the scientific method, including its research methodologies (techniques) and an associated process of professionalization. These provided the intellectual dynamism and contributed to forming a certain broad world view that strongly shaped how medicine would develop. A third factor influencing the direction of medical advance at this time, one that would be progressively eroded in the second half of the century, was the normative expectation inherent in late Victorian and early Edwardian Britain that males would lead the development and dominate the higher grades of what would become a rigidly hierarchically structured profession.

Up to the second half of the nineteenth century women had a respected place at the local level as midwives and as sources of traditional medical advice. Scientific medicine, firmly under middle-class male control, displaced women from healthcare either by direct exclusion or by restricting them to cleaning and nursing roles; roles framed as menial and of little medical value. The promotion of a 'scientific' medicine, often based on overly ambitious promises, and the easy dismissal of most traditional medicine, further masculinised professional medicine

In the early decades of the twentieth century both medical research and medical practice were generally undertaken by the same people but as the century progressed there would be a progressive separation of these – not total, but almost so, especially in areas such as pharmaceuticals, virology, bacteriology, immunology, and in developing the newer technologies such as scanning and bio-investigation techniques. Mechanical technologies also advanced in such areas as surgical instrument design and manufacture, and in life support systems and diagnostic aids such as: kidney dialysis, ex-rays and non-invasive scanning techniques, cardiac pace-makers, defibrillators, ultrasound procedures, along with a range of high-tech intensive care equipment.

In terms of illness and of healthcare in practice, the human being as a 'medicalized' entity emerged from the nineteenth century framed by 'scientific medicine' – echoes of Cartesian dualism – into a machine-like physical body and a non-physical, almost spirit-like, mind. With illnesses being allocated by medical professionals, as relating to one or the other and so treated separately. Indeed, mental illness was not generally recognised unless bordering on or within the category of psychotic; by when it had become more of a social rather than a personal problem.

Clinical psychology would develop along with the science of psychology for the most part separately from mainstream medicine. What treatments were available circa 1900 were delivered in separate 'mental hospitals' (asylums) for the emotional disturbed or the socially problematic. For the better off there were 'convalescent homes' and the comfortable consulting rooms of professional psychoanalysts. Most of these offering the therapeutic approaches suggested by the work of Freud, Jung, or Adler.

For the first half of the twentieth century treatment for serious mental ill-health continued to be mostly based on long-term separation from mainstream society in secure containment and, up to about the 1970s, mostly unsatisfactory drug, electroconvulsive therapy (ECT), and surgical treatments. From when a slow, but progressive change in how mental illness was interpreted saw the development of a range of more humane treatments. In the more enlightened clinical environments more common today the more severe (surgery or drug) treatments are now used sparingly and based on consultation with a patient and their family.

During the nineteenth century the cities and large towns of the industrialising nations had been breeding grounds for diseases such as cholera, smallpox, diphtheria, measles, polio, tuberculosis, and a number of sexually transmitted diseases such as syphilis and gonorrhoea. If anything but straight-forward, then child-birth could quite often be a life-threatening experience. For a more immediate description of nineteenth century living conditions of the masses see Friedrich Engels 'Condition of the Working Class in England' (1846). The outlook for the more commonly experienced unhealthy urban environments would improve (most quite dramatically) during the twentieth century. Even if cities like Liverpool, Glasgow, and Manchester, retained slum localities until well into the century; similar conditions also prevailed across much of Europe.

Along with medical advances there were also improvements in basic living conditions, including in: drinking water, urban air quality (post the 1956 Clean Air Act in Britain), sanitation, and nutrition. Basic improvements in living standards are now acknowledged as together making a significant contribution to improvements to the health of populations.

Some key medical inventions inherited from the 19th century, and improved in the 20th, included the hypodermic syringe 1857, the 'clinical thermometer',[25] the optical microscope, and the stethoscope (1816). The latter allowing potentially diagnostic sounds of the chest cavity to be monitored. The stethoscope was to become a symbolic role-indicator when hung round a doctor's neck.

Although early on recognised as medically relevant, pre-twentieth century attempts to assess blood pressure had not provided accurate instruments for measurement, but in 1896 the invention of the sphygmomanometer by Scipione Riva-Rocci, combined with the pneumatic cuff (invented by the company Dunlop), began a process of gradual improvement in measurement technology. By 2014 blood pressure could be accurately monitored using variations of computer-based 'wireless' devices, accessed via mobile telephone applications.

An important advance in understanding the body's nutritional requirements was the identification by Christiaan Eijkman and some others, of essential food factors. Eijkman, whilst studying beriberi, had identified vitamin A as being the deficiency causing the disease. In 1928 Albert von Szent Gyorgi had identified the substance later identified as vitamin C, the presence of which in fruit and vegetables had for sometime been known as necessary to present the deficiency disease of scurvy. This was a field of study significantly developed by Fredrick Gowland Hopkins, gaining him a Noble prize in 1929 for his discovery of these 'vitamins'; named as such by Casimir Funk. The identification of these essential food factors developed into a more general research-driven undertaking to gain a better understanding of human (and animal) nutrition.

---

[25] One 10" long had been designed but by 1866 Thomas Clifford Allbut had made a significantly shorter and so more practical version – reducing the time to accurately register a patient's temperature from 20 to 5 minutes.

The working conditions of 18th/19th century industry created hazards that caused a range of occupational diseases: lead poisoning of pottery-makers and house painters – phossy-jaw of mainly female match-makers – silicosis of mainly male miners – chest infection by the particle laden atmosphere of the factory and mill, and numerous types of cancers from contact with carcinogenic materials.

There was an increasing awareness of links between living conditions – water quality (typhus and digestive disorders) and air quality (pulmonary illness such as influenza and tuberculosis which was the biggest killer disease of the industrial city) - nutrition, especially vitamin deficiency, and overall inadequate diets – high density living conditions and poor sanitation prevalent in the growing cities - sexually transmitted diseases, especially syphilis – and more generally, the conditions favourable to the rapid transmission of a wide range of infectious diseases.

With much of the above impacting on women's health in relation to childbirth and early years child mortality rates. Most births took place in the home with a friend or neighbourhood 'midwife' in attendance. Child-birth would, during the twentieth century, become much more a medical condition to be managed in a clinical setting rather than to be supported in the locality/home more as a natural function.

Increasingly as the nineteenth century progressed medicine was being focused on large buildings, the 'hospitals'. Hospitals had been established in most leading cities by the late medieval period including: Venice, Rome, Vienna, Paris, St Petersburg, and London – most of these hospitals being funded as religious institutions or by royal patronage. Those who could afford it would mostly opt to have their illness treated in their homes.

Whilst providing places for treatment and recuperation, and with separation from the wider social world reducing the risk of infection to others, nineteenth century hospitals were themselves quite unhealthy places; pyaemia and erysipelas being two types of widespread infections incubated in the hospitals. The later part of the nineteenth century had seen determined attempts to address this issue, with a priority being placed on cleanliness (disinfectants) and the recognition of the value of well-trained nursing staff.

An understanding of causal links between specific bacilli and certain diseases was initially provided by Louis Pasteur who had established causative links between streptococci and staphylococci;

so setting the foundations of bacteriology. Foundations soon built on by researchers including Robert Koch, another pioneering bacteriologist who identified the bacilli causing tuberculosis (1882) and cholera (1883). By the early twentieth century bacilli had been identified for diseases such as: typhoid, diphtheria, gonorrhoea, meningitis, leprosy, tetanus, plague, syphilis, and whopping cough. European typhoid epidemics (caused by the bacteria - Salmonella typhus - mostly spread by lice) were common; ravaging Ireland in a series of epidemics in the first half of the century. In terms of mortality rates, early twentieth century European epidemics were much reduced following the introduction of public health measures and from 1916 vaccination (TAB). By the second decade of the twentieth century a range of microbes involved in diseases had been identified and the specialism of bacteriology had been firmly established. Cities continued to be liable to the multiplicity of types of flu virus; with significant global pandemics in 1918 ('Spanish flu'),[26] 1957 ('Asian flu') and 1968 ('Hong Kong' flu), the worst being the one of 1918 which infected about 500m of which between 20-50m died. Even today the flu virus continues to cause the deaths of about 80,000 per year in the UK alone.

During this period of the early decades of the twentieth century, continuing colonial interests, including the health of businessman, soldiers, white farmers, and the native workforce employed by these, focused medical attention on the parasitic microbes causing tropical diseases. Including elephantiasis caused by a parasite (the nematode worm Filarria) that can be present in the blood-stream of mosquitos. A 'School for Hygiene and Tropical Medicine had been established in London in 1899, and another similar insitute in Hamburg in 1901, to progress a research-based study of cause and treatment of diseases common to the tropics.

Naturally produced quinine continued to be the main treatment for diseases such as malaria, yellow fever, and leprosy but, following intensive research between1918 - 1945 this was gradually supplemented by synthetic derivates of quinine and of other synthetic alternatives: 1943 mepacrine, 1939 chlorquanide, 1946 primaqune,

---

[26] Each pandemic being named after the place where the first recorded cases were identified – as at summer 2020 only Donald Trump in the US has used the term 'Chinese flu' for the current Covid-19 pandemic, and this for his own domestic political interests.

1948 amodiaquine, 1950 hydroxychloroquine, and 1951 pyrimethamine. The widespread spraying of Dichlorodiphenylti-chloroethane (DDT) on breeding grounds was a cheap and effective means of eliminating the mosquito-carriers of malaria and yellow fever; but the malaria carrying anopheline mosquito gradually developed resistance, so new insecticides such as dieldrin and lindane were developed. The over-liberal use of these, whilst having an adverse impact on local environments, has made a significant contribution to reducing the impact of this debilitating condition.

Specialists working in this branch of medicine (parasitology - a sub-specialism of bacteriology) soon identified a number of parasitic organisms responsibly for the spread of diseases: trematode worm-schistosomiasis, amoeba-bilharzia, trypanosome-sleeping sickness, plasmodium (a parasite using the mosquito as a vector)-malaria. Another species of mosquito was identified by Carlos Finlay in 1881 as the carrier of yellow fever. Throughout the century the work of parasitologists made significant inroads into the eradication in some areas, and mitigation in others, of a range of microbe-borne tropical diseases.

An understanding of the immune system progressed in parallel with other aspects of human biology. In 1884 Elie Metchnikoff had observed a phenomenon that he termed phagocytosis ('cell eating') where single cells in lower organisms were seen to engulf and ingest invasive substances. A bit later human white blood cells were seen through the microscope to become attached to and 'eat' harmful pathogens such as anthrax.

Louis Pasteur made the landmark observation (based on a series of carefully conducted experiments) that fermentation depends on the presence of microbes (he termed these 'ferments'), with an implication being that these were the cause of infection in wounds. The search was on to identify more of these disease-causing microbes, a search made possible by a steady improvement in optical microscopes. Robert Kock, and a small number of late nineteenth century researchers, can be identified as setting the foundations of the microbiological revolution that was the central focus of the science of twentieth century immunology. In 1890 Kock had formulated a set of criteria for identifying a causal relationship between a microbe and a disease; these, 'Kock's postulates, were used throughout most of the twentieth century.

It was out of the study of disease-causing microbes that the branch of medicine known as immunology developed. Immunology focuses on the body's own mechanisms for withstanding the various microbes that threaten its integrity, its health. It had been shown by a number of workers in the 18th/19th centuries, most notably Edward Jenner, that there are a range of microbes in the air and water that, if taken into a body, will cause disease. But Jenner and others were also aware that individuals who caught a disease and survived had gained a certain level of immunity on subsequent exposure to the same, and very similar, microbes. Jenner in the 1790s had noticed this with survivors of small-pox (milk-maids exposed to cow-pox exhibited resistance to the more serious small-pox) and he exploited this bodily reaction to produce vaccines for anthrax and rabies. It seemed that exposure had provided (stimulated) the body with some molecular 'memory trace' that could serve to mobilise appropriate immune defences when re-exposed to similar microbial infection.

The technique, prophylactic injection of anti-toxins, was developed by Elizabeth Wright to protect against tetanus and the use of this in WWI contributed to a significant reduction in the mortality rate of British soldiers, but it was not until the 1930s that a vaccine that stimulated the body's own defences was developed.

Bacillus Calmette-Guérin (BCG) vaccination, offering protection against tuberculosis, had already been introduced in Britain and the US by the 1920s. Immunization was extended to protect against diseases such as diphtheria (first developed 1890s) with the mass vaccination of children being adopted by US in the 1930s followed by Britain in the 1940s; in England during 1940 there were 1,830 deaths from diphtheria...... by 1969 this was zero. The first viral vaccines were developed for yellow fever in the late 1930s, influenza 1945, and poliomyelitis 1954. So offering the potential to significantly mitigate the affect of these diseases. In the 1960s vaccinations for measles and rubella were developed, even if their introduction would later on (1990s) reveal the potential for controversy (and the misleading use of scientific data) in medicine involving disagreement over possible side effects. It is now generally accepted that the benefits far outweigh any potential hazards.

In the last quarter of the twentieth century an intense research focus was on the molecular level, including the genetic mechanisms involved in the production of antibodies. The progress of immunology led to a significantly improved understanding of the biologically complex ways in which the body is able to identify and defend against potentially harmful microbial material to, in effect, recognise molecular entities that are self and those that are non-self.

Viral and bacterial infections continue to represent a clear potential to harm human health. Viruses are tiny bodies (approx 1/10,000,000th of an inch), composed mainly of densely packed chromosomes of DNA, or nucleotides of RNA. They have different types of proteins protruding from their bodies that enable a virus to attach to a target cell prior to invasion followed by its then taking control of the target cell's own reproductive bio-mechanisms. Bacterium are also relatively tiny (approx 1/25,000th of an inch) but significantly larger than any virus. To view the latter required an electron microscope to view the former a good quality optical microscope would be adequate. Viral infection can be very difficult to treat, although antiviral drugs have been a significant advance (more recently in treating HIV), much of the treatment for viral infection tends to focus on subsidiary symptoms such as pain, pneumonia, or even organ failure; to allow time for the body's own immune system to respond to the infection. Most bacterial infections respond to antibiotics, although resistance to these drugs is becoming a serious issue. A great deal of public and privately funded pharmaceutical research is directed toward treatments for viral and bacterial illnesses.

By the 1950s and 60s practitioners of scientific medicine had gained a certain confidence in their increasing ability to cure disease, indeed this was a time when scientific medicine was probably at its most optimistic, it seemed that there was no limit to the contribution that advancing scientific medicine could make to the eradication of disease and to the alleviation of most health problems. Claims made by the pharmaceutical companies, leaders of the medical profession, and indeed of government ministers of health, were redolent of an overly optimistic discourse of 'progress'.

The most powerful drugs developed during the post WWII period were the antibiotics. Earlier in the century Alexander Fleming had advanced the understanding of harmful microbes in relation to human health and campaigned for the need to remove dead tissue from wounded soldiers in WWI. His observation in 1928 that microbes could be killed if in 'contact with a contaminating mould' is taken to have launched the development of antibiotics......a development brought to fruition by Howard Flory and Ernest Chain (in the 1940s). It was also in 1928 that Fleming discovered that penicillium mould was able to kill the bacterium staphylococcus, so identifying the potential value for human health of his 'penicillin'. A potential clearly illustrated by the success it had in alleviating infective bacterial conditions, including potentially serious infections of throat, ears, lungs, and skin. The effectiveness of antibiotics was enhanced by the related discovery of streptomycin, a drug that proved to be effective against the debilitating, and often fatal, tuberculosis. By the mid 1960s various types of antibiotics had been made available. The medical profession gave the impression, initially justified, of control over a range of infective conditions, from the relatively trivial to the deadly; few people able to access doctors went without a prescription for one of these new antibiotics and most doctors were prepared to easily prescribe. Vetinary science also soon utilized the power of antibiotics against diseases of animals; by the end of the century animals in the human food chain were being routinely saturated with antibiotics, even to the extent of these being given as precautionary treatments to facilitate high intensity farming.

A feature of certain forms of Streptococcus and Staphylocopccus bacteria highlighted by Joshua and Esther Lederberg as early as 1952, had demonstrated that some bacteria had the inherent ability to develop resistance to anti-bacterial drugs. They found that the administration of high dosages of powerful antibiotics could kill off about 99% of a patient's harmful type of bacteria but could leave the about 1% of the resistant variety. Allowing it to rapidly increase partly due to the elimination (perversely by the dosage of antibiotics) of any other bacterial competition. By the end of the century it had also become clear, not least due to the rapid rise in hospital based infection by bacterium (such as MRSA and C-diff) that the genetic material in bacteria had the potential to respond to the anti-bodies and in turn mutate into forms resistant to the antibiotics that had been used against them.

What had become an antibiotic development and production industry has in the last twenty or so years been engaged in a desperate search for ever more powerful antibiotics, as the agents of infection adapt and increasingly survive. A continuous process of adaptation to antibiotics that are now often administered in multiple forms in an attempt to overcome resistance.

As the century progressed it became clear that the body's immune system was but an aspect of a more extensive biological system monitoring its internal constitution at the cellular and molecular levels and, when required, responding to any threat to the body's biological integrity. With this wider system of identification and communication leading to the mobilisation of appropriate defence responses, involving the traditionally identified immunological system along with the lymphatic, the endocrine, and the nervous systems.

A new (twenty-first century) and very exciting approach to immunology is the application of hybridoma technology - based upon using the secretions of a fusion of two cells, the outcome being contained within one cell membrane – using a particular type of cell (B lymphocytes) from a body's immune system and another from a specific type of cancerous cell (melanoma). The different types of secretion can be used in the treatment of a range of diseases. The ability to clone the fused cell results in offspring that can themselves produce the secretions. Some forms of the hybrid cell can produce the secretion of monoclonal antibodies that can be used for diagnosis, treatment and even for prevention in conditions such as AIDS and a range of cancers, and can also be used to mitigate the effect of immunological rejection during transplantation of organs. The fused (hybrid) cells combine the anti-body producing ability of the B cell with the longevity and rapid reproductive ability of the cancer cell. These monoclonal antibodies can also be developed for use in genetic engineering for example, in identifying and isolating single genes. It seems that, on an almost monthly basis, new medical uses are being found for hybridoma technology. This approach reflects the direction that medical, especially immunological, research has been taking as the twentieth century drew to an end; a focus on the changes that take place at the molecular level that precede the onset of disease.

To illustrate the rapid innovations happening in the field of immunology, in early June 2018 immunologists working at the US National Cancer Institute in Maryland developed a technique involving the removal of white blood cells from a patient with advanced breast cancer (assessed to be terminal), the cells were then 'bred' in laboratory conditions, producing millions of cells, which were then transfused into the patient. The patient's condition began to improve straight away and within a relative short time the symptoms eased then disappeared. This, if quite dramatic, case (if limited to but one individual), reflects the central approach of current research, which is to find ways of more effectively mobilising the body's own immune system.

Immunological action was framed in a discourse of conflict.....as if battle lines were being drawn between the immune system and an 'invading enemy', with defences being 'mobilised' following the 'detection of invasion' – 'battle raged' between two sides – 'invaders' were 'surrounded and attacked, if on occasion the system succumbed to 'attack' ('defeated') it was also at times 'victorious'…etc. A range of simplistic conceptualizations of the processes involved but an understandable way to cognitively contain these.

There are a range of organs directly involved in the immune system: thymus, spleen, tonsils, adenoids, liver, along with bone marrow, lymph nodes, lymph vessels and the skin. But cells throughout the body, both fixed and circulating, also play an important part in the immune system. Today medical researchers roam the whole body searching at the micro (molecular and cellular) level as they continue what has been a productive mapping and interlinking of the structure and function of the macro (whole body level) systems. Invariably, the use of computer modelling is serving to transform the initial stages of research. Utilising programmes that map virtual molecular processes in effect copying 'healthy' or 'sick' processes and then tracking how these respond to virtual antigens and other forms of molecular-level interventions. From about 1985 onwards there has been a shift of research focus towards the identification of the genetic basis of cellular immunity to antigens and cytokins and to understand the other immunological bio-mechanisms.

A landmark step along the road of increasing focus on the molecular level and on genetics had been taken by Linus Pauling who, in an article in *Science* (1949), was able to outline the origin of sickle-cell anaemia and note how a single gene mutation could have a significant impact on the conformation of the three dimensional structure of haemoglobin which could in turn effect oxygen absorption. He also highlighted the role of antigens operating as templates in the formation of the polypeptides constituting antibodies. Pauling's subsequent work drew increasing attention to the importance of changes taking place at the molecular level. Leading him to make the informed prediction that medical science would in due course be able to modify the ways in which genetic predispositions operate and do so in ways that could prevent disease being expressed. Pauling's prediction was at least partly validated, in relation to the treatment of sickle cell when, in 1997, a treatment was developed that could significantly reduce the changes taking place at the molecular level and for at least some sufferers ease the symptoms of this often very distressing condition.

Early in the twentieth century, William Bayliss and Ernest Starling, were working as researchers engaged in the study of proteins and enzymes, when they identified the 'hormones' the '....regulatory messengers travelling from particular organs (ductless or endocrine glands - thyroid, pancreas, sex glands, adrenals) to other parts of the body via the blood stream' (R. Porter, 2002, p95). Diabetes was shown to be a hormone deficiency disease, and the role of the hormone insulin was identified, in 1922, by Fredrick Bunting and Charles Best; who had been able to isolate and extract the hormone. With the first insulin injections being given in the same year to a 14 year old boy, as well as to Best himself.

For the nervous system the role of certain types of enzymes – including acetylcholine, cholinesterase, adrenaline, serotonin, noradrenalin, dopamine – in their initiating the excitatory and inhibitory actions in neuron-based communication and showing their link in helping to maintain the body's healthy function, have been identified. The crippling disease of Parkinson's was found to be related to the reduction of the dopamine level active in the area of the brain called the substania niagra – 'black substance'. And some types of serious depression have been linked to low levels of serotonin, with the drug branded as Prozac, by increasing the level of serotonin, being found to alleviate the distressing symptoms. The story of Prozac (fluoxetine) itself illustrates a problem with the promotion of drugs and the suppression of negative research findings, unfortunately a too-common practice in the industry. Research shows that for some people Prozac can be very effective as a short term treatment for severe depression but has very little effect on mild and moderate depression, and yet is has been widely prescribed for all forms of the condition. With much of the research highlighting this difference being effectively suppressed by the company. This highly profitable drug can have quite significant adverse side effects including the very distressing one of addiction, and of course offering a basically ineffective treatment to some patients.

Within the hospital the surgeon had by 1900 comfortably completed the transformation from 'butcher/barber' to become a more respected member of the medical profession. Surgical interventions had been performed for lung conditions from the second quarter of the nineteenth century (mainly for pulmonary tuberculosis and intraplural sepsis), kidney removal (1876), appendix removal

(1886), operations on the brain (1892), and for a gastric ulcer (1892). Between 1843 and 1883 seventy-eight women in England had been operated on for removal of their ovaries. And, if more as a last resort than a belief of their being an effective treatment, surgical removal of cancers in the large bowel, rectum, and stomach, became a treatment option. In 1908 Ernest Miles carried out a complex operating procedure to remove a cancerous growth from a patient's rectum.

In 1893 surgeons had undertaken an operation for a brain abscess. Other significant advances in neurosurgery were achieved in the US during the first decade of the twentieth century. Harvey William Cushing performed operations for epilepsy, for the very painful condition trigeminal neuralgia, for debilitating pituitary disorders, and to remove brain tumours. These were mostly part of an advancing range of pioneering operations at the horizon of advance - and they clearly illustrate how surgery was going significantly beyond the 'cut and hack' of earlier times. When, even if a patient survived the generally brutal operation they would be fortunate to avoid infection, or death from shock, as they recovered in the hospital ward.

At the turn of the twentieth century three central problems confronted the surgeon: – pain control – infection – shock. As the century progressed each of these would be more effectively addressed. For pain control during operations: by 1900 chloroform had become more generally preferred than ether, although care had to be taken with dosage because an overdose could stop a patient's heart. By 1910 a mixture of nitrous oxide and ether further improved effectiveness and reduced potentially adverse side-effects. Anaesthesia developed into a speciality during the first half of the century as even more sophisticated anaesthetics were introduced. By the 1930s pentothal (thiopental sodium) was being used as a pre-op relaxant. And in the 1940s a purified preparation of curare could be injected to allow muscles to be paralysed and so make operations easier. Increasing knowledge and further development of techniques of anaesthesia gave the surgeon much more time to operate; time required for extensive abdominal, thoracic and heart surgery, and one of the necessary conditions for the transplant surgery that ambitious and skilled surgeons were beginning to undertake during the 1960s. The human heart had been operated on to repair valves (1912 aortic, 1925 mitral) and to remove shrapnel and other foreign bodies. Post WWII specialist cardiac surgeons were operating to repair congenital conditions (such as 'hole in heart' babies), but the sheer volume of blood flowing through what is basically a continuously operating pump impeded what could be undertaken. In 1952 Floyd John Lewis (US) used cooling (induced hypothermia) to lessen the rate of blood flow, and by the 1960s a machine was developed that could be used to circulate a patient's blood via external 'piping'. Making it possible for it to be cooled and oxygenated as it undertook the work of the heart in sustaining the patient's life, allowing the cardiac surgery 'team' (as it had by then become) to operate on a motionless and relatively dry heart.

Kidney transplants had been attempted as early as 1902 but these became more viable from the 1950s, and from the 1960s transplants were also being undertaken of the pancreas, the liver, and the lungs. But the headline transplant was that in 1967 of a human heart by a South African team of cardiac surgeons led by Christian Barnard. These were pioneering operations and there were serious continuing problems of tissue rejection, so the need to identify a best possible donor match. Combined with the heavy use of immunosuppressant drugs (with obvious risks of potentially fatal infections) in order to overcome possible rejection of the new organ by a body's own defence mechanism, its immunological system, deployed to protect it against potential harmful 'foreign bodies'.

For infection more generally, the importance of hygienic conditions in the operating theatre had been realised for some time and, although by 1900 operating instruments had been made of forged steel, with wood or ivory handles, the introduction of effective steam sterilization in 1879 had been an advance; one attributed to Charles Chamberlin with his 'autoclave'. Then followed a series of improved versions, the latest of which, the STATIM, was introduced into the US hospitals as recently as1989. The introduction of stainless steel surgical instruments from the 1920s made the sterilization process even more effective. Rubber gloves, gauze masks, and the meticulous 'scrubbing up', began to be practices taken up by surgeons from the 1890s. At best, the operating conditions, as well as the skill of the surgeons, circa 1900, were far in advance of the conditions that had pertained at the start of the nineteenth century. Post-operative, and more general clinical, pain was alleviated by morphine. Heroin was refined by the chemical company Bayer from 1898, barbiturates (1903), and phenobarbitone (1912).

Shock, both physically and psychologically based, is a serious threat to the recovery process but to even get to the post-operative stage the risk of death caused by shock-induced from significant loss of blood or other fluids during an operating procedure had to be avoided or at least mitigated.

For the physician more generally: in 1897 Walter Bradford (working at Harvard Medical School) had shown how X-rays could be used to provide diagnostically useful images of internal organs. By the end of the First World War X-rays had become a routine way for surgeons to identify the location of invasive objects such as bullets, shrapnel, and calcified gall and bladder stones, as well as enhancing the ability to assess limb fractures and damage to the spine. Enabling surgery to be less of an experience of educated 'digging around', and so allowing the surgeon to cut straight to the primary site of any trauma.

Prior to WWI surgery (and indeed medicine more generally) was consolidating the spread of successful practices, aided by the growing number of students recruited for training in the increasing number of 'teaching hospitals'. During the conflict, the inevitable result of military weaponry and poor living conditions, on human bodies and minds, gave a further impetus to the treatment of injuries caused by a wide range of illnesses as well as wounds, both physical and psychological. The operating conditions of the theatres of war served as intense learning environments for a new generation of surgeons.

Post-war surgery built on the intensified experience of war and was further informed by advances in anatomy, physiology, micro-biology, and pathology. Post-operative shock, and a range of other conditions, were markedly improved by the increasing understanding of blood. In 1901 Karl Landsteiner discovered ABO blood groups and in 1914 sodium citrate was used to prevent the clotting (anti-coagulant) and so improve its keeping ability. A further advance came with the introduction of the continuous drip method, pioneered by Hugh Marriot and Alan Kekwich (in London), to transfuse blood from a donor to a patient. The storage and transfusion of blood had been further developed during WWII and by the War's end had become but another standard medical practice; blood banks were steadily established by the leading hospitals across the civil world. Another contribution to reducing shock was the practice in the 1920s of infusing the patient with a saline solution in order to reduce the debilitating effect of surgery, especially for abdominal operations.

Into the twenty-first century and by now routine surgery can involve such techniques as micro-surgery, robotic surgery, laser-guided surgery. Currently being introduced are techniques of scanner-guided surgery where the surgeon can observe a continuous scan of a patient whilst carrying out an operation. All organs, except the brain, can now be successfully transplanted and many previously inoperable conditions can now be successfully treated. Some conditions remain beyond even the most advanced surgical techniques and the availability of good quality surgery, including even obtaining sterile conditions, remains a serious issue in many parts of the economically developing world.

In relation to the key medical skills of diagnosis: investigation of both how the healthy body functions, and the physical appearance of a sick body, had been based mainly on anatomical inspection and patient self-reports. In addition to these, of paramount importance in terms of more effective diagnosis and so also prognosis and treatment, has been the increasing knowledge of the internal biological conditions (and psychological outlook) of a patient. Verbal reports have always been available as have the 'look' and 'feel' - clammy skin, coating of tongue, areas of redness, swellings and lumps, dilation of eye pupils and colour of the surrounding 'white area' - of a sick person and these clinical signs have over the past two centuries been supplemented by other methods of investigating physiological conditions. These additional diagnostic techniques include use of: the stethoscope – clinical thermometer - blood pressure gauge – X-rays – ultra-sound - microscopy – various fibre optical devices – the tracking of isotopes – electrocardiographs (ECG) – electroencephalographs (EEC) – a range of computerized body scanning techniques and more speciality brain scanning procedures - being just some of the range of 'tools' available to medical professionals in the twenty-first century.

There has also been a steady advance in techniques of examining biological samples such as: blood, nasal secretions, urine, faeces, as well as biopsies and aspirations, manual internal examination and external manipulation. In addition, clinicians potentially have access to their own initial and ongoing medical training and their unique clinical experience, as well as to vast store of accumulated research information gathered over the past 100 or so years; information for which the internet has facilitated more easy access.

The development of new drugs has been ongoing feature of 20th /21st century medicine; if some argue that the big pharmaceutical companies have focused overmuch on potential profitability rather than globally considered clinical priorities. These two are of course not necessary exclusive, but they can be. The point of patient treatment of illness was connected to a massive world-wide medical research (including pharmaceuticals) 'industry'. There is a critical issue with the circumstances surrounding the marketing of new drugs, - not least the issue of placing restrains on, or simply not allowing, the publication of research results showing that a new drug was no better for a condition than a currently available drug or even of a placebo, or has uncomfortable side effects, some of which might even be life-threatening for frail patients. There is a scandal involving the systemic selective publication of research results (even to the extent of refusing access to research data for healthcare regulators). A direct abuse of the ideal of scientific honesty by companies making the spurious claim of necessary commercial confidentiality.

It is an industry (estimate value at 2018 of $1.2 trillion) fiercely determined to use the patent system to prevent generic (much cheaper) versions of their drugs being made available. They often claim that they need high levels of profit in order to fund further research on new drugs. A somewhat dubious claim given that nine out of ten of the biggest pharmaceutical companies spend more on advertising and other forms of sales promotion than they do on research and development of new drugs. In addition, the initial stages of the development of most new drugs is based on freely available research made in, or funded from, the public sector

The trilion-dollar plus global drug industry shares similar potential regulation weaknesses with the global finance industry, the main ones being: working in a political environment reluctant to set a strong regulatory framework and 'soft' on enforcing what regulations are in force; 'regulator capture', as an outcome of too close working with companies, and a the career path that allows some regulatory staff having ambitions to move to, usually much better paid, employment in the private pharmaceutical companies. Numerous books, journals, and web-sites, have revealed the potentially harmful (and expensive) drug production and marketing strategies of 'Big Pharma'. Ben Goldacre, is one noted critic of the ways in which the pharmaceutical industry has been operating, and he has outlined in some detail and at some length the issues involved with 'missing' research data, he writes: 'Everything we thought we knew about whether treatments worked or not was probably distorted, to an extent that is might be hard to measure, but that would certainly have a major impact on patient care.' The outcome being that: '......doctors are kept in the dark, patients are exposed to inferior treatments, ineffective treatments, unnecessary treatments, and unnecessarily expensive treatments that are no better than cheap ones; governments pay for unnecessarily expensive treatments, and mop up the cost harms created by inadequate or harmful treatment......' (Goldacre, 2013, p23 and p28). The industry as a whole, uses a sophisticated strategy involving: financial 'sticks and carrots' on those conducting research, suppressing research that undermines claims for the medical value of new drugs, gaming patenting and national approval systems, prioritising the production of new drugs on the basis of maximising income rather than ones responding to global medical priorities, using misleading advertising and more general healthcare propaganda, at times simply ignoring regulation, along with a continuous and well-targeted process of political lobbying (especially prevalent in the US).

The pharmaceutical industry has the means to do great good; the knowledge, intelligence, and will, to enable this are abundant amongst those working within it. But there is also an abundance of hard evidence to show that it currently engages in a range of scientifically dubious practices and socially dysfunctional business strategies, that together risk causing great harm; and it does so in the relentless task of seeking ever-increasing profits.

Coming back to consider more political trends in the delivery of medicine: as well as accelerating the rate of advance in surgery, and indeed in most other areas of medicine, WWI (reinforced in WWII) also saw a significant increase in the involvement of governments in healthcare – an involvement that had extended to further responsibility for a populations' general health in term of preventative medicine (outlining what is a 'healthy lifestyle'), adequate nutrition, and the 'nudge' effect of using taxation and minimum pricing for products (cigarettes, alcohol, sugary confectionary) deemed to be harmful, as well as using the criminal law to deter use of certain drugs (such as heroin, ecstasy, marijuana).

One darker aspect of twentieth century government involvement in healthcare that would today be considered unethical (and throughout based on an ignorance of genetics) was the promotion of eugenics. At the turn of the century a view was promoted suggesting that the well-being of the population of the industrialized countries was degenerating, both physically and intellectually. That civil life (especially the development of early 'welfare states') was inhibiting the operation of so-called 'Darwinian mechanisms' that were supposed to operate to wean out the weaker members of a species and to enhance the 'survival of the fittest'. More intellectual promoters of eugenics included Francis Galton (a pioneer of intelligence testing) who: '...proposed in the principle of artificial selection or, in other words, a voluntary policy of eliminating the least fittest...' P.Virilio ('The Information Bomb', 2005 ed, p136) Galton wrote '......I object to pretensions of natural equality'. He considered differences in abilities, including intelligence, to be mainly inherited and assumed that the human species could be improved with selective breeding. Four books published: 1869, 1874, 1883 and 1889, were offered by Galton in support of his ideas on eugenics (G.Miller 'Psychology', 1962, p155).

The direction of thought influencing eugenics was at best based upon a misinterpretation of Darwin – of what 'fitness' might mean in a social setting - and at worst a continuation of a view founded on a racist mentality of nineteenth century colonialism. An ideology that promoted the idea of some 'objective measurement' that showed white (Caucasian) upper and middle-class peoples being intellectually superior to others carried on into the twentieth century. Germany had established the 'Archive of Race-hygiene' in1908 and its work would during the 1930s offer some spurious intellectual credibility to Hitler's belief in Aryan racial superiority, and the demonization of a threat to 'racial purity', and so to the ascendancy of the German nation. A demonization by Hitler that included whole groups such as gypsies, Jews, communists, along with those with mental illness and intellectual impairment. But it was mainly qualified doctors who sterilised over a quarter of a million 'social misfits' in the lead up to WWII – culminating in the death camps and the relentlessly efficient (industrialized) murder of millions as part of the 'final solution'. Few in the German medical profession challenged the false medical justifications offered for the social (claimed as biologically hygienic) cleansing of the German population's 'impairments'. It was qualified doctors, most notably Josef Mengel, who conducted a series of cruel and often fatal experiments on children and adults in a number of concentration camps. Including experiments on Roma (gypsies) and Jews, purporting to test race-based reaction to contagious diseases. Paradoxically, aspects of the philosophical mythology created to influence the projection of superior racial types were the ideas of the philosopher Friedrich Nietzsche, who was himself, similar to most

Nazi leaders, very much less than a super-human specimen.

Influenced by a similar misunderstanding of genetics, and mostly lacking any restraining moral sensitivity, a number of governments introduced sterilization laws including – the Swiss canton of Waadt 1928, Denmark 1929, Norway 1934, Sweden and Finland 1935, as well as the notorious Germany 'Hereditary Health Law' of the 1930s. These, and some other ethical issues in medicine, resulted in pressure from the international ethical movement for medicine led to the introduction in 1947 of the 'Nuremberg Code' on this. Although, even as recently as well into the post WWII period, some US states have continued with forced sterilization, and in India pressure was brought to bear on sections of its population to undertake voluntary sterilization (offering free transistor radios as an inducement in one project).

During the twentieth century, governments across the world have sought to distinguish the 'respectable norm' and the 'socially troublesome' within their citizenry, using this distinction to justify economic and social inequality and even expulsion (ethnic cleansing), torture, and killing. Sadly, as members of social communities, medical professionals have on occasion been complicit with such governments in the misuse of science and in activities contrary to traditionally assumed medical ideals.

Other ethical problems have involved psychiatric care. Including an ongoing propensity to apply unproven treatments: surgical, pharmaceutical, and therapeutic. One extreme activity involved Russian psychiatrists being complicit in committing political dissidents to secure psychiatric care (1964 onwards). Such techniques as: chemical 'restraint' - lobotomies and other types of brain surgery – and the use of electric shock treatment have been misused by professionals in mental health-settings. More generally, the use of psychiatric 'labelling' has been deployed to support, or even define, the normative (bourgeoisie) categorization of anti-social behaviour.

Fertility-related medicine became increasingly involved in repro-ductive and recreational sexual activity. Birth control that had been mainly reliant on restraint, couples aligning sexual intercourse with the female reproductive cycle, or on various types of vaginal 'barriers', was revolutionised with the introduction of the female birth-control pill (oral-contraceptive - based on an understanding of the role of the hormones oestrogen and testosterone) from 1959.

Control over fertility was a significant factor in sexual activity becoming more of a recreational activity leading to expectations of an entitlement to pleasure. The internet has made pornography easily available, popular newspapers and magazines, teenage and even mainstream films and T.V. programmes push the boundaries of acceptability further and further toward an outlook run through with infantilism, with sex as but another game having the goal of immediate gratification. Viagra, and other chemical aids to penile erection, allows penetrative sex into male old age and offers heightened sensation to females. But, along with the psychological impact of sexual freedoms and expectations of self-gratification, people place themselves at increased risk of STDs and of some cancers. As well as emotional problems related to performance expectation, body shape, of rejection, and of the self-loathing due to the unappealing emotional shallowness that can for some be an unexpected feature of casual sexual encounters – these can be 'fun' but they can also be emotionally problematic, and a potential risk to health, depending on the individuals involved and the context.

More positively, ways have been found to enable infertile (and same sex) couples and singles to become biological parents, to have some element of their own genetic constitution passed on. Implanting an externally fertilised egg into a substitute womb for gestation (so-called 'test-tube' babies). There is also the use of invitro fertilization techniques (IVF) and, perhaps sometime soon, the possibility of human genetic cloning.

The twentieth century was to see outstanding work on gaining knowledge of the human brain and central nervous system, if the most significant advances came in the fourth quarter of the century from when computer-aided scanning technologies became available. In the 1920s Walter Hess was able to build on past work to design a functional map of the brain in which he identified some links between an organ and a part of the brain involved in its function. A few years on and Hans Berger had devised a way of recording the electrical activity of the brain, leading to the development of the electro-encephalograph (EEG). By 1928 Edgar Adrian had found a technique for monitoring the electrical activity at the level of a single brain cell.

In 1952 Alan Hodgkin and Alexander Huxley confirm that the generation of electrical impulses that are the basis of communication in the nervous system are based upon ions moving across a neuron's membrane. In 1976 Erwin Neher and Bert Sakmann developed a technique for measuring the action of a single 'ionic channel', so enabling a better understanding of the passage of the ions (potassium, sodium, and chlorine) via molecular channels, the action of which is triggered by nerve impulses.

The continuing focus on the cellular level of the nervous system was highlighted by Ulf von Euler's discovery that during the process of nerve-cell communication tiny amounts of chemical substances that, prior to release, accumulate within the cell. With these 'neurotransmitters' being released into the tiny gap, the 'synapse', between connected cells. Further advances in understanding communication between cells in the nervous system were made in 1966 when Bernard Katz, in his book 'Nerve, Muscle, and Synapse', described the cellular mechanism involved in the release of neurotransmitters. Changes taking place at synapses were also the focus for identifying the neurological base for learning and in 1969 Eric Kandel demonstrated that if he interfered with the chemical changes occurring at synapses 'during learning' then this blocked the route to long-term learning; so making a significant contribution to the understanding of the process of memory.

In 1958 Arvid Carlsson discovered that a lack of the neuro-transmitter dopamine was a key factor in Parkinson's disease, a discovery that led to the development of the drug L-Dopa, which has been used to at least somewhat mitigate the affects of the condition. Continuing to outline the functional structure of the brain Roger Sperry, in 1961, established that the brain had a lateral diversity in function embodied in two cerebral hemispheres. In 1962 David Hubel and Torsten Wiesel identified areas of the brain with a central role in the visual system – the neural route too and from the sensory cells to the information processing areas.

Magnetic Resonance Imaging (MRI) introduced in the 1970s allowed access to a detailed, two-dimensional, image of tissue (including internal organs) and bone. By the twenty-first century the advance of computer graphics, allied to improved scanning techniques, made three-dimensional images of the brain (and other organs) available.

The fourth quarter of the 20th, and early decades of the 21st centuries, saw a veritable explosion in gaining knowledge of the structure and function of the brain and nervous system. A process, aided by developments in biochemistry, but one that could not have reached the current level of knowledge without the development of various means of computer-aided electronic scanning. I will be considering the brain in more detail in the psychology section below. For now it is sufficient to note that, even if there is still much to learn about the whole nervous system and its relationship to other bodily systems, knowledge that we have gained has allowed a significant improvement in our understanding of the brain's vulnerability to physical trauma and psychological illness. A knowledge that has led to the improvement in surgical procedures, drug treatments, and also in the design of various therapeutic techniques such as versions of psychoanalysis and cognitive behaviour therapies.

Landmarks on the way to these advances included Hans Selye's highlighting the role of the mind in illness, in particular the contribution of stress in inducing physical symptoms; an aspect of psychiatric research still continuing apace. In the 1950s Abram Hoffer discovered that the urine of schizophrenic individuals contained the oxidative product of certain substances, including adrenaline, and that these products could have a toxic effect on the central nervous system. He offered vitamin-based treatments that were found to alleviate conditions such as schizophrenia.

Globally, the body looked to in relation to healthcare has been the World Health Organization (WHO) officially established on 7th April 1948 (7th April is now set as 'World Health Day' each year). The WHO now has about 7,000 staff working in about 150 countries, with its headquarters in Geneva; it notes its primary role being: '.....the directing and coordinating authority on international health within the United Nations system.' And if inhibited by similar difficulties of its parent body, including addressing varying national interests, the WHO continues as an important organisation in monitoring, data collection, basic in-field research, and managing appropriate healthcare interventions.

There have been various WHO initiatives to eradicate diseases such as malaria and small-pox in the 1950s; the latter being significantly more successfully than the former. Malaria continues to be a serious issue in terms of global health, with over 200m people suffering and deaths running at about 450,000 per year (possible considerably more) – about 90% of the deaths being in rural Sub-Saharan Africa and about 75% being children under 5 years old. The philanthropic charity, the Bill and Malinda Gates Foundation, has been funding and overseeing a well-publicised initiative, initially aimed to eradicate malaria. But, as yet, with only very limited success. The WHO 'World Malaria Report' (2017) noted that what had been a slowly improving situation had stalled, with 5m more suffering from the condition in 2016 than in 2015, and the death rate being similar between these two years.

More generally, WHO data indicates that the primary causes of death differ quite significantly between richer and poorer countries. Unsurprisingly, the main causes of death in the rich countries (with their, on average, much longer-lived citizens) are conditions linked to affluence, whereas those in the poorer are ones are linked to poverty and the lack of adequate healthcare systems. Heart disease, alzheimer's and other forms of dementia, pulmonary conditions, cancers, and diabetes, being the common causes of death in the rich countries. Whereas, heart disease, lower respiratory infections, diarrheal disease, and HIV/AIDs, being more common in poorer countries. Death occurring during pregnancy and in child-birth are also at considerable higher rates in poorer countries than in rich ones.

Even within the economically developed countries there is a marked difference in health outlooks between wealthy and poor; with life-span differences of up to 20 years, favouring the wealthy. In most developing countries many of the senior politicians and business leaders seek healthcare for themselves and their families abroad. Compounding the problems, IMF structural readjustment programmes imposed on developing countries have put already meagre healthcare budgets under increasing pressure. All in all, we have a global picture of markedly unequal provision of healthcare; one highlighted during the current Covid-19 pandemic.

Medical professionals and sociologists who have studied healthcare have, as the twentieth century progressed, placed the sick individual within a wider network of social factors. According to Ashley Crossman (on-line About.com Sociology, accessed 15/06/2012): 'Sociologists have demonstrated that the spread of diseases is heavily influenced by the socioeconomic status of individuals, ethnic traditions or beliefs, and other cultural factors. Where medical research might gather statistics on disease, a sociological perspective of an illness would provide insight on what external factors caused the demographics who contracted the disease to become ill.'

Scientific medicine has considerably advanced the understanding of the human body and how to intervene to prevent or treat illness. But a wider perspective on healthcare gained during the past 200 years has shown that the most effective interventions can often require government action at a fairly obvious and achievable level. Action to ensure such things as: clean drinking water, clean air, efficient sanitation, adequate levels of nutrition, decent housing, and healthy working conditions. If the economically developed civil world were to want to intervene effectively to reduced deaths by illness in the economically developing countries it would work with governments, and if appropriate local communities, to ensure these quite basic (in 'civil' terms) conditions pertain. High profile initiatives such as those taken to combat malaria, HIV, ebola, small-pox, polio, etc. are useful and can save many lives, but in terms of the quality of human lives and improvement in human physical and psychological health, the more mundane improvements in living circumstances could achieve much more both in health and more general social terms.

The dynamism and innovation of scientific medicine is mostly generated in the laboratory, if increasingly determined in political cabinet offices and commercial boardrooms. Political influence is often directed by personal ambition and narrow ideological aims (accepting that this is more often adjusted to suit the pragmatic considerations i.e. electoral prospects), and the wish to pander to public opinion. In the boardroom there is the affective echo of insatiable shareholder expectations of ever higher dividends (and share values) rooted in the commodification of healthcare.

In the civil world the delivery of scientific medicine continues to be focused on large hospitals, some of which are specialist, drawing patients from beyond a locality and others operating as general hospitals serving local populations (usually of about 300,000 people in the UK). In recent years advancing medical technologies and more easily delivered treatments have allowed for the development of more community-based provision in polyclinics. In countries such as Britain the 'General Practitioner' (GP) is usually the first point of contact for a sick person (in effect 'gatekeepers' to the system), although a significant proportion across the civil world can also access the medical care system via 'Accident and Emergency' units, usually attached to general hospitals. More recently health advice (including whether a condition requires hospital treatment) has been made available via telephone advice lines and via a proliferation of medical advice internet web-sites and phone-based applications.

The internet has played a role in providing useful medical information for lay-people, and facilitated access to forums led by suffers of a physical or mental health condition, but it has also served to undermine the authority of medical experts. Nowadays it is feasible to imagine a patient consulting their GP armed with (informed by) a range of information about their symptoms garnered from the veritable mass of medical information available on publically accessible internet sites.

To consider modern medicine at its best – encompassing twentieth century advances in technology, medicines, and specialist medical knowledge - imagine such scenarios as: the intensive care unit of a paediatric ward, as medical staff deploy sophisticated medical equipment and clinical skills to manage very poorly babies and young children - or the semi-lit room in the hospice, as enlightened care skilfully delivered, including effective use of painkillers, eases the passing from life of a terminally ill person whose final years and months have probably been extended and certainly made more comfortable by medical intervention - or the drama of an emergency department as remarkably well-coordinated, multi-skilled, teams set to work on a seriously injured person; with its intently focused professionalism deployed by a highly trained medical team, aided by a range of modern technologies and drugs – or the midwife/nurse travelling, on her well-used motor-scooter, between isolated Indian villages; assisting with difficult births as well as administering life-saving drugs or progressing immunization initiatives.

Just a few 'headline' scenarios that can illustrate the value of human intelligence and individual emotional commitment systematically applied to healthcare.

If we consider the relationship of medicine to human beings today (the place of medicine in society), the social and personal – at least for most people in the economically developed countries, those who are able to access it – it would be reasonable to suggest that we have see the 'medicalization' of the human condition.

Michel Foucault's genealogical approach to understanding social institutions offers an enlightened (if perhaps limited by certain assumptions) perspective on the complexity of stages leading to the social construction of twentieth century medicine – on the social construction of the institution of scientific medicine and the central role that discourse has played in this.

Foucault specifically noted the role of the '.....institutional sites from which the doctor makes his discourse, and from which this discourse derives its legitimate source and point of application...' these sites being for Foucault '....the hospital, a place of constant, coded, systematic observation, run by differentiated and hierarchized medical staff, thus constituting a quantifiable field of frequencies...' Other institutional sites identified by Foucault include the 'laboratory' and the 'library' or 'documentary field.' This latter being the sum-total of the discourse of scientific medicine as contained in books, treatises, medical research papers, press releases, articles, as well as the accumulated mass of statistical information that categorises and records the quantification of illness and more general medical information that is used to inform these serving to provide an informational framework (different, but often closely related to, the social and political) within which healthcare professionals administrate the institutional values and practices. (see Foucault's 'The Archaeology of Knowledge', pp 55-61, 1969, English edition of 1972) he also conceptualises this framework as an '.....horizon of rationality against which the progress of medicine emerged, its efforts to model itself upon the exact sciences....' Foucault's analysis, if perceptive in relation to the construction of medicine as a social institution plays down the human input – the nurses, doctors, porters, and nursing assistants along with the catering, cleaning and administrative staff that support them - each interpreting their role in unique (often quite creative) ways within parameters that allow for compassion as well as professional competence to be expressed.

In relation to the current state of the healthcare industry and the basis for its (progressively commercialised) claims to authoritative priority of knowledge, it would be useful to consider Foucault' two questions that he suggests as being useful for evaluating authoritative claims 1) Who is claiming authority over others? 2) In whose interest is this authority operating?

We can see (throughout the media especially) how we have interiorised the scientific model of medicine to the point where it has become a central part of our conscious lives. There is an expectation that the 'medical' can treat each pain, ache, adverse mood, perceived need to re-shape a body, and of course a whole panoply of suspected more serious conditions that require 'investigation'. Medicine has provided dramatic narratives in which are expressed a wide range of human emotions, romance, violence, empathy, comedy, the drama of birth and of dying, the moral issues associated with aging and terminal illness, the dramatic urgency of the A and E dept. A whole genre of 'medical' novels, newspapers with personal 'How I survived this or that potentially fatal medical condition' stories, and articles on 'latest miracle treatments' in the lifestyle sections of newspapers and magazines (often sponsored by commercial interests). Television programmes have proliferated... in Britain there has been 'Emergency Ward 10' of the 1950s through to 'Casualty' in the 1990s, and Holby City in the 21st century; in the USA there has been 'Dr Kildare' of the 1950s through 'St Elsewhere' and 'ER'' of the 80s to 'House' in the 21st century – With most of these being broadcast (along with national variations on medical dramas) across the world - and these are but the more prominent examples of a continuous stream of T.V. dramas based a range of dramatic medical narratives to entertain and to vicariously highlight the experience of the viewer. Ever available are documentaries: airborne emergency doctors, 24 hrs in an emergency unit, life on a children's ward, etc. With celebrity presenters offering running commentaries on this or that specialist hospital ward, seeking to draw the viewer emotionally into the medical dramas being played-out.

And then there are the many TV programmes that consider a particular condition – heart, kidney, bone problems – childhood illness, recovery from an accident or living with a psychological condition such as autism, stroke, Parkinson's, etc. It does seem that each 'celebrity' has to trawl though their past lives in order to identify some physical or mental health (ideally both) medical condition and to share this with the public via glossy magazines or morning TV chat shows. I would admit to mixed feeling about this in that, whilst I am somewhat sceptical about the motivations involved, it could be the case that non-celebrities suffering from a similar condition might gain some reassurance from learning about recovery and of a celebrity revealing that she/he has a traditionally more embarrassing cancer (bowel, testicular, cervical, prostate, etc.), or sex-related condition; so usefully opening up some public space for these to be discussed.

Advertisers, for private medical services and drug treatments, increasingly push the boundaries of ethics, scientific credibility, and at times simple honesty, as they endeavour to sell healthcare 'products'. Including numerous cosmetic procedures, drugs to improve this or that physical or cognitive performance, drugs to improve mood, new drugs (so patented) that research shows are no better than those (out of patent) currently available, and very expensive insurance to cover these, as well as more serious illness.

The mass media and advertising industry's concentration on the medical aspects of being human has made a significant contribution to the phenomenon of the 'worried well'. Informed estimates suggested that the big drug companies currently spend about twice as much on marketing and product promotion than they do on research. As a related aside we might note that for Goldacre (op.cit 2012) this marketing strategy '.....one might argue, exists for no reason other than to pervert evidence-based decision-making in medicine.'

There are a rising number of individuals who present at the surgeries, clinics and emergency units, across the civil world on a regular basis complaining of various 'symptoms' but, when examined are found to be physically well. Increasingly we see individuals experiencing a personal crisis about this or that aspect of body shape, looks, or this or that aspect of physical, intellectual, or sexual, performance. We are repeatedly being encouraged to compare ourselves with some idealised version of what should be aspired to in terms of looks and health. The advertising industry's general intention, made explicit in healthcare related adverts, is to make us feel bad about ourselves, to stimulate a sense of personal inadequacy.

'Industrial' medicine is intent on framing healthcare in terms of a series of contractual services and purchased products, as healthcare is increasingly marketized. Much more so in the US, but increasingly in the UK and some other European countries. Medical and cosmetic services and products are being advertised in exuberant terms, with the promise of glowing health if taken up, and the unspoken but ever-present threat of vulnerability to illness or social rejection if not. We seem to live lives with a sense of our teetering on the edge of serious illness; an ever-threatening horizon shaping our imaginative lives; tending towards the narrowing of our perspective on over-concern for ourselves and those close to us.

Perhaps even more than most social institutions healthcare has a core function in having the potential to provide considerable benefits to humankind, or at least those people in the world that can gain access. A range of life-threatening diseases can now be cured or their symptoms alleviated. One key consideration for the future of healthcare is the form it should take private (basic US model) public (basic UK model). The alternatives (or balance between) of fully commercialized systems or some form of socialised provision. In

Britain, if we ignore the traditional private medical system,[27] and consider current attempts to change the socialized NHS, we can see mostly negative aspects of moves (by Conservative, Con/Lib Dem coalitions, and New Labour governments) to privatise by stealth. Using such mechanisms as compulsory contracting for services and Private Finance Initiative (PFIs) arrangements for capital investment. Experience as of now (2021) has been overwhelming negative, with private companies attempting to 'cherry pick' what look like the most easily profitable services, and even then failing to fulfil contracts in areas such as GP services and at least one attempt to run a hospital. But then the introduction of private companies into healthcare provision was clearly a political decision and not evidence based, indeed lack of evidence to justify changes in healthcare provision is a disappointing characteristic of most if not all politically motivated changes made to a service whose fundamental work (medicine) should be determined by research- and experience-based evidence; and of course the relevant characteristics of any population.

Throughout the world the now dominant neo-liberal narrative is increasingly commodifying services for which most people would suggest quality of healthcare should be prioritised rather than potential for profit. The primary justifications for privatised provision are that competition offers efficiency in delivery and so stimulates innovation and enables cost saving, but the actual experience is more often of reduced quality of provision and often at higher costs. Provision of healthcare is a challenge for governments with a key role in setting out a policy strategy required for prioritising different areas of medicine, training and support of staff, and the efficient management of large complex organizations, (the UK's NHS is the largest single employer in Europe) and of sourcing the means of paying for any service. On the latter, the main alternatives are direct taxation, a government supported insurance scheme, or by some form of private medical insurance; with some developed countries opting for a mixture of these. The predominantly private insurance based US system costs over twice as much per capita as the UK's (the UK in 2020 is just below the Western European average) and arguably the average person in the UK has a better standard of service than their counterpart in the US. Nor do they have to contend with the on-going

---

[27] Britain has the quaint 'forelock-touching' practice of naming public hospitals after members of its 'royal' elite who themselves never use the public system.

fear of unaffordable insurance premiums or the costs of having to 'top-up' limits on insurance-based funding. There could be advantages in involving private organizations (especially charities and other not-for-profit organizations specialising in particular aspects of healthcare) but the way in which any provision should be delivered would ideally be based on democratic decision-making made by populations informed by facts rather than by sophisticated programmes of misinformation, well-funded political lobbying, or narrow political ideology.

It has been argued that in medicine, as in other social provisions, the motivational dynamism underlying private enterprise would allow medicine to advance more swiftly than any other system. But, as we have seen with other sciences, the education and initial training of practitioners, and much fundamental research, is usually state funded (this is especially so with pharmaceuticals) and made available free to private medical companies.

Some form of socialised medicine, with any society sharing the costs of supporting all of its members, removes the profit motive driving development, but possibly at the cost of incentives that drive innovation. Can service to others, and the motivation of scientific achievement, themselves be sufficient incentives? I think that the UK's experience over the first seven decades of the NHS (to the 2020s) have shown that they can.

Socialised medicine also offers the potential for equality of access, whereas a system based on private medicine (in practice, such as USA, heavily subsidised by government funding in both research and delivery) would find it much more difficult to achieve this. Need socialised medicine be administratively sclerotic? Would security of employment of medical staff and their support workers, lead to a system impossible to efficiently manage? Would free at point of access to healthcare lead to misuse? Would doctors easily refer patients for costly investigative procedures on a 'just in case' basis if they do not have direct responsibility for budgets? Would a socialised system reduce the incentive for people to take personal responsibility to maintain their own health? All significant potentially problematic aspects of a publically funded (free at point of access) system threatening, or perhaps just challenging, this model of healthcare delivery. Clearly each of these can be addressed with enlightened management, well trained and adequately rewarded staff, a properly informed public, and sound political leadership.

Healthcare, with even just a nominal free-market approach (invariably substantially subsidised by governments) opens up the 'space' for its commodification. Of placing a monetary exchange value, on an aspect of the human condition that it seems most people would want to be managed not as a commodity but rather as a collective responsibility based on mutual support and care. A free market approach to healthcare prioritises the profitable, the most accessible, the seemingly novel; the type of healthcare that attends to the medical issues associated with relative affluence. These are the priorities that determine research and the development of drugs and treatments as well as the deployment of resources assigned to technological innovations in diagnostic equipment and treatments. The medical career structures, and associated financial and status rewards, of a system strongly influenced by market priorities also draws expertise towards the generally more profitable 'illnesses' of the relatively affluent in the economically developed countries and the pockets of affluence that provide for elite groups in many developing countries:

Most of those living in the economically developed countries who qualify as 'citizens' can expect to have access to a fairly good level of healthcare, although where (as in the US) there is a significant private sector there can be problems in accessing more expensive treatments.

The provision of healthcare in civil societies, based on some form of democratic governance (or at least to some extent the 'popular will' in non-democracies), include governments assuming responsibility for a range of public heath-issues. Including: setting political priorities for such provisions as; mass immunization policy and a strategy for preventative medicine more generally - air and water quality, regulation of medical training and of the pharmaceutical industry, a range of health and safety measures for the work-place, public spaces (transport), and in the home – as well as lifestyle advice on nutrition, drug-taking, alcohol consumption. smoking, and advice on personal safety.

In terms of its contribution to the 'information' store making up our Reality, medicine not only offers a detailed documentary pattern of a developing history contained in thousands of books, other historical studies, of masses (millions and millions) of research papers and journal articles produced by thousands and thousands of research workers There is also an ever-growing store of more of less useful web-based information on healthcare, including globally accessible patient forums. A mainline web 'Google' search hit numbers (2020): heart problems 300m, kidney disease 36m, depression 280m, malaria 57m, schizophrenia 32m, typhus 4m, rheumatism 7m, cancer 752m.

When programmed appropriately I.T. facilitates the storage of detailed patient records available to inform the health professionals that we come into contact with, and a store of information valuable to medical researchers. But one that also offers a set of surveillance information, potentially useful for governments and medical and life insurance companies, on individuals, groups, and wider populations.

A central tension, exacerbated by increasing public expectations, and the increasing cost of treatment, remains the tension between availability of treatment and to what extent an individual should be responsible both for paying towards treatment (for yourself and your family) and also for endeavouring to maintain your own (and your family's) health. On the latter: at the extremes, should people who have repeatedly chosen (in spite of clear warnings) to continue drinking alcohol to excess be given a liver transplant, or a second transplant if, due to continued drinking, the first fails? To what extend should smokers, other drug-addicts, or gross overeaters being given treatment? Can the reasons for their poor lifestyle itself be the results of 'illness' (mental health) or should people suffer healthcare 'discrimination' if the experience of poor living conditions during childhood could have be a contributory factor to adult ill-health? What about treating people with a genetic predisposition to any disease – to what extent might a predisposition to cancer be morally more worthy of treatment than a predisposition to alcohol inducted liver disease or to the accumulation of fatty tissue? We are not far from being able run a genetic disease 'probability map' for individuals; some healthcare companies are already making quite misleading claims on this. Will this sort of personalised information be used to determine access to state services, or the cost of private insurance premiums?

What about the adventurous: the mountain climbers, sailors, rugby and football payers, recreational divers, or any of the many types of amateur/professional sportspeople more generally – if injured, should they be treated when they have freely chosen to risk their health? And if one of these becomes long-term disabled whilst undertaking their chosen sport, should they be entitled to life-time, state-funded, medical treatment and other forms of financial support?

Would the prolongation of the life of a cancer patient by say three months justify very expensive drug treatment….probably for a 30 year old mother but what about an 80 year old? We might offer a £50,000 heart bypass operation to a woman of 40 but what about one of 90? It is the case that healthcare will become evermore expensive and, on average, more will need to be spent during the final years of an older person's life. A fundamental, but political uncomfortable, issue is to what extent should people be expected to take responsibility for their own physical health and mental well-being?

These will be serious choices that need to be made; if not explicitly by democratic decision-making processes, then implicitly by politicians and those who manage healthcare provision. Presumably, we could simply increase taxation or private insurance premiums to meet the ever increasing costs; which seems unrealistic even for the most idealistic.

All branches of medicine have seen significant advance during the 20th/21st century generating a massive amount of 'information' within the store of human Reality. A key challenge for researchers and clinicians is in determining the most useful diagnostic techniques and the most appropriate treatments. And a key challenge for governments is to ensure access to these for all of their citizens, as well as identifying value for money diagnostic and treatment procedures in order to make the best use of invariably limited resources.

Modern medicine, supplemented by use of proven traditional therapies, and taking a holistic approach in a partnership between patients and clinicians, offers the means to significantly enhance physical and psychological health. In all countries there are serious questions to be addressed in terms of funding and the interface/relationship between access to healthcare and personal responsibility. And currently, access to the best quality healthcare is uneven within the economically developed countries and much more so for most people living in the economically developing parts of the world.

Psychology

Human psychology has drawn the attention of thinkers from the earliest times of civil life, it is an aspect of life that most considers wherein lies the essential core of what it means to 'be' (the home of our being). The Pythagorean physician Alcmaeon of Croton (6th cent

BCE) has been identified as noting '.......thinking or consciousness as the distinguishing feature of man and he [Alcmaeon] localized these functions in the brain; he traced perceiving to specific sense organs and emotions to the heart.' Alcmaen's (and later Aristotle's) early suggestions on human psychology were based on self-reflection and on inferential reasoning on the behavior of others.

Psychologists endeavour to systematically interpret information encompassing a field of study that generates the most complex and dynamic forms of information that we know about – human behavior. A complexity that eludes any relatively straight-forward quantifiable research methods and mostly lacks universally agreed basic theoretical, methodological, and even therapeutic assumptions. Given this, it is understandable that a number of approaches - differing in theoretical frameworks and often in research methodologies - have been developed. I will briefly cover only those that became more prominent during the twentieth century, these being:

Psychodynamics. Behaviourism, Cognitive Psychology, Social Psychology, Humanistic Psychology, Existential Psychology, Biological Psychology, and Neuro-psychology.

I will then move from neuro-psychology into some work in neuroscience that focuses on a consideration of consciousness. This final section will consider ideas that have endeavored to address the implications of the suggestion made over one hundred years ago by William James that: 'The explanation for consciousness is the ultimate question for psychology.'

As the scientific method came to encompass the social sciences so too it impacted on the development of psychology. Its scientific 'coming of age' was, at least partly marked by the establishing of the American Journal of Psychology (1887) and the founding of the American Psychological Association (1892). The latter, with Stanly Hall, who had set up the first US psychological laboratory in 1883, as its first president. By early in the twentieth century there were specialist psychological journals such as 'Journal of Genetic Psychology' (1891), 'Journal of Religious Psychology' (1904), 'Journal of Applied Psychology' (1915). The first 'International Congress of Psychology' was held in Paris in 1889. Psychoanalytic Institutes spread across Europe, the earliest included: Berlin (1920), Vienna (1922), and London (1925).

The primary research techniques applied in psychology have included the systematic observation of behaviour (human and other animals), in both the more controlled conditions of the laboratory, and what are generally considered to be more ecologically valid 'field studies'. Introspection has also been used; if this has been a more contentious method of gaining psychological information. It was one that was a primary method for psychodynamics, and the humanistic and existential approaches.

Psychodynamics, encompassed the work of individuals such as Sigmund Freud, Alfred Adler, Carl Jung, Eric Erickson, Melanie Kline, Erik Fromm, Kate Horney, and many others whose work has enriched psychology, not least by provoking critical reaction and in stimulating debate and reflection. Enlarging our understanding of mental life (expanding the imaginative terrain of mental life), its rootedness in early life experience, and the forms that this can take.

It was out of a background focusing on physiological psychology, that Freud began his own career. His education included eight years as a medical student working in laboratory settings[28] and training in the positivistic tradition that Freud would claim he stayed true too throughout his working life; not a view shared by some others. Even as a newly qualified physician he was able to continue with research focusing on cerebral anatomy, and by the age of 29 he was appointed to the position of Lecturer in Neuropathology. According to the neurologist Oliver Sacks, Freud's work as a neurologist (covering about 20 pre-psychoanalytic years) has been undervalued, or at least understated. He draws attention to such insights as Freud's precocious proposal of thinking in terms of brain centered functional 'processes' (mainly as these relate to learning), and his introduction of the idea of 'cortical fields' as '.....large areas of cortex endowed with a variety of functions, some facilitating some inhibiting each other.' (Sacks, 2017, p87).

On becoming a doctor Freud (1856-1939) moved to Paris where, for five years, he undertook post-doctoral work with Jean-Martin Charcot. Here, in a clinical setting, he encountered the condition of hysteria being treated with techniques involving hypnosis; inducing semi-conscious states and alleviating symptoms in hysterical patients and also, by using suggestion, showing that it was possible to induce hysteria in non-hysterics.

This work suggested to Freud a terrain of unconscious mental life

---

[28] As a medical student he studied at the medical school at the University of Vienna, with Ernst Brucke as his physiology teacher.

of which people are unaware but which can be involved in conscious thoughts, and emotions.

Freud seemed to be an ambitious young man motivated by some long-held belief that he would become famous – he used cocaine to overcome periods of depression and occasional bouts of apathy; he wrote a paper on the drug and recommended its use to family and friends.

Continuing his work on hysteria, Freud co-operated with his supportive older friend Josef Breuer and in 1895 they co-wrote and published 'Studies in Hysteria'. In addition to the use of hypnosis, Breuer had also pioneered a technique involving 'free association' – with hypnotized patients being encouraged to talk about whatever comes into their minds. As Breuer's interest in this technique declined Freud's increased, refining the technique to the point where he felt able to dispense with the use of the hypnosis element. Freud's psychoanalytic theory arose from his clinical experience along with detailed self-reflection that included insightful analysis and studious record keeping.

Freud undertook a wide-ranging self-directed programme of psychoanalysis in which he considered how he had dealt with the mixture of emotions invoked by the death of his father; questioning the intensity of his affection for his mother, guilt at the death of a brother and the emotional consequences of some other events and relationships of his childhood. He also analyzed his own dreams. Dreams were to (famously) become Freud's 'Royal road to the unconscious', and recording these was said to be how he began each day for the rest of his life. Freud's early theoretical (psychodynamic) approach, and his descriptive outline of the structure of the mind, were published in his 1900 book 'The Interpretation of Dreams'. And so, a revolutionary theory-based approach to psychology was announced to the world as the new century began.

The initial reception of Freud's work was mostly quite muted and it took the steady publication of his ideas (including 'Three Essays on the Theory of Sexuality' 1905), along with his growing recognition through contacts in the Vienna Psychoanalytic Society (VPS), for awareness of his work to spread. The VPS was initially founded, by Freud, Adler, and some others in 1902, as the Wednesday Psychoanalytic Society prior to being renamed in 1908.

By 1910, following a visit to America and the enthusiastic promotion of psychodynamics by those working within the field -

including Carl Jung and Alfred Adler - Freud settled down to develop his theory of the mind, including child development, as well as his employing psychoanalysis as a therapeutic technique for the hundreds of patients who consulted him in his clinic. It would be the presence of the Nazis in Austria (The Germans invaded in 1938) that led to Freud moving his family to London where he died in 1939.

During the early period of his psychoanalytic theorizing Freud outlined a topographical 'map' of the mind as being constituted by: an unconscious – a preconscious – and a conscious, as interlinked sets of psychic processes. He suggested that ideas and emotions can be generated in the unconscious and these can impact (in affective ways) on the behavior and the emotional life of an individual. The conscious is the area of material that we are immediately aware of, the subconscious of material in the preconscious and the unconscious. The preconscious contains material that can be deliberately accessed (memories and thoughts), the unconscious contains material that can't be directly accessed but from which 'thoughts' can intrude into consciousness in original (undisguised) forms or taking symbolic (disguised) forms. The unconscious is significantly larger in mental capacity than the two other areas and could be described as containing the emotional accumulation of a person's lived experience. An accumulation that can be blocked from consciousness by different types of repression; one result being that this repressed material can find other ways of intruding into consciousness. This can be in ways that give rise to a strong emotional energy and for some individuals can lead to pathological conditions (especially hysteria). For Freud (and most later psychoanalysts) it is in the experiences of childhood, critically the first five years, that lay the foundations of the adult personality: the emotional resources of the adult are primarily established by the impact of childhood experience.

The task of the psychoanalyst being to help the patient bring the repressed material into consciousness, and this re-presentation of these experiences enables them to be reconsidered as an adult, a process assumed to offer some relief to the pathological symptoms – its entering into consciousness allows the energy sustaining the repressed ideas to be discharged and so lose its power to be a source of disturbance.

The power (energy) that flows, in the form of demands, through the three mental 'levels' (the constituent parts of personality) is generated by an instinctual element of the psyche. Freud terms this element the Id, and suggested that it is commonly linked to sexual (libidinal) needs. The unconscious demands of the Id seek release in pleasurable experience (the 'Pleasure principle'), it takes no account of the external world (its limitations and expectations) – ever seeking the satisfaction of basic demands. It is the role of a second psychic element, the Ego, to mediate between the demands of the Id and the facts of the external reality. Although the Ego also seeks ways of releasing the psychic energy generated by the Id in pleasurable experiences, it endeavours to do so in ways that temper an individual's aims to any social reality ('Reality principle') within which they live. Basically the Ego's primary work is in preserving the self, even in relation to satisfying basic physiological needs such as hunger and thirst. The third element constituting the tri-partite division constituting the personality is termed the Superego. The Superego only develops from the time that a child begins to see itself more clearly as separate from others, the time when a child begins to internalize ('introject' - identify with) the views of parents, usually in early adolescence. The processes involved in the formation of the Superego are the outcome of the socialization experience to which an individual has been exposed. Influencing the means by which a person absorbs and responds to the normative values and moral injunctions of the wider society. Through later childhood and early adolescence a person's personality development is strongly influenced by the internalization of the views of their parents, other significant adults, and the wider society more generally as they increasingly interact with it.

When the Superego is developed it forms the conscience that is, for most people, strongly influential in regulating and directing behaviour. The most fully formed model of Freud's idea of developing personality is set out in his 1923 book 'The Ego and the Id' (1923). In his later book 'Inhibitions, Symptoms and Anxiety' (1926), Freud focused on the interaction of the Id/Ego/Superego and how this can cause psychological conflict, upon which the process of repression operates to reduce anxiety.

For Richard Stevens (1983, p38) 'Freud conceived of development as a complex interaction between a biologically-programmed timetable of development and the environment and social context of the child.' As a child grows a close link between the basic instincts is focused on various physical aspects during psychosocial stages of development – oral, anal, phallic (0-5 years), latency (from about 5 years), genital (from the onset of puberty).

Freud's speculations went beyond individual psychology when he suggested ('Civilization and its Discontents', 1930) that out of the sublimation of innate drives, such as the sexual and the aggressive, came the foremost achievements of civilization itself.

The therapeutic techniques derived from psychodynamics have been subject to a range of attempts to assess their effectiveness as a treatment. These have identified methodological difficulties such as: finding control groups, assessing outcomes, of identifying potentially confounding influences (not least the liability to 'false memory' of subjects), forming testable hypotheses, etc. In his defense, Freud would perhaps echo Wilhelm Dilthey in suggesting that the use of measurement and other quantitative evaluation was unsuitable to the study of human beings, for Freud ' Our consciousness furnishes only *qualities*, whereas (physical) science recognizes only *quantities* ......it is to be expected from the structure of the nervous system that it consists of contrivances for transforming external quantity into quality' (taken from Stevens, 1983, p119, noted as originally in Freud's 'Project for a Scientific Psychology' 1895). The very material considered by psychoanalysis is saturated with subjectively generated and interpreted meanings, and as meanings are negotiable, and can be elusive to clarify, we have to be wary of making any final judgments.

A central weakness of psychodynamic theory (impacting on its therapeutic practice) is that its conceptual framework is composed of a series of generalizations amenable to flexible interpretation including concepts such as: unconscious, pre-conscious, conscious, ego, id, superego, displacement, repressions, penis envy, anxiety, aggression, Oedipus and Electra complexes, castration complex, inversion, introjection, fixation, object, etc Concepts applicable to a range of psychic phenomenon (clinical symptoms) or rather, the phenomena (and symptoms) seem often to be adapted to fit the theoretical assumptions embodied in these formalized concepts.

Reading descriptions of clinical conditions I have strong sense that even if a patient were to object to a psychodynamic interpretation of their condition this could be assumed by their therapist to be merely reflecting their resistance to accepting the ascription of their symptoms, their denial of the outcome of 'objective' mediation. On the other hand, a significant strength of psychoanalytic theory is how it has revealed the depth of non-conscious mental content and processes and how this might impact on an individual's childhood to adult development.

Overall, I think that any claim that classical psychoanalysis is an effective treatment for serious mental health pathologies, has to be placed in the context that suggests patients: have to have some belief in the therapy, she/he has to be cooperative and prepared to discuss very personal, and potential distressing, aspects of their past, and the practitioner has to be of high quality (not all are). It is also a treatment that is usually time consuming and so quite expensive.

Claims to the status of 'scientific' have generated a significant amount of criticism, including those from the philosopher of science Karl Popper, who suggested that the theoretical elements of psychoanalysis are unfalsifiable, and prediction of outcomes open-ended and conceptually imprecise. For Popper these three: falsifiablity, open-ended prediction, and conceptual precision, are important requirements for scientific status - he wryly observed that: 'No description whatsoever of any logically possible human behaviour can be given which would turn out to be incompatible with the psychoanalytic theories of Freud, or of Adler, or of Jung'. (Popper, 'Objective Knowledge', 1972, fn p38).

But as an imaginative theory of the mind, psychodynamic psychology continues to stimulate thinking into that deeply, sometimes darkly, complex terrain of human mental life, and as an aspect of most current psychological counseling procedures it continues as a useful therapeutic technique. From the start of the twentieth century psychodynamics has made a significant contribution to opening up the field of psychology and, in accumulating a body of rich qualitative data, it has served to counterbalance the tendency of some other approaches to narrow the study of human psychology to material that was amenable to more quantitative methods.

Alfred Adler (1870-1937) and Carl Jung (1875-1961) were two other early theorists and practioners taking a psychodynamic approach, They both collaborated with Freud early in their careers but split with him due to significant differences of view; exacerbated by Freud's own sensitivity to criticism. Adler took issue with Freud's emphasis on sexuality as the primary force influencing personality. He felt that there was a much stronger drive for 'power', and that the psychological roots of this lay in the basic sense of inferiority and of inadequacy that are felt from the helplessness experienced by a young child. A key aspect of growing up being the process of coming to terms with this sense of inferiority by a process of compensation, undertaking this by focusing on activities that promote an individual's sense of well-being and the self-esteem (sense of self-worth) that arises from success. For Adler, people engage in a continuous striving for superiority in order to overcome the basic inferiority complex that is the psychological cost of being human. Problems arise if behaviour in pursuit of this drive for superiority goes beyond the bounds of the socially acceptable, or impacts more personally if an individual comes to hold expectations based on unrealistic assumptions of her/his own importance.

Adler emphasized the importance of the whole person and used this perspective for developing a school of individual psychology. With therapy being focused more on conscious processes related to attempting to overcome feelings of inferiority rather than seeking to investigate less easily accessible unconscious elements. In order to understand any adult's behaviour the analyst would need to understand each individual's 'style of life'; the behavioural and personality outcomes related to the ways in which a person seeks to compensate for the sense of inferiority rooted in childhood experience, especially those involving the family. A more general disagreement with Freud was the extent to which personal psychology was influenced by innate or by social factors, for Freud the former were more important, for Adler the latter. In its theoretical parallels to psychoanalysis, Adler's theory had all of the inherent methodological weaknesses as had Freud's.

Carl Jung worked closely with Freud up until 1913 and, as with Adler, Jung took issue with Freud's emphasis on the deterministic links between sexuality and personality. The main motive force within the human psyche was for Jung connected more to the 'will-to-live'. The goal of any individual's development being towards 'individuation'; the processes whereby a person can come to understand and accept their own circumstances and their own limitations. '......the process by which a person becomes a psychological 'individual', that is, a separate, indivisible unity or "whole".' ('Collected Works', Vol. 9 Part1, sec. ed. 1968, p275). The role of the therapist is to support and encourage this process of transcendent unification. A key idea for Jung included the 'self', which is composed of conscious and unconscious elements. This self is distinct from the 'ego' which is that aspect of a person's psychology that provides the conscious aims in life; the ambitions both small and large. The character that an individual knowingly presents to the world is embodied in their 'persona'. Similar to Freud, Jung also places some emphasis on the role of the unconscious, which for him was made up to two distinct types of contents. One type being the accumulation of personal experiences that accrues and lies beneath the level of consciousness (although available to it) made '.......for the most part of *complexes*', the other '....made up essentially of 'archetypes'' (ibid, p42), This last being the innate area of the unconscious as the source of ideas and images shared with all humans. Jung described the latter aspect of the unconscious in terms of rich and vivid imagery as containing 'the whole treasure-house of mythological motifs.....' ('Collected Works', Vol. 8, sec. ed. 1969, p310). Within this 'collective unconscious' are shared 'archetypes' which, although generated in the unconscious, represent psychological structures that organize individual experience; even accepting that for Jung these organizational structures are patterned by collectively shared themes of myths and symbols. He suggests that: '......a child possesses no inborn [formed] ideas, it nevertheless has a highly developed brain which functions in a quite definite way. This brain is inherited from its ancestors; it is the deposit of the psychic functioning of the whole human race.' (ibid, p310)

The collective unconscious consists of pre-existent forms, the archetypes, which can only become conscious secondarily, and so give more definite form to certain psychic contents. This form can be in images, myths, and fantasies that occur in dreams, and in drawings and paintings made by an individual. It can also be found in works of art and in various types of religious symbolism which can be found taking similar (usually ideographic) forms in all, even isolated, cultures.

As with the aspects of the unconscious related to personal experience, the 'collective unconscious' is composed of contents that can also for Jung push up into '......the light of consciousness' (op cit 1968, p305)

The following quotes offer a flavour of Jung's more metaphysical perspective:

'The deeper "layers" of the psyche lose their individual uniqueness as they retreat farther and farther into darkness. "Lower down" that is to say as they approach the mind's autonomous functional systems, they become increasingly collective until they are universalized and extinguished in the body's materiality, i.e. chemical substances........

hence "at bottom" the psyche is simply "world"' and,

'The archetypes are the imperishable elements of the unconscious, but they change their shape continually.' 'Clear-cut distinctions and strict formulations are quite impossible in this field, seeing that a kind of fluid interpretation belongs to the very nature of all archetypes. They can only be roughly circumscribed at best' (these quotes taken from 'Collected Works', Vol 9, 1968m,, p179)

For Jung, pathological conditions can result from the inability of a person's consciousness to control the unconscious; perhaps what we might more simply say was losing touch with everyday reality. 'In all cases of dissociation [between the conscious and the unconscious] it is therefore necessary to integrate the unconscious into consciousness. This is the synthetic process which I have termed the "individuation process".' (ibid, p40)

Given a whole series of possible challenges to Jung's analytic and descriptive theory of the human psyche, especially the more imaginative depictions of the contents of the collective unconscious, his ideas have generally fallen out of favour (along with a great deal of psychoanalytic theory more generally) with mainstream psychology circa 2020. But the very richness, indeed boldness, of Jung's outline of a mental terrain containing some deeply layered, meaning-drenched, psychic constitution, opens up a view of a world of affective symbolism shared by human-beings across the world and throughout time. Jung has determinedly mined motifs from the religions of early civil life, including Christian Gnosticism and the Hinduism of the early Sanskrit texts. Its imaginative ambition and Jung's own sense of certainty in his work gives his writing an interest and aura of authority that allows it to serve as a counterpoint to more mainstream psychology and for me to enrich the subject in helping to expose the complexity of possible interpretation that reflects the enigma that is the human individual and collective psyche.

There are of course other more rational explanations, including those informed by advances in anthropology as well as in psychology, for the links between cultural and individual imagery and myths of the type that Jung delineates. But his work provides a mostly unique perspective for psychology and perhaps also stimulates thinking on aspects of our psychological constitution that we collectively share (can access), even if not in the ways that Jung suggests.

Erik Fromm, Karen Horney and Eric Erickson were members of a new generation of psychologists, taking a psychoanalytic approach in work that would span most of the twentieth century.

Fromm (1900-1980) developed a distinctive type of psychoanalytic theory that included the use of existentialist ideas as a definitive aspect of the human condition. By the age of 22 he had gained a PhD in sociology and during the mid 1920s he undertook training as a psychoanalyst and was in clinical practice by 1927 (in 1930 he was working at the Frankfurt Institute – and contributed to the 'Critical Theory' approach in sociology noted above). Fromm highlighted the role of social context and the interactive relationship between this and any individual as she/he develops and seeks satisfaction of needs. 'Man' is viewed as an animal but one with unique insight into its own situation – he has both an instrumental intelligence and also the ability to reason. But the existential cost of the ability to reason, along with imagination, and the awareness of these in self-refection, the '...life being aware of itself' ('The Art of Loving', 1957, p13), is the loss of '...the harmony that characterizes animal existence' (Fromm quoted by Stevens 1983 p72). As an alternative: 'Man [sic] can only go forward by developing his reason, by finding a new harmony, a human one, instead of the prehuman harmony which is irretrievably lost' (op cit 1957 p13). Unlike other animals, humans are faced with awareness of our own death. Our biological constitution means death is inevitable but our consciousness craves life; just one of a number of dichotomies that a developing person has to face (accommodate themselves too) in a process of individuation, one somewhat different to Jung's. But just as a child gains some sense of autonomy in this process of individuation the uncomfortable feelings of separateness tends towards their seeking union with others; union in groups as well as in family and intimate relationships. Different ways of interpersonal relating form an important part of Fromm's psychoanalysis and, although there are common motivational factors that can be linked to psycho-social stages of development (oral, anal, etc), the more specifically individual experiences and cultural settings also contribute to shape the forms this relating takes.

In a book written late in his life, 'To Have or to Be?' (1976), Fromm separates the psychology of 'having', ownership of possessions, of the consumer society and the commodification of relationships, from the psychology of 'being', and its expression in love. In this book he warns of the power of large corporations, the shallowness of consumerism, the 'contemporary, cybernetic, bureaucratic industrialism (whether capitalist or socialist) and more generally of the malaise increasingly affecting humans that is leading us towards '.......psychologic and economic catastrophe,' (ibid. p165). He also sets out how catastrophe might be averted with some suggestions that reflect an admixture of Marxism, Buddhism, and existential psychology. This being based on an individualism that seeks to promote forms of self-development that plays down the role of possessions and enhances the development of the person as self-aware and self contained, even if open in relationships......the first three on a list of twenty-one primary qualities sought for the 'New Man' (ibid. p167) give a sense of Fromm's approach, these being:

- 'Willingness to give up all forms of having, in order to *be*.'
- 'Security, sense of identity, and confidence based on faith in what one *is*, on one's need for relatedness, interest, love, solidarity with the world around one, instead of on one's desire to have, to possess, to control the world, and thus become the slave of one's possession.'
- 'Acceptance of the fact that nobody and nothing outside oneself give meaning to life, but that this radical independence and no-thingness can become the condition for the fullest activity devoted to caring and sharing'

As can be expected from above, Fromm's approach to therapy is focused on ways of fostering a sense of agency and autonomy in the patient and of opening her/him up to being able to build authentic relationships with others. The ideas set out in his book 'Escape from Freedom' (1941) show Fromm's closeness to the philosophical approach of existentialism. In this book he suggests that the most significant problem confronting any reflective individual (i.e. most individuals at some time in their lives) was freedom; with freedom comes the need to choose, and so uncertainty leading to a sense of being alone, experiencing 'aloneness'. Most people manage to accommodate to the sense of aloneness-induced anxiety by adopting various strategies: non-reflection, social conformity (the most commonly used), authoritarianism (following the direction offered by authority figure/s – most common in religions), and some other more extremist (so destructive) attitudes.

These strategies are dysfunctional, in the sense of denying human potential, and a more productive psychological strategy would be to openly accept the fundamental freedom that is the primary constitutive element of humanness and to define your own life-course. To foster the potential uniqueness of your own self (the potential that freedom allows) in order to achieve 'individuation'.

Karen Horney (1885-1952) was another psychoanalyst on the longish list of those who took issue with Freud. For Horney, it was mainly due to what she fairly considered was his 'male-centered' ideas, especially the suggestion of some female sense of inferiority being based on envy of the male penis. More generally, she challenged Freud's emphasis on biological factors, especially gendered anatomical differences. As is common for psychoanalysts, she recognized the importance of early childhood experience and the child's developing mental capabilities (stages).

For Richard Stevens (1983, p 76) 'What Horney's writings offer are sensitive, descriptive accounts of the neurotic personality'. Horney was in the vanguard of those taking psychoanalysis to the USA – she moved there in 1932. In the clinical context, she considered that, once they have been supported to overcome the defense mechanisms suppressing difficult past experiences, many individuals suffering from mental health problems can go on to develop into autonomous individuals, and so can express a capacity for growth. For Horney, 'basic anxieties' underlie neurotic symptoms and a range of strategies can be deployed to help an individual to cope with these She can fairly be considered to be a link between psychoanalysis and the humanist psychology that was to come to prominence from the 1950s.

Erik Erickson (1902-94) (like Horney an emigrant to US) came to develop an interest in psychoanalysis from a background including work as an artist. Probably more than any other of the leading psychoanalysts, Erickson emphasized the important role played by the cultural setting in the formation of personality. Economic and geographic factors are for him important for providing the main context for any culture. The intermixing of individual psychology and cultural factors was one of the main themes of Erickson's classic book 'Childhood and Society' (1950). In this book Erickson also highlighted the importance of 'identity'; in fact comparing the importance that he held identity for personality formation to the way in which Freud held sexuality. He outlined eight developmental stages during a person's life when an identity-related transition takes place. Each stage is characterized by a quality to be developed during the transition: between stages 0-1 year it is trust vs mistrust – between 13-18 years identity vs role confusion and at 41+ years ego integrity vs despair. Although accepting that childhood experience was important for personality development and how subsequent transitions are coped with, he also emphasized personality as developing (out of identity transitions) throughout life. The dynamic driving developmental change creates a 'crisis', as each transition stage is approached and dealing with this, and the accompanying emotional uncertainty and anxiety, is a normal aspect of life. If, as is usual, a stage is dealt with by resolving the crisis (focused on identity) then healthy development continues, if significant problems are faced during this transition - these can have external, social, causes - then mental health problems can arise.

If we take the 41+ midlife 'crisis' as an example: this is characterized by a sense of life becoming meaningless, the best is behind one, a slow grind towards death awaits, etc. If an individual feels that their life has been wasted, if ambitions have not come to fruition, disillusionment with relationships and perhaps work, can contribute to the erosion of a positive sense of self. If these feelings can't be rationalized and replaced by a sense of acceptance - ideally one informed by wisdom gained from lessons learned - then ego development does not progress. Then despair, depression, resentment, at varying intensities, can become central dysfunctional aspects of personality.

An offshoot of mainstream psychoanalysis (if one prompted by some ideas set out by Freud in his 'Inhibitions, Symptoms and Anxiety' (1926)) has been termed 'ego-psychology'. A type of psychoanalytic theory that prioritizes the idea of an autonomous role for the ego as involved in processes: sensory perception, symbolic and logical thought, speech, the ability to concentrate, and the organization of thought more generally - similar to those suggested by cognitive psychology. Heinz Hartmann, Rudolph Loewenstein, and Ernst Kris, were leading psychologists in developing ego-psychology from about 1939 - late1960s

One variety of ego-psychology developed into 'modern conflict theory', making detailed analytical connections between material social conditions and neurotic symptoms, dysfunctional behaviours, and the underlying roots of these. Rather than treating the mind as if constituted by some more balanced structure of id – ego – superego, modern conflict theory focuses on conflict (internal and social) as the basis of the relationship between the conscious and the unconscious.

Psychoanalysis was also influential in developing a 'Humanistic' approach to psychology. A type of 'third way' between the contrasting theories of psychoanalysis and behaviorism. Whereas psychoanalysis frames (pre-analysis) human personality as basically tending towards the dysfunctional if not the actually pathological, the Humanistic approach emphasizes the potential for human-beings to thrive. It focuses upon individuals as each offering a unique perspective (based on feelings and perceptions) within which lies the meaning of their behaviour. For this approach, the way of understanding behavior is located in the subjective experience of any person. It is an approach that seeks the personhood that lies beyond (behind) the social persona. Unsurprisingly, in the clinical setting this approach to therapy focuses on the person rather than the 'problem'.

The two twentieth century leading proponents of this approach were Carl Rogers and Abraham Maslow. Carl Roger's (1902-87) 'self-theory' views the organism as the source of basic needs (food, drink, sex) but also the source of what he terms the 'actualizing tendency'. Interpreted by William E. Glassman as: '…an innate drive which reflects the desire to grow, to develop, and to enhance one's capacities' (Glassman, 2000, p255) and that this tendency (operating from early childhood) is based on our ability to make choices and for humanistic psychology these choices generally endeavour to prompt a sense of self-worth, fulfillment, and happiness.

For Rogers, the individual engages with the world via a 'Phenomenal Field' that represents their perceptual awareness. For each person to thrive, and so promote the actualizing tendency, there is the need for both conditional and unconditional positive regard (especially from significant others) and for conditions such as – regard, openness, empathy – that promote psychological growth to pertain. For David Brazier, a key to Roger's philosophy: '……was the notion that the person is a living experiencing organism whose basic tendencies are trustworthy.' (Brazier ed., 1993, p7). From a social perspective, Rogers would advocate the construction of social institutions, especially the education system, which would allow this inherent trustworthiness to be brought to bear on influencing the process of individual self-actualization, out of which individuals would gain personal fulfillment and the social would be enriched.

The other leading Humanistic psychologist was Abraham Maslow (1908-70) – working from the 1930s, he set out his ideas in books such as: 'Towards a Psychology of Being' (sec. ed.1968) and 'The Farther Reaches of the Human Mind' (1971). Again, as with Rogers, we see a positive approach to the human-being; emphasizing the potential for creativity, for love, and for personal growth more generally. Although initially sympathetic to psychoanalysis his own approach developed away from this as he came to reject psychodynamic psychology's more deterministic view of human personality formation (especially that of Freud). For Maslow, Freud emphasized the pathological aspects of being human (the 'sick half') rather than the positive aspects (the 'healthy half') and he considered that it was more valuable to focus on providing conditions that enhance the latter – the potential summed up in the concept of 'self-actualization'.

For Maslow, in his posthumously published 'The Farther Reaches of the Human Mind', (1971, p7) 'That society is good which fosters the fullest development of human potentials, of the fullest degree of humanness'. Although Maslow's ideas risk approaching the idealistic, indeed improbable, they have enjoyed quite wide circulation. Especially his commonsense 'hierarchy of human needs', at the bottom of which is the physiological needs, then above this comes needs for safety, love and belongingness, esteem (these four are 'deficiency needs'), and then 'self-actualization (the 'growth need'). The hierarchy of needs is still used (at times misused) in a wide range of management courses, staff training, and therapy settings.

The hierarchy of needs, being relatively easy to explain and being arranged in a progression that makes normative sense, is easily accessible. It offers a rationalizing framework for underperformance but, by also opening the grounds for improvement (for an individual to 'grow'), has been found to be motivational. Maslow did concede that the relative importance of 'needs' is liable to change according to differing social situations – yes if starving the physiological (need to survive) takes priority, but to save their child from starving (the love and belongingness levels) most parents would give up their food (physiological level). Different types of cultural settings can impact on which needs are given priority. For example, in 'modernizing' cultures there is now an emphasis on material needs (for gaining more consumer goods), this tends to inhibit the opportunities for personal growth in the sense of self-actualization.

Maslow highlights a certain type of mental experience that is often associated with self-actualization. He does suggest that only about 1% of people are able to attain the fulfillment of the highest level of need, with most settling (conscious or unconsciously) for seeking to satisfy the lower, deficiency-based, needs. The highest level of the hierarchy of needs is potentially available to human-beings during what he termed 'peak experiences' – the feelings that any person can experience when viewing a work or art, piece of music, birth of ones' child, and similar.[29] The more mundane, but potentially more personally satisfying (as more sustained than peak experiences), implications of self-actualization is in gaining the opportunities to develop any individual's creativity, abilities, and skills.

Maslow outlined the lives of particular individuals, including some of his own teachers as well as more public figures such as Albert Einstein and Abraham Lincoln, in order to illustrate the reality of self-actualization. Glassman writes 'In the end, Maslow's ideas have proved influential more because of their capacity to inspire than for their empirical foundation.' (Glassman, 2000, p278) He also notes that: '......the humanistic approach evolved out of the psychodynamic approach, but it was also a reaction to the more deterministic viewpoint found in psychoanalysis and behaviourism' (ibid p253)

Humanistic approaches to the study of psychology focus on the uniqueness of human-beings, and on positive aspects of their individuality – their uniquely personal existence. It offers grounds for clear theoretical overlap with existential psychology, even accepting that here the focus shifts from personal fulfillment to a search for deeper levels of meaning within a complex reality that involves dealing with often challenging personal and social circumstances. Existential psychology arose from the cross-fertilization of the humanistic approach such as that of Rogers and Maslow (and aspects of its own background in psychoanalysis) and the existential philosophy of those such as Soren Kierkegaard, Friedrich Nietzsche, Karl Jaspers, Gabriel Marcel, Martin Heidegger, and especially John-

---

[29] This seems to be very similar to the idea of 'oceanic' feeling initially suggested by Romaily Rolland in a letter to Sigmund Freud, but also taken up by Arthur Koestler and expressed as a sense of heightened awareness in which the 'I' is absorbed in the universal, for Koestler it is a cathartic experience: '.....a process of dissolution and limitless expansion' – Or within a more sacral context it is perhaps linked to the ecstasy experienced by religious believers when in trance-like states.

Paul Sartre.

Leading psychologists in this tradition were Rollo Mays (1909-1994),[30] Ernest Becker (1924-1974), and Victor Frankl (1905-97). The bleakness of the world of the first half of the twentieth century confronted psychology with challenges related to meaning and purpose, in the absence, for many leading thinkers, of any credibility for religious apologetics. In philosophy, Kierkegaard and Nietzsche had, towards the end of the nineteenth century, set down challenging - metaphor rich in Nietzsche and rather pathetically personal for Kierkegaard – interpretations of the human condition. Frankl had first hand personal experience of the dark side of humanity having, as a Jew, been subjected to three years in concentration camps during WWII; including Auschwitz and Dachau. One of relatively too few concentration camp survivors, having to live on with the memories of evil experienced first hand, as well as the guilt of having survived. He set down some reflections on this experience in his 1959 book 'Man's Search for Meaning'. Ending this book (in a postscript added in 1984) by noting that '…..the world is in a very bad state, but everything will become still worse unless each of us does his best.

So, let us be alert - alert in a twofold sense:

Since Auschwitz we know what man is capable of.
And since Hiroshima we know what is at stake'

The source of his outlook of 'tragic optimism' can perhaps be traced in reflections such as his comment (2005 ed. of 'Man's Search for Meaning', p75) 'We who lived in concentration camps can remember the men who walked through the huts comforting others, giving away their last piece of bread. They may have been few in number, but they do offer sufficient proof that everything can be taken from a man but one thing: the last of the human freedoms - to choose one's attitude in any given set of circumstances, to choose one's own way'. This ability for humankind to choose the morally transcendental action fostered his optimism, but the context for the exercise of choice (a concentration camp) fostered his resignation to the tragic.

---

[30] Working in the second half of 20th century – Mays co-authored, with Ernest Angel and Henri F. Ellenberger, the first American book on Existential Psychology, 'Existence a New Dimension in Psychiatry and Psychology', 1958.

It was the determinism of behaviorism, and to an extent also of psychoanalysis, that Frankl rejected. Post WWII Frankl, having previously gained Doctorates in medicine and in philosophy from the same university, became professor of neurology and of psychiatry at the University of Vienna.

His most significant contribution to psychology - accepting that his more general reflections on human suffering and what man may become could be judged a more lasting contribution - was probably his theory of development and his therapeutic programme. The latter being his 'logotherapy'. Frankl explained that he employed this term in order to express the central place of meaning in human psychology as he wrote:

'According to logotherapy, this striving to find a meaning in one's life is the primary motivating forces in man [sic]. That is why I speak of a *will to meaning* in contrast to the pleasure principle….on which Freudian psychoanalysis is centered, as well as in contrast to the *will to power* on which Adlerian psychology, using the term "striving for superiority" is focused.' (ibid., p104)

Neuroses (or rather noögenic neuroses) are for Frankl the outcome of loss of meaning. He accepted a role for anxiety in causing neuroses but felt that more often the cause was loss of meaning in a patient's life, and he was critical of mainstream psychoanalysis for concentrating on anxiety and ignoring meaning. For Frankl, although meaning was generally realized by an individual taking a positive approach to their life, meaning could also be found in suffering; even in the experience of facing terminal illness a person could find peace and calmness, a sense of coming to oneself in meaningful ways. The promotion of pleasure-seeking that characterizes civil society can itself promote a sense of existential emptiness and out of working through this suffering a stronger sense of a self engaged within a meaningful relationship to life can emerge.

Frankl notes that (ibid. p108): 'Logotherapy regards its assignment as that of assisting the patient to find meaning in his [sic] life' and to do so by '……piloting the patient through his existential crisis of growth and development' even if this piloting could at times involve challenging a patient and: '…if therapists wish to foster their patients' mental health, they should not be afraid to create a sound amount of tension through a reorientation toward the meaning of one's life.' (ibid, p110)

For Frankl meaning is not something 'out there' to be taken in but is rather potentially within the human condition as an ever-present possibility. He suggests that: 'Ultimately, man should not ask what the meaning of life is, but rather he must recognize that it is *he* who has asked. In a word, each man is questioned by life; and he can only *answer to* life by answering for his own life; to life he can only respond by being responsible. Thus logotherapy sees in responsibilities the very essence of human existence.' (ibid, p113)

We might view Existential Psychology as an approach that encourages the individual towards a reflective process focused on self-hood. And so drawing on a resource that could enable a person to come to terms with psychological problems; accessing the positivity of outlook potentially available within. Seeking to achieve a cognitive realignment towards life based on psychologically sustaining meanings; even if this is a concept that requires person-centered re-definition for each unique therapeutic setting.

I think two broad approaches that came to the fore during the twentieth century – behaviorism and cognitive psychology - although themselves based upon significantly different assumptions about what counts as evidence - share an allegiance to the positivistic scientific method, and each has its roots in the psychological laboratory,

Behaviourism was an approach that differed markedly from those of the psychoanalytic, humanistic, and existential approaches. The basic methodological assumption of behaviourism was that there is little to be gained from making suggestions about what is going on in the mind, much better to consider the 'environmental conditions' within which certain behaviors are expressed. What goes in via perception and what comes out expressed in behaviour. Behaviourism eschews introspection; why speculate on a range of complex possible explanations for any behaviour, it's more fruitful to just focus on the obvious and the obviously observable ('parsimony' - aim for the simplest possible explanation – so applying 'Occam's razor'). For behaviourists, past experience (learning by association) is important in shaping current behaviors; early in the twentieth century William McDougall (1905) had defined psychology in terms of the study ('science') of behaviours.

John B. Watson (1876-1958) his major work 'Behaviourism' 1930 (he had already introduced the term 'behaviourism' in a 1913 paper) focused on 'public data', on behaviour that can be observed; assuming that an understanding of the conditions within which a behaviour occurs was sufficient to explain it. Watson's aim was to model psychology on the methods – observable and measurable – that had proved to be successful in the natural sciences. What happens between input and output – as not being amenable to reliable measurement, and introspective accounts being liable to subjective error - are of no consequence for Watson.

Clearly, within the laboratory setting the types and intensity of stimuli and the responses to these could be more easily measured. An example of this being Watson's 'Index of learning', designed to measure response on a learning task; or at least the characteristics of any response that can be agreed and recorded. Learning (similar to any behavior) can be shaped by experience, for example: a child learning a language can initially offer quite garbled translations of words and phrases in the early stages of learning a new language. But, with repeated practice, aided by correction (reinforcement and other types of guided feedback), the child can be stimulated to learn more effectively.

Watson was zealous in his belief in the power of taking a behaviourist approach to learning, indeed he even went so far as to echo the Jesuit claim that if given a child of seven years of age they can give back any type of adult wanted. Watson's version was that if he was allowed to subject a healthy child to behaviourist learning techniques he could produce whatever occupational specialist was required including: teacher, doctor, artist, or even a criminal. For Watson, humans begins life with a mental 'blank slate' (a tabula rasa) and such aspects of personality as '.....talents, temperament and mental conditions...' depend upon training (learning).

During the early period of Watson endeavouring to promote his behaviourism, a series of fairly detailed experiments (or given its ambitions, more an extensive research program) that were taking place in Russia would offer support for his suggestion of focusing on the stimulus/response relationship and the shaping of behavior. Ivan Petrovich Pavlov (1849-1936) was the head of the division of physiology at the 'Imperial Institute of Experimental Medicine', St. Petersburg, 1891-1904 (he considered himself to be a physiologist rather than a psychologist). Pavlov planned and oversaw 1000s of experiments, focused on '....the nervous physiology of digestion.' undertaken by over 100 researchers who were mainly medical students.

According to George Miller (1962, p200) Pavlov focused on only three experimental problems during his working life:

1. '....the function of the nerves of the heart'
2. '....the activity of the principal digestive glands'
3. '....the function of the higher nervous centres of the brain.'

Pavlov's classic experiments were focused on reflexes, using dogs as the principle subjects. A dog naturally salivates at the sight of food (an innate reflex) – if a bell is rung at times when food is delivered, the dog salivates; initially over the food not the bell's tone. After a number of food plus bell events, the bell is rung without the food, and the still dog salivates. The dog has at this stage been 'conditioned' to respond to the sound of the bell. But if a bell but no food event is repeated a number of times the dog gradually ceases to salivate, the link between bell/food has been broken (habituation). For Pavlov, the physiological path of the conditioning must be via a neural connection (the 'central switchboard') based upon an 'engram' being formed.

Pavlov, and a large number of his closely supervised students, undertook a range of experiments (over 20+ years) assuming that their work showed that psychology was amenable to laboratory conditions and so could serve to produce 'objective knowledge' in the positivist tradition. He also speculated about the structure of the human brain, setting out his ideas in the monograph – 'Conditioned Reflex: An Investigation of the Physiological Activity of the Cerebral Cortex' (1926) According to Jon Ager: 'Pavlov's conditioned reflex set the stage for behaviourist psychology in the early 20th century' (Ager, 2012, p76).

Edwin L.Thorndike (1874-1949) was another leading figure within the early behaviourist approach. A part of his work focused on learning, primarily using cats as subjects. In one series of experiments cats were 'trained' to progressively learn to reduce the time taken to escape from a cage. He treated reducing time as an 'index of learning', suggesting that learning occurred (took place) by a process of reinforcing responses (R) to stimuli (S) that had the most favourable consequences. This progressive strengthening of S-R associations was, for Thorndike, the learning process. His 'law of effect' represents this process of animals being more likely to repeat a response that has a satisfying outcome and not repeat one that has an unpleasant outcome. He suggested that the physiological basis for this reinforcement was the strengthening of neural connections (pathways) in the brain. This 'instrumental conditioning' differed from the classic S-R type (Watson and Pavlov) conditioning in that a response was contingent on the animal's own behaviour.

To the classical conditioning of Watson and Pavlov, and the instrumental conditioning of Thorndike, can be added a third type of conditioning – that of 'operant conditioning'. If operant and instrumental conditioning are pretty much synonymous, with any outcome being based on a subject's behaviour, they differ, in that, for operant conditioning it is the subject that in initiating behavior (which is then, if desired, rewarded) whereas, in instrumental conditioning it is the experimenter manipulating the changes. Operant conditioning was the variation of behaviourism adopted by B.F. Skinner (1904-1990). Skinner took Thorndike's work further, not least he devised an experimental technique using a 'Skinner Box' that allowed a significant reduction in observation time[31] achieved by reinforcing responses that were 'successive approximations' towards the desired behavior. For example: if the desired behaviour was to 'teach' a rat to press a lever to obtain food then, as a rat in a Skinner box approached the lever a reward would be offered - a repetition of this but with the food pellet being withheld was used as a strategy for encouraging a closer approach to the lever. A process which continued until the lever was actually touched. The next stage being to progress from just touching to slight pressure required to obtain the food pellet, with this continuing to encourage the rat to increase pressure until a point was reached where the action of pressing was sufficient to release the food without intervention of the researcher. The outcome being that a rat entering an unknown environment had its behaviour 'shaped' to undertake a novel action in order to access food. Food is a strong motivator for rats, and perhaps this simplicity of motivator highlights a potential weakness with extrapolating aspects of conditioning experiments on rats to humanbeings, given the more complex motivational factors underling human behaviour.

The type of conditioning focused on by Skinner is based on reinforcing positive behaviors; those which are deemed likely to increase the probability of a specific intended behavior. But other

---

[31] When compared with the previously favored techniques involving rats negotiating their way through a maze or being observed in Thorndike's 'puzzle boxes'

procedures can use negative reinforcement to change behaviour i.e. introducing an objectional factor such as a loud noise, or mild electric shock, when the experimenter wishes to deter a behaviour. Skinner considered that he had moved beyond the S-R relationship and suggested that this was too simplistic and that it would be better to consider two types of response – elicited and emitted – The 'elicited' response better describe the classic behavourist experiments such as Pavlov's where experimental conditions were manipulated to prompt novel ('unnatural') behaviours and the 'emitted' were behaviours that would be naturally expressed by a subject which were then reinforced in ways that 'shaped' a required behaviour. Skinner took behaviourism to the general public in his influential novel Walden II (pub.1948). In which he wrote about a utopian society built on behavourist principles. He considered that a range of social ills – including crime and urban decay – could be resolved if behavourist principles were applied; primarily based on the idea of shaping people's behaviour by the use of positive reinforcement.

On a simple but obviously relevant level, as people grow up in a civil society they learn the value of money and this can be a significant general reinforcer in eliciting desired behaviours. In reality, it would probably be the case that different people would require different amounts of money to do the same behaviour (or the same person in different circumstances), or even that some people would not be prepared to undertake a behaviour however much money was on offer. The extent of human freedom - along with individual differences, especially in terms of motivation - to chose, is a significant confusing factor reducing behaviourism to a potentially useful practical strategy rather than a comprehensive explanatory theory of human behaviour; Skinner himself claimed that he did not have a theory. William E. Glassman (1995 edition of 'Approaches to Psychology', p119) notes that: 'By insisting that mental states are both inaccessible to study *and irrelevant to understanding behaviour*, Skinner was advocating a point of view which has come to be called **radical behaviourism**'. His ideas do at least suggest a version of a theory, even if its primary assumption is asserted rather than reasoned. A 1975 survey in the US found that Skinner was consider to be the most famous living scientist, due significantly to the extent of the county's then cultural admiration for reductionalist science and, at least in theory, rewarding endeavor.

For Fred Toates and Ingrid Slack (OU 1990 DSE202 Vol.1, p277)

'Acceptance of such a technology of behavior change [positive reinforcement] involves abandoning some of our most cherished ideals, such as the notion that man is a free agent. One of Skinners most famous books 'Beyond Freedom and Dignity' (1971) described the urgent need for such a programme of social change.'

There is clearly an element of credibility in relation to Behaviourist interpretations of behaviour, especially in highlighting the potential influence of the wide range of stimuli that confront us as ever-present aspects of our daily experience. Adapting to the world means reacting to this form of experience; I would note 'processing', rather than 'reacting', but of course Behaviourists would ignore this internal operation as being irrelevant. Being aware of the power of social influences, and their role in tacit and explicit learning, is important to understanding human psychology. Behaviorist techniques for shaping behaviour are still used in areas such as: in training animals, for designing advertisements, government 'nudge' theory, and in classroom management. Even accepting that their use in formal education is based on specific, quite limited, teaching techniques rather than on a fuller implementation of behaviourist learning processes.

The limitations of Behaviourism can most obviously be seen in its explanation for language acquisition – that children learn language by a process of trial and error when exposed to language in use by others and the gaining of reinforcement by the reaction of others. Critics point out that language acquisition (the 100,000 + words and complex, often culturally specific, arrangements of syntax and grammar, of the average adult) happens too quickly for trial and error to explain what is happening. And also that a 'critical period' in a child's early life can be identified when more active learning is taking place; clearly some period of enhanced learning ('cognitive') ability which would be contrary to Behaviourist assumptions.

In the 1950s Behaviourism was the leading approach to psychology, especially in the US (where two-thirds of the world's psychologists were working in this time), due in part to its aura of scientific positivism. Behaviorism can perhaps be rather crudely seen as partly a reaction to the highly subjective introspectionist approach of psychoanalysis in the first half of the twentieth cent. And also to a rising confidence in the value of applying positivist (laboratory-based) methods to the study of the 'science' of psychology.

Today, Behaviourism as a psychological theory can seem

simplistic at best and at worst used in the design of vaguely suspect types of experiments, and attempts at even more sinister political and/or social manipulation ('social engineering'); overall its being based on a dismal consideration of human psychology, especially as this relates to human freedom, dignity, and the potential for human agency in decision-making.

Another significant approach to psychology, given the umbrella term 'cognitive psychology', differed from Behaviourism primarily in its assumption that are there in fact complex mental processes (involving a series of more stable representations) that underlie behavior and that these are amenable to experimental methods. In its most fundamentalist version the assumption is that these mental processes can be explained in terms of information-processing models, as if following identifiable patterns (rules). In recent decades cognitive psychology has been significantly influenced by developments in neuroscience; to the point that 'cognitive neuroscientist' would probably be the self-descriptor used by many researchers in the field today.

These processes include: learning, memory, perception, problem-solving, reasoning and language. With behaviour being the result of an often complex interactive relationship between environmental stimuli and mental processes; the latter serving as mediating agents between S and R.

An early application of this approach can be seen in G.A.Miller's 1956 article 'The Magical Number Seven; Plus or Minus Two', with its focus on information processing. And in the same year (introduced at the same MIT conference) there were a number of landmark publications that were to offer stimuli for a cognitive approach. Including Noam Chomsky's conference paper outlining his theory of language acquisition and, at the same conference, a Bruner, Goodnow, and Austin, paper on concept formation, along with Newell and Simon's paper 'General Problem Solver' offering a computational model of cognitive processes. It was also in the later years of the 1950s that artificial intelligence became established as a science; and this operates on the basis of very simple (linear) 'cognitive-type' processing.

Cognitive psychology and cognitive science (incorporating A.I. and related computing) was established in the second half of the 1950s, with some important books on aspects of cognitive psychology being produced during that time. But it was to take until1967 for the publication of a landmark undergraduate level textbook, written by Ulrich Neisser. It was Neisser who introduced the term 'cognitive psychology' in his book itself titled 'Cognitive Psychology'. Currently, about 60 universities in North America and Europe offer cognitive psychology research programs and I would not think that any undergraduate psychology degree would gain professional recognition (by national psychology associations) unless it had a significant amount of content that included at least some elements of cognitive psychology.

But even before the development of the modern approaches to cognitive psychology there had been attempts to re-direct psychology in a way that would apply the methods of positivistic sciences but in a different form than that taken by behaviourists.

Gustave Fechner (1801-87) had already undertaken experiments to study some thresholds of perception, with similar experiments taking place in most of the new psychological laboratories established in the final quarter of the nineteenth century. This type of research was continued in the laboratory of Wilhelm Wundt and that of James McKeen Cattell. During the final decade of the 19th and early part of the 20th century, William James made a series of insightful suggestions as to the content of the mind. Especially in relation to attention and memory; the latter as being composed of primary (psychologically present) and secondary (psychologically past) aspects, that would today be termed short-term and long-term memory. And his suggestion of thinking as being composed of a 'stream of consciousness' experienced by an enduring mind, highlights the mind as processor.

The work (in the 1930s/40s) of, Edward Tolman can serve as a bridge between behaviourism and the cognitive approach in that, although he considered himself to be a behaviourist, some of his work e.g. his experiments involving rats running mazes were explained by him in terms of learning by mental processes (internal mental structures) involving mental representations and 'cognitive maps'. Given Tolman's credibility within the psychological community his work was influential in advancing the cognitive approach.

It was Max Wertheimer who is generally credited with initiating the approach to psychology that became known as 'Gestalt' ('original wholes', or Gestalten), a suggested feature of thinking clearly related to cognition. The initial insight of this is said to have occurred to Wertheimer in 1910 whilst on a train journey. During the trip he reflected on the perception of motion and how static objects seen through the carriage window can be seen as 'moving' if we allow the reorganization of our perception of the experience of motion. In order to follow this up he bought a toy stroboscope during a brief stop at Frankfurt station. Back aboard the moving train he found that a series of flashing lights within the toy could seem to be in motion – an optical illusion labeled the 'phi phenomenon'. One often used in light displays; as a series of static light bulbs, placed in close proximity and lit-up in sequence suggest a single light source in motion. It is also a similar type of optical illusion that facilitates the 'moving pictures' created from hundreds or thousands of static images. We seek to make sense of what we are experiencing and organize our cognition accordingly.

Werthemier along with two assistants, Wolfgang Köhler and Kurt Koffka, went on to undertake a range of experiments designed to investigate the tendency to organize perception into 'wholes' in line with expectations gained at least partly from past experience. But we can see possible links between Gestalt processing, with its organizing of 'wholes' anticipated from environmental 'cues' (clues), and evolutionary psychology, with its suggestion of the need to be able 'read' the environment as quickly as possible, not least to identify potential dangers; so something more innate as well as being influenced by experience.

As interest in Gestalt psychology grew Wertheimer, in 1921, founded the journal, 'Psychologische Forschung' ('Psychological Research') which became a focus for disseminating research findings. Gestalt theory went on to be applied to areas such as education, therapy, and problem solving. Köhler carried out some notable experiments involving problem solving with chimpanzees, showing how, when presented with a 'problem' e.g. obtaining bananas placed just out of reach, individual chimps would, after a short period of 'reflection', use a stick (left lying in the cage) to reach out and drag the bananas to within arms-reach. The interpretation being that the chimp had reorganized (reconfigured) her perceptual experience in order to achieve an aim. The chimps (and humans), when they 'see' the resolution to a problem experience a variously named 'light-bulb' moment, or 'eureka act' (Koestler 1964); have achieved the kind of 'productive thinking' underlying a range of inventive organising cognitions. Kurt Koffka noted that for Gestalt psychology, the basic premise is that: '…..the whole is something other than the sum of the parts.' Suggesting that we integrate seemingly fragmented perceptual experience in ways that seek to make sense of it.

For Jon Agar the: 'Fundamental claim of Gestalt psychology was that structured wholes were the primary units of mental life; wholes were grasped as wholes, not assembled from bitty sensations.' Ager (op cit, p138) refers to the historian Mitchell Ash who suggested that: '......Gestalt psychology, even while designed to be able to address higher philosophical debate [including ideas of Hume, Kant, and in the 20th century Husserl and Merleau-Ponty] was rooted in a working model of the world'.

When covering Gestalt psychology most introductory textbooks offer numerous examples of simple graphics in order to illustrate how we endveavour to see patterns, wholes, and connections, in seemingly incomplete images. They also present ambiguous figures (e.g. the Necker Cube, Rubin Vase, and similar) that can be seen in two equally stable, but very different, images depending on the viewer's perception as she/he endeavours to 'create' an image that makes sense of the presentation, one that satisfies their expectations.

Gestalt psychology notes a 'law of prâgnanz' ('pithiness'), operating to organize perceptual experience in terms of: order, regularity, simplicity, and symmetry.

Simple examples of this include the type of images noted above, but for Gestalt psychology this perceptual propensity can also operate on the most complicated (information rich) types of perceptual experience. These can include the phenomenon of 'schema', the sets of related stereotypic expectations that we carry with us in the form of organized ideas about specific types of situation.

Gestalt psychology, with its focus on perceptual cognition, influenced a turn towards understanding the psychological influences impacting on how we perceive; the process of selecting from the mass of sensory information we are continuously subjected to. The same type and intensity of stimulus offered to a group of human subjects can elicit quite different responses; related to motivation, social background, individual abilities, etc., suggesting that there must be some intervening influences bearing on perception and outcome; some 'mental/cognitive' processes. And it is these processes and associated mental representations that cognitive psychologists seek to understand.

In terms of adherents, cognitive psychology really began to gain credibility, and increasing popularity within the psychological community in the 1950s/60s, as dissatisfaction with behaviorism was increasing within the psychological community.

Up to the late 1970s the consensus within cognitive psychology was that the processing that took place within the nervous system (centered on the brain) was progressed in a series of sequential stages (Donald Broadbent, 1958). From about the late 1970s a range of experimental findings, and related theorizing, had moved the understanding on to a position describing cognition as involving mental processes that could be top-down (initiated by a subject's conceptualization) or bottom-up (initiated by input from the environment) and that in general thinking was the outcome of interaction between these two. The standard model was one of an 'information-processing' framework, where the information being processed was made up of symbolic and conceptual representations, processed within an underlying intentionality. All taking place within a brain-based system with limited processing capacity impacting on the amount of information that can be processed and the time taken to undertake this. The central research aim being to identify the processing capacity (characteristics) for different types of information (such as in: learning, memory, problem-solving) and the factors that influence performance on a task.

Up to about the 1980s, a popular metaphor for the information processing model of cognitive psychology had been the comparison with a telephone exchange - a central mechanism undertaking the efficient organization of communicating messages - but towards the century's end, this has given way to the metaphor of a computer. Suggesting more complex processing going on, but a model still generally mechanistic and based on linear communication; if with feedback loops, or 'recursions' in computer speak. The comparison of human mental thought processing with computer software has led to the construction of software designed to 'model' thinking – well known examples being chess players ('Deep Blue' - a computer programme that defeated the then world chess champion Garry Kasparov in 1997). But also a range of 'parallel distributed processing' (PDPs) connectionist models which are designed to model human abilities such as learning and memory. Being based on assumptions related to the wider storage of inter-connected information in the brain, and the reinforcement of these connections during repeat learning and recall.

Although sharing basic assumptions of the relationship between thinking and behavior, cognitive psychology had developed into specialist areas. Including research into such aspects of mental activity as: decision-making, memory, concept formation, problem solving, perception, attention, learning, and language. In the latter Noam Chomsky initiated what seemed at the time (1960s) a revolutionary advance in understanding the acquisition of language. Another area of advance has been undertaken by Simon Baron-Cohen (1997) and his use of aspects of the 'theory of mind' to offer some explanation of the increasingly identified condition of autism.

Theory of mind is suggested as being the way by which people's thinking can include an understanding of the thoughts (including beliefs and predictable feelings and behaviours) of others. The article available at holah.co.uk – (accessed 02/01/2013) suggests that: 'Baron-Cohen's study attempts to demonstrate that the central deficit of autism is a failure to fully develop this cognitive process of a theory of mind'.

In relation to therapeutic technique, cognitive psychology assumes that individuals have the power of agency, at least to some extent, and so can influence the focus of their own thoughts. This has led to the development of a therapeutic technique called cognitive behavior therapy (CBT). One that involves a 'therapist/counsellor' assisting a client to re-direct their thinking in ways that frame distressing events and experiences in more positive ways. To understand aspects of their lives in less psychologically 'harmful' contexts. CBT has proven to be a fairly effective approach in alleviating the symptoms of some disabling psychological conditions as it seeks to exploit a person's ability to cognitively adjust the interpretation of aspects of their experience.

The cognitive approach has also been especially applied to childhood development – initially led by the work of Jean Piaget, Lev Vygotsky, and Jerome Bruner.

For Piaget children go through developmental stages, - sensori-motor, pre-operational, concrete operational, formal operational - at each of which they are able to perform a particular level of mental tasks – this developmental process is based on the idea of our having 'schemas' for different situations. We begin to develop these schema from birth and by the stage of infanthood (2-4 plus years) children have accumulated these in a quite developed form; schemas can then be adjusted according to subsequent experience. As a child experiences the world she/he receives information about parts of it, this new information is then aligned with her/his current understanding of the world – a cognitive process Piaget terms 'assimilation'; fitting the new into the old. If new information cannot be aligned with the then currently held schema it would be rejected or the schema itself would be adjusted to incorporate the new information – a cognitive process Piaget terms 'accommodation'. Assimilation and Accommodation represent the two cognitive processes that, for Piaget, take place during learning. For example: a child has a schema of a church as being an old medieval looking building with a square tower (the Anglo-Saxon church of his village) then, on a visit to a neighbouring city, he sees a recently built 'Mosque', with dome and minarets. On asking what the building was he was told that this was a place of religious worship just like the village church. The cognitive process talking place here would result in assimilation, not probably being obvious to the child (the new does not necessarily easily conform to the old), but which can be accommodated. The outcome being an enlargement of the boy's schema for place of worship; learning would have taken place.

For Piaget a schema is '....a psychological structure that represented everything about an object or action built up [initially] from basic reflexes' – some schemas are considered to be innate e.g. human face recognition. More recent work (Margaret Donaldson 'Children's Minds', 1978 and 'Human Minds', 1992) suggests that Piaget underestimated children's ability at each of his 'levels/stages'.

A different cognitive approach to child development was that set out by the Russian psychologist Lev Vygotsky (1896-1934). Vygotsky drew attention to the importance of language development and the social factors influencing this. He distinguished between 'elementary' and 'higher' mental functions. The former being innate capacities such as attention and sensation, and the latter being based upon '....cultural knowledge [which] is the means by which cognitive development takes place' (Glassman, 2000). In his classic book, 'Thought and Language' (1934), Vygotsky endeavoured to highlight the relationship between thinking and language – he suggested that very young children have a 'pre-linguistic' form of thought and that, from about 2 years of age, exposure to social influence fosters the development of more formed language. Initially spoken out-loud by the child and then the gradually, by about the age of 7 years, the use of language (for thought) becomes an 'inner speech'.

Jon Agar (2012, p193) notes that for Vygotsky: '...while a child's pre-linguistic thought might have biological roots, as soon as it intersected with language, a social and historical entity, the two – thought and language – developed dialectically.'

In terms of learning, Vygotsky suggested that children have a 'zone of proximal development '(ZPD) which was '......the distance between a child's current and potential abilities at any given moment in time'. This zone of potential learning can be reached and even enlarged given guidance as in thoughtful child-centered teaching. The key to effective learning being that the educator needs to become aware of an individual child's ZPD prior to designing appropriate lessons. This idea is similar to the strategy of 'scaffolding' suggested by Wood, Bruner, and Ross (1976); with a teacher's role being to construct an intellectual and emotional 'scaffold' that supports the child's passage as it progresses from where it is to the incorporation of new information. .

These types of approach to developmental psychology made a significant contribution to the rise of 'social psychology'. A productive field of psychology, William E.Glassman considers that: 'Together, social cognition and social influence touch on virtually every aspect of the relationship between an individual and society, and thus help to outline the subject-matter of social psychology.' (Glassman, 2000, p320)

Social psychology has developed as a specific area of study. One shown to be amenable to experiment, if sometimes these have been liable to being criticised for lacking ecological validity. We do seem to be intrinsically social animals, with masses of experimental evidence showing that we tend to project human type emotions and motivations in any situation where there is even just a hint of animated interaction. The classic 1944 experiment of Fritz Heider and Marianne Simmel offers a simple example. They presented a short film to a group of people – the animated film involved a small circle and a triangle spinning around each other beside a large rectangle – then a larger triangle is introduced and approaches the small triangle, bumping against and pushing it away – the small circle then slowly enters the rectangle via an open 'door' - the large triangle, after seeming to chase the small triangle away, prises open the door to the rectangle and appears to menace the small circle, the small circle moves rapidly about in the rectangle ('as if' agitated). The little triangle then returns to the scene and is able to open the door of the rectangle, through which the circle quickly passes through, shutting the door firmly behind them leaving the large triangle bouncing about in the rectangle as it also attempts to get out – the small triangle and circle spin round one another, as if happy! Even my attempt to describe the film has included some 'human' characteristics – of bullying, trapping, escape, joy, and, when asked to describe what they had been watching the experimental subjects went even further than I have as they described a narrative of 'a love story, a fight, a chase, and victory' (Eagleman 2015, pp 148/9). Heider and Simmel suggested that this finding illustrates just how social, and indeed socialized, we are.

Just to offer some idea of the scope of social psychology we can note that it can range though the influence of specific social settings, socialization processes, group membership, the influence of the mass media, as well as pressures to conform and obey figures of authority. Also, the counterpart to these as rebelliousness and resistance to the pressure to accept social (group) norms and values. Observation, both 'detached' and 'participant', have formed a primary research method, as has the analysis of data generated by interviews and social surveys.

It was in the 1920s that Floyd Alport challenged what were then conventional ideas about human nature as it is expressed in social interactions. In his 1924 book, 'Social Psychology', he placed an emphasis on the significant contribution individual psychology makes to social relationships and in more general social interactions. Although Alport was liberal-minded on some social issues he was reactionary in areas such as workers rights, race relations, and economic inequality, suggesting the latter as 'natural'. This combination of liberal and reactionary infused his interpretation of social behavior. To a greater extent than other areas of psychology, twentieth century social psychology drew a mix of liberal, reactionary, and activist practitioners; and most of these attitudes were reflected in their choice of research area and in the interpretation of evidence.

Research endeavouring to assess the influence of the social has been applied to such areas as: social and political attitudes, conformity and obedience, public opinion, anti-social behaviour (disorder), along with community and small group psychology. Considering conformity, there have been a range of experiments highlighting the influence of others. The US psychologist, Solomon Asch, undertook a series of experiments roughly similar to the following...... two cards, on one of which, say card A, was a straight line on the other, say card B, were three straight lines of varying length, only one of which is the same length as the line on card A. The task given to participants was to identify which line on card B that was the same length as the line on A (the correct answer was quite obvious). The social setting included a group of 'confederates' primed to strongly assert a line of different length to A to be the correct answer. The outcome being that when asked to identify the correct length line over 30% of participants agreed with the rest of the group (the confederates) in identifying the obviously incorrect line; showing the power of group (social) influence on some individuals (Asch, 1955). Numerous other psychologists have conducted, in principle similar, research and have shown a significant tendency for individuals to conform to group (social) pressure. Since the 1950s psychologists across the world have collectively offered a mass of evidence showing that, whilst the power of social influence can be relatively benign, (as in the simple Asch experiments) it can harden into more extreme behaviour such as collusion in prejudicial acts against minority groups or willing obedience to authoritarian political regimes. Two classic (more perhaps infamous) experiments were the 'prison' experiment of P.G. Zimbardo (1975) and the 'punishing mistakes' experiment of Stanley Milgram (1963) each of which dramatically revealed the extent to which a social role (Zimbardo), or obedience to authority (Milgram), can influence individuals. These two experiments are now also often used to illustrate experimental design based on questionable ethics.

The influence of group membership has been shown by pioneering social psychologists such as Henri Tajfel and John Turner. In the 1970s these two developed an aspect of social psychology, noted as Social Identity Theory. Research related to this theory highlighted the role of group membership, as this contributed to personal identity – the tendency we have to self-identify in relation to group membership, and to be similarly identified by others.

Long after his 'prison experiment,' following decades of further research and reflection on the contribution of situational (social) factors to the expression of evil, Philip Zimbardo outlined a detailed, well argued, exposition highlighting the power of social influences. In his readable book, 'The Lucifer Effect – How good people turn evil', (2007), he noted that there is: '......a substantial body of evidence that counterbalances the dispositional [personal] view of the world and will expand the focus to consider how people's character may be transformed by their being immersed in situations that unleash powerful situational forces.' (Zimbardo, 2007, p8) Powerful forces that, for Zimbardo, are mostly the outcome of socially constructed (political and social) 'systems'. He notes that: 'Systems, not just dispositions and situations, must be taken into account in order to understand complex behaviours' (ibid, p10). But towards the end of his book he gives us grounds for hope with an outline of individuals – from Rosa Parks (opposition to racial discrimination), to helicopter pilot Hugh Thompson (intervened in the My Lai massacre), to the young man who faced-down the tanks in Tiananmen square, and many others - who have bravely resisted powerful situational forces at the disposal of political and social 'systems'. In the final paragraph of his book he writes: 'And so, the parting message that we might derive from our long journey into the heart of darkness and back again is that heroic acts and the people who engage in them should be celebrated. They form essential links among us; they forge our Human Connection. The evil that persists in our midst must be countered and eventually overcome, by the greater good in the collective hearts and personal heroic resolve of Everyman and Everywomen.' (ibid., p488)

Looking around the world today we can find plenty of evidence of both evil social circumstances ('systems') and of heroic resistance to these. But in terms of human lives lost, and lives being lived in degraded conditions, it is the evils that are foremost, with the action of heroes offering but a tiny chink (sliver) of light within an otherwise bleak 'heart of darkness'.

Clearly the influence of social context on individuals, and indeed the influence of individuals on groups, especially those with charismatic personalities or having some form of authority, is especially important in relation to the veritable explosion in the use of social media and populist politics.

Invariably, the role of language is central to considerations of social interaction. The ways in which language can be deployed to frame social roles (e.g. mother, policeman, waiter, teacher) in terms of acceptable behaviour patterns. And also the cultural influence of language in use and how it can shape the interpretative repertoire of individuals; how the mix of social narratives that we are exposed to influences identity and so the contribution they make to social interaction. A sub-branch of social psychology focusing on language, 'discourse psychology', has developed into a specialist area of study.

A central focus of social psychology, in relation to any particular social setting, has been endeavouring to tease out the balance of the influence of other people on individuals and the counter tendency of individuals seeking to maintain their autonomy – a balance affected by the specifics of any situation and the character (and even perhaps more immediate 'mood') of an individual.

Taken overall, the cognitive approach (encompassing the social), combined with increasing advances in understanding the physiological operation of the nervous system (primarily the brain) is probably the most potentially productive of the current approaches to advancing our understanding of human psychology – this does not of course mean understanding 'of the human condition', but it is a key aspect of this. Research in cognitive psychology has traditionally been more about understanding the processing of information rather than the analysis of meaning; although these two are of course inextricable interlinked in our own personal experience. So, in terms of a more holistic understanding of human psychology, the possible weaknesses of the cognitive approach could include:

- being mainly a theory based upon experiments undertaken in 'laboratory' settings there can be a problem with lack of ecological validity.
- assumptions underlying the information-processing model (even in its more complex interactive forms) might be misleading in terms of how the mind manages information.
- it is an approach that makes 'second-hand' assumptions on how the nervous system (mainly brain) operates. Experimental observations are made on stimuli and behaviours and self-reporting are set against the cognitive information-processing theoretical frameworks. In recent years observations of the physical operation of the brain (via various types of 'scan') have changed this situation somewhat – but the conclusions arrived at by experiments are based on correlations between direct observation of behaviours and the indirect representation of this as interpreted from scanning information.
- has traditionally tended to downplay motivational and emotional influences and so some lack of recognition of the differences between individuals.

I think it is fair to suggest that cognitive psychology in its broadest sense (i.e. when it includes significant input from social- and neuro-psychology) has now become the leading approach in psychology; at least in terms of the number of researchers and practitioners, and so with the generation of research findings. Methods of modeling human thinking processes have been enhanced by developments in computer-based technologies; 'brain' processing modeling and the design of algorithms.

The next approach to be considered is neuropsychology; an approach which assumes that behaviour is closely aligned to the physical state of the body; especially of the nervous system (central and peripheral nervous system - CNS and PNS) with its primary organ, the brain.

For many neuropsychologists, the development of the CNS, indeed of the whole organism, is viewed as the outcome of an evolutionary progression; not least in terms of its physiological complexification. In practice neuropsychology can be undertaken without a commitment to this interpretation, or indeed any other marco-theoretical perspective, of development. But there is a branch of more theoretical neuropsychology that incorporates a quite deterministic evolutionary perspective seeking to explain behaviour primarily in terms of the evolution of the brain and of the adaptive value of the whole nervous system.

Even accepting the evolutionary assumption noted above, and different views on localization of function (see below), practitioners in neuropsychology have generally eschewed overmuch concentration on theory. This is partly, I think, due to the principle theoretical question being centered on the conceptually tangled issue of the relationship between the mental and the physiological going beyond the correlational. But is also due to the rapid advance in the technical means of investigating the human brain that, along with increasing understanding of the body's 'communication' systems at the molecular level, offers research opportunities that are exciting in themselves. There being a sense that consideration of theoretical issues beyond those of actual function, location and processes, are just too 'speculative' for our current level of knowledge and so are perhaps best left to philosophers or neurologists with a more specific interest in this area. In order to at least to gain some idea of the mind/body issue, I will, just briefly, consider 'consciousness' and some theoretical perspectives in the final part of this section.

During the last decades of the nineteenth century a focus for research was on the interaction of the psychological and physiological aspects of the nervous system. At the forefront of this research activity was Charles Scott Sherrington (1857 – 1952), who gained experience of human and animal physiology in travels between some European laboratories. After settling back in England he studied the reflex responses of humans (at St. Thomas's Hospital, London), then followed a move to Liverpool where he undertook an extended range of experiments (mainly on dogs) seeking to identify forms of functional integration involving different parts of the nervous system, including the brain. His ideas on this were set out in the collection of Yale lectures published in 1906 as 'The Integrative Action of the Nervous System'. Sherrington applied the term 'synapse' for the gap between neurons and in doing so, in effect, highlighted how the brain is composed of integrated groups of neurons.

There can be no more central behaviour characteristic of humans than the use of language; a behaviour for which the twentieth century began with two main brain areas already having been identified (mapped) as being directly involved. It was in 1861 that the French neurologist Paul Broca had, on autopsy, identified (on a 51 year old patient named Leborgne) a relatively small area in the frontal lobe of the left cerebral brain hemisphere as being directly involved in the production of speech ('Broca's' area). This in a patient who, when alive, was unable to use speech but could easily understand writing and the talk of others. In 1874 the young neurologist Carl Wernicke was to do similar for the comprehension of speech, identifying an area immediately adjacent to the cortical auditory area in the right hemisphere, very close to a number of cortical and sub-cortical regions that are implicated in human memory. Later on, the arcuate fasciculus – a dense elongated bundle of neurons - was identified as linking Broca's and Wernicke's areas via a direct neural pathway. These two discoveries illustrate a more general advance in functional neuro-mapping in the late nineteenth century. The main focus for identifying the localization of function was the linking of neural lesions (traumas) in certain localities with specific behaviors, or known psychological deficits.

In the twentieth century an alternative approach ('equipotential theory') argued for a rather more generalized functionality of the brain. Proponents of this approach, whilst accepting the localized nature of sensory input, suggested that it was the extent of lesions (quantity of cells destroyed) rather than the specific location that impacted on behaviours and that, at least for perceptions and other forms of cognition, the whole brain was involved. Prominent supporters included Kurt Goldstein, Henry Head, and Karl Lashley. Some of Lashley's own research focused on the study of rats, and he found that, in rats that had previously learnt how to run mazes it was the amount of brain tissue removed from the brain, rather than the location of the lesion, that affected their ability to remember how to perform the maze-negotiation task. From this, and similar research, he concluded that each brain region participates in a range of functions rather than having a single autonomous function of its own.

During the twentieth century, in terms of mapping function, advances had been made in the process of identifying cerebral hemispheric specialization. A postwar approach pioneered in the 1950s by Roger Sperry and his students Jerre Levy and Michael Gazzaniga.

Some evidence to support integrated (rather than autonomous) localization in the normal brain came from surgical intervention. Picking up on earlier suggestions about hemispheric localization, Sperry (in the 1950s) surgically separated the two halves of monkey brains. Doing so by cutting through the dense collection of neural fibers (the corpus callosum) that join together each of the brain's hemispheres. Sperry found no significant behavioural differences in the post-op monkeys. The condition of epilepsy was thought to be a condition where during a 'fit' the erratic firing of neurons begins in one hemisphere then rapidly spreads across to the other. Severe epilepsy is a very distressing condition, one that can be life threatening, and the US neurosurgeon Philip Vogel, aware of Sperry's work, decided on the dramatic step of cutting through the bundle of dense neuronal fibers that operates as a communication 'bridge' between the two hemispheres. The first such surgical operation (commissurotomy) was undertaken by Vogel in 1962, with eight more completed by 1968. Although Vogel found that there were some changes in the patients, mainly related to perception, the procedure did prevent the more severe 'grand mal' episodes and significantly reduced the frequency of the less serious 'petit mal' episodes. As well as being a useful last resort procedure at that time, the behavioural changes detected in humans – mainly in relation to hemispherical relations to the left and right side of bodies – subsequently opened up a fruitful research field on the functional operation of the brain.

More detailed 'mapping' of the brain had been made possible by the Camillo Golgi's silver staining process (1873) a technique that revealed the structure of neurons with their intricate network of dentritic and axonal connections. This process remains one of the best histological techniques for revealing the structure of neurons. Golgi had assumed that the neuronal system formed a continuous 'flow' of connectedness. It was Santiago Ramon y Cajal who, in 1888, identified neurons as discrete cells, with no permanent connection to each other, describing these as: '….cells with delicate and elegant forms, the mysterious butterflies of the soul'.

Marcus and Freeman ('The Future of the Brain', 2015) refer to ground-breaking work in brain mapping by Tatsuji Inouye (ophthalmologist), focusing mainly on the visual system by carefully recording the neural and behavioural effect of individuals with gunshot wounds suffered during the Russo-Japanese war of 1904/5.

An important step on the mapping of the brain was the map designed by the German anatomist Korbinian Brodmann early in the twentieth century. Brodmann mapped the cortex in terms of 52 areas, with each assumed to have a specific primary 'function'. In some ways, Brodmann's map served as a model for the endeavours to map the brain that followed. One more recent attempt at mapping has been the project led by neuroscientist David Van Essen, based at Washington Medical School, St Louis, Missouri. This project produced a map of the cerebral cortex with 180 separate areas (97 of these being new) identified according to function, morphology, and connectivity.

Overall, the twentieth century began with neuropsychology and its biological links already established as a legitimate area of work within the broad-based disciple of psychology.

In 1921 Otto Loewi, investigated the action of nerves, especially the propagation of 'messages'. For Jackson Beatty: 'In one single experiment, Loewi had demonstrated three important findings 1) that communication at the gap between nerve and heart muscle was chemical, 2) that each nerve released a different transmitter substance, and 3) that it was the characteristics of these different transmitter substances that caused the increase or decrease in heart rate. A similar gap, with a similar form of message transmission, was later found to characterize synapse-based communication throughout the cells of the nervous system, including those in the brain.' (Beatty, 'Principles of Behavioural Neuroscience', 1995, Chapt. 5, p83)

One of the chemical substances that Loewi found was later (in the 1930s) identified as acetylcholine (ACh); the first identification of a neurotransmitter. ACh is a molecule produced and released by motor neurons in order to activate muscle fibers in the central nervous system (CNS), and subsequently was also found to be involved in learning and memory. Since the 1930s dozens of chemical substances have been identified as being involved in neural transmission systems, related to fairly specific aspects of brain function, including the common ones of:

Dopamine – motor activity, coordination, emotion, and memory
Glutamate – anxiety and mood more generally – the most abundant of the brain's neurotransmitters.
Serotonin – sensory processing including both arousal and sleep
GABA - anxiety, arousal and learning – the second most abundant of the brain's neurotransmitters.

(D.E.Presti 'The Blackwell Companion to Consciousness', 2017, p173 notes about 30-40 different molecular combinations/compounds functioning as neurotransmitters).

A more useful outcome of twentieth century military conflict, especially the two world wars, was in advancing the understanding of brain function. This being due mainly to clinicians being presented with patients suffering from a wide range of brain injuries, and the funding made available for medical research (especially during and following WWII), each of which gave an impetus to neuropsychology, both clinical and experimental.

From the early 1920s the recording of 'brainwaves' offered the opportunity to note the brain's changing patterns of electrical activity (electroencephalograph - EEG) and noting the associated behaviours. The electrical waves produced by the activity of neurons were found to come in five main strengths. The weakest (below 4 Hz) being delta waves, recorded during sleep, the next (4-7 Hz) being theta waves also recorded during sleep, when relaxing, and when 'visualizing'. Then there are alpha waves (8-13 Hz) recorded when calm and relaxed and the beta waves (13-38 Hz) recorded during focused thinking such as problem solving. The strongest are gamma waves (39-100 Hz), these are associated with higher forms of thinking, such as reasoning and planning activities.

In the 1950s the development of the technique of electrical stimulation (ESB) of small clusters[32] of localized brain cells (neurons) became possible and so a method of active intervention (and recording of outcomes) was available to investigators. The neurosurgeon, Wilder Penfold (1891-1976), working at the Montreal Neurological Institute, utilized this method during surgical investigation of conscious patients (most with epilepsy) and was able to make a significant contribution to the 'mapping of cortical function' (Glassman, 2000, p56).

But it was to be the late 1960s when the development of computers, and a bit later on techniques of neuro-imaging were developed, that combined to give extraordinary images of the brain 'at work'. Brain 'scanning' offered non-invasive techniques for investigating the function of the brain and nervous system in a variety of forms including: CAT (1970s turning X-ray images into 3-D pictures), PET where a short-lived radioactive substance (tracer), combined with glucose, is injected into bloodstream. When this reaches the brain its more active areas absorb more of the glucose and so also the tracer which can then be detected, MRI (introduced about the same time as PET, is a technique for recording the response to magnetic fields (resonance) of electrical charges within neurons), fMRI – combined with computing software that can convert the initial two-dimensional images into three-dimensional models of the brain.

We should perhaps be wary of assuming too much about the type of information that current types of neuro-imaging provides – Mitchell G. Ash offered a useful warning: 'Are psychological processes now being made visible by neuroscientific apparatus, as some neuroscientists clearly want to argue, or are pieces of equipment and spectacular images being used as tools in a rhetorical strategy to make people believe that this has happened.'

('History of the Social Sciences Since 1945', eds. Roger E. Blackhouse and Philippe Fontaine, 2010, p25). The imaginative power of increasingly striking representations of the brain's three-dimensional 'connectome' might persuade us to make potentially misleading assumptions, especially that the brain is the sole location of consciousness and so realizing a traditional tendency to downplay the role of the whole body and the environment within which it

---

[32] Perhaps just a few thousand - but the act of inserting an electrode can also destroy hundreds of cells

operates. Neuro-imaging is just one, albeit very useful, means of circumscribing the nexus represented by the archaic idea of 'mind'. But each technique re-presents brain activity in particular forms, each with potential (if overlapping) interpretive frameworks.

In the world of Big Science there are a number of ambitious projects seeking to model, or provide more detailed 'maps' of, the human brain. The European Human Brain Project (HBP), based at the École polytechnique fédérale de Lausanne (EPFL) in Switzerland, is a project coordinating the collection and analysis of data gained from neuroscience laboratories located across the world. The target is to, by 2023, have constructed an amalgam of computer-based hard and software that could be run as a simulation of a whole human brain. But given that each brain is uniquely 'wired' then presumably the modeled brain produced by the HBP will be some 'ideal', and so more functionally useful rather than offering anything novel in relation to what it 'feels like' to be an individual person. Another international project with similar ambitions was the 'Human Connectome Project', began in 2009 intended as a 5 year project. A US/UK collaboration with the aim to produce a three-dimensional network 'map' of the whole human brain. The BRAIN project, launched by President Obama in the US in 2013, is a public/private initiative intended to develop technologies for improving brain mapping, primarily in terms of functionality but with a particular focus on pathologies.

Crudely put, in terms of its evolutionary development, we can view the brain as an organ that has evolved as a series of interlinked 'layers' (but with each development changing the whole) wrapped around a central core formed by a spinal cord surmounted by the brain stem and cerebellum, with the mid-brain above these and the neo-cortex overlying all of this. With each layer a 'higher' level of function (increased information processing capacity expanding the behavioural repertoire) has developed, progressively extending the functional information processing capacity of the system. This crude description reflects an evolutionary approach, so functionally based upon adaptations appropriate to exploit environmental opportunity, at least in terms of structure and function. And if we can picture the CNS of organisms ranging from amphibians, to insectivorous tree-dwellers, to ape and on to humans, we will see clearly, the neuro-anatomical stages that has led to the development of the human CNS, and also illustrate that our place is in rather than outside the animal world. With some variation in detail, the evolutionary explanatory context for the development of the human nervous system is accepted by most working in the neurosciences today. One quite extreme interpretation was offered by Paul D. MacLean ('The Paranoid Streak in Man', 1966, sourced from Koestler and Smythies eds. 1972 ed. p264). Maclean suggested a: 'Schema of 'holonarchic' organization of the three basic brain types which, in the evolution of the mammalian brain, become part of man's (sic) inheritance. Man's counterpart of the old mammalian brain comprises the so-called limbic system which has been found to play an important role in emotional behaviour.'

This idea of a tripartite brain is now generally assumed to be a quite misleading description of the brain's emotive and cognitive processes, as well as its functional topography. But it is based on the more general truth that human behavior is an outcome of a nervous system that has developed over a very long period of time – taking different functional forms in response to adaptive requirements. Humans are very different from the creatures that we have evolved from, but to varying degrees we undoubtedly carry the accretion of the serial species evolutionary experience within ourselves.

Whereas genetic constitution might provide the bio-ground conditions for the brain's development, it is an individual's experience that allows the brain to take shape in terms of capacity of communication complexity. Initially a baby's brain is composed of a limited number of mostly unconnected neurons. But by the age of about two years - when the connections between neurons had been made at a rate of up to two million connections per second – a child has about twice the number of synaptic connections than an adult. Then follows a lengthy process of trimming down to the adult number according to how they are stimulated into taking part in neural circuits, which in turn is strongly influenced by any individual child's experience. Given that no two individuals have the same experience (even identical twins) no two brains have the same synaptic patterning.

Brain mapping (as different from mental 'brain maps' posited as being an aspect of cognition by some theorists) advanced with the identification of parts of the brain such as: cerebellum, hypothalamus, hippocampus, amagdala, and the varied areas of cortex being mapped according to sensory experience, as being involved with various 'mental activities'. These included emotions, memory, sensations, perceptions such as vision and hearing, regulatory functions of the body, as well as cognitive functions. But it is also now accepted, that all but basic reflexes involve regions located across the whole brain, in complex interactive ways.

In terms of shared basic assumptions about mental phenomena, the cognitive and neurological approaches are probably the closest of the primary approaches taken in psychology. The most obvious of these being that 'mental phenomena' seen from these two theoretical frameworks are amenable to positivist experimental methods – amenable to measurement and observation – and the view that thoughts and thinking can be modeled in terms of biological processes.

Neuropsychology focuses closely on how behaviour – involving perception, emotions, remembering, and thinking - can be related to the physiological activity of the brain (and the rest of CNS and PNS) summed up in the view that there are *neural correlates of consciousness*. Neuropsychology has two broad divisions – clinical neuropsychology, which focuses on behavioral and pathological dysfunction as this relates to physiological structure and function – and experimental neuropsychology which focuses on 'normal' behaviour, as related to physiological structure and function. Neuropsychology also overlaps with the rapidly developing neurosciences and to some extent with philosophy; where a central issue is the epistemologically, and indeed ontologically, enigmatic phenomenon of consciousness.

On a simple material level we now understand that the adult human brain is formed within a soft pink/grey lump of jelly-like cellular tissue material, weighing about 1.35 kgs (3 lbs), with a volume of around 1,400 cc.

There are two kinds of specific brain (nervous system) cell, neurons and glia. Neurons are cells that operate primarily as 'signaling' units within an intercommunicating system; having three main forms: motor, sensory, and interneurons; but there are suggested to be between 30-100 different types of neural constitution featured at the cellular level. Indeed, Gary Marcus and Jeremy Freeman (2015) note that: '….the word *neuron* makes it sound like there is only one kind, whereas in fact there are several hundred kinds each with distinctive physical characteristics, electrical characteristics, and, likely, computational functions.' The glial (Greek 'glue') cells are non-neural cells (so not directly involved in electrical conduction) present throughout the central and peripheral nervous systems serving in supportive, protective, and nutritive roles for the neurons; they are quite small cells. Which generally contribute to maintaining homeostasis, and more specifically form the layer of myelin covering (most) neurons in the human nervous system. Neurons whose axons are lined with myelin are able to propagate 'signals' faster than neurons lacking myelin; deterioration in myelin is associated with the progressively disabling condition of multiple sclerosis.

As well as the neurons and glial cells there are also the endothelial cells that are involved in the formation of the pattern of the brain's blood vessels. They form a thin layer of cells that line the surface of blood vessels, providing the tiny capillaries carrying oxygen and nutrients throughout the nervous system.

For much of the past 30 years it has been considered that the human brain has about 90 billion neurons and anywhere between 10-50 times as many glia cells – even as recently as early 2000s the estimated number of glia cells was twice that of neurons. The currently accepted figures – calculated by employing an innovative counting method using an 'isotropic fractionator' - suggests about 86 billion neurons and about the same number of glia cells. Interestingly, estimates are of about three times more neurons (about 60.8 billion) than glia cells (about 16.3 billion) in the human cerebral cortex area of the brain. We need to bear in mind that the neuron-based nervous system interconnects throughout the body (even the heart has about 40,000 neurons) and for some theories of consciousness this is an important factor in locating cognitive processes 'beyond the brain'.

Certain types of neuron ('principal neurons' such as pyramidal neurons) have longer axons that can connect localized brain activities with more distant areas in the CNS and PNS, establishing interacting connections across the brain and wider nervous system. Certain theories of consciousness highlight a possible role for these cells in the integration of the (differentiated) information that facilitates consciousness.

Each neuron receives connections (dentritic) from many other neurons and via its axon in turn connects to many more. In the entire known Universe there are suggested to be 'about' 10 followed by 80 zeros worth of positively charged particles, but the connections possible in the brain are 'hypoastronomical' – of the order of 10 followed by millions of zeros.....If you were to count them, one connection (or synapse) per second, you would finish counting about

32 million years after you began.[33]

The synapse is the location at which neurons are connected to other neurons via the transfer of - electro into chemical (or for some electrical – ionic) energy as the 'signal' passes through the sending neuron and is released into the synaptic gap, taken up as chemical compounds, and turned into electro energy following reception by the receiving neuron. This electro-chemical transmission of 'information' between neurons can be excitatory or inhibitory – and any single activated network can include patterns of activity involving million or tens of millions of neurons. The synaptic cleft itself (along with the presynaptic axon terminal and postsynaptic dentritic area) should be viewed as a key aspect of transmission given the complexity of effects of the multiplicity of neurotransmitters, neuro-modulators, and some other molecules involved in the differentiated 'soup' mediating neural transmission; not least in their role in neuroplasticity, including the strengthening or weakening of synaptic connectivity suggested as underlying both learning and memory. As David E. Presti notes: 'Chemical synapses thus have a stunning capacity to finely regulate the signaling activity between cells.' (op cit. p173)

The neuroscientist Susan Greenfield considers the electrical activity of neurons less important for communication than the release of chemicals (peptides); she views the former as more a means to an end. I think she is drawing attention to the more mundane electrical firing system (basically on or off – excitatory or inhibitory) compared with the massive potential complexity of the range of the neurotransmitters and other molecules involved in transmission. A complexity given molecular substance in the fact that the propagation of action potentials and associated synaptic transmission requires the involvement of hundreds of individual proteins; a complexity able to express the necessary dynamic networking by its vast potential for differentiated neural connectivity. There has been a more recent acknowledgement of the role of astrocytic glia cells in the propagation and transmission of 'waves' of activity in the hippocampus, which has revealed yet another complexity-increasing

---

[33] V.S.Ramachandran (2004, p3) noted that: '......it has been calculated that the number of possible permutations and combinations of brain activity, in other words the number of brain states, exceeds the number of elementary particles in the known universe.'

factor in neural transmission.

A large number of substances[34] have been identified as being involved at different types of synaptic connection. The most obvious difference between their behaviour is the speed at which they operate and how they can influence the strength of a signal by controlling the release of neuro-transmitters. To complicate things further, we can have molecules that act as a neurotransmitter in one part of the nervous system and neuromodulators in another e.g. acetylcholine functions as a neurotransmitter in the brain and as a neuromodulator in the peripheral nervous system. There is still much to learn about the functionality of the various types of neurons (as well as that of glia cells and the range of different enzymes involved in neural transmission), but it is an aspect of neuroscience that is advancing at a rapid pace. A complex electro-chemical symphony being expressed within the performance space locally bounded by the intricate bio-architecture forming the cellular level of the nervous system.

The living neural system is always in a state of continuous discontinuous activity, with each individual neuron having a 'resting state' of -70 millivolts,[35] a rate of activity that rises rapidly to + 40 millivolts when it 'fires' ('spikes' – 'depolarization'), prior to returning to the resting state, with this three-part process taking about 4 milliseconds.

Billions of neurons, with each one connected to as many as 7,000 other neurons (it can take as few as 10-15 incoming 'spikes', to generate an axon potential) and firing at a rate of 2-10 times per second. So, if synaptically connected to 7,000 other neurons, this mean firing at a single neuron can be involved in firing 14,000 - 70,000 times per second! For a single human brain, assuming only 1,000 connections per neuron, there can be as many as 100 trillion synaptic connections (very rough estimate) – but the potential number of neuronal 'firing' patterns makes the generally understandable basic quantification transcend any easy comprehension. Can any form of prose adequately capture the dynamic complexity of the brain's operation: an electro-chemical kaleidoscope of organized wave-like mermerations, in

---

[34] Neurotransmitters and neuromodulators - neurotransmitters such as acetylcholine, y-aminobutyric acid (GABA), glutamate, aspartate, and neuromodulators such as serotonin, dopamine, norepinephrine, epinephrine.

[35] A resting electrical potential of -70 millivolts (there are 1,000 millivolts in one volt)

discontinuous recursive flow, at times overlapping, and at times inter-lapping; an evolutionary unique interpreting, integrating, and signaling biosystem. With a functionality presupposed by the relentless processing of information, some in awareness, some not, and some at the shimmering boundary between these.

As evidence of a 'link' between thoughts and brain-states, often accompanied by the assumption that the latter provides the necessary and sufficient bio-conditions for the former, most neuroscientists support the connected assumption of there being neural correlates of consciousness (NCCs - and presumably, at least theoretically, neural correlates of various types of unconsciousness NCUCs - see below). Susan Greenfield considered neural correlates of consciousness, noting that: 'The idea developed in this [her] book is that because we have only one consciousness at any one moment, then the dominant assembly for that moment would have to be so massive that it precluded the formation of any other sufficiently large rivals.' (Greenfield, 2000, p187). That which is held immediately before the mind in awareness possibly involves 10^7 neurons (probably more) 'in less than 250 milliseconds'.

For Greenfield, classical synaptic transmission would be adequate for explaining the co-ordination of 1,000,000 'or so' neurons for a fraction of a second so probably OK for local circuits (networks). But '....possibly a different process is operational [required] in the more gradual recruitment of very large, global assemblies, that will in turn be necessary for consciousness' - Penrose and Hamecroff (op cit. p189) suggest that the processing power missing from the more standard models of neural processing might be explained by an aspect of quantum theory. But for Greenfield (op cit. p193): 'On my view, quantum theory on its own does not hold the answer to consciousness' (see more below).[36] She concludes: 'Whatever the eventual mechanisms of attaining a transient coherence in a very large assembly of neurons turn out to be, there is no shortage of candidates......The future will no doubt reveal more........and hence the reality of a neural correlate of consciousness that is not just necessary but sufficient.'

The perceiving human brain (as 'embodied') operates by

---

[36] If interested, see the whole of Greenfield's Appendix pps. 187-193 in her book 'The Private Life of the Brain', 2000, on the neural activity required to enable both unconsciousness and consciousness.

translating information from the body and wider environment – visual, sound, smell, touch, spatial awareness, pain, taste, etc. – into electro-chemical signals within complex patternings of neurons. But these neural processes are also informed by emotions, expectations, motivations, and other types of internal influences and editing procedures generated by aspects of genetic constitution and the ways in which an individual brain has accumulated past experience. Without this form of selective processing even the complex human nervous system could not manage to process the sheer volume of information to which its sensory networks are continuously exposed; we move in a world in which we are bathed in a sensory, and indeed a social, environment. Even accepting that this selective bias is a necessary feature of perception, it does provide the neural basis for stereotyping, prejudice, poor decision-making and other forms of narrow thinking, it is a cognitively necessary but potentially socially divisive condition. This allows some understanding of the challenge for computer scientists endeavouring to produce a 'self-conscious' machine; the need for some form of complex 'intentional arc', psychologically much richer than being only functional.

The discrete processes involving the activation of a CNS - some types of reiterative brachiating radiation of activation from numerous variously termed nodes or groups of locally situated specialized neural bundles -. situated within local interconnected networks themselves within wider networks, has been considered in some depth by neuroscientists such as O.Sporns (2011) – V.S.Ramachandran (2004) – G.Edelman (2006) – G.Tononi (2012) – they and others have made their conclusions on these considerations available in reasonably accessible forms for the layperson.

Although the transmission of electro-chemical information between neurons seems linear when described in its simplest form; we loosely note neural 'wiring', as if linear communication. But in order to gain at least some idea of the interconnected complexity we need to retain the idea of 0000s (possibly millions) of cells making up any specifically activated localized 'net' spreading out to other brain areas which are then drawn into a brain-based 'event'; and, of course, the ever-continuous background activity running throughout the brain could have significant but yet largely unknown influences.

In recent decades physiological research at the molecular level has emphasized the interlinking of three intra-body 'communication' systems: the nervous system (CNS and PNS), the immune system, and the endocrine system – that together operate to monitor and regulate the integrity of the body.

Neurons and the white cells of the immune system develop from a common region of the embryo and they also share some of the same types of signaling molecules; since the 1970s there has been a section of interdisciplinary neuroscience named 'neuroimmunology'. It has long been accepted that the immune system has a 'memory' facility (centered on its T-cells - the molecular basis for the effectiveness of vaccination). David Robinson suggested that: '......it is becoming necessary to face the probability that both [nervous and immune systems] are part of a single interactive network, with common evolutionary origins and common cellular and chemical methods of communication.' (Robinson ed. 1996, p95)

Organs of the endocrine system secrete diverse classes of chemical compounds (hormones) into the bloodstream which can then travel throughout the body, having receptors that are able to bind onto target cells and influence the target cell's molecular activity. This system includes a number of neurosecretory organs including: pancreas, thyroid, adrenals, pineal, and gonads that, via the medium of hormones, facilitate a form of communication throughout the body. A key organ of the endocrine system is the pituitary gland – sited just under the brain, protruding from the hypothalamus, and so in direct contact with it. The pituitary organ can interact, via hormones, with the brain, and it has a more controlling role over the endocrine system, releasing hormones that regulate the activity of the other endocrine organs.

To see how the three systems - nervous, immune, endocrine - are interacting we can consider what happens when a individual is under stress, very simply put: The conscious brain is focused on the external stressor (endeavouring to work through it or, if too distressing, to try to take action to alleviate it), the brain 'signals' the stress to the endocrine system and, in response, the adrenal cortex (part of the endocrine system, located just above the kidneys) releases corticosteroid hormones into the blood stream and these bind with cells in the immune system and reduce its effectiveness. The suppression of the immune system during a period of stress can seem counterproductive, but this action significantly reduces metabolic resource use, which in turn is available to be deployed to reduce the impact of stress. For a short period of stress this: brain–endocrine–immune interaction is a useful bio-mechanism but, if continued, it can make the body vulnerable to illness, a known outcome of prolonged stress. This is in fact a bio-system reaction (immuno-suppression) similar to that exploited by surgeons to prevent the rejection of transplanted organs by a patient's own immune system.

Although rather crudely shown above, the interaction of these three systems is becoming a given for neuroscience. Even beyond this tripartite interaction there are a number of other bio-systems – skeletal, muscular, digestive, urinary, reproductive, cardiovascular, respiratory, integumentary (skin, hair, etc.) – in continuous communication; via sensory receptors, hormones, neurotransmitters, and similar entities involved as instigators, receivers, or otherwise operating as a medium of 'messaging'; all operating at a molecular level of bio-organization. The body can be modeled as a macro-system of interacting sub-systems, based on an interconnected dependency – individual behaviour is an outcome of this whole dynamic phenomenon. A phenomenon that is itself situated within both physical and social environments.

An aspect of psychology that throughout the 20th century and continuing into the 21st has maintained the interest of some neuropsychologists and philosophers has been the 'question' (more conundrum?) of consciousness. What is this entity that embodies a range of psychological experiences that we call 'awareness of'. Often categorized as phenomenal ('qualia') that are ontologically subjective and experientially constitutive; as famously framed in 1974 by Thomas Nagel as the 'What it's like to be ......' - the subjective 'sense' we (and for Nagel bats) have of being aware. Although reflection on this preceded Nagel, and we can fairly view Rene Descartes (1596-1650) as loosing this philosophical hare to run on into the modern period with his setting out his intellectual search for the grounds of certainty. This being initially found in his awareness of his own thinking (the 'what its like to be...') – if of the act rather than the content. This was the primary idea leading him into separating the immaterial mind from the material body – the mental from the physical. Descartes reduced the body to the status of a machine, one characterized by being extended in space and capable of motion, with the mind being non-material and characterized by thought (a non-extended 'thing') – one, the body, divisible, the other, mind, non-divisible. These two, mind and body, being linked by interactions taking place, for Descartes, via the pineal gland situated at the base of the brain.

This idea of a disembodied 'mind' has done much to stimulate centuries-long interest about the nature and cause of an entity that we know as consciousness. Even today, the sprit if not the substance of Descartes's idea continues to surface, not least as an intellectual marker, in some commentaries of neuroscience – a presence seen in the latest edition of 'The Blackwell Companion to Consciousness' (2017, eds. S.Schneider and M. Velmans). An almost 800 page-long collection of essays by noted contemporary biologists, neuroscientists, and philosophers. Descartes is referenced in the first essay and in at least three others.

The rise (dramatic progress) of the neurosciences, significantly aided by the development of computer-based imaging techniques, has been a major factor in the declining interest in idealist attempts to subsume the material into the mental; most notably by the philosophers G.Berkeley and G.Hegel. Today most neuroscientists and interested philosophers accept the material reality of the brain (and wider body) and that this is the central organ from which consciousness: 'arises', 'transcends', 'is entailed by', 'emerges', 'is an artifact of', 'supervenes on',........ is a 'spandrel', an 'epiphenomenon', or 'by-product', of the material; some of the variously different ways of phrasing the expression of mind from a material substrate. Phrases acknowledging some amorphous, shifting, boundary between the material and the mental; this vibrant threshold, this elusive 'difference' between two realms (domains) has so far eluded convincing explanation. It seems likely that such an explanation will require as a minimum the radical (and ambiguously qualitative) re-positioning of what we mean by 'material' and probably also what we mean by 'mental', as they are each subsumed within some higher-level constructs; or perhaps sublated in some dialectical movement creating an illuminatingly novel synthesis.

The brain is generally functionally framed in terms of information processing in highly complex non-linear, in variously termed recursive, or reentrant, or recurrent, inter-linked neural networks. With this arrangement providing the necessary and sufficient conditions for some wafer-thin (osmotic-like) neuronal processing activity 'threshold' to be past, allowing human 'self-consciousness' (awareness) as the outcome.

I think it would be helpful if we distinguish, primarily for heuristic purposes (as I don't want to get distracted by an assuredly fruitless philosophical analysis involving ontology), between consciousness and self-consciousness. Both involve 'awareness', and awareness can be usefully framed as operating at different levels, if on an underlying continuum. A continuum assessed by a 'scale' (both quantitative and qualitative – see below) set by information-processing capacity. I feel uneasy with my awkward endeavors to distinguish between 'consciousness' and 'self-consciousness' (with 'awareness' spanning both), but I think that at least some debate on these would be useful and so I press on....... . Defining these two concepts can usefully be viewed within an evolutionary context, one in which the development of organisms can be seen to follow a general path of the appearance of organisms able to process evermore complex information – and so exhibit evermore novel forms of behaviours. A range exhibited by the microscopic worm c.elegans moving away from heat or toward a food source, and homo-sapien building cities and designing space-based telescopes. So, within this wider explanatory framework we have identified a phenomenon termed 'consciousness' (defined by behavioral response), a feature of life-forms that we loosely associate with the presence of biological nervous systems. Given this, consciousness can be defined as a phenomenon of life-forms that requires, in addition to more basic organic structures, the necessary presence of nerve-cells (neurons) – the body of c.elegans has 302 neurons and the body of homo-sapien about 86 billion.

There are micro-organisms, such as the single-celled paramecium, that lack neurons and yet exhibit 'behavours' (including a primitive form of learning), so would not meet even the loose criterion I set for consciousness. But a paramecium does have two nuclei within its single-celled body, one larger than the other that is thought to coordinate the organism's activities, with the smaller one thought to co-ordinate reproduction. The identification of pre-neuronal directed 'behaviours' illustrates the somewhat arbitrary, but I suggest heuristically useful, nature of my definition based on neuronal nervous systems. It might be that the larger nuclei in the paramecium body (or the fusion of the two nuclei) is the cellular precursor to neurons, but here my general speculation becomes complete guesswork.

Accepting that RNA/DNA also 'communicates' information on the body's biological development and maintenance, it is the case that neurons play a key role in coordinating the activities of an organism's nervous system. And even if, in terms of information processing, it does seem to be somewhat arbitrary in making the presence of neurons (as entities involved in information processing) a sign of consciousness (awareness), I feel this does at least offer a marker that we can debate. One that allows a more coherent framework for the range of the forms of consciousness and the behavioural flexibility that we can observe in organisms.

Coming now to self-consciousness, I think we can associate this with 'higher' forms of consciousness[37] (a more reflective mode of awareness) and these having additional elements such as learning, calculating, and judging, as well as feelings, emotions, memory, and intentionality. Again, we can detect the sources of these in organisms with 'lower' forms of consciousness – but they appear more obviously with primates and with a definiteness facilitated by language in humans.

The 'individualizing' characteristics of self-consciousness - as a personalizing supervenience on the underlying constituting consciousness - offers the psychological factors from which our personality is continuously developing. A significant factor in forming 'my own' and 'your own' worlds. For the neuropsychologist Oliver Sacks this provides the thematic and personal continuity of our individual consciousness. An outcome illustrated by Sacks in the passage: '…..I am sitting at a café on Seventh Avenue, watching the world go by. My attention and focus dart to and fro: a girl in a red dress goes by, a man walking a funny dog, the sun (at last!) emerging from the clouds. But there are also other sensations that seem to come by themselves: the noise of a car backfiring, the smell of cigarette smoke as an upwind neighbor lights up. These are all events which catch my attention for the moment as they happen. Why, out of a thousand possible perceptions, are these the ones I seize upon? Reflections, memories, associations, lie behind them. For consciousness is always active and selectively-charged with feelings and meanings uniquely our own, informing our choices and interfusing our perceptions. So it is not just Seventh Avenue that I see but *my* Seventh Avenue, marked by my own selfhood and identity.' (Sacks, 2017, p182)

The current range of neuro-scientific (descriptive) explanations for consciousness do seem to share an agreement on viewing the brain as the central organ of self-consciousness, considered to receive persuasive confirmation in the ever-accumulating evidence from

---

[37] Higher again in terms of information processing capacity – capacity including qualitative novelty as well as quantitative content.

brain imaging technologies identifying 'neural correlates of consciousness' (NCC – see below my own reservations on relying on these) – albeit, as already noted, some do set the brain firmly in the body and both within a physical and social environment; three interacting fields creating a nexus of experience.

Theories of consciousness differ in detail, a situation reflecting the 'hardness' of the central issues, the paucity of appropriate explanatory language, and the need to incorporate the ongoing development of research into the current understanding of the operation of the nervous system. Some posit a form of central executive 'macro'- processor overseeing the brain's activities (Baars 1988, and Dehaene 2014), and others highlighting a more global form of integration that is itself consciousness (Edelman 2007, Tononi 2010, Damasio 2012, Sporns 2011). These two approaches generally share a view of consciousness as a property of the more global integration of information arising in the differentiated sources of neural activity. A common feature of these more cognitive description-based explanations is the idea of brain maps. There being two main types of these brain-maps. Those associated with an individual moving within the physical world – an interactive process begun in the womb continuing throughout life as a fundamental, if mostly unconscious, aspect of our 'being in the world'. Linked to this more proprioceptive experience is the less commonly held view of conceptual maps, again gained through experience, but represented more as ideas, examples might be: schemas (sets of expectations we hold of 'standard' situations), social roles, and assumptions about one's own identity. Conceptual maps help us to interpret our experience, as an aspect of our engagement within the world. Where theorists posit both types of mapping they are usually assumed to be interrelated. Attempts have also been made at theories seeking to model consciousness in terms of quantified/mathematical descriptions (Sporns's Graph Theory (see below), and Tononi's phi as related to his Integrated Information Theory).[38]

Most theories limit their speculations on consciousness to the individual level (although some do acknowledge that any individual functions within a social context) and these are mostly set as an outcome of evolutionary processes (Edelman 2007, Pinker 1998). But

---

[38] Tononi's phi, is a calculation/measure of the potential number of integrated states that any system can assume.

some others posit human consciousness as a manifestation of some form of universal property (Nelson 2015, Tononi 2010, Chalmers 2010, Nagel 2012). Encapsulated in Nagel's suggestion that human beings are but '......part of the lengthy process of the universe gradually waking up and becoming aware of itself.' (Nagel 2012). These more 'panpsychic' views consider information (the content of consciousness) to be a fundamental feature of reality; for some, even more so than time, space, and energy (Nelson 2015). These more speculative endeavours link our own consciousness to an intrinsic feature of the whole universe; with information as the 'medium' by which it is expressed.

Some neuroscientists (famously so with Patricia and Paul Churchland, 1988) deny conventional views of consciousness to the extent that they 'eliminate' most if not all of its essential characteristics as currently understood.

Unsurprisingly, and generally usefully, some philosophers have also approached the issue of consciousness (as self-consciousness) with a closer focus on the language being deployed to explain the phenomenon. Daniel Dennett (1991), challenging the very idea of some phenomenal consciousness, is critical of the term 'qualia' (the subjective qualitative sense of any experience), considering it to be '......a poison gift to neuroscience if ever there was one....' Consequently he also notes his: '....misgivings about the notorious "what it is like"' idiom (noted above) first explored by Brian Farrell (1950) and made famous by Thomas Nagel (1974). Nagel had suggested that: 'There is something that it is like to be a conscious organism'. For Nagel, regarding the '....something that it is like.... We can offer plausible descriptions of the 'like' but cannot explain the 'something'. The 'something it is like' continues to be deployed as some species-specific aspect of experience, one that forms the sense for humans of being self-conscious.

Another philosopher, Colin McGinn, has been critical of attempts to construct theories of consciousness, mainly due to its being a mysterious phenomenon that, in principle, eludes any orthodox explanation. He advocates a 'mysterianism' that '.....acknowledges that human intelligence is a local, contingent, temporal, practical and expendable feature of life on earth – an incremental adaptation based on earlier forms of intelligence that no one would regard as faintly omniscient.' (McGinn, 2018)

I think it might be useful to consider a few theories of consciousness in a bit more detail to allow a 'flavour' of this generally constructive, if multifaceted, debate to be gained, at least in terms of the central ideas being debated.

The neuroscientist Olaf Sporns (2011) has offered a sophisticated description of the working brain. His book, 'Networks of the Brain', brings together his own and some others' similar ideas on: '.......neuroscience and the emerging science of complex networks' - including identifying some emergent properties of these networks.

Sporns's ideas, with their combination of links between neural-architecture, dynamic networks, and systems mathematics, offers some innovative suggestions about network-based communication in the brain. He considers that we need to take into account empirical data and theoretical frameworks, as well as subjective experience, if we are to adequately explain brain-based activity. He goes on to add that if we are to adequately explain the experience of thinking, we would also have to take into account the involvement of the whole of the body, especially the CNS beyond the brain itself, the PNS, the endocrine system, as well as environmental conditions.

He endeavoured to make the case for approaching the study of the brain expressed in the term 'network neuroscience'. For Sporns, a typical neural network is composed of millions of neurons in interlinked (interactive), excitatory and inhibitory, activation across hierarchically arranged but interwoven matrices of neurons. The activity being expressed at each level of neural connectivity is for Sporns appropriate to model in terms of 'graph theory' (a geometry of position devised by Euler) so constituting a mathematical foundation for network science.

When endeavouring to form images of graph theory-based neural networks, we need to consider the possibility of a topological model – of images modeled on spatial separation – in doing so we would be imaging a complex interconnected tracery of dynamic activation. With neurons represented by 'nodes', and nodes interacting within groups composed of other nodes – connection strength within and between nodes can be of high- or low-degree within any hierarchical network of signaling transmission.

So Sporns's theory of neural operation is based on a model of dynamic networks with immediate local networks active within wider local and regional networks. Neural processing is focused on the 'nodes' (dense localities of neurons) which serve to concentrate, co-ordinate, and integrate information in line with functional (in the widest sense) patterning.

The application of graph theory introduces connection-related concepts such as the 'edges' 'paths' and 'walks' characteristic of networks and, whilst admitting the difficulty of offering precise definitions of these, it does seem that he considers that they allow a more useful understanding (by mathematical representation) of neural communication as exhibited/identified by current neuro-imaging techniques. Fairly simply put, for Sporns: 'Nodes can be linked directly by single edges or indirectly by sequences of intermediate nodes or edges. Ordered sequences involving unique edges and their connectedness to intermediate nodes are called paths, while sequences of non-unique edges are called walks. Many of the graph analyses of brain networks highlight a central role in network integration for paths. Paths can re-connect a node to itself, in which case it is called a cycle.'(Sporns, 2011, p9). Edges represent direct connections between nodes and a path is an interconnected set of functionally related nodes.

This outline provides a descriptive representation of the basic neural architecture - constituting the various levels (hierarchically arranged collections of neurons differing in neural density) and patterns of connectedness that form the networks which can in turn be mathematically modeled in line with graph theory.

One quantifiable measure related to neural activation (as modeled by graph theory) is the 'clustering coefficient'. For Sporns (p11) 'The clustering coefficient of an individual node measures the density of connections between the node's neighbours.' And so this offers the potential to measure neural density in local neural groups or wider regions of the brain, at least in relation to their functional role. In doing so this can for Sporns highlight the brain's: '......tendency to form segregated sub-systems within sub-systems with specialized functional properties.' (Sporns, 2011, p13)

The framing of the neural architecture of the human brain in terms of local and regional hierarchies of involvement, suggests three dimensional, lattice-like, arrangements of neurons locally connected in nodes and these arranged in hubs. For Sporns, the concept of node can apply at many levels of neural organization, be this: a single neuron, a population of these, or a brain region. In neuro-imaging, a node can also be applied to represent a single pixel (voxel) or to discrete clusters of these.

'Communities' of nodes are structurally highly interconnected, a modular property that facilitates functional roles. Across the brain these neural communities exhibit variable patterns of connectivity and interaction, allowing for their supporting different processing tasks.

Within the networks 'hub nodes' allow interactive communication between local groups of nodes and between hub nodes in different brain regions and they can '.....engage and disengage across time, as they link different sets of brain regions at different times' (Sporns 2011,p13). But as important as the various levels of hubs are for integration this is not 'realized' as an outcome in any hub network in itself, this takes place in '......the distributed and global dynamics of the brain.' (Sporns, 2011, p125)

The organizational features of networks, based on structural segregation and functional integration, make a significant contribution to the characteristically dynamic operation of neuron-based communication, a dynamism expressed for Sporns in the comment that: '.....we should not think of the brain's endogenous neural activity as a static time-invariant pattern of interneuronal or interregional coupling. Instead, spontaneous dynamics exhibits significant shifts, transitions, and non-stationarity, allowing for rapid reconfigurations of functional interactions at a time-scale of hundreds of milliseconds, even in the absence of exogenous perturbations.' (Sporns, 2011, p168)

In terms of connectivity, Sporns suggests that the brain is composed of three distinct types of networked connectedness. The *structural* (the 'wiring' diagram) and *functional* connectivity noted above (as 'webs of dynamic interaction), but also what he terms *effective* connectivity. This latter type of network is focused on the level of neuron to neuron connectivity and to identifying patterns of causation that they exhibit. I think he means the identification of the underlying neural (molecular) elements allowing neural activity to 'create' a network for this or that function.

Although setting out the various elements of neural networks and their description by graph theory, Sporns placed less emphasis on this more reductionist aspect of networks and instead emphasized the realization of the elements in an integrative hierarchy operating within regional and global brain contexts.

According to Sporns, a neuro-scientific theory would be incomplete if it did not offer some account of subjective experience and so of self-consciousness. For his own theory he describes consciousness as emerging '......from complex brain networks as the outcome of a special kind of neural dynamic'. He suggests that consciousness (or what he terms 'cognitive function') is a product of particularly dynamic networked configurations of neuronal systems with the, functionally local and regional, properties he has assigned to them. He notes that '......cognition is nothing more (and nothing less) than a special kind of pattern formation, the interplay of functional segregation and integration and the continual emergence of dynamic structures that are molded by connectivity and subtly modified by external input and internal state.' (Sporns, 2011, p206)

Although again, similar to other theories, Sporns cannot seem to offer a convincing conceptual 'explanatory bridge' between molecular materialism (or even network properties) and the elusive phenomenon of consciousness as in the infamous 'What it is like.....' (Nagel, 1974) of subjective experience.

A possible advantage of Sporns's 'Graph theory' is its potential for facilitating the quantification of dynamic and hierarchically arranged neural networks and so the prospect this would have for computer-based modeling of neural activity. But he also suggests a certain caution in relation to non-empirical aspects of his approach to modeling communication within the brain – suggesting that certain assumptions are made based on reasonably balanced 'assessment' rather than hard data. Although a work in progress, graph theory does seem to the layperson to offer a potentially useful (and certainly stimulating), if descriptively ambitious, explanation of neural communication.

Another, similar to Sporns, attempt at the quantified modeling of thought processes has been made by William Teed Rockwell with the 'Dynamic Systems Theory' (DST). This is a determinedly non-dualistic, approach to understanding human thinking, echoing ideas of John Dewey, summed up in the comment: '.....I believe that we should conclude that it is the brain, body, and world that embody consciousness and not the brain alone.' (Teed Rockwell 2005, p109). Teed Rockwell is highly critical of both traditional and more recent ideas that focus on brain-based activity 'as if' this alone embodies thinking. He offers an analysis based on considering cognitive systems in process rather than in atomistic (reductionist) terms; the latter framing the mind as '.....manipulating atoms of meaning and/or experience....' A fundamental assumption of DST is the need to focus on mental functions themselves rather than the architecture of the brain. Teed Rockwell considers the word 'brain' to have '......no essential use in neuroscience'. In relation to consciousness, for Teed Rockwell '......it seems sensible to conclude that the supervenience base for all mental events including subjective experiences includes not only the brain events, but events in the rest of body and in those parts of the environment with which the conscious organism maintains a synergetic relationship.' (ibid, 2005, p206) He credits Dewey with laying down the basic principles of a Dynamic System Theory (DST) that can provide a more appropriate model of the processes that form cognition than those currently on offer.

A more radical type of contribution to considerations of consciousness, one that challenges commonsense ways of framing the 'mental', can be traced back to the eighteenth century and the philosophical psychology of David Hume. The more philosophical past traced in these ideas has found modern interpretations in neuroscience. One leading interpretation was given the term 'eliminative materialism' by James Cornford in his 1968 essay ''On the Elimination of 'Sensations' and Sensations''.

Probably the two most prominent proponents of eliminative materialism have been the neuro-philosophers, Patricia and Paul Churchland. For the Churchlands, common-sense narratives of mental processes are framed within a conceptual understanding inherited from the past – concepts such as beliefs, emotions, desires, etc. Epistemologically flawed concepts, that the advance of neuroscience has made redundant, not least due to their conceptual vagueness and the inability to plan a potentially useful research programme to investigate their supposed role in human psychology. In effect, nothing taking place in the brain corresponds to such concepts; they are representative of a variety of 'Folk psychology'. For eliminative materialists, what can be found are 'brain states', the form and function of which are being increasingly revealed by the advance of the neurosciences; encompassing the '..... teeming intricacies of one's inner life within the conceptual framework of a completed neuroscience...' (P.Churchland, 2013 edn., p281)

The content of consciousness takes the form of representations inherent in underlying 'recurrent neural networks'; the 'recurrent' expressing the interactive (the 'dynamic profile') combination of feed-back and feed-forward connectedness within networks able to retain access to memories gained from past experience of the world.

Just digressing slightly from the more reductionist tendencies of eliminative materialism, Paul Churchland offers some more speculative ideas on a universal integration of conscious intelligence that has developed during the evolution of the universe. For Churchland: 'According to a broad and growing consensus among philosophers and scientists, conscious intelligence is the activity of suitably organized matter, and the sophisticated organization responsible for it is, on this planet at least, the outcome of billions of years of chemical, biological, and neurophysiological evolution.' He then goes on to suggest that, given that evolution is an outcome of 'natural laws' it is highly probable that similar types of intelligence would have developed elsewhere in the universe – he even predicts that '.....the evolutionary process is chugging relentlessly away, at *some* stage or other, on at least a million planets within this galaxy [our own] alone.' (Churchland, 2013 edn., p261 – I return to Churchland in the philosophy section of Vol. III)

A more conventional sense of consciousness is that offered by the highly respected neuroscientist Gerald M.Edelman. For Edelman, the adult brain's anatomical structure is quite fixed whereas its neuronal interconnectedness is highly flexible, functioning as a biological medium continuously developing conscious and unconscious messaging systems. A development summed up in the (evolutionary) concept of 'adaptation' taking place within a broader 'econiche'. The messaging systems at their simplest level are centered on the neuron, and the vast multitude of possible electro-chemical excitatory and inhibitory connections formed within populations of neurons. At the next level, these topologically local groups of neurons are in turn located within a wider interconnected and intercommunicating mesh of neuronal material. Edelman (2006, p145) notes the potentially '......hyperastronomical interactions of core neurons.' The flexibility (and indeed plasticity) of local neural groups is expressed in the continuous rate of synaptic change driven by experience and behaviour. These three-dimensional, but locally circumscribed, neural structures communicate either directly or indirectly with other brain areas mostly via reciprocating parallel pathways composed of elongated neurons.

For consciousness, the primary activity generated at the local level is found to be in the thalamocortical system, embodied in two-way primary neural pathways linked to such sub-areas as the basal ganglia, hippocampus and the cerebellum. These thalamocortical pathways convey sensory information to the cortex where it is integrated and interpreted as it is incorporated and reacted to within pre-existing 'information' which it can also alter in turn. The cortex is itself composed of wider processing systems – association, motor, auditory, visual, somatosensory, and emotional - interconnected by other types of neural pathways.

So, for Edelman, we have a brain characterized by a complex interconnected global system composed of billions of neurons within each of tens of thousands of local groups and these groups constituting functionally specialized cortical areas, operating within multiple networks directly or indirectly distributed throughout the brain. Although it seems that all neural groups can be directly or indirectly reciprocally connected, there are groups that are preferentially connected in relation to specific functional processes; the neural processes facilitating vision being an obvious one of these.

There is an additional feature of neural processing that dramatically increases the interpretive ability at all levels of the information processing organism. This is the feature of 'reentrance'. A feature that operates to integrate neural communication at the key higher levels of neural connectedness. I think that for Edelman, this is very different from the 'central coordinating executive' posited as the master integrating mechanism for some other theorists (such as Baars, 1988 'Global Workspace Theory' – a sort of meta awareness of neural representations). Edelman's integration via reentrance is a real-time feature operating 'within' the neural base of conscious experience, not some 'third-person' type of supra integrating mechanism. The dynamic neural mechanism of reentry is a particular feature of the thalamocortical-corticalthamic pathway with its connections to such key brain areas as the cortex, the basal ganglia, and the cerebellum – reentrance is a form of complex and dynamic recursive function.

This outline of the brain's network functionality forms the basis of Edelman's 'dynamic core hypothesis' (DCH). Given that this DCH has the potential to generate predictions it is a theory amenable to empirical investigation. And at the local network level it is amenable (with necessary caveats) to sophisticated computer modeling. Indeed a decade-long research program based at The Neurosciences Institute (founded by Edelman in 1981) has involved the design and construction of a series of evermore powerful 'brain-based devices' (BBDs) from Darwin I to Darwin X. These are not designed to replicate the conditions for some global consciousness (Edelman considers that the complexity of the brain make this 'currently unrealizable' - Edelman, 2006, p139), instead they focus on information processing operating to 'learn' from incoming perceptual information, and the coordination of appropriate motor outputs.

For Edelman, the 'higher-order selectional process', realized via the reentry noted above, with its integrating feature of reciprocal connectedness, 'entails' the experience of consciousness. For Edelman and his colleague Giulio Tononi: '......empirical observations suggest that underlying consciousness are distributed neural processes that, through reentrant interactions, are at once highly integrated but continually changing and thus are highly differentiated.' (Edelman and Tononi, 2000, p74)

The differentiation referred to here was significantly enhanced by the acquisition by humans of linguistic and associated semantic capabilities, including an evolutionary novel form of 'memory', linking self with the past, and so enabling a sense of the future. Memory and language enhance conceptual understanding with the result that, for Edelman and Tononi: 'Consciousness of consciousness becomes possible.' (Edelman and Tononi, 2000, p194). But this is a higher level form of consciousness (self-consciousness) that overlays and reciprocally interacts with a core of unconscious psychic material. I think I am fairly interpreting Edelman if I suggest that he views unconscious and conscious material as a continuum; if one influenced by any particular state of awareness.

The 'qualia' (the qualitative sense of each subjective state) identified as providing the differentiated content of consciousness are formed from the earliest experiences, as firstly an embryo then as the baby adapts, via physical movement, perception, and social interaction, within (not 'too') its 'world'. These early qualia provide the experiential base to which future experiences can be referred, so stimulating the primary processes that allow evermore complex qualia to be formed; evermore differentiated contents of consciousness.

My own very simplified and so selective outline of Edelman's ideas on consciousness is based mainly upon his own popularized version of these as outlined in books such as: Edelman1992, 2006, and Edelman and Tononi 2000. For those motivated to further their understanding of the work of this important specialist practitioner in neuroscience, as well as being an important and inspiring theorist, there are numerous web-sites, and other publications, where more academic papers can be accessed.

The types of neurological analysis seeming to suggest the brain as feeling emotions, pain, remembering, hearing, seeing etc etc – as if some internal third-person 'observer' of brain-based activity is present - have been subjected to considerable criticism. M.R.Bennett and P.M.S.Hacker (essay 'Philosophical Foundations of Neuroscience' from 'Neuroscience and Philosophy', 2007, p47) suggest that: '......by speaking about the brain's thinking and reasoning, about one hemisphere's knowing something and not informing the other, about the brain's making decisions without the person's knowing, about rotating mental images in mental space, and so forth, neuroscientists are fostering a form of mystification and cultivating a neuro-mythology that are altogether deplorable.'

They critically comment on what they term the 'mereological fallacy' – the ascription of psychological attributes, cognitive and perceptive, including remembering, feeling, anger, seeing, hearing, etc. etc. For Hacker and Bennett for example: 'It is not the eye (let alone the brain) that sees, but *we* see *with* our eyes (and we do not see *with* our brain......).' In relation to qualia more generally, if there were such phenomena, they would for Hacker and Bennett be experienced by human beings not brains.

According to Hacker and Bennett the misapplication of attributes stems from conceptual confusion, noting that: '....only when the long shadows cast by conceptual confusions are chased away can the achievements of neuroscience be seen alright.' Given that non-neuronal as well as neuronal elements are involved in synapse-based communication they suggest that it would be '.....wiser to consider the search for the "cellular" rather than just "neuronal" correlates [of consciousness].' (Neuroscience and Philosophy', 2007, p54)

Some more philosophical observations on consciousness unsurprisingly focus on the language used to describe and analyze the phenomenon. It is obvious that language can be used to note entities whose existential states are more imagined rather than real....unicorn, soul, and angels, being more obvious examples. Can the word 'consciousness', and indeed the word 'mind', represent similar unreal (insubstantial) concepts? But what about the sense we all feel of what it's like to be 'me'? Surely to deny reality to the concepts used, even if conceptually inadequate to fully circumscribe this sense of 'like to be', is to deny our intimate experience of self-hood.

It is difficult to know how the conceptual gap between brain (physiological) states and consciousness (mental) states will be bridged, but sophisticated mathematical approaches to modeling the spatial and functional operation of the brain offer an exciting potential. The mathematical modeling will not in itself explain consciousness (indeed Sporns himself describes consciousness as an 'emergent property') but it could offer an explanation of the ground conditions for a conceptual understanding that will advance the progress of analysis. Computer-based mathematical modeling offers the potential for 'capturing' a clear sense of the complex connectivity (spatial and functional) involving a fluctuating range of background activity, overlaid by a more focused patterning of local and global excitatory and inhibitory signally going on in the brain. But even if a similar level of speed and bio-complexity of information processing can be replicated via some computer software, it might still be that consciousness will not be expressed (emerge). At least then it might be acknowledged that the investigation into consciousness will need to be reframed towards some more phenomenological description, rather than using complex information processing models. Or that the persistently elusive 'what it feels like to be' of Nagel (1974) would become even more vulnerable to critical (or 'eliminative') analysis centered on the language used – the 'feels like' – rather than in any material advances in neuroscience.

How about imagining a potentially infinite set of inter-connected micro-systems. Within these systems there is information storage, but information stored in such a way that it can degrade and its accessibility - availability of memories - depends on a number of factors such as: strength of original encoding, the number of times it has been reinforced in the past and the emotional and/or intellectual intensity during each reinforcement, current physiological condition of the system's environment, strength of attention etc. – with both continuous and intermittent feedback loops. Communication within the basic 'cell-based' system being based seemingly on a binary on/off flow of 'bits' of information, but from this binary flow intricate patterns of excitation and inhibition are produced. With the inhibitions being potentially just as 'meaningful' as the excitations in the 'directing/framing' processes.

Step slightly away from this micro-level and imagine nets of these micro-level activities, seemingly three dimensional but, due to intrinsic properties emerging from communication patterns between cells, turned multi-dimensional – a form of bio-informational transcendence. But how does the more material activities taking place in the brain progress to the seemingly bio-transcendent phenomenon of consciousness? One idea (taking various descriptive forms) is of the conscious mind 'arising from' or being an 'emergent property' of the brain's physical activity. Is this merely offering a conceptual mystery to explain a feature of a bio-mechanism we don't yet understand; does it beg the fundamental question of how? Early proponents of the idea of emergence draw parallels with other phenomena of the natural world – steam from heating water and bile from liver function - as similes for the mental emerging from human brain activity. A comparison that ignores the fact that these more mundane emergent properties can be explained by the same physical laws (of molecular chemistry) used to explain the initial material conditions; whereas consciousness arising from the material brain eludes explanation by natural laws (at least as yet).

Accepting this more epistemological reservation, I would suggest that it is useful to consider thoughts 'emerging' from brain activity (within the associated body-environment nexus) in a fairly superficial, more descriptive sense, whilst being aware (or at least hoping) that a more convincing explanation is out there awaiting the advance of neuroscience and a level of intellectual insight informed by this. An explanation that conceptually sublates both material brain and conscious and unconscious mental experience within a unified theoretical frame-work, is awaiting some more precocious thinkers to develop.

Is the mental embodied in the physiological in such ways that current language does not allow of plausible description, or is it simply a mistake in principle to consider that the material substrate is both necessary (which is obvious) and sufficient (which is not) for self-consciousness to be realized. The implication being and that these are categorically different forms of natural phenomenon. A difference illustrated when we consider that human beings are inevitably disconnected by physiology (embodiment) but can be connected by sharing ideas, emotions and an unspoken sense of empathy. The mental seems to be the only feature of the universe that cannot be adequately described in terms of physicality – but it can be experienced and this might be sufficient for widening the boundaries of Reality in qualitatively progressive ways. Ways that lead to our learning more about mind-substrate as physiological and mind-substance as phenomenal, to a stage that allows the social construction of a form of language that can overcome the elusive difference between the two perspectives; perspectives that in principle cannot currently be reconciled.

The conceptual language necessary for resolving the physiological/phenomenological disjunction has not been developed, Any convincing conceptual unification of body and mind would obviously not be reductionist and would instead surely be transcendental, in that it would accommodate the primary characteristics of each in ways that offer more information than when each is considered apart. Such a description would transcend our current understanding of both the material and the mental, reframing properties of each within a new synthesis.

If we accept the brain-mind distinction as expressing some realistic categorization of aspects of being human, a distinction that does at least facilitate an initial introduction to the elusive idea of the relationship between neural conditions and consciousness (the source of the '....epistemic gap between the physical and phenomenal domains' noted by Torin Alter, 2017, p404) then persuasive evidence for their being a confounded phenomenon e.g. that consciousness emerges, or arises from, supervenes on, or is entailed by, the neural constitution of the brain and nervous system, seems to be their correlational relationship.

Correlation is a quantifiable alternative to 'causation' and 'identity' when causation and identity cannot be proven, or when they might involve a number of contributory factors. Susan Greenfield (2000) considered that speed and spread of neural transmission (as conventionally understood) would allow a processing threshold to be past and so provide a sufficient density of electro-chemical transmission for consciousness – for the seat of the neural correlates of consciousness - to be found in transient neuronal assemblies. The basic structure of the developed human brain (especially the experience-shaped networks of associations providing a '....common referent to myriad experiences' (Greenfield, 2000, p186) being the necessary condition, and with certain forms of these 'transient neural assemblies' providing the sufficient condition for self-consciousness. Greenfield is confident enough to define 'mind', and she does so in a fairly conventional neuro-scientific terms, suggesting that: 'My particular definition of the *mind* will be that it is the seething morass of cell circuitry that has been configured by personal experience and is constantly being updated as we live out each moment.' (Greenfield, 2000, p13).

Clearly Greenfield's ideas on the neurological base for consciousness are to some extent speculative, if informed by her extensive experience as a neuroscientist. She also notes the even more speculative ideas of Roger Penrose and Stuart Hameroff based upon aspects of quantum theory – their 'Orchestrated-Objective Reduction' (Orch-OR) theory. Where a quantum characteristic of cellular material is suggested as possibly allowing much faster transmission of information than the more conventional speeds noted above. This characteristic relates primarily to the idea of 'quantum coherence'. A feature of changes taking place in the protein tubulin (a complex molecule present in the tiny microtubules – hollow tubes - of almost all cells in the body) that, in turn, can generate the '.....wavelike signals propagated in accord with quantum theory.' (Greenfield, 2000, p190). Harald Atmanspacher, in brief, suggests that, for Penrose and Hammeroff, the quantum explanation is that '......elementary acts of consciousness are non-algorithmic, that is non-computable, and they are neurophysiologically realized as gravitation-induced reductions of coherent superposition states in microtubuli.' (Atmanspacher, 2017, p302).

Whilst Greenfield's own, fairly mundane, explanation of the bio-chemical mechanisms might provide the necessary and sufficient conditions for consciousness, she does not seem to have the conceptual language that would allow an adequate description of the transitional bio-threshold that elevates molecular activity into consciousness. Her potential candidate for neural correlates of consciousness being the emotion-based special type of 'transient neural assemblies' that she outlines.

Given the importance allowed to NCC in current neuropsychology let's just consider NCC in the context of this imagined scenario:

An artist is connected to a real-time 'super-version' of an fMRI scanner that can accurately record patterns of continuous waves of neural nets at the level of individual (single) neurons. The artist is tasked with painting a portrait of a sitting subject and whilst doing so to provide a continuous verbal report on what is going through her conscious mind as she draws the outlines and paints in the details. A transcript of this verbal activity might go something like:

"I first gaze at the subject endeavouring to take in the detail within the face as well as the overall shape, shaded areas, and occasionally switch attention to assessing the size of the canvas and imagining the line my hand might take as I begin. I hesitate, as I consciously try to imagine the flow of my hand across the canvass. The pencil touches the surface and, decision made, I move on to sketch the outline of the head, taking care to try to capture the shape of the fairly prominent jaw-line. I notice the first attempt is not quite right and so erasure the line and blow the residual rubber from the canvass as I brush the surface clean with the edge of my hand. I begin again on the chin section. I get slightly distracted as I think about the possibility of making a cup of coffee and feel that my right shoe is a little tight. Now I am sketching in eyes, nose, mouth, ears, I notice that the subject's hair is similar to my brother's and that there is a sense of sadness, of a life lived, in his eyes. I try to imagine him as a younger person just as I think of my own daughter who should be having her morning break at school ...." and so on, and on, over the approx. 6 hours taken to complete the portrait.

Even accepting the fMRI recording rate, with its fluctuating activity peaks as recorded from the changing magnetic strengths in the diffusion of the oxygen transporting molecule of hemoglobin (in brain regions associated with emotional reactions), especially during more 'emotional-laden' comments. Each time I ask this, or another artist, to repeat the activity, the pattern of the neural recording will invariably be different in detail, even if similar brain regions show above resting-level activation when such conscious behaviours as: decision-making, emotions being felt, and eye and hand coordination, are repeated. Is any 'measure' of correlation adequate to encapsulate the relationship between the artist's behavior and what has been 'observable' in the brain?

Now imagine a neurosurgeon undertaking a complex and lengthy brain operation and think about the relationship between their verbal outline and the recorded patterns of brain activity. As the artist and surgeon undertake their work their attention would be ever-shifting (both spontaneously - along with their dynamically developing processing of more focused attention) veritable 'waves' of differentiated patterning would characterize neural activity – accepting that the repeatedly active areas show a coherent pattern of regular activity. Fundamentally, each repetition of these (indeed all) types of experience would invariably result in both a differing verbal account for each and, crucially for proponents of NCC as evidence of material explanations for consciousness being sufficient, the transient neural patterns will also be unique each time they are 'measured'. If traced in terms of precise neural patterns then creative originality is the hallmark of human consciousness.

Whilst not of course dismissing the value of NCCs for investigating neural activity, the examples noted above do offer some indication of the complex subtleties of human behaviour (its experientially creative property). NCCs can usefully capture the neurological basis of thinking in fairly static mode, whereas thinking itself is imbued with a mode of originating dynamism. The identification and investigation of NCCs and NCUs (neural correlates of unconsciousness) has made a significant contribution to the functional mapping of the brain, especially in the identification of specialist areas directly associated with consciousness. The value of NCCs can also be seen in their tracking the difference between conscious and unconscious awareness.

In the process of considering the relationship between consciousness and attention Michael A. Cohen and Marvin M. Chun noted research indicating that when subjects were exposed to a 'subliminal' stimulus there was a significant level of neural activity, even in the absence of conscious awareness of the stimulus. The brain activity did not extend to any significant activation of the prefrontal and parietal cortices, areas that are known to be highly activated during conscious experience. It seems that a) the stimulus ('experience'), whilst unconsciously perceived by the subjects, was only associated with sensory level cortical area activity and b) a suggestible assumption being that there must be a mass of material that is continually being 'registered' within the nervous system of which we are not aware c) that fMRI, and other forms of neuro-imaging can identify both conscious (NCC) and unconscious (NCU) processes.

For Cohen and Chun: 'Together, these results demonstrate that information that fails to reach consciousness can still activate high-level neural processes.....' (Cohen and Chun, 2017, p546).

This, along with a mass of related psychological research, highlights an ongoing accumulation of unconscious content that could presumably influence our perceptual and conceptual experience, and our dependent behaviours. And of course this type of research reinforces the long held view that there is the accretion of past experience (not least the 'impact' of the socialization processes) that we unconsciously 'carry' with us. An accretion that in some (known and some as yet unknown) ways shape our approach to life; a relationship that has been identified by most approaches to psychology, not least psychoanalysis. Unconscious psychic material clearly has a key role in various aspects of our conscious lives including: judgments, prejudices, self-identity, and language use. The threshold between unconscious material and conscious awareness is probably best seen as dynamically porous, and so with the potential of the threshold between these being constantly shifting. Identifying the formation and influence of unconscious material is an important on-going area of psychological research.

The very complexity of consciousness suggests that care is required when considering the relevance of NCCs as anything other than conceptual combinations, albeit a very useful theoretical idea and one that some day could be given more substantial empirical confirmation than currently. A time when the continuously propagated traceries of neural activity (at the level of millions/billions of neural connections) that tracks (correlates too) behaviour can be recorded. Daniel Robinson (2007, p181) notes that: 'The living brain is never silent, and therefore the number of possible neural-phenomenal correlates is effectively limitless.' But even if this potential complexity of neural activity could be faithfully recorded (as more dynamic NCCs) this would still exclude the potentially primary role of endocrinal and immunological systems, and a secondary role of the other, seemingly more banal, bodily sub-systems (reproduction, digestion, cardiovascular, etc. in behaviour. Each 'experience' (qualia)[39] is biologically and phenomenologically unique, only being synthetically circumscribed as one experience spills easily into others. No combination of neural patterning, circumstances of the external (world), and internal bodily conditions, are ever repeated. That's not to say that NCCs are of but little value in offering some support to the idea of locating a key aspect of mental activity (behaviour) within patterns of neural constitution, just that we need to be careful in not over-interpreting these.

I can imagine that sometime in the future we will be able to accurately trace the progression of 'evolving' patterns of neural networks as thinking progresses, but even then I do feel that NCCs are more useful constructs for our reflections on mental activity, ones

---

[39] For the philosopher John Searle: '...all qualia are conscious states and all conscious states are qualia'.

constructed for the narrow purpose of proving materialism than offering fruitful ways of understanding thinking. Neurons and other types of cellular material within the brain are a necessary condition for consciousness as are the rest of an organism's bodily bio-systems, organs, etc. and the organism's lived in environment. Each of these: brain, body, and environment, are necessary but all have to be present for the form of sufficiency required for consciousness to pertain.

Max Velmans (1996, p5) compares the neural correlate of consciousness 'issue' to the wave/particle descriptions of the behaviour of sub-atomic particles. The idea that neural correlates and related conscious experience: '......encode identical information that appears to be formatted in different ways because it is viewed from different, third- and first-person perspectives...'

Would the phenomenon of 'entanglement' – the relationship between two synthetic perspectives, mind-brain - be more appropriate to express their relationship than a relationship of correlation? Not least, this would challenge neuroscientists to create new terms for the material and the mental. And would also allow for the involvement of other material factors – immunological, endocrine, and other embodied bio-systems – within the entangled conditions of necessity and sufficiency.

We can realistically only discuss consciousness from the perspective of our own introspective experience and the inferences - gained from neuroscience, philosophy, prose and poetic literature, as well as more direct personal social experience - we make assuming similar processes taking place in others. So we have direct experience of our own consciousness, indirect (inferred) experience of it in others, and an assumption of our shared ability to communicate about it. The idea of a type of interpretive objectivity expressing a shared understanding of 'Reality'.

I think that the brain can be provisionally modeled as a dynamic bio-system[40] constituted by a set of subsystems interconnected by recursive neural pathways, with these subsystems themselves constituted by often dense bundles of more or less transiently connected neurons. The development (evolutionary and phenotypically) of this bio-system suggests its form can be related to a special kind of functionality. Not one operating as some highly

---

[40] The 'bio' is cogent in terms of both evolutionary and epistemological implications.

efficient mechanism with feedback loops allowing continuous appropriate adjustments in response to changing mental, bodily, and environmental (including social) conditions. But a bio-system that, if for most seems to provide sufficient functionality to maintain the integrity of an individual, is liable to somewhat eccentric and at times even seemingly dysfunctional system behaviours. Such is the potentially overwhelming amount of internally and externally generated information available to any human bio-system that processing this is a massive and continuous task such that partiality – to reduce amount and complexity - is a necessary adaptation. If one that has a place in the factors contributing to many of the challenges and problems of the individual human (existential) condition and of our social and political circumstances.

Wolf Singer suggests human consciousness (including 'qualia') is an outcome of a process of meta-cognition arising from social interaction which takes place when: '......cognitive agents share their experiences of the outer and their inner worlds.' For Singer: 'Without the embedding in a differentiated social-cultural environment, without the option to mirror oneself in the perception of others, without the reflexive interactions between persons endowed with a theory of mind, without the exchange of reports about inner states, formulated in a symbolic language system we would probably not be aware of being conscious.'

The epistemic gap between the material nervous system and the phenomenal experience of 'what it's like to be.....' might fascinate the more philosophical inclined, and to be fair it is an interesting problem. But if we consider neuroscience in terms of more obviously tangible benefits we can see that the twenty-first century holds exciting prospects for neuropsychology and for the neurosciences more generally, let's just consider a few areas of potential advance:

- Neuroscience will be closely involved in the advance of the science of genetics, with the possibility of manipulating genetic material in brain cells in order to treat clinical conditions such as the various dementias – and perhaps in enhancing normal cognitive performance.
- Stem cell research – current research is focused on the substitution of the currently used fetal stem cells used to create new brain and other nervous system cells with bone marrow cells.

- The range of older drugs are being refined and new ones being developed to treat brain related illness/dysfunction.
- Related to the last point, a range of 'designer drugs' might be on offer that can enhance (optimizing cognitive abilities) mental abilities 'cogniceuticals' (Tallal, 2012)
- Increasing technical improvements in neuro-imaging and computer based representation of brain function allowing increased access to its complexity.
- In the area of cognitive neuropsychology – the further refining of computational models designed to process information in ways similar to the operation of brain-based processing (reading, spelling, object recognition) so that if purposely disordered the researcher could then observe how the induced disorder has manifested itself in the 'behaviour' of the computational model – and then, if the induced 'symptom' in the model is similar to the symptoms of patients suffering from a particular disorder the researcher could 'map' the induced disruption of the model with what might be happening in the brain of patients.
- We can expect that the range of technological innovations arising from nano-technoloy to include devices that will open up the investigation of the brain and nervous system. Perhaps devices that can be injected into the blood stream to enable tracing neural connections and operation at the tiniest (nano) of scales.
- Increased computing power will also be made possible by nano-technology 'Nanoscale fabrication, superconductivity, and three-dimensional structures, will eventually make possible the building of immensely powerful supercomputers' – Futurologists (such as Martin 2006) have predicted a massive processing capacity shift in the interconnection of networked computers (such that qualitative outcomes might be possible. – Martin p240 notes the current US TeraGrid as being the '...world's most powerful computer network' – with the capacity to perform 20 million operations per second and able to store over 1,000 trillion bytes of data. Martin imagines a 'ZettaGrid - a zetabyte = 1,000,000,000,000,000,000,000 bytes: 'The ZettaGrid would connect millions of zettaflops of supercomputers, each with zettabyte of data. It is in such an environment, with automated evolution, that the Singularity will occur' - Singularity (p239) being the idea of computer

scientist Vernor Vinge, of computers 'feeding' on themselves – Vinge '...uses the term to refer to the curve of technological growth becoming almost vertical' – the point where computers could 'take control' (an evolutionary 'jump') according to Vinge 'There may be an explosion of intelligence far beyond anything that humans can either understand or control' - plus more suggesting supercomputing as having positive as well as threatening prospects. p217 Vinge also suggests a 'new type of intelligence' Non-human-like' (NHL) intelligence 'The growth of powerful NHL intelligence is one of the important momentum trends shaping our future'

- Quantum computing, seems to offer the possibility of a significantly increasing computing power, impacting on a number of neuro-technologies.
- The developing use of the internet to share detailed information from research, according to Paula Tallal (2012) '....The internet will [in 21st century] facilitate communication between scientists across fields and domains, while providing for unprecedented, rapid dissemination of cross-disciplinary scientific information around the world.'

Taking a more metaphysical perspective:

- The advancing descriptive power (and theoretical frameworks) of the neurosciences combined with the potential analytic power of philosophy could see the resolving of the age-old dichotomies nature/nurture, mind/matter, perhaps even normal/abnormal. (these three pairs copied from Tallal (2012) For Tallal: 'With a growing understanding of the mind as a complex, ever-adapting genetic/neural/behavioural/social system, new technological advances will allow us to move toward an increasingly integrated perspective in the 21st century'. Currently various metaphors are used to give cognitive access (allow understanding) of matters that are just too challenging to easily express using the simple language of description but endeavouring to offer adequate (intellectually satisfying) metaphors for the mind seems to be an impossible challenge because there is nothing in the known universe as complex, nothing from which to create and offer an adequate metaphor. Especially ones that can capture the profound complexity of the mind and how physiological (processes/patterning) weaves into consciousness and consciousness in turn objectifies the physiological.

Fifty years ago relatively little was known about the function and structure of the CNS, and indeed how its physiological activity might relate to the mind ('consciousness'). Since then the amount of information (and the conceptualization of this is in descriptive, and analytic explanations) has made a significant contribution to the store of human knowledge and has done so in ways that suggests this is a cutting edge field of novel advance. Information that can significantly contribute to the overall understanding of the human condition.

For the first half of the twentieth century psychology was predominately a European, US, and Russian, social science, but psychology laboratories and university departments have since been establish in almost all of the countries of the economically 'developing world' (Africa, Asia, Latin-America, China, India). Along with the spread of psychology centres, there has been a progressive sub-division of the science in relation to particular specializations including: clinical, experimental, developmental, educational, social, occupational, organizational, criminology, health, marketing, etc. In 1947 the American Psychological Association (APA) first introduced a divisional structure (7 divisions) and by 2010 there were 54 such divisions. By the end of twentieth century over 60% of practicing psychologists were still American.

In the 1970s there were 70,000 psychologists in the US which had reached 150,000 by 2011.

Even in division there has still developed a core of research 'good practice' (methodological conventions) related to such aspects of experimental design as: use of control groups, identification of dependant and independent variables, the use of standardized statistical significance testing to evaluate results, the application of agreed ethical standards..... all contributing to good practice, reliability, ecological validity, and reproducibility.

More recently Asch ('History of the Social Sciences', 2010, p28) highlights the idea of a 'reflexivity' in psychology increasingly since WWII (a practice that had been an integral aspect of psychoanalysis since its early period). For James Capshaw (2007): 'psychologists are themselves part of the subject-matter of their own discipline'.

Two conventional, internationally recognized, diagnostic systems are the standard diagnostic and statistical tool complied and published by the American Psychological Association (APA) 'Diagnostic and Statistical Manual for Mental Disorders' (DSM-5) and the WHO's 'International Classification of Disease' (ICD-10). Although seemingly useful in the clinical context they do in fact endeavour to synthetically categorize many behaviours that are continuous, but of differing 'magnitudes; with any boundary between normal and abnormal being socially rather than empirically defined. As Richard P.Bentall points out: 'The designers of widely used diagnostic manuals such as DSM-5 and ICD-10 simply determined their diagnostic criteria by seeking consensus among their fellow clinicians.' ('The Blackwell Companion to Consciousness', 2017 ed., p157)

The APA's DSM-4 - the Diagnostic and Statistical Manual of mental disorders lists 297 disorders. A fifth edition DSM-V was published in 2013 (with a supplement added in 2017) also listed 297 disorders, in 19 major groups. The first DSM published in 1950 listed only 106 conditions the third, published in 1980, listed 265 conditions. Criticisms have included the contribution this manual has made to the medicalization of 'the normal', if we accept that the normal encompasses a broad spectrum of behaviours. It has been estimated that if the manual's guidance on diagnosis is applied to the population of America then about 50% of its citizens would be labeled as mentally ill at some time during their lives. For Bruce K. Alexander and Curtis P. Shelton: 'The DSM has diverted attention from the dark shadow of psychological misery that hangs over late modernity by chopping it up into supposedly manageable bits. We see heavy attacks from many directions and many professional groups on the new DSM-5 (e.g. Frances, 2013) as a welcome sign of an awakening in the psyc. professions throughout the world.' (Alexander and Shelton, 2014, p485).

The DSM can be a productive generator of work for psychiatrists, as well as a liberal source of profit for the drug companies. Clearly a potentially useful aid for working psychiatrists (fostering consistency of diagnosis) but one with significant social implications, not least on how we frame the normal, and the denial of the opportunities to accrue psychological resilience during bouts of mild-moderated emotional difficulty. In addition the unspoken focus for psychiatric illness is on the individual, so avoiding serious consideration of the contributions of the ever-increasing pressures of a psychological complex, uncertain, and dislocating social environment; considering this could have economic and political implications that most governments seem to want to avoid.

For the public, there are now numerous pervasive psychological narratives for our own lives. Illustrated by the language in which we describe our feelings and emotions and in our constant distraction with identity concerns (which is both stimulated and exploited by the advertising industry) – plus a almost industrial production of self-help books, TV programmes, and newspapers/magazine 'features', informing us how we can be happier, have more attractive personalities, improve memory or our problem-solving abilities. All contributing to create the 'Psychological society' noted by Roger Smith (1998) (see Asch, 2010, p28). This manifestation of the wider consumer-generated ego-centric medicalization of ourselves, can itself become an 'unhealthy' psychological distraction to living a more balanced mental life.

We have no knowledge of any biological entity as complex (in information processing terms) as the human nervous system, and what can emerge from this level of complexity can't always be predicted given our current understanding of bio-chemistry and human psychology. In a sentence we can think of two great areas of mystery, the mind and the universe, the complexity and reflexivity of one allowing, by comparison, a reference for the other. Both share a mystery that is resolving into knowledge and enlightenment as the sciences of psychology and astronomy informed by speculative philosophy advance in relative tandem.

Perhaps even more so than any other of the social sciences, psychology offers exciting prospects for future advance. Even if we accept much of this advance will probably be a product of the 'harder' branches of psychology as these are developing in neuroscience and pharmacology, rather than in the development of theoretical explanations. But in terms of pathology, psychology is progressed in social settings that are becoming evermore stressful, with an ever-increasing number of children and adults experiencing distressing conditions such as anxiety, autism, adhd, stress, depression, eating disorders, and loneliness. Consequently, in terms of clinical value, it does seems that advances in psychology have at best been more about producing coping mechanisms (drugs and/or behavioural strategies) for managing dysfunctional outcomes of lives being lived in confusing social worlds, than implementing the fundamental social changes necessary for more 'healthy/fulfilling' social environments. A change of perspective that would allow psychologists to focus their work on supporting those much smaller in number who would probably suffer mental health issues (such as the schizophrenia, the dementias, and severe depressions) even in less stressful, more human centric, societies. A more profound challenge for psychologists is not to assume that psychological dysfunction is necessarily an individual problem but rather to, when appropriate, highlight any broader social circumstances contributing to ill-health

G.A.Miller in his 1969 presidential address to the APA noted that: 'In my opinion, scientific psychology is potentially one of the most revolutionary intellectual enterprises ever conceived by the mind of man. If we were ever to achieve substantial progress toward our stated aim – toward the understanding, prediction and control of mental and behavioural phenomena – the implications for every aspect of society would make brave men tremble.'

After a sweep through the history of 20th century western psychology, highlighting the diverse perspectives that have accrued in relation to human psychology, the authors Bruce K. Alexander and Curtis Shelton conclude that: 'A psychology of multi-layered perspectives may provide the most precise description possible of today's polymorphic human beings. The arrangement that works for the psychological problems of our time in history, however, remains to be discovered....... A sobering possibility emerges from this line of thought. A creature that encompasses incompatible perspectives is subject to unending conflict......It seems that one of the few areas of consensus that has emerged from 2,500 years of work is that human beings dwell in a state of conflict! Permanent individual serenity and social utopia may be no more a possibility for creatures like us than is flying by flapping our arms, although we may continue trying to achieve both.' (Alexander and Shelton, 2014) A somewhat depressing, if considered, conclusion that I would want to view more as a challenge to be overcome, than an entirely accurate assessment of the human situation.

In order to offer some more detailed sense of how the social sciences have developed I have considered just three social sciences – sociology, medicine, and psychology - but the interrelationship between all branches of social science means that in order to better understand most of the particular social issues a multi-disciplinary approach is necessary. – politics/social policy, anthropology, history, social geography, law, economics, management studies, population studies, statistical analysis and systems theory, ecology and environmental studies - being the more obvious. Interdisciplinary team-working is becoming a common feature of social science studies.

One obvious conclusion to my overview of the natural and the social sciences is that they are in the vanguard of the process of expanding the 'Reality' within which homo-sapien continues its evolutionary journey.

***

Summary of the sciences

The interlinking of science charged with facilitating economic exploitation and addressing perceived social problems, offers the potential for both harms and benefits. To a significant extent research funding is directly linked to the interests of the funder (whether government, corporate, philanthropic, or charity) rather than being offered to support disinterested enquiry into scientifically important areas as assessed by overall benefit to humankind. The direction of scientific advance is mainly determined by some combination of the current state of any science, what any individual scientist or research group considers worth investigating, and the interests of potential funders. Consequently, if we wish to know how any science has developed in relation to 'objective knowledge' we would need to start by teasing out the balance of influence of each of these factors.

In as early as 1929, John Dewey bluntly noted that 'The notion of the complete separation of science from the social environment is a fallacy which encourages irresponsibility, on the part of scientists, regarding the consequences of their work' (McDermott, 1973, p400). Consequences that often get overlaid with considerations of income and career advance within science, both important aspects of being an individual but ones that should be secondary to moral considerations; society should value and support an infusion of morality within science, but systemic reform of institutions would be required to ensure this.

In relation to individual influences, C.H.Waddington noted that for scientists '....such a mind cannot produce a theory which is completely objective, and uninfluenced by the mind's own nature' (Waddington,1961,p124), So highlighting the potential for such personal elements as ambition, prejudice, and other social influences, to influence any individual scientist's approach to their work

According to Hans Christian von Baeyer, Neils Bohr himself expressed doubts about gaining certainty: '....objective reality is an illusion we construct for our own comfort. The best we can do, Bohr came to believe, is to create a coherent model of the world that reproduces its measured properties without claiming to describe reliably what it actually is.' He goes on to quote Bohr on the aim of science: 'Our task is not to penetrate to the essence of things, the meaning of which we don't know anyway, but rather to develop concepts which allow us to talk in a productive way about the phenomena in nature' (von Baeyer 2004, pp64/65)

Even if we ignore the influence of a wider social context (funding sources, institutional traditions, scientific 'fashion') and focus on individual scientists we can find numerous examples of both personal bias as well a subtle and crude forms of cheating in scientific research. Just one controversial research area rife with subjective bias has been 'intelligence' – from overt racist bias inherited from the nineteenth century pioneers to the crude cheating of Cyril Burt, who manipulated data and even 'invented' researchers to ensure that research outcomes supported his own preconceptions. Work, whose influence on intelligence testing had a profound and enduring influence on education in post WWII Britain, work produced by a cheat that tainted IQ meta-studies across much of the civil world.

I am suggesting that objectivity applied by scientists at a 'local' level should be (in fact at best is only) an idealized (guiding) aim within a wider methodological approach constituting the social production process of scientific knowledge; an ideal that scientists themselves should adhere too, and society itself should have the opportunity to express a view about. All of humankind's civil institutions (economic, religious, political, legal, educational...etc) are socially constructed, a fact that roots them into the subjective conditions that are a fundamental aspect of social life. To acknowledge that this is also the case with scientific discovery offers the intellectual justification (indeed imperative) for the wider society to question, and possibly challenge the basis of this or that specific scientific undertaking or claim. In addition to the intellectual justification for evaluating scientific developments there is also a role for scrutiny (and indeed regulation) in terms of any social implications of these.

Judged positively, the scientific method has given us knowledge of the material and social worlds that has allowed a significant proportion of humankind to experience an increasing level of material wellbeing, healthy and prolonged lives, and also the opportunity to gain ever wider perspectives of the Reality within which we experience the world. My strongly anti-military and general anti-corporate attitude in relation to the scientific endeavour, along with a deep-rooted suspicion of government and corporate motivation in relation to science and social policy, might fairly be considered to lack balance. But in the context of the expression of evil strand of my narrative, such is the increasingly pervasive influence of 'inhuman' forces driving scientific advance that any balance has to take into account the overwhelming power of the forces seeking influence and control over our lives (and deaths).

The internationalization of science in bodies like the Pugwash conference programme, 'Scientists for Global Responsibility', UNESCO, and a range of more science–specific organizations such as: 'The International Mathematical Union', 'The International Geoscience Programme', the 'International Primatological Society', the 'Federation of Earth Science Information Partners'...... and about 150 other similar international scientific bodies – does offer some grounds for optimism. As does the innovative use of the internet to foster international co-operation, if more between scientists, and some scientific institutions, rather than between governments and corporates.

Also valuable in terms of the integrity of science are publishing initiatives such as the 'Initiative for Open Citation' (launched with philanthropic financial support in April 2017) with the stated aim of promoting '.....the unrestrained availability of scholarly citation data'. In a similar spirit of open science is the 'Public Library of Science' (also supported by philanthropic funding – from 2001). This library being another not-for-profit organization promoting open access for its 9/10 journals, mainly focused on the biological sciences. Its aim being to progress its belief: '.....that scientific ideas and discoveries are a public good. [That] Their benefit will only be fully realized when scientists have effective means to rapidly communicate ideas, results and discoveries to each other and to the broader public.'

The campaign for open science is gaining both momentum in the scientific community and traction with a wider public. It does face seemingly implacable resistance from the world's military, corporate (and now speculative) interests, as well as those many 'benefit capitalism' supporting politicians. The phrase 'benefit capitalism' is eminently suitable when applied to science given the large amount of public subsidy for educating scientists and for basic research, especially in materials and pharmaceuticals, gifted to private companies for them to exploit. And also as a principle customer for the end products facilitated by scientific advance - not least in computing, communication, weapons systems, and medicine. Where would supposed 'free-wheeling market capitalism' be without over a hundred years of massive public subsidy? Indeed where would science be if it had had to rely solely on private profit oriented research finance? There is the need to recognize the contribution of philanthropic funding (especially in the US) even accepting that this is invariably the recycling of profits from corporate activities that would have benefited from government subsidy...etc....etc.

At the start of the twentieth century the work of a few thousand scientists was funded by institutions disbursing a few million dollars, with results being published in a few hundred printed journals. Currently research funding has reached $1,000 billion globally each year, with millions of scientists able to publish in thousands of journals and on thousands of web-sites. The Science Citation Index lists 8,500 significant scientific journals covering 150 disciples, for both the natural and social sciences. Web sites such as 'Web of Science' and 'SciSearch', offer access (if some by subscription) to masses of scientific research, albeit with probably at least as much made unavailable due to classification by governments or held secret by corporations and other private companies.

At times scientists have raised concerns about aspects of research. The rising concern of some scientists during and just following WWII was initially expressed in the Russell-Einstein manifesto of 1955 'Bulletin of Atomic Scientists'. The manifesto warned of the dangers of the terrible destructive potential of the hydrogen bomb and urged governments to '.....find peaceful means for the settlement of all matters of dispute between them.' The Russell-Einstein manifesto was endorsed by a number of the worlds' leading scientists including Max Born, Linus Pauline and Joseph Rotblat, with a later petition on nuclear weapons being signed by over eleven thousand scientists working in fifty countries.

Russell and Rotblat went on to establish the Pugwash series of conferences (noted above). The first meeting being held in the small Nova Scotian town of Pugwash in 1955, with the sixty-second meeting in Astana, Kazakhstan, in August 2017. The central aim of these gatherings has been to bring together scientists who are collectively determined on the eradication of nuclear and other types of weapons of mass destruction - Rotblat and Pugwash were jointed awarded the Noble Peace Prize.

Pugwash was but one manifestation of a wider set of concerns about the use of science. A concern shared by a large section of the global scientific community, spanning the natural and the social sciences. There are numerous university departments now offering courses on the social implications of the sciences. An aspect of science that has also being institutionalized in the UN and in regional groupings. An example of the latter is the European Commission's 'Horizon 2020' project.

The twentieth century has seen the increasing level (domination) of government and corporate control of science. Crudely put, the focus will increasingly be: on the means of killing and the means of profiting. We rely on government action but most have been shown to be reluctant to act against the twin interests of military and corporates. Public pressure is a potentially powerful source of action but this is currently mostly fractured into single issue groupings. Concerned scientists (and informed lay people) use public platforms to raise issues, more often only seeking further research and modest controls on potentially harmful activities based on the 'precautionary principle' approach; assessing possible risk against potential benefits. They immediately face the relentless mobilization of industrial-strength corporate criticism and disinformation; at times amounting to implicit or explicit intimidation in relation to withdrawal of funding of institutional sponsorship, and the impact on individual career prospects. Industries such as -pharmaceuticals, big-agriculture, tobacco, weapons manufactures, processed foodstuffs, and coal and oil producers – have slick, well-funded, public relations depts. along with thousands of articulate professional corporate lobbyists able to efficiently disburse election funding and negotiate political support in order to prevent or dilute attempts at legislation, or even the application of some modest ethical dimensions to international trade deals, especially in relation to intellectual property rights.

The future of science includes the potential for addressing serious human problems – not least in relation to the environment, biodiversity, healthcare, weaponry, artificial intelligence and, more specifically for the social sciences, problems such as consumer manipulation, and various forms of social policy involving surveillance and control of sections of populations

We are also witnessing the relentless erosion of the 'commons' that should be the WWW, as corporates and governments seek to gain control, manage, manipulate and monetrise, what should be an accessible platform for open science and indeed for participatory democracy.

Seen in a positive light the scientific endeavour, with the aim of pursuing the accumulation of the ideal of unbiased 'objective' knowledge, should retain our respect. Science, subject to the priorities expressed within participatory democratic political contexts (ideally global) - open in sharing knowledge, shaped by and responding to human values, can continue to expand our understanding of the material, social, and personal, aspects of Reality within which we live.

Lightning Source UK Ltd.
Milton Keynes UK
UKHW022037090223
416682UK00015B/1740